Educational Research

A Contextual Approach

KEN SPRINGER

Educational Research

A Contextual Approach

WILEY John Wiley & Sons, Inc.

VICE PRESIDENT & EXECUTIVE PUBLISHER	Jay O'Callaghan
ACQUISTIONS EDITOR	Robert Johnston
PRODUCTION MANAGER	Dorothy Sinclair
SENIOR PRODUCTION EDITOR	Valerie A. Vargas
MARKETING MANAGER	Danielle Torio
CREATIVE DIRECTOR	Harry Nolan
SENIOR DESIGNER	Madelyn Lesure
PRODUCTION MANAGEMENT SERVICES	Sunitha Arun Bhaskar, Laserwords Maine
SENIOR PHOTO EDITOR	Hilary Newman
EDITORIAL ASSISTANT	Mariah Maguire-Fong
MEDIA EDITOR	Lynn Pearlman
COVER PHOTO	StockphotoPro

This book was set in 11/12 Bembo by Laserwords Private Limited, Chennai and printed and bound by RRD-JC. The cover was printed by RRD-JC.

This book is printed on acid-free paper. ⊗

To order books or for customer service please, call 1-800-CALL WILEY (225-5945).

ISBN-13 978-0-470-13132-9

Printed in the United States of America

10 9 8 7 6 5 4 3 2 1

To Cecilia

Brief Contents

Contents

Chapter 3   Research Reports   63

Chapter 4   Ethics and Sampling   91

Chapter 5   Measurement   **121**

Chapter 6 Validity and Reliability **151**

Chapter 7 Experimental Designs **175**

Chapter 8   Single-Participant Designs   213

Chapter 9   Nonexperimental Designs

Chapter 10 Descriptive Statistics

Chapter 11 Inferential Statistics

Chapter 12   Statistical Representation   **345**

Chapter 13 Ethnographies and Case Studies   381

Chapter 14 Content Analysis and Historical Research   417

Chapter 15 Mixed-Methods Designs 435

Chapter 16 Action Research 457

Purpose

This book is suitable for an introductory course in educational research. I wrote the book for students who are learning how to be consumers of research, as well as for those who will be planning their own research project. To be a successful researcher you need a variety of skills. You need to become a critical reader of published work, to learn about research methods and design—*and* to be able to put what you learn to use. I have tried to ensure that students would not only understand what the technical terms and concepts mean, but also be able to apply them.

Context

One of my basic assumptions in writing this book is that the knowledge and skills used by educational researchers are not context-independent. The topics we choose to study, the descriptive frameworks we use, the methods we deploy, and the analyses and interpretations of data we rely on are all informed by historical, political, and social trends. These trends might be thought of as "external" contexts, in the sense that they influence the process of scientific inquiry but are not intrinsic to it. An example would be the federal government's emphasis on using evidence-based research, and randomized trials in particular, as a basis for educational policy and practice. During the past decade, this emphasis has had an impact on the direction and evaluation of educational research. I wanted to give students a glimpse of external contexts such as this, rather than just presenting the material as a compendium of definitions and hypothetical examples.

The practice of educational research reflects a kind of subculture. Researchers are influenced by theoretical and conceptual assumptions that inform our research questions, methods, analyses, interpretations, and approaches to dissemination. These theoretical and conceptual assumptions provide the "internal" context for scientific inquiry. An obvious example is reflected in the differences between the assumptions of quantitative and qualitative researchers. In the book I wanted to draw out some of these assumptions, so that students would more readily understand the material and become acculturated as consumers and perhaps also producers of research.

Finally, educational research is not only influenced by, but also influences, the context in which it is created. The results of our studies influence the way subsequent research is carried out, and our results have an impact on educational policy and practice. Here too I wanted students to see how educational research not only shapes its own progress but also influences policy and practice. In the final chapter I address the issue of whether the research shapes educational practice as much as it should.

Complexity

Another key assumption informing this book is that both consumers and producers of educational research need many different kinds of knowledge, skills, and strategies in order to appreciate the study of educational issues. Educational research is becoming more interdisciplinary and complex. For this reason, quantitative, qualitative, and mixed-methods research are all discussed throughout the book, and I made an effort to be inclusive of a variety of both traditional and contemporary concepts and paradigms.

Organization

Broadly speaking, the book consists of three parts. The first six chapters cover introductory material, the second six chapters focus on quantitative design and analysis, while the final six chapters concern qualitative, mixed-methods, and applied research.

The chapters are also organized into smaller groups of three:

- Chapters 1–3 introduce the field of educational research and address preliminary considerations such as the selection of research topics, the dissemination of research reports, and the literature review.
- Chapters 4–6 introduce methodological concepts of importance in the early stages of a study, including research ethics, sampling, measurement, and reliability and validity.
- Chapters 7–9 introduce quantitative research designs.
- Chapters 10–12 introduce statistical analysis and representation.
- Chapters 13–15 introduce qualitative and mixed-methods research.
- Chapters 16–18 deal with applied research activities, including action research, program evaluation, and strategies for bridging the research–practice gap.

Although there is considerable cross-referencing, each chapter stands alone. If an instructor prefers to introduce statistics before design, for example, the statistical chapters can be read before the chapters on quantitative design.

Distinctive Features

This book contains several characteristics that distinguish it from the current textbooks available for this course.

Contextual Information

Along with the first and last chapters, which provide information about the contemporary state of educational research, contextual information is available through several sources:

- Each chapter has three "Spotlight on Research" features that consist of an excerpt from a published article that illustrates chapter content. As students progress through the book and acquire more capacity for understanding research, the Spotlight features increase in length accordingly.

- There are many discussions of research studies in the main text, along with illustrations and anecdotes that provide a meaningful context for the material.
- Each chapter closes with suggestions for further reading. The Resource Guide on the companion website provides the full text of articles as well as links to other resources that provide contextual information.

Comprehensiveness and Balance

This text is comprehensive, in the sense that it covers all major topics of importance typically covered in books of this genre. In addition, certain topics receive greater coverage than most texts provide. These topics include research ethics (Chapter 4), statistical representation in tables and figures (Chapter 12), and program evaluation (Chapter 17). Statistical material is treated more thoroughly than in most texts, with two long chapters devoted to descriptive and inferential statistics (Chapters 10 and 11), and part of one chapter devoted to advanced statistical modeling (Chapter 12). Chapter 18 provides an extended discussion of the research–practice gap and how that gap might be bridged. Finally, although the book provides a standard, full-length introduction to quantitative research, qualitative approaches to sampling, measurement, and design are discussed throughout the book, and three chapters are devoted exclusively to qualitative and mixed-methods approaches (Chapters 13, 14, and 15).

Applications

Throughout the book I provide students with support for applying their newly acquired knowledge and skills. For example, Chapter 2 provides detailed guidance on using ERIC to conduct a literature review, Chapters 10–12 each lead the student through the process of creating and analyzing a small dataset, and Chapter 18 closes with a summary of how to plan and conduct a study. Each chapter in the book opens with a brief description of learning objectives. At the end of each chapter is a feature entitled "Applications: A Guide for the Beginning Researcher" in which I summarize ideas from the chapter that will help students begin their research. Exercises at the end of each chapter allow students to apply what they have learned, and further exercises and activities can be found in the Study Guide on the companion website.

Supplementary Materials

All of the supplementary materials for instructors and students are available on the companion website at *www.wiley.com/college/springer*.

- The Study Guide contains exercises, problems, and other activities designed to help students apply what they have learned from each chapter.
- The Resource Guide provides both students and instructors with the full text of articles, as well as links and other resources that help provide context for the material presented in the chapters.
- The Instructor's Manual and Test Bank provide tips and strategies for introducing chapter content, as well as handouts and test items for each chapter.

Acknowledgments

Many people offered helpful feedback on drafts of this book. I would like to thank the numerous individuals who reviewed the manuscript, including Fawzy Ebrahim, Florida Atlantic University; Xin Liang, University of Akron; Diana LaRocco, University of Hartford; David Pugalee, University of North Carolina, Charlotte; Lois Trautvetter, Northwestern University; and Paul Erickson, Eastern Kentucky University. In addition, I would like to thank my editor at John Wiley & Sons, Robert Johnston, the development editor, Ann Greenberger, my colleague Jill Allor, and the many MEd and MBE students who took my educational research class and gave me detailed feedback on earlier versions of the book. I am deeply grateful to the students for helping me see both the strengths and the weaknesses of my writing.

My former Dean U. Narayan Bhat, and my current Dean David Chard were extremely encouraging and supportive at various stages of the book's development. Mary Mulley was especially helpful during the early stages, owing to her insights as a teacher and her unstinting encouragement and enthusiasm. I am indebted to the head of the production team, Sunitha Arun Bhaskar, and Kate Boilard, both project managers at Laserwords, Maine, for their patience and thoroughness. And I want to acknowledge Lily Springer for computer support, Deborah Diffily for inspiration and advice, Irene Mitchell and Husein Ebrahim for their assistance in the collation of reference material, Cartwright (Kelley Carter) for her friendship and abiding love, and my daughter Cecilia for being a constant and unqualified source of joy.

CHAPTER 1

Introduction to Educational Research

Image Source/Getty Images

Educational Research: A Historical Introduction

As a student 200 years ago, you would not have encountered anything like this book. Educational research—the scientific study of educational questions—did not exist yet. Educational practice reflected a mix of common sense and tradition, with guidance from authorities such as Aristotle and the Bible. Education itself was still a rare privilege. Most schooling was private, and less than 1% of Americans received more than 6 years of formal education. Had you been among the lucky few, your experience would be very different from that of a contemporary student. As you learned how to read, for instance, you would have been required to memorize sentences such as "In Adam's fall, We sinned all" and, perhaps of more immediate concern, "The idle Fool is whipt at school" (*New England Primer*, 1777 - see Figure 1.1). There was no research at the time indicating whether rote memorization of these sentences is an effective approach to reading instruction.

The Rise of Educational Research

The development of educational research reflects two interrelated historical changes. First was the growing success of scientific inquiry as a source of knowledge. By the 19th century, scientists had come to assume that questions about the physical world were best answered through direct observation rather than tradition, and rapid progress was being made in the understanding of long-standing theoretical and practical problems. In the second half of the 19th century, progress was also being made in the study of mental phenomena such as learning, memory, and intelligence. Links were forged between these research areas, the study of children, and debates among educators about instructional methods and curriculum. Advances in sociology and cultural anthropology provided new methods for the study of educational issues. In short, both researchers and educators began to assume that scientific research might have something useful to say about classroom practice.

The second historical impetus for educational research was the rise of universal education. The industrial revolution created new technologies, and as its mills and factories spread across the United States and other countries during the late

FIGURE 1.1 Excerpt from *The New England Primer.*

In Adam's fall
We sinned all.

Thy life to mend,
This Book attend.

The Cat doth play,
And after slay.

A Dog will bite
A thief at night.

An Eagle's flight
Is out of sight

The idle Fool
Is whipt at school.

As runs the Glass,
Man's life doth pass.

My Book and Heart
Shall never part.

Job feels the rod,
And blesses God.

Proud Korah's troops
Were swallowed up.

The Lion bold
The lamb doth hold.

The Moon shines bright
In time of night.

18th and 19th centuries, governments began to recognize the need for an educated workforce. In addition, rapid population growth and urbanization reinforced the assumption that social stability would need to be maintained through education and other means. The so-called three R's (reading, 'riting, and 'rithmetic) were increasingly considered important not only for the privileged but for all responsible and productive members of society, and the numbers of children attending school gradually increased. By 1918, every state in America had passed laws requiring all children to attend school for at least several years. Concerns about the quality of education stimulated an interest in assessing the quality of schools and curricula, an interest that would gradually be taken up by researchers.

As education became compulsory and class sizes grew, educators quickly realized that not all children could be educated in the same setting. Students with learning disabilities, emotional problems, and poor self-control were among those who struggled to keep up with their peers. In 1904, the French government asked a group of child psychologists to appoint a commission on the problem of identifying students who could not function in regular classrooms, so that alternative education could be provided. Two members of the commission, Theophilus Simon and Alfred Binet, developed a test that could be used to identify such children. (A contemporary version of Simon and Binet's test, referred to as the Stanford–Binet 5, is still a widely used intelligence test.) Simon and Binet's research, along with the efforts of American colleagues such as Lewis Terman, resulted in the intelligence testing movement. Their work can be counted among the earliest examples of educational research, in the sense that the researchers took a scientific approach to the study and resolution of educational problems.

Legislation and Research: The Contemporary Scene

Since the early 20th century, profound changes have taken place in education and educational research. Educational practice is still based in part on common sense and tradition, but the decisions made by educators are also influenced by research conducted in departments of education, educational psychology, and other disciplines at colleges and universities, and the sheer quantity of research is growing. Educational research is not only a new area of scientific inquiry but an expanding one.

Among the influences on both the quantity and importance of educational research in recent years are growing concerns about the academic achievement of American students. Since the beginning of public education, concerns about achievement have been voiced by parents, educators, researchers, and policymakers. Fueling these concerns have been studies indicating that the American educational system is in trouble and, in the words of the influential report *A Nation at Risk* (1983), threatened by a "rising tide of mediocrity."

The most recent responses to concerns about achievement include federal legislation passed during the first few years of the new millennium. A prominent example of the new legislation is the No Child Left Behind Act, signed into law in 2002. As of this writing, No Child Left Behind (NCLB) requires that states conduct annual testing of student progress in grades 3–8, and at least once in grades 10–12. Through NCLB, federal spending on schools is linked to the results of these new tests. Federal spending is also linked to attempts to improve student progress through instructional and curricular changes that are scientifically based. Through NCLB "federal support is targeted to those educational programs that have been demonstrated to be effective through rigorous scientific research" (U.S. Department of Education, 2003, p. 18).

NCLB, as well as other federal legislation such as the Education Sciences Reform Act (ESRA) of 2002, enables federal funding for research, and offers guidelines as to what "rigorous" scientific research would be. In addition, ESRA provided for the creation of the Institute of Education Sciences, a prominent source of support for educational studies. The goal of the Institute of Education Sciences is "the transformation of education into an evidence-based field in which decision-makers routinely seek out the best available research and data before adopting programs and practices that will affect significant numbers of students" (*www.ed.gov/offices/IES/*).

These are just a few examples of how federal legislation has contributed to an environment in which educational practice is increasingly informed by research (see Spotlight on Research 1.1 for further discussion). It may seem obvious that educational practice should be research based. Just as we want pediatricians to treat our children on the basis of scientific evidence and not merely common sense, so we should want teachers to do the same. The story is not so simple, however, and in Chapter 18 you will read about how the relationship between research and educational practice continues to be a source of uncertainty and debate.

Scientific Knowledge and Values

At the outset of this chapter, I defined educational research as the scientific study of educational questions. But what does it mean for educational questions (or any other questions) to be addressed through "scientific study?" Over the past two millenia there have been many answers to this question, each reflecting a particular **epistemology**, or philosophical assumption about the nature of knowledge, how knowledge is acquired, and what constitute valid sources of knowledge. In the next section of this chapter, traditional approaches to the acquisition of knowledge are reviewed, followed by an introduction to the scientific method, which informs a great deal of contemporary research in education and other fields. Some of the core values that inform scientific practice are then identified. Later in the chapter, a fundamental distinction is made between quantitative and qualitative research, two approaches to scientific study that are grounded in different epistemological assumptions.

Scientific Knowledge

There are many sources of scientific knowledge. Two that have been mentioned already are tradition and authority, which are useful when factual knowledge has been clearly established. Scientists rely on star charts, the periodic table of the elements, and many other definitive sources of knowledge rather than taking time to discover these facts all over again. However, tradition and authority can be problematic when the knowledge they provide is incorrect, or incomplete.

DEDUCTION   Aristotle and other ancient Greek thinkers are considered the first to have systematically described the role of logic in the acquisition of knowledge. In the 4th century B.C., Aristotle introduced the deductive method, or **deduction**,

Politics, Research, and Practice: The Contentious Case of Literacy Instruction Reform

As you will see in Chapter 5, one of the prominent applications of educational research is standardized testing conducted at the state and national levels. Owing to federal legislation such as the No Child Left Behind Act, the extent of standardized testing for basic skills such as literacy has increased in recent years, as have efforts to improve the quality of literacy instruction.

In a 2005 article in *Policy Review**, David Davenport and Jeffery Jones describe how literacy instruction became part of the national political agenda only recently, during the presidencies of Bill Clinton and George W. Bush. Davenport and Jones explain how the politicization of literacy instruction provides a context for debates about the results of educational testing.

Once you begin to quantify a policy matter such as literacy, as is now done through standardized testing, warring camps line up with differing interpretations of the data. This has certainly been the case as literacy has moved onto the political stage, with some arguing that literacy is now a problem of crisis proportions, whereas others read the testing data with less alarm. Further complicating matters, there are now three major reading assessments of school-aged children: the National Assessment of Educational Progress (NAEP), the Program for International Reading Literacy Study (PIRLS), and the Program for International Student Assessment (PISA). NAEP . . . examines reading results on both a national and state basis at different grade levels, providing an opportunity to examine changes in

reading achievement over time. Both PIRLS, which targets fourth-graders, and PISA, which looks at 15-year-olds, provide useful comparisons between U.S. students and their international peers.

One reading of the tests suggests fairly consistent results. Both NAEP and PISA indicate that only three out of 10 U.S. students are proficient readers—that is, they competently read and understand texts. A significant number of children read at a level below basic: 36 percent of fourth-graders, 25 percent of eighth-graders, and 26 percent of twelfth-graders. . . . Internationally, PIRLS and PISA indicate that early on U.S. schoolchildren are near the top in reading achievement compared with students of other countries. But their performance slips significantly between fourth grade and high school, and by age fifteen U.S. students are just average.

From these testing data, a highly influential coalition of politicians, business leaders and conservative academics argues that the U.S. is suffering from a debilitating literacy crisis. Pointing to statistics showing poor overall reading performance, racial disparity, and declining performance relative to international peers, the group pushes for major literacy reform, especially greater accountability and school choice. . . . Another camp, largely supportive of the public school system, believes the rhetoric about a literacy crisis is overblown. . . . Supporters of the present school system examine literacy data over a longer period of time and find test scores mostly flat over the last 30 years. . . . They argue for increased resources and greater investment in teacher training and development.

(continued)

through which specific conclusions are drawn from generalizations. An example of a deductive syllogism would be:

Major Premise: Every kindergarten student is a child.
Minor Premise: Lily is a kindergarten student.
Conclusion: Lily is a child.

The deductive method is useful because it allows conclusions to be drawn from what is already known. As you can see from this example, deduction yields conclusions that are necessarily true, but only if the premises are true. Hence, one limitation of deduction is that the conclusions are only as good as the premises—faulty premises yield faulty conclusions. Another limitation, evident from this example, is that deduction does not expand our knowledge very much.

The debate over whether there is a literacy crisis is further complicated by attacks on the tests themselves. One criticism is that the tests and resulting data are not legitimate because the standard for proficiency can be manipulated up or down, especially in the state testing schemes. The fudging is apparent when state test results are compared to NAEP results for the same state. Other concerns include whether literacy testing encourages gamesmanship, teaching to the test, and outright cheating. Researchers continue to debate the merits of testing, and both Democrats in Washington and state legislators have expressed reservations about participating in the No Child Left Behind programs in part because of concerns about the pervasive testing scheme. . . .

Davenport and Jones argue that further reform of literacy instruction practices is needed, and that any reform should be based on scientific research—a belief that is widely held, though controversial (see Chapter 18 of this book).

The debate over whether test scores indicate a crisis is not terribly useful. Instead, let us agree that where we now stand—regardless of how it compares across the years—is unacceptable. Public policy should bring the communities of interest together to target realistic gains at each level of proficiency. There is ample evidence that the achievement gap is real and must be addressed. The testing process itself can be improved by breaking results down to the state and local levels. . . . Additionally, test results should be packaged so they can give teachers useful information for addressing areas of need.

Reform should continue along the lines of what scientific research shows best teaches children to read. Much work

remains before we can say we have a science of reading development and comprehension. . . . If a teacher's classroom must be based on scientific research, then we must fund the research and train the teachers in what the research shows. As new teaching techniques, curricula, and educational structures are developed, they will help challenge and improve existing methods. After a decent interval, we must test the effectiveness of new federal initiatives such as Reading First in the No Child Left Behind Act.

Only a few years ago, an examination of "the politics of literacy" would have made no sense. Literacy was an educational issue, not a matter of public policy, and any politics that attended the discussion would have been inside the academy. Now both Democrats and Republicans alike have indicated a willingness to federalize literacy policy. . . . Literacy is of fundamental importance, and it seems important to take advantage of this opportunity for some consensus on literacy policy and renewed efforts to improve the ability of our children to read.

Davenport and Jones's article illustrates some of the connections between educational research, instructional practice, and political policy. The results of educational testing have increased concerns in some quarters about the academic preparedness of students, and some educators and policymakers believe that the solution to inadequate preparedness is to link instructional methods more closely to the results of educational studies.

*Davenport, D., & Jones, J. M. (2005, April/May). The politics of literacy. Policy Review, pp. 45–57. Quoted with permission from the publisher.

INDUCTION In the early 16th century, Francis Bacon criticized the use of deduction in science on the grounds that the premises were often erroneous expressions of traditional dogma. Bacon argued that scientists had been "imprisoned in the writings of certain authors," including Aristotle, rather than acquiring knowledge through observation (Bacon, 1620/1963, p. 234). Bacon (1620/1963) developed a new approach to obtaining knowledge that is referred to as **induction**, or the inductive method. Whereas deduction proceeds from general to specific, induction proceeds in the opposite direction from specific to general. For example, from the observation that several infants crawled before beginning to walk, you might conclude through induction that all infants crawl before they walk.

As you can see from this example, induction relies on experience as a source of knowledge. Induction is appealing because the starting point—the premises—consist of observations rather than on assumptions or traditional ideas. Induction is also appealing because the knowledge acquired can extend far beyond prior knowledge. However, assuming that your premises are correct, inductive inferences are not as certain as deductive ones. The fact that many infants crawl before walking suggests but does not prove that they all do. (As it turns out, a small percentage of infants never crawl.) Moreover, induction by itself is not a focused source of knowledge. The same set of observations can lead to many different conclusions, and there is no guarantee that any one conclusion will be more correct or relevant than the others. For example, imagine using a purely inductive method to figure out what "geniuses" have in common. If you begin with no preconceived ideas, but simply observe various geniuses, your conclusion will include the fact that geniuses tend to have two eyes, 10 fingers, and two legs. Nothing about inductive inference per se makes this conclusion less valid than any other you might draw.

In the 19th century, the deductive and inductive methods were first linked and applied to scientific questions through the work of Charles Darwin. Darwin was interested in knowing, among other things, why some kinds of species characteristics are passed from generation to generation, while others disappear. Darwin's first approach to this question was purely inductive, in that he gathered as many facts as he could in hopes that the facts would lead to a general conclusion. As Darwin himself put it, "I worked in true Baconian principles, and without any theory collected facts on a wholesale scale" (1899, p. 68). This approach was not very effective until Darwin developed a hypothesis, based in part on the ideas of another scholar, to account for the facts he was observing. Briefly, Darwin's hypothesis was that characteristics that are more adaptive—that is, more useful to the organism's survival—are more likely to be passed from generation to generation. From this hypothesis, Darwin made deductions that could be tested through further observation. These further observations provided strong inductive support for Darwin's hypothesis, although not the logical certainty of deductive inference.

The Scientific Method

Darwin's combination of deduction and induction illustrates the modern approach to scientific inquiry. The scientist first establishes a hypothesis. The scientist then deduces specific predictions from the hypothesis and tests those predictions through careful observation. Finally, the scientist determines through induction whether the initial hypothesis was supported.

This approach to scientific inquiry has been formalized by John Dewey (1938) and others as the **scientific method**, and in slightly more elaborated form it consists of the following steps:

1. *Identify a question.* Most research studies address a clearly stated, testable question, known as the **research question**. The research question may pertain to the characteristics of some population, such as learners, teachers, or schools. The research question may require a comparison between two or more theories, programs, or groups of people. Whether the research question is motivated by theoretical or practical concerns (or both), the research that is conducted to answer the question is usually also intended to contribute to existing research on a topic.

In a given study, researchers may focus on several research questions, or one complex question. In some cases, the research question is relatively straightforward. In a recent study by Angela Duckworth and Martin Seligman (2006), for example, the researchers focused on the question of why girls tend to make better grades than boys.

2. *Develop a hypothesis.* A **hypothesis** is an informed guess. The hypothesis provides guidance as to the types of observations that should be made, and it can be expressed as predictions about the results of observation. Hypotheses are suggested by theories and/or prior research findings. Prior research tends to provide specific guidance as to what the researcher might expect to find. For example, in the study by Duckworth and Seligman (2006), the researchers hypothesized, on the basis of prior findings, that girls make better grades because they have greater self-discipline than boys do. This was one of several hypotheses explored by the researchers.

3. *Collect and analyze data.* This step begins with systematic observation, the heart of the scientific method. The term "**data**" refers to units of information. Examples of data include a person's height, a set of IQ scores, the numbers of students absent from a particular school in a given month, and the percentages of male elementary school teachers nationwide. Anything that can be measured constitutes data. ("Data" is the plural form of "datum." Although researchers sometimes refer to data in the singular tense [e.g., "the data on this topic is clear"], the correct usage is plural.) Much of this textbook focuses on the collection and analysis of data in educational research.

In the study by Duckworth and Seligman (2006), eighth graders at a large northeastern school were sampled. These data were obtained from measurements of students' self-discipline, IQ and achievement test scores, overall GPA, and final grades in algebra, English, and social studies. Statistical analyses, the focus of Chapters 10 through 12 in this book, were used to identify patterns in the data.

4. *Formulate a conclusion.* The results of data analysis suggest conclusions. Researchers seek conclusions that allow them to evaluate their original hypotheses. Sometimes, data analysis yields pleasant (or unpleasant) surprises that suggest conclusions more or less unrelated to the researcher's original interests. For example, Duckworth and Seligman (2006) found, as predicted, that girls made better grades than boys, girls performed better than boys on a test of academic achievement, girls were more self-disciplined than boys, and differences in self-discipline predicted differences in grades. However, the researchers were also surprised to discover that girls scored lower, on average, than boys on an IQ test. This finding was not consistent with recent research on gender differences.

5. *Evaluate original hypothesis.* Finally, the researcher judges the extent to which the data support the original hypothesis. On the basis of inductive inference, the original hypothesis may be rejected, or the researcher might argue that the results support the hypothesis to a greater or lesser extent. For example, Duckworth and Seligman (2006) concluded that their results strongly support the hypothesis that gender differences in grades are due in part to gender differences in self-discipline. The researchers also noted that one of their measurements of self-discipline did not yield strong effects, and that future studies with a modified version of this measurement could provide further support for their original hypothesis. This is one example of how researchers evaluate a hypothesis in a more subtle way than simply concluding that the hypothesis is "right" or "wrong."

The five steps of the scientific method are summarized in Figure 1.2.

FIGURE 1.2 Steps of the scientific method.

1. Identify a question.
2. Develop a hypothesis.
3. Collect and analyze data.
4. Formulate a conclusion.
5. Evaluate original hypothesis.

Scientific Values

The scientific method is not a "recipe" that researchers use for scientific inquiry. Most researchers would not say that they begin with the first step, and then proceed, one-by-one, through each step until they find themselves evaluating their original hypothesis. Because the actual practice of scientific research tends to be more tentative, repetitive, and messy, the scientific method can be thought of as an ideal that is reflected with more or less clarity in specific research activities. In addition, there is much more to research than the scientific method. Scientific inquiry is based on fundamental assumptions, or values, that inform the way research studies are conducted and interpreted. Six of the more important assumptions that I will discuss here are empiricism, conditionality, precision, parsimony, objectivity, and theoretical motivation. This list is not complete, and the six assumptions overlap somewhat, but it does convey part of the foundation on which science is constructed.

EMPIRICISM   As noted earlier, modern scientific inquiry is based on the assumption that observation is the primary source of knowledge. The idea that knowledge is grounded in observation is referred to as **empiricism**. (The term "empirical" means "based on experience.") This is a very different assumption from that reflected in a 15th century dispute, recounted by Francis Bacon, about the number of teeth in a horse's mouth (Bacon, 1620/1963). For 13 days, a group of friars argued about this topic, each buttressing his argument with complex arguments and references to ancient books. On the 14th day, a young friar suggested that someone open a horse's mouth and take a look. According to Bacon, the friar was attacked, physically and verbally, for his unorthodox method of seeking knowledge, and his colleagues later concluded that since no answer could be found in the historical or theological record, the number of teeth in a horse's mouth would remain an eternal mystery. Whether true or not, Bacon's story reflects something like the opposite of the empirical attitude that characterizes modern science.

CONDITIONALITY   Because observation is the primary source of knowledge, it is always possible that new observations will conflict with existing knowledge. Scientific knowledge is therefore conditional, in the sense of always being open to revision. Of course, not all knowledge seems equally conditional. Knowledge obtained from a descriptive study of first-graders' spelling errors will seem more conditional than, say, the knowledge that Mercury is the planet closest to the sun. However, it is always possible that future research will continue to yield the same results about early spelling errors. At the same time, even the most widely accepted facts may need to be revised. We may always consider Mercury a planet, but the "official" number of planets in our solar system has dropped recently from nine to eight (and, meanwhile, some astronomers raise the possibility of an additional planet beyond the orbit of Pluto).

If all knowledge were considered highly conditional, it would be difficult for scientists to understand the world. Scientists accept key facts as "givens" on which knowledge and theory are constructed, even though in principle all facts are conditional. However, a single research study is rarely considered sufficient to establish a finding as given. The finding must be replicated, or repeatedly observed (preferably by different scientists using somewhat different methods) before it is widely accepted. Researchers thus refer to **replicability** as a prerequisite of knowledge in science.

PRECISION   Scientific research is based on precise measurements, as well as careful use of logic to derive predictions and interpret results. Technical terms are used in order to convey precise meanings. In addition, **operational definitions** may be used for broad concepts such as "intelligence," "motivation," "instructional method," and so on. Defining a concept operationally means defining it in terms of how it is measured. For example, in a particular study, "intelligence" may be operationally defined in terms of scores on a particular IQ test. By using this definition, the researcher ensures that others understand what is meant by "intelligence" in his or her study. Operational definitions are inherently limited, in that they tell us very little about the nature of the concepts measured. A researcher who claims to be studying intelligence, but only says that intelligence is what is measured by a particular IQ test, seems to be side-stepping the question of what intelligence is. However, through this operational definition, the researcher gives us a precise and understandable meaning to work with. We know at least what intelligence means in the context of the researcher's study. As you will see, many debates in science are created or resolved by a careful look at the way broad concepts are operationalized.

Another sense in which precision can be observed in scientific research is through the requirement of **falsifiability**. A good hypothesis will be falsifiable, meaning that it is expressed clearly and specifically enough that we know what kinds of evidence would refute it. It is not falsifiable to simply predict that learning how to read results in larger vocabulary size, because children who are learning how to read will be acquiring new vocabulary anyway from both written texts and verbal interactions. A falsifiable hypothesis would be that children who are better readers at the end of first grade will acquire more vocabulary by the end of second grade than children who are poorer readers. This hypothesis is falsifiable, because the relationship between reading and vocabulary development is expressed clearly enough that we could imagine how to design an experiment that could yield contradictory results.

Because precision is valued, scientific research tends to be highly specialized—a point that I will revisit in Chapters 2 and 18.

PARSIMONY   **Parsimony** refers to simplicity. The desirability of parsimony can be seen when researchers choose the simpler of two explanations for a particular result. Considerations of parsimony also inform research in a more fundamental sense. One of the basic goals of science is to identify the simplest concepts through which the complexity of phenomena can be understood and predicted. This idea is illustrated by research and theory concerning the nature of intelligence. There are thousands of behaviors that could be classified as "intelligent," but most researchers believe that what underlies these behaviors is something between one and nine distinct types of intelligence. Although there are lively debates about the number of "intelligences," the range of possibilities is vastly smaller than the number of intelligent behaviors that can be observed.

OBJECTIVITY   Ideally, researchers do not let personal biases influence their interpretations of research findings. A researcher may be passionately committed to improving instructional methods in computer classes, and the researcher may have strong opinions about which method is preferable, but the researcher should be receptive to results of studies comparing methods, even if the preferred method makes a poor showing. (As you can see, the ideal of objectivity follows from empiricist assumptions.) Although objectivity is a fundamental ideal, it is just that—an ideal. Researchers disagree about the extent to which objectivity is achievable, or even desirable, given the fact that decisions about which topics to research and how to interpret the results will always be influenced by a researcher's background, interests, and values. The role of subjectivity in scientific inquiry is revisited later in this chapter, and in Chapter 13, in the context of qualitative research designs.

THEORETICAL MOTIVATION   Although science is grounded in empirical observation, facts alone are meaningless unless they are organized and interpreted. Ultimately, the goal of science is not mere observation but the creation and refinement of theories. A **theory** is a set of interrelated concepts that are used to explain and make predictions about specific phenomena. A theory provides us with a general explanation of why certain phenomena are the way they are, and it allows us to make predictions about how those phenomena are interrelated, and what will happen to those phenomena under various circumstances. For example, one of the prominent classical theories of learning, known as cognitive social-learning theory, holds that children learn a great deal simply by watching others, interpreting what they see, and then imitating the same behaviors (Bandura, 1965). This is called observational learning, and it helps explain why children acquire the mannerisms, eating habits, and other social behaviors of their parents and other individuals in their culture. Cognitive social-learning theory posits that children acquire both desirable and undesirable behaviors through observation. One set of predictions fostered by the theory is that children can learn aggressive behavior by watching violent role models in real settings, as well as on television and in video games that contain violent content—predictions supported by numerous research studies.

Some theories, like cognitive social-learning theory, are very broad, whereas others are more narrow in focus. Regardless of breadth, theories play a variety of roles in research. They generate hypotheses and predictions. They suggest new areas of research. They provide a basis for integrating existing results. And they provide frameworks in which new results can be interpreted.

The scientific values discussed in this section are summarized in Table 1.1.

The Purpose of Studying Educational Research

Why study educational research? In other words, why do the faculty at your college or university require you to take an educational research course? Here are two answers to the question.

TABLE 1.1 Fundamental Scientific Values

Value	Brief Definition
Empiricism	Scientific knowledge should be grounded in observation.
Conditionality	Scientific knowledge should remain open to revision.
Precision	Scientific research should be based on precise measurements, hypotheses, operational definitions, and inferences.
Parsimony	Scientific explanations should be as simple as possible.
Objectivity	Interpretations of research should not reflect personal biases.
Theoretical motivation	The goals of research should include the creation, refinement, and evaluation of theories.

First, educational research now has a substantial impact on educational policy, administration, and practice. We have come a long way from colonial times, when teachers needed no particular qualifications, and children were taught to read by means of the New England Primer and its cheerful rhymes ("Time cuts down all, Both great and small"). Currently, most researchers and many practitioners assume that research has at least something of value to contribute to educational practice. The influence of research on practice is relatively direct when research reports are studied and put to use by teachers, counselors, principals, writers of curricular materials, local and national policymakers, and so on. By studying educational research, you will acquire a better understanding of why things are the way they are in our educational system—and how they might be improved. Educational research has something to say about students, families, teachers, instructional materials, programs, schools, and administrators. The focus of the research ranges from highly specific processes in the brains of individual students to international trends in school administration. Although educational practice has never been influenced by research to the extent that some feel that it should be (see discussion of the research–practice gap in Chapter 18), the extent of influence is growing as a result of recent social and political trends.

A second reason for studying educational research is the less direct but nonetheless important influence of the media and other indirect sources of information about research. Educational practice and research are frequently discussed in both print and electronic formats, and these discussions impact parents, policymakers, and educators in numerous ways. A grasp of the basic principles of educational research will help you understand where media reports come from, and how they should be evaluated. In addition, as discussed in Chapter 3, there are numerous sources of information about educational research that fall somewhere between the scientific publications written by researchers and popular media reports. For example, on the day I drafted this paragraph, the Internet website *insidehighered.com* posted a story on the growing trend for colleges and universities to make SAT and ACT scores optional rather than mandatory for undergraduate applicants. This story contained the following statement:

> *Mount Holyoke, which dropped the SAT in 2001, is wrapping up one of the most extensive studies done of such a shift—a research effort financed by the Andrew W. Mellon Foundation. [Jane] Brown, who is leading the study, said that "each year of data confirms the trend: We are able to make very good admissions decisions without the use of standardized tests." By all measures of academic performance, she said, high school grades and courses selected are sufficient to predict who will succeed and who won't.*
>
> *(www.insidehighered.com/news/2006/05/26/sat)*

After studying educational research, you will be able to answer many of the questions a passage like this one might raise. For example, in what sense might a study be "extensive?" What are foundations, and what does it mean for one of them to "finance" a study? How can grades and coursework, or anything else, "predict" success? What criterion is used to determine that the capacity for predicting success is "sufficient?" What does existing research actually suggest about how well SAT scores predict later success, and where can these research studies be found?

Types of Educational Research

In the inaugural edition of the *Journal of Educational Psychology*, the editors observed that "educational practice is still very largely based on opinion and hypothesis, and thus it will continue until competent workers in large number are enlisted in the application of the experimental method to educational problems" (1910, p. 2). In the century since that observation was made, large numbers of researchers have studied educational problems. Differing theoretical perspectives and goals have led to the creation of different types of educational research, and the evaluation of any give study is influenced in part by the type of research it represents. Many different types of research can be identified, depending on whether we are considering the purpose of the study or the types of methods used.

Basic Versus Applied Research

First, if we consider the immediate purpose of a study, a distinction can be made between basic and applied research. The purpose of **basic research** (also called "pure" or "fundamental" research) is to acquire concrete knowledge, and ultimately to contribute to theory. Although the knowledge gained through basic research may have practical benefits at some point in the future, the most immediate goal of the research is knowledge rather than practical application. Examples of basic research questions include:

- How does attention span change during early childhood?
- What is the relationship between gender and self-esteem?
- Why do many autistic children have difficulty making eye contact?
- Which countries have the most rigorous high school science and math curricula?

Through basic research on these and other topics, educational researchers are able to provide descriptions and explanations that build on existing knowledge.

In contrast to basic research, **applied research** focuses on questions of immediate practical interest. Most educational research studies are applied, in that they address topics of practical importance in education, such as developing better instructional methods, learning how to increase student motivation, documenting problematic attitudes and behaviors, assessing student learning, evaluating educational programs, and so on. (Since it is often possible to glean information from basic research and apply it to educational problems, the distinction between basic and applied research should not be considered clear-cut.) Two of the major types of applied research—action research and program evaluation—are discussed in Chapters 16 and 17. Examples of applied research questions include:

- How can first-graders' reading comprehension be improved?
- Does a particular intervention program reduce absenteeism and delinquency?
- When does a particular student give up when solving difficult math problems?
- Do teachers prefer pay raises to be accompanied by additional responsibilities?

Through applied research on these and other topics, educational researchers are able to directly address issues of relevance in the classroom and in other educational settings.

Quantitative Versus Qualitative Research

Along with considerations of purpose, educational research can be distinguished by its epistemological and methodological assumptions. Throughout this book you will encounter many distinctions between quantitative and qualitative research.

Quantitative Research

Quantitative research is based on numerical data. In quantitative research, the information obtained is numerical, or converted to numerical form, and then analyzed. The scientific method is used, in the sense that research questions are posed, hypotheses are formulated to guide the collection of data, and conclusions are drawn from data analysis. The immediate purpose of quantitative research may be basic or applied.

Four different types of quantitative research can be identified on the basis of how variables are treated. A **variable** is any dimension on which different values can be measured. Age, gender, intelligence, grade point average, and the number of A students in a particular class are all examples of variables. Research studies generally focus on more than one variable, but what constitutes a variable will vary from study to study. For example, studies have shown that attention span increases from ages 4 to 7, and that at any age girls have better attention spans than boys. In these studies, gender and age are the main variables. However, other studies have looked at gender differences in attentional skills among 4-year-olds. In these studies, gender is a variable, but age is not. Age may vary in the "real world," but in a study of 4-year-olds it is not a variable because the focus is on only one age group.

In this section, the four types of quantitative research that I will discuss are experimental, causal–comparative, correlational, and descriptive.

EXPERIMENTAL RESEARCH   In the quantitative approaches known as **experimental research**, one or more variables are manipulated, and their effects on other variables are measured. The variables that are manipulated are called **independent variables**, while the variables that may be affected are called **dependent variables**. For example, a common approach to the study of reading instruction is to randomly assign elementary school students to one of several instructional groups. Suppose that for an entire semester, Group A is instructed as they normally would be, while Group B is instructed by means of a new method designed by the researcher. Imagine too that the reading comprehension of each group is measured at the beginning and end of the semester. In a study such as this, the independent variable is the instructional method, and the dependent variable is reading comprehension score. The researcher would be interested in the extent to which reading scores are differentially affected by the instructional method used with Group B. Some other examples of independent and dependent variables are given in Table 1.2.

Experimental studies are characterized by the control that researchers have over independent variables and other aspects of the research. In the previous example, the researcher would carefully choose who participates in each group, and then

TABLE 1.2 Examples of Independent and Dependent Variables

Study Description	Independent Variable(s)	Dependent Variables(s)
Half of the incoming freshmen at a university participate in a new alcohol awareness program during orientation. The other half participate in an older alcohol awareness program at the same time. Drinking behavior of all students is surveyed at the end of the year.	Type of program	Drinking behavior
Two months into the semester, 25 students taking algebra in high school are asked to visit a math skills-building website. Another 27 algebra students from the same high school are asked to read a pamphlet that offers tips on building math skills. A third group of 22 students is asked to watch a short video designed to build math skills. Understanding of math concepts among all three groups is measured by means of the MCT, a test developed by the researchers and administered at the beginning and the end of the semester. Student interest in the extra instructional materials is also gauged at the end of the semester by means of a survey that the researchers call the MCIS.	Type of extra instruction	MCT results MCIS results
Teachers in each of three school districts participate in either a 1-day or a 5-day in-service program. This results in six groups of teachers (i.e., one group of teachers in each school district participates in the 1-day in-service program, and one group participates in the 5-day program). The attitudes of all six groups toward in-service training are measured before and after their participation in one of the programs.	School district Length of program	Teacher attitudes

attempt to ensure that the only difference between the groups pertains to the instructional methods used to teach reading. This careful manipulation of variables would allow the researcher to demonstrate a cause–effect relationship between instructional method and reading scores. If the students in Group B tended to improve more on the test of reading than Group A students, and the only difference between the groups was in the instructional methods they received, the researchers could conclude that Group B's greater improvement in test scores was caused by the intervention they received. As discussed in Chapter 7, experimental research is highly respected for its potential to demonstrate cause-effect relationships. Spotlight on Research 1.2 provides a closer look at one such study.

CAUSAL–COMPARATIVE RESEARCH   A second type of quantitative research is known as **causal–comparative research** (or "ex post facto" research). Causal–comparative studies are like experimental studies, except that the researcher does not manipulate independent variables. Rather, the effects of naturally occurring differences in variables are studied. For example, in a study on gender differences in spatial skills, the researchers would compare the spatial skills of boys and girls, but,

Does Training in Self-Regulated Learning Help Students Learn from Hypermedia?: An Example of Experimental Research

Hypermedia environments such as websites have great potential as learning tools. Owing to the variety of text, pictures, videos, and other resources embedded in these environments, students often find them more engaging than traditional, linear sources such as textbooks. Hypermedia information is readily available, and users have substantial control over the flow of information. Unfortunately, a number of studies suggest that students working on their own with hypermedia do not acquire a deep conceptual understanding of their topic. Commentators often point out that the strengths of hypermedia environments—including nonlinearity and user control over information—also undermine their effectiveness as educational tools.

In a 2004 article in the *Journal of Educational Psychology**, Roger Azevedo and Jennifer Crowley examined whether college students would benefit more from hypermedia-based learning if they are trained first in self-regulated learning strategies. Using an experimental design, the researchers looked at how well non-biology majors could learn about the human circulatory system given 45 minutes to study the encyclopedia portion of the Microsoft Encarta Reference Suite 2000 hypermedia environment.

In Azvedo and Crowley's study, 63 undergraduates were assigned to an experimental condition in which they were taught strategies for self-regulated learning (SRL). An additional 68 undergraduates participated in a control condition. Students took a pretest prior to participating in each condition.

There were four parts to the pretest: (a) a sheet on which students were asked to match 16 words with their corresponding definitions related to the circulatory system (matching); (b) a color picture of the heart on which students were asked to label 20 components (labeling); (c) an outline of the human body on which students were asked to draw the path of blood throughout the body, ensuring that the path included the heart, lungs, brain, feet, and hands (flow); and (d) another

sheet which contained the instruction "Please write down everything you can about the circulatory system. Make sure you learn about the different parts and their purpose, how they work both individually and together, and how they support the human body" (essay).

Following the pretest, each student participated in an experimental or a control condition. The experimental condition lasted 30 minutes and focused on teaching students to consciously use self-regulatory strategies such as planning their learning goals, monitoring the progress of their learning, and deploying effective learning strategies:

Prior to the experiment, we designed a four-page script for the SRL training condition. It contained a table showing phases and areas of SRL, a diagram illustrating a simplified model of SRL, and a table with a list of SRL variables. . . . Subsequently, students were given a general learning goal and were allowed to generate their own learning goals during learning. . . .

The SRL variables include planning (planning, subgoals, prior knowledge activation), monitoring (feeling of knowing, judgment of learning, self-questioning, content evaluation, identifying the adequacy of information), strategies (selecting new informational source, summarization, rereading, and knowledge elaboration), task difficulty and demands (time and effort planning, task difficulty, and control of context), and interest. . . .

In the control condition, students were merely introduced to the task. Both experimental and control group participants were given the same general learning goal:

Your task is to learn all you can about the circulatory system in 45 minutes. Make sure you learn about the different parts and their purpose, how they work both individually and together, and how they support the human body. We ask you to "think aloud" continuously while you use the hypermedia environment to learn about the circulatory system . . .

as you know, the researcher could not assign children to different genders. Other variables that cannot be manipulated by the researcher include grade, ethnicity, birth order, school district, and so on. (Although the fact that a variable cannot be manipulated means that it does not fit the strict definition of an independent variable, the results section of causal–comparative studies sometimes include references to

Finally, each group took a posttest, which consisted of exactly the same questions as the pretest. Data analysis focused on two questions: (1) Did the experimental group acquire a more sophisticated mental model of the circulatory system than the control group did? and (2) How did SRL training affect the experimental group's ability to regulate their hypermedia learning?

With respect to the first question, Azvedo and Crowley found that from pretest to posttest, the experimental group showed significantly more improvement than the control group did in their mental models of the circulatory system, as reflected in the flow diagrams and essays. The researchers also found that while both groups improved from pretest to posttest on the matching and labeling tasks, the extent of improvement for labeling was significantly greater among the experimental group (32.6% vs. 19.3%).

With respect to the second question, Azvedo and Crowley found that compared to the control group, a significantly larger number of students in the experimental group used planning strategies, monitored their learning, and engaged in learning strategies such as drawing, taking notes, and coordinating sources. In other respects too, the experimental group showed more self-regulated learning at posttest.

In Azvedo and Crowley's terms, the experimental group benefited from SRL training owing to an increased focus on their own goals, plans, strategies, and specific progress. In contrast, the control group was more externally focused on qualities of the hypermedia environment:

In our study, allowing students to use hypermedia without SRL training led to them attempting to regulate their learning by using inefficient planning activities (e.g., recycling goals in their memory), monitoring the content of the hypermedia system . . . using a variety of inefficient strategies to learn about the circulatory system (e.g., engaging in free search), and handling task difficulties and demands by focusing on features of the hypermedia environment to enhance the reading and viewing of information. That is, poor learners were externally focused, as opposed to self-regulating

learners, who monitored their own cognitive systems and their progress toward goals.

Based on their results, Azvedo and Crowley noted several implications for educational usage of hypermedia:

One direct application of these results would be for teachers to train their students to regulate their learning with hypermedia by using our SRL script. By doing this, they might facilitate their students' learning of complex science topics when hypermedia environments are used in the classroom or at home for researching topics for school assignments.

A second application would be for instructional designers to incorporate specific embedded scaffolds in hypermedia environments designed to foster students' conceptual understanding of complex topics. The hypermedia environment could present several questions (similar to our pretest measures) at the onset of the learning task to measure students' current understanding and to activate any prior knowledge. This type of testing would need to be repeated during the learning task to continually monitor students' understanding and to periodically activate their prior knowledge. A planning net could be included to allow students to plan their learning activities by accessing . . . learning goals and corresponding instructional hypermedia material. During learning, students would be able to access the two lists and compare them with their current goal(s). As for monitoring, the system could encourage a student to engage in two specific monitoring activities (i.e., feeling of knowing and judging their learning) related to knowledge and monitoring progress toward goals. A more demanding challenge would be to have the hypermedia environment facilitate a student's SRL by monitoring his or her progress toward goals.

In sum, the use of an experimental design allowed Azvedo and Crowley to directly demonstrate the effectiveness of a brief instructional intervention designed to improve self-regulated learning strategies.

*Azvedo, R., & Cromley, J. G. (2004). Does training on self-regulated learning facilitate students' learning with hypermedia? Journal of Educational Psychology, 96(3), 523–535. Quoted with permission from the American Psychological Association.

independent and dependent variables, in order to indicate the causal relationship being studied. A comparison of boys' and girls' spatial skills in which gender is treated as the independent variable is based on the assumption that being male or female may impact performance on the dependent measure [i.e., a particular test of spatial skills].)

As discussed in Chapter 9, causal–comparative research is a common approach, because there are many comparisons of interest between preexisting groups. However, the convenience of causal–comparative research is balanced by the possibility of preexisting differences between the groups that limit what we can conclude from the results. Imagine, for example, that you want to know whether students in the urban high schools of a particular state are more likely to apply to vocational colleges than their peers in rural high schools. Any differences between the two geographic groups (urban vs. rural) may be attributable to differences in affluence, access to vocational colleges, advice from counselors, educational levels of parents, and so on. Geography, in short, may not be the only difference between the two groups, and so the possibility of inferring causality is somewhat limited. Casual–comparative researchers attempt to overcome such limitations through their approaches to sampling (Chapter 4) and/or statistical analysis (Chapter 11).

CORRELATIONAL RESEARCH   A third type of quantitative approach, known as **correlational research**, explores the relationship between variables. Two variables may have a positive or a negative relationship. This is referred to as the direction of the relationship between variables. A positive correlation indicates that as the values of one variable increase, the values of the other variable tend to increase as well. For example, Byrnes (2003) found that the number of math classes that high school seniors had taken was positively correlated with the seniors' grades on a math test (i.e., the more classes the seniors had taken, the higher their grades on the test). Two variables may also have a negative relationship, meaning that as the values of one variable increase, the values of the other variable tend to decrease. Byrnes found that the extent to which students agreed with the statement "Math is mostly memorizing facts" was negatively correlated with grades on a math test (i.e., the more that a student agreed with this statement, the lower the student's test score tended to be). Finally, correlational studies may show that two variables have no relationship at all. Byrnes found that the extent to which seniors agreed with the statement "Math is useful for solving everyday problems" was unrelated to their scores on the math test.

Correlational research not only indicates the direction of the relationship between variables, but also the strength of that relationship. For example, Byrnes (2003) found that the extent to which seniors agreed with the statement "I like math" was positively correlated with their scores on the math test, but that the number of algebra courses that seniors took was more strongly correlated with their scores on the test. As discussed in Chapters 9 and 10, the strength of the relationship between correlated variables is expressed mathematically.

A key difference between experimental and correlational research is that correlational studies are not designed to reveal cause–effect relationships. You may have heard the phrase "correlation does not equal causation," or some equivalent thereof. The meaning of the phrase is that establishing a correlation between two variables does not allow us to conclude that one variable casually influences the other one. Correlational studies have shown that academic achievement is positively related to high self-esteem. One interpretation of this result is that higher achievement leads students to have more positive feelings about themselves. An alternative interpretation is that having positive feelings about themselves helps students achieve more. (Yet another possibility is that there is some third variable, such as emotional closeness with parents, that is responsible for both high self-esteem and high academic achievement.) In Byrnes (2003), the positive correlation between math scores and agreement with the statement "I like math" could result from the fact that the better students are at math, the more they like it. Alternatively, the positive correlation could result from the fact that the more students like math, the more diligently they study the subject.

DESCRIPTIVE RESEARCH   **Descriptive research** reflects the fourth type of quantitative approach. As the name suggests, descriptive studies provide numerical characterizations of phenomena, often on the basis of surveys. Some of the earliest examples of educational research, arising from the child-study movement of the late 19th century, consisted of descriptive studies on children's knowledge and interests (e.g., Hall, 1883), and this approach continues to maintain a significant presence in the field.

Although purely descriptive studies provide no direct information about either causal or correlational relationships between variables, these studies can provide useful insights into peoples' attitudes, beliefs, intentions, and actual behaviors. For example, much has been learned about the prevalence of bullying from studies on the various forms of victimization experienced by students. Moreover, the results of some descriptive studies do at least point to associations between variables that merit further study through experimental, causal–comparative, or correlational methods, as when it was noticed that bullying tends to be more prevalent in certain schools and among certain groups. Descriptive studies, and other types of nonexperimental quantitative research, are discussed further in Chapter 9.

The differences in how variables are treated in each of the four types of quantitative research described here are summarized in Table 1.3.

Quantitative versus Qualitative Epistemologies

Although quantitative, qualitative, and mixed-methods studies have been conducted on educational topics since the early 20th century, the distinction between quantitative and qualitative approaches has been discussed (and debated) most openly over the past few decades.

Philosophically, quantitative and qualitative research are grounded in somewhat different epistemological assumptions. Quantitative research tends to reflect **positivism**, the assumption that reality consists of facts and causal processes that are independent of observers and thus can be revealed through scientific observation. For example, positivism is reflected in descriptive studies of motivation in which surveys are administered to students in order to measure, in numerical terms, the extent of their motivation for academic achievement in specific subjects. The positivist assumption here is that each individual's motivation exists prior to

TABLE 1.3 Treatment of Variables in Each Type of Quantitative Research

Type of Quantitative Research	Treatment of Variables
Experimental	Independent variable is manipulated. Effects on dependent variable are measured.
Causal–comparative	Effects of naturally occurring differences in the independent variable are measured.
Correlational	Extent of association between two or more variables is quantified.
Descriptive	Quantitative information about variables is measured.

administration of the survey, and will be knowable insofar as the survey is well designed.

Qualitative research tends to reflect **constructivism**, the assumption that realities are constructed by individuals rather than objectively observed. Researchers are individuals too, of course, and so just as participants in their studies construct particular views of reality, so the researchers must in turn reconstruct the participants' views. Indeed, reconstructing the perspectives and meanings that individuals create is the fundamental goal of qualitative research, and in doing so researchers may acknowledge their own subjective contributions to the process. For example, a qualitative approach to the study of motivation might consist of a narrative description of the experiences of two inner-city students during their first month in a new high school, with emphasis on their beliefs about the importance of academic success, their interests in succeeding in particular classes, and their emotional ups and downs during the week. The constructivist assumption here is that the motivational states of the students must be constructed through a subjective process of interviewing each student, encouraging them to reflect on their experiences, and creating a narrative that may be influenced by the researcher's own values and assumptions pertaining to inner-city high schools. The process of reconstructing the students' motivational states is inherently fallible, according to a constructivist view, whereas the positivist view would hold that any fallibility would reflect limitations in the specific way that motivation is measured and the data are analyzed.

Qualitative Research

Qualitative research, as the name suggests, is based on nonquantitative methods and assumptions. The information obtained from qualitative studies is not expressed in numerical terms, but rather in the nonmathematical terms and concepts of social science. Qualitative studies can be described as more or less **phenomenological**, a philosophical term indicating a focus on subjective experience. The goal of the research tends to be holistic, in the sense of attempting to provide comprehensive descriptions of peoples' experiences and the meanings they construct from interactions with other people and things in their environments. In order to create these in-depth descriptions, qualitative studies are often based on multiple methods.

There are many ways to classify the different approaches to qualitative research. In this section you will read about two approaches to the study of individuals in natural settings (ethnographic research and case studies) followed by two approaches that focus on documents and other materials (content analysis and historical research).

ETHNOGRAPHIES AND CASE STUDIES   **Ethnographic research**, based on methods developed by cultural anthropologists, consists of attempts to describe cultural or social groups. An ethnographic study is based on extensive fieldwork in which the researcher converses with group members at length, and perhaps also lives and works among them, in order to acquire as much information as possible through various methods. The goal of ethnographic research is to reconstruct, in extensive detail, the behaviors, worldviews, and subjective experiences of people in a group, and to describe the group in a way that reflects their cultural context. The resulting description—called an "ethnography"—is expressed in narrative as opposed to quantitative terms. The focus of an ethnography tends to be holistic, rather than restricted to a few details. Typically, the ethnography acknowledges the researcher's impact on the group during the process of observation, and considers the ways that the researcher's own cultural background may influence his or her observations of the group. In a **realist ethnography**, the researcher attempts to be as impartial as possible in describing the group, while in a **critical ethnography** the researcher both describes and advocates for the group rather than trying to minimize the impact of his or her own values on the research process.

Although some ethnographies pertain to other societies, the group under study is often a subculture within the researcher's own society. There is substantial ethnographic research focusing on the educational experiences of different groups in the United States. For example, in one study on preadolescents' experiences with racism, the site director at an after-school program observed eight African American, Asian, and Latina children interacting with peers, tutors, mentors, and staff over a period of 1 year (Masko, 2005). The director also interviewed children individually and in groups, and collected samples of their drawings and writings. The results were presented narratively, with extensive quotations from the children, and the researcher also attempted to classify different responses to racist episodes. One of the main findings was that although the children frequently reported racist acts to teachers and administrators, the adults were not very supportive. Often, the adults ignored the racist acts, or counseled the children to ignore them.

In contrast to ethnographies, **case studies** focus more directly on individuals. The "individuals" may be people, programs, or institutions—anything that can be treated as a single unit (Merriman, 1998). Although quantitative methods are sometimes used, case studies tend to be qualitative in focus. For example, Choi and Park (2006) documented the experiences of a college instructor who was in the midst of teaching an online course for the first time. The instructor's activities were observed on five separate occasions, and interviews were conducted with the instructor, her teaching assistant, one of her students, and a professional colleague. Choi and Park found that the instructor's experience was more negative than positive, in that she experienced a heavy workload, some degree of student apathy, and difficulty multitasking during synchronous online teaching sessions.

CONTENT ANALYSIS AND HISTORICAL RESEARCH   Ethnographies and case studies, the focus of Chapter 13, tend to be grounded in observations of and interactions with people in natural settings. Other types of qualitative research are based on written records and other materials. **Content analysis** focuses on the interpretation of materials such as textbooks, films, diaries, e-mails, and blogs, while **historical research** relies on such materials as well as interviews in order to describe and interpret past events. These two qualitative approaches are the focus of Chapter 14.

Content analysis, which is also known as document analysis, constitutes an important part of the qualitative study described in Spotlight on Research 1.3.

Other Types of Research

Along with the quantitative and qualitative approaches described above, I discuss three additional types of educational research in this book: mixed-methods research, action research, and program evaluation.

MIXED-METHODS RESEARCH   Chapter 15 focuses on **mixed-methods re-search**, an increasingly common, labor-intensive approach in which quantitative and qualitative methods are combined in a single study. Depending on the relative importance of each method, three kinds of mixed-methods research can be distinguished. In a **triangulation design**, qualitative and quantitative data

Helping Models and Referrals: A Qualitative Research Study

Teachers refer students to school counselors for a number of reasons. In a qualitative study reported in *Professional School Counseling* in 2000*, Shelley Jackson explored how the tendency to make referrals is influenced by the assumptions that teachers make about the helping relationship that should exist between counselor and student. Based on prior work, Jackson referred to these assumptions as "models," and contrasted four different models that teachers have about the responsibilities of helpers (i.e., counselors) and the students they help. As you will see, each of the four models—moral, compensatory, medical, and enlightenment—reflects a different philosophical perspective on people.

The first model of helping is described as the moral model. In the moral model, people are responsible for creating and solving their problems. The process of helping in the moral model involves reminding people that they are responsible for their own fate, and that it is important for them to take responsibility for themselves. School counseling interventions would stress student empowerment but the child would be blamed for causing the problem.

The second approach is the compensatory model. In the compensatory model, people are not responsible for creating their problems, but they are responsible for solving their problems. Helpers in this model see themselves as compensating for resources or opportunities that the recipients of the help deserve but somehow do not have. Advocacy would be stressed in school counseling interventions in addition to student empowerment.

In the medical model, people are not responsible for creating their problems nor are they responsible for solving their problems. The helper is viewed as an expert who has been trained to recognize what the problem is and then to provide appropriate treatment and service. A medical model would support and perpetuate students' weaknesses and promote the counselors' expertise.

In the enlightenment model . . . people are responsible for creating their problems, but they are not responsible for solving their problems. Helpers are seen as stern or sympathetic

disciplinarians who seek to correct a problem that the individual has created. Students remain powerless over their own problems in this model of helping while the school counselor assumes a powerful authoritarian role . . .

Jackson studied the counseling referrals at an elementary school in a large, southeastern U.S. city. Most of the 430 students at the school are African American, Hispanic/Latino, or European American, and virtually all come from low-income families.

A sample of 313 referral documents was selected for this study. Seven years ago the counselor developed an individual counseling referral form to be used by teachers and parents to request counseling for individual children. . . . For this study, 190 of these forms were randomly selected from the primary researcher's collection. In addition, the counselor also received requests for counseling that were not on the formal request for individual counseling form. In order to add depth to this study, the researchers also examined 123 of these additional informal requests.

In addition to document analysis, two focus group interviews were held with 10 elementary school teachers. . . . The first interview explored (a) the participants' personal experiences with counseling referrals including their expectations of the counselor; (b) the problems that students have that they do or do not refer to the counselor; and (c) their descriptions of a typical counseling referral. During the second interview, teachers helped the researcher to confirm and better understand what was discussed in the first interview or areas of interest that were discovered during the examination of the referral forms to the school counselor. The purpose of the second interview was also to discuss the impact of the interview process on the participants and the researcher. Each interview was approximately one hour long. . . .

Through the process of document analysis, Jackson found that referrals reflected the medical model more frequently than the other three models.

Sixty-one (45%) of the referral documents indicated the medical model, in which both problems and solutions to problems are attributed to others. For example:

collection take place simultaneously. In an **explanatory design**, quantitative data are collected first and play a more central role, while in an **exploratory design** qualitative information is gathered first and then predominates in analysis and

Formal Referral 96. *"Amy is currently seeing an outside counselor but mother feels she would benefit from seeing you as well. She has been to a variety of schools."*

Here, the referral agent assumes that the child is neither responsible for her problem (*"she has been to a variety of schools"*), nor is she responsible for the solution to the problem (*"she would benefit from seeing you"*).

Forty-three (31%) of the referrals indicated the enlightenment model in which problems are attributed to the child and solutions to problems are attributed to others. For example:

Formal Referral 41. *"Jeff needs counseling because he is uncooperative and sometimes appears socially maladjusted."*

In this example the referral agent assumes that the child is responsible for the problem (*"he is uncooperative"*), and the solution to his problem is attributed to others (*"Jeff needs counseling"*).

Twenty-three (17%) of the referrals indicated the moral model in which problems and solutions are attributed to the child. For example:

Formal Referral 122. *"Ricky never accepts fault for his actions. It is always someone else. Would it be possible for you to meet with Ricky to discuss alternatives to hurting others?"*

The referral agent, in this instance, assumes that the child is responsible for both the problem (*"Ricky never accepts fault for his actions"*), and the solution (he needs to *"discuss alternatives to hurting others"*).

Finally, 10 referrals (7%) indicated the compensatory model (i.e., problems are attributed to others and solutions are attributed to the child). For example:

Formal Referral 162. *"Please talk to Andrew to make sure he knows what to do in the afternoons when he is by himself so that he is safe. His mother works until 6 P.M."*

Here the referral agent assumes that the child is not responsible for his problems (*"His mother works until 6 P.M."*), but he is responsible for the solution to the problem (*"make sure he knows what to do in the afternoons when he is by himself so that he is safe"*) . . .

The medical model was also apparent in the first group interview. The participants were asked to talk about their expectations when they referred a child to counseling.

Researcher: *"So, What are your expectations when you refer someone?"*

Teacher 1: *"The counselor should heal all pain in the world."*

Although this comment generated a lot of laughter, it illustrates the assumption that the counselor is viewed as an expert who has been trained to solve problems. The responsibility for prescribing the solution and for judging whether it has been successful rests with the expert (Brickman et al., 1982). Marilyn, one of the teachers, goes on to describe a situation in which she felt the counselor did *"fix"* the problem:

Teacher 2: *"In my case, I referred someone for hygiene problems, you fixed . . . well you didn't fix it everyday (laughs), but . . . you talked to somebody else who went out to the family and talked to the family and told them this is what you need to do, otherwise the kid is going to be made fun of everyday because she doesn't bathe, she needs to bathe and, so you, I mean you took it further . . . you fixed it."*

These comments illustrate the assumptions of the medical model; that is, the child is not responsible for the solution to the problem. Instead, the counselor is called in to remedy the situation. . . .

Jackson concluded that both document analysis and group interviews revealed the prevalence of the medical model. Building on prior work, Jackson noted that one problem with the medical model is that it fosters dependency in helpees, because it presents them as ill and in need of help from a responsible expert. Jackson presented a number of suggestions to promote more helpful assumptions and practices among teachers and counselors.

*Jackson, S. A. (2000). Referrals to the school counselor: A qualitative study. *Professional School Counseling, 3*(4), 277–287. Quoted with permission from the American School Counselor Association.

interpretation. Regardless of the particular design, the purpose of conducting mixed-methods research is to take advantage of the respective strengths of each approach—the numerical precision of quantitative methods and the narrative richness of qualitative methods—and to use the results of one method to corroborate or extend the results obtained by the other.

ACTION RESEARCH   Chapter 16 concerns **action research**, an applied approach in which practitioners conduct studies in their own educational settings and make immediate use of the results. There are two main types of action research: The goal of **participatory action research** is to empower individuals who have been exploited or marginalized, in part by actively involving these individuals in researching the challenges they experience; the goal of **practical action research** is for the practitioner to create improvements in his or her immediate educational setting. Often the practitioners are teachers attempting to address an educational problem in their own classrooms, such as poor motivation or difficulties with challenging material.

Action research tends to be iterative, in the sense that practitioners identify problems, make changes, reflect on the results of those changes, make further changes, and so on, in a cyclical process. As one researcher put it, in describing practical action research:

> *Action research differs from other types of educational research in that it is carried out in the context of an ongoing class. The researcher is the classroom teacher, who may have no opportunity to set up true experiments. . . . In action research, the cycle of curriculum innovation is iterative and may never be complete. . . . Action research requires that teachers . . . consciously analyze results with the intention of making adjustments as the course proceeds.*

> *(Clement, 2004, pp. 343–344)*

PROGRAM EVALUATION   Finally, Chapter 17 focuses on **program evaluation**, an applied approach to judging the merit and effectiveness of educational programs. Program evaluation is often quantitative but may be carried out through qualitative, mixed-methods, or action research designs. Historically, program evaluation was motivated by a desire to judge the effectiveness of school-based reforms, but it is now used in a variety of educational settings.

Broadly, two types of program evaluation can be distinguished: **Formative evaluation** takes place as programs are being developed, whereas **summative evaluation** is carried out on existing programs. Formative and summative evaluations may focus on one aspect of a program (e.g., the written materials used in a bully prevention program), the entire program, or a set of programs implemented on a large scale. In each case, the goal of the evaluation is not just to understand the program but to arrive at a judgment about its merit and effectiveness. Merit and effectiveness are judged in many ways. Summative evaluation of a school-wide intervention program designed to prevent bullying, for example, might focus on one or more of the following questions:

- How closely are the materials used in the program aligned with recommendations made by national organizations such as the National Association of School Psychologists?
- How much did students enjoy and learn from the program?
- How much did the incidence of bullying at the school change following implementation of the program?
- What additional personnel, resources, and procedural changes would the program need to achieve its stated goals?

TABLE 1.4 Major Approaches to Educational Research

Approach	Examples
Quantitative	Experimental, Causal–comparative, Correlational, Descriptive
Qualitative	Ethnography, Case study, Content analysis, Historical
Mixed-methods	Explanatory, Exploratory, Triangulation
Action research	Participatory, Practical
Program evaluation	Formative, Summative

- What is the ratio between the cost of the program (in terms of time and resources required for implementation) and its effectiveness (e.g., the extent to which it fosters a decline in bullying)?

A Caveat

You have now read about several different types of educational research (as summarized in Table 1.4). These are perhaps better described as different approaches to research. Some studies are based on more than one approach, while others are difficult to classify. For example, just as ethnographies sometimes focus on individuals, case studies may consist of ethnographic descriptions of an individual group. In such instances, there may not be a sharp distinction between ethnographic and case study research. More broadly, in the interest of doing better science, researchers often use methods that incorporate elements of other approaches without relying heavily on the methods and assumptions of those approaches. Quantitative laboratory studies may include collection of qualitative data, only some of which is converted to quantitative form for analysis. Ethnographies sometimes include quantitative information, information obtained from documents, and so on. The boundary between a qualitative study that incorporates some quantitative data collection (or vice versa) and a true mixed-methods study may be difficult to discern. In short, Table 1.4 is meant to provide you with an introduction to different approaches to educational research rather than a definitive typology.

A Look Ahead

This book provides an introduction to the principles and practice of educational research. The title of the book, *Educational Research: A Contextual Approach*, reflects the fact that some attention is paid to the contexts in which educational research takes place. You have already read a little bit about the historical and political contexts that gave rise to educational research. The specific concepts and methods of educational research have their own particular histories as well, some of which you will read about in later chapters.

Closely related to the historical background for educational research is the scientific subculture in which it is carried out. This subculture is distinguished by some of the assumptions and values you read about in this chapter. In Chapters 2 and 3, I provide more information about the subculture of science and its conventions for obtaining and disseminating knowledge.

Educational researchers, like other scientists, are part of a broader culture in which the links between research findings and classroom practice are complicated and diverse. In some cases, teachers, administrators, and policymakers are influenced by research reports created by educational researchers themselves. In other cases, educators are influenced by summaries of research, or by media reports, which vary in their degree of accuracy. Individual teachers and administrators may institute changes on the basis of what they have learned. As you will see in Chapter 16, individual teachers sometimes conduct action research and put the results to immediate use. At the same time, school boards, state legislatures, and other policymaking bodies may institute widespread changes on the basis of research findings. Finally, keep in mind that the relationship between educational research and educational practice is not unidirectional. Just as research influences practice, so the interests and challenges facing practitioners influence the kinds of research that are conducted. These are just a few general illustrations of the idea that educational research takes place in a historical, cultural, and political context. These ideas will be taken up more specifically at various points in each of the subsequent chapters and revisited at length in the final chapter.

Applications: A Guide for Beginning Researchers

Here are some ideas from the chapter that will help you plan your research:

- There are many different approaches to conducting research. One decision you will be making is whether to adopt a quantitative, qualitative, or mixed-methods approach.
- Most quantitative approaches, and some qualitative approaches, call for you to have an impartial, objective attitude toward the research topic.
- Most quantitative approaches, and some qualitative approaches, are based on clearly stated, falsifiable hypotheses and precise measurements. You will need to operationally define the key variables that interest you.
- Regardless of what approach you take, your research activities will be grounded in observation.

Chapter Summary

Educational research originated in the 19th century amid increasing confidence in science as well as concerns about academic achievement. Federal legislation such as the No Child Left Behind Act has had a powerful influence on contemporary educational research.

Scientific knowledge about education is acquired through deduction, induction, and the application of the scientific method. Educational research is informed by key assumptions, including empiricism, conditionality, precision, parsimony, objectivity, and theoretical motivation.

The purpose of studying educational research is to better understand how research has influenced—and can influence—educational practice, both directly and indirectly.

Distinctions can be made between basic and applied research, and between quantitative and qualitative research, which are grounded in different epistemologies. The major approaches to quantitative research are experimental, causal–comparative, correlational, and descriptive, while the major qualitative approaches include ethnographies, case studies, content analyses, and historical research. Also discussed in this book are mixed-methods approaches, action research, and program evaluation.

Key Terms

Epistemology	Quantitative research	Case studies
Deduction	Variable	Content analysis
Induction	Experimental research	Historical research
Scientific method	Independent variables	Mixed-methods research
Research question	Dependent variables	Triangulation design
Hypothesis	Causal-comparative research	Explanatory design
Data	Correlational research	Exploratory design
Empiricism	Descriptive research	Action research
Replicability	Positivism	Participatory action research
Operational definitions	Constructivism	Practical action research
Falsifiability	Qualitative research	Program evaluation
Parsimony	Phenomenological	Formative evaluation
Theory	Ethnographic research	Summative evaluation
Basic research	Realist ethnography	
Applied research	Critical ethnography	

Exercises

1. Which of the following most clearly reflects an operational definition for test anxiety?

a) A researcher observes that ninth graders in her study experienced a great deal of anxiety before an algebra test.

b) A researcher states that in his study, the extent of test anxiety will be predictable based on information about students' prior academic performance.

c) A researcher asserts that test anxiety in her study will be measured by State scores on the State–Trait Anxiety Inventory.

d) A researcher claims that in a particular study, sixth graders were clearly more anxious than fifth graders before their first science test.

2. "Experienced teachers who transfer to a new school district will experience changes in the learning environments they encounter." What is the main problem with this hypothesis?

a) It is not sensible.

b) It is not objective.

c) It is not empirical.

d) It is not falsifiable.

3. A researcher randomly selects a group of third graders for participation in an environmental awareness program. Later, this group's knowledge of environmental issues is compared to that of a group of third graders who did not participate in the program. What type of research design does this description imply?

a) Experimental

b) Causal–comparative

c) Correlational

d) Ethnographic

4. Which of the following sounds like an ethnographic research study?

a) "The researchers looked at gender differences in scores on a standardized test of mathematics achievement administered to three different primary schools in England."

b) "The researchers calculated the relationship between the number of years an individual had served as principal of a school and the overall extent of teacher satisfaction expressed on a survey."

c) "The researchers described the experiences of immigrants from Southeast Asia who had been enrolled in ESL classes at a local community center."

d) "The researchers documented the number of education classes taken for elective credit by athletes versus nonathletes at a large state university."

For questions 5–6, refer to the description below:

> *Eight- and ten-year-olds listened to a series of short stories that either did or did not contain inconsistencies, and then indicated after each story whether it was easy to understand or they had some problem understanding it. . . . Some of the students . . . received brief examples of how to detect inconsistencies. . . . Other students did not receive these examples.*
>
> *(Mayer, 2003, pp. 105–106)*

5. If the only hypothesis of the study was that 10-year-olds would be better than 8-year-olds at detecting inconsistencies, what type of research would the study represent?

a) Experimental

b) Causal–comparative

c) Correlational

d) Ethnographic

6. In this study, which of the following does *not* appear to be an independent variable?

a) The age of the students

b) Story content (consistent vs. inconsistent)

c) Support for students (examples provided vs. no examples)

d) Detection of inconsistencies

7. *Critical thinking question:* Why do you suppose researchers might disagree about how to operationally define concepts such as "gifted," "learning disability," and so on?

Answers to Exercises

1. c   **2.** d   **3.** a   **4.** c   **5.** b   **6.** d

7. *Possible answer*: Concepts such as "gifted" cannot be defined as objectively as characteristics such as age, gender, or class ranking. However, when exploring what criteria to use for giftedness, or studying individuals who have been labeled as gifted, researchers must be concrete and specific about what they mean by these terms. Through operationalization, researchers define giftedness in terms of meeting certain criteria, such as minimum scores on particular tests. Researchers may disagree with each others' operational definitions, because concepts such as "giftedness" mean different things to different people. Each researcher has his or her own sense of what the concept means, based on personal experience as well as knowledge of prior research and theory on the concept.

Suggestions for Further Reading

Research Article: Allan, E. J., & Madden, M. (2006). Chilly classrooms for female undergraduate students: A question of method? *Journal of Higher Education*, 77(4), 684–711.

This mixed-methods study distinguishes clearly between the quantitative and qualitative methods that are used, and the methods themselves are described in relatively accessible terms.

Application Article: Duncan, T., Kemple, K., & Smith, T. (2000, Summer). Reinforcement in developmentally appropriate early childhood classrooms. *Childhood Education*, pp. 194–199.

This narrative report describes some of the concrete ways that classroom management strategies are influenced by prior research and theory.

Extension Article: Schaefer, S. A. (2001). *Understanding research: Top ten tips for advocates and policymakers*. Washington, DC: National Association of Child Advocates.

This narrative report provides an accessible introduction to evaluating research, and covers material discussed in Chapter 1 as well as in later chapters.

CHAPTER 2

Research Topics

Thomas Barwick/Getty Images

After studying this chapter, you will be able to answer the following questions:

- What are the major sources of research topics?

- What is a literature review?

- Where can research reports be found?

- How are specific research questions formulated?

This chapter will prepare you to do the following:

- Identify a research topic

- Conduct a literature review

- Develop a research question

Introduction

Research begins with the choice of a topic to investigate. Although the late George Carlin suggested many interesting topics (a few of which are quoted above), researchers are typically more discerning in what they choose to study. For an experienced scientist, the choice may be relatively easy. The quantitative researcher who has developed curricular materials for first-year algebra may choose to expand these materials for use in more advanced algebra classes. The qualitative researcher who has written an ethnography about the effects of immigration on local schools may begin a case study of one particular teacher. The action researcher who has modified her writing instruction for third-graders might try out the same modification with her second-grade class. When a researcher has published numerous, thematically related studies on a particular topic, the research is described as "programmatic," and reference is made to the individual's **research program**.

Well-developed research programs provide a steady supply of topics for future study. At the other end of the spectrum, the student who has never conducted research before may find it daunting to choose a topic. There are so many potential topics and methods. Searches of library or Internet sources reveal a seemingly endless succession of studies, and the focus of each study seems narrow—perhaps much narrower than the student's initial interest. When students explore published research for the first time, they often describe feeling lost, confused, or unable to link their particular interests to what has already been studied.

This chapter focuses on the process by which research topics are chosen and refined. It is both a description of what experienced researchers actually do, as well as a guide to what you can do in order to select a topic.

Areas, Topics, Questions, and Hypotheses

If we were to ask an educational researcher what she plans to study next, we might receive one of the following answers:

- "Reading comprehension"
- "How to improve the reading comprehension of struggling readers."
- "The effects of a new direct instruction intervention on the oral reading comprehension of first- and second-graders identified as poor readers."

All three answers may be accurate, but they differ in specificity. The first answer identifies an area (or "field") of research. The second answer describes a topic of study within that area. The third answer describes the topic more specifically, and constitutes a **research question**. (As noted in Chapter 1, a research question is a clearly stated, testable question, usually focusing on relationships between variables.)

Although the boundaries between research "areas," "topics," and "questions" are not clear-cut, these categories can be related hierarchically: Within a given area of research, there are many different topics, and under the heading of each topic there are many different research questions. Most of this chapter focuses on the selection of a research topic. The first section of the chapter describes the various sources from which topics are drawn. The second section describes the role of the literature review as a way of both selecting and refining a topic, a process that ultimately results in the creation of research questions. The final section offers some guidelines for how research questions can be developed and evaluated.

When prompted to tell us more about her work, our fictional researcher might go on to say: "I hypothesize that my direct instruction intervention will benefit oral reading comprehension, but the benefits will be greater among first-graders than among second-graders." As noted in Chapter 1, a hypothesis is an informed guess about the results of a study—it is a prediction, in other words, about the answer to the research question. Hypotheses typically embody predictions about relationships between variables. For example, our researcher has expressed a hypothesis concerning three variables: the effects of (1) a particular intervention on (2) oral reading comprehension, and how the strength of those effects will be influenced by (3) students' grade in school. Both the number of variables and the number of hypotheses vary from study to study. Some hypotheses are deduced from prior theory or empirical findings, while others represent an inductive leap. What all good hypotheses have in common is that they are clearly stated, testable, and informed by prior research and/or theory (as opposed to being purely speculative).

In the preceding example, the researcher stated a hypothesis prior to the collection of data that will be used to evaluate the hypothesis. This is a typical approach in quantitative research (see Chapter 1 for discussion of the quantitative–qualitative distinction). In a qualitative study, the researcher may allow hypotheses to emerge as the study progresses, rather than specifying them in advance. Although the qualitative researcher begins with a **focus of inquiry**, or general topic of interest, the process by which research questions and hypotheses are formulated tends be more or less inductive, in the sense of being constructed as data are gathered As Bogdan and Biklen (2007) put it in their advice to a qualitative researcher: "You are not putting together a puzzle whose picture you already know. You are constructing a picture that takes shape as you collect and examine the parts" (p. 6).

Further information on qualitative hypotheses is given in Chapter 13, while a discussion of hypothesis testing in quantitative research can be found in Chapter 7.

Sources of Research Topics

Although educational research tends to have an applied focus, many educational studies reflect a combination of theoretical, empirical, and practical interests. In the following section I discuss six sources of research topics: theory, informed opinion, prior research, practical concerns, policy, and, finally, curiosity and chance. Keep in mind as you read this section that any given study will probably be motivated by more than one source.

Theory

As noted in Chapter 1, a theory is a set of interrelated concepts that are used to explain and make predictions about specific phenomena. Theories vary in scope (i.e., in the breadth of phenomena they account for). The broadest theoretical formulations may stimulate a variety of research over time and across areas. Well-known examples include Jean Piaget's theory of cognitive development, Albert Bandura's social learning theory, and the sociocultural theory of learning developed by Lev Vygotsky in the late 1920s and early 1930s, which continues to influence both quantitative and qualitative studies of teacher–student interactions, reciprocal teaching, cooperative learning, and related topics.

Other theories foster a variety of research through their focus on more specific phenomena. A classic example is Robert Rosenthal and Lenore Jacobs's (1968) theory of "Pygmalion effects" in education. Rosenthal and Jacobs proposed that over time, a student's academic performance may become increasingly consistent with his or her teacher's expectations. According to the theory, teacher expectations function as self-fulfilling prophecies: A student who is expected to succeed will show gains in achievement, while a student who is expected to do poorly will make less progress. Over the past four decades, educational research has documented the existence of Pygmalion effects, described the conditions under which these effects are more or less likely, and evaluated models of why these effects occur (e.g., Brophy, 1983; Jussim, Smith, Madon, & Palumbo, 1998; Rosenthal, 1974, 2003).

Finally, some theories are developed to account for highly specific phenomena and are thus quite narrow both in scope and in the research they foster. An example would be the proposal that phonological processing is "modular," or independent of higher-order cognitive skills such as intelligence (Stanovich, 1988). This is a highly specific "microtheory," in the sense that it focuses on one specific cognitive process and its independence from other cognitive skills. We can deduce from this theory the prediction that variability in phonological processing skills across individuals should be generally unrelated to variability in intelligence. (A number of studies have indeed supported this prediction; e.g., Siegel, 1988.)

THEORETICAL PERSPECTIVES   A good theory generates clear, testable predictions, and a close connection can be observed between the theory and the studies it gives rise to. However, some studies can be said to reflect theoretical assumptions rather than explicitly testing predictions from the theory. In such cases, the studies are informed in a broader way by a theoretical perspective that suggests the kinds of research questions worth studying, as well as the methodological approaches that would be most suitable. This type of broader influence is illustrated by research on emergent literacy. The phrase "emergent literacy" refers to the development of literacy prior to formal instruction (Sulzby & Teale, 1991; Whitehurst & Lonigan, 1998). In contrast to older views, the emergent literacy perspective assumes that prereading activities and interests are part of a continuum that eventually includes mature reading. When prereaders retell familiar stories, for example, or pick up books and pretend to read each page, they are not just having fun but also practicing important skills that contribute to the further development of literacy. This assumption gives rise to research questions such as how early reading skills are influenced by interest in books, spontaneous retells, and concepts of print (e.g., the fact that printed text consists of words arranged from left to right and top to bottom). Prior to the development of the emergent literacy perspective, researchers rarely considered such questions worthy of study, because it was assumed that most prereading behaviors are not relevant to the effectiveness of reading instruction. The emergent literacy perspective thus guides research in both general and specific ways.

The relationship between theory and research is never static. Over time theories inform research questions, and the results of research studies lead to the refinement or rejection of existing theories as well as the formulation of new ones. In qualitative research, the interplay between theory and research may be ongoing within a single study. The **grounded theory** approach was developed as an alternative to the standard method of conducting research in which preexisting theories are tested. In grounded theory studies, theories are not developed prior to data collection. Rather, the researcher attempts to set aside any preconceived ideas so that theoretical explanations can be constructed from the ground up, so to speak, as data are collected (Glaser & Strauss, 1967; see Chapter 13, this volume, for further details).

Informed Opinion

Some studies are motivated by ideas, speculations, or hunches that stem from prior experience. These "informed opinions" may be held by the researchers themselves, or they may reflect the thinking of teachers or some other group who play a central role in the educational process. Although philosophers of science have articulated numerous distinctions between scientific theory and informed opinion, there is not always a consensus as to where the boundaries exist in actual practice. This point is illustrated by reactions to Howard Gardner's widely known theory of multiple intelligences, or MI theory, which holds that there are at least eight distinct types of intelligence. Supporters of MI theory consider it an innovative, if not revolutionary theoretical perspective, while detractors have described it as a poorly substantiated theory and, in some cases, not a theory at all but an assemblage of interesting ideas and opinions. Regardless of how it is characterized, MI theory has stimulated a variety of research since Gardner's earliest formulation in 1983, including the development of assessments to measure various types of intelligence, the evaluation of curricula intended to serve students who show strengths in particular intelligences, case studies of individuals who excel in one particular intelligence, and explorations of additional intelligences. MI theory has also given rise to numerous studies and research-based commentary criticizing the various claims of the theory (see, e.g., an exchange between Gardner and critics in the Fall 2006 issue of *Educational Psychologist*, as well as the 2006 book *Howard Gardner Under Fire*).

In qualitative research, the investigator's opinions may provide a starting point for research, but they are considered a potential impediment to progress. Recall from Chapter 1 that qualitative studies such as ethnographies are intended to reconstruct the beliefs and perspectives of people in their particular cultural contexts. In the process of doing so, qualitative researchers attempt to acknowledge and then look beyond their own assumptions, values, and opinions. In contrast to the quantitative researcher who may test an informed opinion, qualitative researchers try to keep their opinions, informed or otherwise, from interfering with their appreciation of other perspectives.

Prior Research

Just as it is rare for someone to participate in a conversation without acknowledging what has previously been said, so virtually all scientific studies are connected in specific ways to prior research. This section describes how new studies can replicate earlier ones, address disagreements, fill gaps, introduce new distinctions, and integrate prior theory and/or findings.

REPLICATION RESEARCH   In the simplest case, the goal of a study will be to replicate a prior finding. Recall from Chapter 1 that replication is essential to the establishment of scientific knowledge. Researchers may attempt to replicate a new study if the findings contradict or challenge existing beliefs. Classic studies may be replicated in order to determine whether the findings still hold after decades of historical change. Student projects often consist of replications, since retracing someone else's steps is not only easier than designing an original study, but also a desirable hands-on approach for learning how to conduct research. However, published replications are rarely identical to the original studies. Replication studies usually extend prior research through the use of new methods or different populations. If a new, 50-minute test of verbal intelligence appears to be as reliable and valid as existing tests, a researcher might study whether a 15-minute version of the test could be equally effective. If a bully prevention program has been found to work with sixth through eighth graders, a researcher may examine whether the program is effective with third through fifth graders. Typically, a study will extend prior research in more than one way.

RESEARCH THAT ADDRESSES DISAGREEMENTS   Not all studies that attempt to replicate prior findings actually do so. When findings conflict, as is often the case, researchers conduct new studies in order to decide between divergent findings, or at least shed light on the issues. Spotlight on Research 2.1 introduces a study that addresses conflicting findings with respect to early gender differences in verbal skills.

RESEARCH THAT FILLS GAPS   Some studies are conducted because there is little or no existing research on a particular topic. For example, over 2,000 studies have looked at how undergraduate course evaluations are influenced by characteristics of teachers (e.g., gender, seniority, enthusiasm), characteristics of students (e.g., gender, major expected grades), and the nature of the classes themselves (e.g., size, subject area, level). Building on these studies, Safer, Farmer, Segalla, and Elhoubi (2005) explored one particular variable that had never been considered before—proximity between student and teacher—and found that when other variables are held constant, evaluations are slightly less favorable in classrooms in which students tend to be more physically remote from their teachers.

RESEARCH THAT INTRODUCES DISTINCTIONS   It is common for a study to extend prior research by introducing new distinctions. The results of a study may call for a distinction between subsets of a previously undifferentiated group (e.g., individuals with a disorder such as autism), or a distinction in the way that two or more variables interrelate. For instance, in studies on the relationship between praise and motivation, Dweck and others have shown that praise per se is not helpful in motivating children to attempt challenging tasks (e.g., Dweck & Leggett, 1988). Rather, praise for effort motivates children to do so, while praising children for their intelligence encourages them to choose easier tasks on which they can appear intelligent. Such findings tell us that a distinction is needed between praise for effort versus praise for intelligence when considering what motivates children to perform challenging tasks.

Gender Differences in Literacy: A Case of Conflicting Findings

For many decades, researchers in psychology, education, and related fields have disagreed about whether there are gender differences in early literacy skills. This topic is addressed in a study by Douglas Ready, Laura LoGerfo, David Burkam, and Valerie Lee, published in the *Elementary School Journal* in 2005*.

A substantial body of research has suggested that gender differences are not present in the early grades (e.g., Davies & Brember, 1999; Entwisle, Alexander, & Olson, 1997). In these studies, girls exhibited either no advantage or a slight, essentially trivial edge in literacy over boys. Conversely, numerous studies have claimed that, on average, young girls possess more literacy skills than boys.... Scholars who have reported a female advantage have offered a variety of explanations, ranging from biological differences in cognitive development and physical maturation (Maccoby, 1990) to the disparate cultural expectations placed on males and females (Sommers, 2001). Another popularly accepted explanation—and the focus of this study—is that differences in school behavior explain any gender differences in young children's school performance.

In general, two limitations have hampered previous research on this topic, leading to these contradictory results. First, nationally representative data on young children were unavailable. Instead, most researchers used small, local samples of unknown generalizability. Second, many studies investigating gender differences in early literacy were cross-sectional and rarely accounted for the fact that girls may enter school with stronger literacy skills. . . .

Fortunately, a new longitudinal study with data compiled by the U.S. Department of Education allows researchers to investigate the literacy development of a nationally representative sample of kindergartners. In this study we addressed three important questions: (1) Are there gender differences in literacy skills as children begin their formal schooling? (2) If so, does the gender gap widen during the kindergarten year? and (3) Are any gender differences in literacy learning explained by boys' and girls' classroom behaviors?*

Ready and colleagues observed that research has consistently shown gender differences along five dimensions of school behavior. Compared to kindergarten and first-grade girls, boys of the same age exhibit less positive learning approaches (e.g., persistence), less self-control, less prosocial behavior (e.g., cooperation), more externalizing behaviors (e.g., fighting), and internalizing behaviors such as solitary play that are more likely to be considered problematic by teachers. Prior research suggests that lower achievement among boys is attributable to the relatively high incidence of these problematic behaviors. Ready and colleagues argue that studies should explore the influence of these behaviors on learning skills—the precursors to achievement—rather than on achievement itself.

[G]irls and children with better behavior may enter school with more advanced academic skills. As a result, claims that young boys' lower achievement is due to specific classroom behaviors may be unwarranted. Instead, research should focus on classroom learning and how behavior may influence that learning and not on cross-sectional relations between achievement and behavior. In this study we sought to remedy this problem in the research base.

Ready and colleagues used data on literacy and classroom behavior from 16,833 kindergartners available

(continued)

RESEARCH THAT INTEGRATES Finally, some studies extend prior research by integrating concepts and ideas, and perhaps even developing a new concept. Many of the concepts you may be familiar with through education classes—conservation, learning styles, reinforcement, learned helplessness, and so on—were developed in part on the basis of research evidence. To take an emerging example, Hoy, Tarter, and Hoy (2006) explored the characteristics of schools other than SES that have a direct impact on student achievement. Hoy and colleagues noted that prior research and theory have implicated three characteristics: academic emphasis, collective efficacy (teachers' beliefs that they can positively impact students), and trust in through a Department of Education dataset called the Early Childhood Longitudinal Study, Kindergarten Cohort of 1998–1999 (ECLS-K).

The literacy assessment was designed to measure both basic literacy skills (print familiarity, letter recognition, beginning and ending sounds, rhyming sounds, word recognition) as well as advanced reading comprehension skills (initial understanding, interpretation, personal reflection, and ability to demonstrate a critical stance). . . .

We focused on the same five areas of children's classroom behavior discussed earlier: learning approaches, self-control, interpersonal skills, and external and internal behavior problems. At two points during the school year (fall and spring), ECLS-K teachers were asked to indicate how often individual children exhibited various behaviors on a scale of one (never) to four (very often). . . .

For each behavior, we created a five-level categorical variable that indicated whether a child displayed poor, medium-poor, medium, medium-good, or good behavior in that area.

Ready and colleagues' findings revealed clear answers to their first two research questions:

On average, girls entered kindergarten with better-developed literacy skills. Just over 6 months later, at the time of the spring literacy assessments, the female advantage widened. . . .

In order to address their third research question, Ready and colleagues used statistical analyses to determine how strongly gender and classroom behaviors influenced literacy skills. The researchers found that one set of classroom behaviors, learning approaches, was especially influential, although they also found that this variable did not completely explain the gender gap in literacy skills:

Children's learning approaches (attentiveness, task persistence, eagerness to learn, learning independence, flexibility, and organization) were the most important of the five behaviors considered here. Children with "poor" learning approaches scored on average…lower on the spring literacy test than those with "medium" learning approaches, even after taking into account their literacy achievement in the fall. For children's external and internal problem behaviors, only the presence of "poor" school behaviors was related to literacy learning [and the effects were less than for learning approaches]. . . .

Behaviors that are most directly related to learning best explain gender differences in literacy-skill development during kindergarten. The notion of "boys being boys"—boys' stereotypically rambunctious behavior—as an explanation for this gap is not as important as popularly believed. Our results suggest that kindergarten teachers might best assist boys academically by focusing on their approaches to learning, including their organizational skills and ability to pay attention.

In sum, Ready and colleagues' response to conflicting findings in the literature is that girls do indeed begin kindergarten with more advanced literacy skills, and during the kindergarten year their advantage over boys increases, but this gender difference is largely attributable to a difference in learning approaches.

*Ready, D. D., LoGerfo, L. F., Burkam, D. T., & Lee, V. E. (2005). Explaining girls' advantage in kindergarten literacy learning: Do classroom behaviors make a difference? *Elementary School Journal*, *106*(1), 21–38. Quoted with permission from the University of Chicago Press.

students and parents on the part of teachers. Hoy et al. hypothesized that these three characteristics reflect a single dimension, which they labeled "academic optimism," and that academic optimism directly impacts student achievement. Their results supported these hypotheses, and extended prior research on school achievement and related topics by showing that academic optimism can be considered a distinct variable among the many others that impact achievement.

Practical Concerns

Educational research addresses practical concerns about the quality of schools and educational programs, the preparation and professional well-being of teachers, the effectiveness of instructional methods and materials, and the academic, social, and emotional development of students. A teacher might conduct action research in order to help him improve his instructional approach in a particular class. An educational administrator might choose to evaluate the impact of a state-level policy on teacher training that will be implemented in her particular school. A researcher might decide to begin a case study on the educational experience of her own child as he enters kindergarten.

In the preceding examples, the researchers are motivated by immediate, highly personal concerns. Not all practical concerns are quite so immediate or personal. Educational research is deeply connected to both short- and long-term needs of students, families, teachers, administrators, and community. Some studies focus directly on educational problems (e.g., finding the best way to promote writing skills among high school students), while other studies focus on methodological precursors to the study of educational problems (e.g., determining the best way to evaluate high school students' writing; e.g., Espin, Weissenburger, & Benson, 2004). Some studies take a proactive approach, in the sense of introducing and then evaluating the impact of some intervention or change. Other studies focus on describing the variables that are associated with, or have contributed to, particular experiences. For example, McHatton, Zalaquett, and Cranson-Gingras (2006) examined the characteristics of students from migrant farm families who had overcome various obstacles and successfully enrolled in college. McHatton and colleagues reported that these students were able to achieve postsecondary success through a combination of personal strengths (e.g., self-determination) and encouragement from parents, in spite of the fact that they received little informational support from parents, and almost no support from their high schools.

Policy

Both quantitative and qualitative studies focus on the impact of education-related policies, including those implemented by schools and school districts, as well as local, state, and federal governments. The influential journal *Educational Evaluation and Policy Analysis*, for example, publishes articles on topics ranging from changes in teacher certification to school finance reform to the impact of school drug searches. Policy-oriented studies may examine the effects of specific policies, broad trends, or both. For example, using a content analysis approach (see Chapter 1 for definition), Hiebert (2005) studied the impact of reading reform on the content of first-grade textbooks used in California and Texas. Hiebert found that policy reforms in these two states during the past two decades resulted in first-grade textbooks that differed from older books in ways that both were and were not directly mandated by policy. In accordance with specific reforms, newer textbooks contained a higher proportion of decodable (i.e., phonetically regular) words. However, one change not directly mandated by policy was that the textbooks became more difficult, in the sense of containing a higher percentage of new words, as well as less repetition of these words. In discussing the results, Hiebert traced changes in the content of first-grade textbooks to state-level policy reforms as well as broader national trends.

In Spotlight on Research 2.2, some of the relationships between federal legislation, research, and efforts to achieve equal educational opportunity are described in the context of an influential study known as the Coleman Report.

Curiosity and Chance

Given that research is time-consuming and, in the case of educational research, motivated by practical concerns, it is not surprising that researchers tend to choose topics of interest to them. Although the curiosity that drives the choice of topics tends to be informed by some combination of prior research, theory, and

Equal Educational Opportunity: The Coleman Report and the Role of Educational Research

The interplay between research, policy, and educational practice can be seen in efforts to understand and address the negative effects of segregation in American public schools.

In 1954, the Supreme Court ruled in *Brown v. Board of Education* that separate educational facilities for blacks are "inherently unequal" and damaging to black students, and that mandatory segregation of American schools is unconstitutional. The *Brown* decision was based in part on testimony from Kenneth Clark and other social scientists, who cited research attesting to the harmful effects of segregation. Although some of these studies have been criticized on methodological grounds, scholars have pointed out that since the *Brown* decision, educational research has played an increasingly influential role in legislative and judicial debates about equal opportunity in education. This change is attributable in part to increasing receptivity among the judiciary to scientific research. In the Civil Rights Act of 1964, for example, a call was made for a survey "concerning the lack of availability of equal educational opportunity by reason of race, color, religion, or national origin in pubic educational institutions at all levels" (Title IV). The immediate consequence of this part of the Civil Rights Act was a congressional mandate that such a survey be completed within 2 years. A large-scale survey, known as the Coleman Report, was carried out by James Coleman and Ernest Campbell. The results of their work, although not without critics, fostered additional research on the causes and effects of unequal opportunity in education, and influenced educational policy and legal decisions over the next several decades.

In a 2004 article in the *Peabody Journal of Education**, Kenneth Wong and Anna Nicotera point out that the Coleman Report "not only reshaped the way in which social scientists design and conduct research but it transformed how educators think about the purpose of education and significantly informed the policy arena" (p. 126). Regarding the influence on research, Wong and Nicotera note that Coleman and Campbell's research was innovative in several ways, including its focus on distinguishing schools not just by facilities and other resources, but also by student achievement:

The Coleman report was monumental in terms of its research design. The sample included around 600,000 students, 60,000 teachers, and 3,100 schools across the nation, which was the second largest social science research project ever conducted in the United States. . . .

The research design and analytical strategies of the Coleman report allowed Coleman to ask new research questions regarding the nature of equal educational opportunities. In a 1983 interview, Coleman stated

Ordinarily, quality of schools had been defined in terms of inputs to the schools [e.g., facilities]. We asked about outputs, using achievement outputs as criteria for judging the relative quality of schools. . . .

Although the validity of the methods used in the Coleman report have been critically analyzed by social scientists (Hanushek & Kain, 1972; Heckman & Neal, 1996),

practical considerations, the influence of seemingly random influences should also be acknowledged.

Although quantitative research methods tend to be less spontaneous and flexible than qualitative methods, the history of science is filled with important discoveries made while quantitative researchers were studying a different topic. Ivan Pavlov, for instance, was a physiologist who won the Nobel Prize in 1904 for his research on digestive processes in dogs. While conducting this research, which required the collection of saliva, Pavlov noticed that some of his dogs began to salivate even before being fed (e.g., when an assistant merely approached with a container of meat powder). Based on such observations, Pavlov began a new line of research and developed the theory of learning known as classical conditioning. Although Pavlov's discovery is sometimes described as accidental, this portrayal fails to acknowledge *the research question posed by Coleman went nearer to replicating the intentions of Brown by going beyond assumptions that increases in school resources, such as separate but equal facilities, would improve educational opportunities. Rather, the Coleman report was designed to systematically measure the types of inputs that impact educational outputs.*

Wong and Nicotera point out that the two major findings of the Coleman Report were surprising to education researchers and had a significant impact in both the educational and legal systems:

The Coleman report found two significant results that changed the notion of equal educational opportunities and consequently impacted the interpretation of the Brown ruling.... First, the Coleman report found that school resources, including school facilities, curriculum, and teacher quality, do not show statistically significant effects on student achievement. Second, the most significant effect on student achievement was the background characteristics of other students....

Though Coleman clearly establishes the general insignificance of school resources, the caveat to the research is that among the school resources that do show a slight relationship to student achievement, such as science laboratories, the variations in the facilities of Black students did create differences in student achievement. The Coleman report claimed, "Again, it is for majority whites that the variations make the least difference; for minorities, they make somewhat more difference" (Coleman et al., 1966, p. 22). The Coleman report may not have found statistically significant school effects on student achievement. Nevertheless, the findings suggest school resources have differential impacts on White and Black students.

In terms of the effects of teacher characteristics ... teachers' family education, teachers' own education, and teachers' score on a vocabulary test show a weak impact on student academic achievement. Overall, the Coleman report found that differences in teacher quality have a cumulative effect on student achievement over the years and those differences influence the academic achievement of disadvantaged minority groups more than the achievement of White students....

Although the Coleman report found a relationship between...teacher quality...and student academic achievement, the second major finding of the report was that the background characteristics of students in the school have a larger statistically significant effect on student achievement.... This second finding indicates that the social composition of schools is critical to providing equal educational opportunities, which validates the Brown ruling for desegregation of public schools. Furthermore, the Coleman report makes clear that the social composition of a school impacts student achievement through the student body's educational background and aspirations rather than the racial composition....

Wong and Nicotera observe that the Coleman Report, and the testimony of James Coleman himself, influenced a number of subsequent legal cases, and helped strengthen the legal grounds for busing. They note too that although *Brown v. Board of Education* has experienced significant legal setbacks in recent years, the legacy of the Coleman Report includes a closer relationship between education-related research and educational policy.

*Wong, K. K., & Nicotera, A. C. (2004). Brown v. Board of Education and the Coleman Report: Social science research and the debate on educational equality. Peabody Journal of Education, 79(2), 122–135. Quoted with permission from the publisher.

that Pavlov himself had to notice the association between fluctuations in salivary output and changes in the dogs' immediate environment. As Louis Pasteur put it, "chance favors the prepared mind." The simultaneous contributions of informed opinion, curiosity, and chance are illustrated by one of the earliest explorations of the neurological basis of dyslexia. The story begins with the brain of an individual with dyslexia who had died in the 1970s. The brain had been preserved in a laboratory for several years when Albert Galaburda, a neuroscientist who had not been studying dyslexics, obtained access to it in 1978 and tested a simple hypothesis suggested by one of his colleagues. The hypothesis was that dyslexics have less brain tissue devoted to language than nondyslexics, and yet there will be no differences between the two groups in the amount of brain tissue devoted to other skills. Galaburda's case study did not support this hypothesis. Instead, he was

TABLE 2.1 Sources of Research Topics

Theory
Informed opinion
Prior research
Practical questions
Policy
Curiosity and chance

surprised to find something else distinctive about the dyslexic individual's brain: certain brain cells in the cortex (the outermost surface of the brain) were out of place. This observation fostered a substantial number of studies, continuing through the present, exploring the possibility that dyslexia is associated with an abnormality in the migration of certain brain cells to their proper locations during early development.

The sources of research topics discussed in this section are listed in Table 2.1.

The Literature Review

This discussion thus far was informative, you might be thinking, but where do I start? What specific steps should I take in formulating a research topic? It should be clear now that besides thinking about the topics that might interest you, you should look at what researchers have already done. In some cases, the researchers themselves suggest topics for research. In books, book chapters, reviews, and discussion sections of articles, limitations in existing research are often acknowledged, and suggestions for future research are sketched in. In other cases, it is up to you to review existing research and determine what should be done next. Even if your interests are motivated by practical concerns, policy, and/or curiosity, you will need to study existing research on your topic. This part of the chapter focuses on both how and where to look for published research.

Scientists often refer to the "literature" on some topic, as in the literature on phonics instruction, the literature on gender differences in self-esteem, or the literature on factors that influence absenteeism among high school students. A **literature** consists of research and theory that address a particular topic. The studies that make up a literature refer to each other, and a historical progression can be seen as each new study attempts to qualify or extend its predecessors. A study may address a debate, test a theory, provide new knowledge, or contribute to practice, but whatever it does, it will relate to some literature or literatures in a specific way. Thus, before designing a study, researchers conduct a **literature review** in order to find out exactly what has been studied and proposed with respect to a topic of interest. The literature review helps researchers accomplish several important goals:

- To avoid needless repetition of well-established findings
- To identify issues that are in need of further study
- To refine connections between planned and existing research
- To obtain guidance as to the methods that are most (and least) suitable for studying particular topics

Although the selection of a research topic may take place prior to the literature review, the latter process is necessary in order to refine the topic. In quantitative research, the literature review typically takes place prior to the collection of data. Qualitative researchers, in contrast, may consider it desirable to avoid plans and preconceived notions at the outset of a research project, so that they can discover through the study itself what questions and issues are most germane. Ultimately, qualitative studies include literature reviews and research questions, but in a way that is integrated with rather than antecedent to the research process.

A Terminological Note

The phrase "literature review" is commonly used in reference to both a process and a product. Throughout most of this chapter, the term refers to the process of reviewing, evaluating, and synthesizing prior research. In Chapter 3, I use the term in reference to the product—the part of a scholarly publication in which prior research on a topic is reviewed. Put simply, a literature review (in the sense of a published product) is the outcome of many hours spent conducting a literature review (in the sense of the process discussed in this chapter).

Primary and Secondary Sources

Each publication identified in a literature review can be classified as a primary or a secondary source. A **primary source** is a firsthand report created by the individuals who actually conducted the research. Because this textbook is mainly concerned with educational research (as opposed to educational theory, practice, or policy), most of the primary sources I discuss are research studies. However, theoretical papers, school district reports, and summaries of federally funded research also constitute primary sources, and in ethnographies and other forms of qualitative research, primary sources include interviews, cultural artifacts, political documents, and so on.

Primary sources of research studies include monographs, books, and professional journals. As discussed later, peer-reviewed professional journals are the most primary of primary sources, in the sense that journals often contain the first authoritative reports of original research. Table 2.2 lists some of the influential journals in which educational research can be found.

TABLE 2.2 Examples of Peer-Reviewed Journals in which Educational Research is Reported

American Educational Research Journal	*Journal of Adolescent Research*	*Psychological Bulletin*
Anthropology and Education	*Journal of Contemporary Ethnography*	*Psychological Review*
Applied Measurement in Education	*Journal of Educational and Behavioral*	*Qualitative Family Research*
Child Development	*Statistics*	*Qualitative Research*
Educational Administration Quarterly	*Journal of Educational Measurement*	*Reading Research Quarterly*
Educational and Psychological Measurement	*Journal of Educational Psychology*	*Research in Higher Education*
Educational Evaluation and Policy	*Journal of Experimental Education*	*Research Quarterly for*
Analysis	*Journal of Research in Music Education*	*Exercise and Sport*
Harvard Educational Review	*Journal of Research in Science Teaching*	*Sociology of Education*
Intl. Journal of Qualitative Studies in	*Journal of School Psychology*	*Theory and Research in Social*
Education	*Learning and Instruction*	*Education*

Although research topics are very specific and the studies that compose a literature may be tightly connected, the research reflecting a particular literature will not usually be found in just one or two journals, but rather in many. Each researcher may have his or her own preferred outlet for publication, and most researchers also hope to reach the broadest possible audience. To revisit an earlier example, if you were interested in research on early reading comprehension, you would find studies in journals that span a broad range of fields such as developmental psychology (e.g., *Child Development*), educational psychology (e.g., *Journal of Educational Psychology*), school psychology (e.g., *Journal of School Psychology*), and education (e.g., *American Educational Research Journal*). You would also find research in specialist journals focusing on your age group of interest (e.g., *Early Childhood Research Quarterly*), on the specific topic of literacy (e.g., *Reading Research Quarterly*), and on issues of interest to particular audiences such as practitioners (e.g., *The Reading Teacher*). As you focused your research questions, you might find additional studies in these as well as more specialized journals. For example, if you became interested in how to help students with significant problems in reading comprehension, you might consult journals such as *Annals of Dyslexia*.

A **secondary source**, as the name suggests, provides a secondhand description of a primary source. The secondary source might be quite technical and published in a review written for researchers. It might consist of a long abstract printed separately from the original publication. Or, it might be written in lay terms and published in a magazine or newsletter intended for teachers. Regardless of format, the secondary source reduces longer, more complex primary sources into a simpler form, and often provides commentaries on primary sources. In these characteristics you can see both the strengths and the weaknesses of the secondary source. The simplifying, time-saving quality of secondary sources is useful, especially to teachers and other professionals with highly practical interests. At the same time, secondary sources may oversimplify results and contain misleading commentary.

Secondary sources can be especially helpful as you search for a research topic and attempt to identify the key primary sources in a literature. Review articles are published in numerous journals, and some journals, most notably *Review of Educational Research*, are restricted to reviews. Annual reviews of the literature, such as *Review of Research in Education*, are useful, as are handbooks that are printed every several years, as well as encyclopedias such as the American Educational Research Association's *Encyclopedia of Educational Research*, or the *Encyclopedia of Special Education*. Finally, the *Mental Measurements Yearbooks* is one of the many secondary sources that provide lists and critical reviews of measurements used for research in social science and education. These and other examples of recent secondary sources are listed in Table 2.3. (This list is meant to provide you with a few examples rather than being comprehensive.)

The Meta-Analysis

A relatively new type of study that blurs the distinction between primary and secondary sources is the **meta-analysis**, a statistical summary of quantitative research on a topic. Meta-analysis is an alternative to the narrative evaluation, in which a set of studies is analyzed and evaluated qualitatively. Narrative evaluation—the approach to reviewing material that you have been familiar with since elementary school—is now, and will probably always be, the most common type of literature review. However, an obvious limitation of the narrative review is its subjectivity. The reviewer must decide which studies to include, how to evaluate those that are included, and how to draw conclusions from the results. These are

TABLE 2.3 Examples of Secondary Sources in Educational Research

Reviews

Review of Educational Research. Washington, DC: American Educational Research Association.

Review of Research in Education. Washington, DC: American Educational Research Association.

Handbooks

Anfara, V. A. (Ed.). (2001). *Handbook of research in middle level education*. Greenwich, CT: Information Age.

Denzin, N. K., & Lincoln, Y. S. (Eds.). (2000). *Handbook of qualitative research* (2nd ed.). Thousand Oaks, CA: Sage.

Eisner, E. W., & Day, M. D. (Eds.). (2004). *Handbook of research and policy in art education*. Mahwah, NJ: Erlbaum.

Richardson, V. (2001). *Handbook of research on teaching* (4th ed.). Washington, DC: American Educational Research Association.

Smart, J. C. (Ed.). (2004). *Higher education: Handbook of theory and research*. New York: Kluwer.

Encyclopedias

American Educational Research Association. (2001). *Encyclopedia of educational research* (7th ed.). Farmington Hills, MI: Macmillan.

Reynolds, C. R., & Fletcher-Janzen, E. (2004). *Concise encyclopedia of special education: A reference for the education of the handicapped and other exceptional children and adults* (2nd ed.). Hoboken, NJ: Wiley.

Walberg, H. J., & Haertel, G. D. (Eds.). (1990). *The international encyclopedia of educational evaluation*. Elmsford, NY: Pergamon.

formidable challenges, given that there may be hundreds or even thousands of studies on a particular topic, and given that many of the studies differ in their methodological approach. Which fruit should be chosen, we might ask, and how should we compare the apples to the oranges? During the 1970s, researchers became increasingly interested in developing a more objective, quantitative approach to creating a literature review, and by the end of the decade Gene Glass and colleagues had published some highly influential discussions of meta-analysis as a solution to the problem (e.g., Glass, 1976; Smith & Glass, 1977).

The meta-analysis begins with a review of primary sources, and in this respect meta-analyses tend to be more inclusive than narrative reviews. All known studies on a particular topic may be included. Or, inclusion may be based on relatively objective criteria (e.g., all studies conducted in the past 10 years, or all studies that were published in a particular journal, etc.). By reviewing multiple studies, the meta-analysis may reveal patterns that are not evident, or not clearly represented, in individual studies.

The most distinctive aspect of meta-analysis is the statistical approach used to compare individual studies. This approach transforms the results of each study into an **effect size**, a number that indicates the strength of the relationship between variables. (The mathematical basis and interpretation of effect sizes is discussed in Chapter 11.) Once the effect size for each study has been determined, an average can be taken of the effect sizes for all studies reviewed. This overall effect size is the goal of the meta-analysis. Suppose, for instance, that a meta-analysis focuses on studies of the relationship between exposure to a particular curriculum and mathematical achievement. An effect size would be calculated for each study, and these individual effect sizes would then be averaged to determine how strongly exposure to the curriculum influences mathematical achievement.

In meta-analyses, effect sizes can be computed for almost any quantitative study, regardless of the study's methodological and statistical approach. Calculation of effect size thus allows the researcher to compare apples and oranges (and bananas, and most other kinds of fruit). However, meta-analysis is not uncontroversial. Meta-analyses often include unpublished studies, under the assumption that because it is often difficult for studies to be published unless significant effects are identified, published work might overestimate the extent to which two variables are related, or one variable impacts another. Critics argue that the inclusion of unpublished studies opens the door to low-quality research and compromises the results of meta-analysis. In spite of these criticisms, meta-analysis is becoming an increasingly prominent approach to the literature review. Spotlight on Research 2.3, which appears later in this chapter, provides an example, as does Spotlight on Research 7.2 in Chapter 7.

Where to Find Research

Whether your goal is to browse through published studies and get ideas for a research topic, or to conduct a full-fledged literature review and refine an existing topic, there are numerous resources you can turn to in order to find primary and secondary sources. In this section, I discuss libraries, online databases, professional organizations, and other Internet sources.

Libraries

Perhaps the best place to start when searching for educational research is to consult with the reference librarian of your college or university. Most academic libraries have online catalogs (in place of the card catalog) that allow you to search the library's resources. Information on resources available at other local libraries should be available, as should a process by which you can obtain resources through interlibrary loan. Finally, your library should provide access to many of the sources noted in Tables 2.1 and 2.2 and in the remainder of this section.

Online Databases

When conducting a literature review, it is common for researchers to use **databases** that provide searchable access to a variety of primary and secondary sources.

The largest database of educational research in the world is the Education Resources Information Center, or **ERIC**. ERIC was established in 1966 through the U.S. Department of Education (ED) in order to help keep track of the rapidly growing number of education-related documents, some of which had disappeared after being submitted to the ED. Funded by the National Library of Education and the ED, ERIC currently provides access to over a million bibliographic citations, as well as over 100,000 nonjournal primary sources. ERIC is free to use, relatively easy to search, and can be accessed through the Internet at *www.eric.ed.gov*. As with other online databases, an ERIC search can be carried out for particular authors, titles, and keywords, as well as for other kinds of criteria such as journal name, publication type, and source institution. ERIC provides a thesaurus of search terms that can be browsed or used as a source of suggestions for terms that the user inputs. ERIC also provides a search field that allows the user to evaluate the quality of identified sources (e.g., in terms of relevance to education, and whether or not the source is peer-reviewed). Of particular relevance to students is that an ERIC search can be limited to just those resources that are directly available through ERIC.

Other widely used databases include the Current Index to Journals in Education, which includes abstracts from over 1,000 journals from 1969 to the present, and the Education Index, which includes bibliographic information for educational articles published since 1929. These two databases are specific to educational research. Other databases are broader in scope but include sources of relevance to education. For example, in 2004 Google introduced Google Scholar, a free search engine that provides access to downloadable primary and secondary sources in a variety of fields, including education (see *http://scholar.google.com*).

Although some databases only provide bibliographic information and/or abstracts, your academic library should have access to databases containing the full text of scientific publications. Many of these databases can be accessed from any computer with an Internet connection (ask your librarian, or consult your university or college website, for details). For example, Academic Search Complete provides access to full-text articles in nearly 5,000 peer-reviewed journals, including many of relevance to education. Academic Search Complete is one of the databases available through EBSCO information services (*www.epnet.com*). Like most full-text databases, Academic Search Complete requires a subscription but is available at no cost to many faculty and students through their academic library. Other examples are PsycINFO, a database that includes summaries of psychological research and theory, including some material of relevance to education (*www.apa.org/psycinfo*), as well as InfoTrac and Web of Science (*www.isinet.com/products/citation/wos*).

SEARCH ENGINES   A **search engine** is the software that allows the user to search a database for sources that fit particular criteria. Although there are many different kinds of search engines, all of them allow users to narrow the scope of a search. Depending on the particular search engine, a search can be narrowed to particular authors, topics, methods, samples, dates, and types of publication, as well as to other characteristics and combinations of characteristics. As you may know, general search engines such as Google will search for a term anywhere in a document, while search engines associated with scholarly databases (e.g., ERIC and Academic Search Premier) will allow you to specify where the term appears, and will allow you to restrict your search along other dimensions (such as peer review).

Although no single set of instructions can be used for all search engines, each one should have a help function with instructions for use. Moreover, virtually all search engines allow searches to be narrowed by means of keywords and Boolean operators. A **keyword** is simply a distinctive word or phrase that appears in a document. A **Boolean operator** (named for the 19th century mathematician George Boole) is a term such as AND, OR, or NOT that allows keywords to be used in ways that either narrow or expand a search. For instance:

- A search for "fluid intelligence" AND "creativity" will yield sources that refer to both concepts.
- A search for "fluid intelligence" OR "creativity" will yield sources that refer to either concept.
- A search for "fluid intelligence" NOT "creativity" will yield sources that refer to fluid intelligence only, but not creativity.

As you can see from these examples, the Boolean operators AND and NOT provide different ways of narrowing searches, while OR broadens a search.

EXAMPLE OF AN ONLINE DATABASE SEARCH   To illustrate the use of search engines in online databases, imagine that you are interested in recent studies on music education for elementary school students. Using the Internet to access ERIC at *www.eric.ed.gov*, you would arrive at the home page shown in Figure 2.1. Since you already have an idea for a topic, the next thing to do is to click on the Advanced Search button. You will now see the screen shown in Figure 2.2.

One way to proceed at this point is to consult the ERIC thesaurus for appropriate descriptors to use. Clicking on the Thesaurus tab will lead you to the screen illustrated in Figure 2.3. Clicking on the Search & Browse the Thesaurus tab, you will see, among other things, a row of letters that allows you to browse the thesaurus alphabetically. The "M" option leads to the descriptor "Music Education." Once you have clicked on "Music Education" you will see the screen reproduced in Figure 2.4. Notice that this Descriptor Details page suggests other descriptors that may or may not be more relevant to your search—depending on your interests, you might decide to use a descriptor such as "Music Techniques," "Piano Lessons," "Music Activities," or some other term on this page.

Returning to the Advanced Search page (by clicking on the Start an Eric Search icon), you would now take the following steps:

1. Change the second field from Keywords (all fields) to Descriptors (from Thesaurus) and enter the phrase "Elementary School Students." including the quotation marks. (You can verify independently that this is an ERIC descriptor.)

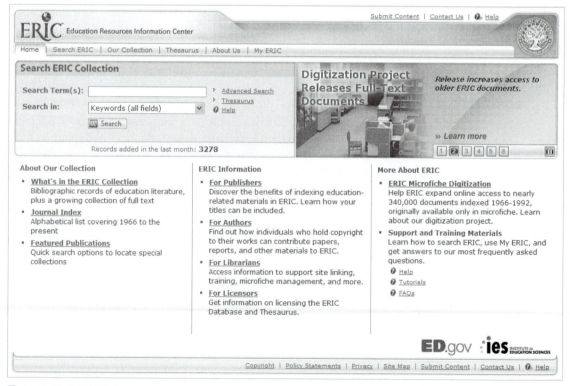

FIGURE 2.1 ERIC home page.

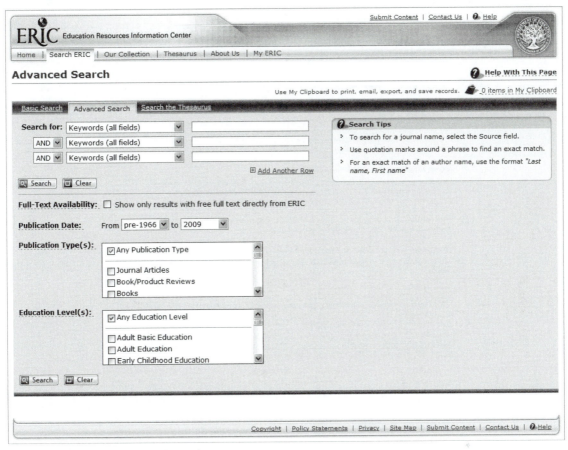

FIGURE 2.2 ERIC Advanced Search page.

2. Specify publication date and publication type. For example, restrict your search to journal articles published between 1997 and 2007.

Once you have entered this information, you will see the screen illustrated in Figure 2.5. If you then click on the Search button, bibliographic information will be listed for all articles in the ERIC database that meet the search criteria. At the time I wrote this chapter, 56 citations meeting these criteria were available. Figure 2.6 shows the first page of these 56 "hits," and Figure 2.7 illustrates the full entry for the first article cited on the list (at the time).

Professional Organizations

Professional organizations, such as the International Reading Association (IRA), the National Science Teachers Association (NSTA), the National Council for the Social Studies (NCSS), the Association for Supervision and Curriculum Development (ASCD), and many others, publish journals and newsletters, and host websites containing reports of research as well as links to research resources. For example, the National Council of Teachers of Mathematics (NCTM), founded in 1920, is currently the largest organization in the world devoted to mathematics education. The NCTM offers several annual membership options and, like other organizations, provides discounts to students. Members gain access to peer-reviewed

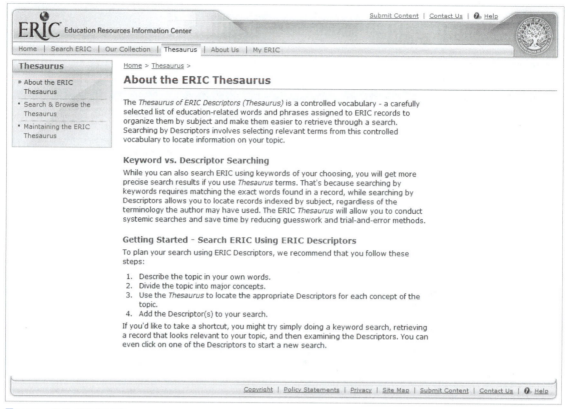

FIGURE 2.3 ERIC Thesaurus page.

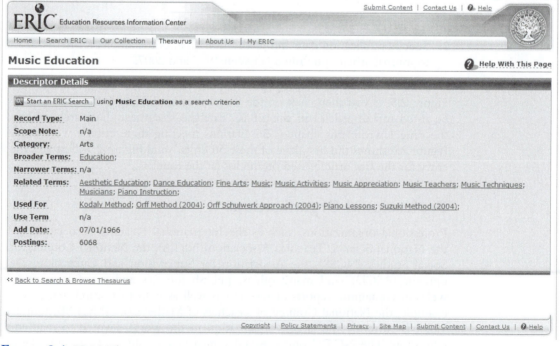

FIGURE 2.4 ERIC Thesaurus Music Education Descriptor Details page.

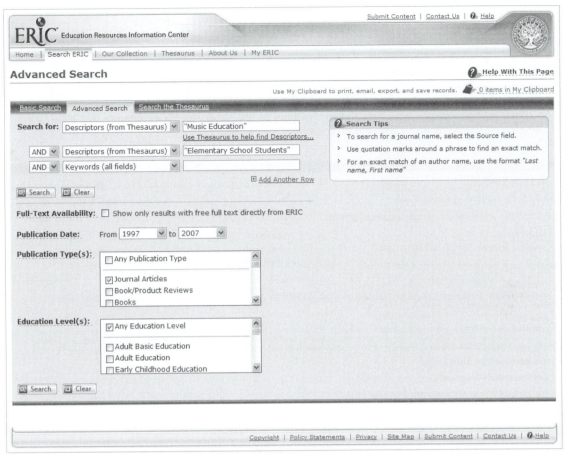

FIGURE 2.5 ERIC Advanced Search page with search criteria filled in.

journals published by NCTM, as well as to professional development opportunities, instructional resources, and discounted or free access to conferences that NCTM sponsors. (For more information, visit *www.nctm.org*.)

Other Internet Sources

The U.S. government maintains a number of websites that provide important information for prospective researchers. For example, the U.S. Department of Education website (*www.ed.gov*) contains links to databases, research articles, summaries, and educational organizations. The National Center for Education Statistics (*www.nces.ed.gov*) provides a searchable collection of statistics, research reports, and other information pertaining to the state of education at the local and national level.

E-mail is a quick and relatively focused way of interacting with experts in a particular field. For example, by subscribing to an **electronic mailing list**, you can receive announcements, post questions, and interact with members of an organization or group who have common interests. These electronic mailing lists are often referred to as "listservs" or "listserves." (The origin of these terms is LISTSERV, the trademarked name of the oldest and still most widely used of such lists.) Electronic mailing lists such as the American Educational Research Association (AERA) Communication of Research List are useful in that a free

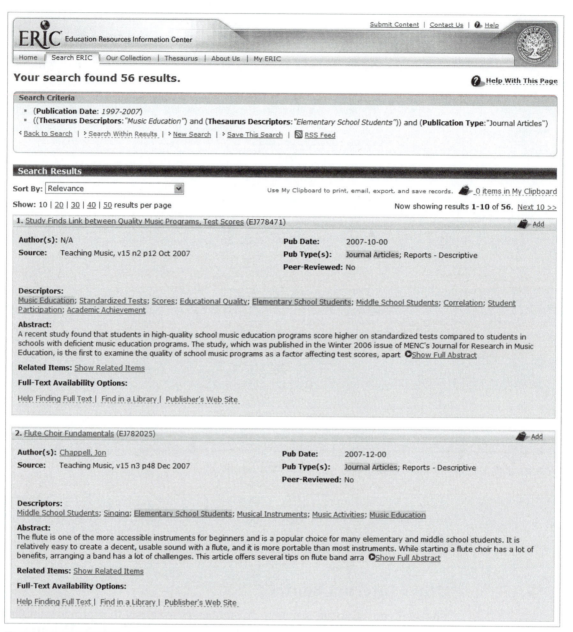

FIGURE 2.6 ERIC Results page.

subscription provides opportunities to interact with experts as well as other students in a particular area, and perhaps obtain advice about research topics. The AERA-CR list is available at *http://aera-cr.asu.edu/listserv*. An extensive catalog of electronic mailing lists pertaining to a variety of topics, including education, can be found at *www.lsoft.com/lists/listref.html*.

Increasingly, scholarly journals are available online exclusively. The Communication of Research SIG, a special interest group of the American Educational Research Association, provides links to online educational journals "that are

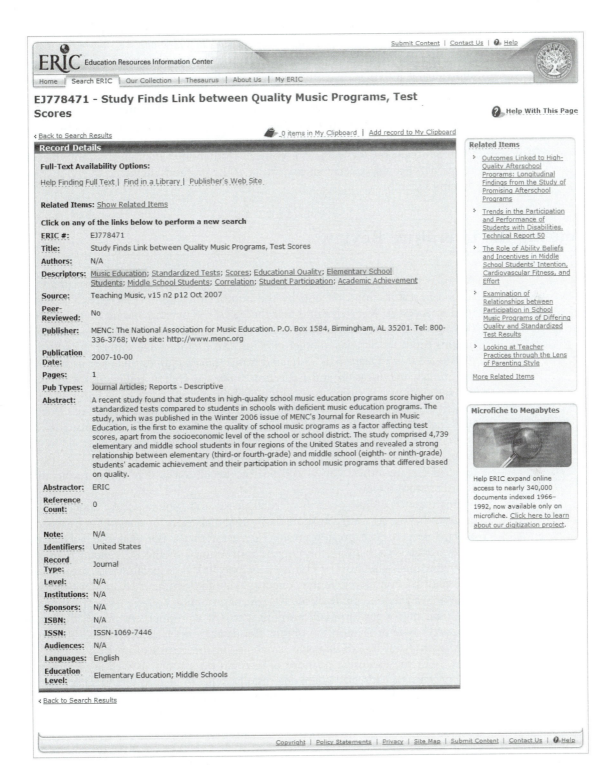

scholarly, peer-reviewed, full text and accessible without cost." This list of e-journals is available on the Internet at *http://aera-cr.asu.edu/index.php.*

Finally, the websites of private organizations, foundations, and centers, as well as individual researchers, may provide helpful information as you search for a research topic. Some of these resources are free, while others require paid subscriptions. For instance, the website *www.edweek.org* offers paid as well as free trial subscriptions to *Education Week* and *Teacher Magazine,* two helpful sources of information about educational policy, research, and practice.

In Spotlight on Research 2.3, you can read about a meta-analysis in which the researchers provide a detailed description of the methods they used to conduct their literature search.

Focusing the Literature Review

At some point, you may feel daunted not only by the quantity of primary and secondary scholarship, but also by the number of different resources that can be used to access it. Keep in mind that there is some overlap among these resources. For example, for someone interested in research on early reading fluency, a study on this topic by Schwanenflugel et al. in the October–December 2006 issue of *Reading Research Quarterly* is abstracted in secondary sources such as Current Index to Journals in Education and Education Index, as well as online at ERIC and at the International Reading Association website (*www.reading.org*). The full text of this article is available online through databases such as Academic Search Premier, InfoTrac, and PsycInfo. In short, there are several different paths through which you could discover this article. At the same time, a thorough search would identify thousands of other studies on the development of reading fluency, and so for this topic, as for any other, you would need to decide on which studies to include in your literature review.

Apart from the sheer quantity of available research, you may have concerns about quality. (If you do not, you should!) Print sources vary in quality, and the extent of variability is even greater among Internet sources. For example, a December 2006 Google search using the phrase "instructional methods" yielded more than 2 million hits. The first 10 consisted of one link to a professional organization, one scholarly conference report, one 15-year-old document created by scholars as a public service, one guide created as part of an online course, and six commercial sites (i.e., sites whose primary purpose is to sell a product). Although the quality of sources would be more consistent if a database such as ERIC had been used, there would still be considerable variability in the results of an ERIC search. In short, both the extensive quantity of research on a topic, as well as variability in quality, must be addressed when determining what to include in a literature review. Following are three of the most important general prerequisites for selection. These prerequisites—authoritativeness, relevance, and timeliness—are "general" in the sense of applying to virtually any kind of quantitative or qualitative study.

Authoritativeness

The authoritativeness of a source is determined by many factors, including the affiliation and reputation of the author as well as the reputation of the source. Sources that contain no information about authorship, are not edited, do not include citations, and/or exist for a commercial purpose tend to be less authoritative than

Intervention Strategies in Special Education: A Literature Search and Meta-analysis

Self-determination has been defined as "a combination of skills, knowledge, and beliefs that enable a person to engage in goal-directed, self-regulated, autonomous behavior." An example would be choosing to read several pages in a textbook every evening during the week before a test, so that you need not cram the night before.

The teaching of self-determination strategies has played a role in special education for many years. Individuals with mental retardation, learning disabilities, and other special needs may benefit from interventions that help them make decisions, set goals, and achieve those goals. Until recently, however, there has not been much research on the success of these interventions in special education settings. In a 2001 study published in *Review of Educational Research**, Bob Algozzine, Diane Browder, Meagan Karvonen, David Test, and Wendy Wood conducted a meta-analysis on studies of this topic. In the following passage, Algozzine and colleagues described the methods they used for their literature search.

Narrative reviews have traditionally been used by researchers to integrate empirical studies. These reviews sometimes lack focus and have been criticized as limited and biased, and quantitative methods have often been used to supplement the findings from these conventional reviews. . . . Meta-analysis *is a widely accepted quantitative method for systematically combining outcomes in efforts to provide a comprehensive evaluation of a domain of interest. . . . The accepted strength of meta-analysis, in addition to its inclusive orientation, is that findings from different studies are reduced to a common metric (i.e., effect size) that provides an estimate of comparability and importance of outcomes. No one has yet used quantitative review methods to summarize research on self-determination interventions. . . .*

A wide variety of electronic and print resources was screened to identify articles (published or in press) for possible inclusion in this study, including ERIC, EBSCO-Host, PsycInfo, Dissertation Abstracts International, and the Council for Exceptional Children databases. Twenty-nine search terms (e.g., self-advocacy, problem solving, student-directed learning) were each used in conjunction with the word "disabilities" to narrow the search. Recent issues of relevant journals . . . were searched manually to identify references not yet included in databases. In addition, the reference sections of included articles as well as position papers, chapters, and books on self-determination were reviewed to identify potentially relevant research. Finally, nearly 200 researchers and practitioners widely recognized as active in the field of special education were asked to identify and submit additional studies. . . .

(continued)

others. Typically, many or all of the useful research studies identified through a literature review are published in "refereed" or "peer-reviewed" publications. **Peer review** refers to the process by which experts in a particular field review scientific manuscripts and make recommendations about whether or not each manuscript should be published. A journal editor, for example, will usually ask two to four experts to review a manuscript and provide written feedback. Once the reviewers have responded, the editor will examine their feedback and make a decision about whether or not the paper should be accepted for publication, revised and resubmitted, or rejected.

Peer review can be a highly rigorous process. Among the most selective journals in education and related fields, the rejection rate exceeds 90%. The importance of peer review is that it confers a degree of authoritativeness on those research reports that actually do get published. Publications in journals that do not employ peer review rarely make significant contributions to scientific knowledge. On the other hand, peer review does not automatically guarantee widespread respect for a scientific report. Peer-reviewed journals vary widely in quality, and thus their impact on the science varies too. The more experienced you become as a researcher,

Algozzine and colleagues noted six criteria for the inclusion of a study in their meta-analysis.

First, the article had to be published or in press in a peer-reviewed journal between 1972 and 2000. . . . Second, the subjects had to be individuals classified with one of the disabilities recognized by the Individuals with Disabilities Education Act or nonspecified developmental disabilities. Third, studies involving individuals from age 3 to adulthood were included. Fourth, the article had to report the results of a data-based intervention. The article did not have to demonstrate experimental control and could be a report of a teaching intervention or a qualitative study. Fifth, the intervention had to be one in which participants learned new skills or acquired new opportunities. . . . Sixth, the intervention had to focus on a component of self-determination. Excluded were reviews, position papers, or expository articles that did not report first-hand data, as well as research that did not involve direct interventions to promote self-determination (i.e., correlational and descriptive studies). The application of these criteria yielded 51 studies for inclusion in this review. . . .

Following the calculation of effect sizes and other statistics, Algozzine and colleagues offered several generalizations about the literature:

The most common interventions teach choice making to individuals with mental retardation (N = 15 studies) or self-advocacy to individuals with learning disabilities or mild mental retardation (N = 19 studies). . . .

Self determination is being taught using a variety of methods . . .

Almost half the studies (N = 22) included observations of the participants using self-determination skills in vivo [i.e., in naturalistic rather than laboratory environments]. . . .

The researchers also reported that very few studies looked at quality-of-life outcomes after the self-determination interventions—a major gap in the research literature, in their view—and that self-management interventions, although excluded from their meta-analysis, have been shown to be effective.

On the basis of their meta-analysis, Algozzine and colleagues concluded that at least some kinds of self-determination can be taught to at least some kinds of special needs individuals. They recommended that future research consider other kinds of self-determination and other groups, and that future studies also pay more attention to the effects of interventions on the lives of individuals with disabilities, rather than just showing that they are capable of learning the strategies taught to them.

*Algozzine, B., Browder, D., Karvonen, M., Test, D. W., & Wood, W. W. (2001). Effects of interventions to promote self-determination for individuals with disabilities. *Review of Educational Research*, 71(2), 219–277. Quoted with permission from the publisher.

the more clearly you will be able to ascertain distinctions in the authoritativeness of both journals as well as specific articles—and the more disagreements you will find among researchers on these issues.

When conducting a literature search, peer review is ordinarily considered a minimum requirement for the inclusion of a research report. Two exceptions to this principle are worth mentioning. First, as discussed earlier in the chapter, meta-analyses may include unpublished studies, under the assumption that strict reliance on published data may artificially inflate effect sizes. Second, although dissertations are not peer reviewed, they are evaluated and approved by faculty committees, and in some cases they make a contribution to a specific literature. Information about dissertations can be obtained through a database called *Dissertation Abstracts International* (DAI), which contains bibliographic information extending back more than a century, and includes abstracts from 1980 through the present. Print versions of DAI are available at most academic libraries and, for a fee, online.

Relevance

The ultimate goal of a literature review can be described as the identification of studies of specific relevance to a specific topic of interest. As your topic becomes more narrowly focused, you will find that fewer studies are directly relevant. There are tens of thousands of peer-reviewed studies on aggression, for instance, but only a handful on gender differences in relational aggression among middle school students. You may find a dialectical relationship between the progress of your literature review and the identification of research topics and questions, in that refining your topic and developing research questions influences the studies you include in your literature review, and that as you review published studies your topic and research questions change.

Because research studies are narrowly focused, determining the relevance of a study to your literature review depends on a careful examination of the content. The focus of any given study will be highly specific in terms of the ages of participants, the skills or characteristics studied, the types of measures used, and many other variables. The specificity of educational research is illustrated in Figure 2.8, which contains a sample of article titles from one of the most prestigious outlets for educational research.

As you read through these titles, notice the implicit distinctions that indicate the topic of each study. The first study, for example, pertains to bilingual rather than monolingual children. The focus is not on bilingual children in general but rather on a comparison between those who are versus are not at risk for reading disabilities. The development of literacy and cognition among these two groups appears to be the primary basis for comparison. If this title suggests to you an article of potential relevance, your next step would be to read the abstract and/or skim the text of the article, in order to figure out the age range of the children, the two languages they speak, the types of literacy and cognition measured, the types of measures used, and so on.

Although the topics of the various articles in Figure 2.8 may be unfamiliar to you (as they might be to educational researchers in other fields), prior experience reading research pertaining to one of these articles might allow you to recognize the specific literature that its title alludes to, and perhaps even give you a sense of the research questions that are explored. As with authoritativeness, the more experience you have with reading research articles, the better you will become at determining relevance.

Timeliness

Because each research study connects in specific ways with its predecessors, it is important for a literature review to include the most recent research on a topic. Browsing recently published secondary sources and the current issues of journals can be a helpful approach, particularly if you already know your area of interest.

FIGURE 2.8 Titles of selected articles from the *Journal of Educational Psychology,* May 2006

"Growth in Literacy and Cognition in Bilingual Children at Risk or Not at Risk for Reading Disabilities"

"The Influence of Phonological Processing and Inattentive Behavior on Reading Acquisition"

"A Portrait of Benchmark School: How a School Produces High Achievement in Students Who Previously Failed"

"Selecting At-Risk Readers in First Grade for Early Intervention: A Two-Year Longitudinal Study of Decision Rules and Procedures"

"Effects of Instructional Support within Constructivist Learning Environments for Elementary School Students' Understanding of Floating and Sinking"

"Task Values and Ability Beliefs as Predictors of High School Literacy Choices: A Developmental Analysis"

In addition, the Social Sciences Citation Index (SSCI) may be of use. The SSCI is published each year and contains, among other things, a list of every journal citation of a particular author's works in that year. For example, if you find an interesting article written by John Doe in 1998, you can use the SSCI to identify other articles that have cited Doe's study up through the present. At least some of those articles may be extensions of Doe's work that are relevant to your topic. The SSCI is available in print at most academic libraries. Paid subscriptions to the SSCI or to the Web of Science, which also allows researchers to identify citations of a particular source, allow users to search online for citations.

Developing a Research Question

As your literature review becomes more focused, your research question may become more clearly articulated as well. The many criteria that must be considered in order to develop a good research question can be boiled down to two dimensions: testability and connectedness.

Testability

Testability refers to the need for a research question to be stated in such a way that it can be evaluated through empirical research. Several requirements must be met in order to achieve testability:

- The research question should be expressed in clear and highly specific terms.
- Value judgments (e.g., as in the distinction between "good" and "bad" students) should be avoided.
- If there is a hypothesis, it should be falsifiable (see Chapter 1 for definition).
- The research needed to address the question should be logistically feasible and ethically appropriate (see Chapter 4 for details).

Again, one of the key differences between quantitative and qualitative research is that quantitative research questions are formulated in advance, while the qualitative researcher may begin with a focus of inquiry that is gradually narrowed as research questions and hypotheses are developed and refined. Thus, there will be some differences between quantitative and qualitative research in what constitutes adequate testability. A qualitative research question may not, at the outset of the study, be highly specific or accompanied by a hypothesis, although there is a need for clarity, logistical feasibility, and ethical appropriateness.

Connectedness

Connectedness refers to the relationship between the research question and whatever theoretical, empirical, and/or practical concerns give rise to it. As with testability, two requirements must be met in order for a research question to be "connected":

- The relationship between the research question and whatever concerns gave rise to it should be clear and specific.
- The research needed to address the question should be able to contribute something of theoretical and/or practical importance to an existing literature.

To illustrate connectedness (and some of the other concepts introduced in this chapter), consider a study by Hong and Raudenbush (2005) on the effects of kindergarten retention on reading and mathematical skills. Retention—requiring students to repeat a grade—is a controversial practice. Proponents argue that retaining students who are struggling academically allows them to catch up, and ultimately results in classrooms with a more homogeneous mix of ability levels. Critics of retention argue that it is ineffective and stigmatizes retained students. Hong and Raudenbush's research question was not simply whether retention is generally good or bad. Rather, on the basis of their literature review, the researchers developed three specific questions pertaining to retention at the kindergarten level.

First, because prior studies typically focused on individual students, Hong and Raudenbush explored the average, school-wide effects of kindergarten retention, focusing in particular on effects that could be observed after schools change their retention policy. Second, because prior studies tended to make broad comparisons between retained and promoted students, Hong and Raudenbush focused more specifically on low-performing students who would be (just barely) promoted if retention policies were adopted in their schools. Finally, through methods that were intended to improve upon existing approaches, Hong and Raudenbush explored the effects of retention on students who were actually retained. In sum, the three research questions were as follows:

- What are the effects of retention policies on entire schools?
- What are the effects of retention policies on low-performing students who would be promoted?
- What are the effects of retention policies on students who are retained?

For each research question, the researchers focused on reading and mathematical skills (as opposed to other academic skills, emotional development, or other variables known to be affected by retention). As you can see, each research question extended prior studies in a different way.

Hong and Raudenbush (2005) found that the school-wide effects of retention were small or nonexistent, that low-performing students who would be promoted according to their schools' retention policies would not benefit, and that students who are actually retained lose ground in their reading and mathematical development. Thus, the researchers did not present evidence that retention per se is simply bad. Rather, for a particular age group (kindergartners) and a particular set of skills (reading and math), the researchers showed that on average, retention has either no effects or negative effects on students. The specificity of the results follows from the specificity of the research questions, and in the future, researchers studying the effects of retention will develop specific research questions that are informed by the findings of Hong and Raudenbush as well as others.

A Look Ahead

In this chapter, you have read about what motivates educational research, where research can be found, and how to develop a research question. Chapter 3 provides a detailed look at the different types of research reports, in which research questions have already been articulated and addressed. The next chapter also provides some guidance in the creation of research reports, ranging from class projects to dissertations to peer-reviewed journal articles.

Applications: A Guide for Beginning Researchers

Here are some ideas from the chapter that will help you plan your research:

- As you think about choosing a research topic, you will have many sources to draw from, including theory, opinion, practical concerns, policy, and curiosity. Most educational research is guided at least in part by practical concerns.

- As you develop a research question, you should be familiarizing yourself with prior research through a literature review.

- Your research question needs to be testable, and to reflect a specific connection between your research and prior studies. Ask yourself, what could my research contribute to the existing literature on a topic?

- Prior research is described in many kinds of primary and secondary sources available in print and online. Review this chapter for details on some of these sources and where to find them.

Chapter Summary

A research study begins with the selection of a topic in a given area of inquiry, followed by the development of specific research questions (or foci of inquiry) and hypotheses.

Research topics are selected on the basis of theoretical claims, informed opinion, prior research, practical concerns, policy, and/or curiosity and chance.

Selection and refinement of a research topic depends on conducting a literature review of primary sources, secondary sources, and/or meta-analyses. Resources for conducting literature reviews include libraries, online databases, professional organizations, and other Internet sources. Decisions about what publications to include in a literature review are based on considerations of authoritativeness, relevance, and timeliness.

The quality of a research question depends on its testability as well as its connectedness to issues of importance to researchers as well as practitioners.

Key Terms

Research program	**Primary source**	**Search engine**
Research question	**Secondary source**	**Keyword**
Focus of inquiry	**Meta-analysis**	**Boolean operator**
Grounded theory	**Effect size**	**Electronic mailing list**
Literature	**Databases**	**Peer review**
Literature review	**ERIC**	

Exercises

1. Which of the following appears to be a primary source?

a) A review of research on dyslexia published in the past 5 years.
b) Commentary on a highly influential study of undergraduates with dyslexia.
c) A report of survey results obtained from a group of children with dyslexia.
d) An annotated bibliography of classic studies of dyslexia.

2. In question #1, which option is most likely to indicate a meta-analysis?

3. Which of the following can a search engine do for you?

a) Rank articles on the topic of juvenile delinquency according to the quality of the research.
b) Identify numerous correlational studies on a particular topic published in peer-reviewed journals since 2000.
c) Indicate which of a set of published studies on gender differences in spelling is most relevant to a particular research question.
d) All of the above

4. When you read a research report published in a journal that is not peer reviewed, what aspect of the report should you be most concerned about?

a) The length of the report
b) The quality of the research
c) The practical importance of the research question
d) The author's sincerity

For questions 5-6, refer to the description below:

Researchers agree that drawing evolves from scribbling. . . . Scribbling in its initial phases is viewed as a motor activity, unguided by visual planning, and determined mainly by the mechanical functioning of the motor system of the arm, wrist and hand. Children show only transient interest in their own scribbles, and often readily move from one scribble to the next. . . . With increasing perceptual–motor coordination, the scribbles become complex patterns, guided by visual attention, and determined by esthetic considerations like that of balance.

(Adi-Japha, Levin, & Solomon, 1998, p. 26)

5. In light of the claims made in this passage, which of the following research questions best meets the criteria of testability and relevance?

a) Do children who begin to draw earlier than their peers eventually achieve greater aesthetic competence?
b) Do children value their drawings more than their scribbles?
c) When children make marks on paper, do those who can draw spend proportionally more time looking at their paper than children who can only scribble?

d) Compared to children with above-average perceptual–motor coordination, do children who have below-average perceptual–motor coordination show a greater tendency to omit key aesthetic features from their drawings?

6. Where would be the best place to find additional research on the development of drawing?

a) A large database such as ERIC

b) A large meta-analysis of peer-reviewed studies on the development of drawing

c) A large electronic mailing list consisting of researchers who study the development of drawing

d) All of the above

7. *Critical thinking question:* If peer review is a rigorous process involving expert oversight, why is it possible for published research to contain flaws and errors?

Answers to Exercises

1. c **2.** a **3.** b **4.** b **5.** c **6.** d

7. *Possible answer:* Peer review typically relies on a small number of experts. If the experts fail to detect an error, or if they believe that the merits of the study outweigh its flaws, they might still recommend the study for publication. In some cases, a flaw is only discernible in light of subsequent research.

Suggestions for Further Reading

Research Article: Andrews, M. L., & Ridenour, C. S. (2006). Gender in schools: A qualitative study of students in educational administration. *Journal of Educational Research, 100*(1), 35–43.

This qualitative study illustrates several concepts from the chapter and is explicitly motivated by theory, research, and practical need.

Application Article: Rosselli, H. C., & Irvin, J. L. (2001, January). Differing perspectives, common ground: The middle school and gifted education relationship. *Middle School Journal*, pp. 57–62.

This literature review illustrates how research bears on the ways that middle schools should serve gifted students.

Extension Article: Brophy, J. & Bawden, D. (2005). Is Google enough?: Comparison of an internet search engine with academic library resources. *ASLIB Proceedings, 57*(6), 498–512.

This case study provides further information on the strengths and weaknesses of using Google versus academic databases for scholarly searches.

CHAPTER 3 Research Reports

ColorBlind Images/Getty Images

After studying this chapter, you will be able to answer the following questions:

- What are the different types of research reports?

- What information does each part of a journal article provide?

- How are research reports created and published?

- What determines the quality of a research report?

This chapter will prepare you to do the following:

- Find key information in a journal article

- Begin a thesis or dissertation proposal

- Begin to write a research report for publication

- Evaluate the quality of a research report

- Become a better scientific writer

Introduction

As you develop a research question, the literature review is your closest ally. By carefully studying what is already known about a topic, you will come to see what is not known yet, and you will be prepared to fill that gap in existing knowledge through new research. But simply conducting a study is not enough. Your research could not be considered "successful" unless the results were communicated to others—to other researchers, to practitioners, and to anyone else with an interest in the educational system. In short, you would need to disseminate a report of your research. This chapter leads you through the process by which research reports are created and communicated to others. The information in this chapter will help you understand the research reports you encounter in your coursework and in literature reviews for more advanced projects such as theses or dissertations. This chapter will also help you plan and then write a research report, thesis, or dissertation. In short, this chapter is written for both consumers and producers of research.

Types of Research Reports

Researchers communicate with each other in many different ways. We have informal conversations via e-mail, listservs, and face-to-face interactions. We communicate more formally through presentations at conferences and departmental colloquia, and through peer-reviewed materials published in print or on the Internet. What these methods of communication have in common is that each allows for many different forms of expression. A peer-reviewed journal article, for instance, may consist of any one of the following:

- A theoretical framework
- An informed opinion
- A book review
- A narrative literature review
- A meta-analysis
- A report of original research

This section of the chapter focuses on research reports. I discuss five different types of research report here: conference presentations, journal articles, professional reports, theses and dissertations, and secondary sources.

Conference Presentations

The academic or professional conference consists of a gathering of experts, practitioners, students, and other interested parties. The research presented and discussed at the conference may be diverse or limited to a highly specific area. The conference may last half a day or an entire week, and the number of attendees may range from a few dozen to tens of thousands. Two of the largest conferences of relevance to educational research are the annual meeting of the American Educational Research Association (AERA), which lasts for 5 days, and the biennial meeting of the Society for Research in Child Development (SRCD), which lasts for 3 days. At each of these conferences you would find several thousand research reports, delivered in formats ranging from symposia to poster sessions to invited speeches. These conferences also host presentations and workshops pertaining to professional development, dissertation support, grant writing, and publishing. (Additional details can be found at *www.aera.net* and *www.srcd.org*.)

Most academic conferences have a review process that begins with a "call for proposals" well before the conference is scheduled. Calls for proposals appear in journals and on the websites of professional organizations. Each call for proposals includes information about format and content requirements for submissions. In most cases, the quality of each submission is evaluated too, and thus each conference provides a more or less selective venue for the presentation of research reports. However, a conference presentation does not have the same impact on the state of knowledge in a discipline as a peer-reviewed journal article. Conference presentations are typically the first step in the process of publication. The researcher hopes to obtain feedback at the conference, and then expand his or her presentation into an article-length manuscript. For this reason, conference presentations are often considered preliminary—they attract interest as reports of the most cutting-edge findings, but they lack the authoritativeness of results that have been published in peer-reviewed journals and replicated over time.

The two main types of conference presentation are the conference paper and the poster.

CONFERENCE PAPERS   The **conference paper** is read before an audience during an allotted time period (often between 15 and 30 minutes). It may be a theoretical paper, an opinion piece, or, most commonly, a report of original empirical research. The audience includes experts interested in the particular area of research, as well as practitioners who find the topic relevant to their work. Audience members are able to locate presentations of interest because the conference schedule is available in advance. The schedules at larger conferences are a source of both enthusiasm and frustration, since many presentations are scheduled concurrently. To give you a sense of what this means, some of the concurrent presentations scheduled for 8:15 in the morning of one day during a recent meeting of the AERA are reproduced in Figure 3.1. (Keep in mind that this figure shows fewer than a quarter of the presentations available at that time.)

Conference papers on a related theme may be presented in a **panel** format, in which each of a small number of presenters read their papers, after which a commentator offers feedback and coordinates questions from the audience. This type of format may be called a panel session, a paper session, or a symposium. Presenters often make hard copies of their papers available to the audience, or at least provide the address of a website where the paper can be downloaded. An example of a conference paper available online is presented in Spotlight on Research 3.1.

22.002. AERA Web Content Management System Training for Division and SIG Web Managers - Session 1. AERA
Hilton New York, Concourse H, Concourse Level
8:15 am to 9:45 am
Chair:
Phoebe H. Stevenson, American Educational Research Association

22.010. Assessing Hurricane Katrina's Impact on Urban Education.
Presidential Session
Hilton New York, Sutton Complex, Sutton Center, 2nd Floor
8:15 am to 10:15 am
Chair:
Tondra L. Loder-Jackson, University of Alabama
Participants:
On Indignation, Hope, and a Call to Action: Assessing Hurricane Katrina's Impact on Urban Education. *Tondra L. Loder-Jackson, University of Alabama*
Out of New Orleans: The Katrina Diaspora and the Implications for Educational Research in the U.S. South. *Jerome E. Morris, University of Georgia*
Surviving Katrina: The Strengths of Legacy and Tradition in Historically Black Colleges and Universities. *Renee Akbar, Xavier University - Louisiana; Michele Jean Sims, University of Alabama*
Hope for an Uncertain Future: Recovery and Rebuilding Efforts in New Orleans's Schools. *Karen Ann Johnson, University of Utah; Ken Johnson, University of Utah*
Documenting Tragedy and Resilience: The Importance of Spike Lee's "When the Levee's Broke." *Kevin M. Foster, University of Texas - Austin*

22.011. The Educational Pipeline and Its Consequences for Students: Realizing Bakke's Legacy. Presidential Session
Hilton New York, Murray Hill Suite B, 2nd Floor
8:15 am to 10:15 am
Chair:
Patricia Marin, University of California - Santa Barbara
Participants:
O'Connor's Claim: The Educational Pipeline and Bakke. *John T. Yun, University of California - Santa Barbara; Chungmei Lee, The Civil Rights Project*
Educational Attainment in the States: Are We Progressing Toward Equity in 2028? *Donald E. Heller, The Pennsylvania State University*
Bakke Beyond College Access: Investigating Racial/Ethnic Differences in College Completion. *Michal Kurlaender, University of California - Davis; Erika Felts, University of California - Davis*
Is 1500 the New 1280? The SAT and Admissions Since Bakke. *Catherine L. Horn, University of Houston; John T. Yun, University of California - Santa Barbara*
Discussants:
Shaping the Equity Agenda: Bakke's Contribution to the Next 30 Years of Research. *Gary A. Orfield, University of California - Los Angeles*
Realizing the Benefits of Bakke: Setting a Policy Agenda for the Next 30 Years. *John Payton, NAACP Legal Defense and Educational Fund*

22.012. Building on the Past and Transforming the Future: STEM Education Research at the National Science Foundation. AERA Sessions
Hilton New York, Sutton Complex, Sutton South, 2nd Floor
8:15 am to 10:15 am
Chair:
Cora Marrett, National Science Foundation
Participants:
NSF's Involvement in Educational Research: A Retrospective Look. *Joan Ferrini-Mundy, National Science Foundation*
STEM Education Research to Inform Practice. *Janice H. Earle, National Science Foundation*
STEM Education to Inform Methods. *Anthony E Kelly, National Science Foundation; James Dietz, National Science Foundation*
STEM Education Research to Inform Policy. *Larry E. Suter, National Science Foundation*

Discussion: Reflections on the Three Cases and Thoughts About the Future. *Marcia Linn, University of California - Berkeley; Robert Boruch, University of Pennsylvania*

22.013. AERA Committee on Scholars of Color in Education, Awards and Early Bird Reception.
Committee on Scholars of Color in Education Sheraton New York Hotel & Towers, Empire Ballroom, Empire West, 2nd Floor 8:15 am to 10:15 am
Chair:
Stephen D. Hancock, University of North Carolina - Charlotte

22.014. Developing Cross-Cultural Parental Influence Instruments for International Applications.
International Relations Committee Sheraton New York Hotel & Towers, Liberty Suite 5, 3rd Floor
8:15 am to 9:45 am
Chair:
James Reed Campbell, St. John's University
Participants:
Summarizing 25 Years of Quantitative/Qualitative Research with Effective Parents. *James Reed Campbell, St. John's University*
Behavioral Home Environment and its Relation to Motivation and Achievement for High School Students in Cyprus. *Michalis Koutsoulis, Intercollege - Cyprus; James Reed Campbell, St. John's University*
Cross-National Comparison of Specific Environmental, Educational, Demographic, and Motivational Factors Affecting German High School Students Achievement. *Sharon Anne O'Connor-Petruso, Brooklyn College - CUNY; Marilyn A. Verna, Saint Francis College*
Family Influences and Academic Achievement in China. *Annie Xuemei Feng. The College of William & Mary*
Parents Know Best: Italian Students Excel in Academic Achievement. *Marilyn A. Verna, Saint Francis College; Sharon Anne O'Connor-Petruso, Brooklyn College - CUNY*
Discussant:
Seokhee Cho, St. John's University

22.015. GSC Chair Fireside Chat. Taking Youth and Adult Leadership Development From the Academy to the Community: Actively Engaging Communities in Collective Leadership Social Justice. Graduate Student Council
Sheraton New York Hotel & Towers, New York Ballroom, New York Ballroom West, 3rd Floor
8:15 am to 9:45 am
Chair:
John A. Oliver, Michigan State University
Participants:
Maenette K. P. Benham, Michigan State University
Matthew C. Militello, University of Massachusetts - Amherst
Anna M. Ortiz, California State University - Long Beach
Patrick Kim Halladay, Michigan State University

22.016. What a Wonderful World: Gender Equity, Research, and Building Civic Capacity. Committee on Scholars and Advocates for Gender Equity (SAGE)
Hilton New York, Murray Hill Suite A, 2nd Floor
8:15 am to 10:15 am
Chair:
Adrienne D. Dixson, The Ohio State University
Participants:
James Earl Davis, Temple University
Sofia A. Villenas, Cornell University
Venus E. Evans-Winters, Illinois Wesleyan University
Stacey J. Lee, University of Wisconsin - Madison
Kevin K. Kumashiro, University of Illinois - Chicago
Edward Fergus, New York University
Lisa W. Loutzenheiser, University of British Columbia

22.017. Developing Principals, Developing Practice. Division A-Administration, Organization, and Leadership
Hilton New York, New York Suite, 4th Floor
8:15 am to 9:45 am
Chair:
Jonathan A. Supovitz, University of Pennsylvania

FIGURE 3.1 Excerpt from the AERA 2008 Annual Meeting Program showing some of the presentations scheduled for 8:15 A.M. on March 25. (Copyright 2008 by the American Educational Research Association; reproduced with permission from the publisher.)

Participants:

School Leaders As Learners: Acquiring Expertise for Improving Instruction and Achievement in High-Poverty Schools. *Carol A. Barnes, University of Michigan; Eric M. Camburn, University of Wisconsin - Madison; Beth Rachel Sanders, University of Michigan; Jimmy Sebastian, University of Wisconsin - Madison*

Exploring the Relationship Between Professional Development Program Implementation and School Leadership Change. *Joy Lesnick, Vanderbilt University; Ellen B. Goldring, Vanderbilt University*

School Principals' Work Practice: Days of Their Lives. *James P. Spillane, Northwestern University; Spyros Konstantopoulos, Northwestern University*

How Principals Enact Instructional Leadership. *Jonathan A. Supovitz, University of Pennsylvania; Phillip Buckley, University of Pennsylvania*

Discussants:

Hilda Borko, Stanford University
Michael S. Knapp, University of Washington - Bothell

22.018. Extending the Debate on the Ed.D. in Educational Leadership: Transmission Versus Transformation. Division A-Administration, Organization, and Leadership
Hilton New York, Holland Suite, 4th Floor
8:15 am to 9:45 am

Chair:

Ted R. Purinton, National-Louis University

Participants:

Introduction: Parsing the Educational Leadership Ed.D. Debate. *Ted R. Purinton, National-Louis University*

Transmission Versus Transformation: The Student Perspective. *Mary Ann Kahl, National-Louis University*

Marketing Touches Versus Substantive Changes in Colleges of Education via the Ed.D. *Linda S. Tafel, National-Louis University*

Rethinking the Profession Through Its Training: The New Ed.D. As a Vehicle for Leadership Change. *Olivia Watkins, National-Louis University; Linda S. Tafel, National-Louis University*

Addressing the Doctoral Dilemma: Why a Doctorate for Transformation and Disposition? *Ted R. Purinton, National-Louis University*

22.019. International Perspectives on Education. Division A-Administration, Organization, and Leadership
Sheraton New York Hotel & Towers, Riverside Ballroom, 3rd Floor
8:15 am to 9:45 am

Chair:

Candace Head-Dylla, The Pennsylvania State University

Participants:

Is Education Fever Treatable? The Impact of Culture on Korean Students' College Choices. *Soojeong Lee, Korean Educational Development Institute; Roger C. Shouse, The Pennsylvania State University*

Lessons From India: Community-Based Rehabilitation As a Model for Educational Inclusion and Community Empowerment. *Laura Desportes, James Madison University*

Post-Soviet Societal Changes and Impact on Schools and Teacher Collaboration in Ukraine. *Benjamin Kutsyuruba, University of Saskatchewan*

Discussant:

Benjamin Levin, OISE/University of Toronto

22.020. Offsite Visit to the Middle College-Early College High Schools at LaGuardia Community College. Division A-Administration, Organization, and Leadership
Off Site Visits, LaGuardia Community College
8:15 am to 12:30 pm

Participants:

Elisabeth Barnett, Teachers College, Columbia University
Haiwen Chu, Graduate Center - CUNY
Cecilia Cunningham, Middle College National Consortium

22.021. Critical Multiculturalism From Theory to Practice: A Division B Equity Session. Division B-Curriculum Studies
Sheraton New York Hotel & Towers, Central Park East, 2nd Floor
8:15 am to 10:15 am

Chair:

Stephen A. May, University of Waikato

Participants:

Introduction and Overview: From Principles to Practices. *Stephen A. May, University of Waikato*

Critical Multicultural Approaches to Mathematics Education in Urban, K-12 Classrooms. *Eric H. Gutstein, University of Illinois - Chicago*

Critical Multiculturalism and Physical Education: Complexities, Contradictions, and Potential for Resistance. *Katie Fitzpatrick, University of Waikato*

The Arts and Social Justice in a Critical Multicultural Education Classroom. *Mary Stone Hanley, George Mason University*

Sustaining a Critical, Culturally Responsive Pedagogy of Relations. *Russell Bishop, University of Waikato - New Zealand*

Radicalizing Language Teacher Education: Infusing Critical Multicultural Principles and Practices Into the Curriculum. *Lilia I. Bartolome, University of Massachusetts - Boston*

Discussant:

Christine E. Sleeter, California State University - Monterey Bay

22.022. EcoJustice Education: A Commons-Oriented Curriculum. Division B-Curriculum Studies
Sheraton New York Hotel & Towers, Madison Suite 3, 5th Floor
8:15 am to 9:45 am

Chair:

Kelly A. Young, Trent University

Participants:

James Joss French, University of Connecticut
Kurt Love, University of Connecticut
John Joseph Lupinacci, Eastern Michigan University
Andrejs Kulnieks, York University
Sean Blenkinsop, Simon Fraser University
Kelly A. Young, Trent University

Discussant:

Rebecca Martusewicz, Eastern Michigan University

22.023. Effectiveness of Mathematics Curriculum and Programs. Division C-Learning and Instruction
Hilton New York, East Suite, 4th Floor
8:15 am to 9:45 am

Chair:

Jae Meen Baek, Arizona State University

Participants:

A Study of the Effectiveness of the Louisiana Algebra I Online Course. *Laura M. O Dwyer, Boston College; Rebecca A. Carey, Education Development Center, Inc.; Glenn M. Kleiman, North Carolina State University*

Effects of a Reformed Curriculum on Student Learning Outcomes in Primary Mathematics. *Yujing Ni, Chinese University of Hong Kong; Qiong Li, Beijing Normal University; Jinfa Cai, University of Delaware; Kit-Tai Hau, Chinese University of Hong Kong, Zhonghua Zhang, Chinese University of Hong Kong*

Classroom Connectivity in Promoting Mathematics and Science Achievement: Year One Results. *Stephen J. Pape, University of Florida; Douglas Owens, The Ohio State University; Karen E. Irving, The Ohio State University; Christy Kim Boscardin, University of California - Los Angeles; Vehbi Sanalan, The Ohio State University; Louis Abrahamson, Better Education Foundation; Sukru Kaya, The Ohio State University; Hye Sook Shin, University of California - Los Angeles*

Using Computerized Adaptive Testing and an Accelerated Longitudinal Design to Index Learning Progressions in Early Mathematics Development. *Joseph Betts, University of New Mexico; James R. McBride, Renaissance Learning*

The Vermont Mathematics Initiative: Student Achievement From Grade 4 to Grade 10. *Herman W. Meyers, University of Vermont; Douglas Harris, Vermont Institutes; Kenneth Gross, University of Vermont*

Discussant:

David C. Webb, University of Colorado - Boulder

FIGURE 3.1 (continued)

Academic Progress in Untracked Classrooms: An Example of a Conference Paper

Many schools make use of ability grouping, or "tracking," a practice in which students with similar abilities are placed in the same classroom so that teachers can cover the same material to the same degree of rigor with all students in the class. Tracking is a controversial practice, in part because studies show that student achievement is influenced by diversity on other dimensions besides academic ability. A number of studies have also shown that students in lower track classes may achieve less and experience lower self-esteem as compared to students in higher track classes.

These problems with ability group tracking inspired an ethnographic research study on untracked classrooms by Sarah Freedman, an academic researcher, and Verda Delp, an experienced classroom teacher. Freedman and Delp reported some of their research findings as a conference paper at the 2006 American Educational Research Association meeting.* A longer version of the paper, available online at *www-gse.berkeley.edu/faculty/SWFreedman/aeratracking2006.pdf*, contains references and other details not provided in the actual conference talk, and portions of the paper appeared in a 2005 publication in the journal *Research in the Teaching of English*. In short, the paper introduced in this Spotlight on Research is a report of research from a larger, ongoing project.

In the introductory section of their paper, Freedman and Delp spell out the theoretical foundations of their study, which includes the assumption that effective teaching occurs in Vygotsky's zone of proximal development (ZOPED), where students cannot yet complete a task on their own but may do so with the help of more experienced individuals. Teaching within the ZOPED is desirable in untracked classrooms, in part because less advanced students can turn to both the teacher as well as more advanced students as a source of support.

Freedman and Delp describe their methodological approach as follows:

What we report here is part of a larger study looking at both teaching and learning in untracked English classes and at teaching beginning teachers to teach in these settings (Freedman, Delp, & Crawford, 2005). For the larger study two research assistants observed, took field notes, and videotaped Delp's second-period, eighth-grade class during the

first three weeks of school and during three of six literature studies: The Light in the Forest *across eight weeks in the fall,* The Autobiography of Miss Jane Pittman *across eleven weeks in the winter, and* A Lesson before Dying *across seven and a half weeks in the spring. In addition, Freedman observed and took field notes once or twice a week during the data collection periods. In all, we collected 111 videotapes representing 26 weeks of class time. We also collected all teaching materials related to the tapes, including books and short stories the students read and handouts Delp distributed.*

The research team, including Delp, Freedman, and the two research assistants, met weekly to review the videotaped data and add information about Delp's intentions and her sense of her students' progress to the field notes. Besides the videotapes, audiotapes, and associated materials and notes, Delp wrote daily field notes about her teaching during the research year and audiotaped several one-on-one conferences that occurred outside of class.

Freedman and Delp noted that because the research team included themselves, as well as six research assistants, and because at any given time at least two observers were present in the classroom, the conclusions drawn from the data represent multiple perspectives. After transcribing 34 of the 111 class periods in full, and partially transcribing 25 additional classes, Freedman and Delp coded the verbal interactions in the transcripts and began to make sense of the data. They noted that Delp made use of highly structured and routinized activities, such as keeping logs and creating resource maps. Since these activities were repeated for each literature study, students became very familiar with the routine and could focus on the content of the studies rather than the directions for how to proceed.

The authors observed that over time, Delp created an academic community in her classroom.

The community functioned according to a set of moral values and a community ethos in which diverse views and approaches to learning were both valuable and valued. To teach diverse groups of students so that they have opportunities to choose to work within their ZOPED, the community must feel supportive and safe; working in the ZOPED implies a willingness on the part of individual students to take risks and to struggle to learn . . .

Across time, the community's moral values and the classroom ethos were addressed during each literature study and helped students understand and make personal connections with the literary themes and characters they studied. Community and curriculum mutually reinforced each other.

The community further was held together with a set of common stories and shared ideas. All students and the teacher were responsible for contributing ideas and taking on the ideas of others. Contributing ideas was something all students could do and something others could value. Further, Delp structured activities so that the ideas of others became useful and were worth collecting.

Delp began the year by getting her students to agree to live according to a common moral and ethical code. She, too, agreed to abide by the code. Over time, members of the class grappled with how to "respect" and "trust" one another, act with "integrity," "dignity," and "compassion," examine and "reflect" on the "perspectives" of others, "contemplate" across time, and take "responsibility" for their actions. They also considered what it meant to be "mindful" of others and themselves, show their "vulnerability," and be willing to engage in the inevitable "struggle" associated with learning and growth. Delp spent time helping her students understand the values connoted by these words and why such values were important to building an equitable intellectual community . . .

Delp also used the moral code to teach about her behavioral expectations. As she explained to her students on the first day of school, "[I] expect everybody to be wonderful and kind to each other and respectful." Her expectation and assumption was that all students were committed to respectful behavior. At the same time, Delp realized that she played a critical role in reminding students to act respectfully. Indeed in most middle-school classes, and Delp's was no exception, student behavior must be carefully managed, and Delp told her students that she understood that there would be times when a student might forget to behave respectfully.

Finally, across the year the moral code permeated the literature Delp taught and the vocabulary study associated with the literature. Students explored these moral values through the actions of the characters in the stories they read and through ongoing discussions of these same concepts in relation to characters' lives and their own lives . . .

As she worked to bind her class into an academic community of learners, Delp focused on equalizing academic respect and opportunity for her students. She did this primarily by promoting a culture that at its center valued sharing ideas (Bakhtin, 1981).

She believed that all students had good ideas to share and that students could benefit by giving and taking ideas from her and from their classmates. Even if their skills differed, all were on level ground with respect to their ideas. Indeed, a diverse group was valuable because the ideas they came with were diverse as well. Delp told her students the first day she met them:

> *"So we're going to be building a community of, well I call it a classroom community of learners. That is, we're going to be a group of people where we've shared our ideas together. This class will be very different than my first-period class and very different than my third-period class because of the ideas that we have in here. You will have a distinctive community in here, because of your ideas."*

A few weeks later she elaborated on her philosophy of idea sharing and idea generating:

> *"You're taking the ideas that you already have, and you're listening to other ideas, and then you're negotiating your thinking. So you may take on some new thinking. Or you might even feel more strongly about what you already think. That's good. But it's hard work. And I know that."*

Toward the end of the year, when Delp's students were used to sharing and using one anothers' ideas, she reminded them of what they gained from sharing and encouraged them to choose to share broadly with their classmates as they read each others' logs . . .

The authors concluded that heterogeneous students in untracked classrooms can flourish in the kind of academic community that Delp enabled.

*Freedman, S. W., & Delp, V. (2006, April). Students "latch on": Rethinking applications of Vygotskian and Bakhtinian theories for teaching and learning in an untracked English class. Paper presented at the annual meeting of the American Educational Research Association, San Fransisco. Quoted with permission from the author. For additional details, see Freedman, S. W., & Delp, V. (2007). Conceptualizing a whole class learning space: A grand dialogic zone. *Research in the Teaching of English*, 41(3), 259–268, and Freedman, S. W., Delp, V., & Crawford, S. M. (2005). Teaching English in untracked classrooms. *Research in the Teaching of English.40(1)*, 62–126.

POSTERS The **poster** consists of a research report attached to a large bulletin board. A **poster session** consists of a group of posters displayed in a designated room. During a poster session, each presenter stands beside the bulletin board containing his or her poster and engages in discussion with passersby who express interest. The poster contains minimal text—just the highlights or main points of the study—presented in large font, so that people can see the poster from several feet away. The presenter may also provide hard copies of the poster, or a longer manuscript if available, and may take contact information for individuals who wish to receive the poster by mail or e-mail. As you can imagine, the poster presentation is less formal and more interactive than the conference paper. From the researcher's perspective, the poster session provides an excellent opportunity for acquiring feedback from colleagues on preliminary findings. From the audience's perspective, the poster session provides an excellent opportunity for "grazing," in that one has some control over how deeply to delve into any given study.

Both posters and conference papers will be available from the authors. Also available may be **conference proceedings**, which consist of abstracts and perhaps also entire presentations organized by session. The proceedings of major conferences such as the AERA and SRCD meetings can be found at a university library or downloaded from the Internet.

Journal Articles

Research reports in peer-reviewed journals are the heart of scientific knowledge. (See Chapter 2 for discussion of peer review.) Articles in the most highly respected peer-reviewed journals tend to have the greatest impact on knowledge in particular disciplines. Their impact is attributable to several interrelated factors:

- The editors and editorial board members tend to be leading researchers.
- The submissions are reviewed by experts through a rigorous process.
- The acceptance rates for submissions is very low.
- The articles ultimately published are narrow in focus but have important theoretical implications.
- The articles ultimately published are cited frequently in other publications.
- The journals themselves are widely available, both in print and online, and are indexed in many databases.

The major parts of the research article published in a scholarly journal are described below. My emphasis in this section is on quantitative reports. Although the structure of qualitative articles tends to be very similar, some key differences will be noted later in the chapter.

TITLE PAGE The title page of a journal article is reproduced in Figure 3.2. Although the exact format varies from journal to journal, this example is fairly typical. The top of the page contains the name of the journal (*Applied Measurement in Education*) along with bibliographic information and publisher. Below that you will find the title of the article, the authors' names, and their affiliations. Next is the abstract and the first few lines of the introduction. At the bottom of the page is contact information for the first author. (In some journals certain details, such as contact information, may be provided elsewhere in the article.)

APPLIED MEASUREMENT IN EDUCATION, *17*(1), 25–37
Copyright © 2004, Lawrence Erlbaum Associates. Inc.

Effect of Extra Time on Verbal and Quantitative GRE Scores

Brent Bridgeman
Educational Testing Service
Princeton, New Jersey

Frederick Cline
Educational Testing Service
Princeton, New Jersey

James Hessinger
Educational Testing Service
Princeton, New Jersey

The Graduate Record Examination General Test (GRE) is a measure of academic reasoning abilities that is intended to be a power test in which speed of responding plays at most a minor role. To test this assumption, we experimentally administered both the verbal and quantitative sections of the GRE with standard time limits and with 1.5 times the standard time limit (e.g., 45 min for a 30-min section). Participants volunteered to take an extra section with the experimental timing at the end of their regular GRE test; their incentive was eligibility for a cash payment if they did as well on the experimental section as on their operational sections. Usable data were obtained from 15,948 examinees. Results indicated that extra time added about 7 points to verbal scores and 7 points to quantitative scores (on the 200–800 score scale). Results were comparable across gender and ethnic groups, but quantitative scores were slightly higher for lower ability examinees.

Time limits on tests may serve at least two important functions. They may be needed if speed of performance is presumed to be related to the construct of interest. This is clearly the case on tests such as clerical coding speed in which the task

---

Requests for reprints should be sent to Brent Bridgeman, Educational Testing Service, M/S 09-R, Rosedale Road, Princeton, NJ 08541. E-mail: bbridgeman@ets.org

FIGURE 3.2   Title page of a peer–reviewed journal article. (Reproduced with permission from the International Reading Association.)

ABSTRACT Most research reports contain an **abstract**, a summary of what the researchers found. The abstract is typically one concise paragraph. From the abstract you can get a sense of the main research question and hypotheses, the general design (e.g., quantitative or qualitative), the nature of the participants and procedure, the main findings, and the main implication of the findings. In the abstract in Figure 3.2, you can see that the research question is, roughly, whether individuals will score higher on the GRE given substantially more time. You can see that two sections of the GRE were administered under standard conditions or with 50% more time, and that on average the extra time resulted in a 7-point increase per section. (The implications of these findings are not discussed in this particular abstract, perhaps because the issues are complex and easily misrepresented in a brief summary.)

INTRODUCTION The **introduction** provides an overview of the study. A typical introduction will consist of three more or less distinct parts. The first part contains a description of a problem, including some explanation of its importance. The second part consists of a literature review, in which the authors review prior research and theory of relevance to the problem. In the third part, links between prior research on the problem and the current study are articulated, and the design of the current study is sketched in. (Hypotheses about the results of the study might also be expressed at this point.) The three parts of the introduction may not be clearly demarcated or arranged in any particular order, but information pertaining to each part is usually available.

In the Bridgeman, Cline, and Hessinger (2004) study (see Figure 3.2), the problem described in the introduction is that the role of time limits in GRE CAT administration is ambiguous. (The GRE CAT is the computer-adaptive GRE General Test currently administered by computer.) Time limits may be necessary because one of the skills being tested is the ability to answer GRE questions rapidly. On the other hand, speed of response may be unimportant, in which case time constraints are justifiable only insofar as they make administration of the GRE CAT more convenient. Bridgeman and colleagues reviewed prior studies suggesting that performance on older forms of the SAT and GRE increases substantially when test-takers are given more time. Their rationale for conducting a new study is that it is unclear whether the earlier results generalize to the GRE CAT:

> *None of these results is directly applicable to this GRE CAT because of content and timing differences with the SAT (and earlier versions of the GRE) and because of differences between CAT and paper-and-pencil administrations. Several of these differences in administration mode could affect reactions to time limits. First, the CAT does not allow item review, so the examinee does not have the option of skipping an item and returning to it if time permits. Second, reading long passages on screen, especially if those passages require scrolling, is more time-consuming than reading on paper. Third, on a paper-and-pencil test, easy items often can be answered quickly and very difficult items may be skipped by lower ability examinees; a CAT attempts to select items that are neither very easy nor impossibly difficult for a given examinee, so very few items might be answered quickly. This study is intended to determine the extent to which the findings related to extended time on paper-and-pencil tests do or do not generalize to the GRE CAT.*
>
> *(Bridgeman et al., 2004, pp. 26–27)*

METHOD The **method** section provides information on how the study was conducted. The information is concrete and specific—a well-written method section would allow a reader to replicate the study.

The first part of the method section provides information on participants, including sample size, demographic mix, and any other distinctive characteristics. The second part describes the measures that were used—formal tests, unstructured observation, or however else the researcher gathered information. Procedural details may be provided in a third part of the method section, or combined with a discussion of the measures. Figure 3.3 contains the method section of the Bridgeman et al. (2004) study (which is shorter than what you would find in most articles):

RESULTS The **results** section provides information about the outcome of data collection. In a quantitative study, numerical results are provided, while in qualitative studies and action research, a narrative is developed. Regardless of type of design, the authors will be as specific as possible in their descriptions of findings.

The results of the Bridgeman et al. (2004) study were analyzed by means of complex statistical techniques discussed in Chapters 10 and 11. The main findings are summarized in Table 3.1. In this table, the average GRE CAT scores are given for three different ranges of scores: low, mid, and high. Within each range, average scores are given for the standard administration of the GRE CAT as well as the administration with extra time. As you can see, the more poorly students did on the standard administration of the test, the more they benefited from extra time. Other analyses suggested that there were no differences across gender or ethnicity in the effects of additional time.

DISCUSSION In the **discussion** section, the results of the study are summarized, interpreted, and evaluated. This section may be folded into the results section or stand alone. It may be called the "conclusion" or "summary" section, or the author might provide a separate, brief conclusion.

The typical discussion section consists of three parts. First, the authors summarize the most important results and tease out the implications for the original research question. Next, the authors develop conclusions about whether their hypotheses were supported, and about how the results contribute to the existing literature. Finally, the authors may point out the strengths and weaknesses of their study, and suggest avenues for future research. The three parts of the discussion section may or may not be clearly demarcated.

In the conclusion section of the Bridgeman et al. (2004) study, the authors noted that the effects of additional time had little influence on GRE CAT scores, and that these effects did not differentially affect the performance of women and minorities. These findings point to the conclusion that speed is not part of the skill set measured by the GRE CAT. At the same time, the researchers cautioned against overgeneralizing the results, noting that on other tests, or with certain groups who take the GRE CAT, there may be substantial gains in performance if additional time is given. Finally, the authors suggested that one topic for future research would be to determine how to help low-performing students manage their time more efficiently, since in this study they experienced, on average, a 21-point gain as a result of extra time—a small but not trivial increase.

OTHER COMPONENTS Most journal articles contain tables and/or figures to help convey essential information (see Chapter 12 for details). Information that is too extensive for a table or figure may be included in an appendix immediately

METHOD

Participants

Examinees who took the GRE General Test over a 2-month period were invited to participate in a research project that would require them to take an additional test section. At the end of the regular test, a screen appeared that invited voluntary participation in a research project and offered an incentive not only to participate, but to perform well on this research section. The instructions stated,

> It is important for our research that you try to do your best on this section. The sum of $250 will be awarded to each of 100 individuals testing from September 1 to October 31. These awards will recognize the efforts of the 100 test takers on the research section. Only test takers who meet the following criteria will be eligible for the award. Awards will be given to those 100 test takers who score the highest on questions in the research section relative to how well they did on the preceding scored sections. In this way, test takers at all ability levels will be eligible for the award. Award recipients will be notified by mail.

A total of 29,962 examinees volunteered to participate and at least started to answer questions in the research section. However, about half of this number spent so little time on this extra section that they were apparently not making a serious effort. We decided to screen out examinees who did not spend at least 30 min on the quantitative section (which has a standard time limit of 45 min) or at least 20 min on the verbal section (with a standard time limit of 30 min). Although we may have screened out some test takers who were simply exceptionally fast, this seemed preferable to having large numbers of unmotivated examinees in the sample. As a check on the reasonableness of this screening, we compared the regular operational scores of the examinees who were screened out with the scores of the examinees who passed the screen.

Of the 14,633 examinees who started the quantitative section, 7,653 passed the screen. In the screened-out sample, the mean score on the operational section was 617 whereas on the research section the mean for these same people was 450. The correlation of the scores on the research and operational sections was just .34. The picture was quite different in the sample that passed the screen. Scores on the operational and research sections were 657 and 667, respectively, and the correlation between sections was .90. Thus, for examinees who passed the screen, performance on the research and operational sections was virtually indistinguishable.

Screening results for the examinees with a verbal research section were comparable to the quantitative results. From an original sample of 15,329, the screened-in sample numbered 8,295. Means in the screened-out sample were 498 and 387 for the operational and research sections, respectively, and the correlation was .42. For the screened-in sample, the means were 454 and 457, with a correlation of .80. All further analyses use only the sample that passed the screen.

FIGURE 3.3 Method section of a peer-reviewed journal article. (Reproduced with permission from the International Reading Association.)

TABLE **3.1** Summary of GRE Results from Bridgeman, Cline, and Hessinger (2004)

Ability Level (GRE score range)	Average Score		Improvement
	Standard time	Extra time	
Low (200–500)	449	470	21
Mid (510–700)	630	643	13
High (710–800)	756	762	6

following the discussion section. In educational research, appendices often contain a partial or complete set of items drawn from the measures that were used. Following the discussion section (and appendix, if included) will be the reference section, which provides bibliographic information for all sources cited in the main body of the article.

Journal Articles Reporting Qualitative Research

The structure of some qualitative articles is very similar to those that report quantitative research: the abstract and introduction are followed by detailed descriptions of methods and results, then by a concluding section and a list of references.

One difference between quantitative and qualitative articles is in the terminology used. Whereas the quantitative researcher speaks of "data," the qualitative researcher may use terms such as "findings." The quantitative researcher refers to "data collection," while the qualitative researcher may speak of "gathering information." Many other differences in terminology will be evident in later discussions of quantitative and qualitative designs (Chapters 7–9 and Chapters 13–14, respectively).

Another difference between quantitative and qualitative articles is that the latter may exhibit a less clearly distinguishable structure. Whereas the quantitative research report is typically divided into sections ("Method," "Results," etc.), with relatively clear boundaries between the type of information presented in each section, the qualitative article may include a mix of procedures, findings, and interpretive reflections on both the procedures used to gather information as well as the meaning of that information. As a reader you may be able to distinguish clearly between the "methods," "results," and "interpretations" in a qualitative article, but the writers of the article may present the information somewhat concurrently, in order to convey how their procedures and their understanding of the findings evolved during the course of the study.

Professional Reports

The **professional report** is a description of research written for parents, teachers, school administrators, policymakers, or the agencies that funded the research. Professional reports (sometimes called "technical reports") are not peer reviewed in the formal sense, but they may reflect the thoroughness and quality of peer-reviewed publications. Their impact tends to be restricted to local educational practices. (In some cases, a professional report will influence the way research rather than education is practiced, as in the case of technical reports about psychometric tests.)

Since they are created for highly specific audiences, professional reports do not contribute directly to scientific knowledge, but they are typically part of research activities that lead to publications in peer-reviewed outlets. That is, the same researchers who generate conference presentations, journal articles, books, and so on may also produce professional reports as part of their scholarly activities.

The professional report often begins with a brief executive summary. The body of the report will be concise and specific, with attention to the practical applications of the research. It is important for writers of professional reports to be clear and cautious in explanations of their results, given that the audience may not be well versed in research methods. Because the audience may use the results to directly modify educational practice, authors of professional reports should also be very clear about the practical applications that are and are not suggested by the data.

Examples of professional reports are discussed at length in Spotlights on Research 6.3 and 9.3.

Theses and Dissertations

A **thesis** is the document submitted for a master's degree, while a **dissertation** is the document submitted for a doctorate.

The master's thesis may consist of a report of original research conducted by the student. Alternatively, it may consist of a literature review and/or research proposal—the exact requirements vary from university to university, as do format requirements such as minimum length. In some cases, students are required to submit thesis proposals that must be approved by the student's advisor and/or committee before work on the actual thesis can commence.

In education and related fields, the dissertation is almost always a report of original research. A dissertation proposal must be submitted in advance of the final product, so that the student's advisor and/or committee can ascertain whether the student is on the right track and offer feedback as needed. The proposal conveys a formal, detailed plan for conducting the dissertation research. Included in the proposal will be the theoretical and empirical background for the study, the research question (or focus of inquiry), a detailed description of the methods (including design, sampling strategy, measures, procedures, and any preliminary results), and a timeline. Although format requirements vary across universities, the final dissertation will have roughly the same organization as a journal article.

Traditionally, the literature review presented at the outset of a dissertation was required to be extensive—much longer than appropriate for a research report in a scholarly journal. Students who became professors or took other research-related jobs would then attempt to publish their dissertations piecemeal, perhaps submitting a revised version of their introductions as a review paper, and then attempting to create one or more research reports from the core of the dissertation. Although this practice still occurs, it is becoming more common for doctoral programs to encourage dissertations that are publishable with minimal revision. Doctoral students may write literature reviews as part of their doctoral requirements, but the dissertation itself will contain the focused, somewhat shorter review of the publishable journal article. As noted in Chapter 2, the dissertation abstract becomes part of a database called *Dissertation Abstracts International* (DAI), which is available online and in print form.

Secondary Sources

Research studies may be described in a fairly detailed way in **monographs** (books by a single author or group of authors focusing on a specific topic), edited volumes, handbooks, or one of the other authoritative secondary sources described

FIGURE 3.4 Excerpt from position paper on teacher certification for art students.

> *Generally speaking, based on their studio abilities, writing skills, overall interest, and attitude, it has been my experience that undergraduate and graduate art education majors are much better pre-pared than certification-seeking students to teach art in our public schools. We should not, there-fore, advise students to get an art degree first and then add on certification. This inherently devalues preparation in how to teach and may have a detrimental effect on student learning.*
>
> *Teacher preparation policy — an emphasis on what or how to teach — changes on a daily basis, but I try in this article to provide a good overview of the topic [and] I conclude with a list of policy recom-mendations. (Brewer, 2003)*

in Chapter 2. Although monographs and other kinds of books are peer reviewed before publication, reviewers may not evaluate descriptions of research as rigorously as they would for a journal article, since the research is not described in as much detail—and since most of the research reported in books has already been published. Although books are not as authoritative as journal articles as sources of original research, they may have an equal or greater impact on scientific knowledge because the authors are given more space to elaborate on theoretical perspectives, synthesize and critically evaluate the literature, and so on.

Media outlets such as *Time* magazine, *The Economist*, and *The New Yorker*, as well as professional publications designed for educators, are among the sec-ondary sources that provide in-depth discussions of educational research. The online version of *Education Week*, for example, contains a section for subscribers entitled Report Roundup, which consists of summaries of recent studies (see *www.edweek.org/ew/news/report-roundup*). Like other professional publications and academic journals, *Education Week* also publishes position papers. The **position paper** consists of a closely reasoned argument for a particular idea, usually of immediate relevance to educational practice. Although some position papers consist of little more than an airing of the authors' scholarly biases, others provide a good look at pertinent research studies and constitute useful secondary sources. To give you a sense of how a position paper sounds, an excerpt from the outset of one such paper in which research is cited is given in Figure 3.4.

Spotlight on Research 3.2 describes a secondary source published by AERA that provides in-depth summaries of research for policymakers.

Format of Research Reports

The format of research reports varies somewhat depending on whether they appear in books, journals, websites, or some other outlet, and there is variability within each type of outlet. Moreover, the format of a published research report differs from the format in which it is submitted for publication. To take just one example, whereas tables and figures appear throughout the text of a published journal article, at the time of submission these materials are placed at the end of the manuscript.

APA Style

Most educational journals require that manuscripts be submitted in "APA style"—in other words, in conformance with the requirements of the *Publication Manual of the American Psychological Association, 5th Edition* (2001). For over a half century, the APA

Spotlight
on
Research
3.2

Cognitive Demand and Math Education: A *Research Points* Report for Policymakers

The AERA publishes a series of articles for policymakers entitled *Research Points*, available on the Internet at *www.aera.net/publications*. Here is how this secondary source is described on the AERA website:

AERA's quarterly series, Research Points, *connects research to education policy. The series was established to help ensure that decision-makers have accessible sound and important research on timely education topics.*

Each issue brings essential information on education research to public policy-makers in Washington, D.C., and to education leaders and policy-makers in the 50 states. Information on current research is highlighted. In addition, several actions that policy-makers should take are outlined, and a bibliography is included.

The Fall 2006 *Research Points,** for example, focuses on the problem of increasing American students' achievement in mathematics—a problem the authors of this *Research Points* believe to be exacerbated by the practice of tracking (see Spotlight on Research 3.1 for definition):

[T]his Research Points *tackles the challenge of ensuring that whole groups of students are not excluded from higher mathematics learning.*

In our global economy and democratic society, limiting math education to select students is unacceptable. A recent ACT study provides evidence that college and the workforce require the same levels of readiness in mathematics. One implication: All students require a greater level of "cognitive demand" in mathematics than once was considered appropriate . . .

The term "cognitive demand" is used in two ways to describe learning opportunities. The first way is linked with curriculum policy and students' course-taking options—how much math and which courses. The second way relates to how much thinking is called for in the classroom. Routine memorization involves low cognitive demand, no matter how advanced the content. Understanding mathematical concepts involves high cognitive demand, even for basic content. Both types of cognitive demand are associated with student performance on achievement tests, but they are not substitutes for each other.

The *Research Points* authors go on to observe that both types of cognitive demand are diminished by the practice of tracking:

Course-taking options in the United States are organized according to curricular and ability tracks. Most students are sorted into tracks involving specific course sequences and, ultimately, different opportunities to learn mathematics. Traditionally, high schools have had three curricular tracks—college preparation, vocational, and general education. The college preparation track has top status and provides greater opportunity to learn more demanding mathematics.

Although many schools have done away with such three-track sorting, hidden forms of tracking persist. In one common situation, students are divided by perceived ability under the same course label. For example, an algebra course might sort students into fast and slow speeds of learning, so that by the end of the year students in the same class have not had the same opportunity to learn. Another sorting strategy offers different entry points into college-preparatory coursework (e.g., freshman versus junior year). For students who enter the college-preparatory track late in high school, it might be too late to learn enough mathematics to pursue higher-level college courses . . .

In theory, tracking helps all students by providing instruction suited to their ability and learning styles. However, research strongly suggests that not all students are benefiting. . . . Instead, the positive effects of tracking on overall achievement are associated most with a small minority of students assigned to high-status tracks. . . . We still need to prepare many more students in elementary and middle school to handle high-demand courses in high school, and we need to figure out how to keep the positive trends moving forward.

The *Research Points* authors illustrate some of the specific limitations in the cognitive demand of American mathematics classes by contrasting them with math classes in higher-achievement countries:

Traditionally, American mathematics teaching has emphasized whole-class lectures with teachers explaining a problem-solving strategy and students passively listening. The lecture usually is followed by students working alone on a large set of problems that reflect the lecture topic. . . . In contrast, high cognitive demand mathematics programs generally deviate in important ways from the "normal" approaches to mathematics instruction and classroom practice. The 1999 Trends in International Mathematics and Science Study looked at the ways that mathematics instruction differs among seven countries. . . . It found that although effective teaching varies from culture to culture, the key difference between instruction in the United States (the lowest performer in the study) and the other countries was the way teachers and students work on problems as a lesson unfolds . . .

While higher achieving countries did not use a larger percentage of high cognitive demand tasks compared to the United States, tasks here rarely were enacted at a high level of cognitive demand. High-performing countries avoided reducing mathematics tasks to mere procedural exercises involving basic computational skills, and they placed greater cognitive demands on students by encouraging them to focus on concepts and connections among those concepts in their problem-solving.

Other research found that in classrooms in which instructional tasks were set up and enacted at high levels of cognitive demand, students did better on measures of reasoning and problem-solving than did students in classrooms in which such tasks were set up at a high level but declined into merely "following the rules," usually with little understanding. . . . In successful classrooms, task rigor was maintained when teachers or capable students modeled high-level performance or when teachers pressed for justifications, explanations and meaning through questioning or other feedback.

International comparisons also have shown that some top countries teach fewer concepts in greater depth, while U.S. math curriculum is "a mile wide and an inch deep . . .

Following is the conclusion of this *Research Points* article:

Learning math can be tough. Not learning it is tougher. Many students lack access to higher-level mathematics courses and teaching at all levels of precollege schooling. This is unacceptable in the face of the ever-expanding technical demands posed by higher education and the 21st-century job market. Research reveals that strong academic experience is needed for both college and the workforce. Raising the

cognitive demand in the curriculum is necessary for enhancing students' career prospects.

Recent trends show progress, such as growth in the number of minority students taking higher-level mathematics classes and earning degrees in mathematics. Still, there is much work to be done. Curriculum policies that limit course options restrict opportunities to learn for traditionally underserved students. This problem is compounded by the sorting of students according to ability within the same mathematics classes and the low quality of some mathematics instruction in elementary and middle schools . . .

If we teach math at a higher level of cognitive demand, even in the early grades, we can look forward to a future in which high mathematics achievers better reflect the country's diverse population. To accomplish this, schools need to be staffed by well prepared teachers, and high curriculum standards should be a priority. Teaching in high-performing schools requires a learning environment that supports sustained student engagement on both basic skills and cognitively demanding conceptual mathematics tasks.

The *Research Points* article closes with a table of practical recommendations for policymakers, under the heading "What should policymakers do?"

First, *embrace high expectations for all students in mathematics. Informed civic engagement and a competitive, global economy demand higher levels of technical skill.*

Second, *institute curriculum policies that broaden course-taking options for traditionally underserved students. This includes avoiding systems of tracking students that limit their opportunities to learn and delay their exposure to college-preparatory mathematics coursework.*

Third, *raise cognitive demand in mathematics teaching and learning in both elementary and secondary schools. Elevated thinking processes come into play when students focus on mathematical concepts and connections among those concepts. High cognitive demand is reinforced when teachers maintain the rigor of mathematical tasks, for example, by encouraging students to explain their problem-solving.*

*Do the math: Cognitive demand makes a difference. (2006), *Research Points, 4*(2), 1–4. Quoted with permission from the American Educational Research Association.

TABLE 3.2 Some APA Publication Manual Requirements
for the Reference List

- For each entry in the reference list, all lines after the first line should be indented half an inch from the left margin.
- Authors' names should be inverted, so that the last name appears first, followed by the initials. The last names and initials of all authors of a work should be given, unless there are more than six authors. If there are more than six authors, the first six should be listed, followed by the phrase "et al."
- The entire reference list should be alphabetized by the last names of the first author of each work.
- If the reference list includes more than one article by the same author, and/or multiple-author references that present the same authors in the same order, these entries should be listed by year of publication, from earliest to latest.
- When referring to a book chapter or a journal article, capitalize only the first letter of the first word of the title and subtitle. The first word after a colon or a dash in the title, as well as any proper nouns, should also be capitalized. The first letter of the second word in a hyphenated compound should not be capitalized.
- All major words in journal titles should be capitalized.
- The titles of shorter works such as journal articles or essays in edited collections should not be italicized, underlined, or framed by quotations.

Publication Manual has provided highly specific guidelines on format (including information about organization, citations, and punctuation), stylistic requirements (e.g., rules governing the use of nondiscriminatory language), and ethical standards for the reporting of scientific results. Information about APA format can be found online at *http://apastyle.apa.org*. Table 3.2 provides one example illustrating the specificity of APA format—this table lists a subset of the requirements that are specific to the listing of references. (Check the reference list of this textbook to see illustrations of each bullet point in the table.)

Other manuals that are used sometimes for educational research publications include the *Chicago Manual of Style*, the Modern Language Association's *MLA Handbook for Writers of Research Papers*, and *A Manual for Writers of Term Papers, Theses, and Dissertations*. You may find, when writing your thesis or dissertation, that your graduate department or school has additional requirements over and above those specified in the manual they follow.

Spotlight on Research 3.3 provides a detailed look at the process of submitting research reports to scholarly journals, beginning with the formulation of a plan for writing and continuing through the process of peer review.

Evaluating Research Reports

Some of the advice in Spotlight on Research 3.3 can help you evaluate the quality of the research reports you encounter. But it would be impossible to briefly summarize every consideration of relevance. Since all of the information in this book, and more, bears on the evaluation of research reports, this section simply

How to Publish in Scholarly Journals: A Guide for Beginning Researchers

The process of creating a research report for publication in a peer-reviewed journal is described in a 2005 article by Janette Klingner, David Scanlon, and Michael Pressley, published in the Research News and Comment section of *Educational Researcher*.*

This article is about writing an article for a scholarly journal. We begin at the planning stages and end by describing what can be done if a journal rejects your manuscript. We consider many issues along the way, from conception to finally seeing the work in print. This article is based on an invited talk entitled "Getting Published While in Grad School," which was presented for the AERA Graduate Student Council at the association's 2005 annual meeting. Thus we address young scholars directly, although we invite others to read on for a refresher or to consider using this as a mentoring tool. We ground our advice in our experiences as journal editors and authors. We each have experienced the joy of acceptance, the distress of rejection, and the uncertainty of "revise and resubmit".

Klingner and colleagues discuss four components of article writing: planning before writing, writing the manuscript, submitting the manuscript, and the review process. Although their focus is on writing for peer-reviewed journals, much of what the authors advise is relevant to scientific writing of any sort, including research papers for classes, theses, and dissertations.

Planning before Writing

Good writing begins with planning. Consider first your purposes for publishing and the audience for whom you are writing. A thorough deliberation on why you wish to publish should guide this process . . .

The main reason to publish is that you have something to say. Scholars contribute to their profession's dialogue by publishing. Contributions should be timely in relation to contemporary dialogues and should add new ideas . . .

An even more practical reason to publish, however, is that many professional opportunities follow directly from publications. Academic job-seekers are at a competitive advantage when they can demonstrate a record of productivity with publications in an area of claimed expertise . . .

Once you have established a focus for your research and you are clear about your reasons for publishing, then you can address the scope of your manuscript. Some scholars are overly ambitious, trying to share too much in a single article. A manuscript should have a specific focus so that the author can write in depth about the target topic . . .

When planning your manuscript, reflect about the content available to support your intended points. If your data cannot stand alone, do not try to publish them alone. If your theory and/or evidence only weakly support what you claim, do not overextend your findings; instead, dare to ask yourself critically if you can support your claim at all . . .

The introductory section of an article includes a review of related literature. . . . [R]eviews of the literature should be thorough and up-to-date. . . . Do not cite it all; instead, cite what is most relevant. . . . Avoid citing as evidence of a claim an article that only weakly supports it or, even worse, that offers only speculation about it, which you proceed to claim as fact. To avoid misrepresenting other researchers' work, read the sources you cite . . .

The closing discussion section of an article should also connect the manuscript to the larger field. A common error is to write a very brief discussion that inadequately ties the reported work to the larger professional dialogue(s), thereby not allowing the article to contribute everything it could. In the discussion, you should come full circle, connecting your research findings to the body of work that you described in your review of the literature . . .

One common error is neglecting to research the appropriateness of a journal before submitting a manuscript. For example, the Review of Educational Research *(RER) accepts only comprehensive, critical reviews and never publishes single studies. Yet the journal frequently receives single-study submissions. Likewise,* Educational Researcher *does not publish single studies but often receives single-study manuscript submissions, which it rejects without sending out for external review because such manuscripts do not fit the scope of the journal. To avoid making this mistake and annoying editors and reviewers, be sure that you have actually read articles in the journal to which you are submitting and have determined that your manuscript is a good fit for that journal . . .*

If you are considering targeting a journal with a very high rejection rate, you should read a few articles in the journal with an eye to answering the question, "Is my article as well-reasoned and does it make as great a contribution as the articles this journal publishes?" With respect to a very selective outlet, it also makes sense to ask a senior colleague to read your work and evaluate whether it has a chance of being accepted.... Even if your manuscript is not accepted, one reason to favor the best journals is that they tend to provide feedback of the highest quality, which can be quite helpful to you as you work to improve your manuscript ...

Writing the Manuscript

All writers have their own style and approach to the task of writing. Even so, there are conventions that must be observed if you are going to publish. Some of these conventions pertain to substance, others to the organization of the manuscript, and others to basic style rules ...

Early in the manuscript you should establish its intended contribution to the professional literature: Clearly state the topic of the manuscript, as well as the particular problem or questions you will address and why the problem or questions are important. The introduction to your manuscript does not need to be limited to the professional literature. Links to larger social and political phenomena, such as legislation and societal trends, can be appropriate. Perhaps most important, good work makes a contribution to theory. Atheoretical manuscripts rarely get published in the social sciences ...

Whether you conducted a research study (which may have used quantitative, qualitative, or multiple methods), prepared a comprehensive review of the literature, or developed a theoretical piece, you must report the methods you used. Your research methods should be aligned with your theoretical framework, purpose statement, and research questions.... A common error, one that some editors consider fatal, is to write a vague and too-brief methods section. Methods can never be as specified as a cookbook recipe, but the reader should be well informed about your process of inquiry. Without sufficient detail, the reader cannot judge your findings and discussion and has no reasonable basis for trusting you ...

Describe your results as succinctly as possible, providing analyses that support the conclusions you wish to draw. You do not need to report every analysis you carried out! Hard thinking is required to develop a results section that flows logically and is written so that the most important results are memorable. If the result is a new theory (e.g., a grounded theory; Glaser & Strauss, 1967), the most logical possible version of the theory should be presented, one that provides enough detail to be clear but not so much as to bore readers or

render the article much longer than is justified for the problem studied. In other words, be parsimonious ...

Once you have fully reported your findings, discuss the importance of what you have done and relate your new findings to broader issues. The caution in "going broad," however, is to avoid going too far, drawing implications from findings not sufficiently supported by data or claiming that the findings are relevant to issues beyond those that the study was designed to inform. Avoid undue speculation and keep the discussion consistent with both the purpose of the manuscript and what you reported in each prior section. Do not report new data in the discussion ...

There are a number of basic style rules that should be followed. The targeted journal's information for contributors will likely name several that are specific to that journal (e.g., word count). It will also name a stylebook to follow; most commonly in education this will be the Publication Manual of the American Psychological Association (APA, 2001), currently in its fifth edition. Make certain that you adhere to these guidelines. Stylebooks contain many helpful writing hints; time spent with them can be time well spent ...

There are a few stylistic devices that we, as editors, wish authors would use more often:

- *Make sure transitions are succinct, with one section naturally flowing into another. A weak form of transition is to flag what is going to be said in the next subsection or section. Although advance organizers can be helpful, unneeded repetition should be avoided.*

- *When in doubt, spell it out. Acronyms should be used sparingly and should be defined at first use unless they are ubiquitous (e.g., TV, U.S.).*

- *Avoid the passive voice. Write, for example, "The teachers told us ..." instead of, "We were told by the teachers that ..." The active voice focuses the reader more on the participants and/or the action.*

- *Do not anthropomorphize (i.e., give human-like characteristics to a nonhuman form). Your study did not conclude anything—you did ...*

- *Stay away from wordiness and jargon. Awkward sentences only distract the reader from your message. Let your content dazzle your readers, not your convoluted syntax or use of terms that are unfamiliar to readers because they are vague. Define terminology that is specific to a field.*

- *Avoid using "this" as a stand-alone pronoun; rather, use it to modify a noun. Too often, the antecedent for "this" is not clear.*

Submitting the Manuscript

Once you complete a manuscript, you may have misgivings about whether it makes sense to submit it to the journal that you originally targeted. This is an opportune moment to tap the most distinguished person in your field who is willing to appraise your manuscript and ask for a read and a recommendation about whether the journal you have in mind makes sense for your manuscript. Ask for suggestions for other journals if the targeted journal does not seem quite appropriate. You can also ask the journal editor if you are unsure about the appropriateness of your manuscript for that journal. Virtually all journal editors will look at the abstract to make an initial judgment about the fit and scope of the manuscript for their journal . . .

When you have made your decision, you must send out your manuscript to only one journal at a time. It is a serious ethical violation to submit simultaneously to more than one journal. If an author is caught doing this, all of the receiving journals may summarily reject the manuscript. We have seen it happen!

Make certain that your manuscript has been scrupulously written in the style required by the journal to which you are submitting. Double-check and triple-check that your manuscript is as error-free as possible. . . . There are a few style violations that particularly annoy reviewers, and, thus, authors are well-advised to make certain they do not offend with respect to these points:

- *Do not use condensed character spacing or a font smaller than 12-point to make it appear that your manuscript is shorter than it is.*
- *Similarly, be sure to double-space throughout (including in the reference list, indented quotations, and tables). Tighter spacing is harder to read.*
- *Use flush-left alignment for the body of the text rather than both right and left justification.*
- *Number pages and use specified margins (usually 1 inch, though sometimes wider).*
- *Make sure that your citations and reference list match. Double-check that your references and bibliographic style are correct and complete.*
- *Be fastidious in correcting typographical and grammatical errors before submitting, for they really irritate some readers. As you make such corrections, use your software's spelling check and grammar check, but keep in mind that by themselves these are insufficient for proofreading purposes: Some errors are real words that are not caught.*

When you submit your manuscript, carefully follow submission guidelines. Generally, these guidelines are available both in the journal and on the journal's website. When viewing a copy of the journal, be sure to use the most recent issue. . . . If you are not sure what the journal requires, contact the editors and ask them. If the journal calls for masking the submission, carefully do so (i.e., remove all references to your name and other information that would reveal your identity), following, for example, the guidelines in the APA manual (APA, 2001) . . .

The Review Process

The review process varies somewhat depending on the journal and on whether the submission and review process is handled manually or on-line. Generally, however, the steps are the same. First, an editorial assistant acknowledges receipt of the manuscript, assigns it a number, and assigns it to one of the editors (or the editorial team decides who will handle which manuscripts). Once the manuscript is in the editor's hands, she or he conducts a preliminary editorial review and decides whether the manuscript is appropriate to send out for review. Some manuscripts are rejected at this early stage in the process because they fall outside the purview of the journal or they are not considered to be of sufficient quality to send out for review. When the editor determines that the manuscript is appropriate to send forward, he or she generates a list of possible reviewers with expertise relevant to the focus of the manuscript. . . . For some journals, the minimum number of external reviewers is two. AERA requires its journals to use a minimum of three. Sometimes there are more. . . . Many editors aim for diversity in critical and theoretical perspectives, gender, nationality, ethnicity, methods, and methodology . . .

Once reviewers have been identified, the editorial assistant sends the manuscript to the reviewers and notifies you that the submission is "in review." Many journals use a "double-masked" review process; that is, the reviewers do not know the identity of the author of a manuscript and the author does not know the identity of the reviewers. Virtually all journals keep the identities of reviewers unknown to authors, although individual reviewers sometimes sign their reviews with the intent of identifying themselves to the authors and many editors pass on those identities . . .

The length of time for the review process varies, depending on whether the journal uses an on-line submission system, how quickly the editorial team can find reviewers, and, more than anything, how promptly the reviewers send their reviews back. Typically, editors ask reviewers to complete their review in about 4 weeks. However, reviewers often take longer . . .

The editor carefully reads all reviewers' comments and (re)reads the manuscript before making a decision and might also confer with others on the editorial team. Consulting is particularly important if the reviewers' comments are ambiguous or their suggestions appear contradictory. After reaching a decision, the editor writes a letter to the author that includes the decision, a summary of the reviewers' comments, and any further suggestions. The editor's decision may include one of the following: (a) Accept the manuscript as is; (b) accept it pending the completion of specific revisions; (c) invite a revision and resubmission; or (d) reject. These first-round decisions are not equally probable. Immediate acceptance is extremely rare. The most common decisions are "revise and resubmit" and "reject." If your manuscript is not rejected, the most likely sequence of events is that you will first be asked to revise and resubmit and then may receive an acceptance pending minor revisions. For a revise and resubmit decision to become an acceptance, the revisions must respond constructively to the reviewers' concerns . . .

What if your manuscript is rejected? First, you should recognize that many eventually published pieces were rejected somewhere before they found a publication home. Second, know that there are responses to the rejection that can go far in assuring a more favorable outcome in the future. Carefully

read all the paperwork that you received from the rejecting journal, including the letter from the editor and the reviews, noting and reflecting seriously on any revision suggestions in their comments. Keep reading and processing these remarks until you are certain that you understand them. . . . Once you understand the reviewers' remarks, revise the manuscript on the basis of their suggestions. . . . You may need to do substantially more work before submitting the manuscript elsewhere . . .

Finally, sometimes a rejection decision and the associated reviews compel the conclusion that additional effort on the manuscript would be a waste of time. If that is the implication, take the possibility seriously and reflect carefully on whether that may be the case. If it is, move on. Focus in directions more likely to pay off rather than in ones with little likelihood of success.

Our journals are the major forums for communication in our profession. Their quality and integrity must be maintained. With some effort on your part, you can reap the professional rewards that come with making valuable contributions to professional dialogues by publishing.

*Klingner, J. K., Scanlon, D., & Pressley, M. (2005). How to publish in scholarly journals. *Educational Researcher, 34*(8), 14–20. Quoted with permission from the publisher.

touches on some of the questions worth keeping in mind as you conduct a research-oriented literature review. These questions pertain to type of source, quality of source, importance of research, thoroughness of presentation, and quality of writing.

Type of Source

Even before reading a research report, you can identify the type of source it represents. Following are some key questions to ask:

- How recently was the research report published?
- Is the research report a primary source, or does it consist of a description of research in a secondary source such as a book, meta-analysis, or media report?
- If the research report is a primary source, is the description of the study condensed or presented in its entirety?

Keep in mind that secondary sources provide more theoretical integration and critical evaluation of research, while primary sources describe studies in greater detail and are thus more authoritative with respect to the details of the research. Recent reports may be more relevant than older ones, but recency per se does not guarantee high quality.

Quality of Source

Prior to reading a research report, there are also several questions worth asking about the quality of the source:

- Is the research published in a peer-reviewed source?
- Is the source widely respected in the field?
- Are the editors well known?
- If the source is a journal, what is the rejection rate for submitted articles and the citation rate for those that are published?

Although it can be difficult to evaluate the quality of a source (and somewhat misleading to evaluate its overall quality given the variability of individual contributions), a primary source is probably quite authoritative when the editors are prominent researchers, and when both the rejection and citation rates are high.

Importance of Research

As you read a research report, you can ask yourself several questions about its apparent importance:

- Does the research make a theoretical contribution?
- Does the research address a problem raised by prior studies in the field?
- Do the results have concrete implications for educational practice?
- How feasible would it be to implement any of the changes in educational practice called for by the results?

Research reports vary in the extent of their theoretical focus, their links to prior research, and their capacity to address highly practical concerns. It is important for research reports to be closely connected to *something*, whether it be theoretical, empirical, and/or practical concerns. Ideally, a research report makes a contribution in all three areas.

Thoroughness of Presentation

The thoroughness of a research report can be evaluated by means of the following questions:

- Is each component of the research thoroughly described?
- In the case of a journal article, does the introduction contain a statement of the problem, a literature review, and a research question with an overview of the study?
- Does the method section provide detailed information about participants, materials, and procedures?
- By reading the method section, could another researcher replicate the study?
- Are the results clearly described and pertinent to the research question?
- Does the discussion section link the results to the original research question and hypotheses as well as to prior research, and does it provide commentary on the strengths and weaknesses of the study?

Compared to the other dimensions on which a research report can be evaluated, it is relatively easy to assess the thoroughness with which the different components are described.

Quality of Writing

Finally, as you read through a research report, you can ask yourself about the quality of the writing. This dimension is reflected not only in writing style but also in the clarity, informativeness, accuracy, coherence, and other aspects of the report.

- Is the writing clear, detailed, and free of jargon?
- Are definitions provided for key terms and concepts?
- Do the definitions and other technical information appear to be accurate?
- Do the authors avoid biased language?
- Are the tables and figures informative and easy to read?
- Are the conclusions of the study warranted by the results?

The questions point to some of the principles of good writing that apply to any type of research report. Other general considerations are discussed in Spotlight on Research 3.3. At the same time, what constitutes good writing depends to some extent on the type of report. In a poster, for example, conciseness is essential, and brief summations are preferable to the detail that would be expected of a journal submission. There are also differences in how one should evaluate the writing in quantitative versus qualitative studies. A simple example would be differences across the two types of studies in assumptions about objectivity. The author of a quantitative article is expected to maintain an impersonal, nonjudgmental tone when describing his or her research. Although active voice is preferred, the passive voice may be acceptable if it allows the author to forego use of the personal pronoun "I"—instead of saying, "I asked each participant to fill out the questionnaire," the author might write, "Each participant was asked to fill out the questionnaire." In contrast, a semblance of objectivity would be problematic in certain kinds of qualitative research reports. In an ethnography, for example, it would be critical for the writer to acknowledge personal biases and reactions, weaving these into the description of the culture. Use of the pronoun "I" is commonplace, and it would not be desirable for the ethnographer to rely heavily on the passive voice when describing interactions with participants. (I will provide more information about the evaluation of both qualitative and quantitative research reports in later chapters.)

GOOD SCIENTIFIC WRITING Building on the previous discussion as well as Spotlight on Research 3.3, here are some recommendations that may help you become a better scientific writer.

- *Know your audience.* Be sure you are following the format and content requirements of the outlet for your research report. Be sure there is a stylistic fit between your writing and the writing of the reports that appear in the intended outlet. Overall length, length of particular sections, and conventions of expression that differ across quantitative and qualitative reports are three dimensions of style that you should consider.
- *Write clearly.* Be concise, define key terms and concepts, and avoid slang and other informal expressions. Avoid repetition. When referring to a previously discussed idea or finding, paraphrase the information as briefly and clearly as possible. Good scientific writing is very detailed and specific.
- *Use correct verb tense and point of view.* Most research reports are written using simple past tense. Thesis and dissertation proposals are written in future tense.

Active voice is preferred, although, as noted earlier, passive constructions may be acceptable in quantitative research reports in order to avoid excessive use of the pronouns "I" and "we." Qualitative and mixed-methods reports, as well as action research, tend to require a more personal voice.

- *Use correct grammar, spelling, and punctuation.* Proofread your writing carefully, use the grammar- and spell-check functions provided with your word processing software, and make sure that you are following the conventions of your intended outlet. APA style, for example, consists of extremely detailed guidelines.

- *Use nondiscriminatory language.* Consult the APA manual's guidelines for language that respects particular individuals, groups, and settings.

- *Read published research reports.* Much can be learned from how experienced writers handle each section of a report.

- *Solicit feedback.* Ask your advisor, other professors, and fellow students for critical commentary on your writing.

- *Edit, and then edit some more.* Most writers do not produce their best work on the first try.

A CAVEAT When you evaluate a research report, never forget to be a critical reader of content. The quality of a report is not solely a function of thoroughness and good writing, as illustrated by the thorough, well-written summary of a recent study reproduced in Figure 3.5.

FIGURE 3.5 A media report of a Department of Education study on the influence of books. (From *The Onion*, December 16, 1997, Issue 32-19. Reprinted with permission from the publisher.)

WASHINGTON, DC—A study released Monday by the U.S. Department of Education revealed that, contrary to the longtime claims of librarians and teachers, books do not take you anywhere. "For years, countless educators have asserted that books give readers a chance to journey to exotic, far-off lands and meet strange, exciting new people," Education Secretary Richard Riley told reporters. "We have found this is simply not the case."

According to the study, those who read are not transported to any place beyond the area in which the reading occurs, and even these movements are always the result of voluntary decisions made by the reader and not in any way related to the actual reading process.

"People engaged in reading tend to be motionless," Riley said. "Not moving tends to make it easier to read."

In various field experiments, the study found that young readers are particularly susceptible to the reading–travel myth. One test subject, 11-year-old Justin Fisher of Ypsilanti, MI, began reading a fantasy novel by C.S. Lewis under close observation. After 40 minutes, the only trip Fisher took was to the bathroom, a journey he himself initiated because he "had to go." Further, at no point did Fisher's voyage to the bathroom involve evil witches, messianic lions or closet portals to other universes.

"I just stayed in my chair without moving that much," Fisher said. "I think I scratched my head a couple of times." . . .

The study did note one exception to the findings, citing situations in which people read on buses, cars, trains or planes. Even in these cases, however, the reading–travel link is tenuous at best.

"Many people enjoy reading while traveling," Riley said. "But it is important to note that the traveling always results in the reading, and never the reverse."

As a result of the study, it is expected that many young people will call into question what Riley termed "the empty promises of library posters and other pieces of pro-reading propaganda."

A Look Ahead

The first three chapters of this book provided a general introduction to educational research, as well as some information on how researchers select topics to study and communicate their results. In the next set of chapters, I introduce the steps that researchers take when planning and conducting their studies, beginning with the selection of participants, the focus of Chapter 4.

Applications: A Guide for Beginning Researchers

Here are some ideas from the chapter that will help you plan your research:

- As you review the literature, make note of the type and quality of each source, the importance of the research, the thoroughness of the presentation, and the quality of the writing.
- Since you will be creating a written description of your research plan, and perhaps also of the finished product, you should start thinking about who your audience will be.
- Keep in mind that whether you are writing a research plan or a research report, each potential outlet will have specific format and content requirements.

Chapter Summary

Research reports include conference presentations, journal articles, professional reports, theses and dissertations, and secondary sources. Peer-reviewed journal articles, which tend to be most authoritative, are divided into sections including title page, abstract, introduction, method, results, and discussion. Qualitative reports often reflect less sharply bounded divisions.

Format requirements for research reports vary from outlet to outlet. The format required for submission differs from that used in the final publication. Often, APA format is required for submissions.

The quality of a research report can be evaluated on the basis of type and quality of source, importance of research, thoroughness of presentation, and quality of writing.

Key Terms

Conference paper	**Abstract**	**Professional report**
Panel	**Introduction**	**Thesis**
Poster	**Method**	**Dissertation**
Poster session	**Results**	**Monograph**
Conference proceedings	**Discussion**	**Position paper**

Exercises

1. In what part of a journal article would you expect to find a detailed description of the two main tests that were used to measure problem-solving skills?

a) Introduction

b) Methods

c) Results

d) Discussion

2. Where would you expect the authors of a journal article to describe alternative interpretations for their findings?

a) Introduction

b) Methods

c) Results

d) Discussion

For questions 3–6, refer to the (fictional) abstract below.

This study attempts to show that instructional methods emphasizing scientific thinking have a more positive impact on student achievement in science than methods that focus on conveying scientific facts. Participants in the study consisted of all 49 students in two fifth-grade science classes at a rural middle school. Both classes consisted of primarily Caucasian students with a fairly even distribution of gender within each class. One class received an intervention that focused on scientific thinking, while the other class received an intervention that focused on scientific facts. We found that students who received the scientific thinking intervention showed greater progress on a test of scientific knowledge than students who received the scientific fact intervention. We also found that the difference in extent of progress was roughly the same regardless of students' initial achievement levels. The results are consistent with recent research on instructional methods in secondary-level science classes. We conclude that in all subject areas, students would be better served by instructional methods that focus on critical thinking rather than those in which the mere accumulation of facts is emphasized.

3. In what type of research report would you expect to find this abstract?

a) Monograph

b) Journal article

c) Position paper

d) Poster

4. Which of the following seems *least* adequately described in the abstract?

a) The research question

b) The composition of the sample

c) The materials and procedure

d) The general implications of the results

5. What aspect of the first sentence most clearly needs to be edited?

a) The term "study" should be replaced by a phrase such as "research report," "research study," or "empirical investigation."

b) More information should be provided in this sentence about the content of each type of instructional method.

c) The phrase "This study attempts to show … " should be replaced by a phrase that is not anthropomorphic (e.g., "In this study, we attempt to show … ").

d) The entire sentence should be replaced by a statement explaining what relevance the research question has to middle school science teachers.

6. What seems to be most problematic about the logic of the final sentence?

a) The conclusion is overgeneralized.

b) The conclusion is incoherent.

c) The conclusion has no connection whatsoever to the findings.

d) The conclusion makes no reference to comparisons across gender.

7. *Critical thinking question:* Suppose that you find an interesting research report on the Internet but do not recognize the organization that posted it. How would you go about evaluating the quality of this source?

Answers to Exercises

1. b **2.** d **3.** b **4.** c **5.** c **6.** a

7. *Possible answer:* Ask an experienced professor, or an expert available through a listserv, what they know about the organization. Check the organization's website for professional affiliations, names of editorial staff, and criteria for posting research reports (e.g., check whether the reports are written for the organization or previously published in some other venue). Search the websites of established organizations such as AERA, as well as databases such as Academic Search Premier, for information about the organization. Contact the organization directly for additional information.

Suggestions for Further Reading

Research Article: Stipek, D. (2004). Head Start: Can't we have our cake and eat it too? *Education Week, 23* (34), 43–52.

This narrative article, a research-based call for Head Start reauthorization, illustrates a well-written position paper.

Application Article: Uchiyama, K., Simone, G., & Borko, H. (1999). *Publishing educational research: Guidelines and tips.* Washington, DC: American Educational Research Association. Available at *https://www.aera.net/uploadedFiles/Journals_and_Publications/Journals/pubtip.pdf*

This narrative article provides information for graduate students and new faculty on publishing research reports.

Extension Article: Tierney, W. G. (2002). Get real: Representing reality. *Qualitative Studies in Education, 15*(4), 385–398.

This narrative article describes recent controversies about the writing strategies most appropriate for use in qualitative research reports, and develops a philosophically motivated view of the issue.

CHAPTER 4

Ethics and Sampling

Sean Justice/Getty Images

After studying this chapter, you will be able to answer the following questions:

- What are the ethical guidelines for conducting research?

- How do researchers obtain ethical approval to conduct their studies?

- What are the major types of sampling in quantitative research?

- What are the major types of sampling in qualitative research?

- What constitutes an acceptable sample?

This chapter will prepare you to do the following:

- Evaluate the adequacy of sampling in research reports

- Obtain approval for your study from an ethics board

- Select an appropriate sampling strategy for your study

The voluntary consent of the human subject is absolutely essential.

THE NUREMBERG CODE (1949)

The subjects must be volunteers and informed participants in the research project.

WORLD MEDICAL DECLARATION OF HELSINKI (1964)

Respect for persons requires that subjects, to the degree that they are capable, be given the opportunity to choose what shall or shall not happen to them. This opportunity is provided when adequate standards for informed consent are satisfied.

THE BELMONT REPORT (1979)

Introduction

Any researcher who wishes to study people must obtain permission from an ethics board, select a group of people to study, and then obtain permission from the people themselves. These preliminary steps, carried out before the research begins, are my focus in this chapter. The chapter addresses the implications of two simple ideas:

- Most educational studies require interactions with people—students, parents, teachers, educational specialists, administrators, policymakers, and so on.
- Most educational studies cannot include every relevant person but only a subset of those people—a sample of first-graders, for example, rather than all first-graders in the United States.

The fact that educational research often requires interactions with people raises ethical issues. How researchers deal with these issues is the focus of the first part of the chapter. As you will see, sampling cannot begin until you have demonstrated that your methods meet a set of ethical guidelines embodied in federal law.

The fact that educational researchers typically study subsets of groups rather than entire groups raises methodological issues. Who should be chosen for participation in the study? How should these individuals be sampled? What are the advantages and disadvantages of various methods of sampling? These and other questions are addressed in the second part of the chapter, in which I discuss the principles and types of sampling at length.

In sum, the purpose of this chapter is to introduce the ethical and methodological principles that guide the selection of participants for a research study.

Research Ethics

Current rules governing the ethical treatment of research participants were motivated by a variety of 20th century studies in which participants were treated unethically. Following is a description of one such study.

Historical Impetus

In 1932, a treatment program was introduced in Macon County, Alabama. The purpose of the program was to treat "bad blood," a phrase used at the time to describe physical problems such as syphilis, anemia, and general fatigue. Six hundred black men were invited to participate in the program, and over the next 40 years these men were periodically examined and treated. The men, mostly poor sharecroppers, were happy to participate, because they were offered free medical care. They did not know that the true purpose of the study was to document the effects of syphilis on black males. Three hundred and ninety-nine of the men had been diagnosed with syphilis but not informed about their diagnosis. The other 201 men, who did not have syphilis, were included as a control group. Although effective treatments for syphilis were available, the 399 men who had the disease received no treatment until the study ended in 1972.

The study described here was conducted by the U.S. Public Health Service in conjunction with the Tuskegee Institute, and hence it is commonly referred to as the Tuskegee Syphilis Study. In 1972, stories in the *Washington Star* and the *New York Times* prompted the federal government to shut the study down. In 1973, the NAACP won a class action lawsuit resulting in compensation for surviving participants and relatives, and in 1997 President Bill Clinton issued a formal apology to these individuals on behalf of the U.S. government. The Tuskegee Syphilis Study remains both a symbol and a concrete reminder of the potential abuses that can occur when research is conducted with humans. However, it is not the only study in which the rights of participants have been violated. Medical experiments conducted by Nazi doctors during World War II, as well as experiments in social psychology conducted by American researchers in the 1960s, are among the other infamous examples of ethical violations in research. These studies are the basis for the federal legislation that currently protects research participants. Research with humans in the field of education, as in other fields, must comply with this federal legislation.

Federal Response

In 1974, in response to the Tuskegee Syphilis Study and other ethically problematic experimentation, the U.S. government passed the **National Research Act**. This act led to the establishment of a national commission charged with the development of ethical guidelines for research with humans. The commission's primary work was to create the Belmont Report (1979), an important foundation for current legislation. The Belmont Report describes three ethical requirements that all human subjects research must conform to:

- Participants must be informed in advance about the nature of a study, and must be allowed to either give or withhold consent to participate without coercion. (This requirement is referred to as **informed consent**.)
- The potential risks and benefits of the research must be evaluated. Risks to participants must be minimal, and justified by the potential benefits of the research.
- Participants should be selected fairly, without singling out individuals or groups for either potential benefits or potential exposure to risks.

The National Research Act also requires that all research involving humans be approved in advance by an authorized body. Specifically, the act requires that institutions sponsoring human subjects research maintain an **Institutional Review Board** (IRB) that reviews and approves each study. Each IRB must consist of at least five members, including one individual not affiliated with the institution. By law, no research with humans may be conducted unless an IRB certifies that it meets ethical standards.

45 CFR 46

Currently, the ethical standards and related guidelines for research that IRBs follow are embodied in the Code of Federal Regulations for the Protection of Human Subjects (**45 CFR 46**), which was developed by the Office of Human Research Protections (OHRP) as a means of extending the National Research Act and unifying existing regulations maintained by numerous federal agencies. 45 CFR 46 encompasses the basic principles of the Belmont Report, as well as other formal responses to ethical violations in research. The regulations laid out in 45 CFR 46 place great emphasis on minimizing risk to research participants, obtaining informed consent, avoiding any actual or perceived coercion to participate in a study, and protecting the privacy of participants. In Figure 4.1, you can see some of the general guidelines that 45 CFR 46 outlines for IRB approval of research. Figure 4.2 presents some of the general guidelines that 45 CFR 46 specifies for informed consent. (The full details of 45 CFR 46 can be found on the Internet at *www.hhs.gov/ohrp/humansubjects/guidance/45cfr46.htm*.)

IRB Approval

Educational researchers may not be intimately familiar with the details of the National Research Act or 45 CFR 46, but they do know that they must submit an application or proposal to their IRB before they can begin a research study. Although the exact questions on an IRB form vary from institution to institution, all of these forms request information that allows the IRB to determine whether the requirements of 45 CFR 46 are being met. This information includes a description of basic methods, evidence that potential risks are minimized, the methods for obtaining informed consent, and so on. Thus, as in other fields of inquiry, educational researchers must comply with legal standards for protecting the well-being of participants.

FIGURE 4.1 Excerpt of General Guidelines for IRB Approval of Research from 45 CFR 46

(1) *Risks to subjects are minimized: (i) By using procedures which are consistent with sound research design and which do not unnecessarily expose subjects to risk, and (ii) whenever appropriate, by using procedures already being performed on the subjects for diagnostic or treatment purposes.*

(2) *Risks to subjects are reasonable in relation to anticipated benefits, if any, to subjects, and the importance of the knowledge that may reasonably be expected to result ...*

(3) *Selection of subjects is equitable. In making this assessment the IRB should ... be particularly cognizant of the special problems of research involving vulnerable populations, such as children ...*

(4) *Informed consent will be sought from each prospective subject or the subject's legally authorized representative ...*

(5) *Informed consent will be appropriately documented ...*

(6) *When appropriate, the research plan makes adequate provision for monitoring the data collected to ensure the safety of subjects.*

(7) *When appropriate, there are adequate provisions to protect the privacy of subjects and to maintain the confidentiality of data.*

FIGURE **4.2** Excerpt of Guidelines for Informed Consent from 45 CFR 46

[N]o investigator may involve a human being as a subject in research covered by this policy unless the investigator has obtained the legally effective informed consent of the subject or the subject's legally authorized representative. An investigator shall seek such consent only under circumstances that provide the prospective subject or the representative sufficient opportunity to consider whether or not to participate and that minimize the possibility of coercion or undue influence. The information that is given to the subject or the representative shall be in language understandable to the subject or the representative. No informed consent, whether oral or written, may include any exculpatory language through which the subject or the representative is made to waive or appear to waive any of the subject's legal rights, or releases or appears to release the investigator, the sponsor, the institution or its agents from liability for negligence . . .

(a) *. . . [I]n seeking informed consent the following information shall be provided to each subject:*

(1) *A statement that the study involves research, an explanation of the purposes of the research and the expected duration of the subject's participation, a description of the procedures to be followed, and identification of any procedures which are experimental;*

(2) *A description of any reasonably foreseeable risks or discomforts to the subject;*

(3) *A description of any benefits to the subject or to others which may reasonably be expected from the research;*

(4) *A disclosure of appropriate alternative procedures or courses of treatment, if any, that might be advantageous to the subject;*

(5) *A statement describing the extent, if any, to which confidentiality of records identifying the subject will be maintained;*

(6) *For research involving more than minimal risk, an explanation as to whether any compensation and an explanation as to whether any medical treatments are available if injury occurs and, if so, what they consist of, or where further information may be obtained;*

(7) *An explanation of whom to contact for answers to pertinent questions about the research and research subjects' rights, and whom to contact in the event of a research-related injury to the subject; and*

(8) *A statement that participation is voluntary, refusal to participate will involve no penalty or loss of benefits to which the subject is otherwise entitled, and the subject may discontinue participation at any time without penalty or loss of benefits to which the subject is otherwise entitled . . .*

Other Ethical Constraints

In addition to the legal standards of 45 CFR 46, researchers may also consult ethical guidelines published by major professional organizations. Two organizations that have the greatest influence in educational research are the *Ethical Standards of the American Educational Research Association* (1992), and the *Ethical Principles of Psychologists and Code of Conduct* (American Psychological Association, 2002). These publications address the use of human subjects, as well as other ethical issues that arise in research, including intellectual ownership, plagiarism, and conflict of interest. By way of illustration, Figure 4.3 reproduces one section from the *Ethical Standards of the AERA* concerning professional responsibility. (The *Ethical Standards of the AERA* can be found at *www.aera.net/aboutaera/?id=222.* The American Psychological Association Code of Conduct can be found at *www.apa.org/ethics/code2002.html.*)

Consent and Assent

Educational research is distinctive in that a large number of studies include families and children. Families and children who participate in research are protected by various federal legislation, including the Family Educational Rights and Privacy Act of 1974, as well as 45 CFR 46, which contains special guidelines for research with these and other vulnerable populations. For instance, recall that 45 CFR 46 requires informed consent from individuals prior to their participation in research.

FIGURE 4.3 Responsibilities to the Field Section of the *Ethical Standards of the AERA* (Reprinted with Permission from the American Educational Research Association)

A. *Preamble. To maintain the integrity of research, educational researchers should warrant their research conclusions adequately in a way consistent with the standards of their own theoretical and methodological perspectives. They should keep themselves well informed in both their own and competing paradigms where those are relevant to their research, and they should continually evaluate the criteria of adequacy by which research is judged.*

B. *Standards.*

1. *Educational researchers should conduct their professional lives in such a way that they do not jeopardize future research, the public standing of the field, or the discipline's research results.*

2. *Educational researchers must not fabricate, falsify, or misrepresent authorship, evidence, data, findings, or conclusions.*

3. *Educational researchers must not knowingly or negligently use their professional roles for fraudulent purposes.*

4. *Educational researchers should honestly and fully disclose their qualifications and limitations when providing professional opinions to the public, to government agencies, and others who may avail themselves of the expertise possessed by members of AERA.*

5. *Educational researchers should attempt to report their findings to all relevant stakeholders, and should refrain from keeping secret or selectively communicating their findings.*

6. *Educational researchers should report research conceptions, procedures, results, and analyses accurately and sufficiently in detail to allow knowledgeable, trained researchers to understand and interpret them.*

7. *Educational researchers' reports to the public should be written straightforwardly to communicate the practical significance for policy, including limits in effectiveness and in generalizability to situations, problems, and contexts. In writing for or communicating with non-researchers, educational researchers must take care not to misrepresent the practical or policy implications of their research or the research of others.*

8. *When educational researchers participate in actions related to hiring, retention, and advancement, they should not discriminate on the basis of gender, sexual orientation, physical disabilities, marital status, color, social class, religion, ethnic background, national origin, or other attributes not relevant to the evaluation of academic or research competence.*

9. *Educational researchers have a responsibility to make candid, forthright personnel recommendations and not to recommend those who are manifestly unfit.*

10. *Educational researchers should decline requests to review the work of others where strong conflicts of interest are involved, or when such requests cannot be conscientiously fulfilled on time. Materials sent for review should be read in their entirety and considered carefully, with evaluative comments justified with explicit reasons.*

This means, in effect, that participants must have a sense of what the research entails—their time commitment, the kinds of tasks they will be doing, any risks the research poses over and above those incurred during daily life, and so on. Typically, the researcher will give potential participants a written description of the study, and require a signature from the individual before participating (see Spotlight on Research 4.1 for a sample consent form).

In research with children, informed consent must be obtained from both children as well as their parents or guardians. Since children may not be able to understand written descriptions of research, it is permissible for researchers to obtain a child's **assent**, or oral agreement, to participate in research. (Spotlight on Research 4.1 also contains a sample assent script.) However, 45 CFR 46 stresses that all aspects of research with children, including the process of obtaining assent, must take into account "the ages, maturity, and psychological state of the children involved." Thus, for example, assent must not be equated with a mere failure to object to participation, since young children may be shy or feel compelled to agree to whatever an adult requests.

Example of Consent Form and Assent Script Used in a Research Study

The process of conducting a classroom study typically requires permission from the school district, principals, parents or guardians, and the students themselves. In a study currently underway at the time of this writing, Patricia Mathes and her colleagues are studying the effectiveness of a computer-based assessment of reading progress among students ranging from kindergarten through third grade. Following is the consent form that Mathes distributed to parents after she obtained permission from the school district and school principal for her study*:

Dear Parent/ Guardian:

I, Dr. Patricia Mathes, am faculty from the Institute of Reading Research at Southern Methodist University (SMU). This year I am conducting a project in your child's after school program, which has the support of the principal and school district officials. The purpose of this study is to examine how a new computer-administered assessment program performs in comparison to a commonly used teacher-administered assessment of early reading progress. This letter provides you with information about the study. Please read the information below and ask questions about anything you don't understand before deciding whether or not to take part. Your participation is entirely voluntary and you can refuse to allow your child to participate without penalty or loss of benefits to which you are otherwise entitled.

If you allow your child to participate, your child will participate in seven 15 to 30 minute sessions. Four of these sessions will be conducted on a computer while being supervised by a graduate student from SMU. Three of these sessions will be administered one-on-one by a graduate student from SMU. These students will have been trained to administer each set of assessments and will have passed a careful background check before being allowed to work on this project. During each session your child will be asked to identify letters, read words, and read stories. The sessions conducted on the computer will be delivered in a game-like

format that most children find highly enjoyable. The seven sessions will be held on different days over a 4 to 6 week period. Your child will never have more than 2 sessions in any one week.

Only you, the child's parents, and appropriate school officials, like your child's teacher, will have access to the information we collect about your child. Nobody else will be given this information, unless specifically asked to do so by you, the child's parents.

To ensure confidentiality, your child's name will be removed from all test forms and will be replaced by a number. Further, we will keep all project information in our locked offices at SMU. Following completion of the project, all identifying materials will be destroyed. Only summarized group information will be used in reports of our project, so your child's name will never be identified.

We see no risk associated with your child's participation, and your child may benefit by the fact that we will continually monitor his/her progress in reading and will give this information to you and to his/her teacher.

Participation in this project is <u>voluntary</u>. You have the right to withdraw your child from this project at any time without penalty. If you would like additional information about the project, please call Dr. Mathes at (214) 768–8400.

Finally, if you agree to have your child participate, please complete the form on the next page, and ask your child to return it to his or her teacher. Thank you very much.

Sincerely,

Patricia Mathes, Ph.D.
Director, Institute for Reading Research
Professor of Literacy, Language and Learning
School of Education and Human Development

CONSENT FORM

I understand that the purpose of this project is to compare an early reading assessment administered on the computer to one administered by an adult.

I understand that my child's participation is voluntary, and that I may withdraw my child from the project at any time without penalty.

If, during the course of the study, I have any questions about the study, my child's participation in it, or my child's rights as a research subject, I may call Dr. Patricia Mathes (214) 768–8400 or the chair of the SMU Institutional Review Board at (214) 768–3829.

I agree to have my child _____ participate in this project. (Please print first and last name of child)

_____   _____

Print Parent's or   *Signature*
Guardian's Name

_____

Date

Once parents returned an appropriately signed consent form, a graduate student examiner approached each child to inquire whether he or she would be willing to participate in the study. Since the children in Dr. Mathes's study were very young, oral assent was obtained. The examiner made use of the following assent script when interacting with each student:

Directions:

Before working with each child, explain the project to the child using the following script. If a child states that s/he would prefer not to participate, walk him or her back to class. Be sure to assure the child that the decision not to participate is acceptable, that s/he has "not let you down," and that s/he is not in trouble.

Script:

I'm (examiner's name) and I'm from Southern Methodist University. We call it SMU for short (discuss briefly if the child knows anything about university life—or if he/she knows of a university close by). One of the things we do at SMU is teach people how to be teachers. We want them to be the very best teachers they can be. One of the things we do is show them how to teach reading. That's why we're here. We want to show teachers how to teach reading, and we would like your help. We have already asked your parents, and it's OK with them. I want you to know that this is your choice. You don't have to help if you don't want to. Your parents know that too.

If you agree to help, you will do some reading activities to help us understand more about how kids learn to read.

Some of these activities are games on the computer. Other activities you will do with an adult. If you agree to help, me or one of my friends from SMU will visit you once or twice a week for the next few weeks to complete these activities. Each time we do this, it will take 20 to 30 minutes. In total we will visit you seven times. Four times will be on the computer, and three times will be with me or one of my friends from SMU.

These reading activities have nothing to do with your grades here at school. The only people who will see the results are the people here now and the people learning to teach reading.

Before you tell me if you want to be a part of these reading activities, I want you to think about everything I've said. Do you have any questions?

[Answer honestly using age-appropriate language.]

If you would rather not be a part of these reading activities, I will ask another girl or boy. You will not get in any kind of trouble. Do you have any other questions?

[Answer honestly using age-appropriate language.]

What do you think? Will you be a part of the reading activities?

1. *Child indicated [ ] Yes (initials of examiner _____).*
2. *Child indicated [ ] No (initials of examiner _____).*

*Consent form and assent script quoted with permission of author.

Permission

According to 45 CFR 46, Institutional Review Board approval is not required for certain kinds of research involving humans. Studies of publicly available documents are exempt from review by an IRB, as are studies that make use of test scores if the tests were administered as part of regular school procedure (assuming that the scores are recorded anonymously). However, in most cases a required step between the planning of a study and the sampling of participants is to obtain approval from an IRB.

Once IRB approval has been obtained, the next step for many educational researchers is to obtain permission from school administrators and the participants themselves (whether administrators, parents, teachers, and/or students). Obtaining permission can be quite a challenge, logistically speaking. Teachers and students are busy, and administrators may have concerns about research activities disrupting routines, invading privacy, or revealing something unfavorable about their schools. Each organization will have its own particular bureaucratic procedure for approving research, and in some cases the process is grindingly slow. Some parents are reluctant to participate in research, or to allow their children to participate, because they feel busy or have concerns about what participation in a study would entail. Students themselves may have similar concerns. The extent to which these problems are an impediment to conducting research varies according to the nature of the study. A study of computer use in which grant money allows the researcher to provide participants with access to appealing software is more likely to attract participants than an ethnographic study on the experiences of illegal aliens in our educational system. Regardless of the nature of the study, researchers need to be both patient and persistent in their search for participants. For ethical as well as practical reasons, researchers should be fully cooperative with administrators and ensure that everyone involved in the research is adequately informed.

Introduction to Sampling

The first part of this chapter introduced to you the legal, ethical, and logistical prerequisites for conducting research with humans. In the remainder of the chapter, I focus on a methodological prerequisite: obtaining an adequate sample of participants.

Populations versus Samples

To understand how and why individuals are selected for participation in a study, we need to distinguish between populations and samples. A **population** is the entire group of individuals that a study is intended to investigate. A **sample** consists of those individuals who actually participate in the study. A sample, in other words, is a subset of a population. Sampling is an essential part of research because it is usually not possible to study entire populations. A study on gender differences in the attention spans of 6-year-olds will not include every 6-year-old in the world, but rather a sample of children of this age.

Although it is convenient to define "populations" and "samples" as groups of people, these terms could apply to groups of anything, including organizations, documents, and behaviors. Here are some examples:

- A descriptive study based on samples of urban middle schools drawn from the larger population of urban schools.

- A content analysis based on samples of a school district's internal documents, under the assumption that the samples are reflective of the entire set of documents created in the district.

- The number of aggressive acts exhibited by students during recess recorded in an observational study, under the assumption that these acts are samples of the entire population of aggressive behaviors exhibited by each individual over time and across settings.

In each of these examples, the goal of sampling would be to learn something about the populations from which the samples are drawn.

The population of interest identified in a particular study is called the **target population**. In some cases, a target population will be large, as in the testing conducted by the National Assessment of Educational Progress (NAEP), which takes place periodically in order to record student achievement in various subject areas. The NAEP tests are conducted with about 100 public schools per state in order to yield generalizations about the achievement of all American fourth-, eighth-, and twelfth-graders.

In other cases, target populations are relatively small, as in a study on the effects of starting the high school day an hour later in one particular school district. Although the researcher usually specifies a target population, others may interpret the results of the study more or less broadly than the researcher intended. For example, a study on the effects of starting the high school day 1 hour later might be based on a sample of 35% of the students in a large urban school district. The researcher who conducts the study might indicate that the target population is high school students in urban school districts. However, some researchers might feel that the results generalize to all high school students, and to middle school students as well, whereas others might argue that the results do not generalize beyond the one school district in which the study was conducted. (These interpretive issues will be revisited in the discussion of population validity in Chapter 6.)

Representativeness, Sampling Bias, and Sampling Error

At the outset of a quantitative study, the researcher identifies a target population and then chooses a sampling procedure. In quantitative research generally, and in some qualitative studies, the goal of sampling is to obtain a **representative sample**—that is, a sample that accurately reflects the characteristics of the population from which it is drawn. Representativeness is highly prized in most research studies.

A sample that systematically fails to be representative of the target population is said to reflect **sampling bias**. This term does not mean that the experimenter has some sort of personal bias, but simply that sample characteristics systematically diverge from population characteristics. In a study on the effects of in-service training on middle school teachers, the sample would be biased if it only consisted of male fifth-grade teachers in their first year of teaching. In a study on the effects of starting the high school day 1 hour later, the sample would be biased if it only consisted of students in remote locations who live 45 minutes to an hour from school, but whose school day begins relatively early in the morning. (Presumably these students would benefit more from the extra hour than students in most school districts.)

Sampling bias can be contrasted with **sampling error**, or random divergences between sample and population characteristics. Sampling error, as discussed in Chapter 11, can be dealt with statistically but not prevented, since it results from chance variation. It is always possible that in a sample of 10,000 undergraduates, 9,900 will be women—an unlikely outcome, but possible in theory. If you conduct a study at a large university that has a roughly equal mix of male and female students but discover that 99% of your sample is female, then you are the unlucky victim of sampling error. Sampling bias, in contrast, is preventable. If you wish to test a hypothesis about the undergraduate population in general but choose to obtain a sample from a women's college, then your study will be flawed owing to sampling bias.

SOURCES OF SAMPLING BIAS   Broadly, there are three sources of sampling bias:

1. The individuals whom the researcher attempts to sample are not representative of the target population. If a researcher wants to gauge the effectiveness of an alcohol abstinence program among adolescents in general, sampling bias would be evident if the researcher only approached teenagers who were currently participating in Alcoholics Anonymous owing to prior experience with alcohol abuse. This kind of sampling bias is most readily avoided, since researchers typically have control over the selection of potential participants.

2. The individuals who agree to participate in the study are not a representative sample. In a study on the general effectiveness of an abstinence program, sampling bias would occur if the only individuals who volunteered had already firmly committed to abstinence. Generally, the smaller the percentage of potential participants who actually agree to participate in a study, the greater the likelihood of sampling bias in this sense.

3. The extent of attrition is substantial. **Attrition**, or the loss of participants from a study, creates sampling bias when the remaining participants are not representative of the population. If the aforementioned abstinence program required 1 hour of participation after school every day for 6 weeks, one might expect a great deal of attrition. The students who actually complete the program would probably be an exceptionally motivated group. Or, they may be the group taking the easiest classes and therefore receiving less homework over the course of the study. These and other possibilities illustrate the idea that deciding whether or not sampling bias exists in a study is often a matter of subjective interpretation. Researchers may claim that sampling bias exists in a particular study, because the sample is small, exhibits distinctive characteristics, or has been diminished by substantial attrition. However, the researchers who actually conducted the study may claim that sampling bias is unlikely, either by providing evidence that the sample has the same characteristics as the population, or by arguing that any differences between the sample and the population are not relevant to the variables being studied.

Types of Sampling

In the following sections I introduce some of the major quantitative and qualitative approaches to sampling. As you will see, quantitative and qualitative researchers differ somewhat in their goals and methods for sampling. The quantitative researcher studies a particular sample in hopes that the results can be generalized to the rest of the population. Quantitative researchers are therefore careful to rely on methods of sampling and statistical analysis that increase the plausibility of their generalizations. Qualitative researchers tend to study smaller samples, and may not wish to make generalizations beyond the particular individuals and contexts being researched.

Sampling in Quantitative Research

In quantitative research, a distinction between probability and nonprobability sampling can be made on the basis of whether the researcher knows anything about the likelihood that each member of the population will be selected.

Probability Sampling

Probability sampling includes all approaches to sampling in which each member of a population has a known probability of being chosen. The nature and importance of these approaches will become clearer by means of a further distinction between four types of probability sampling: simple random sampling, stratified sampling, cluster sampling, and systematic sampling.

SIMPLE RANDOM SAMPLING   **Simple random sampling** is a procedure in which each member of the population has an equal and independent chance of being selected for participation in the study. "Independent" means that the selection of one participant does not influence the likelihood that any other individual will be selected. For example, if participants in a study of the general fifth-grade population were asked to invite their siblings to participate, the independence criterion would not be met, because fifth-graders who have siblings would have a greater chance of being sampled than would fifth-graders with no siblings.

Simple random sampling is carried out by some method that guarantees that chance rather than any other factor, such as experimenter preference, determines which members of a population are sampled. For example, suppose that researchers are interested in measuring the attitudes of the 320 elementary school teachers in a particular school district. Assuming that the researchers want to interview half of the teachers, one method of simple random sampling would consist of the following steps:

- Obtain an alphabetized list of all teachers in the district.
- Take the first 160 odd numbers and the first 160 even numbers from a random number table.

- Go down the alphabetized list and write each number next to a teacher's name.
- Select all the teachers who have been assigned odd numbers.

Whatever particular method the researcher uses, simple random sampling is considered the most rigorous and desirable approach to sampling. However, it does not guarantee that a representative sample will be obtained. It is entirely possible that, by chance, random sampling will yield a nonrepresentative sample through sampling error (see earlier definition). In the study on elementary school teachers described above, it is possible that the sample would contain too many highly experienced teachers, too many second-grade teachers, or too many teachers from one particular school district in order to be considered truly representative. Generally speaking, the larger the sample (relative to population size), the greater the likelihood that a random sample will be a representative one.

Although simple random sampling does not guarantee a representative sample, it does guarantee that any sampling errors are truly random. In a sample of elementary school teachers, for instance, it is just as likely that too many highly experienced teachers will be chosen as it is that too many highly inexperienced teachers will be chosen. One implication of this idea is that multiple studies based on simple random sampling should not yield systematically distorted findings. If sampling error occurs, the direction of the error will vary randomly from study to study in which it occurs. Replication of findings (discussed in Chapter 1) helps to minimize the likelihood of sampling error distorting our understanding of some phenomenon.

STRATIFIED SAMPLING   **Stratified sampling** is a procedure in which strata (i.e., subgroups) of a population are identified, and random sampling is carried out within each subgroup. When distinctions between subgroups are important to a study, stratified sampling may be preferable to simple random sampling. For example, in a school district in which 91% of the elementary level teachers are female, a simple random sampling method, particularly for a small sample, might not yield any males. However, the representativeness of the sample would be improved if at least some males were chosen. In fact, the representativeness would be ideal if exactly 9% of the sample were male. This example illustrates one case in which a slight modification of pure random sampling would be desirable.

In some cases, the goal of stratified sampling is for the proportion of each subgroup in the sample to be the same as the proportion in the population. This is called **proportional stratified random sampling**. In the previous example, researchers would randomly sample members of each gender until a balance of exactly 91% females and 9% males was obtained. The researchers might or might not choose to stratify their sample on the basis of additional variables. For instance, if each teacher is classified as either "experienced" or "inexperienced," and it was found that 54% of female teachers and 61% of male teachers are experienced, the researchers would ensure that their sampling within each gender reflected these proportions.

In other cases, researchers use **nonproportional stratified random sampling** when the goal is to simply represent different subgroups. This is a common approach when the researcher's interest is to compare groups of individuals who differ in achievement, demographic background, or some other variable of interest. To use the previous example, the researchers might simply ensure that both males and females are randomly sampled, without attempting to include specific proportions of each group. Further discussion of nonproportional stratified sampling is provided in Spotlight on Research 4.2.

Purposive and Stratified Sampling in a Study of Bullying Over Time

Different approaches to sampling are often combined in a single study. For example, in a 2005 study published in the *International Journal of Behavioral Development**, Mechthild Schäfer, Stefan Korn, Felix Brodbeck, Dieter Wolke, and Henrike Schulz combined a purposive approach to sampling with a nonproportional stratified strategy. ("Purposive" refers to a sample that is chosen because it appears to be representative, based on informal considerations.)

Schäfer and colleagues were interested in how the social environments of primary schools influence the stability of bully and victim roles from primary to secondary school. In this study, which was conducted in Germany, "primary" refers to first through fourth grades, while "secondary" refers to fifth through twelfth grades. Prior research has shown that victim roles become more stable in secondary school, meaning that as students get older, those who are victims of bullying will be more likely to continue to be victimized. (Some research has also shown comparable trends among bullies.) Schäfer and colleagues argued that increases in stability over time can be attributed to increasingly structured social hierarchies. Because young children have less differentiated hierarchies, bullies move from victim to victim and are less likely to consistently target specific victims. By secondary school age, the more structured social hierarchies that emerge allow students in the lowest status positions to be easily identified and consistently bullied. Schäfer and colleagues also suggested that this trend is stronger in schools with clearer social hierarchies.

On the basis of these and other considerations, Schäfer and colleagues developed four hypotheses about the stability of bully and victim roles over time:

- **Hypothesis 1:** *The degree of hierarchical structuring is higher in secondary school than in primary school.*

- **Hypothesis 2:** *From primary to secondary school bully roles are more stable than victim roles.*

- **Hypothesis 3:** *High levels of hierarchy in primary school predict victim role stability from primary to secondary school while no such moderating effect exists for bullying role stability.*

- **Hypothesis 4:** *In primary school bullies are more rejected than victims and vice versa in secondary school.*

Schäfer and colleagues conducted their study with seventh- and eighth-graders who had participated in another study of theirs conducted 6 years earlier. In the prior study, each child was labeled by the researchers as either a bully, a victim, a bully/victim (i.e., both), or neutral (i.e., neither). The researchers' sampling strategy consisted of a purposive approach to the identification of students who represent one geographic region, as well as a nonproportional stratified sampling of students who represent the groups of interest.

One thousand five hundred and twenty-two primary school children (51% male) from the second and third grade from 67 schools in Munich and its surrounding area formed the primary school sample that is regarded as representative for South Bavaria (see Wolke et al., 2001). From this sample, 61 victims, 39 bullies, and 74 bully/victims, identified as being involved in bullying following a commonly agreed procedure (Olweus, 1989) were available for the follow-up study 6 years later.... In addition to [these] children ... another 133 children identified as being of neutral status while in primary school were added....

In secondary school, 2958 seventh and eighth graders (50% male) from 114 classes at 89 schools of all school types formed the second sample. Altogether 283 children were identified in both samples and thus were available for longitudinal comparisons contributing a full data set from assessment in primary and secondary school. Based on the whole data set it was determined that classmates from primary school classes were generally not transferred into the same classes at secondary school.

By combining purposive and stratified sampling, Schäfer and colleagues were able to obtain what appeared to be a representative sample of bullies, victims, bully/victims, and neutral students from one particular geographic area.

Schäfer and colleagues measured status as bully, victim, bully/victim, or neutral by means of slightly different methods depending on whether students were in primary or secondary school.

In primary school bullying experiences were assessed by several questions adapted from the BVQ (Olweus, 1989). First, children were asked whether they had experienced any of six behaviours in the last 6 months that had upset them: having been called bad or nasty names; having belongings taken; having lies told about them; having nasty tricks played on them; having been threatened or blackmailed; having been hit or beaten up. If the child answered that he or she had experienced any of these six behaviours, the child was asked to give examples, to ascertain that the behaviours experienced were carried out with intent by the perpetrator(s) to upset the child and the child felt unable to defend her/himself, rather than having occurred by accident or during play fighting. Those children who had experienced one or more of these behaviours were asked how frequently these incidents had happened in the previous 6 months (never; seldom—1 to 3 times; frequently—4 times or more; very frequently—at least once per week). . . . The six behaviours were then repeated and the child responded to the question whether they had used these behaviours to upset other children and how often they had done this over the previous 6 months in the manner described above.

A set of dichotomous variables were created by classifying those children who reported being bullied "frequently" (equals more than 4 times over the period covered) or "very frequently" during the last term as victims and those children who reported bullying others "frequently" or "very frequently" during the last term as bullies. Children who were identified as both victims and bullies were classified as bully/victims. Children who were not identified as victims, bullies, or bully/victims were labelled neutral children.

In secondary school classes, pupils responded to a modified version of the BVQ [which] consists of 24 questions about children's experiences of being the victims of bullying and of bullying other children within the previous 3 months. Children were provided with a definition of bullying and then asked "whether they had been bullied within the last 12 weeks. . . ." Children responded on a 5-point scale from 0 (I wasn't bullied at all) to 4 (several times a week). In the manner described, children also responded to the question "whether they had bullied others or took part in bullying others within the last 12 weeks. . . ."

A set of dichotomous variables were created by classifying those children who reported being bullied "sometimes or more frequently" during the previous term as victims and those children who reported bullying others "sometimes or

more frequently" during the previous term as bullies. As in primary school, children who were identified as both victims and bullies were classified as bully/victims. Children who weren't identified as victims, bullies, or bully/victims were labelled neutral children . . .

Schäfer and colleagues measured how structured the students' social hierarchies were by asking each student in a class to name the students they liked most and liked least. The assumption underlying this method is that the more consistently particular students are named as most or least liked, the clearer the social hierarchy that exists in the particular school.

The results of the social hierarchy measure supported the first hypothesis, in that the degree of social structure was found to be higher in secondary school than in primary school.

Regarding the second hypothesis, Schäfer and colleagues found that 32% of students labeled as bullies in primary school continued to be labeled as bullies in secondary school, while only 20% of victims and 12% of bully/victims continued to receive these labels. These results show that from primary to secondary school bully roles are more stable than victim roles.

Regarding the third hypothesis, Schäfer and colleagues found victim role stability from primary to secondary school for students who had attended primary schools with high levels of social structure. No such stability was observed for students who had attended primary schools with relatively little structure. Bullying status was generally stable from primary to secondary school, regardless of whether the primary school had been low or high in social structure.

Finally, with respect to the fourth hypothesis, Schäfer and colleagues found that in primary school, bullies experienced a greater degree of social rejection, while in secondary school victims experienced more rejection.

In sum, through the use of purposive and stratified sampling, Schäfer and colleagues were able to demonstrate some of the complexities of both consistencies and shifts in bully and victim status from primary to secondary school.

*Schafer, M., Korn, S., Brodbeck, F. C., Wolke, D., & Schulz, H. (2005). Bullying roles in changing contexts: The stability of victim and bully roles from primary to secondary school. *International Journal of Behavioral Development, 29*(4), 323–335. Quoted with permission from the publisher.

CLUSTER SAMPLING   **Cluster sampling** is a procedure in which entire groups rather than individuals are sampled. If you look back at Spotlight on Research 1.2, for example, you will see that cluster sampling was used to identify three classrooms of students.

A major impetus for the clustering procedure is its relative convenience. Simplified random and stratified sampling are powerful ways to obtain representative samples, but they pose a variety of logistical challenges. In order to obtain a representative sample of elementary school teachers in a particular school district, researchers would have to include teachers from all or at least many of the schools in the district. This will be difficult to carry out in large school districts. For example, as of this writing the Dallas Independent School District (DISD) contains 155 elementary schools distributed over a wide radius. Rather than traveling all over DISD to obtain random or stratified samples of elementary school teachers, researchers might sample all of the teachers in five schools in one particular area of Dallas. The relatively small number of schools, as well as their geographic proximity, makes this cluster sampling approach more convenient. In addition, the researchers would not have to deal with potential problems arising from the need to sample only one or a few teachers from given schools, as might be the case if random or stratified procedures were used. (It can be difficult to obtain permission from school administrators to conduct a study in which one or a few teachers are sampled from a school, because someone will have to justify the choice of teachers, and it is conceivable that some teachers would resent being—or not being—chosen.)

One disadvantage of cluster sampling is the possibility of nonrepresentativeness. Clusters are usually defined in terms of physical units (classrooms, schools, neighborhoods, school districts, cities, etc.), and thus it is possible that the particular physical unit chosen is not representative. A common problem is that the schools or geographic regions chosen for a study turn out to be distinct in terms of demographic characteristics (e.g., particularly high or low in socioeconomic status, or distinct in racial or ethnic composition). One way to deal with this potential problem is to sample more than one cluster. As with other approaches, the larger the size of a cluster sample, the greater the likelihood of representativeness.

SYSTEMATIC SAMPLING   **Systematic sampling** is a procedure in which every Nth individual is selected from a list of the population. For example, if the population consists of 630 school administrators and the researcher intends to sample 20% these individuals, then every fifth administrator would be chosen from a list.

Judging from this example, systematic sampling sounds identical to random sampling, but it would not be identical unless the list of names were in a truly random order. An alphabetized list of last names is not randomly ordered. People of certain nationalities have last names that tend to begin with certain letters of the alphabet. Thus, these individuals might have more or less of an opportunity of being sampled than people of other nationalities (depending on the intended sample size and other factors). From this example, you can see that random sampling is preferable to systematic sampling.

Keep in mind as you read about different approaches to sampling that particular studies may combine approaches, or use more than one approach (as in Spotlight on Research 4.2). Random sampling is often used in conjunction with other methods, as when researchers randomly sample within strata or clusters, for example. A combination of stratified and systematic approaches is reflected in a study on the health habits of undergraduates by von Bothmer and Fridlund (2005), who obtained a list of students in each department of a Swedish university and selected every 10th student on each list for participation. By sampling 10% of the students in each department of the university, von Bothmer and Fridlund were using a stratified sampling method (assuming that the entire university represents the target population), while by selecting every 10th student from the lists, the researchers were using a systematic sampling method. (The researchers could just as well have used a random sampling method for selecting students from each department, in which case random and stratified approaches to sampling would have been combined.)

Nonprobability Sampling

When a probability sampling approach cannot be used, the researcher may rely instead on **nonprobability sampling**, in which the likelihood that each member of a population will be chosen is unknown. I describe three types of nonprobability sampling here: convenience sampling, purposive sampling, and quota sampling.

CONVENIENCE SAMPLING   **Convenience sampling** (also called "haphazard" or "opportunistic" sampling) is a procedure in which sampling focuses on whoever is available in a particular place at a particular time. Most research is based to a greater or lesser extent on convenience, since researchers tend to obtain samples from groups they have ready access to.

It is sometimes said in jest that social science research consists of the study of undergraduates. This comment refers to the fact that a substantial amount of research in psychology and other social sciences is conducted with undergraduate students, the population closest to and most easily accessed by professors who conduct research. In the same way, a great deal of research in education and other social sciences is conducted wherever the researcher has existing connections, or is otherwise able to obtain permission. Although a convenience sample is clearly at risk for nonrepresentativeness, researchers can circumvent at least some potential problems by being clear about the target population, as well as the characteristics of the sample, so that others can judge whether generalizations from sample to population are warranted.

PURPOSIVE SAMPLING   **Purposive sampling** is a procedure in which the researcher samples whoever he or she believes to be representative of a given population. The difference between purposive sampling and probability sampling approaches is that purposive sampling is based on the researcher's informal ideas about representativeness. For example, if researchers know in advance that 82% of elementary-level teachers in a particular school district are female, the researchers could use a stratified sampling technique to ensure that 82% of their sample is female. However, if the researchers are unwilling, or are unable, to determine the gender distribution in advance, they could simply ensure that a majority of their sample is female, under the assumption that elementary teachers tend to be women. Although probability sampling is clearly preferable to purposive sampling, the latter is often used when population characteristics cannot be precisely determined.

QUOTA SAMPLING   **Quota sampling** is a procedure in which exact numbers of individuals who reflect certain characteristics are sampled. A simple example would be a sample consisting of 30 boys and 30 girls in each grade from fifth through eighth. When researchers are interested in studying specific types of people, such as elementary school teachers with over 20 years of experience, immigrant parents who are attending ESL classes, or curriculum specialists at liberal arts colleges, quota sampling may be used to ensure that specific groups are adequately represented. Quota sampling is a common approach in survey research, particularly when it is not possible to create a list of all members of the target population. Quota approaches are also common when participants are relatively difficult to obtain and researchers wish to identify minimum sample sizes needed for particular statistical tests. The difference between quota sampling and stratified sampling hinges on whether random sampling procedures are used (see Spotlight on Research 4.2). The main limitation of quota sampling is the potential for nonrepresentativeness. For example, as the researcher seeks to meet the quota for a particular group, individuals who are most readily accessible, or most willing to participate, may be most likely to be chosen.

Evaluation of Quantitative Sampling Approaches

Table 4.1 summarizes the various approaches to sampling in quantitative research designs. The approach to sampling most suitable for a particular quantitative study depends on the goals that frame the study. If representativeness is a goal, then simple random sampling is the most powerful method, but proportional stratified sampling may be needed instead in order to ensure that particular subgroups are represented. Probability sampling of any sort may be more desirable than nonprobability sampling, but there are often logistical barriers to probability approaches. When the requirements of probability sampling cannot be met, a purposive approach is preferable to simply ignoring the issue of representativeness. Systematic or quota sampling might turn out to be adequate ways of obtaining specific numbers of individuals representing particular characteristics. In sum, the sampling procedure

TABLE 4.1 Approaches to Sampling Commonly Used in Quantitative Research Designs

Approach to Sampling	Simple Definition
Probability	
Simple random	Each member of the population has an equal and independent chance of being sampled.
Proportional stratified	The proportion of each subgroup in the sample is exactly the same as in the population.
Nonproportional stratified	Each subgroup of the population is represented in the sample, but not proportionally.
Cluster	An entire, intact group is sampled from the population.
Systematic	Every *N*th member of the population is selected from a list.
Nonprobability	
Convenience	The sample consists of whoever is available and readily accessible.
Purposive	A group believed to be representative of the population is sampled.
Quota	Exact numbers of individuals who reflect certain characteristics are sampled.

most appropriate for a quantitative study will be determined by a combination of theoretical and practical considerations.

Sampling in Qualitative Research

In qualitative research, sampling is informed by the ultimate goal of obtaining rich descriptions of peoples' beliefs, behaviors, and experiences. Sample sizes, for instance, tend to be smaller than they are in quantitative studies. The information gathered from each participant in a qualitative study tends to be more extensive and requires more contact with the participants—in short, more information is collected from fewer participants.

Because qualitative studies often place more emphasis on describing particular individuals and groups than on generalizing to broader populations, there is correspondingly less emphasis on random assignment and other approaches intended to create representative samples. Qualitative sampling is often described as "purposeful," because the goal is to deliberately identify individuals, organizations, and/or materials that are informative. An informative sample is not necessarily a representative sample.

In a sense, however, qualitative researchers are as deeply concerned with representativeness as quantitative researchers. The difference is that the representativeness sought by qualitative researchers tends to be highly focused. In an ethnographic study of a particular family, the researcher hopes to spend enough time with family members to obtain a "representative" sample of each individual's beliefs, concerns, and responses to everyday situations—that is, a sample that is representative of the individual (rather than some larger group).

Types of Qualitative Sampling

Some of the more commonly used approaches to sampling in qualitative research include typical case sampling, extreme case sampling, intensity sampling, critical case sampling, homogeneous sampling, and snowball sampling (Patton, 1990, 2002).

TYPICAL CASE SAMPLING   **Typical case sampling** is a procedure in which the researcher seeks cases that are typical of the phenomenon under study. Imagine, for instance, that you wish to know more about the experiences of Hispanic teachers in predominantly white high schools. A typical case sample might consist of several experienced Hispanic teachers at predominantly white public high schools in a local district. At the same time, you might exclude from your sample Hispanic teachers in their first year, those who teach at small private schools, or those who teach racially balanced groups of students. Your approach to determining typicality may be informal, or it may be based in part on formal quantitative criteria (e.g., you might decide to restrict the sample to Hispanic teachers who have more than 5 consecutive years of experience teaching in public high schools where the student and teacher populations are each at least 90% white).

EXTREME CASE SAMPLING   **Extreme case sampling**, as the name suggests, is a procedure in which the researcher seeks cases that are unusual in some respect. In the previous example, your sample might consist of Hispanic teachers at predominantly white high schools who have a long history of winning local and regional teaching awards and otherwise being recognized for exemplary teaching. Or, you might choose to study Hispanic teachers at these schools who have had more than 30 years of experience. What constitutes an "extreme" example can also be defined informally or formally.

INTENSITY SAMPLING   **Intensity sampling** is a procedure in which the researcher selects participants who allow the research question to be studied from different perspectives. The participants represent clear but not extreme differences on some dimension of interest. For instance, you might compare the experiences of Hispanic teachers at predominantly white schools who differ in how long they have been in the profession. The selection of teachers along this dimension might be informal, or you might sample within specific strata of experience (e.g., 0–5 years vs. 10–15 years). The stratified sampling that you subsequently carry out may be proportional or nonproportional. This example illustrates one of the many ways in which quantitative and qualitative approaches to sampling may be combined.

MAXIMUM VARIATION SAMPLING   **Maximum variation sampling** is a procedure in which the researcher selects participants who reflect the entire range of variation on some dimension of interest. For example, you might compare the experiences of Hispanic teachers at predominantly white schools who have been teaching for 0–5 years, 5–10 years, 10–15 years, 15–20 years, and so on.

CRITICAL CASE SAMPLING   **Critical case sampling** is a procedure in which the researcher selects a single case, such as an individual, document, program, event, or organization, or a small number of highly similar cases. The term "critical" means that the case is likely to be especially informative about the phenomenon or perspectives under study, and may enable the researcher to put a particular theory or hypothesis to the test. For example, suppose that you choose to interview one experienced Hispanic teacher at a predominantly white high school. If your teacher happens to be highly articulate, proud of his or her ethnicity, and active in promoting the interests of minorities at his or her school, then you have a critical case—an individual who is likely to be more informative than most people about his or her particular experiences. If you happen to theorize that minority teachers experience racially based resistance when they promote their own interests in predominantly white schools, your teacher will be a critical case in the sense of providing a test for your theory.

Spotlight on Research 4.3 provides an extended look at a study in which critical case sampling was used.

HOMOGENEOUS SAMPLING   **Homogeneous sampling** is a procedure in which the researcher selects individuals who are highly similar in background, experience, and/or other characteristics. For example, you might choose to study a group of several young Hispanic teachers from urban backgrounds in their first or second year of teaching at a rural, predominantly white high school. The difference between homogeneous and typical case sampling is that a homogeneous sample is not presumed to be typical (except in the limited sense that each individual in the sample typifies the set of characteristics exhibited by the rest of the sample).

SNOWBALL SAMPLING   **Snowball sampling** is a procedure in which the researcher approaches a few individuals, and then asks for help from these individuals in order to obtain additional participants. This approach, also called "chain

Parent Involvement in Children's Education: A Critical Case Study

As noted in the text, the purpose of critical case sampling is to identify a particular case or cases that are highly informative. In a 1996 study published in *Educational Review**, Gill Crozier described a small group of African-Caribbean parents who were exceptionally knowledgeable about educational issues, deeply involved in their children's education, and somewhat dissatisfied with their children's schooling.

Crozier was explicit in the rationale for sampling:

[W]e present here a case study of a small sample of black parents' experiences with their child's school. These parents are taken as a "critical case," in that . . . they have an understanding of the educational process, some understanding of the education system and parental rights and an understanding of pedagogical issues; also they have some involvement with education . . .

[The study is based on the] accounts of six black parents. Five of them are of African Caribbean origin and one of Indian origin. In order to characterise the respondents' "racial" origins we have used the term "black." All six respondents are women. They are members of Community Groups, a Supplementary School and a Community Centre . . .

The features that justify [calling this] a case study are: the experience of the parents as black parents, in that they have a shared experience of racism and discrimination; they were all contacted through community organisations; they all share an experience of concerns about their children's education which most attribute to being black. They are a critical case rather than a representative sample, as explained above. All of them also place a high value on education and they are active in supporting their children's education; as part of this

they are prepared to intervene on their behalf to ensure their child's needs are met.

Interviews with parents revealed that they were deeply interested and involved in their children's education, but experienced obstacles, particularly as the children reached secondary school age. Some of the parents had difficulties finding enough time to be as involved as they would like, while other parents indicated that racism was a problem. All of the parents had general concerns about the quality of their children's education.

All of the parents interviewed placed importance on their child's education. They all said they helped their children with homework, particularly those with primary aged school children. Some of the parents spent a considerable amount of time with their children after school or at the weekends, reading to them or playing games with them, giving them mathematics work to do or helping them with spelling . . .

Half of the parents spoke about how they needed to rely on the school to carry out their role in fulfilling the high expectations that they held, since they did not have the time to give the children additional support themselves, as Shehnaz Chaudhuri explained,

> *"I would like to have more to do with my child's education, time permitting. It doesn't and I think that is the biggest hindrance rather than anything else. Because if I had more time I would read more about parents' rights and the Parents' Charter. I just have to entrust my children to the school and hope they do their best . . . "*

Three of the parents also believed that black children were negatively stereotyped by schools and teachers and that this disadvantaged them . . .

(continued)

sampling," is common in ethnographic research. For example, Rosenthal (1995) studied some of the differences between Haitian students living in the New York City area who do versus do not complete high school. Recognizing that it is difficult to find students who leave school (since the names of dropouts do not appear in any list or directory), Rosenthal approached individuals familiar with the Haitian community and asked them to identify Haitian youths in their late teens and, in particular, teens who had not graduated from high school. The teens that were identified in this way, both graduates and nongraduates, were asked to identify

The other parents, although not making a link between their child's "race" and their academic performance, were critical of the educational experience that their child was receiving. We have already seen that some parents' views of what they regard as "good" teaching was not taking place. In addition, some of the primary school parents were not satisfied they were receiving adequate information about their child's progress or how they could help their child at home.

In discussing the results, Crozier contrasted the attitudes and behaviors of these parents with those of upper-middle-class white parents in an earlier study.

The views of a group of black parents on their children's education and their own relationships with their children's schools have been described. Most of these parents have educational knowledge and awareness. In addition, they are parents who are involved and highly interested in their children's education, in terms of supporting them at home, expressing concern about what schools should be offering and providing supplementary education. Some parents with primary aged children are, at various times, quite involved in school or classroom activities. . . . There is also evidence indicating parents' commitment to engaging with the education system and/or process in order to secure for their children a form of education which they, themselves, deem appropriate.

Such behaviour is in many ways similar to the kind of behaviour displayed by the "upper middle class" white parents in Lareau's (1989) study. Lareau describes these parents as having educational knowledge, an interconnectedness between family life and school life and a belief that education is a shared responsibility between the teacher and the parent. She also goes on to say that whilst these upper middle class parents are critical of the teachers, there,

nevertheless, is a display of consonance between them and their child's teachers and school . . .

This is not the case amongst the parents in our sample. Distrust of teachers' judgments and the state education system is expressed by these parents, together with frustration at getting teachers to engage with them in dialogue about their children's needs. However, the distrust does not entirely lie in their lack of respect for the teachers' professionalism per se, but rather in the system that the teachers represent . . .

The dissonance experienced by these black parents, together with a wider view and experience of the education system, including that of their own schooling, as black people, has, it is suggested, led these parents to lose confidence in the schools. If black children, particularly those children of African-Caribbean origin, are failing in examinations and are disproportionately being excluded from school, then schools must realise that their parents are going to be concerned. The parents in our case study indicate a desire to work with teachers and schools in order to improve their children's life chances and yet this apparent dissonance would seem to be interfering with the development of a fruitful partnership. If schools are to address satisfactorily the unsatisfactory school experience of black children, there seems to be no alternative, at the very least. than to involve the parents in a manner more meaningful to them.

In sum, by obtaining a critical case sample, Crozier was able to identify some important and distinctive characteristics of one group of parents who were deeply committed to their children's education but not satisfied with the current system of delivery.

*Crozier, G. (1996). Black parents and school relationships: A case study. *Educational Review, 48*(3), 1–14. Quoted with permission from the publisher.

classmates who had not graduated, and those students were asked in turn to identify other individuals who had left school.

Evaluation of Qualitative Sampling Approaches

Table 4.2 summarizes the various types of qualitative sampling. The approach to sampling most suitable for a particular qualitative study depends on the researcher's interests, as is the case with quantitative designs. The difference between typical, extreme, and critical case sampling, for example, corresponds to different goals that a study might have. Thus, it is too simplistic to say that one approach to sampling is generally better than another.

TABLE 4.2 Approaches to Sampling Commonly Used in Qualitative Research Designs

Approach to Sampling	Simple Definition
Typical case	The researcher seeks cases that are typical.
Extreme case	The researcher seeks cases that are unusual.
Intensity	The researcher seeks cases that represent different perspectives.
Maximum variation	The researcher seeks cases that represent the entire range of a dimension.
Critical case	The researcher seeks cases that are highly informative.
Homogeneous	The researcher seeks cases that are highly similar to each other.
Snowball	The researcher seeks help from participants to identify additional participants.

As in quantitative research, qualitative studies are sometimes based on a mix of sampling methods, and random assignment could be combined with any method. Convenience sampling is also common in qualitative designs. Since the focus of a qualitative study may emerge during the process of data collection, the researcher may adjust the sampling method, or take advantage of unanticipated sampling opportunities, in the midst of the study. It may be difficult to know in advance what type of sample will result from a snowball method. As in quantitative research, the approach to sampling that a qualitative researcher ultimately relies on is determined by the research questions that either guide the design of the study or emerge during the gathering of information.

General Principles of Sampling

Most samples are based to a greater or lesser extent on convenience. Researchers tend to conduct studies in their own communities, or wherever they have established connections with schools and other organizations. As a result, sampling is often constrained by local availability. Other logistical considerations influence researchers' sampling strategies too. For instance, if population characteristics are not precisely known, a quantitative researcher will have to rely on nonprobability sampling approaches.

In spite of these constraints, researchers tend to choose the sampling strategies that best fit their particular research questions. Several "principles" guide the selection of samples as well as the evaluation of samples used in other studies. These principles can be illustrated through the impact that size and representativeness have on the adequacy of a sample.

Sample Size

In quantitative research, larger samples tend to be more desirable than smaller ones. Because the goal of sampling is to enable inferences about populations, a larger sample (relative to population size) is more likely than a smaller one to be representative of the population from which it is drawn. This does not mean that larger samples are inherently preferable to smaller ones. Conducting a study can be expensive, time-consuming, and difficult to complete if people are not readily available or willing to participate. When determining sample size, the quantitative researcher must balance the need for representativeness with the "costs" of carrying out the study. Ideally, the researcher will have some sense of the minimum sample size needed in order to have some degree of confidence about the representativeness of the sample.

There have been many recommendations but no consensus as to what constitutes minimally acceptable sample size. Some of the recommendations made by researchers and statisticians are highly specific, in the sense of indicating minimum sizes for different types of statistical tests and desired outcomes. **Power analysis**, for example, is a way of identifying the exact group sizes needed to obtain certain amounts of statistical power and desired effect sizes for particular analyses. (As explained in Chapter 11, statistical power refers to the likelihood that a researcher's analyses will detect an actual difference between groups, or an actual association between variables. The strength of the difference or association can be expressed as an effect size.) Power analysis tables are available for researchers to consult for specific needs. Other recommendations about sample size are more broad. For instance, for large populations, and for experimental and causal–comparative designs, a minimum of 30 participants per group is sometimes recommended, while for correlational studies, a minimum of 30 participants per variable is considered advisable.

Most researchers would agree that there is no simple rule for minimally acceptable sample size that can be applied in all situations. Rather, what constitutes acceptability is influenced by several factors, including the importance of the study, the design of the study, and the size of the target population.

IMPORTANCE OF THE STUDY   Studies of comparable scientific importance may vary in ethical sensitivity and in the potential impact of their results on the lives of participants. For research on sensitive topics such as the safety of a new medication for treating attention-deficit/hyperactivity disorder, or the validity of a method for assigning children to remedial programs, large sample sizes are imperative in order to maximize confidence about any conclusions drawn. Specific sample sizes may be recommended in order to achieve a certain degree of statistical power, or it may be simply assumed that the more participants there are, the stronger the study will be.

DESIGN OF THE STUDY   Minimally acceptable sample size is influenced by the design of a study, including the number of key variables, the number of measurements per variable, and, if applicable, the number of groups. As the number of groups and variables increases, sample size must increase in order to maintain statistical power. As the number of measurements per variable increases, smaller sample sizes may be acceptable.

SIZE OF THE TARGET POPULATION   Generally speaking, the smaller the target population, the larger the percentage of the population that should be sampled. For small populations, sampling the entire population may be desirable.

As noted earlier, sample sizes in qualitative studies are often small, so that researchers can provide an in-depth look at the lives and perspectives of a small number of individuals. Larger sample sizes are often undesirable (and may even be counterproductive if the focus is to learn much about a few people, as opposed to a little bit about many). Whereas quantitative researchers have some sense before beginning their studies of the sample sizes needed in order to achieve adequate statistical power, qualitative researchers may continue to sample until data saturation is achieved. (**Data saturation** means simply that the information being obtained has become redundant—it does not appear, for instance, that interviewing one more member of a group will yield new information.)

Representativeness

Large sample size is not desirable as an end in itself, since larger samples require more time and resources to study. In quantitative research, large samples are desirable as a means of enabling more powerful and flexible statistical analyses, and as a way of achieving greater representativeness. In qualitative research, as noted earlier, sample sizes tend to be smaller, and what determines "representativeness" is the way information is gathered rather than the number of participants.

A CAVEAT   Although size and representativeness tend to go together in quantitative studies, the relationship is not infallible. This point is illustrated by a well-known historical anecdote. From 1916 through 1932, a magazine called the *Literary Digest* correctly predicted the winner of every presidential election. The *Digest*'s predictions were based on public opinion polls conducted during each election year. In 1936, the *Digest* polled roughly 10 million Americans and predicted that Alf Landon would defeat Franklin Delano Roosevelt by a decisive margin. George Gallup also conducted a public opinion poll that year. Although Gallup only polled about 3,000 people, he correctly predicted that Roosevelt would win the election decisively. Given that larger sample sizes tend to be more representative than smaller ones, it seems surprising, at first glance, that Gallup was right and the *Literary Digest* was wrong.

A second glance reveals that although the *Literary Digest* polled a large number of Americans, their sample was only based on names drawn from automobile registration lists and telephone directories. In essence, the *Digest* staff engaged in convenience sampling. Perhaps they also assumed that what they were doing amounted to a purposive approach. In any case, what the *Digest* ended up with was not a representative sample. In 1936, cars and telephones were primarily owned by middle- and upper-class Americans, who were predominantly Republican and would have voted for Landon. However, during the depression most Americans were Democrats and favored Roosevelt. Thus, the *Literary Digest* obtained a large but nonrepresentative sample. Gallup, on the other hand, used a quota sampling method. His team polled specified numbers of individuals representing different demographic characteristics (socioeconomic status, gender, and so on). Despite the fact that Gallup's sample was orders of magnitude smaller than the *Literary Digest*'s, the representativeness of the sample allowed him to correctly predict Roosevelt's victory.

Representativeness is an ideal that is never achieved with certainty. Even if the demographic mix of a sample seems to be a perfectly accurate subset of the target population, the sample may tend to differ from the population on variables that were not measured. The list of potentially relevant variables is endless. For example, a researcher may determine that the distribution of gender, ethnicities, and political affiliations in a sample of teachers matches that of the population, but we might ask whether the sample is representative in terms of experience, interest in teaching, and education level. The mere willingness of participants to be involved in a research study is a potential source of bias. Recall from the beginning of this chapter that individuals cannot be forced to participate in research, but must give consent after being informed about the nature of the study. This requirement, which is absolutely essential on ethical grounds, allows for the possibility of sampling bias in most studies, simply because some people are more likely to volunteer than others. Studies suggest that volunteers in research, compared to those who choose not to volunteer, tend to be more educated, more sociable, more arousal-seeking, and more unconventional (Rosenthal & Rosnow, 1975). These are just a few of the characteristics that distinguish volunteers from nonvolunteers, and introduce the possibility, in theory, of bias in almost any sample.

A Look Ahead

In this chapter you have read about two important sets of preliminaries for conducting research: obtaining permission from an Institutional Review Board as well as from potential participants, and identifying the sample of participants that will be included. The next chapter focuses on basic concepts of measurement that are essential to both the planning of a research study as well as the evaluation of completed studies.

Applications: A Guide for Beginning Researchers

Here are some ideas from the chapter that will help you plan your research:

- Before conducting your research, you will need to obtain permission from the Institutional Review Board at your institution. Check with your advisor, or the professor you work with, for more information about how to proceed.

- Your Institutional Review Board application will include information about how you plan to obtain informed consent and, if necessary, assent. Be sure that your procedures for obtaining consent and assent are in compliance with the federal guidelines.

- Once you have identified a population of interest for your study, you will need to target a particular sample.

- There are many different approaches to sampling. Review the different types described in this chapter and choose the approach that seems most suitable to your particular goals.

- Your specific plan for sampling will be influenced by logistical constraints and, in most cases, by the need for suitably large and representative samples.

Chapter Summary

A preliminary step in conducting a study is to ensure that participants will be treated ethically. Owing to abuses in prior studies, research participants are currently protected under federal law. The National Research Act requires that all research receive prior approval from an Institutional Review Board, which operates under the requirements of 45 CFR 46. Other ethical guidelines for research are disseminated by professional organizations.

Once a researcher has obtained IRB approval for a study, permission must be sought from potential participants by means of informed consent. Assent is required when the participants are children.

Participants in a study typically must be sampled from a population. The goal in most research is to obtain a representative sample. Nonrepresentative samples may result from systematic bias or from random sampling error.

In quantitative research, probability sampling procedures include simple random sampling, proportional and nonproportional stratified sampling, cluster sampling, and systematic sampling, while nonprobability procedures include convenience sampling, purposive sampling, and quota sampling. Qualitative procedures, which tend to yield smaller samples, include typical case sampling, extreme case sampling, intensity sampling, critical case sampling, homogeneous sampling, and snowball sampling.

The sample size appropriate for a particular study is determined by practical and statistical considerations, the importance and design of the study, and the size of the population.

Key Terms

National Research Act	Probability sampling	Purposive sampling
Informed consent	Simple random sampling	Quota sampling
Institutional Review Board	Stratified sampling	Typical case sampling
45 CFR 46	Proportional stratified sampling	Extreme case sampling
Assent	Nonproportional stratified sampling	Intensity sampling
Population		Maximum variation sampling
Sample	Cluster sampling	
Target population	Systematic sampling	Critical case sampling
Representative sample	Nonprobability sampling	Homogeneous sampling
Sampling bias		Snowball sampling
Sampling error	Convenience sampling	Data saturation
Attrition		

Exercises

For questions 1–6, identify the type of sample implied by each description:

1. In order to test the effectiveness of an anger management program, a researcher samples 30 bullies and 30 victims from local schools.

2. A researcher wishes to know more about the subjective experiences of high school students whose families had been displaced by Hurricane Katrina. To obtain more information, the researcher interviews several students, including some who had to relocate to different schools for a month or two, some who relocated for a year, and some whose families relocated permanently to a different state.

3. In order to study gender differences in preschool aggression, a researcher observes most of the children enrolled at her university's day care center.

4. A researcher wants to survey the political beliefs of the 12th-graders in a particular city. The researcher obtains the names of all 387 12th-graders in the city, cuts the names out, places them in a box, and then draws out the names of 70 students who will receive the survey.

5. Knowing that 11 different languages are spoken at home in a particular school district, a researcher who is studying student achievement in the district creates a sample that includes students representing each of the 11 languages.

6. In order to study gang activity in a local high school, the researcher asks each gang member who agrees to participate in the study for names of other members of the gang who might be willing to talk with her.

7. Which of the following approaches to sampling seems most appropriate for learning about the lives and emotional experiences of Laotian children whose parents immigrated to the United States when the children were already in middle school?

a) Simple random sampling

b) Probability sampling

c) Typical case sampling

d) Stratified sampling

8. A researcher studying the development of self-esteem from kindergarten through second grade only has enough resources to interview 35 students in each grade. Which of the following approaches to sampling is the researcher most likely to use?

a) Extreme case sampling

b) Cluster sampling

c) Nonproportional random sampling

d) Quota sampling

9. Which of the following approaches to sampling seems most appropriate when precise information is available about the distribution of gender and ethnicity in a particular city, and researchers wish to obtain a sample that will sustain accurate generalizations about gender and ethnic differences in scores on a standardized test?

a) Systematic sampling

b) Proportional stratified sampling

c) Snowball sampling

d) Critical case sampling

10. *Critical thinking question:* Given the cognitive limitations of young children, what kinds of information should be provided to them in order to obtain their assent for participation in a study?

Answers to Exercises

1. Quota sample   **2.** Intensity sample   **3.** Convenience sample

4. Simple random sample   **5.** Nonproportional stratified sample

6. Snowball sample   **7.** c   **8.** d   **9.** b

10. *Possible answer*: Children should be provided with the same kinds of information that adults would receive, expressed in terms appropriate to their age. For instance, children need to know that they can refuse to participate in the study, or stop at any time, without getting in trouble or disappointing anyone. They need to know how much time will be required for participation and what classroom activities they might miss. They need to be told where they will be, who they will be with, and what they will be doing when they participate in the study. They should understand that what they say or do in the study will be kept private. They should also be invited to ask questions before agreeing to participate.

Suggestions for Further Reading

Research Article: Brechling, V., Day, J., & Cantillon, D. (2006). Consent form return rates for third-grade urban elementary students. *American Journal of Health Behavior, 30*(5), 467–474.

This quantitative study examines methods of increasing consent form return rates among third-graders.

Application Article: Carreón, G. P., Drake, C., & Barton, A. C. (2005). The importance of presence: Immigrant parents' school engagement experiences. *American Educational Research Journal, 42*(3), 465–498.

This ethnographic study makes use of several qualitative sampling concepts in exploring how three immigrant parents attempt to involve themselves in their children's education.

Extension Article: Cawthon, S. W. (2006). Pebbles in the stream: How do we find them? *American Annals of the Deaf, 151*(2), 105–113.

This action research study explores the efficacy of different approaches to obtaining samples in deaf education research, and provides deeper discussion of several concepts introduced in this chapter.

CHAPTER 5 Measurement

After studying this chapter, you will be able to answer the following questions:

- What is the difference between measures and scales?

- What are the major types of quantitative measures?

- What is educational testing?

- What types of educational tests are available?

- What are the major types of qualitative measures?

- How should measures be chosen or created?

- What are the strengths and weaknesses of different measures?

This chapter will prepare you to do the following:

- Understand the measures used in research reports

- Evaluate the measures used in research reports

- Select appropriate measures for a study

Adam Gault/Photo Researchers, Inc.

In Chapter 4, you read about the process by which researchers obtain permission for their studies and select participants. These are essential prerequisites to conducting a research study, but they are only prerequisites. The researcher still needs to determine what will happen during the study. Specifically, the researcher must choose or create a set of measures for collecting information from participants, regardless of whether the participants happen to be educators, parents, students, or a set of documents. In this chapter and the next one I introduce the topic of measurement.

Historical and Conceptual Background

Since 1966, the American Educational Research Association, the American Psychological Association, and the National Council on Measurement in Education have collaborated on a slim but authoritative volume titled the *Standards for Educational and Psychological Testing*. The most recent edition of the *Standards*, published in 1999, reflects a degree of professional consensus about test construction, administration, and interpretation. Along with the *Standards*, there are many lists of specific tests available in hard copy (*Tests in Print, Mental Measurements Yearbook*, etc.) and online (*Test Locator, Buros Center for Testing*, etc.). Given all of these resources, it might seem at first glance that measurement is a relatively simple part of the process of conducting research. All you have to do, it seems, is to identify a research question, choose a test that addresses the question, and make sure that the administration and interpretation of the test are consistent with the *Standards*. However, you will find that measurement is a bit more complicated than this:

- There are many types of measures other than tests.
- Researchers sometimes need to create their own measures.
- Measures may have poor reliability or validity, or be limited in other ways.
- It is often challenging to interpret the results of a measure.

Generally, there is much more to the process of measurement than simply handing out a test and scoring the results.

Key Definitions

Traditionally, measurement was defined in terms of quantification, or numerical descriptions of phenomena (Stevens, 1951). In this chapter, a more inclusive definition will be assumed. **Measurement** can be thought of as the recording of information. The information may be recorded in numerical terms, as in quantitative

Some Units of Measurement

Quantity	Unit of Measurement
2 monologues	1 dialogue
1 million microphones	1 phone
1 million phones	1 megaphone
1 millionth of a fish	1 microfiche
2 wharves	1 paradox

studies, or it may be recorded in some non-numerical format such as a narrative, as in qualitative research. Scores on an IQ test, numbers of absences in a school year, and reaction times on a word recognition task are examples of quantitative measurement. Transcripts of conversations with an administrator, field notes on interactions among a clique, and videotapes of a classroom activity all illustrate qualitative measurement.

A distinction is commonly made between measurement and assessment. **Assessment** is the more inclusive process of gathering, recording, analyzing, and interpreting information. Assessment activities include the creation and administration of a measure, the scoring and interpretation of whatever information the measure yields, and the formulation of conclusions about what to do with the information. Measurement is thus a central part of assessment. This chapter and the next one focus on measurement, but you will find discussion of many assessment-related issues.

The first sections of this chapter introduce the topic of measurement in quantitative research. Although qualitative studies sometimes make use of quantitative measures, approaches to measurement in qualitative research are discussed separately near the end of the chapter.

Scales of Measurement

In this section you will learn about the scale, an abstract concept of critical importance in understanding how variables are measured.

Measures versus Scales

In Chapter 1, a variable was defined as any dimension on which values can be measured. The tools that researchers use to measure variables are referred to as instruments, or **measures**. Measures may be elaborate, as in the case of a timed aptitude test consisting of 160 questions that vary in format and difficulty, or they may be as simple as a checklist used to record whether a child exhibits a particular behavior in class.

A distinction can be made between an entire measure and the scale (or scales) it makes use of. A **scale** is what structures the way a variable is recorded by a measure. Consider, for example, a paper-and-pencil survey in which high school students are asked to circle response options that indicate gender, grade (the options are "9–10" and "11–12"), political affiliation (the options are "Democrat," "Republican," and "Other"), and preferred candidate for president (the options are three prominent politicians and "Other"). In this example, the *measure* consists of a sheet of paper with instructions on how to answer the four questions, followed by the questions themselves and a set of options for students to circle indicating their responses. The four variables of interest (gender, grade, political affiliation, and preferred candidate) are measured by means of four *scales* in which responses are treated categorically (i.e., students are given discrete options to choose from). Another version of this survey might ask for a narrative description of political affiliation, and for exact age rather than grade. In this alternative version, the same four variables are studied, but two of them (*political affiliation* and *age*) are measured by means of a different scale than the original version. This example illustrates the sense in which measures are based on scales. It also illustrates the idea that although variables such as gender may be measured with only one kind of scale, most variables can be measured in a variety of ways corresponding to different types of scales. As you can see, each type of scale corresponds to a somewhat different operational definition (see Chapter 1 for discussion of this important concept).

Notice that although the term "scale" may seem to imply a particular kind of measure, such as a paper-and-pencil test or survey, all quantitative measures consist of scales. Thus, in an observational study of personality in which the experimenter classifies each child as "inhibited" or "uninhibited," the scale is based on judgments about a particular dimension of personality (inhibition) and there are two possible scores (inhibited or uninhibited).

Types of Scales

In quantitative research, and in some qualitative studies, each variable is measured by means of one or more scales. Stevens (1951) identified four major types: nominal, ordinal, interval, and ratio.

NOMINAL SCALES   **Nominal scales** yield categorical data, which means that (1) the values of the variable have no quantitative meaning, and (2) the values are distinct from each other, with no intermediates. Gender, for example, is a variable that has two values—male and female—but one value is not "higher" or "lower" than the other, nor in most studies is there an intermediate value between male and female. Rather, each participant is simply classified as male or female. Other examples of nominal measurements include race, ethnicity, religious affiliation, and the city in which an individual resides.

ORDINAL SCALES   **Ordinal scales** yield ranked data, which means that each value of the variable represents a different position on some ordered dimension. Ordinal scales are like nominal scales in the sense of yielding discrete (i.e., categorical) data, with no intermediate values. The key difference is that each value on an ordinal scale is clearly higher or lower than other values on the scale. Class ranking, for instance, is naturally ordinal. Socioeconomic status would be an example of a variable that can be measured on an ordinal scale (e.g., high vs. middle vs. low) or with one of the other kinds of scales that are discussed below.

Although the values on an ordinal scale provide information about rank, it may not be possible to tell how much each value differs from the others. For example, the person ranked fourth in her graduating class has a higher GPA than the person ranked fifth (and there is no intermediate between the fourth and fifth positions), but it is not clear from class ranking how much higher the person in fourth place is. For the same reason, we cannot conclude that the person ranked fourth did twice as well as the person ranked eighth, any more than we could say that the runner who finishes fourth in a race ran twice as fast as the runner who finished eighth.

INTERVAL SCALES   **Interval scales** also yield ranked data, but they differ from ordinal scales in that the underlying dimension is continuous, and the intervals are equal (i.e., the difference between any two adjacent points on the scale is the same). On a 7-point interval scale, a score of 6 is just as much higher than a score of 4 as a score of 3 is compared to a score of 1. By definition, interval scales lack a true zero point. Whereas a variable such as annual income has a true zero value, a variable such as intelligence does not, because we assume that the lowest possible score on an IQ test would not imply a total lack of intelligence. Because interval scales lack

FIGURE 5.1 Example of Likert-Scaled Survey Question

> Circle the option that indicates the extent of your agreement with the following statement:
>
> *The teachers at my school respect me.*
>
> Strongly disagree   Disagree   Undecided   Agree   Strongly agree

a true zero point, scale values cannot be expressed as ratios. We cannot say that a score of 6 on an interval scale is twice as high as a score of 3.

Although interval scales are quite common in educational research—the tests of aptitude, personality, motivation, and emotional functioning that educators are most familiar with tend to rely heavily or exclusively on interval scales—it is unclear in some cases whether the intervals are equal in a psychological sense. For example, consider the survey item in Figure 5.1.

Likert-scaled questions, discussed later in the chapter, are quite common in educational research. Responses to the item in Figure 5.1 might be recorded on an interval scale in which the "Strongly disagree" option is scored with a 1, the "Disagree" option is scored with a 2, and so on up to a score of 5 for "Strongly agree." This is a sensible approach, but it is uncertain whether the extent of difference between a 2 and a 3, for example, would be the same as the difference between a 1 and a 2. A student who circles the "Strongly disagree" option may have much more negative feelings about school than the student who circles the "Disagree" option, while the difference between students who circle "Disagree" versus "Undecided" may be considerably smaller. In short, the requirement of equal differences between each point on an interval scale is not always unambiguously met, and in some cases it might be more appropriate to treat a particular scale as ordinal. (The significance of this idea will become clearer in my discussion of inferential statistics in Chapter 11.) Interval scales are nonetheless widely used and respected tools in research.

RATIO SCALES **Ratio scales** are simply interval scales that contain zero points. Examples of ratio scales include measurements of height, GPA calculations, and the numbers of absences during a school year. Because a ratio scale is based on equal intervals and contains a true zero value, we can say, for instance, that a score of 160 on a ratio-scaled test is twice as high as a score of 80 on the same test, just as a classroom consisting of 24 students is twice as large as a classroom consisting of 12 students.

Table 5.1 summarizes the four types of scales discussed in this section.

Scales and Scores

The quantitative data obtained by means of a scale are called **raw scores**. Examples of raw scores for one individual would be the numbers of items the individual answers correctly on a test, the numbers of altruistic behaviors the individual exhibits

TABLE 5.1 **Four Major Types of Scales**

Type	Underlying Dimension	Example
Nominal	Categorical	Gender
Ordinal	Categorical	Class ranking
Interval	Continuous	IQ
Ratio	Continuous	Height

in a contrived setting, or the set of ratings that the individual provides in response to a survey of attitudes toward private schools. Because raw scores in themselves may be meaningless or difficult to interpret, numerous methods are used to convert them to more useful form. Raw scores may be converted to **age equivalents**, which indicate the average score on a test obtained by individuals of a particular age, or to **grade equivalents**, which indicate the average score obtained by individuals of a particular grade. A score of 117 obtained by a particular 12-year-old on a 130-point test is difficult to interpret, but if the average score for 12-year-olds is 100, we can assert that a score of 117 is above average, and, as discussed in Chapter 10, we may be able to calculate a percentile ranking that tells us exactly how far above average the student is. (Other types of raw score conversions are discussed in Chapter 10, as are the sets of scores, or **distributions**, that researchers study.)

Scales versus Variables

As noted in Chapter 1, an operational definition is one that defines a variable in terms of how it is measured. One reason to pay close attention to the operational definitions used in a study is that the scale used to measure a particular variable may not be consistent with our informal understanding of the "true" nature of the variable. For example, most people would agree with the following ideas:

- The extent to which parents are responsive to their children's emotional needs is a continuous dimension.
- Greater responsiveness is preferable to lesser responsiveness.
- It is possible in the rare case for a parent to be totally nonresponsive to his children.

We might be tempted to conclude that responsiveness must be measured on a ratio scale, because it is a continuous dimension with a true zero point. We would find, however, that in some studies parents are classified through observational methods as either "responsive" or "unresponsive." In these studies, responsiveness is measured on an ordinal scale. We may dislike this particular operationalization of responsiveness, but we cannot understand how data are collected and analyzed in these studies unless we keep in mind that the scale is ordinal. Likewise, we might find it overly simplistic to label students as either at risk or not at risk for academic failure, but if this is the distinction made in a particular study we will not be able to understand the results unless we remember that for the purposes of the study, at-risk status is treated categorically rather than as a matter of degree.

The preceding discussion illustrates a subtle but important difference between scales and variables. A researcher might choose to measure the variable of parental responsiveness by means of ordinal, interval, or ratio scales (or all three), but the dimensions of the scale need not match the dimensions of the underlying variable. The researcher might be perfectly willing to acknowledge that responsiveness is a continuous variable, and that total nonresponsiveness is possible, and yet not hesitate to use an ordinal scale that distinguishes "responsive" from "unresponsive" parents. There are a number of reasons why a researcher would do so, including the assumption that by creating this artificial dichotomy, something can be learned about the effects of parental responsiveness on children's development. (Some studies of parenting style do in fact rely extensively on categorical distinctions within dimensions that are assumed to be continuous, analogous to the way other kinds of studies are based on classifications of subjects as "high," "medium," or "low" on continuous variables such as socioeconomic status, reading skill, risk of academic failure, and so on.) The relationship between measurements and the variables they are intended to measure is discussed further in the next chapter, under the heading of construct validity.

Types of Measures

For purposes of convenience, the various measures used in quantitative educational research can be divided into four categories: performance measures, personal measures, behavioral measures, and archival measures.

Performance Measures

A **performance measure**, as the name suggests, records how an individual performs on a test, or in some situation in which specific behaviors are elicited. Performance measures are typically based on interval- or ratio-scaled questions designed to allow inferences about underlying characteristics. For example, the number of questions answered correctly on an IQ test is the observable "performance" used to make inferences about the test-taker's intelligence.

Most of the tests of aptitude and achievement I discuss later in this chapter are performance measures. Such measures also include the creative activities and products that students generate in specific, real-life contexts. **Performance assessment** (also known as authentic assessment) focuses on activities and products such as term papers, drama recitals, science fair projects, artworks, and portfolios, all of which may be evaluated in quantitative or qualitative terms. The usefulness of performance assessment is illustrated by the testing required to obtain a driver's license. Although we would want drivers to do well on the two performance measures (written test and eye exam), it would be unwise to award a driver's license to anyone who does not also do well on the performance assessment (i.e., the road test).

STRENGTHS AND WEAKNESSES OF PERFORMANCE MEASURES   The strength of performance measures is their relative impartiality. If we want to measure the mathematical competence of a particular group of students, we could interview their teachers, their parents, or the students themselves, but we might obtain less biased information about competence by using a standardized test of mathematical achievement. Of course, our test could turn out to be too short, too long, confusingly worded, measure skills that we do not intend to study, or fail to test the full range of mathematical skills that interest us. These are among the potential shortcomings of performance measures discussed at length in Chapter 6. In addition, as you will see, obtaining certain kinds of information requires other kinds of measures.

Personal Measures

A **personal measure** records information about attitudes, beliefs, or feelings with respect to specified topics, or about individual characteristics such as demographic background, motivation, or personality. The difference between performance and personal measures is that performance measures ask individuals to "perform" by demonstrating knowledge, expressing creativity, and so on, while personal measures ask individuals to describe something about themselves. Whereas an IQ test is a performance measure, a survey in which respondents rate their own intelligence in different domains would be a personal measure (focusing on self-efficacy, or confidence about skills in different domains). Like performance measures, personal measures may be administered orally, in writing, or online.

Personal measures are sometimes referred to collectively as "personality" or "attitudinal" measures, but neither term is sufficiently inclusive, given that educational researchers study many other characteristics beyond personality and attitudes. Personal measures are sometimes called "survey" measures, but this term is limiting too, because not all personal measures consist of surveys. A rough distinction can be made between descriptive surveys of attitudes and opinions versus inferential and more psychometrically complex measures of dimensions such as personality.

STRENGTHS AND WEAKNESSES OF PERSONAL MEASURES   The strengths and weaknesses of personal measures stem from the same sources.

First, personal measures allow beliefs, attitudes, and feelings to be precisely quantified. Although precision is generally desirable, neither researchers nor subjects may be satisfied with the practice of assigning numbers to internal states such as beliefs and feelings. Indeed, philosophical reservations about the quantification of internal states represents one of the fundamental motivations for qualitative research methods.

Second, personal measures tend to reflect self-report methodologies. Although some kinds of information (e.g., attitudes about teacher salaries) are most accurately obtained by direct questioning (e.g., Do you think teachers are paid enough?), people may misrepresent themselves, either inadvertently, or due to a **self-presentation bias**, which motivates them to wish to appear differently than they know themselves to be. When responding to a personal measure, an individual may wish to magnify his honesty (or his deviousness), his liberal attitudes (or his tough-mindedness), and so on. People may engage in self-presentation bias consciously or unconsciously. The range of possible inaccuracies is as broad as the range of attitudes, beliefs, and other personal characteristics that people consider desirable.

Some examples of performance and personal measures are listed in Table 5.2.

Behavioral Measures

A **behavioral measure** consists of observations made by the researcher. Observations may be made in completely naturalistic conditions, or in situations that are more or less contrived. Behavioral measures are widely used in both quantitative and qualitative research. In quantitative studies, observation tends to be systematic. Researchers determine in advance what behaviors should be observed, and they develop consistent methods for identifying and recording the behaviors. In the simplest case, the observer uses a **checklist** to indicate whether or not each behavior on a list is observed (e.g., Does a particular child exhibit any aggression during a 20-minute recess?). An ordinal **rating scale** may be used, in which particular behaviors are rated along some dimension of interest (e.g., How aggressively, on a scale from 1 to 7, does the child behave toward peers during recess?). Finally, a more elaborate **coding scheme** may be developed. The coding scheme may or may not incorporate checklist and rating scale information (e.g., During recess, how many acts of verbal and physical aggression does a particular child exhibit, and what is the severity of each act as rated on a 7-point scale?).

TABLE 5.2 Some Examples of Performance and Personal Measures

Examples of Performance Measures	Characteristic Measured	Interpretation of Scores
Stanford–Binet Intelligence Scale Graduate Record Exam (GRE)	Aptitude	Norm-referenced
Iowa Test of Basic Skills (ITBS) Stanford Achievement Tests (SAT)	Achievement	Norm-referenced
California Achievement Test (CAT) Comprehensive Test of Basic Skills (CTBS)	Achievement	Norm-referenced and criterion-referenced
Examples of Personal Measures		
Myers–Briggs Type Indicator (MBTI) Minnesota Multiphasic Personality Inventory (MMPI)	Personality	Criterion-referenced
State–Trait Anxiety Inventory (STAIC) Beck Depression Inventory (BDI)	Affect/Personality	Norm-referenced and criterion-referenced
Strong Interest Inventory Kuder Occupational Interest Survey	Vocational interests	Criterion-referenced

STRENGTHS AND WEAKNESSES OF BEHAVIORAL MEASURES   Behavioral measures may be the best approach to recording information about certain kinds of behaviors. How aggressively a kindergartner behaves toward other kindergartners, for instance, is a question that might be most accurately addressed by simply watching the child interact with peers on a playground. Another advantage of behavioral measures is that they may allow individuals to express themselves more naturally than they would in responding to a test. Of course, when individuals know they are being observed, they may alter their behavior out of shyness, malice, or self-presentation bias. A further disadvantage of behavioral measures is that they may not be well controlled. A study of aggressive behavior in playground situations may distort the actual extent of differences across children in their aggressive tendencies. Some children may be quite enthralled with playground activities and ignore behaviors that would otherwise cause them to retaliate. Other children may feel quite uninterested in the playground and thus be more prone to aggression. An additional concern is that the behaviors targeted through behavioral measures may be ambiguous. Imagine, for example, trying to record individual acts of aggressive behavior among a barely differentiated mass of preschoolers racing around a playground, bumping into each other, wrestling playfully, and tripping over each other's feet. (Approaches to addressing this kind of ambiguity are discussed in Chapter 6 in the section "Reliability.")

Archival Measures

What can be called an **archival measure** relies on information obtained from inanimate, preexisting materials. These materials include artifacts, historical documents, census records, old photographs, and video footage, and they provide information that may not be obtainable through any other means. The information that researchers obtain may be recorded in quantitative or qualitative terms.

Content analysis (discussed in Chapter 14) is the form of research grounded in archival measures.

STRENGTHS AND WEAKNESSES OF ARCHIVAL MEASURES An advantage of archival measures is that the materials are sedentary—unlike people, they do not move around, lose interest, change their minds, or otherwise prevent themselves from being studied. A key disadvantage of archival measures is that they are representations from the lives of people rather than the people themselves. Many topics of relevance in educational research, such as attention span, learning, and the efficacy of particular instructional methods, are best studied through measurement of actual individuals.

Tests and Testing

Educational and psychological testing represents one of the most important contributions of behavioral science to our society . . . [and] has been the target of extensive scrutiny, criticism, and debate both outside and within the professional testing community.

(Standards for Educational and Psychological Testing, 1985, p. 1)

The most common type of measure used in quantitative educational research is the **test**, a systematic method of obtaining data from individuals. Although test results are scored numerically, the content, format, and underlying scales vary widely from test to test. An individual may take a test by responding orally or behaviorally to an examiner. Alternatively, the test-taker may write answers down, speak into a tape recorder, or enter responses on a computer. A particular test may be composed of one or any combination of the four scales described earlier. The SAT Reasoning Test, for example, uses nominal and ordinal scales to obtain background information on variables such as gender and grade, while the scores obtained on each major section of the test reflect interval scales, and the new essay requirement is graded on a 6-point ordinal scale. Some tests fall under the heading of performance measures, others can be classified as personal measures, while still others may include a behavioral component. Most of the discussions in this section pertain to tests that are performance measures or, less frequently, personal measures.

The Use of Tests in Educational Research versus Educational Testing

A rough distinction can be made between the use of tests in educational research versus the practice of educational testing. In educational research, a test is one of many types of measurements that can be used in a study. Testing in this sense contributes to the goals of each study. In contrast, **educational testing** refers to the use of tests for evaluating aptitude, achievement, and other academically relevant characteristics of students. The goals of educational testing tend to be more immediately and narrowly practical than the use of tests in educational research.

Historically, many factors contributed to the rise of educational testing in the 19th and early 20th centuries, including dissatisfaction with semi-structured oral examinations used for advancement in secondary school, as well as the development, mostly within psychology, of tests designed to measure intelligence and other capacities of educational relevance (Gallagher, 2003). From the beginning, educational tests have served two practical purposes (Haertel & Herman, 2005).

- Test results are used to compare, sort, and place students. The tests that are used range from screening tools for determining kindergarten readiness to college entrance exams such as the SAT and ACT.

- Test results are used to evaluate the quality of educational experience. The tests that are used range from teacher assessments of individual student progress to state, national, and international tests of achievement.

Educational testing has become a pervasive element of our educational system, owing in part to the demand for relatively convenient, systematic, and "objective" ways of assessing students, particularly in group settings. The use of tests and other measurement tools to evaluate programs has also burgeoned, as I discuss in Chapter 17.

Since the results of educational testing typically serve practical needs rather than addressing scientific questions, the organizations and individuals who administer the tests may not disseminate the results as research studies. Their results will be shared instead with parents, teachers, curriculum specialists, school administrators, and/or legislators. However, there are many points of overlap between the use of tests in educational research and educational testing. The same tests are often used. The same principles of creating and administering tests, as well as analyzing and interpreting the results, tend to be assumed. In a broad sense, the ultimate goal of administering tests is the same: to improve the educational experiences of everyone who participates in the educational system.

In the next two sections I describe some of the different categories and types of tests commonly used by educational researchers (and, in some cases, by professionals who conduct educational testing).

Categories of Tests

The scoring and interpretation of a test is dependent on whether the test is standardized or experimenter-designed, and on whether an individual's test score is interpreted with respect to norms, standards, or the individual's own performance at some earlier time.

STANDARDIZED TESTS   **Standardized tests**, developed over time by experts, are administered and scored in the same way across test-takers. Examples of standardized tests include the WISC and SAT tests, the ITBS (Iowa Test of Basic Skills), the MMUT (Modern Math Understanding Test), and the STAIC (State–Trait Anxiety Inventory for Children). The key advantage of standardized tests is their standardization—they are administered in the same way to all test-takers, with the same instructions, format, content, and time restrictions, all of which make comparisons across individuals more consistent. The disadvantages of standardized tests are also linked to their standardization. These tests cannot be readily modified to fit the backgrounds and characteristics of individual test-takers, and thus they may misrepresent the performance of certain individuals and groups. Studies have suggested the following concerns:

- Since most standardized tests are timed, they tend to be biased against slow test-takers.

- Since the language and content of the questions in a standardized test are always the same, they may be biased against English language learners, or those who speak dialects of English that differ from the language of the test.
- Some standardized tests of aptitude and achievement are biased against individuals from disadvantaged backgrounds.

These are just a few of the limitations of standardized tests that have been discussed and debated over the past century.

EXPERIMENTER-DESIGNED TESTS   The main alternative to standardized tests are **experimenter-designed tests**, which are created by researchers for particular studies. The advantage of such tests is that they can be tailored to specific research questions and environments. At the same time, the results of experimenter-designed tests may be difficult to interpret, owing to poor construction, or to insufficient information about reliability and validity (two concepts discussed in Chapter 6).

Any test, whether standardized or experimenter-designed, can also be classified as norm-referenced, criterion-referenced, or individual-referenced, depending on how the results are interpreted (Glaser, 1963).

NORM-REFERENCED TESTS   A **norm-referenced test** is one in which raw scores can be compared to **norms**, or information from a large group that has already taken the test. "Norming" a test refers to the process of administering the test to a large group and recording the distributions of scores along dimensions such as age, grade, gender, and/or geographic location. Once a test has been normed, the raw score of each individual who takes the test can be interpreted by comparing it to the norm for that individual's age (or gender, etc.). Norms for some tests are simply the mean scores obtained by students at particular grades, information that can be used to determine the percentile ranking represented by each particular raw score. The test score obtained by a particular 9-year-old, for instance, can be transformed into that student's percentile ranking among others of the same age.

Since educational experience and other aspects of culture change over time, norm-referenced tests may be periodically renormed. For example, in response to rising test scores across generations, the Wechsler Intelligence Scale for Children (WISC) has been renormed three times since it was first developed in 1949. Following revision of the third edition, the fourth edition of the test (WISC-IV) was administered to 2,200 children ranging in age from 6 to 16, along with a number of special populations, in order to obtain the set of norms currently used. Through proportional stratified sampling (see Chapter 4 for definition), census data were used to identify desirable proportions of age, sex, race/ethnicity, parent educational level, and geographic region in the sample used to create norms.

The main advantage of norm-referenced tests is that they allow raw scores to be interpreted comparatively. Each raw score (or group of raw scores) can be converted to a number (or numbers) indicating how well the individual (or group) is performing in comparison to some larger group. The main disadvantage of norm-referenced tests is that they may not provide information on individual strengths and weaknesses, or on the extent to which individuals meet definable standards of performance.

CRITERION-REFERENCED TESTS   A **criterion-referenced test** is one in which raw scores are compared to some predetermined standard, or criterion, rather than to the performance of other test-takers. Whereas the purpose of a norm-referenced test is to determine where an individual stands with respect to comparable individuals, the purpose of a criterion-referenced test is to determine whether an individual meets some standard of performance. A criterion-referenced test might be used to determine whether a student has mastered a particular body of knowledge, or to decide whether the student should be allowed to participate in a particular program (e.g., for gifted students). In such cases, a yes–no decision is made depending on whether the individual's score meets a preestablished criterion. In the case of high school graduation exams, currently administered in about two-thirds of American public schools (Center on Education Policy, 2006), the criteria for passing vary from district to district. In the case of standards-based testing mandated by the No Child Left Behind Act, each state sets the criteria for passing that all districts in the state must adhere to.

In practice, a test may be both norm-referenced as well as criterion-referenced. The study described in Spotlight on Research 5.1 includes such a test, the *Early Reading Diagnostic Assessment* (2nd edition), as well as several experimenter-defined tests and behavioral measures.

INDIVIDUAL-REFERENCED TESTS An **individual-referenced test** is one in which the score that an individual obtains at one point in time is compared to the score that the individual obtains at a different point in time. The purpose of this comparison is not to evaluate the reliability of the test, but rather to monitor changes in the individual. For example, individual-referenced tests can be used to track changes in academic progress as a student progresses through a curriculum. Reading teachers often use running records to evaluate individual student progress and make informed decisions about instructional methods.

An example of a running record is provided in Figure 5.2 (see page 136). In this particular example, the teacher has gathered data on one student's oral fluency while reading the first three pages of the story *The Cat in the Hat*. The teacher filled out the running record while the student read the pages out loud. (The teacher also repeated this running record later in the semester in order to evaluate the student's progress). A check mark above a word indicates that the student read the word correctly. A standard coding system was used to mark the student's errors and self-corrections. Here is an explanation of the codes used in this particular running record:

- **SC** means "self-correction." The student misread the word, then corrected herself.
- **T** means "teacher." The teacher supplied the word after the student asked for help.
- **R** means "repeated." The student repeated the previous word.
- −means "omission." The student skipped the word.
- ^ means that the student interpolated a word (which is written on the record).
- If the student substitutes in a different word, the incorrect word is recorded above the correct one.

Errors and self-corrections are distinguished on the running record. Repetitions and slight pauses are not counted as errors. Errors include instances when the teacher has to correct or inform the student, or when the student skips, interpolates, or substitutes in a word. (Other types of errors may be coded too.) In the rightmost column of the running record in Figure 5.2, a distinction is made between errors and self-correction that pertain to meaning (M), structure (S), and visual cues (V). At the bottom of the running record, the teacher calculated the percentage of

Multiple Measures in Quantitative Research: An Example from the Literacy Intervention Literature

Studies have shown that economically disadvantaged children lag behind their more affluent peers in vocabulary development. In a study published in the *Journal of Educational Research* in 2006*, Helen Apthorp explored the effectiveness of a supplemental vocabulary program among third-graders in Title I schools. Eight language arts teachers were randomly assigned to the program (experimental group), while another seven language arts teachers made no changes to their instructional routine (control group). The supplemental vocabulary program, called *Elements of Reading: Vocabulary*, consisted of scripted activities carried out for 20 minutes per day over a 24-week period. Various quantitative measures were administered to teachers and students both before (pretest) and after (posttest) the 24-week intervention. In addition, throughout the study teachers in the *Elements of Reading: Vocabulary* condition kept a weekly activity log and responded to a Likert-scaled survey—two examples of what are referred to in this chapter as personal measures. Behavioral measures were also used to conduct observations of teachers in each condition. The main purpose of these personal and behavioral measures was to document fidelity, or the extent to which teachers in the *Elements of Reading: Vocabulary* condition implemented this program the way it was originally intended:

> [T]he weekly *Elements of Reading: Vocabulary* activity log [was used] to assess treatment fidelity and capture implementation variations; for these logs, teachers recorded the date, the Elements of Reading: Vocabulary *lesson number and story title, and the extent to which they implemented each of five major instructional components. . . . As part of the activity log, treatment teachers also responded to an open-ended question regarding the helpfulness of the* Teacher's Guide *and lesson materials.*

The teacher survey asked about frequency of classroom practices and activities for developing vocabulary (e.g., "In my classroom, students write about their own experiences in relation to vocabulary words" and "In my classroom, students practice new words through discussion"). Teachers recorded the frequency of various activities with one of five response options, ranging from never or almost never to daily.

The research team developed and used classroom observation protocols to record the nature (grouping, type of student activity, materials used, etc.) and content of instruction in treatment and control classrooms . . .

The results of these personal and behavioral measures suggested good treatment fidelity: teachers in the experimental condition implemented the *Elements of Reading: Vocabulary* guidelines, materials, and activities in an appropriate way. Control condition teachers varied in their approaches to teaching vocabulary (if any approach was used) but generally differed from the experimental group in vocabulary instruction.

In order to measure students' oral and sight vocabulary skills, Apthorp's team used the *Early Reading Diagnostic Assessment* (ERDA; 2nd edition). The ERDA can be considered a norm-referenced test, because grade norms have been established that allow a raw score on the test to be converted to a percentile ranking indicating how well the student performed in comparison to other students of the same grade. At the same time, the creators of the test identified ranges of percentiles corresponding to criteria such as "proficient," and thus the ERDA can also be treated as a criterion-referenced test:

The research team used the Early Reading Diagnostic Assessment (ERDA, 2nd ed.; The Psychological Corporation, 2003) to measure the pre- and [posttest] oral and sight vocabulary. The ERDA is an individually administered

words read correctly, as well as the rates of errors and self-corrections. (The ratio of self-corrections is based on the number of errors plus the number of self-corrections divided by the number of self-corrections, thereby yielding a measure of how often the child made a mistake and then self-corrected.)

One, two, or several different types of tests and other measures may be combined in order to address a research question. For example, McCall, Beach, and Lau (2000) *assessment that diagnosis early reading and reading-related skills of students in kindergarten through third grade. The assessment provides percentile scores. . . . The ERDA also defines three performance categories: below basic, basic, and proficient. According to the ERDA manual, children whose scores fall in the below basic range (below the 30th percentile) are considered "at risk of not meeting grade-level expectations for reading proficiency" (The Psychological Corporation, 2003, p. 37). Children in the basic range "can be expected to achieve grade-level expectations" with regular, systematic instruction, and children in the proficient range are considered "highly skilled readers" (p. 37).*

Apthorp's team also used a norm-referenced test to measure reading vocabulary and comprehension at posttest:

The team evaluated reading vocabulary and comprehension with a norm-referenced test, the Gates–MacGinitie Reading Test (GMRT; 4th ed.) Level 3 (MacGinitie, MacGinitie, Maria, & Dreyer, 2000). The reading vocabulary subtest of the GMRT measures knowledge of printed word meaning. The reading comprehension subtest of the GMRT assesses reading comprehension with grade-level passages and questions that students should be able to answer from their reading . . .

The specific measures that Apthorp chose and, in some cases, created, were relevant to both her main research question (was the intervention effective?) and to some key preliminary questions (was there good fidelity in the intervention condition?) Apthorp found that the *Elements of Reading: Vocabulary* program benefited the oral vocabulary as well as the reading vocabulary and comprehension of the third-graders at one of the two sites where the study was conducted. From pre- to post-test, students in the experimental condition showed significantly greater progress than the control group on the oral vocabulary sections of the ERDA. Apthorp also found that the experimental group at one site showed higher GMRT scores at post-test, indicating greater progress in reading vocabulary and comprehension. She noted that this finding replicated three prior studies, two of which were based on experimenter-designed reading

tests. In discussing the differences in her results at the two sites, Apthorp made the following observations:

[I]n Site A, Elements of Reading: Vocabulary had significant and positive effects on measures of children's oral vocabulary and reading achievement. In Site B, however, the positive effects of Elements of Reading: Vocabulary were not replicated. Such a pattern of results may be entirely consistent with the different contexts of the experiment. In Site A, according to diagnostic assessment in oral vocabulary, 78% of the children were at risk for not meeting grade-level expectations. Also, according to school enrollment data, over 90% of children in Site A received free or reduced-price lunch rates. As a supplemental program in Site A, Elements of Reading: Vocabulary may have provided children with exposure to language and content that otherwise was missing in their in- and out-of-school experiences. In Site B, the context of the experiment was different. Over 70% of the children performed at grade level or above when the study began, and only a minority (24% to 35%) received free or reduced-price lunch rates. As a third-grade supplemental program in Site B, Elements of Reading: Vocabulary may not have enriched children's prior language experience . . .

Notably, despite the significant impact on vocabulary and reading comprehension in the present study, Site A children in treatment classrooms still achieved below end-of-grade-level expectations. To bring economically disadvantaged children up to grade-level expectations, the magnitude of the effect of the Elements of Reading: Vocabulary intervention would need to increase. Extrapolating from present findings, three times the magnitude of Elements of Reading: Vocabulary's effects may be necessary for students such as those in Site A to reach grade level on tests of reading vocabulary and comprehension. Researchers need to help identify how best to increase the magnitude of the effects of research-based vocabulary instructional programs, such as Elements of Reading: Vocabulary.

*Apthorp, H. S. (2006). Effects of a supplemental vocabulary program in third-grade reading/language arts. *Journal of Educational Research*, *100*(2), 67–79. Quoted with permission from publisher.

conducted a longitudinal inquiry into the characteristics of underachievement among elementary school children in Hong Kong. The researchers conceptualized underachievement in terms of the discrepancy between academic ability and grades. They measured academic ability by using a standardized, norm-referenced test (The Hong Kong Attainment Test), while the grades they obtained from teachers

Student's Name _____ Mary Jones _____   Age (Yrs/Months) __6/2__   Date ____9/22/07____

Story _____ The Cat in the Hat _____   Number of Words ____86 (pp. 1–3)____

	E			SC		
Page	M	S	V	M	S	V

1 The sun did not ✓✓✓✓ SC shine. → SC: 1

It was too wet to play. ✓✓✓✓✓✓

So we sat in the house ✓✓✓✓✓✓

All that cold, cold, – wet day. → E: 1

2 I sat there with ✓✓✓✓ R T Sally. → E: 1

We sat there, we two. ✓✓✓✓✓

And I said, "How I wish ✓✓✓✓✓✓

We had SC something to do!" → SC: 1

Too wet to go out / outside → E: 1

And it's too cold to play ball. → E: 1

So we sat in the inside house. → E: 1

We did T nothing at all. → E: 1

3 So all we could do is was to → E: 1

Sit! ✓

Sit! ✓

Sit! ✓

And we did not like it. that → E: 1

Not one little bit. ✓✓✓✓

Error rate: 1:11   Self-Correction rate: 1:5   Accuracy rate: 92%

FIGURE 5.2 Example of a Running Record

had been recorded on the usual criterion-referenced scale that ranges from 0 to 100%. The researchers then used an individual-referenced statistical measure to calculate discrepancies between academic ability and grades that emerged over time. A combination of standardized and experimenter-designed measures was used to measure student characteristics. These measures included questionnaires on which parents and teachers were asked to describe the students on dimensions such as competitiveness, impatience, and aggressiveness. McCall and colleagues found, among other things, that underachievers are recognized as such by parents and teachers (while not recognizing their own underachieving tendencies), that underachievement increases during the elementary school years, and that teachers become less supportive of underachievers in the late elementary school years as the children become more impatient and aggressive.

Specific Types of Tests

Thousands of different tests are used in educational research. Four of the more prominent types are achievement tests, aptitude tests, attitudinal tests, and personality tests.

ACHIEVEMENT TESTS   **Achievement tests** measure how well an individual has mastered some particular knowledge or skill. Most achievement tests tend to fall under the heading of performance measures. Examples include the California Achievement Test (CAT), the Iowa Test of Basic Skills (ITBS), and the state-specific, "high-stakes" tests mandated by the No Child Left Behind Act. In the state of Texas, for instance, students are required to take the Texas Assessment of Knowledge and Skills (TAKS) tests beginning in the third grade in order to measure their yearly academic progress. The TAKS tests are criterion-referenced, because they evaluate the extent to which students have mastered a set of curriculum standards and objectives known as the TEKS (Texas Essential Knowledge and Skills). The results of TAKS testing are used to determine whether or not individual students should be retained, and to evaluate the annual performance of entire schools and school districts. One of the reasons the TAKS tests are controversial among Texas educators is that it is unclear how well these tests truly evaluate mastery of the TEKS. (The question of whether a test measures what it is intended to measure is discussed in the next chapter under the heading of construct validity.)

APTITUDE TESTS   **Aptitude tests** (also called ability tests) measure how well an individual is likely to perform in the future on some particular dimension(s). Like achievement tests, aptitude tests typically fall under the heading of performance measures. Examples include the Wechsler Intelligence Scales, the Kaufman Assessment Battery for Children (K-ABC), and the Columbia Mental Maturity Scale (CMMS), all of which are standardized, norm-referenced tests. The WISC-IV, for instance, is an IQ test administered to children during a one-on-one session lasting about 60 to 90 minutes. Children obtain an overall score, as well as scores on each of four indices and subtests (see Table 5.3 for details).

Tests for obtaining admission to undergraduate and graduate programs, such as the SAT, MAT, and GRE, are also designed to be aptitude tests, although that assumption has been called into question in recent years (see Chapter 6 for further discussion). Spotlight on Research 5.2 presents a discussion of some of the concerns that arise from the traditional distinction between tests of achievement versus aptitude.

TABLE 5.3 WISC-IV Indices, Subtests, and Item Descriptions

Index	Main Subtests*	# Items	Competency Tested
1. Verbal comprehension			
	a) Similarities	23	Recognition of similarities among concept pairs
	b) Vocabulary	36	Understanding of word meanings
	c) Comprehension	21	Knowledge of general principles and social situations
2. Perceptual reasoning			
	a) Block design	14	Ability to construct three-dimensional forms given models
	b) Picture concepts	28	Ability to choose conceptually related pictures from larger sets
	c) Matrix reasoning	35	Ability to complete visual matrices given partial information
3. Working memory			
	a) Digit span	36	Ability to recall in forward and backward order sets of digits presented orally
	b) Letter–number sequencing	10	Ability to recall letters or numbers in order from mixed set presented orally
4. Processing speed			
	a) Coding	59–199	Ability to learn associates of visual symbols
	b) Symbol search	45–60	Ability to locate targets through visual scanning

*Additional subtests are available if problems arise in administering the basic set, or if additional information is needed.

Test-takers receive scores for each subtest that are combined into four index scores, and then combined into one overall score.

ATTITUDINAL TESTS   **Attitudinal tests** measure individuals' beliefs, attitudes, or feelings about a specific topic. These tests fall under the heading of personal measures. As with other kinds of personal measures, three of the scales commonly used in attitudinal tests are Likert scales, semantic differential scales, and Guttman scales.

The **Likert scale**, developed in 1932 by Rensis Likert, allows respondents to indicate the extent of their agreement with a series of statements. Agreement is expressed on what appears to be an ordinal or interval scale. For example, imagine that you wish to study how teachers feel about implementing a new, federally mandated educational policy in their classrooms. By means of Likert scaling, you could ask teachers to indicate the extent of their agreement with a series of statements about the new policy. Examples are given in Figure 5.3 (see page 140).

For the first item in Figure 5.3, which is framed in positive terms, a score of 1 would be assigned to the "Strongly disagree" option, a score of 2 to the "Moderately disagree" option, and so on all the way up to a score of 7 for the "Strongly agree" option. For the second item, which is framed in negative terms, the scoring would be reversed: a score of 7 would be assigned to the "Strongly disagree" option, and so on down to a score of 1 for the "Strongly agree" option. Notice that disagreement with a negative statement is equivalent to agreement with a positive statement. By reversing the scoring for negative statements, we ensure that across the entire test, higher scores indicate a more positive attitude. This allows us to combine groups of scores for related items.

Spotlight on Research 5.2

Aptitude or Achievement?

In theory, the distinction between aptitude and achievement tests is straightforward: aptitude tests measure what students are capable of accomplishing, whereas achievement tests measure what students have already accomplished. Not all educators and social scientists are comfortable with this distinction, however. In a 1999 article in *American Educator**, Robert Sternberg articulates some of the sources of concern.

When we give an achievement test, we accept the idea that we are testing a form of expertise, but this is equally true when we administer an IQ test. What differs is the level of expertise we measure and, probably more important, the way we perceive what we are measuring. The familiar IQ/ability model creates a certain expectation: that one kind of accomplishment (IQ test scores) will predict—and, in fact, lead to—another kind of accomplishment (grades or scores on achievement tests). And of course we use different words to describe the two kinds of accomplishment.

But this way of looking at the two kinds of test scores is a familiar convenience rather than a psychological reality. Solving problems on a verbal-analogies test or a test of mathematical problem solving, which are supposed to test a child's abilities, calls for expertise just the way so-called achievement tests do: You can't do well on these so-called tests of ability without knowing the vocabulary or having some familiarity with problem-solving techniques. The chief difference between ability [i.e., aptitude] and achievement tests is not what they measure but the point at which they measure it. IQ and other tests of ability are, typically, administered early in a child's school career, whereas various indications about school performance, such as grades or achievement test scores, are collected later. However, all of the various kinds of assessments are of the same kind, psychologically. They all test—to some extent—what you know and how well you can use it. What distinguishes ability tests from the other kinds of measurements is how the ability tests are used (usually, predictively), rather than what they measure. There is no qualitative distinction.

But if the distinction between what these tests measure does not exist, how do we come to make it? The answer is a complicated story, but the principal reason is historical accident. Briefly, the two kinds of testing were developed separately and used on different groups of people. IQ/ability testing, which originated in Alfred Binet's testing of young children, focused on exceptionally low levels of performance and came to be viewed primarily as predictive. Early studies of expertise were done with adults. They focused on exceptionally high levels of performance and came to be viewed as measures of achievement.

(continued)

Likert scales may be modified to elicit responses other than extent of agreement. For example, Figure 5.4 contains an alternative question for measuring teachers' attitudes toward the new policy (see page 141).

Seven-point and 5-point Likert scales have been used in these examples. The number of points used depends on whether researchers believe that each point on the scale represents a meaningful distinction. Odd-numbered scales are common, so that respondents have the option of choosing a middle value.

An alternative to Likert scaling is the **semantic differential scale**, in which an individual's attitudes, beliefs, or feelings are represented by a set of continua. The extremes of each continuum are marked by bipolar adjectives. For example, Figure 5.5 presents three questions that could be used to survey teachers' attitudes toward the new educational policy (see page 141).

Other alternatives to Likert scales include the **Guttman scale**, which consists of a set of unidimensional statements. The statements are arranged hierarchically, so that if an individual agrees with a particular statement, he or she should agree with all previous statements (assuming that the underyling construct is truly unidimensional). Examples that could be used to measure attitudes toward the new educational policy are provided in Table 5.4 (see page 141).

Sternberg notes that the traditional distinction between aptitude and achievement tests presumes that aptitude is innate while achievement is acquired. This leads to the pessimistic view that abilities such as IQ are fixed at birth—a view that leads in turn to inaccurate and damaging labels, as when children who do poorly on aptitude tests are labeled as having low potential. However, if we assume that these tests measure "what you know and how well you use it," it is less likely that the tests measure innate aptitude, and we have grounds for a more positive view. As Sternberg puts it:

The idea that abilities are a form of developing expertise offers a more flexible and optimistic view of human capabilities, and more in line with what we are discovering about human intelligence. Children become experts in the skills needed for success on ability tests in much the same ways that they become experts in doing anything else—through a combination of genetic endowment and experience . . .

Tests measure both explicit and implicit knowledge: knowledge of the subject matter and knowledge about how to take a test. This is as true of ability tests as it is of achievement tests. A verbal-analogies test, for example, measures explicit knowledge of vocabulary and a student's ability to reason with this knowledge, but the test also measures implicit knowledge of how to take a test. Thus, the student has to

work within certain time limits and choose the best answer from a list of answers no one of which is exactly right.

From these and other considerations, Sternberg draws a number of implications for educators:

First, teachers and all who use ability and achievement tests should stop distinguishing between what the two kinds of tests assess . . .

Second, tests measure achieved levels of developing expertise. No test—of abilities or anything else—can specify the highest level a student can achieve.

Third, different kinds of assessments—multiple-choice, short answer, performance-based, portfolio—complement each other in assessing multiple aspects of developing expertise. There is no one "right" kind of assessment.

Fourth, instruction should be geared not just toward imparting a knowledge base, but toward developing reflective analytical, creative, and practical thinking with a knowledge base . . .

*Sternberg, R. (1999). Ability and expertise: It's time to replace the current models of intelligence. *American Educator, 23*(1), pp. 10–13. Quoted with permission from the American Federation of Teachers.

Please circle the option that indicates the extent of your agreement with each of the following statements:

1. *The new educational policy will have a beneficial influence on classroom practice.*

   Strongly disagree   Moderately disagree   Slightly disagree   Undecided   Slightly agree   Moderately agree   Strongly agree

2. *The new educational policy will have a harmful influence on classroom practice.*

   Strongly disagree   Moderately disagree   Slightly disagree   Undecided   Slightly agree   Moderately agree   Strongly agree

FIGURE 5.3 Examples of Likert-Scaled Questions about a New Educational Policy

PERSONALITY TESTS   **Personality tests** measure one or more dimensions of personality, a tendency to act in similar ways over time and across situations.

Objective personality measures ask individuals to describe themselves on specific dimensions of interests. The items on these measures tend to be forced-choice (yes/no or multiple choice) rather than open-ended. What makes the measures "objective" is not that the results are unambiguous, but simply that people are being asked to describe themselves, as opposed to being described by the researcher. For example, the Minnesota Multiphasic Personality Inventory (MMPI-2), widely used in education and psychology, consists of more than 200 descriptive statements

FIGURE 5.4 Additional Likert-Scaled Question about a New Educational Policy

> Please circle the option that indicates the extent of your agreement with the following statement:
>
> *How fair do you consider the new educational policy?*
>
> Completely unfair   Somewhat unfair   Undecided   Somewhat fair   Completely fair

FIGURE 5.5 Examples of Semantic Differential Scale Questions Concerning a New Educational Policy

> *How would you characterize the new educational policy?*
>
> | Useful | −3 | −2 | −1 | 0 | 1 | 2 | 3 | Useless |
> |--------|----|----|----|----|----|----|----|---------|
> | Fair | −3 | −2 | −1 | 0 | 1 | 2 | 3 | Unfair |
> | Wise | −3 | −2 | −1 | 0 | 1 | 2 | 3 | Unwise |

TABLE 5.4 Examples of Guttman Scale Questions Concerning a New Educational Policy

1. *Would you like the new educational policy to be implemented in the U.S.?*
2. *Would you like the new educational policy to be implemented in your state?*
3. *Would you like the new educational policy to be implemented in your city?*
4. *Would you like the new educational policy to be implemented in your child's school?*

written as if they had been made by the test-taker (e.g., "Criticism or scolding hurts me terribly"). Test-takers mark each statement as true, false, or "cannot say." The MMPI-2 measures numerous dimensions of personality, and contains items that attempt to catch both positive and negative self-presentation bias. For example, one set of items consists of statements about tendencies that most people would admit to if they were responding sincerely (e.g., "At times I feel like swearing"). A high number of "false" responses to these statements implies positive self-presentation bias.

Projective personality measures provide ambiguous stimuli for individuals to interpret, under the assumption that their underlying beliefs, desires, and anxieties will be unconsciously projected into their interpretations. In the Thematic Apperception Test (TAT), for example, people are shown pictures and asked to tell a story about each one (see top of Figure 5.6 for an example). In the Rorschach Inkblot Test, one of the most famous and widely used projective measures, people are asked to describe each of a set of inkblots (see bottom of Figure 5.6 for an example). There are no right or wrong answers on tests such as the TAT and the Rorschach. Rather, each person's descriptions are examined for evidence of projections of their underlying cognitive and emotional states.

Test Selection and Test Construction

Researchers may choose from thousands of existing tests. The selection of a particular test will be guided by the type of information that the researcher wishes to obtain. There are tests corresponding to almost every imaginable characteristic (intelligence, learning style, creativity, motivation, self-esteem, etc.), tests that are intended to serve almost every conceivable function (diagnosis, screening,

FIGURE 5.6 Images Comparable to those Used in the Thematic Apperception Test (top of figure) and Rorschach Inkblot Test (bottom of figure)

tracking, etc.), and tests that are used to make almost every conceivable comparison (individual, gender, state, international, etc.). When searching for a test or other measure that suits your needs, a good resource is the *Mental Measurements Yearbook* (MMY), which contains descriptions of more than 2,000 tests and is updated every 6 months. The MMY provides information on the purpose of each test, the target population, the publisher, and the price, and includes a highly focused narrative review of the test.

Two sources that are more comprehensive than the MMY, although providing less information on each test, are *Tests in Print*, and the *ETS Test Collection Database*. The latter, a fully searchable database, is available on the Internet at *www.ets.org/testcoll*. Research and theory pertaining to tests, testing, and other measurement issues are the focus of peer-reviewed journals such as *Educational and Psychological Measurement*, the *Journal of Educational Measurement*, and the *Journal of Applied Measurement*. Finally, there are several sources that provide more comprehensive guidance for those involved in educational testing. Most prominent among these is the *Standards for Educational and Psychological Testing* (1999), mentioned at the outset of the chapter as an authoritative guide to the principles underlying

TABLE 5.5 General Principles of Test Construction

Principle	Explanation
1. Clarify purpose of test.	Determine what the test is intended to measure, and what population will be suitable for the test.
2. Review relevant research.	By means of a literature review, determine whether similar tests exist, and whether prior studies offer specific guidance on test format, content, and/or administration.
3. Evaluate preliminary version of test.	Obtain feedback from experts on the test, and conduct pilot research to identify problems with test format, content, and/or administration.
4. Revise and readminister test.	Conduct item analyses, collect reliability and validity data, and revise the test as needed (see Chapter 6).

test construction, administration, and interpretation. The professional and ethical responsibilities associated with testing are described in the *Standards*, as well as in two other guides for practitioners, the *Code of Professional Responsibilities in Educational Measurement* (1995) and the *Code of Fair Practices in Education* (2004).

Often, researchers find that existing tests are not ideal for addressing their particular research questions. Differences in format, content, length, and/or difficulty level may be needed, and thus it is fairly common for researchers to create their own tests. The best of these experimenter-designed tests are carefully constructed and provide useful data. Some basic principles of test construction are summarized in Table 5.5.

Measurement in Qualitative Research

Although qualitative studies sometimes make use of quantitative measures such as surveys and observational checklists, the ultimate goal of data collection in qualitative studies is not quantitative measurement but rather rich narrative description. In fact, some qualitative researchers might object to the use of the term "measurement" to describe what they do. This objection is understandable if measurement is defined as the recording of numbers. As I noted at the outset of this chapter, "measurement" can refer more inclusively to the recording of any sort of information, quantitative or qualitative.

Types of Measurement in Qualitative Research

Described below are four common approaches to measurement in qualitative studies: nonparticipant observation, participant observation, open-ended interviews, and the use of archival measures. Each approach reflects a different kind of interaction between researchers and participants. (Further discussion of the concepts introduced here can be found in Chapters 13 and 14.)

NONPARTICIPANT OBSERVATION   **Nonparticipant observation** consists of the recording of information by a researcher who does not interact with participants in the study. The researcher looks and listens (and perhaps also tastes, smells, and touches) without conversing or sharing activities with the individuals who are being observed. During the course of the study, the researcher may gather information unobtrusively, or the individuals may be aware of the researcher's presence but have no meaningful interaction with him or her.

The main advantage of nonparticipant observation is that it provides firsthand information about "natural" behavior. The best way to characterize interactions between teachers and parents at a PTA meeting, for instance, would be to observe an actual meeting. An obvious disadvantage of nonparticipant approaches is the possibility that the participants may know they are being studied and become uncomfortable and/or behave "unnaturally." **Observer effects** occur when knowledge of the researcher's presence causes individuals to change their behavior. (Comparable effects in quantitative research are discussed in Chapter 7.) Even if the researcher is discreet, participants may be aware of being studied simply because informed consent is a prerequisite for their participation in the research. Although informed consent is not a legal requirement if a researcher studies certain kinds of public behavior (e.g., crowd behavior at a park or shopping mall), educational research often requires observation of behavior in private settings. A classroom, for instance, is a private setting, and in most cases students who participate in research are aware that they are being studied.

PARTICIPANT OBSERVATION   **Participant observation** occurs when the researcher has meaningful interactions with the individuals being observed. For example, Russell (2006) used participant observation and other methods to learn about the cultural meanings of songs created by the Inuit. Russell's participation in Inuit life ranged from social activities such as dinner and dancing to interactions with future teachers enrolled in three music courses she taught. Over time these interactions provided a rich source of information about Inuit culture that allowed Russell to understand how their songs served a "decolonizing" function by expressing a mythological closeness to the earth characteristic of Inuit tradition.

The advantages and disadvantages of participant observation stem from the same source: By interacting with people, the researcher may be able to put them at ease and obtain more information, but at the same time the likelihood of observer effects increases. It is important for qualitative researchers to be flexible about adapting their measurement strategies to each situation as it changes over time. Qualitative researchers may change the nature of their participation, or shift from participant to nonparticipant approaches (or vice versa) if doing so will help make participants more comfortable with being studied, or otherwise facilitate the collection of useful information.

OPEN-ENDED INTERVIEWS   **Open-ended interviews** consist of verbal interactions in which the topics of discussion are not formally constrained. Whereas a survey containing multiple-choice questions formally constrains how individuals respond (i.e., you have to choose among the available options), an open-ended interview allows more freedom in the quantity and content of what respondents say, and reduces the likelihood of the researcher imposing his or her perspective. As one team of qualitative researchers put it in describing their approach to interviewing:

[E]ach researcher recognized the limitations in his or her experience and background and diligently sought to privilege the participants' perspective throughout all aspects of the study. For example, we employed very open-ended questions during the focus groups to enable participants to navigate us through their worlds. We attempted to ensure that we were really "listening" to students' words, facial expressions, and their use of material culture, without interjecting our personal views.

(Sirin, Diemer, Jackson, Gonsalves, & Howell, 2004)

Notice that the researchers refer to "very" open-ended questions. Open-ended questions are indeed a matter of degree. Interviews may consist of completely unstructured conversations, or they may be guided by means of specific topics and questions. They may be carried out in person (one-on-one or in groups), over the phone, by mail or e-mail, or through an interactive online environment. In the study by Russell (2006) described earlier, the researcher engaged in casual conversations with Inuit people, scheduled interviews, and created focused interactions guided by questions that the researcher had formulated in advance.

In the process of observing or conducting interviews, the researcher may generate **field notes**, which are written or audiotaped records of the researcher's impressions. Field notes may record details about the appearance and behaviors of individuals, the content of their conversations, background information, and the researcher's own subjective reactions to what is observed. The researcher takes concrete and highly specific notes, and attempts to ensure that the note-taking does not distract the individuals being studied. (See Chapter 13 for further discussion and examples.)

Through observational and interview approaches, the researcher pieces together the situations and perspectives of an individual or group. The researcher reflects on his or her own assumptions in order to help prevent them from influencing his or her understanding of participants, an attitude known as **reflexivity**. The researcher is likely to do some comparing and contrasting of views in attempting to reconstruct participants' experiences. Additionally, the researcher may make use of **triangulation**. Triangulation refers to the use of more than one source of information in order to establish a fact (Bogdan & Biklen, 2007). Researchers sometimes use the term more broadly to refer to the consideration of multiple perspectives in order to better understand a phenomenon. Russell (2006) engaged in triangulation in this broader sense, in that she interviewed Inuit administrators, staff, teachers, students, and others, in order to acquire a deeper understanding of Inuit culture.

ARCHIVAL MEASURES   Qualitative research may incorporate **archival measures**, in which information is obtained from diaries, letters, blogs, artifacts, historical documents, public records, audio recordings, photographs, films, and so on. What all of these materials have in common is that they are representations from the lives of individuals rather than the individuals themselves. Along with her participant observation and interview methods, Russell (2006) examined Inuit songbooks and song sheets, watched videos, created her own video footage, and did considerable background research.

In Spotlight on Research 5.3 you can read about a qualitative study in which several different approaches to measurement were used.

Multiple Measures in Qualitative Research: Literacy Revisited

In Spotlight on Research 5.1, an example of literacy research was described in which several quantitative measures were most suitable for addressing the research question. Here, a different type of literacy study illustrates the idea that some kinds of questions are most aptly addressed by means of qualitative measures.

In a 2006 study published in *Reading Research Quarterly**, Wanda Brooks explored how African American students interpret literary depictions of their ethnic group. In order to conduct this research, Brooks focused on 28 eighth-graders in a reading class in one urban public school. With assistance from the teacher and the school librarian, Brooks selected three novels written by prominent African American writers, *Scorpions* (Myers, 1988), *Roll of Thunder, Hear my Cry* (Taylor, 1976), and *The House of Dies Drear* (Hamilton, 1968). Brooks chose these novels in part because the authors "embedded various depictions of cultural practices into their books, and these depictions help to characterize the stories as culturally conscious African American children's literature." Brooks then joined an eighth-grade reading class and participated in discussions of the three novels over a 6-month period, using a mix of participant observation, interview, and archival approaches to measurement:

The class held 18 literature discussions, each of which I audiotaped and fully transcribed. Talk during the discussions followed a pattern whereby Rhonda [the teacher] led and facilitated and the participants responded to her and one another. . . . She posed planned questions and discussion starters and also facilitated the talk based on student-initiated queries and comments. Some questions and discussion starters evoked predictable responses, and others did not. Because of the teacher–student and student–student literature discussion process, collective influences shaped the data.

To ensure that students who spoke sporadically or not at all during the class discussions . . . were fairly represented in the data, I collected 270 written artifacts, consisting of 7 to 10 responses [to prompts] from about 74% of the participants. Written responses were typically one to two paragraphs in length and addressed the recently read chapters. In addition, about half of the prompts asked participants to react to a wide range of issues . . .

Rhonda facilitated the classroom discussions, and I assumed a participant-observer role (Hammersley & Atkinson, 1996). In this capacity, I assisted Rhonda with developing discussion prompts and questions about the novels. I also

provided regular feedback on the written artifacts. As the participants wrote their responses, they sometimes asked for my assistance. My particularly active role during times of writing likely derived from the teacher and student relationship they also shared with me. As a former teacher at JEM, I had taught this cohort of students in language arts during the previous two school years. I provided reactionary rather than leading responses to the students' requests, which often included grammatical/editorial concerns or minimal amounts of assignment clarification.

Finally, I recorded field notes during each visit. The notes were descriptive (Patton, 1990) and designed to provide a broader contextual picture of the school, classroom literacy environment, and participants' literary experiences, because reading and responding to the African American novels constituted just one component of Rhonda's literacy curriculum. The field notes were later transferred to a computer. At this time, I also inputted interpretive and reflective comments about my observations.

Brooks also developed an informal method of tallying the frequencies of student responses to different features of the novels. The results of the tallies showed that students responded most frequently to five textual features, although there was considerable diversity across student responses:

[The five textual features] that the students responded to most frequently included three recurring themes (forging family and friend relationships, confronting and overcoming racism, and surviving city life), one linguistic pattern (AAVE [African American Vernacular English]), and one ethnic group practice (beliefs in the supernatural) . . .

The multiplicitous nature of the students' responses provides an in-depth look at how culture contributes to the construction and understandings of story worlds. Even for children of a similar ethnicity who read representations of themselves, cultural complexity must be acknowledged from the beginning.

Brooks's descriptions of both the similarities and differences across students were facilitated by the use of multiple qualitative methods, and could not have been achieved with a purely quantitative approach.

*Brooks, W. (2006). Reading representations of themselves: Urban youth use culture and African American textual features to develop literary understandings. *Reading Research Quarterly*, 41(3), pp. 372–292. Quoted with permission from the publisher.

A Look Ahead

Both quantitative and qualitative studies typically rely on multiple measures. And just as qualitative studies may contain some quantitative measures, it is fairly common in quantitative research for qualitative measures to be included as supplementary sources of information. A survey consisting of true–false items, for example, might contain several open-ended questions in which respondents are allowed to expand upon prior responses. At the same time, as I discuss in Chapter 15, some studies represent genuinely mixed-method approaches, in which quantitative and qualitative measures each play an important role. In the end, the most important consideration in evaluating a study is not which categories of measures are used, but simply that the researcher's approach to measurement is suitable for addressing the research questions of interest—and that the specific measures chosen are of good quality. The next chapter introduces validity and reliability, two concepts of particular importance in evaluating the content and use of a measure.

Applications: A Guide for Beginning Researchers

Here are some ideas from the chapter that will help you plan your research:

- There are many different types of existing measures that you can use in your research. Look back at this chapter for some examples.
- If you create your own measures, you will need more guidance than can be provided in this book.
- You will need to use measures that provide information about the variables that interest you.
- The measures (and underlying scales) that you use will reflect operational definitions of your variables of interest. These operational definitions should be consistent with your research question.
- As discussed in Chapter 6, you will need to consider the reliability and validity of the measures you use.

Chapter Summary

Measurement is carried out through measures that record quantitative and/or qualitative information. Each measure is based on nominal, ordinal, interval, and/or ratio scales. The major types of measures include performance measures, personal measures, behavioral measures, and archival measures.

Tests, the most common type of educational measure, play an important role in both educational research and educational testing. Tests may be standardized or experimenter-designed. Depending on how the results are interpreted, each test can be classified as norm-referenced, criterion-referenced, or individual-referenced. In terms of content, each test can be thought to measure aptitude, achievement, attitudes, or personality. There are many sources for existing tests, and many guidelines for test construction.

Qualitative studies make use of nonparticipant observation, participant observation, open-ended interviews, and/or archival measures. Both quantitative and qualitative studies tend to rely on multiple measures.

Key Terms

Measurement

Measures

Scale

Nominal scales

Ordinal scales

Interval scales

Ratio scales

Raw score

Age equivalents

Grade equivalents

Distributions

Performance measure

Performance assessment

Personal measure

Self-presentation bias

Behavioral measure

Checklist

Rating scale

Coding scheme

Archival measure

Educational testing

Test

Standardized tests

Experimenter-designed tests

Norm-referenced tests

Norms

Criterion-referenced tests

Individual-referenced tests

Aptitude tests

Achievement tests

Attitudinal tests

Likert scale

Semantic differential scale

Guttman scale

Personality tests

Objective personality measures

Projective personality measures

Nonparticipant observation

Observer effects

Participant observation

Open-ended interviews

Field notes

Reflexivity

Triangulation

Archival measures

Exercises

For each measure described in questions 1–4, indicate whether the scale is nominal, ordinal, ratio, or interval.

1. A request for principals to describe their high schools as either public, private, or charter.

2. A difficult spelling test consisting of 26 words.

3. A list of four subjects (English, math, science, social studies), accompanied by a request to assign a 1 to the most enjoyable subject, a 2 to the second-most enjoyable subject, and so on.

4. A measure of annual income, expressed in dollars.

For each measure described in questions 5–8, indicate whether the type of measure is performance, personal, or behavioral.

5. A measure of moral development in which individuals are surreptitiously recorded during a card game in order to determine whether they will look at their opponents' cards when presented with an opportunity to do so.

6. A creativity measure consisting of 10 questions asking students to describe their own creativity on various dimensions.

7. A measure consisting of 25 questions about material that eighth-graders studied during their prior 6 weeks in biology class.

8. An open-ended measure in which parents describe their level of engagement in their children's education.

9. Self-confidence could be most directly measured by which of the following types of tests?
a) Aptitude test
b) Archival test
c) Attitudinal test
d) Achievement test

10. The likelihood of academic success in a college English class could be most directly measured by which of the following?
a) Personality test
b) Aptitude test
c) Projective test
d) Attitudinal test

11. A researcher obtains permission to sit in an elementary school parking lot and take notes on the behaviors of children as they approach the carpool line. What type of qualitative measurement does this illustrate?
a) Nonparticipant observation
b) Participant observation
c) Open-ended interview
d) Archival measure

12. A reconstruction of the experiences of public school students in late 19th century America would rely primarily on which of the following approaches to measurement?
a) Nonparticipant observation
b) Participant observation
c) Open-ended interview
d) Archival measure

13. *Critical thinking question:* In a study that incorporates both quantitative and qualitative measures, should the researcher expect to find consistency across the results of these measures?

Answers to Exercises

1. Nominal   **2.** Ratio   **3.** Ordinal   **4.** Ratio   **5.** Behavioral   **6.** Personal

7. Performance   **8.** Personal   **9.** c   **10.** b   **11.** a   **12.** d

13. *Possible answer*: Yes, but the extent of consistency that can be expected depends on the nature of the study and the particular measures being compared. For example, in a study on the effects of a financial crisis on a particular school district, quantitative data indicating the timing and extent of the crisis and its impact on teacher salaries and funds for supplies should be consistent with teachers' recollections about their experiences from year to year. In other studies—or in other comparisons across measures within a study—quantitative and qualitative results can be expected to complement each other, but they might be consistent only in a very general way, because fundamentally different variables were measured. For example, demographic variability in a school district that experiences financial crisis may be relevant to understanding the teachers' situations, but the teachers' recollections might be so strongly influenced by the district's financial instability that very little of what they say reflects quantitative variability in their demographic background or that of their students. (Further discussion of the issues can be found in Chapter 15.)

Suggestions for Further Reading

Research Article: Hamre, B. K., & Pianta, R. C. (2005). Can instructional and emotional support in the first-grade classroom make a difference for children at risk of school failure? *Child Development, 76*(5), 949–967.

This quantitative study on the role of teacher support in moderating risk of school failure includes concrete and relatively thorough descriptions of many different types of measures.

Application Article: Crothers, L. M., & Levinson, E. M. (2004). Assessment of bullying: A review of methods and instruments. *Journal of Counseling and Development, 82,* 496–503.

This literature review evaluates various measures used to assess bullying and notes implications for counselors.

Extension Article: Van Meter, P., Yokoi, L., & Pressley, M. (1994). College students' theory of note-taking derived from their perceptions of note-taking. *Journal of Educational Psychology, 86*(3), 323–338.

This ethnographic study illustrates a relatively involved approach to measurement based on interviews with undergraduate focus groups and content analyses of their notes.

David H. Wells/Age Fotostock America, Inc.

CHAPTER 6   Validity and Reliability

After studying this chapter, you will be able to answer the following questions:

- What is validity and why is it desirable?

- What are the main types of validity and how are they determined?

- What is reliability and why is it desirable?

- What are the main types of reliability and how are they calculated?

This chapter will prepare you to do the following:

- Evaluate the validity and reliability of measures in research reports

- Select appropriate measures for a study

- Use and interpret measures in a valid and reliable way

In Chapter 5 you studied the major types of scales and measures used in educational research, and you learned some of the basic concepts that inform the use of these materials. This chapter focuses on validity and reliability, two concepts of particular importance to researchers when they create, use, and evaluate quantitative measures.

Validity: An Overview

Imagine taking a test that included the following questions:

- Why are beer cans tapered on the ends?
- How many piano tuners are there in the world?
- If you could remove any one of the 50 U.S. states, which would it be?

These questions have been used in job interviews conducted by Microsoft Corporation (Poundstone, 2003). Clearly, a set of questions like these would not be a good test of general knowledge. Correct answers to the first two questions would depend on knowledge of some fairly obscure facts, and it is difficult to imagine how the third question could have a correct answer. Even so, from the perspective of an interviewer, these questions might constitute a good test of creativity when solving unusual problems in stressful situations.

This example illustrates the idea that the interpretation of a measure is influenced not only by the content of the measure but also how the results are put to use. **Validity** refers to the extent to which interpretation of test scores is appropriate, in light of existing evidence and theory. In the *Standards for Educational and Psychological Testing* (1999), validity is defined as "the degree to which evidence and theory support the interpretation of test scores entailed by proposed uses of tests" (p. 9). An important part of this definition is the idea that validity is not a characteristic of tests themselves but rather of the way test scores are interpreted. The "Microsoft test," in itself, is neither valid nor invalid. But it is arguably more valid as a test of creativity than as a test of general knowledge. Both evidence and theory suggest that answers to unusual, unexpected questions require creative thinking, but we would probably find neither evidence nor theory suggesting that answers to such questions accurately reflect general knowledge.

Because validity is not an inherent quality of a measure, the extent of validity will change when the same measure is interpreted in different ways, administered to different samples, or administered in different settings. A test of algebra skills administered to students after 1 year of high school algebra may be quite valid if administered appropriately to students in a particular school district. However, the results of this test would be less valid if administered to the same students in a hot, cramped room, or if administered to students from a different school district in which a different algebra textbook is used, the level of mathematics instruction is demonstrably lower, or a relatively high percentage of students are not native English speakers.

Sources of Diminished Validity

Although researchers sometimes speak of "good" or "poor" validity, or use phrases suggesting that it is an all-or-none quality, the extent to which a test is valid should be thought of as varying on a continuum. Researchers seek to develop and use measures

TABLE 6.1 Sources of Diminished Validity

Source	Definition
Construct underrepresentation	A test fails to measure everything it is intended to measure.
Construct-irrelevant variance	Test results are influenced by variables that were not intended to be measured.

with the greatest possible validity, and to avoid factors that might reduce validity in their studies. Broadly, two sources of diminished validity are construct underrepresentation and construct-irrelevant variance (Messick, 1995, see Table 6.1 above.).

Construct underrepresentation occurs when a test fails to measure part of what it is intended to measure. For example, imagine that scores on the Peabody Picture Vocabulary Test (PPVT-III), a norm-referenced test of vocabulary comprehension, were treated as a measurement of general linguistic skill. Since the PPVT-III only measures vocabulary comprehension, it does not provide data on a variety of other linguistic skills such as oral fluency and grammatical competence, and thus it would have limited validity if it were assumed to measure all of those skills.

Construct-irrelevant variance occurs when test results are influenced by variables that the test was not intended to measure. Imagine that a mathematical achievement test is administered to students who are poor readers or have limited English skills. Since reading comprehension as well as mathematical competence will influence the performance of these students, the test will have poor validity. Among students who are fluent in English, the test may be more valid. However, even among good readers, construct-irrelevant variance could occur if, for example, the word problems on the test are framed in excessively complex language.

Types of Validity

It is essential to consider validity when creating or evaluating a measure. In 1954, the American Psychological Association Committee on Psychological Tests published an influential report, referred to as the APA Technical Recommendations, that included a distinction between several types of validity. Based in part on this report, on further discussion by Cronbach and Meehl (1955), and on the *Standards for Educational and Psychological Testing* (1999), contemporary researchers in fields such as psychology and education continue to distinguish between three interrelated types: content validity, criterion-related validity, and construct validity.

Content Validity

Content validity is the extent to which a test measures the content it is intended to measure. In order for a test to have good content validity, the items on the test must be relevant to the content area, and must represent the entire content area rather than some aspect or aspects of it. Like many other students, you may be able to recall a class you took in which the content validity of a test seemed poor.

Content validity is a particularly important consideration when designing and evaluating achievement tests. An achievement test given to 10th-graders after their first chemistry class will have good content validity if the questions are carefully drawn from textbooks and other curricular materials used in the class, and if the main topics and instructional objectives of the course are evenly reflected in the questions. Insofar as the questions pertain to topics that students did not study (construct underrepresentation), or the questions fail to cover material that students did study (construct-irrelevant variance), content validity will be diminished.

DETERMINATION OF CONTENT VALIDITY   Content validity is most commonly determined by asking experts to judge the degree of correspondence between a measurement and the content it purportedly measures. The experts may complete a rating scale indicating the extent of correspondence between a test and an independent description of its content, or they may indicate the extent of agreement in some other way. Although content validity may not be expressed numerically, the determination of this form of validity is a systematic, empirical process.

A common approach to determining content validity is illustrated in a study by Sireci, Robin, Meara, Rogers, and Swaminathan (1999) focusing on the 1996 National Assessment of Educational Progress (NAEP) for eighth-grade science. The NAEP is a periodic assessment of American students' functioning in eight academic areas, including science. Each item on the NAEP eighth-grade science test was intended to measure one content area (earth science, life science, or physical science) and one cognitive level (practical reasoning, conceptual understanding, or scientific understanding). In the Sireci et al. study, 10 science teachers selected as experts were given descriptions of these content areas and cognitive levels. The experts were also given about a third of the actual items from the NAEP and asked to assign each item to one of the content areas and one of the cognitive levels. Content validity was reflected in the extent to which the experts and the NAEP agreed on the assignment of each item. The researchers found that for area, the extent of agreement ranged from 76 to 90%, while for level, the extent of agreement ranged from 50 to 70%. It was concluded that this particular NAEP test had good content validity for subject area but less-than-ideal content validity for cognitive level.

FACE VALIDITY   In some cases, researchers simply make an informal judgment about content validity. This judgment is sometimes referred to as **face validity**, or the extent to which a test seems to measure what it intends to measure. Good face validity can be a useful prerequisite to determining content validity, but content validity is more desirable because it is empirically determined. The perils of reliance on face validity are illustrated by a case in which the Wechsler Adult Intelligence Scale (WAIS) was modified for use in Canada (Stanovich, 2004). One of the WAIS subscales had been criticized as biased in favor of U.S. citizens, owing to items such as a request for the names of four men who have been U.S. presidents since 1950. Such questions seem to undermine the validity of using the WAIS in Canada, and thus the U.S. presidents item was changed to a request for the names of four men who have been prime minister of Canada since 1900. Changes such as this increased the face validity of the WAIS. However, it turned out that Canadians were more accurate about U.S. presidents than they were about prime ministers. This example illustrates the idea that face validity, like other types of common sense, is fallible.

Criterion-Related Validity

The extent to which test scores are related to another measurement of relevance, known as the criterion, is referred to as **criterion–related validity**. There are two types: concurrent validity and predictive validity.

CONCURRENT VALIDITY   **Concurrent validity** is the extent to which scores on a test are related to scores on a similar, previously validated measure administered at the same time. The previously validated measure serves as the criterion. Ultimately, the purpose of examining concurrent validity is to determine whether a test measures the same characteristic as the previously validated measure. The researcher may want to use the new test in place of the previously validated one because it is shorter, or more easily administered, or more desirable in some other way. For example, standard assessments of intelligence such as the WISC-IV typically require over an hour to administer, but for both practical and theoretical reasons it has been desirable to create comparable tests that can be completed in a shorter time. The Kaufman Brief Intelligence Test, the Slossen Intelligence Test—Revised, the Wide Range Intelligence Test, and the Wechsler Abbreviated Scale of Intelligence are examples of relatively short intelligence tests that have good concurrent validity with respect to longer, established tests. (This is not to say that good concurrent validity allows the shorter tests to be used in place of the longer ones in every possible circumstance. Some of the shorter tests are less valid when used with certain groups, or for making especially important decisions such as a diagnosis of mental retardation.)

Concurrent validity is expressed as a correlation coefficient. That is, scores on the previously validated test are correlated with scores on the new test. (Correlation is discussed in Chapters 1, 9, and 10.) The higher the coefficient, the closer the relationship between the new and previously validated tests, and the more confident the researcher can be that the two tests measure the same construct. The tests themselves may or may not be similar in format. For example, if concurrent validity is established for a shortened version of an IQ test, the formats of the short and long versions of the test may be essentially the same. However, researchers might evaluate the concurrent validity of a test of math achievement by measuring the correlation between scores on the test and grades in math classes. In this example, the formats of the two measures will be quite different.

PREDICTIVE VALIDITY   The second type of criterion-related validity is **predictive validity**, or the extent to which scores on a test are related to some variable that will be measured in the future. Here, some future outcome serves as the criterion. The purpose of evaluating predictive validity is usually to determine how well performance on one measure predicts future performance on a different measure. As with concurrent validity, the two measures may or may not have the same formats, and a correlation coefficient is often used to express the extent of predictive validity. For example, many studies have looked at the predictive validity of college admissions tests such as the SAT. Although the correlation between SAT scores and first-year college GPA varies from study to study, one optimistic, large-scale analysis suggested that in most studies, the correlation ranges from .44 to .62 (Hezlett et al., 2001). This range indicates moderately good predictive validity and reflects one reason many colleges and universities require applicants to provide SAT scores. In recent years, however, the predictive validity of the SAT has been questioned. The correlation between high school GPA and college GPA is higher than the correlation between SAT score and college GPA. The correlation between SAT score and college GPA after the first year is low at best. The correlation between SAT score and professional success following graduation is virtually nonexistent under most operationalizations of "professional success." (These concerns are revisited in Chapter 12 following the discussion of more advanced statistical techniques; see Spotlight on Research 12.1.)

The SAT example illustrates the idea that the predictive validity of a measure is influenced by the criterion one chooses. The predictive validity of the SAT varies depending on whether the focus is on predicting freshman GPA, later GPA, professional success, or some other variable. Like any other measure, the SAT does not have fixed predictive validity. Rather, how predictively "valid" it is depends on what one wishes to predict.

Construct Validity

The earliest theoretical approaches to validity treated it as a criterion-based concept (Kane, 2001). Validity was equated with how well a test predicted some criterion, and the criterion was assumed to provide the best possible measurement of some variable. This way of thinking about validity is appealing, so long as we believe that the criterion provides an accurate measurement. In some cases, however, we may question how well the criterion measures the underlying variable. By the 1950s, researchers had begun to explore this question more systematically, and for this reason authoritative sources such as the APA Technical Recommendations (discussed earlier) introduced and elaborated on the notion of construct validity.

Construct validity is the extent to which a test measures the construct it is intended to measure. A **construct** is an unobservable psychological entity that is proposed in order to account for observable behavior. Intelligence, memory, self-esteem, motivation, and mood would be examples of constructs. We cannot directly observe memory, for instance, but we hypothesize that such an entity exists, because it explains consistencies in how accurately people recognize or recall numbers, words, and other kinds of information.

Content and criterion-related validity represent the strength of the relationship between observable variables, such as tests, curricula, grades, and so on. In contrast, construct validity represents the strength of the relationship between something observable (test results) and something unobservable (a construct). Construct validity is the most fundamental type of validity, in the sense that it is presupposed by each of the other types. If a researcher finds close correspondence between the content of a particular achievement test and a particular curriculum, the researcher may speak of good content validity, but it is implied that the test taps into mastery of certain facts and principles (mastery being a construct). If a researcher argues that good concurrent validity justifies use of a new IQ test in place of an established one, the researcher is assuming that the established test genuinely taps into the construct of intelligence. Likewise, if the researcher finds a high correlation between scores on the IQ test and later achievement, the researcher may speak of good predictive ability, but the researcher is most probably assuming that the test measures a construct (intelligence) that is responsible for the later achievement. (Further interpretive issues are discussed in Chapter 18.)

DETERMINATION OF CONSTRUCT VALIDITY   Since constructs are by definition unobservable, construct validity is not as readily determined as content and criterion-related validity. Often, more than one approach is used, and the measurements that are widely assumed to have good construct validity will have been validated across multiple studies. Following are two of the main sets of approaches to determining construct validity:

1. Owing to the interrelationships between the different types of validity, measurements of content and/or criterion-related validity are often used as indicators of construct validity. For example, using a content validity approach, a researcher who is developing a new self-report measure of adolescent depression may consult with a panel of experts to determine whether the measure seems to genuinely tap into depressed mood. Through concurrent validity calculations, the researcher might compare results on the new measure to established measures of depression such as the Beck Depression Inventory. Through a predictive validity approach, the researcher might determine whether scores on the new measure are related to incidence of treatment for adolescent depression over a 2-year period. At the same time, the researcher might also examine whether results will be different when the new measure is compared to measures that tap into different constructs. The correlations between tests of different constructs should be low or nonexistent, if different constructs are truly being tested. Thus, scores on a test of depression should not be correlated with scores on a test of autism, since it is assumed that depression and autism are different constructs.

2. The internal structure of the measure may be analyzed, under the assumption that if items on the test measure a particular construct, responses to those items will be highly similar. For example, imagine a survey of students' motivation for success that contains three sets of items pertaining to academics, sports, and peer interactions. One possible outcome is that each student responds consistently across all items—some students report high levels of motivation across the board, some report medium levels of motivation, and so on. In this case, we might hypothesize that motivation for success is a single, undifferentiated construct. If each student responds consistently within each set of items, but a student's responses to one set of items are not closely related to his or her responses to the other two sets of items, we might hypothesize that each set of items taps into a different construct. A third possible outcome is that there are no similarities in student responses to related items, a result that does not bode well for the construct validity of the survey in this case. A statistical approach known as **factor analysis** allows researchers to identify those items (i.e., factors) on a test for which responses tend to be relatively similar and thus imply an underlying construct. Spotlight on Research 6.1 describes a study in which factor analysis and other approaches are used to establish the three types of validity discussed here.

In some cases, questions about construct validity are not easily resolved by analyzing item structure or considering other types of validity. This point is illustrated by the history of the SAT's name. When this test was introduced in 1926 by the College Board, the acronym SAT stood for "Scholastic Aptitude Test," under the assumption that the test measures innate mental abilities of relevance to college performance. In the 1990s, in response to evidence that SAT scores can be raised through extra preparation, the College Board changed the name to "Scholastic Assessment Test." Shortly thereafter, this name was dropped, and the acronym "SAT" became the official name of the test, an implicit acknowledgment of some uncertainty about what construct the test measures. Upon substantive revision of the content, the test was once again renamed. It is now called the "SAT Reasoning Test"—a designation that is neutral with respect to whether aptitude, achievement, or some combination of the two are measured, although it does at least acknowledge that the test taps into one cognitive construct (reasoning).

The three types of validity discussed in this chapter are summarized in Table 6.2.

Validation of a Questionnaire on Motivation to Learn Science

Although educational researchers have developed many tests of motivation, not many of these tests focus on motivation within specific academic content areas. In a 2006 study in the *International Journal of Science Education**, Hsiao-Lin Tuan, Chi-Chin Chin, and Shyang-Horng Shieh described how they created a questionnaire for measuring students' motivation toward science learning. This questionnaire, which the researchers refer to as SMTSL, contains six subscales, each corresponding to a different aspect of motivation toward learning science identified in prior research:

1. *Self-efficacy.* Students believe in their own ability to perform well in science learning tasks.
2. *Active learning strategies.* Students take an active role in using a variety of strategies to construct new knowledge based on their previous understanding.
3. *Science learning value.* [Students perceive that the] value of science learning is to . . . acquire problem-solving competency, experience the inquiry activity, stimulate their own thinking, and find the relevance of science with daily life.
4. *Performance goal.* The student's goals in science learning are to compete with other students and get attention from the teacher.
5. *Achievement goal.* Students feel satisfaction as they increase their competence and achievement during science learning.

6. *Learning environment stimulation.* [T]he learning environment surrounding students, such as curriculum, teachers' teaching, and pupil interaction influences students' motivation. . . .

The SMTSL consists of 35 items. Respondents are asked to indicate the extent of agreement with each item on a Likert scale ranging from 1 (strongly disagree) to 5 (strongly agree). Following are example items drawn from each of the six subscales.

1. *Self-efficacy*
   - *Whether the science content is difficult or easy, I am sure that I can understand it.*
   - *I am not confident about understanding difficult science concepts.*
2. *Active learning strategies*
   - *When learning new science concepts, I attempt to understand them.*
   - *When learning new science concepts, I connect them to my previous experiences.*
3. *Science learning value*
   - *I think that learning science is important because I can use it in my daily life.*
   - *I think that learning science is important because it stimulates my thinking.*

TABLE 6.2   Three Major Types of Validity

Type	Definition	Common Method of Determination
Content	Extent to which test measures content it is intended to measure	Expert judgment
Criterion-related	Extent to which test results relate to results on other measurement	Correlation
Construct	Extent to which test measures construct it is intended to measure	Multiple methods

Reliability

Whereas validity pertains to the interpretation of test scores, **reliability** refers to consistency of measurement. A test is reliable to the extent that it yields consistent results. Like validity, reliability is a desirable quality.

4. *Performance goal*
   - *I participate in science courses to get a good grade.*
   - *I participate in science courses to perform better than other students.*

5. *Achievement goal*
   - *During a science course, I feel most fulfilled when I attain a good score in a test.*
   - *I feel most fulfilled when I feel confident about the content in a science course.*

6. *Learning environment stimulation*
   - *I am willing to participate in this science course because the content is exciting and changeable.*
   - *I am willing to participate in this science course because the teacher uses a variety of teaching methods.*

Tuan and colleagues used a stratified random sampling procedure in which one class of seventh- eighth-, and ninth-graders was randomly selected from each of 15 high schools in Taiwan to complete the SMTSL. The researchers' approach to validation was as follows:

Messick (1989) identified that three types of validity need to be addressed in developing a questionnaire. These were content validity, construct validity and criterion-related validity. [To determine content validity] we used previous case studies from different settings and different students' learning motivation and also used existing questionnaires to design the questionnaire items. . . . Six experienced science teachers, three educational psychologists and five science *educators reviewed all the test items. Construct validity was verified by factor analysis. . . . A science attitude test (Fraser 1981) and students' science achievement scores from the previous semester and the current semester were used to assess the criterion-related validity of the SMTSL questionnaire.*

With respect to content validity, Tuan and colleagues indicated that on the basis of prior research, the items on the SMTSL adequately reflected the motivation to learn science (although the researchers did not describe the feedback they received from the experts).

With respect to construct validity, the results of a factor analysis suggested that a test-taker's responses to items from any one subscale tended to be more similar to each other than they were to responses to items from any of the other five subscales. This finding suggests that the six subscales correspond to six different constructs.

With respect to criterion-related validity, each subscale was found to be significantly correlated with the established science attitude test. Moreover, each subscale except for "learning environment stimulation" was significantly correlated with science achievement scores from the previous semester. The researchers concluded that the SMTSL is a psychometrically valid measure.

*Tuan, H-L., Chin, C-C., & Shieh, S.H. (2006) The development of a questionnaire to measure students' motivation towards science learning. International Journal of Science Education, 27(6), 639–654. Quoted with permission from the publisher.

Types of Reliability

Six different kinds of reliability can be distinguished, each corresponding to a different type of consistency: test–retest reliability, equivalent-forms reliability, equivalence and stability reliability, internal consistency reliability, interrater reliability, and standard error of measurement.

Test–Retest Reliability

Test–retest reliability refers to consistency over time. A measurement will have good test–retest reliability if repeated administration of the measurement yields the same results.

As the name suggests, test–retest reliability is measured by administering a test to a particular group, retesting the same group with the same test at a later point in time, and then determining the correlation between the two sets of test results. Test–retest reliability is thus expressed as a correlation coefficient, known as a **coefficient of stability**. (Researchers often simply use the term "test–retest reliability" to name this coefficient.) The higher the coefficient of stability, the greater the test–retest reliability—and, as you can guess, higher coefficients are more desirable than lower ones. A thermometer is not very useful if it yields a different number each time you take your temperature (assuming your actual temperature has not changed). Likewise, a test of verbal fluency is not very useful if the score varies each time you take it (assuming your fluency has not changed). So long as a characteristic remains unchanged, measures with good test–retest reliability will yield highly similar results each time they are administered to the same group of test-takers.

When a coefficient of stability is provided in a research report, the implication is that the characteristic being measured did not change between the time it was tested and the time it was retested. There is no simple rule for deciding when retesting should take place. Readministering the same test too soon is problematic if some of the test-takers remember their original responses, whereas waiting too long is problematic if some of the test-takers actually improve or otherwise change on the dimension being measured. However, if all test-takers are influenced in the same way by the time between tests—for example, if all test-takers improve by 20% on the retest—then the coefficient of stability may still be high.

Naturally, some characteristics do change over time, and if they do, good test–retest reliability is a prerequisite for measuring those changes. In order to detect time-related changes in verbal fluency, for example, we need a test that only reveals such changes when verbal fluency has actually changed. In actual practice, it can be difficult to tell whether differences in test results over time are attributable to actual changes, or to measurement error. There may be differences from one test administration to the next in the conditions under which the tests are administered, as well as other sources of error discussed later in this chapter.

A recent study by Brand, Felner, Shim, Seitsinger, and Dumas (2003) illustrates the use of test–retest reliability, as well as other forms discussed below. The purpose of this study was to develop a measure of how middle-school students experience the social climate of their schools. Based on prior research and theory, Brand and colleagues created a survey, the ISC-S, and administered the survey to students in the spring semesters of 3 consecutive years at the same school. (A key assumption was that each student's impressions of social climate would not change much from year to year.) Students' responses to initial administration of the ISC-S were correlated with their responses a year later, and, separately, with their responses 2 years later. These correlations were computed for each of the 10 subscales of the ISC-S, which covered dimensions such as peer interactions, teacher support, disciplinary harshness, and safety. Each correlation, in other words, was a coefficient of stability for a particular subscale over a 1- or 2-year period. The researchers obtained correlations of .67–.91 after 1 year, and slightly lower figures after 2 years. Based on these findings, the researchers argued that the ISC-S has good test–retest reliability.

Equivalent-Forms Reliability

Researchers and practitioners often find it necessary to measure the same characteristic over a relatively short period of time. Self-reported test anxiety among a group of adolescents might be obtained several times over a 1-year period. Or, the reading comprehension of elementary school students might be measured before and after a semester-long literacy intervention. In such cases, repeatedly administering the same measurement is problematic, because participants might show practice effects, or be less enthusiastic about taking the same test more than once, or respond in some other problematic way once they recognize a test they have already taken. To help prevent such problems, researchers often create **equivalent forms** of measurements that will be administered more than once.

When creating equivalent forms (also called "parallel forms" or "alternate forms"), the goal is to develop two or more alternate versions of a test that measure the same characteristic to the same degree of precision. These alternate versions will contain different questions but be identical in other respects, including content, difficulty, format, time limits, and instructions.

Equivalent-forms reliability refers to the extent of consistency in responses to alternate forms of the same measurement. In order to calculate equivalent forms reliability, alternate versions of a measurement are given to the same group on one occasion, and the scores on the two versions are correlated. The resulting correlation coefficient, known as a **coefficient of equivalence**, reflects the extent of equivalent-forms reliability. If the coefficient of equivalence is sufficiently high, it is concluded that the two forms can be used interchangeably. Thus, in a study of reading comprehension before and after a literacy intervention, students can take one test of comprehension before the intervention, and an equivalent form of the test following the intervention.

Although equivalent forms of tests are often needed, it is sometimes difficult to create forms that are truly equivalent. When the focus of a test is relatively narrow, there may not be much flexibility in the content of the questions. For example, there are not many ways to ask students about their impressions of the difficulty level and relevance of a particular class. In contrast, it is easier to create equivalent forms for a test of mathematical computation, since there are so many specific problems one could develop to measure the same computational skill. The most widely respected tests of aptitude, achievement, personality, emotional functioning, and so on tend to have equivalent forms.

Equivalence and Stability Reliability

If two forms of a test are administered to the same test-takers at different times, the resulting **coefficient of stability and equivalence** indicates both test–retest reliability and equivalent forms reliability. This coefficient provides the most rigorous indicator of reliability, because it shows the extent to which two forms of a test consistently measure the same characteristic over time.

Internal Consistency Reliability

Test–retest, equivalent-forms, and equivalence and stability reliability pertain to consistency when testing occurs more than once. When a test is administered once, it is not possible to measure those types of consistency—nor is it possible to find measurement errors resulting from practice effects, maturation, and other sources. However, the administration of a test on a single occasion does not rule out consideration of other types of reliability. It is often important to measure the extent to which items on a test, or subtest, are consistent among themselves. For example, on a test of long division, in which each problem is comparably difficult and students have sufficient time to complete the test, we would expect some consistency in the quality of each student's responses to all of the problems. Or, on a math test in which one section pertains to long division and the other section pertains to fractions, we would expect some consistency in the quality of each student's responses to the problems in each section (although we might not see quite as much consistency in how well each student responds across sections). If we did not find these kinds of consistency, we might suspect that the tests are not very consistent in measuring what they are supposed to measure.

Internal consistency reliability refers to the extent of consistency observed in response to related items on a test. The three main types of internal consistency estimates are the split-half reliability coefficient, the Kuder–Richardson formula, and Cronbach's alpha. The following discussion of these estimates is phrased in terms of entire tests. However, these calculations can be applied just as readily to subscales of tests. (In fact, internal consistency estimates are often reported for subscales.) Thus, the term "subscale" can be substituted for "test" in the following discussion.

SPLIT-HALF RELIABILITY COEFFICIENTS   The first step in calculating a **split-half reliability coefficient** is to correlate responses to half of the items on a test with responses to the other half of the items. Often, responses to odd items are correlated with responses to even items. The resulting coefficient is, in effect, a coefficient of equivalence, because the two halves of the test are treated like two different tests administered on the same occasion. The second step in the calculation of a split-half reliability coefficient is to modify the coefficient already obtained by means of a correction known as the Spearman–Brown formula. Because split-half reliabilities provide information about the internal consistency of only half the test, and because longer tests tend to be more internally consistent than shorter ones, the Spearman–Brown formula is used to provide an estimate of the split-half reliability coefficient for the entire test.

Split-half reliabilities are only appropriate if test items are equal in difficulty, and if respondents are able to respond to all items on the test. This type of internal consistency calculation is considered best suited for relatively long tests.

KUDER–RICHARDSON 20   The **Kuder–Richardson 20** is an estimate of internal consistency that is, in effect, the average correlation of all possible split-half correlations for responses to a particular test administered on one occasion. This formula is only appropriate when responses to test items are scored dichotomously—correct versus incorrect, yes versus no, and so on. Also available is the Kuder–Richardson 21, a simpler version of the Kuder–Richardson 20 that assumes equal difficulty of items.

CRONBACH'S ALPHA   Since the Kuder–Richardson formulae have limited applicability, Cronbach (1951) developed a broader method for calculating internal consistency. Like the Kuder–Richardson formulae, **Cronbach's alpha** (also called coefficient alpha) describes the average correlation of all possible split-half correlations. However, Cronbach's alpha can be applied when there are more than two response options to each item on a test, and thus it has wider applicability in research.

The use of internal consistency estimates is illustrated by the Brand et al. (2003) study described earlier. Coefficient alphas were computed for each of the 10 sub-scales for each administration of the ISC-S, as well as for other measures used in the study, including measures of academic expectations, attitudes toward substance use, and so on. Coefficient alpha values for the 10 subscales ranged from .63 to .81, and the alphas for the other measures tended to be as high or higher, suggesting good internal consistency within each subscale or measure.

Interrater Reliability

Some measurements are relatively objective. On a survey in which each question must be answered by circling "yes" or "no," there is generally no ambiguity in what respondents circle for each question. Other measurements are more subjective, in the sense that people might disagree about quantification. Essay tests, projective tests, and observational methods would be examples of subjective measurements.

In some cases, subjectivity results from concrete, physical impediments to measurement of some variable. For example, imagine an observational study in which the number of aggressive acts committed by preschoolers in a playground setting is recorded. Even if the preschoolers are videotaped, it will be somewhat difficult to discern from the melee of running, jumping, spinning, twisting bodies which instances of physical contact are aggressive or not. As a result, observers who watch the videotape might not agree on the number of aggressive acts observed.

In other cases, subjectivity is inherent to the variable being measured. Imagine, for example, that the writing skills of a sample of sixth-graders are measured by asking each student to write an essay about his or her summer activities. Although it might be useful to count the number of words in each essay, or to evaluate the essays along other relatively objective dimensions, researchers might also measure subjective characteristics such as quality of handwriting, thematic coherence, and overall skill. It would be difficult to establish completely unambiguous criteria for measuring these characteristics, and thus people might disagree in their ratings of each essay.

Interrater reliability reflects the extent to which two or more individuals are consistent in their observations of some variable. Interrater reliability (also referred to as intercoder agreement, scorer agreement, etc.) is expressed as a simple correlation coefficient or percentage. This correlation coefficient or percentage reflects the extent of agreement between individuals who make independent observations and generate a score or rating. For example, two individuals might watch videotapes of preschoolers interacting on a playground, and then count the number of aggressive acts committed by each child. Or, several individuals might be given a definition of thematic coherence, and then asked to score the thematic coherence of a set of essays.

In the Brand et al. (2003) study, the researchers were interested in knowing whether the students within each school were consistent in their impressions of the school climate. The researchers divided the ISC-S data by demographic character-istics such as gender, and calculated interrater reliabilities within each demographic group. The median correlations were all above .8, which the researchers took as evidence of "high" interrater reliability. Brandt and colleagues concluded that their ISC-S survey is a highly reliable measure, owing to its good test–retest reliability, internal consistency, and interrater reliability.

Standard Error of Measurement

The types of reliability discussed so far all pertain to consistency within groups. We can also consider the extent of individual consistency. In the discussion of test–retest reliability, it was noted that repeated administration of the same test might yield different results, owing either to practice effects or to maturation. If we exclude those sources of error, repeated administration of the same measurement might still yield some variability in an individual's responses. That is, a person's attentiveness, enthusiasm, effort, and so on may vary each time he or she is tested. In light of these and other sources of error, we can see that a person's score on some measurement, obtained on one occasion, is not necessarily their true score.

Standard error of measurement is an expression of how much an obtained score is likely to differ from an individual's true score. It is an estimate, in other words, of how much variation in obtained scores would be observed if an individual took the same test repeatedly. The higher the standard error of measurement, the greater the variability likely to be observed, and hence the lower the reliability.

The calculation of standard error of measurement is based on the assumption that if we could somehow administer the same test many times to an individual, we would obtain a distribution of scores, and variability in that distribution would provide an estimate of how accurate any single administration of the test is likely to be. A lot of variability in the distribution (i.e., a large standard error of measurement) would suggest that any single administration of the test would be more prone to inaccuracy. Little variability in the distribution would suggest that a single administration of the test would be relatively accurate.

Standard error of measurement (SE_M) is estimated by considering the standard deviation (SD) and the reliability coefficient for a set of scores (r). The standard deviation, which is formally defined in Chapter 10, tells you the average amount of variability in a distribution—in other words, the average amount that each value in the distribution varies from the mean. The formula for standard error of measurement is as follows:

$$SE_M = SD\sqrt{1 - r}$$

You can see from this formula that as the standard deviation increases, the standard error of measurement increases. This means that as the variability in a distribution increases, we will find that our estimate of variability in individual performance will increase. You can also see from the formula that as the reliability coefficient increases, the standard error of measurement decreases. If the reliability of some measure were perfect, the reliability coefficient would be 1.0 and the standard error of measurement would be 0.

Interpretation of Reliability Coefficients

As with validity, it is essential to consider reliability when creating or evaluating a test. The lower the reliability, the greater the inconsistency, or **measurement error**. Measurement error can result from many factors, including inappropriate testing conditions such as extraneous noise, extremes of temperature, and inadequate spacing of desks. Measurement error results from variability in how tests are administered and/or scored. Lack of heterogeneity in sampling is a source of measurement error. At the same time, variability among individual test-takers contributes to measurement error too, because people may differ from each other (and, over time, from themselves) in their motivation, alertness, physical comfort, stress levels, and recent life events. Finally, the content of the test can be a source

TABLE 6.3 Six Major Types of Reliability

Type	Alternative Name	Dimension Measured
Test–retest	Stability	Consistency across time
Equivalent-forms	Equivalence	Consistency across forms of test
Equivalence and stability	–	Consistency across forms of test over time
Internal consistency	–	Consistency across items of test or subtest
Interrater	Agreement	Consistency across raters
Standard error of measurement	–	Consistency of individual responses

of measurement error, as, for example, when items vary in familiarity or difficulty to a greater extent than anticipated, or when the test itself is too short.

The concept of measurement error stems from classical test theory, which was developed during the first half of the 20th century and integrated in Gulliksen (1950). Classical test theory provides the basis for distinguishing among the types of reliability discussed in this chapter. A key assumption of the theory is that each individual has a "true score" on a test that will be obscured to a greater or lesser extent by measurement error. Thus, measurement error and reliability are two ends of the same spectrum: The more reliable a measure, the less measurement error it reveals. Classical test theory also assumes that measurement error is random, but whether the source of error is random or systematic, the reliability of a measure will be diminished. (Contemporary alternatives to classical test theory, such as item response theory [IRT], are beyond the scope of this book, but are essential topics for the student or researcher pursuing a deeper understanding of measurement.)

As with validity, researchers sometimes characterize reliability in qualitative terms through distinctions such as "high" versus "low" or "good" versus "poor." In other cases, measurements are simply described as "reliable" or "unreliable." This is a convenient way of speaking, but it is always worthwhile to consider the actual coefficients when interpreting reliability. Although a reliability coefficient of, say, .98 is clearly high, and a coefficient of .14 is clearly (and unacceptably) low, there are no objective boundaries for "high" versus "low" reliability, nor is it possible to say what would constitute "enough" or "minimally acceptable" reliability, although there are some conventions. For instance, it is often recommended that when test scores are used to make important decisions (e.g., academic placement), reliability should exceed .90. Ultimately, the most important consideration to keep in mind when interpreting reliability coefficients is the purpose of the study.

The six types of reliability discussed in this chapter are summarized in Table 6.3.

Validity and Reliability in Qualitative Research

In this chapter my focus was on validity and reliability in quantitative research. Although these concepts receive less explicit attention among qualitative researchers, both concepts are relevant to the design and interpretation of qualitative studies—and both are as desirable in a qualitative study as they are in quantitative research. To take one example, in Chapter 5 you read about

Qualitative Evaluations of Validity and Reliability: A Standard-Setting Example

Academic standard-setting is based on input from researchers, educators, parents, and state agencies. In the case of high school graduation tests, the goal is to identify standards of achievement in particular subject areas.

For a 2005 article in *Applied Measurement in Education**, Dixie McGinty conducted a qualitative study of two 2-day meetings in which panels of teachers and administrators were asked to develop standards for graduation that would be recommended to the state board of education. The panelists' focus at one meeting was to recommend standards for high school science, while the focus of the other meeting was to recommend social studies standards.

Prior to collecting data at these meetings, McGinty critiqued existing research on evaluating the quality of standard-setting activities. She noted that although reliability and validity are important to such evaluations, researchers have not applied these concepts adequately.

The most frequently employed techniques for evaluating the quality of standard setting are found somewhere beneath the conceptual umbrella of reliability. Most of our efforts have been directed toward determining the consistency of the ratings or the replicability of the result over different sets of panelists, different occasions, and so on. Specifically, the reliability-related methods for evaluating standard-setting outcomes have included measures of interjudge consistency, applications of generalizability theory (Brennan, 1995), and measures of intrajudge consistency. Examples of the last category include . . . a method used in a study by Plake, Impara, and Irwin (2000) in which panelists rated the same set of items twice, and the mean absolute differences between the first and second ratings were computed for each item. Much effort has been directed toward refining standard-setting procedures with the goal of achieving more reliable results, as evidenced by more desirable values on these measures. These efforts make an important contribution to the confidence we have in standard setting, but they are far from sufficient.

One of McGinty's concerns is that reliability does not guarantee validity. Test results may be very consistent over time, across observers, and so on, but the test may not be measuring what it needs to:

These reliability measures, individually and collectively, constitute, at best, severely inadequate evidence of the appropriateness of a performance standard. Reliability of a test's scores, although necessary, does not guarantee that its results are appropriate for a given purpose; reliability tells us nothing about the meaning of the scores, although it mediates the interpretation of the scores by establishing the level of confidence. Similarly, reliability of standard-setting judgments is clearly not a sufficient condition for concluding that the standard is appropriate, as many other researchers have emphasized (e.g., Kane, 1994; Linn, 1998; Plake et al., 2000). This is especially troubling in standard setting because researchers know so little about how panelists make their decisions, and consequently so little about what the resulting performance standard really means, without solid validity evidence.

Of the measures listed previously, interjudge consistency is particularly problematic. In evaluating standard-setting quality, the measurement community has relied more heavily on this criterion than on any other; in fact, "convergence" of the ratings often acquires, at least implicitly, the status of the "goal" of a standard-setting process. However, interjudge consistency may be overvalued by the standard-setting community. First, very little is known about the reasons for the variability in panelists' ratings. Consistency can be—and, in my experience, often is—"artificially" achieved through iterative processes and the use of normative data by panelists. However, I do not advocate abandoning these two practices. In other situations, high consistency might occur for other undesirable reasons (e.g., if most panelists were operating on the same misconception about the process or if one judge exercised undue influence over the others, in the case of standard-setting procedures that include group discussion between successive rounds). Second, interjudge consistency should not be considered a sine qua non for "good" standard setting. Individuals are expected to differ in their opinions on policy issues, such as the decision about a desired performance standard, as noted by Kane (1994). As Messick (1995) suggested, differences in opinion seem particularly likely when the panelists represent very diverse backgrounds, as may be the case when various stakeholders are involved in the process. Messick drew a distinction between this type of variability (i.e., variability resulting from values or viewpoints that are consistently different) and random variability around the consensus.

Whereas the latter indicates a lack of reliability, the former is, in Messick's view, not necessarily undesirable.

Certainly, it is important to be as confident as possible about the reliability and replicability of standard-setting results. Yet, no matter how much reliability evidence is amassed, the most important stone is left unturned if we fail to devote equal or greater efforts to standard-setting validity.

McGinty expressed more serious concerns about the consideration of validity in evaluative research on standard-setting, arguing that its importance is acknowledged yet "all but ignored" in both research and practice. She considers this a serious problem, particularly in the context of determining cut scores—the scores below which test performance is unacceptable:

The lack of serious attention to validity is especially disturbing in the context of standard setting (as opposed to the validity of a test score itself) because the argument supporting the appropriateness of a specific cut score involves more steps, and therefore more possibilities for gaps in validity evidence. If, for example, one wants to claim that a particular cut score is appropriate for a particular test, one must assume that there is validity evidence that links the test scores to the domain of interest and that there are measurement opportunities in the test to support the desired use of the scores. In addition, one must assume that the location of the cut score (determined through the standard-setting process) is logically connected to the policy definition for which the cut score is set. Put more simply, standard setting compounds the already troublesome problem of test score validity. In a climate of high-stakes accountability, the measurement community cannot afford to leave its tests unprotected against validity threats.

McGinty recommended that the validity of standard-setting efforts should be evaluated through consideration of four kinds of data: inputs (e.g., the information and training received by panelists), standard-setting processes (the panelists' decision-oriented activities), outputs (e.g., cutoff scores), and consequences (e.g., the resulting passing rates).

McGinty's interest in observing the two standard-setting meetings was sparked by her observation that there is very little research on the standard-setting process. Her approach to collecting data at these meetings was based on nonparticipant observation (see Chapter 5 for definition). Although barred from taking notes, she observed that three validity-related themes emerge across meetings. The first is what she called the "should/would problem." Panelists were asked to consider the minimally competent high school graduate, and to indicate the

probability that this hypothetical person would answer particular questions correctly. In spite of their training, the panelists were often confused as to whether they should judge what a minimally competent graduate *should* answer correctly, versus what such an individual *would* answer correctly on the test. This is a validity issue, in the sense that two very different ideas could potentially inform decisions about cutoff scores. As McGinty put it:

In reality, the task requires both a value judgment and a prediction. The value judgment lies in envisioning a minimally competent examinee; each judge will have his or her own conception of what constitutes minimal competence. The prediction involves estimating how difficult the item would be for this examinee. The panelists, however, often seemed to have lost the sense in which the value judgment is inherent in this task. . . . As one participant said during the second round of standard setting, "I'm still struggling with the word 'probability.' Are we supposed to estimate what they will do or what they should do?" Another participant asked, on the second day of the meeting, "Are we ever going to get to the should? I thought we were here to set standards."

The second theme expressed by panelists was a tension between wanting to set high standards and wanting to be perceived as effective teachers. Higher standards would result in lower passing rates and suggest to the public that the teachers were not doing their job. McGinty had some questions about how to interpret the tension she observed:

It is clear to me that any such conflict of interest has implications for validity, yet I am unsure as to what those implications are. We want panelists to consider consequences when they make their judgments. . . . If some panelists ideally want to raise standards, but lower their ratings out of desire to protect their own interests for reasons suggested previously, does this constitute bias, or, instead, a desirable consideration of reality? The answers to this question would have implications not only for standard-setting validity, but also for education policy in a broader sense.

Finally, a theme that emerged from both meetings is that many panelists became skeptical that their "recommendations" would affect the actual formulation of standards. Although McGinty did not find evidence that negativism on the panel's part affected their decisions, she noted:

It is reasonable to hypothesize that, if present, such attitudes might affect the seriousness with which panelists approach their task, which in turn affects the validity of the resulting standard.

In sum, McGinty's research points to the importance of carefully considering validity and reliability when evaluating the process of standards-setting. Although her study was based on qualitative methods, the conclusion is relevant to both quantitative and qualitative researchers.

*McGinty, D. (2005). Illuminating the black box of standard setting: An exploratory qualitative study. *Applied Measurement in Education, 18*(3), 269–287. Quoted with permission from the publisher.

triangulation, the use of more than one source of information in a qualitative study in order to establish a fact. Triangulation is an essential part of qualitative research, and as a form of corroboration it can be thought of as a qualitative assessment of interrater reliability. (Alternatively, one could say that interrater reliability is a particular kind of triangulation.) What the quantitative researcher who calculates interrater reliability and the qualitative researcher who engages in triangulation have in common is the appreciation that for certain kinds of observations, more than one observer may be needed to establish a fact. If there is a difference between the two researchers, it would be that the quantitative researcher may assume that facts are objective phenomena that can be established, while the qualitative researcher assumes that the facts are constructed to some extent through the process of triangulation (see discussion of positivism and constructivism in Chapter 1).

Quantitative approaches can also be used to establish interrater reliability in a qualitative study. That is, in any qualitative study that relies on observational methods, the researcher can calculate interrater reliability as described earlier in the chapter. This is a fairly common approach in mixed-methods research that relies on qualitative observation (see Chapter 15 for details).

An important concept in qualitative research is that of **social validity**, or the extent to which the results of a study are relevant to audiences beyond the scientific community. Social validity is of importance to both quantitative and qualitative researchers, but qualitative researchers often take the lead in calling for greater social validity, particularly as a way of empowering educational practitioners and connecting research with practice. As discussed in Chapter 18, one way of promoting social validity is to involve practitioners in the planning of a study, so that the results more closely match the needs and resources of the practitioner in his or her educational setting.

Spotlight on Research 6.2 contains further discussion of the role of validity and reliability in qualitative research.

The Relationship Between Validity and Reliability

Although discussed separately in this chapter, validity and reliability are not conceptually independent. Reliability is a prerequisite for validity, in the sense that the results of a measurement cannot be valid if they are not reliable. If someone's scores on an IQ test were quite different each time the person took the test, we would have no basis for saying that the test taps into intelligence (since we believe IQ is fairly stable over time). Thus, we can say that the extent to which a test is valid is limited by its reliability. (This is one of the key points raised in

Spotlight on Research 6.3

Determining the Psychometric Properties of an IQ Test

The Wechsler Intelligence Scale for Children (WISC-IV) is one of the most widely used IQ tests in educational research. Normed for use with children between the ages 6 and 16, the WISC-IV is administered during a single session, and it is believed to measure verbal comprehension, perceptual reasoning, working memory, and processing speed (see Table 5.3 in Chapter 5 for more information on this test).

In a 2003 technical report introducing the WISC-IV (a revision of its predecessor, the WISC-III), Paul Williams, Lawrence Weiss, and Eric Rolfhus described research on the psychometric properties of the test, including internal consistency and test–retest reliability as well as content validity.*

The evidence of internal consistency reliability for the normative sample was obtained using the split-half method for all subtests except the speeded tasks . . . for which the test-retest coefficients were used. . . . The reliability coefficients for the WISC-IV composite scales range from .88 . . . to .97 (full scale). The reliability coefficients of the WISC-IV composite scales are identical to or slightly better than corresponding composite scales in the WISC-III.

That these results can be appropriately generalized is supported by information obtained from the special and clinical samples. Evidence of reliability was obtained utilizing the split-half method from a sample of 661 children from 16 special and clinical groups. . . . The majority of the subtest reliability coefficients across special groups are similar to or higher than those coefficients reported for the normative sample, suggesting that the WISC-IV is an equally reliable instrument for assessing children who are developing typically and children with clinical diagnoses.

The evidence of the WISC-IV's test–retest stability for subtest and composite scales was evaluated with information obtained from a sample of 243 children. Participants were administered the WISC-IV on two separate occasions, with a mean test–retest interval of 32 days. . . . [T]he data indicate that the WISC-IV scores are stable across time. . . .

The actual test–retest correlations ranged from .67 to .93 (full scale). Overall, then, the WISC-IV was found to have good internal consistency and test–retest reliability.

Content validity was evaluated by determining the relationship between the WISC-IV and the WISC-III.

Of particular interest was the relationship between two pairs of subscales that had been revised. First, the VIQ subscale of the WISC-III was replaced on the WISC-IV by the VIQ (Verbal Comprehension Index). Second, the PIQ (Performance IQ) subscale of the WISC-III was replaced on the WISC-IV by the PRI (Perceptual Reasoning Index). The new subscales differed somewhat in content. For example, whereas the PIQ contained primarily spatial and visual tasks, the PRI provides a more direct test of fluid reasoning. Finally, the researchers were interested in the relationship between the WISC-III and WISC-IV in overall score (Full Scale IQ, or FSIQ for short).

Both the WISC-IV and the WISC-III were administered in counterbalanced order to 244 children from ages 6–16; the test–retest interval was 5 to 42 days. . . .

The corrected correlation between the WISC-III VIQ and WISC-IV VCI is .87 and .74 between the WISC-III PIQ and the WISC-IV PRI. The lower correlation between PIQ and PRI reflects important changes made to this composite in WISC-IV. . . . The WISC-III FSIQ and the WISC-IV FSIQ correlate highly (r = .89).

As anticipated, the older WISC-III norms provided slightly inflated estimates for today's children. The overall difference between the WISC-III and WISC-IV FSIQ scores is 2.5 points, with WISC-III scores the higher of the two. . . .

Practitioners should keep in mind that these are average differences, and that an individual child who has been administered the WISC-III and is retested with the WISC-IV may score more or less than 2.5 points lower on the WISC-IV FSIQ, as compared to his or her previous WISC-III scores. When retesting clinical or special education students, many factors can contribute to score differences (for example, the compound effects of the disorder or disability with increased educational and environmental demands as the child ages).

Data reported elsewhere also indicate strong correlations between WISC-IV scores and scores on standardized tests such as the WPPSI-III and the WAIS-III. The researchers concluded that the newest version of the WISC has good content validity.

*Williams, P. E., Weiss, L. G., & Rolfhus, E. L. (2003). WISC-IV Technical Manual #2. Quoted with permission from The Psychological Corporation: A Harcourt Assessment Company.

Spotlight on Research 6.2 with respect to qualitative studies, but the idea applies with equal force to quantitative designs.)

At the same time, a highly reliable measurement is not necessarily a highly valid one. A test might yield extremely consistent results, and yet be consistently measuring a variable that the researchers do not intend to measure. In later chapters, you will read about historical examples of educational research in which the findings were quite reliable, but turned out to be invalid upon closer scrutiny of the purported construct validity. Thus, we can say that the extent of a test's reliability offers no guarantee as to its validity. Large reliability coefficients can, at most, only hint at good validity.

In spite of the conceptual links between validity and reliability, they tend to be measured and reported separately, as illustrated in Spotlight on Research 6.3. The report discussed in this Spotlight draws together several of the concepts discussed throughout the chapter.

A Look Ahead

In Chapters 5 and 6, some of the basic concepts of measurement were discussed. In the next set of chapters I introduce the principles of research design. Chapters 7 and 8 focus on the design of experimental research. In later chapters I introduce nonexperimental quantitative designs, as well as the designs of qualitative, mixed-methods, and action research studies.

Applications: A Guide for Beginning Researchers

Here are some ideas from the chapter that will help you plan your research:

- If you use standardized measures in your research, be sure that your use of the measures as well as your interpretation of the results are valid.
- If you create your own measures, you will need to determine that your intended use and interpretation of the results are valid.
- You may need to consider one, two, or all three types of validity in your research.
- Whether you use standardized or experimenter-designed measures in your research, you will need to ensure that your results are reliable.
- You may need to consider one or more than one type of reliability in your research.

Chapter Summary

Validity and reliability are essential to evaluating the quality of specific measures and their use. Validity is not inherent to a measure but reflects the appropriateness of the way the results are interpreted. Two sources of diminished validity are construct underrepresentation and construct-irrelevant variance.

Three major types of validity are content validity, criterion-related validity (which subsumes concurrent and predictive validity), and construct validity. The extent of each type of validity is determined empirically through different methods.

Like validity, reliability is a desirable quality. Six forms of reliability, each corresponding to a different type of consistency, include test–retest reliability, equivalent-forms reliability, equivalence and stability reliability, internal consistency reliability, interrater reliability, and standard error of measurement.

Although this chapter has a quantitative emphasis, validity and reliability are important in both quantitative and qualitative research. Reliability is a prerequisite for validity, although a highly reliable measure is not necessarily a highly valid one.

Key Terms

Validity	**Construct**	**Internal consistency**
Construct	**Factor analysis**	**reliability**
underrepresentation	**Reliability**	**Split-half reliability**
Construct-irrelevant	**Test–retest reliability**	**coefficient**
variance	**Coefficient of stability**	**Kuder–Richardson 20**
Content validity	**Equivalent forms**	**Cronbach's alpha**
Face validity	**Equivalent-forms**	**Interrater reliability**
Criterion-related	**reliability**	**Standard error of**
validity	**Coefficient of**	**measurement**
Concurrent validity	**equivalence**	**Measurement error**
Predictive validity	**Coefficient of stability**	**Social validity**
Construct validity	**and equivalence**	

Exercises

For questions 1–2, refer to the passage below:

Phonics achievement in this study was measured using an 81-item multiple-choice group-administered test developed by one of the authors. We examined the validity of the test against the criteria [suggested by prior research] for acceptable testing of graphophonics skills, that is, the reading of nonsense words in a list. The items in this measure required students to identify which nonsense word read by the teacher matched one of four possible nonsense words on their answer form. Students indicated their choice by selecting one word. The test was scored by summing correct answers.

(Eldredge, Quinn, & Butterfield, 2001, pp. 205–206)

1. What type of validity appears to have been examined?

a) Content

b) Construct

c) Predictive

d) Concurrent

2. What type of reliability would probably be *least* important to consider when evaluating this test?

a) Test–retest

b) Internal consistency

c) Interrater

d) Standard error of measurement

For questions 3–4, refer to the passage below:

> *A particularly important aspect of social behavior is the quality of the behavior. . . . Quality of social behavior, however, must be judged by others. This can be accomplished by exposing judges to video-taped . . . samples of social behavior and having them rate its quality.*
>
> *(Gresham, 2001, p. 337)*

3. In a study on the quality of children's social behavior, what type of reliability would be especially important to consider?

a) Equivalent forms

b) Interrater

c) Standard error of measurement

d) Internal consistency

4. In the type of study described, which of the following approaches could be used to evaluate concurrent validity?

a) The judges' ratings are correlated with ratings of social competence obtained from teachers 1 year later.

b) Experts in social behavior are asked to evaluate the instructions given to judges, as well as some of the videotaped samples and the judges' ratings for those samples.

c) The judges' ratings are correlated with ratings obtained by means of a widely respected quality-of-behavior scale.

d) The researcher makes an informal judgment about the sensibleness and coherence of the judges' ratings, in light of the instructions given to them.

For questions 5–6, refer to the passage below:

> *The assessment of . . . content validity plays a critical role in establishing the validity of scores obtained from any test of achievement. The most common content validation technique involves the use of a rating scale to quantify the level of expert agreement concerning how well each item's content matches the content domain specified by the test developer. . . . Although a variety of statistical methods have been proposed for summarizing content validation ratings . . . the mean content rating . . . receives widespread use. . . .*
>
> *Although the mean rating is widely used to assess the content validity of items, limited research has been conducted on developing inferential procedures that can provide information concerning (a) how stable the sample mean rating is expected to be, (b) how close the sample mean rating is expected to be to the unknown population mean rating.*
>
> *(Penfield & Miller, 2004, pp. 359–360)*

5. Which of the following types of reliability seems to be implied by the phrase "how stable the sample mean rating is expected to be"?

a) Internal consistency

b) Equivalent forms

c) Split-half

d) Test–retest

6. What population is alluded to in the phrase "how close the sample mean rating is expected to be to the unknown population mean rating"?

a) The population of experts from which a sample was drawn in order to gather content ratings.

b) The population of individuals that the test was designed for.

c) The population of items from which a sample was drawn in order to create the particular test.

d) All of the above

7. For a given test, which of the following is most closely associated with measurement error?

a) Low scores

b) High internal consistency

c) Low standard error of measurement

d) High construct-irrelevant variance

8. On a 50-item spelling test administered to students individually, with each response scored as either "correct" or "incorrect," would you expect the split-half reliabilities to be higher if (a) students respond to all of the items regardless of their performance, or if (b) the test ends when a student makes two consecutive errors?

9. What type of validity is least directly quantifiable?

a) Content

b) Concurrent

c) Construct

d) Predictive

10. *Critical thinking question:* If a test contains many items that are too difficult for virtually all test-takers, why might the test appear to have good reliability?

Answers to Exercises

1. a **2.** c **3.** b **4.** c **5.** d **6.** a **7.** d **8.** b **9.** c

10. *Possible answer*: Internal consistency will be high because most test-takers will have answered most items incorrectly. Equivalent forms reliability will be high because the test-takers will do comparably poorly on a truly equivalent alternate form of the test. Test–retest reliability will be high (assuming that the test-takers are not able to master the content in between test administrations) because the test would be inordinately difficult each time it is taken. For similar reasons, low standard error of measurement would be expected.

Suggestions for Further Reading

Research Article: Canivez, G. L. (2000). Predictive and construct validity of the Developing Cognitive Abilities Test: Relations with the Iowa Tests of Basic Skills. *Psychology in the Schools, 37*(2), 107–113.

This quantitative study of the psychometric properties of the DCAT makes use of numerous validity and reliability concepts discussed in this chapter.

Application Article: O'Neil, T., Sireci, S. G., & Huff, K. L. (2003). Evaluating the consistency of test content across two successive administrations of a state-mandated science assessment. *Educational Assessment, 9*(3), 129–151.

This quantitative study focuses on the content validation of a science achievement test and demonstrates the importance of state-mandated standards tests having good psychometric properties.

Extension Article: L'Engle, K. L., Jackson, C., & Brown, J. D. (2006). Early adolescents' cognitive susceptibility to initiating sexual intercourse. *Perspectives on Sexual and Reproductive Health, 38*(2), 97–105.

This quantitative study explores the psychometric properties of a cognitive susceptibility index, illustrating many chapter concepts and extending the discussion of how construct validity can be established.

CHAPTER 7 Experimental Designs

PRNewsFoto/Autodesk, Inc/NewsCom

After studying this chapter, you will be able to answer the following questions:

- What are the elements of experimental design?

- What is internal validity?

- What are the major threats to internal validity and how can they be avoided?

- What is external validity?

- What are the major threats to external validity and how can they be avoided?

- What are three main types of experimental design?

- What are the advantages and disadvantages of each type of experimental design?

This chapter will prepare you to do the following:

- Understand experimental research reports

- Evaluate the internal and external validity of experimental research

- Choose the experimental design that best suits your research question

- Design an experimental study

175

Research Design

You have read about how an investigator formulates a research question (Chapter 2), identifies measures that address the question (Chapter 5), and obtains the sample that will be measured (Chapter 4). One more element is needed before data collection can begin: The researcher must formulate a **design**, or general plan for carrying out the study. Knowing the research design of a study gives you some sense of the overall procedure, as well as the kinds of relationships between variables that will be investigated. Well-designed studies are the foundation of scientific knowledge about education and have the greatest benefits for educational practice.

In this chapter, and the two that follow, I introduce the major types of designs used in quantitative research. The focus of the present chapter is on experimental designs, which are highly respected for their superiority in revealing specific cause–effect relationships.

Introduction to Experimental Design

Experimental designs were developed and refined in the 19th and 20th centuries, mostly by experimental psychologists, but some of the basic concepts are grounded in common sense and have probably been familiar to people for millenia. For example, the book of Daniel relates that during the Babylonian occupation, a group of talented young Israelites, including Daniel, was to be nourished with the king's meat and wine for 3 years prior to appearing before the king. Daniel objected to this practice, and asked that he and four others be allowed to stick to a vegetarian, nonalcoholic diet. By way of a test, the king allowed the five children to abstain from meat and alcohol for 10 days, while not permitting the rest of the Israelite children to abstain. The results of the test were clear: "And at the end of ten days their countenances appeared fairer and fatter in flesh than all the children which did eat the portion of the king's meat" (Daniel 1:15). In light of these results, the king allowed the five children to continue their vegetarian diet, and at the end of the 3-year period further benefits were observed. Although historically not all approaches to the acquisition of knowledge assume that observation is the best method (see discussion in Chapter 1), it is not difficult to understand the basic rationale of this 10-day "experiment" once it is explained, or why it made sense to compare the appearance of the five children to those who continued to eat meat. As you read this chapter, it should become clear that several elements of an experimental design are reflected in this story.

The Logic of Experimental Design

In an **experimental design**, one or more independent variables is manipulated, and the effects of the manipulation on one or more dependent variables are measured. There are many ways to manipulate an independent variable. In educational research, manipulation often involves dividing participants into groups that are treated in systematically different ways. For example, suppose that a researcher wants to know whether a new bully prevention program will reduce the extent of bullying initiated by first-grade participants. The researcher could randomly assign one group of first-graders to the new program, while assigning a separate group of first-graders to an older program. The researcher would try to ensure that the only change to each group's daily routine would be participation in a bully prevention program, and that each group spends the same amount of time in their respective program. The researcher would also measure, as carefully as possible, the incidence of bullying among each group before and after participation in a program. By means of this design, the effectiveness of the new program would be seen if the incidence of victimization declines among children who participated in this program, while staying the same (or not declining as much) among children who participated in the older program.

Groups and Conditions

The logic of experimental designs is not difficult to grasp, but the terminology may seem awkward at first. In this example, the incidence of bullying is the dependent variable, and the independent variable is the type of bullying prevention program (new vs. old). The group assigned to the new program is called the experimental group (or "treatment group"), while the group assigned to the old program is called the comparison group. Generally speaking, an **experimental group** experiences one change introduced by the researcher, while a **comparison group** experiences a different change introduced by the researcher. Often the experimental group experiences the change most relevant to the research question—in this example, assignment to the new program, since the main goal of the study is to determine the effectiveness of the program.

By definition, the experimental group participates in the **experimental condition** (or "treatment condition," or "intervention"), while the comparison group participates in the **comparison condition**. In our example, the new bully prevention program constitutes the experimental condition, while the old program is the comparison condition. You can also see that "manipulating the independent variable" in this case means assigning each student to one of the two conditions.

In order to evaluate the effects of the independent variable, the researcher must compare the experimental group to some other group of participants. The options are a comparison group (as in this example) or a control group. A **control group** consists of participants in a study who experience no change whatsoever. If a researcher were to compare the effects of participating in a new bully prevention program versus the effects of not participating in any program whatsoever, those children who do not participate in any program would be the control group. The incidence of bullying would be measured in both groups, but the control group would not "do" anything. That is, each student's ordinary routine at school would constitute the **control condition**. Some studies include an experimental group, a comparison group, and a control group, or more than one of any (or all) of these groups. The three types of groups are summarized in Table 7.1.

Comparison groups are more common than true control groups in educational research, because it may be impossible or unethical for the nonexperimental group to "do nothing." Consider, for example, a recent study in which an attempt was made to improve comprehension of theme among second- and third-graders (Williams, Lauer, Hall, Lord, Gugga, Bak, Jacobs, and deCani, 2002). Students in the experimental condition received two 40-minute lessons per week for a 7-week period. During each lesson, the teacher focused on a specific story and attempted

TABLE 7.1 Definitions of Experimental, Comparison, and Control Groups

Group	Definition
Experimental group	Experiences key change introduced by researcher
Comparison group	Experiences different change introduced by researcher
Control group	Experiences no change to ordinary routine

to teach students simple organizational strategies for identifying themes. What, then, could this experimental condition be contrasted with? Reading books and discussing how to analyze the components of stories are essential components of early literacy instruction. It would have been neither realistic nor ethical for this study to include a control group in which no formal reading activities take place for a 7-week period. Instead, the researchers examined a comparison group who also received two 40-minute lessons per week, but whose lessons were based on a traditional approach to instruction that emphasizes vocabulary and plot rather than higher-level theme identification. The researchers found that the experimental group did indeed learn and benefit from the theme identification strategies, but that the extent to which they could generalize these strategies to unfamiliar stories and themes was somewhat limited.

Random Assignment

In the biblical story at the outset of the chapter, the "independent variable" is the children's diet, while the "dependent variable" is their appearance. The "experimental condition" consists of the meat-and-wine diet, which the children had never experienced before, while the "comparison condition" consists of a vegetarian diet that Daniel and his four friends had always consumed and continued to consume during the 10-day period. (In this story, a difference was observed between the experimental and comparison groups, but it was one that favored the comparison group.)

There is one element missing from this story that prevents it from illustrating experimental research in the strictest sense. A true experimental design is characterized by **random assignment**, which means that each participant is equally likely to be assigned to the experimental or the comparison group. Participants do not choose their group, nor does the researcher systematically assign participants to each group. Rather, the researcher uses some simple method, such as a coin toss, in order to divide participants randomly. As the size of the sample increases, random assignment is more likely to ensure that participants in each group are comparable with respect to other variables.

For centuries scientists have made use of what we now call experimental and control groups, but it was not until the early 20th century that Roland Fisher and others formalized the practice of random assignment. The importance of this practice becomes clear if we imagine alternative methods of assigning individuals to groups. To use the bullying program example, imagine that the experimental group consists of all first-graders at the school who had been identified by their teachers as the most active and aggressive bullies, while the control group consists of the other first-graders at the school. As a result of this nonrandom division of participants into experimental and control groups, any outcome will be ambiguous:

1. If the incidence of bullying among the experimental group declines following participation in the new bully prevention program (while remaining the same among the control group), we might conclude that the new program is effective. An alternative explanation would be that because the experimental group consists of the most extreme bullies, they would benefit from any bully prevention program regardless of quality. (Or, perhaps the teachers unconsciously identified a group of bullies who were not only extreme but also seemed most likely to be receptive to intervention.) Thus, the researcher's new program might actually be stronger, weaker, or no different in effectiveness than most programs. If, on the other hand, random assignment had been used, the most extreme bullies would probably be distributed roughly equally across groups, and the effectiveness of each program could be measured independently of the composition of each group (since each group would probably be very similar in composition).

2. If the incidence of bullying among the experimental group stays the same, or increases (while remaining the same among the control group), we might conclude that the new bully prevention program is ineffective. However, it is conceivable that the new program would help students who occasionally engage in bullying, but that extreme bullies are a special group who cannot be helped much by any program that has been developed thus far. Once again, if random assignment had been used, the effectiveness of the program could be evaluated independently of the composition of the groups.

Pretesting and Posttesting

Notice that in our example, the dependent variable (incidence of bullying) is measured before and after students participate in a prevention program. This is a common—although not universal—practice in experimental research: A **pretest** is administered to the experimental and control (or comparison) groups before the experimental manipulation, and a **posttest** is administered to each group after the manipulation. Pretesting is desirable in order to determine whether the groups differ at the outset of the experiment, and to allow researchers to calculate changes in the performance of individual participants following the manipulation. Posttesting is also needed to calculate those changes, and the researcher may administer more than one posttest if there is some interest in tracking the duration of changes that result from the manipulation.

The Randomized Pretest–Posttest Control Group Design

What I have described thus far is a type of experimental research design called a **randomized pretest–posttest control group design**. Below, the steps that researchers follow when implementing this type of design are summarized in Table 7.2. (Note that the structure of this design is the same regardless of whether the alternative to the experimental group is a control group or a comparison group.)

TABLE 7.2 Steps in Carrying Out a Randomized Pretest-Posttest Control Group Design

1. Pretest all participants.
2. Randomly assign participants to experimental and control groups.
3. Administer the experimental and control conditions.
4. Posttest all participants.

Experimental Design: The Gold Standard in Applied Literacy Research?

As discussed throughout this chapter, experimental designs—particularly the randomized pretest–posttest control group design—are widely considered the most suitable for identifying cause–effect relationships between well-defined variables. However, some researchers question whether such designs are truly the "gold standard," or the most ideal approach for addressing every important research question. One source of concern pertains to classroom applications of the results of experimental studies. This is illustrated in a 2003 article published in *The Reading Teacher**, in which Michael Pressley expresses both enthusiasm and concern about the use of experimental designs in research on early literacy instruction.

I am confronted almost daily by the 2001 No Child Left Behind (NCLB) legislation and its demand that reading instruction be scientifically evidence-based. Assertions are also being made that reading instruction provided to children in the United States should be evaluated in randomized experiments, especially reading instruction supported by public funds, such as those provided by the Reading First program.

As an experimental psychologist, I have conducted many "true" experiments (i.e., experiments with random assignment to condition) to the scientific literature. I am proud that I have mastered the ability to conduct research experiments. I am also proud that as part of my education I learned a great deal about the strengths and weaknesses of experimentation—when experiments are credible and useful and when they are not . . .

I present in this article 12 points about experimentation that I think all teachers concerned with evidenced-based reading instruction should keep in mind as they evaluate the flurry of assertions that are overflowing the marketplace of ideas in literacy education.

Pressley's article is based on the premise that experimental designs are indeed superior in some respects:

There is no doubt that experimentation, when it is possible to randomly assign participants to differing forms of instruction, permits insights on instruction as a cause of achievement better than any other methodology. There is no substitute for the randomized experiment as a powerful window on cause–effect relationships.

For example, if a researcher is interested in testing some new type of phonemic awareness instruction against an existing type and can randomly assign kindergarten classrooms to receive either the new type of instruction or the existing one, it is possible to decide whether the new type of instruction is more effective. To do this, we assess phonemic awareness at the beginning of the kindergarten year, before students have experienced any instruction, with some formal instrument. If at that point phonemic awareness is equivalent in the two classrooms, an interpretable experiment can begin. After students received instruction (i.e., in the late spring of the kindergarten year), if phonemic awareness is greater in classrooms receiving the existing instruction, the best bet is that the new type of phonemic awareness instruction caused the difference.

Although Pressley is clearly an advocate of experimental designs, one of his concerns is that when properly

To illustrate how the steps in Table 7.2 are carried out:

1. Measure the incidence of bullying in a sample of 100 first-graders during a 2-week period.
2. Randomly assign 50 of the first-graders to a new bully prevention program that lasts 20 minutes per day for 1 week. Assign the other 50 first-graders to a new "fun science" program that lasts 20 minutes per day for 1 week.
3. Carry out the bully prevention and fun science programs.
4. Measure the incidence of bullying among all 100 first-graders during a 2-week period after the programs have ended.

The randomized pretest–posttest control group design, sometimes referred to as a "randomized controlled trial," is widely considered the most desirable type of experimental design. As far as experimental designs go, it is clearly superior conducted, experimental studies take too long to be useful in the evaluation of programs that are constantly updated:

> *[Some say that if] comprehensive reading instructional pro-grams want to be considered scientifically based, they should be evaluated in randomized true experiments. I do not agree. The design, execution, and reporting of such experiments would take a minimum of two to three years, maybe longer. By the time such experiments were concluded, the specific published programs under evaluation would be out of print, replaced by revised and new comprehensive reading instruc-tional programs. The net effect would be well-controlled evaluations of products that were disappearing from the mar-ketplace.*

Pressley also warns that because literacy instruction programs may combine a number of components, exper-imental studies that demonstrate the benefits of such programs may not allow us to discern which component is most important:

> *One such study comes to mind again and again. It involved a comparison of four beginning reading instructional pro-grams, each of which included some form of word-recognition instruction, literature, writing, and so on. Only one program included synthetic phonics. When that program produced greater effects than the other three, the researchers concluded it was due to the synthetic phonics. The problem, of course, was that the students in that treatment also received literature and writing instruction unique to that instructional program, along with a number of other bells and whistles not in the other packages. There was no way to isolate the effects of the synthetic phonics component. In general, that is typical when a large program is evaluated in an experiment. It is*

> *impossible to know which of the program's many components produced effects that are observed.*

Since experimental designs include a small num-ber of control and/or comparison groups, Pressley also expresses concern about researchers overstating the case when they find that an experimental intervention is effective:

> *What can an experimenter conclude when a new type of instruction produces positive achievement relative to existing instruction . . . [T]he best bet is that the new form of instruc-tion caused the achievement difference. Sometimes, however that claim is broadened—either by the experimenter or some-one else—to state that the new form of instruction is the best one. It is impossible to decide that some form of instruction is the best unless it is tested against all possible alternative forms of instruction that exist right now or might exist in the future. When an experimenter claims that a form of instruc-tion produces superior achievement, demand a comparison. If a claim is made that the instruction is superior to every other form of instruction, then reject the claim as impossible.*

Other concerns that Pressley raises pertain to experi-menters who are insufficiently versed in the instructional methods they study, and to experiments that do not readily generalize to classroom settings—the problem of limited external validity discussed in Chapter 6. In the end, Pressley is confident that experimental research can have a positive impact on literacy instruction, but he warns against numerous kinds of misuse or misinterpre-tations of the findings of pertinent studies.

*Pressley, M. (2003). A few things reading educators should know about instructional experiments. *The Reading Teacher, 57*(1), 64–71. Quoted with permission from the International Reading Association.

to others at revealing specific cause–effect relationships. Some researchers and policymakers go a step further, asserting that it is preferable not only to other kinds of experimental designs, but to other kinds of designs in general. Others question the assumption that the randomized pretest–posttest control group design should be the "gold standard" in educational research (see Spotlight on Research 7.1, as well as the discussion in Chapter 18). As you will find in later chapters, nonexperimental designs may be more suitable for addressing certain kinds of research questions.

At this point, you might be wondering: What are the other types of experimental designs? How do these designs differ? What makes one type more desirable than another? Why would a researcher make use of anything less than the best possible design? The answers to these questions, provided later in the chapter, will make more sense after further discussion about why experimental designs are structured the way they are.

Experimental Validity: An Overview

The general purpose of experimental design is to help researchers make inferences about cause–effect relationships (i.e., relationships between independent and dependent variables). There are many obstacles to making these inferences, and the details of experimental design are intended to help overcome the obstacles. This section of the chapter focuses on the concept of experimental validity, which is essential to the process of making accurate and useful inferences about cause–effect relationships. I will discuss the two major types of experimental validity at length, because they are essential to both planning the design of an experimental study as well as evaluating the designs of published studies.

For the purposes of simplicity, the following discussion assumes a randomized subjects, pretest–posttest control group design involving one independent variable and one dependent variable. Unless otherwise indicated, the discussion applies equally well to designs in which there is more than one independent and/or dependent variable, as well as to designs in which either comparison or control groups are used.

Control of Extraneous Variables

Experimental research provides evidence of causality by showing that the dependent variable is affected by the independent variable, and not by any other variable. Any variable other than the independent variable that affects the dependent variable is an **extraneous variable**, and is by definition an undesirable source of ambiguity. (Extraneous variables are sometimes referred to as "confounds," and reference is made to the "confounding" of an independent variable with some extraneous variable.)

Anything the researcher does to exclude the effects of an extraneous variable is referred to as **control**, and thus it is common to speak of "controlling" or "controlling for" extraneous effects. For example, researchers will try to ensure that individuals in the experimental and control groups are as similar as possible in personal characteristics, and that their experiences (other than participation in each condition) are as similar as possible too. Differences in characteristics such as age or gender are relatively easy to spot, while other differences between groups cannot be readily anticipated. Random assignment is one way to diminish the likelihood of such differences. The researcher may also choose to measure variables that would be obvious sources of extraneous effects. For example, before comparing the effectiveness of two methods for reading instruction, the researcher will probably test the experimental and control groups to ensure comparable reading skills. If extraneous effects do occur, they may be minimized or excluded by altering the composition of the sample, or by statistical analyses (as discussed in Chapter 11).

Internal Validity

The extent to which a dependent variable is affected by manipulation of the independent variable alone is referred to as **internal validity**. Internal validity is desirable—the more the better, so to speak—although it cannot be directly quantified. Rather, the more confident we are that change in a dependent variable can be attributed to the influence of an independent variable, the more internal validity we can assume.

Types of Internal Validity

By definition, extraneous effects lower the internal validity of an experimental study. In a classic paper, Campbell and Stanley (1963) described eight threats to internal validity that result from extraneous variables: history, maturation, testing, instrumentation, statistical regression, differential selection, attrition, and selection-maturation interaction.

History

History refers to unexpected events that are not part of the experimental manipulation but influence the dependent variable. History, in this sense, does not refer to prior events, but rather to events that occur while the experiment is in progress. During an experiment comparing the effectiveness of different methods of science instruction, for example, history effects could occur if a new television show on science is aired for the first time and becomes popular, or if some of the participating students are inspired by field trips to the local zoo and planetarium, or if some of the participants simply happen to have greater access to science-related materials in their classrooms. In each of these examples, internal validity would be compromised, because the researcher could not tell whether student progress was due to the methods of science instruction that were used, to the influence of the historical events, or to some combination of both. That is, if the researcher found that the experimental group progressed more than the other group(s), it would be unclear whether the methods used in the experimental condition were responsible, or whether history effects selectively favored the experimental group. On the other hand, if all groups progressed equally, the researcher could not rule out the possibility that the experimental condition had an influence that was masked by history effects that benefited all participants equally (e.g., all students went on field trips to the planetarium and learned something about science there).

The longer the duration of an experiment, the greater the likelihood of history effects. To prevent such effects, researchers attempt to make the experiences of experimental and comparison groups as similar as possible (although control over their lives outside the experimental setting tends to be neither possible nor ethically desirable).

Maturation

Maturation refers to changes that naturally occur in participants over time. A participant may acquire study-related knowledge between pretest and posttest. A participant's mental or physical health may change during this time period. Or, a participant's interest in the study may change before posttesting is completed. Maturation effects undermine internal validity when changes such as these rather than the experimental manipulation influence the outcome of an experiment. As with history effects, maturation effects become increasingly likely as the experiment increases in duration, and thus one way to diminish the likelihood of either effect is to avoid prolonging studies needlessly.

Maturation effects are especially problematic in research with children, owing to the relative speed with which they develop. It is difficult to study the effects of interventions on characteristics such as early verbal skills, reasoning abilities, and peer interactions, because children are changing along these dimensions anyway, and the extent to which the changes are due to the intervention, as opposed to maturation, may be unclear. Generally, researchers assume that that if participants were initially assigned to groups on the basis of random assignment, maturation effects will tend to either affect both groups comparably (e.g., all participants increase in verbal skills from pretest to posttest, owing to natural language development) or to be randomly distributed across groups (e.g., a small number of participants in each group become less interested in the study from pretest to posttest). Essentially the same assumption is made with respect to history effects.

Testing

Testing refers to improvement in performance resulting from familiarity with a test. Testing effects threaten internal validity, owing to uncertainty as to whether improved performance is due to the experimental manipulation, to familiarity with the test, or to some combination of both. This threat is especially problematic when the dependent measure focuses on factual knowledge, concrete skills, or other variables that are readily influenced by repeated exposure to test questions. One approach to preventing testing effects, as discussed in Chapter 6, is to create two different but comparable versions of a test that can be used as the pretest and posttest. Another approach is to skip the pretest altogether, so that following the experimental manipulation the dependent variable is measured for the first time. Although this approach offers complete protection against testing effects, it is problematic for other reasons noted later in the chapter (see the discussion of posttest-only control group designs).

As you read through this list of threats to internal validity, keep in mind that more than one may be operative in a single study. For instance, imagine that in order to study the impact of in-service workshops on social studies instruction, a researcher measures students' knowledge before and after their teachers participate in a workshop. Student performance on the posttest could be influenced by external events following the pretest (history effect), increasing interest in geography (maturation effect), and/or similarities between the second test and the first one (testing effect).

Instrumentation

Instrumentation refers to changes in performance resulting from changes in the measurement used. Internal validity will be undermined if the measurement changes in length, difficulty, or interest to participants. For example, a posttest that is longer, more difficult, or less interesting than a pretest could mask the benefits of an experimental intervention, while a shorter, easier, or more interesting posttest could result in overestimation of the experimental effects.

Instrumentation effects are especially problematic in observational studies. Observers who are recording the instructional methods of teachers, for example, may expect to see improvement (or some other sort of change) and their expectations, whether conscious or unconscious, may alter the criteria they use when making key observations. The calculation of interrater reliabilities, as described in

Chapter 6, may or may not catch this problem. The main strategy for preventing instrumentation effects is to avoid any unwanted changes in the measurement of the dependent variable.

Statistical Regression

Statistical regression refers to the tendency for participants who make extreme scores on pretest measures to score nearer to the mean at posttest. The theory behind statistical regression (also known as "regression to the mean") is that performance on certain measures reflects a combination of both true abilities and chance. On an achievement test, for instance, extremely high scores tend to reflect genuine achievement as well as good luck. Many kinds of good luck are imaginable. Perhaps an unusually high percentage of guesses turn out to be correct. Or perhaps there is an especially close match between the test questions and the test-taker's personal interests. On the other hand, extremely low scores reflect poor achievement as well as bad luck—perhaps the test-taker feels ill or fatigued on the day of the test, or guesses badly, etc. Put simplistically, the idea behind statistical regression is that participants with the highest pretest scores have nowhere to go but down, whereas participants with the lowest scores can only improve.

The concept of statistical regression is familiar to sports fans, who know that athletes tend to follow an unusually good or poor game with a more typical performance. In experimental studies, statistical regression poses a threat to internal validity when the research focuses on extreme groups. Early literacy researchers, for example, are interested in developing better remedial programs for struggling readers, and in creating more stimulating activities for gifted readers. Owing to statistical regression, the lowest scorers on a test of reading skills will tend to show some improvement when retested, regardless of whether they have benefited from an experimental treatment in the interim. Likewise, the highest scorers may not score as highly when retested, even if additional stimulation were genuinely beneficial. A common approach to minimizing the possibility of statistical regression effects when studying extreme groups is to sample a relatively large number of participants representing a range of extreme scores.

Differential Selection

Differential selection refers to preexisting differences between experimental and comparison groups. The groups may differ in ability level, demographic characteristics, or some other variable of pertinence to the study, and the threat to internal validity arises from the possibility that posttest results are driven by initial group differences rather than the independent variable. For example, suppose that the experimental group is older on average than the comparison group. Any benefits of an experimental manipulation could be attributed in part to greater compliance, better attentional skills, or superior knowledge on the part of the experimental group. If the manipulation were not successful, it could be argued that the experimental group, being older, was less interested in participation. The results would be just as ambiguous if the experimental group were younger than the comparison group. In this case, it could be argued that any benefits of the experimental manipulation would be underestimated. If the manipulation were unsuccessful, it could be argued that the experimental group was not old enough to benefit. Differential selection may be attributable to sampling bias or sampling error (see Chapter 4 for discussion).

Random assignment is the most fundamental method for preventing differential selection effects. (Another method, known as matching, is discussed later in this chapter, and statistical methods are discussed in Chapter 11.) Once random assignment has taken place, researchers may then compare the experimental and comparison (and/or control) groups in order to check for specific differential selection effects. For example, in the classic High/Scope Perry Preschool Project, 128 children were randomly assigned to either a High/Scope Perry Preschool program, or to a no-program control condition (Schweinhart et al., 1993; Schweinhart & Weikart, 1980). Once random assignment took place, researchers compared the program and no-program children on variables such as the socioeconomic status and size of their families, as well as the age, employment status, and educational levels of the parents. Through these comparisons, the researchers were able to rule out many possible differential selection effects that might have undermined the internal validity of their results. For example, the effectiveness of the High/Scope Perry Preschool program, as compared to the no-program condition, was apparently not attributable to greater affluence or educational levels among the families of children who participated in the program.

Attrition

Attrition (also known as "mortality") refers to the loss of participants from a study. Participants may withdraw from a study for a number of reasons, including illness, relocation to a new city, declining motivation, or resentment at being assigned to a particular condition. Although a small amount of attrition is common in research, internal validity will be compromised if attrition is extensive, or if there is a selective loss of participants across groups. For example, if one of the conditions is more difficult or less interesting than the other one, attrition may be greater for that condition and make the results ambiguous. Suppose that a researcher is comparing the effectiveness of two alcohol awareness programs, one of which is held during study hall, while the other requires attendance after school. Because attrition is more likely for the after-school program, students who stick with this program are likely to be an especially motivated group. If the after-school program turned out to be more effective, the researcher would not know whether the benefits were due to the content of the program, or to the fact that the students who participated in it were especially motivated (or some combination of content and motivation levels).

The most straightforward approach for dealing with attrition is to monitor it, in order to ensure that the loss of participants is due to chance rather than attributable to some characteristic of the participants and/or the study. For example, researchers determined that attrition in the High/Scope Perry Preschool Project did not undermine the internal validity of the findings, because the extent of attrition was fairly low, fairly evenly distributed across the program and no-program groups, and did not result in significant changes in group characteristics.

Selection–Maturation Interaction

Selection–maturation interaction refers to differential selection effects that result specifically from maturation. For example, suppose that a researcher is comparing the effects of two sets of instructional materials, each used in a different first-grade classroom. If one of the first-grade teachers is more effective than the other one, the students in her class may progress more rapidly from pretest to posttest, and it will be difficult to tell whether their progress is attributable to maturation or to the particular instructional materials they are exposed to. In this example, the difference between the teachers represents an initial group difference (a differential selection effect) that creates a difference in student progress (a maturation effect).

In an influential paper, Cook and Campbell (1979) discussed three additional threats to internal validity: experimenter effects, subject effects, and diffusion.

Experimenter Effects

Experimenter effects refer to any unwanted influence the researcher has on a study, whether or not the researcher is aware of the influence. Experimenter effects include expectations that bias the researcher's observations, as well as experimenter characteristics and behaviors that affect the way participants respond. In either case, internal validity is compromised insofar as the experimenter rather than the experimental manipulation influences the results. Suppose that in order to evaluate a new method of art instruction, a researcher asks two kindergarten teachers to implement the new method in their classrooms. The researcher visits these classrooms, as well as two classrooms in which an old method is used, in order to observe the effects on students. In this scenario, the researcher and/or the teachers might create experimenter effects through their interaction with the children. Here are some ways this could happen:

- The researcher (perhaps unconsciously) asks more experienced teachers to implement the new method.
- During classroom visits, the researcher interacts more frequently, and/or more favorably, with teachers who are implementing the new method.
- During classroom visits, the researcher unconsciously tends to view student responses to the new method more favorably.
- The teacher who is implementing the new method realizes that it is a new method and feels especially enthusiastic (or timid) about being an innovator.

Experimenter effects have been implicated in classic studies on the relationship between modeling and prosocial behavior. In the course of a typical study, children earn a prize, observe a model, and are then asked to make a donation to a needy child. Half the children observe a model behaving prosocially (experimental condition), while the other half observe a model behaving selfishly (comparison condition) or observe no model at all (control condition). Some studies have shown that the experimental group is not more likely to make a donation than the comparison or control groups. However, as Eisenberg and Fabes (1998) point out, the lack of experimental effect could be due to children in the other groups feeling pressure from the experimenter. That is, children who observed a selfish model, or no model at all, might still have wanted to make a donation to the needy child because they felt that this is what the experimenter wanted them to do.

Subject Effects

Subject effects are changes in participant attitudes and behavior that result from participation in the research. Many types have been described. Participants may attempt to please the experimenter, respond in a way that they think conforms to the hypothesis, or endure greater stress than usual because they consider the experiment to be important. The mere fact of participating in an experiment and being treated differently from usual may influence participants. In the late 1920s and early

1930s, at the Western Electric Company's Hawthorne plant, researchers studied the relationship between levels of lighting and employee productivity. The researchers increased the lighting in the workplace and found that productivity increased. The researchers increased the lighting again and found that productivity still increased. Then, when they dimmed the lights, productivity continued to rise. The researchers realized that it was the attention they were giving the employees, rather than the change in lighting per se, that was leading to increases in productivity. The term **Hawthorne effect** is now used to refer to any changes in behavior that occur when individuals are aware of receiving special attention during their participation in an experiment. Internal validity is compromised because it is the awareness of being treated specially, rather than the experimental manipulation, that causes a change in participant behavior.

In addition to the Hawthorne effect, there are three types of subject effects that are specific to the control or comparison group:

1. **Compensatory rivalry** occurs when control or comparison group participants perform above their usual level because they believe they are in competition with the experimental group.

2. **Compensatory demoralization** occurs when control or comparison group participants become discouraged and decline in performance because they feel that the experimental group is receiving more desirable treatment.

3. **Compensatory equalization of treatments** occurs when the control group's behavior is influenced by resources they receive that are intended to be similar to what the experimental group receives. For example, control group schools in educational intervention research sometimes receive funding that balances what the experimental group schools receive. Although the control group schools do not receive the educational intervention programs that experimental group schools receive, extra funding may allow them to improve the quality of their educational offerings, thus masking any effects of the experimental intervention (Cook & Campbell, 1979).

Diffusion

Diffusion occurs when communication between groups results in sharing of information and resources between them. Diffusion is most likely when experimental and control or comparison groups are in close proximity, and when the experimental group is perceived as having access to more desirable resources. In a literacy intervention study conducted in one school, for instance, the experimental group teachers may have access to books and other curricular materials that are unavailable to the comparison group teachers. Diffusion would occur if the comparison group teachers borrow some of the curricular materials from the experimental group. This would undermine internal validity by diminishing the differences between the two groups.

It is difficult to guarantee that experimenter effects, subject effects, and diffusion will not diminish the internal validity of a study. Awareness of the possibility of these effects allows researchers to do what they can to prevent them from occurring. For example, one stipulation in the High/Scope Perry Preschool Project mentioned earlier was that siblings were always assigned together to either the program or no-program condition. The reason for doing so was the concern that diffusion effects would be likely if siblings were assigned to different conditions.

The 11 threats to internal validity discussed in this section are summarized in Table 7.3.

TABLE **7.3** Threats to Internal Validity, and the Source
of Each Threat

Threat	Source
History	Unexpected events
Maturation	Change in participants
Testing	Familiarity with measure
Instrumentation	Change in measure
Statistical regression	Shift to more typical performance
Differential selection	Preexisting group differences
Attrition	Withdrawal from study
Selection–maturation	Selection-driven participant change
Experimenter effects	Presence of experimenter
Subject effects	Participation in research
Diffusion	Sharing of resources or information

External Validity

Control is essential to experimental designs, but it can be a mixed blessing. On the one hand, a carefully controlled experiment permits inferences about cause–effect relationships. On the other hand, a controlled environment is inherently unusual. The manipulation of independent variables creates unique situations, and the participants themselves may be unique or atypical in some respects. Thus, we should ask whether the results of an experiment tell us anything about cause–effect relationships beyond the particular situations and samples that were studied.

External validity refers to the extent to which experimental findings can be generalized beyond the original study. Like internal validity, external validity is a desirable quality. Although each study focuses on specific participants, settings, and methodologies, researchers typically hope to identify more general cause–effect relationships. This illustrates one sense in which scientific activity is inductive (see Chapter 1): The generalizations that researchers make from experimental findings may be strongly supported by various evidence, but they never attain the certainty of deductive inference.

Types of External Validity

Extending the work of Campbell and Stanley, Bracht and Glass (1968) distinguished between two types of external validity, population and ecological, and discussed the conditions under which each type is threatened.

Population Validity

Population validity is the extent to which experimental results can be generalized to a larger group of individuals. In a study of the effects of reward on motivation, for instance, researchers might sample kindergarteners from a middle-income urban district in Boston, but the researchers will want to draw conclusions about the effects of reward among all middle-income kindergartners—or all kindergartners, or perhaps even young children in general. The greater the extent of generalizability to one of these larger groups, the greater the population validity of the research.

Researchers often raise concerns about population validity in their own studies, and in others, because (1) it is difficult to obtain truly representative samples, and (2) most samples are based to an extent on convenience (see Chapter 4 for discussion). When experimental effects are obtained with samples representing one gender, one socioeconomic group, one school, or one region, population validity may be questioned. Thus, the anger management strategy that benefits male high school students raises the question of whether female high school students, or middle school students of either gender, would benefit too, and further research will be needed to determine the extent of population validity. As noted in Chapter 2, it is fairly common for new research to be motivated by the desire to extend prior findings to different samples.

Population validity is primarily influenced by the characteristics of a sample, including heterogeneity (in many cases, the more heterogeneous the sample, the greater the generalizability) and representativeness (by definition, the more representative a sample, the greater the generalizability to the population from which it is drawn).

Ecological Validity

Ecological validity is the extent to which experimental results can be generalized to a broader set of environmental conditions. Any study conducted in a laboratory, or under special conditions created by the experimenter, is potentially limited in ecological validity. In the reward-motivation study described earlier, researchers might look at how kindergartners' motivation to complete a drawing task during free play is influenced by whether or not they are promised a sticker for completing the task. Consistent with prior work on this topic, researchers might find that preschoolers who receive a sticker for completing the drawing task will be less motivated in the future to engage in drawing than preschoolers who were never rewarded. In other words, it might be found that preschoolers are more motivated when they perform a task for its own sake as opposed to doing it for a reward. Given this finding, we would want to raise several questions about the ecological validity of the study:

- Does the type of reward matter?
- Does the nature of the task matter?
- Does the amount of effort required for the task matter?
- Does it matter whether the children are in the classroom or at home?

The answers to these and other questions would tell us whether the study reveals something about the general relationship between reward and motivation (a desirable outcome), or whether it simply tells us something about the use of stickers in contrived tasks and artificial settings (an undesirable outcome). As with population validity, new research is often motivated by the desire to extend a published finding to new materials and situations.

Threats to External Validity

Although researchers recognize a distinction between population and ecological validity, the more inclusive term "external validity" is often used instead. Along with sampling limitations, threats to external validity include the experimenter and subject effects noted earlier. For instance, if the experimenter's presence influences the success of an intervention program, the results will not generalize as readily to situations in which someone besides the experimenter (e.g., a teacher) administers the program. **Novelty effects**, in which new experiences in the experimental condition create a sense of enthusiasm, may threaten external validity. Also included among these threats are three types of interactions involving the experimental manipulation (Cook & Campbell, 1979; Parker, 1993):

1. **Selection–treatment interaction** refers to interaction between participant characteristics and the experimental treatment. In theory, the effects of almost any intervention depend on the nature of the participants. For example, Belsky (1985) and others have pointed out that parenting interventions that have been found to benefit low-income families sometimes show no effects among middle-class families because the latter are already relatively advantaged.

2. **Setting–treatment interaction** refers to interaction between the experimental setting and the experimental treatment. As with selection-treatment interactions, it is possible in theory for the effects of almost any intervention to be influenced by the nature of the experimental setting. Academic enrichment programs, for instance, may be more effective among students in low-income school districts than among students from more affluent districts.

3. **Pretest–treatment interaction** refers to interaction between participation in the pretest and the experimental treatment. Exposure to a pretest may change participants' responses to experimental treatment in ways that do not generalize to individuals who are not pretested. Imagine, for example, that an intervention program is found to change high school students' attitudes about risky behavior. If the researchers pretest student attitudes about drinking, driving, and related issues, it is conceivable that the pretest sensitizes students to their own behaviors and makes them more receptive to the intervention program. Students who do not participate in the study might therefore not benefit as much from the program if it is presented to them with no pretest.

Test Validity, Internal Validity, and External Validity

The type of validity discussed in this chapter is a characteristic of experimental design, and thus it is referred to as "experimental validity" in order to distinguish it from the type of validity discussed in Chapter 6, which pertains to the way tests are interpreted (and can therefore be called "test validity").

Experimental and test validity are fundamentally different, although one can imagine specific points of connection. For example, if an alternate form of a test has poor content validity (as defined in Chapter 6), then using the original form at pretest and the alternate form at posttest might result in poor internal validity, owing to instrumentation effects.

Although internal and external validity are fundamentally different too, there is, to some extent, a tradeoff between them. Insofar as an experimental study is carefully controlled, internal validity will be strong. But the more extensive the control, the more artificial the experimental conditions may be, and thus the weaker the ecological validity of the study. This is not a necessary consequence of experimental control, but an outcome that becomes increasingly likely as control increases.

Two points of similarity between internal and external validity are also worth noting:

1. Both types of experimental validity represent continuous rather than categorical dimensions. Unfortunately, researchers often speak of internal and external

validity as if they were categorical. References are made to "good" or "limited" validity, or to the fact that validity has been "established," as if there were a sharp distinction between having versus not having this quality. This is a convenient way of speaking, but we assume that each type of validity varies on a continuum. There are no clear criteria for distinctions such as "good" versus "adequate" versus "poor" experimental validity.

2. Both types of experimental validity are critical to the design and evaluation of experimental research. It is not uncommon for a study to be limited in one or both types (see Spotlight on Research 7.2). In a sense, internal validity is the more basic of the two, since accurate generalization of results is impossible if the results are attributable to extraneous variables rather than to the independent variable of interest. As Campbell and Stanley put it, "Internal validity is the basic minimum without which any experiment is uninterpretable" (1963, p. 5). For this reason, experimental researchers may acknowledge internal validity limitations in the discussion sections of their publications, but they will typically not develop extensive arguments for the effects of extraneous variables. (If they seriously doubted the internal validity of their studies, they probably would not attempt to publish them!) It is the critics of a particular experimental study, or group of studies, who will develop arguments for poor internal validity, and their doing so is often the fuel for subsequent debates.

On the other hand, experimental researchers often comment on potential limitations in the external validity of their studies. For example, in summarizing the results of a quasi-experimental study on the effectiveness of a computer-assisted approach to line-graph instruction, a pair of researchers offered the following conclusion:

The limitations that affect the results of this study include the following: (1) One teacher and 45 students participated in the study. One teacher taught the instructional treatments to the groups. It would have been desirable to have 45 classes as compared to 45 students in the study. A sample size of 45 was small and limits generalizing of results . . . (2) The number of formal reasoners in treatment groups was very small. The reader should exercise care in interpreting the results related to formal reasoners. (3) The computer technology used in this study is just one of many computer applications. The reader needs to be aware of this fact and avoid over-generalising from the study. Statements regarding the general effectiveness (or ineffectiveness) of computers to improve instruction should be guarded. (Ates & Stevens, 2003, p. 63)

Points (1) and (2) focus mainly on the possibility of limited population validity. Point (3) reflects caution about the extent of ecological validity.

Experimental Validity and Ethics

In this chapter, internal and external validity are described as essential to the design and interpretation of experimental research. Experimental validity is also intimately related to a variety of ethical considerations. Here are three prominent examples:

- Control of extraneous variables is especially critical when the experimental condition includes administration of psychoactive drugs, the implementation of substantial curriculum change, or any other ethically sensitive manipulation.

Spotlight on Research 7.2

Experimental Validity and Interventions for Learning Disabilities: A Meta-analysis of Experimental Findings

Experimental studies have shown that some interventions for learning disabilities (LD) are more effective than others. In a 2001 meta-analysis published in the *Journal of Learning Disabilities**, Susan Simmerman and H. Lee Swanson investigated the impact of internal and external validity limitations on the effectiveness of published interventions. (Refer back to Chapter 2 for extended discussion of meta-analysis.)

Simmerman and Swanson searched for experimental studies by means of three online databases (PsycINFO, MED-line, and ERIC), requests to experts for unpublished and ongoing studies, manual searches of key journals (including generalist journals such as *Journal of Educational Psychology* as well as specialist journals such as *Learning Disability Quarterly*), and requests for technical reports from state departments.

The resulting pool of relevant literature was narrowed down to studies that involved an experimental design in which children or adults with learning disabilities received treatment to enhance their academic, social, or cognitive performance. This procedure narrowed the search to 913 data-based articles or reports that appeared potentially acceptable for inclusion in the quantitative review. After a review of these studies, each data-based report was evaluated on five additional criteria for study inclusion. First, the study had to include at least one . . . comparison condition . . . involving participants with LD. Thus, studies that included a pretest and posttest without an instructional control condition of participants with LD were excluded. Second, the study had to provide sufficient quantitative information to permit calculation of effect sizes. . . . Third, the recipients of the intervention were required to be identified as children or adults with average intelligence but with problems in a particular academic,

social, or related behavior domain. . . . Fourth, the treatment group had to receive instruction, assistance, or therapy over and above what they would have received during their typical classroom experience. . . . Finally, the study article had to be published in English.

On the basis of these criteria, Simmerman and Swanson selected 180 studies for analysis. These studies looked at the effectiveness of various interventions on the academic, social, and/or cognitive functioning of individuals with LD. In most cases, the dependent variables were literacy-related. In the process of reviewing the 180 studies, Simmerman and Swanson coded numerous variables relevant to internal and external validity. For example, with respect to whether internal validity had been compromised by Hawthorne effects, the researchers coded each study on a 4-point scale as either "yes," "no," "not stated," or "not applicable." Other threats to internal validity that were coded include attrition, experimenter effects, testing effects, and statistical regression. The researchers also examined or calculated effect sizes indicating how strongly the interventions benefited participants. (See Chapters 2 and 10 for discussion of effect sizes.) The researchers found, among other things, that effect sizes were smaller for studies in which there were Hawthorne effects, experimenter effects, and testing effects. In other words, the interventions appeared to be less beneficial when these internal validity problems were present. Regarding experimenter and testing effects, the researchers noted:

Those studies that used different experimenters or teachers in administering treatments yielded larger effect sizes than studies that used the very same experimenter or teacher for treatment and control in administering treatments . . . Larger

(continued)

• In any kind of experimental study, compensatory demoralization, as well as certain kinds of experimenter effects, must be avoided if the outcome would be experienced by participants as embarrassing or demeaning.

• It is critical to ensure appropriate population validity before generalizing the results of an ethically sensitive manipulation beyond the original sample. Likewise, ecological validity is essential when generalizing from curricular materials and other interventions to classroom settings, individual students, and special groups.

Although researchers cannot prove that these ethical conditions have been met, we are obligated to try our best to meet them.

effect sizes emerged for studies that used alternative forms compared with studies that used the same test. . . .

External validity effects were also found. The researchers assumed that if effect sizes were higher in studies for which specific information was lacking about the sample and/or the materials, then limitations in the population validity of the sample and/or the ecological validity of the materials may have artificially magnified the effect sizes:

[W]e found that the value of a set of studies for generalizing to individuals, settings, or procedures was related to the underreporting of information. No doubt the underreporting of information may be related to several factors (e.g., authors' writing style and thoroughness of description; authors differed in what they viewed as important; information was not collected); nevertheless, this underreporting clearly biased the magnitude of treatment outcomes. Underreporting of information was also related to ethnicity (studies that reported ethnicity yielded smaller effect sizes than those that did not), locale of the study (larger effect sizes occurred when no information was given about the locale of the study), psychometric data (larger effect sizes occurred when studies did not report psychometric information), and teacher applications (studies that provided minimal information in terms of teacher implications yielded larger effect sizes than those that yielded more information). The magnitude of effect sizes was also related to the use of the federal definition of LD (studies that did not report using the federal definition yielded larger effect sizes than those that did), and to the use of multiple definitional criteria in sample selection (studies that included multiple criteria in defining their sample yielded smaller effect sizes than those that did not report using multiple criteria).

Simmerman and Swanson drew several conclusions from their meta-analysis:

What implications do our findings have for interpreting treatment outcomes for students with LD? First, extreme caution must be used in efforts to convert or transfer research outcomes to classroom practice. Studies that reflect the violations we have outlined should not be included in dissemination efforts. . . . At the very least, efforts should be made to replicate their treatment outcomes. For example, we think that studies that compare different treatments, but in which those treatments are directly tied to different teachers in the administration of the conditions, should not be included in dissemination efforts . . .

Second, although the list of threats that we have identified is relevant to synthesizing research on LD, it certainly is not definitive. All threats are probably empirical questions, and we have only identified a few of the variables. Experienced researchers who carry out interventions correct many inadequacies in their studies and realize, when they generalize from other studies, that caution must be used . . .

Finally, the most important point of this study is that not all methodological variables are as influential as others. This does not imply that the variables that emerged as nonsignificant in our analysis should be overlooked when designing intervention studies; rather, because no perfect study can be designed that controls for all potential noise in the treatment outcomes, particular attention must be directed toward those variables that create the greatest threat to conclusions that we can draw from intervention studies for students with LD.

*Simmerman, S., & Swanson H. L. (2001). Treatment outcomes for students with learning disabilities: How important are internal and external validity? *Journal of Learning Disabilities, 34*(3), 221–236. Quoted with permission from the publisher.

Types of Experimental Design

Broadly, there are three types of experimental design: true experimental, quasi-experimental, and pre-experimental. Each type can be understood and evaluated in terms of how well it handles threats to internal and external validity.

True Experimental Designs

True experimental designs are based on random assignment of participants to an experimental group and at least one control and/or comparison group. In this section I will describe some of the most prominent examples of true experimental designs.

RANDOMIZED PRETEST–POSTTEST CONTROL GROUP DESIGN   The randomized pretest–posttest control group design, described at length at the outset of the chapter and summarized in Table 7.2, begins with random assignment of participants to experimental and control (or comparison) groups, followed by pretesting of each group, administration of each condition, and then posttesting of the groups. The extent of control inherent in this design is greater than in others, because in the ideal case, the only difference in the experiences of the two groups would be the experimental manipulation. The use of a pretest helps identify differential selection effects (although one potential risk of this design is the possibility of pretest–treatment interaction). Random assignment helps prevent differential selection effects from occurring in the first place. Moreover, certain kinds of subject effects and selection–treatment interactions are less likely when random assignment is used.

RANDOMIZED POSTTEST-ONLY CONTROL GROUP DESIGN   The **randomized posttest-only control group design** is simply a randomized pretest–posttest control group design without the pretest. When using this design, researchers assume that randomization will prevent any differences between the groups that would result in selection effects. One strength of this design is that it excludes the possibility of pretest–treatment interactions, since the dependent variable is measured only once. A disadvantage is that there is no way of knowing whether randomization truly prevented initial differences between the groups. Consider the following anecdote from an 11th century Chinese medical text:

> It was said that in order to evaluate the effect of genuine Shangdang ginseng, two persons were asked to run together. One was given the ginseng while the other ran without. After running for approximately three to five li [equivalent to 1,500 to 2,500 meters], the one without the ginseng developed severe shortness of breath, while the one who took the ginseng breathed evenly and smoothly.(Ben Cao Tu Jing, 1061)

Even if the choice of who received the ginseng was made at random, it is entirely possible that the second runner was in better physical condition to begin with. Differential selection effects are always a possibility if pretesting is not carried out, although the likelihood of such effects varies from study to study. An example of a posttest-only study in which differential selection seems quite unlikely is summarized in Spotlight on Research 7.3.

TRUE EXPERIMENTAL DESIGNS WITH MATCHING   The **matched subjects, pretest–posttest control group design** and the **matched subjects, posttest-only control group design** correspond to each of the two true experimental designs discussed above, except that matching is used to divide participants into groups. Generally speaking, **matching** is a way of creating groups that are comparable with respect to some variable(s). For example, in a study on the effects of different types of advanced computer science instruction, researchers would want to ensure that the experimental and comparison groups are comparable in mathematical skills. One way to do that would be to administer a math test to all participants, identify pairs of students who obtain the same score on the test, and then randomly assign one member of each pair to the experimental group and the other member to the comparison group. Although matching may include an element of random assignment, as in this example, it is based on a nonrandom

Promoting Inquiry Learning: A Posttest-Only Control Group Study

Beginning in elementary school, science instruction incorporates the practice of inquiry learning, in which students are taught how to formulate empirical questions, design studies that address their questions, gather evidence, and critically evaluate the explanations and predictions they infer from the evidence. In a 2005 article in *Psychological Science**, Deanna Kuhn and David Dean explored whether a simple intervention could make inquiry learning more productive among a sixth-grade sample:

Participants were from a population of sixth-grade students at a low-performing inner-city public middle school where the large majority of students are academically at risk. In contrast to their counterparts (and even younger students) from more advantaged populations, students from this population had shown the ability to make only limited progress in developing inquiry skills through engagement and exercise (Keselman, 2003), and we contemplated introducing some more structured intervention, which we ultimately did (Kuhn, 2005; Kuhn & Dean, 2005). We speculated, however, that offering the students a modest initial suggestion might make their inquiry activity more productive, and this is the effort we report on here.

In particular, weaknesses in the inquiry process arise long before students get to the phase of designing and interpreting experiments. A first, critical phase is formulating a question to be asked. . . . But it is not sufficient simply for the student to understand the need to formulate a question; the student must also be able to formulate effective questions. In a context of multiple variables potentially affecting an outcome, students who have developed an understanding of the need to access an available database as a source of information may nonetheless still initially pose ineffective questions, in particular because they aim to discover the effects of all variables at once. It may be this ineffective intention that leads them to simultaneously manipulate multiple variables (in effect, over-attending to them, rather than underattending by failing to

control them, as is typically assumed). In the present study, therefore, our intervention was simply to suggest to students that they try to find out about only one thing at a time.

Kuhn and Dean described their design and procedure as follows:

Because previous work had repeatedly established poor pretest performance in this population, a posttest-only design was employed. Students in the experimental group participated in twelve 45-min sessions over 8 weeks, working in pairs with the Earthquake Forecaster inquiry software during their science period (as did students in the alternative control condition, who worked with Earthquake Forecaster during the same period without the additional intervention the experimental group received). Students in the main control group remained in their regular science classes. At the end of this period, students in all groups underwent an individual assessment with this same program.

Initial Assessment. Earthquake Forecaster asks students to investigate five binary variables—water pollution (high or low), water temperature (cold or hot), soil depth (deep or shallow), soil type (igneous or sedimentary), and elevation (high or low)—and ascertain their role in earthquake risk. In each of four cycles of investigation during a session, students choose which of the variables they want to find out about (with the option of choosing one or more) and then are able to select a site that reflects a combination of variable levels of their choice (e.g., they choose whether they wish to see a site having high or low water pollution, high or low elevation, and so forth for the other three variables). An outcome appears, in the form of a gauge displaying the risk level (one of four alternatives, from low to extreme). Students are then asked to draw an inference regarding each of the five variables, indicating whether it does make a difference in earthquake risk, it does not make a difference, or they are unsure whether it makes a difference. Students are then prompted to make any notes they wish to in an electronic notebook.

approach to the assignment of participants to groups, and thus it represents an alternative to pure random assignment as a way of ensuring experimental control.

The advantage of matching is that if properly done, researchers can be confident that the experimental and comparison and/or control groups are comparable with respect to a variable of importance. At the same time, matching does not rule out all

At this point, a second investigation cycle begins, with the variable levels and outcome from the preceding cycle remaining displayed in a corner of the screen. The process is repeated for the third and fourth cycles. At the end of the fourth cycle, students are thanked for participating, and the program shuts down.

Second and Subsequent Sessions. The researcher introduced the second and subsequent sessions with this additional suggestion:

> "Today let's try to find out about just one feature to start. A lot of you disagree about the soil type whether it makes a difference if it's igneous or sedimentary. Today let's all try to find out for sure about the soil type to figure out if it has anything to do with the earthquake risk."

At each session, a different variable was suggested as the focus of investigation.

Immediate Assessment. At a final session with this program, students worked alone on Earthquake Forecaster. The suggestion to focus on a particular variable was not included.

Transfer Assessment. At the next session, students worked alone on a parallel inquiry program, Ocean Voyage. This program is structurally identical to Earthquake Forecaster and varies only in content. In Ocean Voyage, students investigate whether variables such as crew size and sail type affect a ship's progress toward its destination.

Delayed Assessment. Three months following the transfer assessment, students again spent an individual session working with Earthquake Forecaster.

Students in the main (assessment-only) control group engaged in only a single individual session working with Earthquake Forecaster. This was their only assessment.

In the alternative (practice) control group, participants were involved in the same weekly engagement with Earthquake Forecaster as participants in the experimental group, but did not receive the suggestion to focus their investigations on a single variable. The purpose of including this alternative control group was to establish that any superiority of the experimental group was attributable to the manipulation itself, rather than to the practice provided by engagement with the program. This group received the immediate assessment.

Kuhn and Dean found that their intervention was successful:

> The results were clear-cut. At the immediate assessment, each student participated individually in four cycles of Earthquake Forecaster, and in each cycle, every participant indicated only a single variable as the one he or she intended to find out about. By contrast, students in the main control group intended to find out about a single variable only 11% of the time, and 83% of the time they intended to find out about three or more variables in a single comparison. The mean number of variables a student in the control group intended to find out about was 3.1. (Results were comparable in the alternative control group.)
>
> Of ultimate interest, however, was the effect of the manipulation on students' ability to investigate effectively and draw valid inferences as a result of their investigations. We took valid inferences to be the ultimate indicator of successful investigation, defining a valid inference as a determinate inference (i.e., the variable makes a difference or the variable does not make a difference) that the evidence generated supports adequately. Given four instances to compare across four investigative cycles in a session, a student was able to make a maximum of three valid inferences at each assessment . . . 75% of students in the experimental group made mostly or exclusively valid inferences at the immediate assessment on Earthquake Forecaster. In contrast, no students in the main control group did so. In the alternative control group, inference performance was also poor, confirming that the superiority of the experimental group was not attributable to engagement with the activity itself.

*Kuhn, D., & Dean, D. (2005). Is developing scientific thinking all about learning to control variables? *Psychological Science, 16*(11), 866–870. Quoted with permission fro the publisher.

possible differential selection effects, because it is impossible to match participants on every dimension. A disadvantage of matching is that if it is done as rigorously as possible, using matched pairs as in the example above, there will inevitably be a loss of participants (i.e., if only one participant obtains a particular score, that participant will have to be dropped from the study). In order to prevent the loss of participants, researchers may relax the criterion for matching so that instead of pairing individuals who have the same score, individuals falling within the same range of scores can be matched. Insofar as the criteria are relaxed, the comparability of the experimental and comparison groups will be diminished.

OTHER TYPES OF TRUE EXPERIMENTAL DESIGNS   Other types of experimental designs include single-participant experimental designs (the focus of Chapter 8), and the **Solomon three-group design**, which is based on random assignment of participants to one experimental group and two control groups. The experimental group and one control group are pretested and posttested, while the other control group does not receive a pretest. The Solomon three-group design can be thought of as a randomized pretest–posttest control group design, to which a control group that only takes the posttest is added. The purpose of adding such a group is to help discern whether there are testing or pretest–treatment effects.

Quasi-Experimental Designs

Random assignment has obvious benefits, but it may not be desirable—or even possible—when a researcher obtains permission to study entire groups, such as school districts, schools, or classrooms. In such cases, the researcher may use a quasi-experimental approach, in which each district, school, or classroom is assigned to a single condition. **Quasi-experimental designs** are like true experimental designs, except that the experimental, comparison, and/or control groups reflect preexisting differences. In this sectionI discuss the four major types of quasi-experimental designs.

NONEQUIVALENT CONTROL GROUP DESIGN   The most common type of quasi-experimental design, the **nonequivalent control group design**, is simply a randomized pretest–posttest control group design in which participant groups are based on preexisting differences rather than random assignment. For example, suppose that a researcher has permission to work with six classrooms of third-graders in a study comparing the effectiveness of two new, semester-long interventions for improving mathematical skills. Intervention A is the experimental condition in this study, while Intervention B is the comparison condition. The researcher's first inclination might be to carry out a randomized pretest–posttest control group design in which half of the students from each classroom are assigned to each condition. This kind of design would provide the most control over extraneous variables, but the researcher would immediately encounter logistical challenges. Where, for example, would the interventions be carried out? Would students assigned to Intervention A move to one side of the classroom, out of earshot of the students in Intervention B? Would they have to leave the classroom, or participate in their intervention condition on a different day than the Intervention B students? And once these questions are addressed, how would the researcher prevent diffusion and compensatory effects, since the students interact with each other everyday? A nonequivalent control group design would help alleviate these problems. The researcher could simply assign three classrooms to one method of literacy instruction, while assigning the other three classrooms to the other method. This would be much easier, logistically speaking, and perhaps diminish the effects of student interaction.

Although the assignment of classrooms could be made randomly, an obvious disadvantage of the nonequivalent control group design is the possibility of differential selection—one classroom or set of classrooms may be different from others, owing to the composition of the students, the preexisting instructional methods of the teacher, and so on. For the same reason, the possibility of selection–maturation and selection–treatment effects is increased. (A carefully conducted nonequivalent control group study that addresses some of these potential problems is described in Chapter 5; see Spotlight on Research 5.1.)

STATIC GROUP COMPARISON DESIGN   The **static group comparison design** is identical to the posttest-only control group design described earlier, except that random assignment is not used. The appeal of this design lies in its convenience. A researcher might administer an algebra test to students in two different school districts in order to compare their performance. Or, the teaching evaluations of history professors in several different universities might be compared. At this point, you should be able to recognize some of the limitations of this design. As with nonequivalent control group designs, differential selection effects cannot be ruled out. Static group comparison designs also fail to control for maturation, history, selection–maturation, and selection–treatment effects.

TIME-SERIES DESIGN   The **time-series design** is a quasi-experimental approach in which pretesting and posttesting are carried out repeatedly. The researcher might be interested in studying the effects of a stress management program, and will thus be more confident about baseline levels of stress, as well as the effectiveness of the program, if stress is measured repeatedly before and after participation in the program. Both the advantages and the disadvantages of time-series approaches result from the repetition of testing: Although repeated testing may provide more accuracy with respect to the effects of each condition (since minor fluctuations in each person's performance will be diluted across testings), it also increases the likelihood of history and maturation effects (since more time is required), as well as the likelihood of pretest–treatment interactions.

COUNTERBALANCED DESIGN   In a **counterbalanced design**, all groups receive each treatment and are posttested after each one. Two or more groups may be used. In the case of two groups, the counterbalanced design can be schematized as follows:

- Group A participates in the experimental condition first and is posttested, then participates in the comparison condition and is posttested again.
- Group B participates in the comparison condition and is posttested, then participates in the experimental condition and is posttested again.

The advantage of counterbalanced designs is that they tend to rule out differential selection and testing effects, since all participants participate in each condition. Intuitively, this seems appealing. An obvious disadvantage of counterbalancing is the potential interference resulting from participation in more than one condition. Once you have participated in a experimental condition, for instance, you may have been affected in ways that cannot be reversed prior to your entry into the other condition.

A counterbalanced design is illustrated in a study by Albus, Thurlow, Liu, and Beilinski (2005) on the effects of dictionary use among eighth-grade English language learners. Albus and colleagues administered tests of reading comprehension and other measures to Hmong ELL students as well as to their regular education peers. The reading comprehension of each participant in the study was measured four times: twice while the participant had access to a dictionary while reading, and twice while the participant had no dictionary. Counterbalancing is evident in this study because each group was posttested after participating in the experimental

TABLE 7.4 Types, Examples, and Key Features of Experimental Designs⋆

Type	Examples	Key features
True experimental	Randomized pretest–posttest control group	Randomization, control group, pretest and posttest
	Randomized posttest-only control group	Randomization, control group, posttest
	Matched subjects posttest-only control group	Matching and randomization, control group, posttest
	Solomon three-group	Randomization, two control groups, pretest and posttest
Quasi-experimental	Nonequivalent control group	Control group, pretest and posttest
	Static group comparison	Control group, posttest
	Time-series	Control group, repeated pretest and posttest
	Counterbalanced	Each participant in experimental and control group, pretest and posttest
Pre-experimental	One-shot case study	One group, posttest
	One group pretest–posttest design	One group, pretest and posttest

⋆The term "comparison group" could be substituted for "control group" anywhere in this table.

condition (use of dictionary) and the control condition (no dictionary). Albus and colleagues found that for the most part the dictionary was not very helpful.

Pre-experimental designs

Pre-experimental designs are experimental designs that are based on a single group. For example, in a **one-shot case study**, a single group is exposed to an experimental treatment and then posttested.

A more preferable alternative is the **one-group pretest–posttest design**, in which the group is pretested, exposed to an experimental treatment, and then posttested in order to measure the effects of the treatment. Although pre-experimental designs are relatively convenient, the lack of a comparison group does not allow researchers to rule out history, maturation, testing, instrumental, or statistical regression effects.

Pre-experimental designs may be appealing when the researcher's goal is simply to demonstrate that an experimental intervention has an impact, and it can be argued that the influence of extraneous variables is unlikely. Imagine, for example, a study on the effects of instruction in a foreign language that students would otherwise have no exposure to. If the researcher simply wishes to show that competencies acquired during instruction in the spring are maintained over the summer vacation, the researcher can focus on one group of students who are tested at the end of the spring semester, and then retested when they return to school in the fall.

The various types of experimental designs discussed in this chapter are summarized in Table 7.4.

Factorial Designs

All of the research designs you have read about so far were described in terms of the effects of a single categorical independent variable. Focusing on one independent variable at a time made it easier to distinguish between each design. However, any one of these designs could be based on two or more independent variables—in fact, most experimental studies do consider at least two independent variables, since the dependent variables of interest to researchers (achievement, motivation, aggression, etc.) tend to be influenced by multiple causes. **Factorial designs** are experimental designs in which the effects of two or more categorical independent variables are studied. To reiterate, any of the designs listed in Table 7.4 could be single-variable or factorial in nature.

Factorial designs have become widely used in experimental research since they were first developed by Roland Fisher in the 1920s. In a factorial design, the effects of one independent variable on the dependent variable are referred to as **main effects**, while the combined influence of two or more independent variables on the dependent variable are referred to as **interactions**. Saying that one group benefited more from an intervention than another one would indicate a main effect. Saying that one group benefited more from an intervention than another one, and that the boys in the first group benefited more than the girls, would indicate one type of interaction. These concepts are described more fully below.

Main Effects

The concept of a main effect can be illustrated by a study on the effects of an alcohol awareness program among high school students. In this study, each student either views a multimedia show during a school assembly or watches a video during class, and afterward the student is either given a packet of statistical information about the consequences of alcohol use, or receives no further information. This procedure yields four groups:

- Group MS participates in the multimedia assembly and receives statistical information.
- Group MN participates in the multimedia assembly but receives no follow-up information.
- Group CS watches the classroom video and receives statistical information.
- Group CN watches the classroom video but receives no follow-up information.

The extent to which students resist peer pressure to drink alcohol is measured by means of a survey administered at the beginning and end of the study. The survey consists of several Likert-scaled questions. A 7-point scale is used for each question, with higher numbers indicating greater resistance to peer pressure. The questions are closely related, so that each student receives an average "resistance" score.

In this study, the two independent variables are type of presentation (multimedia assembly vs. classroom video) and follow-up materials (statistical information vs. no information). For convenience, we can call these two independent variables "presentation" and "materials." We would describe this as a 2×2 factorial design, which indicates two independent variables with two levels apiece. (Had there been a third type of presentation, for instance, we would speak of a 3×2 factorial design. If gender had also been considered, we would speak of a $3 \times 2 \times 2$ factorial design.) The dependent variable is resistance to peer pressure, as measured by the survey. If the results show that extent of resistance is affected by type of presentation, the researchers would say there is a main effect of presentation. There are only two possible main effects for this variable, only one of which could actually be observed.

- *Main effect 1:* Students who participate in the multimedia assembly show greater resistance to peer pressure on average than students who watch the classroom video.

- *Main effect 2:* Students who watch the classroom video show greater resistance to peer pressure on average than students who participate in the multimedia assembly.

The phrase "on average" is used here because means are being compared. (As discussed in Chapter 10, the mean is the mathematical average of a set of numbers—in this case, a set of scores.) A main effect of presentation tells us that the mean resistance scores for the MS and MN groups combined were either significantly higher than the mean resistance scores for the CS and CN groups combined (Main effect 1), or significantly lower than the mean resistance scores for the CS and CN groups combined (Main effect 2). Analogously, a main effect for materials would tell us that the mean resistance scores for the MS and CS groups combined were either significantly higher or lower than the mean resistance scores for the MN and CN groups combined.

If the study showed that the type of presentation had no effect on resistance, the researchers would conclude that there is no effect (i.e., no main effect) of presentation. It is conceivable that both, one, or none of the independent variables would have a main effect. That is, in a study with two independent variables, it is possible to find zero, one, or two main effects.

A statistical caveat before continuing: The discussion of main effects and interactions in this section and the next one assumes that the means have been compared through statistical analysis. Strictly speaking, main effects and interactions are defined in terms of statistically significant differences—that is, differences we believe to be genuine, to a high degree of confidence. In the discussion of statistical significance in Chapter 11, you will find that the magnitude of difference between two means does not indicate with certainty whether or not they are significantly different.

Interactions

We say there is an interaction between two or more independent variables when the effects of these variables together cannot be reduced to the separate effects of each one. When examining the effects of a pair of categorical independent variables, we will find either one interaction between them, or no interaction. Whether or not the variables interact, it is possible for there to be zero, one, or two main effects. In other words, the number of main effects we observe does not tell us anything about whether or not we will find an interaction.

Recall that in our alcohol awareness study, resistance to peer pressure is measured at pretest and posttest. By subtracting each participant's pretest score from his or her posttest score, we obtain a "difference score." The difference score tells us how much his or her resistance changed from pretest to posttest. The higher the difference score, the more the student's resistance to peer pressure increased from pretest to posttest. (From an educator's perspective, high difference scores would be desirable.)

ONE MAIN EFFECT, NO INTERACTION   One possible result that we could obtain is one main effect but no interaction. The lone main effect could be for either presentation or materials. A main effect of presentation is illustrated in Figure 7.1, which presents the mean difference scores for each group and also shows the same data in graphic form.

FIGURE 7.1 Main Effect of Presentation, with No Interaction

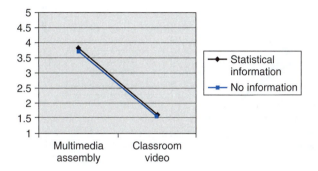

Group	Mean Difference Score
MS	3.8
MN	3.7
CS	1.6
CN	1.5

Figure 7.1 shows a main effect of presentation, in that the mean for the two multimedia assembly groups (3.75) is greater than the mean for the two classroom video groups (1.55). There is no main effect of materials, because the mean for the two statistical information groups (2.7) is almost identical to the mean for the two no-information groups (2.6). (You can check that for yourself by averaging the values for the MS and CS groups combined, and then for the MN and CN groups combined.) Nor is there an interaction, because the effects of presentation are not influenced by the type of materials. From the data in Figure 7.1, we would conclude that multimedia presentations are more effective than classroom videos at increasing self-reported resistance to peer pressure concerning alcohol, but that the type of follow-up information provided has no effect on resistance.

ONE MAIN EFFECT PLUS INTERACTION   Another possible outcome of our study would be one main effect and an interaction. Assuming a main effect of presentation, this outcome is illustrated in Figure 7.2.

We can see a main effect in Figure 7.2, in that the mean difference scores were greater for the two groups who participated in the multimedia assemblies than for the two groups who viewed the classroom videos (3.5 vs. 1.3, respectively). There is no main effect of materials, because the mean for the two statistical information groups is the same as the mean for the two no-information groups (2.4). However, there seems to be an interaction between the two independent variables. Among the multimedia assembly groups, students who received no follow-up information had higher mean difference scores than students who received statistical information (3.7 vs. 3.3, respectively). Among the classroom video groups, this pattern is reversed: Students who received statistical information had higher mean difference scores than students who received no information (1.5 vs. 1.1, respectively). We can speak here of an interaction, because there are effects on the dependent variable that cannot be predicted from the separate effects of each independent variable. Type of presentation influences resistance, but the direction of influence depends on the materials.

The data in Figure 7.2 suggest that multimedia presentations are more effective than classroom videos at increasing self-reported resistance to peer pressure concerning alcohol. The data also suggest that the type of follow-up information provided

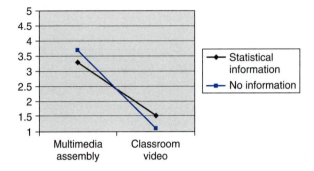

FIGURE 7.2 Main Effect of Presentation, with Interaction between Presentation and Materials

Group	Mean Difference Score
MS	3.3
MN	3.7
CS	1.5
CN	1.1

does not in itself affect resistance. However, the positive effects of multimedia presentations are diminished somewhat when follow-up statistical information is provided (perhaps because students feel that the presenters are trying too hard), while the positive effects of classroom videos, although not as strong as those of multimedia presentations, can be increased by the presentation of statistical information (perhaps because the students were not paying attention especially well in class).

TWO MAIN EFFECTS, NO INTERACTION Figure 7.3 illustrates main effects for both independent variables but no interaction between them.

Figure 7.3 shows a main effect of presentation, because the mean for the multimedia assembly groups is higher than for the classroom video groups (3.75 vs. 2.25, respectively). A main effect of materials is also seen, in that the mean for the

FIGURE 7.3 Main Effects of Presentation and Materials, with No Interaction

Group	Mean Difference Score
MS	3.0
MN	4.5
CS	1.8
CN	2.7

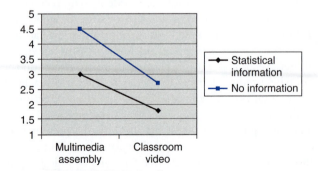

no-information groups is higher than for the statistical information groups (3.6 vs. 2.4). But there is no interaction between the two independent variables. Among students in each presentation group, having no follow-up information increased the difference scores by exactly 50%. (That is, among students who viewed the multimedia assemblies, the no-information group mean of 4.5 is 50% higher than the statistical information mean of 3.0. Likewise, among students who viewed the classroom videos, the no-information group mean of 2.7 is 50% higher than the statistical information group mean of 1.8.) Thus, there appears to be no interaction, because we cannot see any effects on the difference scores other than the separate effects of each independent variable. The data in Figure 7.3 suggest that multimedia assemblies are more effective than classroom videos (perhaps because multimedia shows are more engaging), and that providing no follow-up information is more effective than providing statistical information (perhaps because high school students find statistical material off-putting).

TWO MAIN EFFECTS PLUS INTERACTION   Figure 7.4 shows main effects of both independent variables and an interaction between them.

Figure 7.4 reveals a main effect of presentation, in that the mean score for the multimedia assembly groups is much higher than for the classroom video groups (4.5 vs. 1.5, respectively). There is a main effect of materials, because the mean score for the two no-information groups is higher than the mean for the statistical information groups (3.4 vs. 2.6). There is also an interaction, of the same sort shown in Figure 7.2. That is, although the means in Figures 7.2 and 7.4 are different, and although there is no main effect of materials in Figure 7.4, the patterns of interaction are the same: In Figure 7.4, the positive effects of multimedia assemblies are diminished when statistical follow-up information is presented (or, to say the same thing differently, the positive effects of multimedia assemblies are enhanced when no follow-up information is presented). At the same time, the lesser but still positive effects of classroom videos are enhanced when statistical follow-up information is presented. A possible interpretation of these findings is that the multimedia assemblies were extremely convincing, but some of the students who received statistical information afterward felt they were being pressured, and so for

FIGURE 7.4 Main Effects of Presentation and Materials, with Interaction

Group	Mean Difference Score
MS	3.3
MN	5.7
CS	1.9
CN	1.1

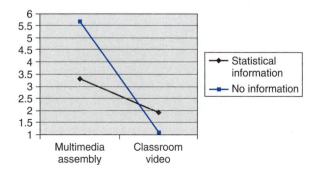

them the benefits of the multimedia show were diminished. The classroom videos were much less convincing, but a few students did not pay very close attention, and so they found the statistical information new and interesting.

Figures 7.2 and 7.4 present one kind of interaction, but there are others, such as the interaction that is depicted in Figure 7.5.

Figure 7.5 depicts a main effect of presentation, in that the mean score for the multimedia assembly groups is higher than the mean for the classroom video groups (4.5 vs. 1.5, respectively). There is a main effect of materials too, because the mean score for the two no-information groups is higher than the mean for the statistical information groups (3.6 vs. 2.4). There is also an interaction, but the pattern is different from what was observed in Figures 7.1 and 7.3. Here, among students who attended the multimedia assembly, those who received no follow-up information showed a much greater increase in resistance than those who received statistical follow-up information. However, among the classroom video groups, there was no difference between the statistical information and no-information groups, perhaps because the classroom video was simply not very convincing.

Factorial designs are appealing because we recognize that in the real world, most cause–effect relationships of relevance to education involve more than one cause. However, researchers cannot consider every possible independent variable of interest. When factorial designs are used, researchers typically focus on the variables that are most likely to be influential, or have the greatest relevance to the study, and control for the rest through random assignment or matching. For example, in a study on the factors that promote classroom engagement among kindergartners, Finn and Pannozzo (2004) examined the effects of three classroom-level independent variables—length of day, class size, and presence of aide—as well as demographic variables such as type of community (urban vs. mid-size vs. rural). Although these are not the only variables that influence engagement, they are important ones, as Finn and Pannozzo demonstrated in their literature review. The researchers found main effects of length of day and class size: Half-day students were more engaged than full-day students, and students in smaller classes (less than 20 students) were more engaged than students in larger classes (more than 20 students). No main

FIGURE 7.5 Main Effects of Presentation and Materials, with Interaction

Group	Mean Difference Score
MS	3.3
MN	5.7
CS	1.5
CN	1.5

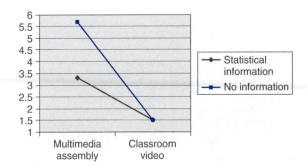

effects of presence versus absence of teacher aide were found. However, there were a number of interactions, such as an interaction between class size and community: The benefits of small class size were greater in large urban and rural schools than they were in mid-size communities.

A Look Ahead

You might infer from this chapter that each experimental study is based on a single type of design. Although this is often true, some studies rely on one type of design while incorporating elements of others, and in recent years the prevalence of research designs that incorporate both experimental and nonexperimental methods has been increasing. It might also appear that internal and external validity are only associated with experimental designs. Clearly, there are exceptions. Attrition, for example, is problematic in any type of research if the loss of participants is not random. With respect to attrition, the difference between experimental and nonexperimental designs (the topic of Chapter 9) is simply that the accuracy and usefulness of the results will be undermined for different reasons.

In the next chapter, the principles of experimental design are applied to studies that focus on individual participants.

Applications: A Guide For Beginning Researchers

Here are some ideas from the chapter that will help you plan your research:

- Choose an experimental design if you are interested in identifying specific cause–effect relationships, and you have sufficient time and resources.
- Choose the type of experimental design that is most rigorous and best addresses your research question, given your available time and resources.
- Review the threats to internal and external validity discussed in this chapter and minimize these threats to the greatest extent possible in the design and implementation of your research.

Chapter Summary

Experimental research design, the most highly respected approach to identifying specific cause–effect relationships, consists of assignment of participants to experimental and comparison and/or control conditions, and may include pre- and/or posttesting.

The experimental researcher attempts to control for the effects of extraneous variables, which threaten internal validity. The main threats to internal validity consist of history, maturation, testing, instrumentation, statistical regression, differential selection, attrition, selection–maturation interaction, experimenter effects, subject effects, and diffusion.

The experimental researcher also attempts to maximize population validity and ecological validity. Threats to these two types of external validity include some of the internal validity threats as well as novelty effects, selection–treatment interaction, setting–treatment interaction, and pretest–treatment interaction.

Internal validity and external validity share similarities as well as a reciprocal relationship, and can be distinguished from the test validity discussed in Chapter 6.

The main types of true experimental design include the randomized pretest–posttest control group design, the randomized posttest-only control group design, the matched subjects pretest–posttest control group design, the matched subjects posttest-only control group design, and the Solomon three-group design. The main types of quasi-experimental design include the nonequivalent control group design, the static group comparison design, the time-series design, and the counterbalanced design. The main types of pre-experimental design include the one-shot case study and the one group pretest–posttest design.

Regardless of specific design, each experimental study will be single-variable or factorial. Factorial designs are more common and allow for any combination of main effects and interactions to be identified.

Key Terms

Design

Experimental design

Experimental group

Comparison group

Experimental condition

Comparison condition

Control group

Control condition

Random assignment

Pretest

Posttest

Randomized pretest–posttest control group design

Extraneous variables

Control

Internal validity

History

Maturation

Testing

Instrumentation

Statistical regression

Differential selection

Attrition

Selection–maturation interaction

Experimenter effects

Subject effects

Hawthorne effect

Compensatory rivalry

Compensatory demoralization

Compensatory equalization of treatment

Diffusion

External validity

Population validity

Ecological validity

Novelty effects

Selection–treatment interaction

Setting–treatment interaction

Pretest–treatment interaction

Randomized posttest-only control group design

Matched subjects pretest–posttest control group design

Matched subjects posttest-only control group design

Matching

Solomon three-group design

Quasi-experimental design

Non-equivalent control group design

Static group comparison design

Time-series design

Counterbalanced design	One-shot case study	Factorial design
Pre-experimental designs	One group pretest–posttest design	Main effects
		Interactions

Exercises

For questions 1–5, refer to the description below:

One intact kindergarten class was provided 300 minutes of intensive instruction in PA. Results indicate that students who received [this instruction] made significant growth in word reading when compared to a cohort of kindergarten students who received general kindergarten instruction.

(Leafstedt, Richards, & Gerber, 2004, p. 252)

1. What appears to be the dependent variable in this study?

a) Kindergarten students

b) PA

c) Word reading

d) Type of instruction

2. Which of the following best characterizes the independent variable mentioned in this description?

a) Kindergarten students

b) PA

c) Word reading

d) Type of instruction

3. Assuming that the word reading skills of all kindergartners were measured before and after instruction, what type of experimental design appears to have been used?

a) Randomized pretest–posttest control group design

b) Nonequivalent control group design

c) One group pretest–posttest design

d) Counterbalanced design

4. If the kindergartners who did not receive the intensive instruction were aware of it and believed that it consisted of especially fun activities, what type of internal validity problem is most likely to have influenced the results?

a) Differential selection

b) Experimenter effect

c) Instrumentation

d) Compensatory demoralization

5. Based on this description alone, does the study appear to be factorial?

a) Yes

b) No

For questions 6–8, name the type of experimental design implied by each description.

6. The critical thinking skills of all 37 undergraduates in an introductory philosophy class were tested at the beginning and end of the semester.

7. A new curriculum unit on reproductive health is incorporated into an eighth-grade health class. Knowledge about reproductive health is measured at the end of the semester among this class and among an eighth-grade class at another school after the latter was exposed to a different curriculum unit on the topic.

8. One hundred and twelve history teachers are randomly assigned to either an in-service presentation that relies heavily on video presentations, or to an in-service presentation that covers the same content through primarily verbal and written materials. Knowledge of the content covered by the presentations is measured before and after the presentation.

For questions 9–11, describe the type of internal or external validity limitation implied by each criticism.

9. By means of a randomized pretest–posttest control group design, a researcher demonstrates the effectiveness of a new instructional method in promoting better laboratory safety in high school chemistry classes. Critics point out that the students in the instructional condition had higher grades, on average, than students in the comparison condition.

10. A researcher studies the effectiveness of a new conflict resolution training program for graduate students in educational administration. The researcher finds that the new program is highly effective. Critics point out that the program lasts for 12 weeks and requires 6 hours per week of additional training over and above what the graduate students already receive.

11. A researcher makes use of two kindergarten classrooms in order to test the effects of a new classroom management strategy. The teacher in the experimental group classroom professes to being much more of a constructivist than the teacher in the control group classroom. Although a pretest reveals no differences between the two classrooms in various manifestations of management style, critics argue that the effectiveness of the experimental manipulation at posttest is related to the difference in constructivist tendencies between the two teachers.

12. *Critical thinking question:* What kinds of research questions of interest to educators might *not* be most effectively addressed by experimental designs?

Answers to Exercises

1. c   **2.** d   **3.** b   **4.** d   **5.** b

6. Pre-experimental (one group pretest–posttest design)

7. Quasi-experimental (static group comparison design)

8. True experimental (randomized pretest–posttest control group design)

9. Differential selection

10. Limited ecological validity

11. Selection–maturation

12. *Possible answer*: Research questions about personal experiences (e.g., among classroom teachers) would be more effectively addressed by descriptive or ethnographic studies. Research questions about whether or not particular variables tend to be associated (e.g., affluence of school and number of available extracurricular activities) would be more effectively addressed by correlational studies. Research questions about naturally occurring differences between groups (e.g., gender differences in spatial reasoning) would be more effectively addressed by descriptive or causal–comparative studies. Generally, research questions pertaining to the way things are, as opposed to the way things could be, tend to be less suitable for experimental designs.

Suggestions For Further Reading

Research Article: De La Paz, S., & Graham, S. (2002). Explicitly teaching strategies, skills, and knowledge: Writing instruction in middle school classrooms. *Journal of Educational Psychology*, *94*(4), 687–698.

This empirical study provides a thorough and accessible illustration of a quasi-experimental design.

Application Article: Freeman, G. D., Sullivan, K., & Fulton, C. R. (2003). Effects of creative drama on self-concept, social skills, and problem behavior. *Journal of Educational Research*, *96*(3), 131–138.

This empirical study makes use of a Solomon four-group design to study the influence of creative drama on the psychological and behavioral functioning of third- and fourth-graders.

Extension Article: Barry, A. E. (2005). How attrition impacts the internal and external validity of longitudinal research. *Journal of School Health*, *75*(7), 267–270.

This empirical study elaborates on chapter concepts through discussion as well as a simple meta-analysis.

CHAPTER 8

Single-Participant Designs

Gabe Palmer/©Corbis

After studying this chapter, you will be able to answer the following questions:

- Why is single-participant research conducted?

- What are the three main types of single-participant research designs?

- What are the strengths and weaknesses of single-participant research designs?

This chapter will prepare you to do the following:

- Understand and evaluate single-participant research reports

- Choose the single-participant design that best suits your research question

- Design a single-participant study

Introduction to Single-Participant Designs

When you saw the title of this chapter, you may have wondered: How is this possible? How can the concepts of experimental design be applied to research with *one* participant? What about the need for representative sampling discussed in Chapter 4? What about the assignment of participants to experimental and comparison groups discussed in Chapter 7?

Single-participant research is based on the assumption that although experimental designs are valuable, in some cases it may be difficult or undesirable to conduct a group experiment. Single-participant designs may be preferable for studying an individual who is unique in some respect, such as an ELL student, a student with learning differences, or a student with severe behavioral problems. A research question about the influence of a particular intervention on a particular child is best evaluated by means of a single-participant design. Moreover, since there is no assignment to groups, single-participant designs rule out some of the threats to internal validity discussed in Chapter 7, including differential selection, selection-maturation, and diffusion.

Historically, single-participant research was inspired by the animal learning studies of B. F. Skinner, in which participants consisted of a single animal whose behavior across different experimental conditions was carefully and repeatedly measured. The legacy of this approach is that in education and other social sciences, single-participant research continues to rely heavily on repeated measurements of behavioral change.

Characteristics of Single-Participant Designs

Single-participant designs tend to share four general characteristics: a focus on individual participants, the application of experimental concepts, the use of repeated measurements, and the reliance on time-dependent data analysis.

Focus on Individual Participants

Single-participant studies—no surprise here—focus on individual participants. As you will see, more than one participant may be studied, but the focus of data analysis is always on patterns of change in the individual. The case study approach described in Chapter 13 also focuses on individual participants. The difference is that whereas case studies tend to rely on qualitative methods, single-participant studies are structured by the principles of quantitative experimental design.

Application of Experimental Concepts

Single-participant designs are a form of experimental research. The term "group designs" is used sometimes for the experimental designs introduced in Chapter 7, in order to distinguish them from the single-participant variety.

Single-participant designs consist of baseline and treatment phases. The term **baseline** refers to the natural characteristics of an individual prior to experimental intervention. Baseline measurements in single-participant research are thus analogous to the pretest in a true experimental design. The term **treatment** refers to a change introduced by the researcher. This is roughly analogous to the independent variable manipulation in experimental research. In single-participant designs, the individual serves as his or her own control group, in the sense that measurements are taken at baseline and during treatment (and, in many cases, afterward). The variable that gets measured is referred to as the dependent variable.

Use of Repeated Measurements

In order to increase both reliability and validity, single-participant designs include repeated measurements of the participant before, during, and after treatment. Measurements focus on a single variable, or on one variable at a time. Validity is enhanced through detailed descriptions of measures and procedures. Reliability is enhanced by a systematic approach to measurement.

Reliance on Time-Dependent Data Analysis

Data analysis in single-participant studies focuses on change in the participant's behavior over time. The frequency and/or duration of particular behaviors during specific time periods are recorded and analyzed. Figures are created in which behavioral changes during and after treatment are graphically represented, and visual inspection of the figures plays a central role in making sense of the data.

Types of Single-Participant Designs

There are three main types of single-participant designs: baseline–treatment, multiple–baseline, and alternating treatments.

Baseline-Treatment Designs

A **baseline–treatment design** is composed of two parts, referred to by convention as "A" and "B." **A** consists of measurements taken at baseline, while **B** consists of a treatment, during which measurements are also made. Depending on the number of baseline and treatment phases, three major types of baseline-treatment designs can be distinguished: A-B, A-B-A, and A-B-A-B.

A-B DESIGNS   The **A-B design** consists of measurements of the participant at baseline (A), and then again during the treatment (B). For example, Norris and Datillo (1999) studied the effects of a social story intervention on a mildly autistic 8-year-old girl who attended general education classes. During the baseline period, which lasted 5 days, an 8- to 10-minute sampling of the girl's behavior was recorded each day while she was having lunch with her classmates. The researchers coded the number of appropriate and inappropriate social behaviors exhibited by the girl in this setting. The treatment period lasted for 13 days. Prior to lunch on each of these days, the girl read one of three social stories. (Social stories are personalized stories for autistic individuals that explain how and why to behave appropriately in particular social situations.) During the treatment period, the girl's lunchtime behaviors were recorded in the same way as they were during the baseline period. Thus, there were five measurements of social behavior at baseline, and 13 measurements during the treatment. Norris and Datillo found that the extent of the girl's inappropriate behaviors generally declined after the fourth day of treatment, while there were no changes in the extent of appropriate behaviors (see Figure 8.1 for details).

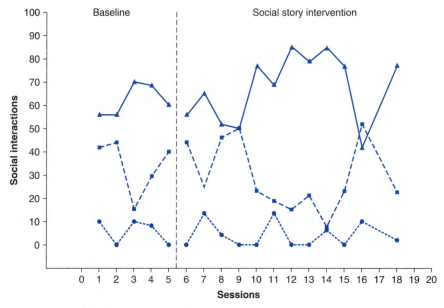

Percentage of Jennifer's appropriate (●), inappropriate (■), and no (▲) social interactions (SIs) during lunch.

A-B-A DESIGNS   The **A-B-A design** is the same as the A-B design, except that after administering the treatment the researcher withdraws the treatment and measures the participant again. In other words, the first "A" is the baseline phase, the "B" is the treatment phase, and the final "A" is a **withdrawal phase** in which the participant is measured under the same conditions as baseline. For example, in the Norris and Datillo (1999) study, if the researchers had recorded the autistic girl's lunchtime behavior for an additional week following the 13th day of treatment, without using social stories, the result would be an A–B–A design.

In some cases, A–B–A designs are preferable to A–B designs because they provide evidence about the persistence of treatment effects. **Carryover effects**—effects that continue to be observed during the withdrawal phase—hint that the treatment has an enduring influence. Effects that disappear after the treatment has been withdrawn may not be reproducible without constant presence of the treatment.

Note that carryover effects are not always desirable. If the researcher hopes that a one-time intervention can create permanent changes, carryover effects are welcome because they show that treatment-related changes persist even after the intervention is withdrawn. For example, carryover effects are desirable for studies in which the goal is to foster more socially appropriate behavior (as in the Norris and Datillo [1999] study). On the other hand, if the researcher wishes to demonstrate that behavioral change is wholly contingent on treatment, carryover effects will be problematic because they weaken the connection between treatment and change. One approach to addressing this internal validity problem is to ensure that the treatment phase is short. Another approach, discussed later in the chapter, is the use of an alternating treatments design.

A-B-A-B DESIGNS   The **A-B-A-B design** is the same as the A-B-A design, except that the researcher adds a final treatment. (The resulting design may be referred to as A_1-B_1-A_2-B_2 in order to distinguish between each baseline and treatment phase.)

The main advantage of the A–B–A–B design is that it yields more data than A–B or A–B–A designs. Confidence in the effectiveness of a treatment will be increased if we find the same effects each time the treatment is introduced, and the effects diminish or disappear each time the treatment is withdrawn. (According to this logic, an A–B–A–B–A–B design would be even better, but increasing the number of baseline-treatment alternations increases the likelihood that a design will be ethically inappropriate, pose logistical challenges, and suffer from testing, instrumentation, and/or subject effects.) An example of an A–B–A–B design is discussed in Spotlight on Research 8.1.

Multiple-Baseline Designs

The A–B–A and A–B–A–B designs make use of more than one baseline so that the effects of treatment can be more clearly observed. These designs are based on the assumption that the effects of a treatment will disappear once it is withdrawn, so that in each "A" phase after treatment, baseline functioning will be restored. This assumption is not always warranted. In the first place, it may not be possible to withdraw the effects of treatment. The child who has learned a particular skill in the treatment phase may not forget the skill, just as a child who has recovered from a minor ailment through treatment may not develop the ailment again once treatment ceases. Second, even if it is possible to reverse the effects of treatment, doing so may be ethically unacceptable. An example would be a study in which the treatment consists of a therapeutic intervention that appears to be helping the individual. In short, there may be logistical and ethical obstacles to the restoration of baseline in A–B–A and A–B–A–B designs. These obstacles can be overcome by means of a **multiple-baseline design**, in which additional participants are added to the study, or additional variables are measured, so that more than one baseline is available.

Bliss and Skinner (2006) conducted a multiple-baseline study that focused on whether a taped-word intervention would help an ELL student improve his sight-word reading. The student in question was a fifth-grader from Russia who was making slow progress toward acquiring basic reading skills in English. The baseline period consisted of the measurement of the student's sight-word reading on 3 consecutive days, with one word list (A, B, or C) being used each day. During the treatment period, a taped-word intervention was used in which the student received word list A and an audiotape. The student was instructed to read each word before hearing it on the tape, and then to correct his reading of the word, if necessary, after hearing it. Once the student could read 25 of the 30 words on list A correctly, the researcher then started the taped-word intervention for list B, and no longer conducted any treatment for list A. The taped-word intervention was then used for list B until the student read 25 of the 30 words on that list correctly, at which time the process was repeated for list C. Although treatment for each list ended once the student reached the 25/30 accuracy criterion for that list, the student's ability to read each list was measured once per week until 77 school days after the experiment had begun. Bliss and colleagues found immediate gains in sight-word reading accuracy for each list immediately following the baseline period. The researchers also found that sight-word accuracy gains lasted throughout the duration of the study. The findings for each list are summarized in Figure 8.2. The dotted lines in the figure serve to identify the boundaries between baseline, intervention, and maintenance phases, since each phase had to begin at a different time for each list. (List D was used for assessment purposes only.)

Maternal Speech Rate Influences Children's Speech Rate: Evidence from an A-B-A-B Study

Parents of stutterers have been advised to speak more slowly to their children, under the assumption that the children will in turn speak more slowly and thereby become more fluent. In a 2001 study published in the *Journal of Speech, Language, and Hearing Research**, Barry Guitar and Lisa Marchinkoski sought to evaluate this assumption.

Guitar and Marchinkoski noted that prior research has not clearly shown a connection between the speaking rates of parents and children, in part because group designs were used. If some parents who had been asked to speak more slowly failed to do so, than the benefits of those parents who did speak more slowly might have been masked in the group data. For this reason, Guitar and Marchinkoski chose to use a single-participant design, so that more focused attention could be paid to individual differences.

The participants were recorded during normal play and conversation in four (A1, B1, A2, B2) 10-minute segments completed within one session. The mothers' normal speech rates were used in the A conditions, and slower speech rates used in the B conditions. Thus, the independent variable was the mothers' speech rates and the dependent variable was their children's speech rates.

Six mother–child dyads were used as participants for this study. They were recruited from among the experimenters' friends and acquaintances. The children were 3 boys and 3 girls between the ages of 3 and 4 who were considered normal speakers by parental report. Language samples taken from children in the baseline condition indicated they were all within 1 SD of their predicted MLU for their age in years and months (Miller & Chapman, 1981). There was no history of communication disorders in the families and no concern about any aspect of the children's development, hearing, or middle-ear status or history.

Each phase of the design was 10 minutes long to approximate the time that parents are often asked to set aside daily for practice of slow speech with their child. Thus, changes between phases were made not on the basis of the data, but when 10 minutes of interaction had elapsed. When

recruited, the mothers were told only that the purpose of the study was to learn more about how mothers and children talk to each other when they play. For the first A conditions, mothers and children were taken to a room containing a variety of toys as well as two audio recorders and a video camera. They were asked to play together and converse in their typical, natural manner. During this time, the experimenters monitored their activities through a one-way mirror. After the session was recorded for 10 minutes, the child was left in the original room to play with a graduate clinician while the mother was taken into another room and informed about the nature of the slow rate condition. She was then trained by the experimenters in a style of slow speaking commonly used when working with preschool children who stutter. This consisted of lengthened vowels, slightly stretched consonants, and lengthened pauses. Prosody was kept as natural as possible so that the mothers' speech sounded slow but not staccato or monotone. Training each mother, via modeling and reinforcement, took approximately 10 minutes. Each mother was trained to speak at approximately one half her normal rate, as judged by the clinicians' online perceptual judgment. When each mother achieved a satisfactory rate, she was asked to speak at this rate for one minute so that clinicians could ensure she could maintain it without feedback.

For the first B condition, the mother was reintroduced into the playroom and requested to use the slow rate while interacting again with her child. During this condition, as during subsequent conditions, the experimenters monitored the mothers' rates throughout, prepared to interrupt if her rate should change noticeably. All mothers maintained relatively consistent rates in all sessions, so no interruptions were necessary.

Following the first B condition, each mother was then taken into a separate room and asked to practice speaking at her normal rate while the experimenters assessed her speech to ensure that it sounded normal and was close to the rate in the A1 condition. The mother and child were then recorded during the second A condition. Following this, another training period ensured that the mother could reestablish her slow speech at approximately the rate used before. Then the final B condition was carried out.

Audio recordings were made of mother–child interactions, and data analysis focused on 8 minutes of conversation (the first and last minutes of each 10-minute segment were excluded). Speech rates were calculated by dividing the total number of syllables each individual uttered by the total amount of time the individual spoke. Interrater reliability for the measurement of speech rates was high, and the results of the study were straightforward:

Mothers reduced their speech rates by an average of 51% (range = 44% to 62% reduction).

Children reduced their rates by an average of 15% (range = 4% to 28%) in the two B conditions compared to the two A conditions. Further support of the hypothesis that children slowed their speech rates when their mothers did is provided by the results of tests comparing children's mean speech rates for the two A conditions and the two B conditions. . . . Mean speech rate values . . . indicate that all of the children had lower mean speech rates in the two conditions when their mothers slowed their speech rates . . .

It can also be discerned that some children's speech rates decreased and increased in conjunction with the mothers' speech rate changes in the B1, A2, and B2 conditions. This is most evident in Dyads 2, 4, 5, and 6. Pearson product moment correlations . . . were used to examine the association between each mother's and child's speech rates across the entire course of the four A-B-A-B phases. With the exception of the first mother–child pair, all correlations were positive and significant.

The figure below presents the results for Dyad 2. The x-axis in the figure presents four sets of 8-minute intervals since, as noted earlier, the first and last minute of each 10-minute interaction were excluded. The association between the speech rates of mother and child are illustrated by the rough convergence between the lines in the graph representing each speech rate (i.e., number of syllables spoken per minute).

In sum, children's speech rate was linked to that of their mothers. When the mothers spoke more slowly, the children's speech rates slowed too. Use of an A-B-A-B design allowed the researchers to see fluctuations in children's speech rate as their mothers began to speak more slowly than usual, returned to a normal rate of speech, and then once again spoke more slowly.

*Guitar, B., & Marchinkoski, L. (2001). Influence of mother's slower speech on their children's speech rate. *Journal of Speech, Language, and Hearing Research, 44*, 853–861. Quoted with permission from the publisher.

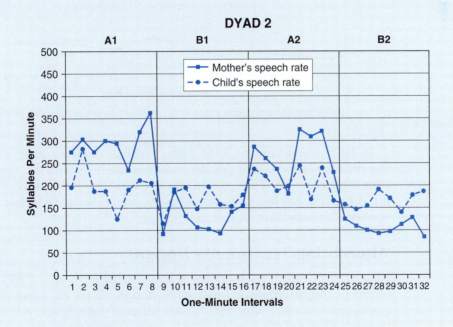

DYAD 2

FIGURE 8.2 Main Results of Sight-Word Reading Intervention (Adapted from Bliss and Skinner, 2006)

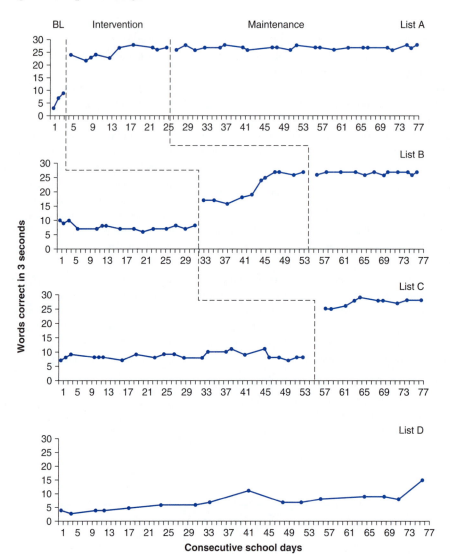

Words read correctly across baseline (BL), intervention, and maintenance phases.

In the Bliss and Skinner (2006) study, a multiple-baseline design was created by the inclusion of more than one dependent variable—specifically, the use of more than one reading list. There was in effect one baseline period associated with each list. A multiple-baseline study that relies on the inclusion of additional participants is described in Spotlight on Research 8.2.

Alternating Treatments Designs

All of the single-participant designs discussed so far focus on the effects of a single treatment. An **alternating treatments design** allows the effects of more than one treatment to be compared. One advantage of these designs is that they do not require withdrawal of treatment. The fact that multiple treatments can be compared is advantageous, but problematic too given the possibility of interference effects resulting from participation in more than one treatment. Spotlight on Research 8.3 contains a description of an alternating treatments study.

Teaching Writing to At-Risk Second Graders: A Multiple-Baseline Design Study

Writing is one of the more challenging skills learned in elementary school, and many children struggle to acquire the basics. In a 2006 study published in the *Journal of Special Education**, Torri Lienemann, Steve Graham, Beth Leader-Janssen, and Robert Reid attempted to improve the story writing of a small group of second-graders by means of an instructional intervention called self-regulated strategy development, or SRSD.

SRSD involves explicitly teaching students strategies for accomplishing specific writing tasks, such as composing a persuasive essay. Students are also taught any skills or knowledge (e.g., the attributes and elements of a convincing argument) needed to apply the strategies effectively. Students further learn to use a variety of self-regulation procedures (self-instructions, goal setting, self-monitoring, and self-reinforcement) to enhance motivation and regulate their use of the target strategies, the writing task, and their behavior during writing. The emphasis of this instruction is on students' independent, effective, and flexible use of the target strategies. Consequently, procedures for promoting maintenance and generalization are embedded throughout the instructional regime.

Lienemann and colleagues focused on four girls and two boys who had been identified by their teachers as at risk for writing failure, and who had scored below the 25th percentile on a normed test of written story construction. The children were evenly divided into two cohorts of three students apiece. Baseline writing performance for each of the six children was measured by means of three to four stories. Three to four stories written by each child were also evaluated immediately after instruction ceased (independent performance), and then again 2 and 4 weeks later (maintenance):

During baseline, each child wrote three or more stories to establish pretreatment performance.

Instruction was initiated for the first student in each cohort after the children established a stable baseline for number of elements in their stories. Instruction continued until the first child in the cohort demonstrated independent mastery of the strategy, resulting in a story with all of the basic story elements. Instruction did not begin for the next child in the

cohort until the first student's independent or posttreatment performance reached a criterion level of 5 story elements (out of a possible 7). These same procedures were used with the third student in each cohort.

Each student wrote three to four stories immediately following SRSD instruction. These writing probes were completed under the same conditions as during baseline.

Maintenance probes were conducted 2 and 4 weeks after the end of the independent performance phase. These writing probes were completed under the same conditions as baseline and independent performance.

Lienemann and colleagues focused on three dependent variables: number of story elements, number of words, and overall quality.

Number of story elements was scored by tabulating students' inclusion of the following 7 common elements in their papers: main characters, locale, time, what the main characters want to do, what they did, how they felt, and how it all ended (see Stein & Glenn, 1979). Students were taught to generate ideas for these elements or parts during instruction. Consequently, we used this measure to make decisions about when to start and end instruction for students . . . [see above]. Interrater agreement (agreements divided by agreements plus disagreements) for two independent raters was .93.

Each story was entered into a word processing program. Spelling and punctuation were corrected. The number of words written was computed by using the word processing program's word count function. Because this measure was machine scored, no reliability was computed.

Raters evaluated quality of stories using a 7-point holistic scale (with a score of 1 representing the lowest quality and a score of 7 the highest quality). They were asked to read each paper attentively, but not laboriously, to obtain a general impression of overall writing quality. To guide the raters in the scoring process, we used anchor points for second grade developed by Saddler et al. (2004). These anchor points provided a representative paper for scores of 2, 4, and 6 for both stories and personal narratives. Two raters independently scored each paper for overall quality. The raters were graduate students (one at the master's level and one at the doctoral level), and both were unaware of study hypotheses. Before papers were scored, they were typed and entered into a

(continued)

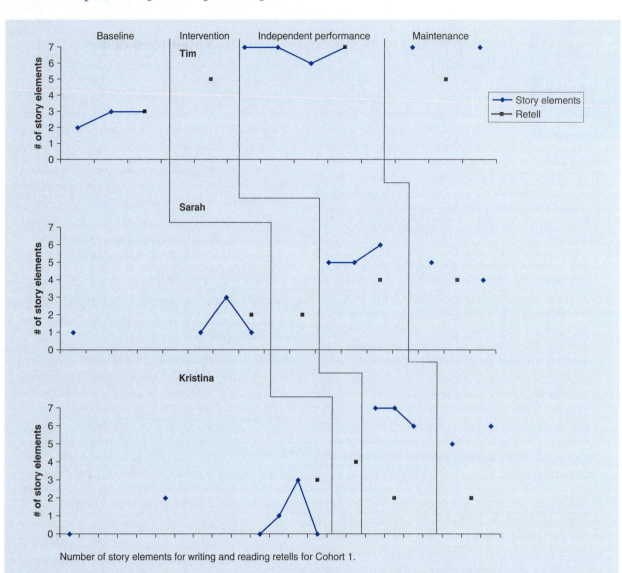

Number of story elements for writing and reading retells for Cohort 1.

word processor. All spelling and punctuation errors were corrected prior to scoring. Interobserver agreement for the stories was .83.

The researchers found that compared to baseline, five of the six students showed dramatic gains on all three dependent variables during independent performance:

Prior to instruction, students' compositions were short, incomplete, and of poor quality.... They contained an average of only 2.1 story elements and 28 words, and they scored an average of 1.8 on a 7-point quality scale. None of the students showed any evidence of planning, as they immediately began writing as soon as the directions for the story prompt were finished ...

Following instruction, all students' stories improved markedly on the independent performance writing probes.... Four students (Trevor, Skylar, Tim, and Kristina) included all 7 story elements in all or all but one of their independent performance stories. Tim included all 7 elements in three out of four independent performance stories. His stories became almost 4 times longer, and his quality scores improved nearly threefold. Kristina's stories included all 7 elements in two out of three stories. Her stories were also 2.5 times longer, and the average quality of her stories more than doubled. Skylar included all 7 story elements in each of her independent performance stories, nearly doubled the average length of her stories, and made a 168%

improvement in her mean quality scores. Trevor's stories included all 7 story elements in two out of three independent performance writing probes. In contrast to the other students, however, his story length stayed about the same and the quality of his stories improved only slightly.

Although Sarah and Katie did not include all 7 story elements in their independent performance stories, they still made improvements (see figures on the previous page). Sarah went from a mean of 2 elements in baseline to a mean of 5.3 elements during independent performance; the length of her stories nearly doubled, and story quality improved by 1 point on a 7-point scale. Katie's stories went from a mean of 2 elements in baseline to a mean of 4.8 elements during independent performance. Her stories became more than 6 times longer, and quality scores improved nearly threefold.

The story elements results for three of the students (the first cohort) are included in the figure on the previous page. The differences between baseline and independent performance for each student can be seen quite clearly in the figure.

The researchers also found strong effects of their intervention at maintenance:

Four of the six students (Skylar, Tim, Sarah, and Kristina) maintained improvements in the number of story elements across the 2- and 4-week maintenance probes.... Katie returned to baseline levels on her first maintenance probe but increased above baseline levels on the second one. Trevor included all 7 elements at the first maintenance probe but decreased markedly to baseline levels on the second probe. All but one student maintained improvements in the length of stories.... The exception was Trevor, whose average story length dropped below baseline levels. Nevertheless, the quality of all students' stories was above baseline levels at maintenance. For three students (Trevor, Skylar, and Sarah), there was little change in story quality from independent performance to maintenance. For two other students (Tim and Kristina), story quality improved at maintenance, but it declined for Katie, staying only marginally better than baseline. There was little overt evidence that the students used the story-planning strategy at maintenance, as only Katie and Trevor wrote the story part reminder at the top of any maintenance story (this occurred on the first maintenance story).

In sum, by using a multiple-baseline design in which each of six second-graders provided baseline data, the researchers found that the SRSD writing intervention had a positive impact on the students' writing.

*Lienemann, T.O., Graham, S., Leader-Janessen, B., & Reid, R. (2006). Improving the writing performance of struggling writers in second grade. *Journal of Special Education, 40*(2), 66–78. Quoted with permission from the publisher.

Experimental Validity in Single-Participant Research

Internal and external validity are essential to the evaluation of a single-participant study for the same reasons that they are essential to the evaluation of group designs. Failure to control for extraneous variables undermines the conclusions drawn from an experimental study, regardless of sample size.

To some extent, single-participant and group designs face the same kinds of threats to validity. Experimenter effects, for example, are a threat to any design. At the same time, single-participant research can be characterized by some unique strengths and susceptibilities with respect to each type of experimental validity.

Internal Validity

As noted at the outset of the chapter, single-participant designs tend to automatically rule out the possibility of internal validity problems associated with differential selection, selection-maturation, and diffusion. Repeated measurements help rule out statistical regression effects and other problems associated with one-time pretesting in experimental designs. At the same time, the emphasis on repeated measurements in single-participant designs raises the possibility of testing effects (if the same measures are used repeatedly) or instrumentation effects (if the measures

Visual Cues Improve Autistic Children's Comprehension: Evidence from an Alternating Treatments Study

Central to the diagnosis of autism is impaired communication. Although both the diagnostic criteria and the research evidence focus on verbal expression, studies show that autistic children may also have difficulties with comprehension. Since many autistic children learn most effectively when information is presented visually, it is sometimes recommended that any communication-related instructional program developed for them should incorporate visual cues.

In a 2006 study published in *Focus on Autism and Other Developmental Disabilities**, Janet Preis examined the comprehension skills of five autistic children ranging in age from 5 to 7 years. The focus of the study was on whether the children could understand simple requests better when the requests are accompanied by pictures. Preis explored three research questions:

1. *Will verbal requests presented in conjunction with picture communication symbols result in a higher number of correct responses for following directions than verbal requests alone?*

2. *Will the commands achieved generalize to a novel therapist under those same conditions?*

3. *Will the commands achieved maintain over time?*

These research questions correspond to the three phases of the study: treatment, generalization, and maintenance.

The five children that Preis studied had all received a professional diagnosis of autism, and had scored below the 10th percentile on the Peabody Picture Vocabulary Test–III. Prior to the treatment phase, a "preintervention commands assessment" determined the types of verbal commands that the children were and were not capable of following. These commands were drawn from six norm-referenced tests and could therefore be arranged in order of difficulty (with difficulty being defined in terms of the age at which children typically perform the command correctly). The easiest commands that each of the five autistic children were unable to follow were used as part of the treatment phase. The goal of treatment was to teach children how to follow these commands. Two alternating treatments were used: commands with pictures (Treatment A) and commands without pictures (Treatment B). Each child received commands representing each treatment:

The alternating treatments, which were counterbalanced, involved the presentation of verbal commands with an associated picture symbol (Treatment A) and without picture symbols (Treatment B). The picture symbols used in Treatment A were commercially produced 4-in (10-cm) black-and-white line drawings (Mayer-Johnson Company, 1994) with text accompanying each drawing. Each picture symbol represented a key element of the verbal direction (e.g., a picture of a ball was presented with the command "get the ball," and a picture of jumping was presented with the command "jump"). Cards depicted more complex directions with two and three picture symbols per 10-cm area (e.g., the two-step command "stand up and push the car" was represented by two picture symbols contained in a single frame).

Both treatment conditions consisted of verbal commands involving body movements, manipulation of materials, or identification of pictured items; examiners presented the conditions in alternation during the same session. Each condition contained an equal instructional set and consisted only of items found not to exist in the participant's repertoire as established by the preintervention commands assessment. Maintenance probes conducted throughout the intervention monitored the performance of each participant over time.

Examiners presented the commands in the order of their developmental sequence . . . as reflected in the order of the preintervention commands assessment . . . with the "easiest," or those expected at the youngest age, presented first. Commands were randomly but evenly assigned to a treatment condition after having been grouped according to the age equivalence expectations established through the previously noted standardized assessments. For example, if a participant had been unable to complete some of the commands in Item 6, which are typically demonstrated by ages 18 months to 23 months (i.e., "touch head," "touch hair," "touch ears," "touch ball"), these commands would be included in the intervention and randomly assigned to either Treatment A with pictures or Treatment B without pictures in equal distribution . . .

Examiners considered a command to be mastered when a participant was able to follow the command for five consecutive trials at the independent level (i.e., no prompts, gestures, or cues) during three consecutive sessions without requiring any repetitions, gestures, or physical prompts.

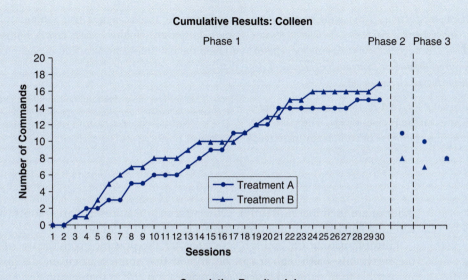

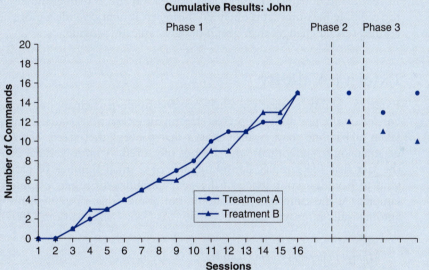

Following the treatment phase, a generalization phase was initiated in which each child's ability to follow the same commands from a different examiner was evaluated. The maintenance phase consisted of probes that were conducted at the beginning of every sixth treatment session, and then again at 10 and 20 weeks following the generalization phase.

The results for each of the research questions are as follows:

The results of the study indicated that there was no therapeutic difference between treatments for the participants' response to verbal requests ...

The generalization of acquired commands to a novel examiner was greater, with borderline significance ... when the clinician presented participants with a picture symbol rather than a verbal directive alone ...

The most visible differences between the treatment conditions occurred in the long-term maintenance sessions. ... The participants retained a significantly greater number of commands under Treatment A at both the first ($z = -2.06$, $p = .02$) and second ($z = -1.83$, $p = .03$) probes. Examiners conducted long-term maintenance probes at approximately 10 and 20 weeks following the intervention phase in order to assess the participants' retention of acquired commands *over an extended period of time. Each participant, with the exception of Kristen, received two probes. Treatment A was significantly more effective for the maintenance of the acquired commands at each of the probes. Individually, Treatment A was also most effective for all participants . . .*

The overall results for two of the students are presented in the figures on the previous page. The *y*-axes in these figures pertain to numbers of commands mastered.

In sum, the results suggest that although pictures do not help autistic children learn new commands, they do help the children generalize and maintain commands that they have already learned.

Preis, J. (2006). The effect of picture communication symbols on the verbal comprehension of commands by young children with autism. Focus On Autism and Other Developmental Disabilities, *21*(4), 194–210. Quoted with permission from the publisher.

differ or are used inconsistently). Observational measures that are unobtrusively and carefully applied minimize these threats to internal validity.

History, maturation, and subject effects are also possible given the use of repeated measurements—although it can be argued that single-participant designs are less susceptible to undetected history and maturation effects than group designs, because the multiple measurements obtained during treatment provide a more detailed look at time-related changes than group designs typically provide.

External Validity

External validity is clearly a challenge for single-participant research. A specific concern is the possibility of pretest–treatment interactions, since the measurements taken at baseline may create changes that prevent the effects of treatment from generalizing to individuals who are not measured. A more general concern is that the fact that the samples consist of one or a small number of participants. We tend to have less confidence in the generalizability of results obtained with small samples. At the same time, we should not assume that sampling more participants automatically improves external validity. As Gall, Gall, and Borg (2007) put it:

> *[M]any studies that employ samples . . . do not involve random selection of the sample from a defined population. Rather, the particular sample is chosen because it is readily accessible, and then the results are generalized through logical inference to a larger population having similar characteristics.*
>
> *In balance, it appears that both single-case and group experiments can be criticized on similar grounds for limited external validity. The real issue is how to increase the external validity of each type of experiment, rather than rejecting one type in favor of the other. (Gall et al., 2007, p. 437)*

In the case of single-participant research, external validity is increased by the use of carefully chosen materials and repeated measurements, and by thorough descriptions of all materials and procedures. The small number of participants is balanced, to an extent, by the detail with which changes in individual behavior can be recorded and analyzed. External validity is also enhanced by creating a suitable match between the research question and the choice of participant(s) and treatment(s).

A Look Ahead

This chapter can be thought of as an extension of Chapter 7, in that I described how the basic concepts of experimental design can be applied to studies focusing on single participants. In the next chapter, I discuss nonexperimental approaches to quantitative research.

Applications: A Guide for Beginning Researchers

Here are some ideas from the chapter that will help you plan your research:

- Choose a single-participant experimental design if you are interested in identifying specific cause–effect relationships, and you wish to focus on one or a small number of participants.
- Choose the type of single-participant design that best addresses your research question, given your available time and resources.
- Make note of the threats to internal and external validity that single-participant designs are especially susceptible to, and minimize these threats to the greatest extent possible in the design and implementation of your research.

Chapter Summary

Single-participant experimental designs are characterized by their focus on individual participants, application of experimental concepts, use of repeated measurements, and reliance on time-dependent data analysis. The three main types of single-participant designs are baseline-treatment, multiple baseline, and alternating treatment designs. Each type of design has unique advantages and disadvantages. In general, single-participant designs are susceptible to some kinds of threats to experimental validity while inherently resistant to others.

Key Terms

Baseline	**B**	**A-B-A-B design**
Treatment	**A-B design**	**Multiple-baseline**
Baseline-treatment	**A-B-A design**	**design**
design	**Withdrawal phase**	**Alternating treatment**
A	**Carryover effects**	**design**

Exercises

For questions 1–4, identify the type of design implied by each description.

1. An 11th-grader's algebra skills are measured on two separate occasions before he participates in a curricular intervention designed to enhance algebraic reasoning. The student's algebra skills are then retested immediately following the intervention, and then again 2 weeks later. The students' attitudes toward algebra, and toward math generally, are also measured each time his algebra skills are tested.

2. A history major is asked to record the amount of time she spends reading or watching news reports (a) on 7 consecutive days before participating in a 3-day current events seminar created by researchers, (b) on each day of the seminar, and (c) on 7 consecutive days following the seminar.

3. A researcher plans to observe a third-grade boy diagnosed with attention-deficit/hyperactivity disorder (ADHD) while the boy is at recess. Observations will take place once per day during 2 consecutive school weeks. The researcher knows that prior to school on Thursday of the first week, the boy will begin to take a new medication for his ADHD.

4. A first-grader whose reading skills are extremely poor participates in two phonics instruction programs. The student participates in program A for 15 days, participates in no program for 5 days, and then participates in program B for 15 days. The students' reading skills are measured on multiple occasions before and after participation in each program.

For questions 5–9, refer to the following figure:

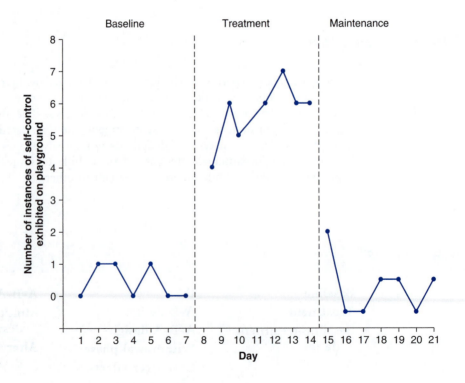

5. What is the dependent variable in this study?

6. What type of design appears to have been used?

7. Does the treatment appear to have been effective while it was being administered?

8. Does the treatment appear to have long-lasting effects?

9. What appears to be a strength of the procedure?

10. *Critical thinking question:* A researcher wishes to demonstrate that a brief motivational talk during morning assembly will improve the attentiveness of students throughout the day. The researcher uses an A-B-A-B design, in which students receive no talk on Monday, a talk on Tuesday, no talk on Wednesday, a talk on Thursday, and no talk on Friday. The attentiveness of three students from a fifth-grade class is measured throughout the week by means of a checklist filled out by their teacher at the end of each school day. What are some potential limitations of this particular design?

Answers to Exercises

1. Multiple-baseline design   2. A-B-A design   3. A-B design

4. Alternating treatments design   5. Self-control   6. A-B-A design   7. Yes   8. No

9. Numerous, consistently obtained measurements

10. *Possible answers*: (a) Few measurements are taken. For example, the first baseline consists of a single measurement obtained on Monday. This increases the likelihood of maturation effects—in particular, student attentiveness may ordinarily wax or wane as the week progresses. History effects are possible too, since the students' attentiveness may vary according to classroom activities. (b) The effects of the motivational talk may not be reversible. It is possible that student attentiveness for the remainder of the week will be influenced by Tuesday's talk. (c) Teacher effects are possible, in the sense that the teacher's ratings may be influenced by the day of the week, or by increasing familiarity with the study protocol.

Suggestions for Further Reading

Research Article: Stahr, B., Cushing, D., Lane, K., & Fox, J. (2006). Efficacy of a function-based intervention in decreasing off-task behavior exhibited by a student with ADHD. *Journal of Positive Behavior Interventions, 8*(4), 201–211.

This empirical study makes use of an A-B-A-B design to evaluate the efficacy of a behavioral intervention for keeping an ADHD student on task.

Application Article: Montarello, S., & Martens, B. K. (2005). Effects of interspersed brief problems on students' endurance at completing math work. *Journal of Behavioral Education, 14*(4), 249–266.

This empirical study illustrates the use of an alternating treatments design in studying a practical classroom problem.

Extension Article: Horner, R. H., Carr, E. G., Halle, J., McGee, G., Odom, S., & Wolery, M. (2005). The use of single-subject research to identify evidenced-based practice in special education. *Exceptional Children, 71*(2), 165–179.

This review article provides detailed discussion and empirical examples of many of the concepts introduced in this chapter.

CHAPTER 9

Nonexperimental Designs

Betsie Van Der Meer/Getty Images

After studying this chapter, you will be able to answer the following questions:

- What are causal–comparative research designs and why are they used?

- How can threats to the validity of causal–comparative designs be addressed?

- What are correlational research designs and why are they used?

- What are the two major types of correlational designs?

- What are descriptive research designs and why are they used?

- What are the three major types of descriptive designs?

- What are the strengths and weaknesses of each type of nonexperimental design?

This chapter will prepare you to do the following:

- Understand and evaluate nonexperimental quantitative research reports

- Select the nonexperimental design that best suits your research question

- Design a nonexperimental study

231

> *The U.S. Department of Education recently proposed that, when considering funding for educational practices or programs, priority be given to programs supported by research that uses an experimental design under which participants—e.g., students, teachers, classrooms, or schools—are randomly assigned to participate in the project activities being evaluated or to a control group that does not participate in the project activities being evaluated.*
>
> *The assertion that education can be investigated using randomized experiments is not uncontroversial; the literature of this debate starts as early as the nineteenth century . . . , and proponents of experimental research in education acknowledge the challenges presented by the field.*
>
> (Zucker, 2004, p. 4)

Introduction: Why Non-Experimental?

In Chapter 7 you read that experimental research designs are superior for discerning causality. If that is the case, and if the primary goal of science is to illuminate cause–effect relationships, why would any other type of design be used? Why would you be reading a chapter entitled "Nonexperimental Designs"? The three types of quantitative research designs covered in this chapter—causal–comparative, correlational, and descriptive—each provide a different answer to these questions.

Consider the following research findings:

- Children who attend Head Start full time enter kindergarten with more advanced preliteracy skills than children who do not attend a preschool program.
- The higher a student's SAT score, the higher the student's first-year college GPA will tend to be.
- The incidence of ADHD is greater among boys than among girls.

Each of these findings reflects one of the nonexperimental quantitative designs that will be discussed in this chapter. What these findings have in common is that they provide information of great importance to educators that could not be obtained through an experimental design. Specifically, they provide information about existing relationships rather than the effects of an intervention or some other independent variable manipulated by the researcher. Because these findings were obtained from studies that do not involve assignment to conditions, the designs of each study are also simpler and, in some cases, more easily replicated than the typical experimental design. For these and other reasons, nonexperimental quantitative designs are widely respected alternatives to experimental research.

Causal-Comparative Designs

In experimental designs, independent variables are manipulated so that their influence on dependent variables can be measured. However, many variables that have a causal influence cannot be manipulated. We know that the socioeconomic level of a school district has some impact on the academic achievement of its students, but we cannot randomly assign districts to socioeconomic levels. Nor can we assign a child to a particular age, gender, or district, in spite of the fact that prior research attests to the influence of each variable on achievement.

In some cases, a variable cannot be manipulated because it would be impossible to do so. Examples include personal characteristics such as gender and intelligence, family characteristics such as birth order and number of parents living at home, and environmental characteristics such as place of residence and school district. In other cases, variables cannot be manipulated because it would be unethical to do so. We know that nutrition is critical for early neurological development, and we could learn more about the brain by manipulating this variable, but it would be terribly unethical to deprive children of adequate nutrition in order to create a comparison group for an experimental study. The various practical and ethical barriers to manipulating variables are among the challenges to experimental research designs alluded to in the second quotation at the outset of this chapter.

One alternative to manipulating variables is to make use of a **causal–comparative design,** in which the effects of naturally occurring differences in categorical variables are studied. Rather than manipulating an independent variable and measuring the effects, the researcher measures the effects of a categorical variable that naturally varies. Thus, researchers can study the brain development of toddlers who differ in nutritional levels, the academic achievement of students in different school districts, differences in verbal skills between males and females, and attitudes toward college expressed by parents from various ethnic backgrounds. In these examples, nutritional level, school district, gender, and ethnicity function as independent variables, but they are not manipulated by researchers. Rather, the researchers look for evidence of causal influence that these variables may have already exerted. (For this reason, causal–comparative designs are sometimes called *ex post facto*—the Latin phrase for "originating after the fact"—because the goal is to describe causal relationships that have already occurred. Later in the chapter, limitations on our ability to infer causality from causal–comparative designs are noted.)

Discussions of causal–comparative designs incorporate some of the terminology used in experimental research. For example, Hewitt and Smith (2004) looked at how evaluation of a trumpet student's performance is influenced by two independent variables: the evaluator's career level (in-service teacher vs. upper-level undergraduate music education student vs. beginning music education student) and the instrument on which the evaluator had been trained (brass vs. other). Each evaluator was asked to rate six trumpet performances on a variety of musical dimensions. Surprisingly, Hewitt and Smith found virtually no main effects or interactions for their main independent variables. One exception was a main effect of career level on judgments of intonation, with less experienced evaluators generating higher scores than more experienced ones. Another exception was an interaction between career level and student performer, with upper-level music students rating one performer more highly than lower-level students and in-service teachers did. As you can see from this example, discussion of independent and dependent variables, as well as main effects and interactions, is common in causal–comparative research. (You can also refer back to Spotlight on Research 2.1 in Chapter 2 for a more detailed description of a causal–comparative study.)

Causal–Comparative and Quasi-Experimental Designs

Students are sometimes confused by the distinction between causal–comparative and quasi-experimental designs. As discussed in Chapter 7, quasi-experimental designs involve intact groups that are assigned to conditions. An intervention designed to encourage attendance might be implemented at one school, while another school serves as a control group, and the two schools' rates of absenteeism are later compared. Causal–comparative designs also involve intact groups, but the experimenter does not assign the groups to conditions before they are compared. Rather, the groups are directly compared on variables of interest. If two schools already differ in their approaches to encouraging attendance, and if researchers find a difference in absenteeism between the two schools, the researchers might infer a causal relationship.

Internal Validity in Causal–Comparative Research

Recall from Chapter 7 that internal validity is the extent to which a dependent variable is affected by the independent variable(s). When internal validity is poor, our ability to infer a causal relationship between independent and dependent variables is undermined.

Using the language of experimental research, we can say that differential selection is a major threat to the internal validity of causal–comparative designs. Because random assignment is not used to create groups in causal–comparative studies, the groups may differ on any number of dimensions of importance. Imagine a study showing that the college grade point average (GPA) of students who had attended private high schools was higher than that of students from public schools. This main effect could reflect a difference in the educational quality of the schools. However, it is conceivable that the private school students came from more affluent families, or that the private school sample contained a higher percentage of girls, or that parents of private school students tend to put more pressure on their children to succeed. In other words, the results might be attributable to extraneous variables such as affluence, gender, or parental pressure, rather than to some intrinsic difference between schools. This study only shows that college GPA is associated with type of high school attended. The study does not definitively show that the type of high school one attends has a causal influence on college performance.

The preceding example illustrates the belief, held by some researchers, that the causal–comparative study is ultimately just another form of correlational research. Even if that is the case, distinguishing between these approaches is helpful when reading published studies. Causal–comparative researchers discuss causal relationships. Their studies are framed in terms of the effects of categorical independent variables (i.e., group membership) on continuous dependent variables. As you will see later in the chapter, correlational researchers discuss the extent to which variables are associated, and their focus will be on any combination of categorical and continuous variables.

Several approaches can be taken to minimize threats to the validity of causal–comparative research. Each of the five approaches discussed in this section helps prevent extraneous effects by increasing the likelihood that the groups differ only on the variable of interest.

INCREASING SAMPLE SIZE   If a small sample of private schools happens to contain several all-girls schools but no all-boys schools, increasing the sample size would increase the likelihood that the sample will yield a more even distribution of gender. But increasing sample size will only be useful in the event of sampling error, as in this example. If the variable of interest and the confounding variable are truly linked, larger samples will continue to reflect that linkage. Because families with children in private school tend to be more affluent, for example, obtaining a large sample will probably not reduce mean differences in socioeconomic status between private versus public school families.

OBTAINING HOMOGENEOUS OR STRATIFIED SAMPLES   In our example, differences in socioeconomic status could be controlled for by means of a homogeneous sample focusing on just those private and public schools that are quite affluent, or by means of a stratified sample in which high- and low-socioeconomic-status schools are sampled from each population. These approaches to sampling increase internal validity but may decrease population validity, owing to their focus on particular segments of the private and public school populations.

COMPARING HOMOGENEOUS SUBGROUPS   Once a sample has already been obtained, the researcher could identify "high," "medium," and "low" socioeconomic levels and then compare the public and private school students at each level. This strategy can be carried out through analysis of variance and other statistical techniques discussed in Chapter 11. Such strategies are useful only insofar as the researcher is sure that the right extraneous variables have been identified. In other words, statistical strategies can only minimize threats to validity for those extraneous variables that have been anticipated and measured.

MATCHING   As discussed in Chapter 7, matching allows groups to be equated with respect to some variable(s). In our example, after obtaining an initial sample of schools, the socioeconomic level of each school would be measured, and pairs of schools (one public and one private) that reflect the same socioeconomic level would be retained for the final sample. Although matching is a powerful strategy, it can only rule out differential selection effects for the matching variable (in this case, socioeconomic level), and it will result in a loss of participants each time a particular value on the matching variable is represented by a participant from only one group (refer back to Chapter 7 for more extensive discussion).

CONTROLLING FOR GROUP DIFFERENCES   Initial group differences in causal–comparative and experimental studies can be removed (i.e., controlled for) through statistical procedures. For instance, a comparison of the academic achievement of public and private school students can be made after controlling for the effects of an initial difference in socioeconomic status between the groups. In Chapter 11 I briefly describe the analysis of covariance techniques and other statistics that could be used to modify achievement scores so that the effects of private versus public schools can be measured independently of the effects of socioeconomic status. Again, the utility of such methods depends on identifying and measuring those variables that may create extraneous effects.

Spotlight on Research 9.1 presents an extended look at a causal–comparative study in which gender, grade, and ethnicity are treated as the independent variables.

Creativity and Deafness: A Causal–Comparative Study

Because the development of communication skills is somewhat different for deaf children than it is for children with normal hearing, researchers have studied the possibility that the cognitive development of deaf children is unique in certain ways. With respect to creativity, the results of prior research have been mixed. Some studies suggest that deaf children are less creative than children with normal hearing, while other studies have shown that the creativity of deaf children is comparable to—and in some cases exceeds—that of peers with normal hearing.

In a 2006 study published in *Roeper Review**, Fawzy Ebrahim addressed these discrepancies in the literature by means of a larger-than-usual sample of deaf students. Ebrahim sampled 210 deaf 8- to 11-year-olds, as well as 200 students of the same age who had normal hearing. Students in each group were administered two tests. The first was a standardized test of nonverbal reasoning called the Matrix Analogies Test—Expanded Form (MAT-EF), which consists of four subtests:

1. *Pattern Completion: This subtest requires that students choose one of four options that accurately complete a pattern. These items require the individual to examine the directions and shapes in the diagram presented to determine which option fits the pattern and belongs on the question mark. The correct option should continue the pattern without interruption in a manner similar to that found in the rest of the diagram . . .*

2. *Reasoning by Analogy: This subtest of items requires that the examinee investigate how the change(s) in one figure is (are) analogous to the change(s) in another. These items require the individual to analyze a matrix on the basis of specific variables (i.e., shape, size, shading) and determine*

how changes in two or more variables converge to result in a new figure . . .

3. *Serial Reasoning: This subtest of items requires the student to discover the order in which items appear throughout a matrix. The boxes in the items included in this group have a specific order in which they appear, and the student has to decide which option completes the matrix according to the specific order . . .*

4. *Spatial Visualization: This subtest of items requires the student to imagine how a figure would look when two or more components are combined.*

Ebrahim also administered the Torrance Tests of Creative Thinking—Figural (TTCT-F, Form A), the most widely used standardized measure of creativity. The TTCT-F consists of three parts: (1) The Picture Construction task requires the participant to create an imaginative story about a single curved shape; (2) the Picture Completion task requires the participant to complete ten incomplete figures; and (3) the Lines task (Form A) requires the participant to make an original picture out of each of 30 pairs of parallel lines. Ebrahim noted that these three parts of the TTCT-F tap into five norm-referenced creative thinking abilities, and one crtierion-referenced skill, "creative thinking strengths," which has 13 components:

These three activities provide scores for five norm-referenced creative thinking abilities and 13 criterion-referenced abilities. Norm-referenced creative thinking abilities are fluency, originality, abstraction of titles, elaboration, and resistance to premature closure. Fluency refers to the number of ideas a person expresses through interpretable responses that use the stimulus in a meaningful manner. Originality refers to the infrequency and unusualness of the response. Abstractness of titles refers to the ability to produce good

Correlational Designs

Experimental and causal–comparative designs focus on establishing causal relationships. In contrast, the immediate purpose of a **correlational design** is to quantify the extent of association between variables. The magnitude of association may be of interest for its own sake, or because it allows researchers to use information about one variable or variables to predict the values of others. Although correlational designs date back to the late 19th century, they have become increasingly popular *titles and involves the thinking processes of synthesis and organization.*

In scoring elaboration, credit is given for each pertinent detail (idea, piece of information, etc.) added to the original stimulus figure, its boundaries, and/or its surrounding space. Resistance to premature closure refers to the ability of a creative person to keep open and delay closure long enough to make the mental leap that makes possible original ideas. This is measured by the individual's tendency to close or not to close the incomplete figures immediately with straight or curved lines (Torrance, 1998).

In scoring for the criterion-referenced creative thinking strengths, any genuine appearance of a strength is indicated by a plus sign (+). If the strength appears three or more times, this is indicated by two plus signs (+ +). These creative strengths include: emotional expressiveness (e.g., in drawings, title); storytelling articulateness (context, environment); movement or action (e.g., running, dancing, flying, falling); expressiveness of titles; synthesis of incomplete figures (e.g., combination of 2 or more); synthesis of lines (e.g., combination of 2 or more); unusual visualization (above, below, at angle, etc.); internal visualization (e.g., inside, cross section); extending or breaking boundaries; humor (e.g., in titles, captions, drawings); richness of imagery (e.g., variety, vividness, strength); colorfulness of imagery (e.g., exactingness, earthiness); and fantasy (e.g., figures in myths, fables, fairly tales, science fiction).

Ebrahim found no overall differences between deaf and hearing children in their MAT-EF and TTCT-F scores, indicating that on the whole they have comparable nonverbal reasoning and creativity skills. At the same time, there were specific differences between the groups. Hearing children scored higher than deaf children on Pattern Completion, Reasoning by Analogy, and Serial Reasoning, while deaf children scored higher on Spatial Visualization. In addition, children with normal hearing scored higher on the abstractness of titles variable of the TTCT-F. Ebrahim did not consider interactions with gender or age over and above these main effects.

Ebhraim noted that group differences in the abstractness of titles may be attributable to differences in the early language experiences of deaf and hearing children. In the discussion section, Ebrahim also acknowledged that the study has four limitations:

1. *No attempt was made to determine if any of the participants (deaf and hearing) had training in reasoning or in creative thinking.*
2. *Hearing children were selected on the basis of convenience sampling procedures. It would be more beneficial if these children were selected by random sampling procedures.*
3. *No attempt was made to investigate language variability among the deaf children. Further investigation will be made on the same sample of deaf children concerning the language variable and its relation to reasoning and creative thinking abilities.*
4. *... If each group was divided into subgroups based on the age of the participants, it might reveal more significant underlying constructs that could provide more insights about the relationship between reasoning abilities and creative thinking abilities.*

As you can see, each limitation has some bearing on the validity of this particular comparison between deaf and hearing children. Most of the concerns here pertain to preexisting differences between groups and limitations in population validity.

*Ebrahim, Fawzy. (2006). Comparing creative thinking abilities and reasoning ability of deaf and hearing children. *Roeper Review, 28*(3), 140–147. Quoted with permission from the publisher.

during the past four decades, owing in part to the development of computer programs for analyzing large numbers of variables (some of which are discussed in Chapters 10 and 11).

Correlation Coefficients

The magnitude of correlation between two variables is expressed by a **correlation coefficient,** which ranges from—1.0 to 1.0. (In this chapter, I discuss correlation coefficients and other concepts of relevance to correlational designs in largely nonmathematical terms. Chapters 10 and 11 each provide some of the mathematical foundation of correlational research.)

Positive Correlation

When the value of the correlation coefficient is positive, we speak of the variables as being directly or positively correlated, and we understand that as the value of one variable increases, the value of the other variable tends to increase. (We could just as well say that as one variable decreases, the other one tends to decrease too.) The higher the value of a correlation coefficient, the more closely related the two variables are. For example, since the WISC-IV and the Stanford–Binet both measure general intelligence, the correlation between scores on these tests is highly positive—the higher a person's score on one of the tests, the higher their score will tend to be on the other. A correlation coefficient of exactly 1.0 would mean that the variables are perfectly positively correlated, an outcome that is rarely observed in meaningful correlational analyses. The correlation between people's height in meters and their height in inches is 1.0, but there would be no point in calculating that particular correlation (unless one is uncertain about the accuracy of one of the measuring instruments).

Negative Correlation

A negative correlation coefficient means that the variables are indirectly (or inversely, or negatively) correlated, so that as the value of one variable increases, the value of the other variable tends to decrease. For example, studies have demonstrated a negative correlation between the amount of TV that adolescents watch and the amount of time they spend on outdoor activities. This finding makes sense in light of the fact that people only have a finite amount of leisure time—the more time spent watching TV, the less time available for being outside. A correlation coefficient of exactly—1.0 would mean that the variables are perfectly negatively correlated. This too is rarely observed in correlational studies.

No Correlation

A correlation coefficient of 0 (or close to 0) means that there is no relationship between the variables, so that variability in one will be unrelated to variability in the other. For example, Fox and Boulton (2006) showed that the correlation between the extent to which children are bullied and the number of best friends they have is virtually zero (−.05). At the same time, the extent to which children are bullied is highly positive correlated with the extent to which other children view them as having poor social skills (.91), and moderately negatively correlated with the extent to which they are liked by other children (−.44). (Terms such as "highly" and "moderately" are subjective, and the same correlation coefficient may be evaluated differently depending on the nature of the study. In a study in which interrater reliabilities are computed, a correlation of .5 would probably be considered low, whereas the same value would be considered alarmingly strong if it represented the correlation between absenteeism and the number of miles students live from school.)

Specific Coefficients

The correlation coefficient that expresses the strength of association between two variables is named by a lowercase, italicized r. Thus, the phrase "$r = .87$" tells

TABLE 9.1 Some Commonly Used Correlation Coefficients

Nature of Variables	Coefficient used
Both variables continuous	Pearson product–moment coefficient
Both variables ordinal	Spearman rho
Both variables dichotomous	Phi coefficient
One dichotomous variable, one continuous variable	Point biserial correlation

you that the correlation between the variables in question is .87. When the two variables are continuous, the researcher calculates a **Pearson product–moment correlation coefficient.** This has been the most widely used type of correlation coefficient following its introduction by Karl Pearson in the 1890s. Other coefficients may need to be calculated depending on the scale used to measure each variable (see Table 9.1 for examples).

Representing Correlations

There are three ways to represent correlations between variables: coefficients, correlation matrices, and scatterplots.

Coefficients

As discussed earlier, the correlation coefficient is a numerical estimate of the strength of the relationship between the variables. As a rule, coefficients are provided in research reports when correlations are described.

Correlation Matrices

When numerous variables are intercorrelated—that is, when correlations between numerous variables are calculated two variables at a time—the resulting coefficients may be presented in a table known as a **correlation matrix.** Table 9.2 provides an example. Each number at the upper right-hand side of the table corresponds to one of the variables in the left-hand side column. (The number 1 stands for teachers' perceptions, the number 2 stands for students' performance, and the number 3 stands for students' feelings.) The dashes in the table illustrate the obvious point that a variable cannot be correlated with itself. You should be able to see, for example, that the correlation between teachers' perceptions and students' performance is .35.

TABLE 9.2 Correlation Matrix (Adapted from Schappe, 2006)

Measure	1	2	3
1. Teachers' perceptions	–	.35	.08
2. Students' performance		–	.02
3. Students' feelings			–

Scatterplots

A correlational relationship can also be depicted visually by means of a **scatterplot,** a simple graph in which the *x*-axis corresponds to one variable, the *y*-axis corresponds to the other variable, and each point represents one individual's score on both variables. Scatterplots illustrating three different types of correlational relationships are shown in Figure 9.1. The scatterplot in the upper left of the figure illustrates a positive correlation, in that as the *x*-axis values increase, the values on the *y*-axis tend to increase too. The scatterplot in the upper right illustrates a negative correlation—as the *x*-axis values increase, the values on the *y*-axis tend to decrease. The scatterplot at the bottom of the figure illustrates no correlation, because there is no consistent tendency for *y*-axis values to either increase or decrease as the *x*-axis values increase.

Linear and Curvilinear Relationships

The positive and negative correlations discussed thus far, and depicted at the top of Figure 9.1, illustrate **linear relationships** between variables, meaning that the more positively (or negatively) the two variables are associated, the more closely the graph of their relationship will approximate a straight line. (Correlations of—1.0 and 1.0 would be represented as perfectly straight lines.)

A linear relationship is not the only kind of systematic association between variables, however. Pairs of variables sometimes reflect **curvilinear relationships,** meaning that for one range of values they exhibit a positive correlation, while for a different range of values they exhibit a negative correlation. Figure 9.2 depicts a famous curvilinear relationship known in psychology as the Yerkes–Dodson law. This law expresses the relationship between physiological arousal and performance on complex tasks. Up to a point, the more aroused you are, the better your per-formance on a task, presumably because alertness and concentration are enhanced. In other words, at low levels of arousal, there is a positive correlation between arousal and performance. However—as you may know if you have experienced test anxiety—there is a point at which arousal begins to become counterproductive.

FIGURE 9.1 Scatter-plots Depicting Positive Correlation, Negative Correlation, and No Correlation

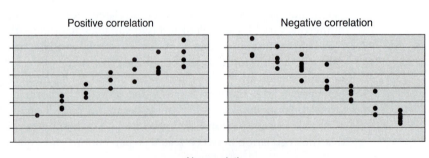

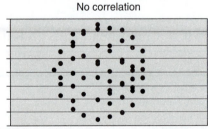

FIGURE 9.2 Representation of Yerkes–Dodson Law

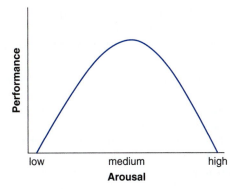

Beyond this point, arousal and performance are negatively correlated—the more aroused you become, the less well you perform, presumably because the symptoms of anxiety, such as shaking, butterflies in the stomach, and "brain freeze," are increasingly distracting.

Curvilinear relationships may be relatively simple, as illustrated by the Yerkes–Dodson law, or they may reflect more complex patterns of positive, negative, and/or zero correlations for particular ranges of values. For example, Figure 9.3 represents a hypothesized relationship between the number of introductory algebra classes a group of college students have attended during a particular semester and their performance on a test consisting of simple algebra problems. During the first few classes, there would be no correlation between these variables, because the students are reviewing prerequisite skills and would not be very skilled yet at solving even simple problems. Then, a positive correlation would emerge as students become increasingly able to apply what they are learning in class. Finally, the correlation would disappear as students achieve perfect, or near-perfect, scores on the test, because they will have mastered the skills required to solve simple problems and will have already begun to learn more advanced content.

Deciding How to Represent Correlations

One or more approaches to representing correlations will be used in a particular study, depending on the researcher's needs.

Because a correlation coefficient is a numerical estimate, it represents the strength of association between two variables more precisely than a scatterplot does, and thus correlation coefficients, singly or in matrices, are most commonly reported in

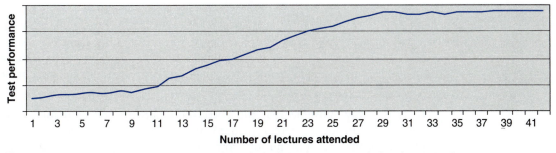

FIGURE 9.3 Relationship between Number of Algebra Classes Attended and Test Performance

published research. Scatterplots are nonetheless important in correlational studies, because they provide information that cannot be acquired by means of correlation coefficients, including the presence of outliers and the possibility of a curvilinear relationship between variables.

First, any set of values for a particular variable may contain an **outlier,** a datapoint that does not fit the overall pattern. If the dependent measure in a study happens to be test scores, for instance, then one extremely high or extremely low score would constitute an outlier—it would lie far outside the range in which the rest of the scores are found. The presence of outliers cannot be detected by means of correlation coefficients, but they can lower the absolute value of the coefficient, thereby causing the researcher to underestimate the extent of association between variables. Outliers may need to be removed before final data analysis gets underway. In a study on the relationship between IQ and reaction time, in which reaction time is measured by how long it takes to push a button when a light flashes, most people would respond in under a second, and the researcher would exclude data from someone who took 9 seconds, for instance, under the assumption that the person was not paying attention, or the equipment was malfunctioning, or there was some other problem.

Second, a curvilinear relationship between continuous variables may result in a Pearson correlation coefficient that is very close to zero. In the case of the Yerkes–Dodson curve, for example, we could say, informally, that the positive correlation for one half of the values would be cancelled out by the negative correlation for the other half of the values. But it will be inaccurate to conclude that the variables are unrelated, even though the correlation coefficient would suggest as much. Simple coefficients such as Pearson's are not sensitive to curvilinear relationships. By examining a scatterplot, the researcher can tell whether there are nonlinear relationships between variables that merit further analysis with *eta,* a correlation coefficient that is appropriate for curvilinear relationships—or whether Pearson correlation coefficients can be used for certain subsets of the total range of values in which linear relationships occur. For example, some studies have identified a negative correlation between the amount of television children watch and their grades in school. However, this relationship is only observed among children who watch more than one hour of TV per day. Data from children who watch less than one hour per day must be excluded in order for the negative linear relationship to be observed.

Correlation and Causation

It is sometimes said that correlation does not imply causation. Taken literally, that statement is untrue. Correlation does *imply* causation to greater or lesser extent, depending on the study, and researchers sometimes take a hint from the results of correlational analyses to design experimental studies. A more accurate statement would be that correlation does not *prove* causation. Broadly, there are three reasons for this.

1. It is always possible that the correlation between two variables can be attributed to coincidence rather than to an actual relationship between them. Sampling error may result in spurious correlations. Likewise, the more correlational analyses a researcher runs, the greater the likelihood of a fluke.

2. The direction of causality between correlated variables may be ambiguous. Studies show that self-esteem is positively correlated with peer acceptance, but this correlation is consistent with two diametrically opposed interpretations:

- The better you feel about yourself, the more positively you interact with others.
- The more your peers like you, the better you feel about yourself.

Many researchers on this topic would advocate a somewhat more complicated alternative:

- Throughout childhood, there is an ongoing interplay between self-esteem and peer acceptance, such that better self-esteem leads to more peer acceptance, which in turn boosts one's self-esteem, which in turn makes one more confident in social interactions, and so on.

Although, strictly speaking, the direction of causality implied by a correlational relationship is ambiguous, in many studies it is quite clear which variable is the one that would exert a causal influence. Distance from school is positively correlated with absenteeism, but there is no question that insofar as these variables are causally related, absenteeism does not cause a student to live farther away from school. Rather, greater distance from school results in greater absenteeism. Still, we should be careful in how we apply common sense. There are many instances in which the direction of causality between correlated variables seems obvious, but actually run in the opposite direction upon closer scrutiny. For example, a number of studies have shown a negative correlation between parental supervision of homework and student achievement. Does this mean that the more parents supervise their children's homework, the more poorly the children do in school (owing to frustration, a sense of incompetence, and/or misinformation from parents)? Some researchers have drawn that conclusion. But studies also show that when children are doing poorly in school, their parents respond by monitoring their homework more closely (Larzelere, Kuhn, & Johnson, 2004). So increasing supervision does not cause performance to falter. Rather, declining performance causes supervision to increase.

3. The third, and perhaps most fundamental reason that correlation does not prove causation is the possibility that the relationship between correlated variables is created by a third variable. The third variable is related to each of the two variables of interest and creates the apparent association between them. This is sometimes called the **third-variable problem,** and it is a key reason to be cautious about inferring a causal relationship from a correlational one.

The Third-Variable Problem

When it seems inconceivable that correlated variables are causally related, we suspect the presence of a third variable. For example, in some coastal cities we would find a positive correlation between ice cream consumption and incidence of shark attacks, but it is hard to imagine either variable having much causal influence on the other. Rather, each of these variables is separately associated with a third variable—season—that creates a spurious correlation between them. Ice cream consumption increases in the summertime, as does the number of swimmers (and, therefore, the likelihood of shark attacks). In other words, warmer weather stimulates more ice cream consumption and more exposure to shark attacks, and for that reason a positive correlation is observed between the latter two variables when in fact they are not directly related.

In some cases, the presence of a third variable is not suspected until one is suggested by later research. For example, a 1999 study showed that babies younger than 2 years of age who sleep with a light on have an increased risk of myopia (i.e., nearsightedness). This finding is consistent in a general way with research on the sensitivity of the developing visual system to ambient light. However, Zadnik and colleagues (2000) argued that owing to shared genes, parents with myopia tend to have children with myopia, and that parents with myopia are more likely to use nightlights in their children's rooms, owing to their own poor vision. Thus the original relationship between lighting and childhood myopia can be attributed to a third variable, the quality of the parents' vision.

Although in theory the number of potential third variables is limitless, theoretical considerations and common sense motivate researchers to try to exclude those that seem most plausible. For example, students in health classes are taught that cigarette smoking causes lung cancer, because the literature shows not only that the number of cigarettes people smoke per day is positively correlated with the incidence of lung cancer, but that the incidence of the disease is not related to third variables such as a tendency for people who live in cities with extensive air pollution to smoke more.

Partial Correlation

One approach to addressing third-variable problems is a statistical technique known as partial correlation. A **partial correlation** yields a correlation coefficient between two variables after the effects of a third variable or variables have been statistically removed. Consider the relationship between the quality of instruction students receive in their high school math classes and their performance on a mathematics achievement test administered at the end of their senior year. One of the third variables that would affect this relationship is mathematical intelligence: students who are better at math will tend to understand and retain more of the information their math teachers present, and they will tend to do well on mathematical achievement tests. As a result, the simple correlation between instructional quality and student learning will be artificially inflated. Their relationship will be measured more accurately if differences in student IQ are controlled for (i.e., eliminated) through partial correlations. (Partial correlations yield the same kind of coefficient as the other types of correlations discussed in this chapter. Thus, the latter are often referred to as "simple" or "zero-order" correlations, in order to distinguish them from partial correlations.)

When the effects of a third variable are controlled for, the partial correlation will tend to be smaller than the original, zero-order correlation (as in the previous example). In some cases, the partial correlation will be larger than the original one. When this occurs, the third variable is said to exert a **suppressor effect** on the two variables of interest, meaning that the two variables are more closely related than indicated by the simple correlation between them. In educational research, suppressor effects are sometimes observed when the third variable is reading ability. For example, the relationship between instructional quality and scores on a timed achievement test will be weakened somewhat by variability in how quickly and accurately students can read the test. Even though better instruction might be associated with higher test scores, the strength of the relationship will be weakened by the fact that poor readers, even if instructed well, will experience some difficulties in understanding test questions. Partialling out differences in reading ability will allow a stronger relationship between instruction and test scores to be revealed.

(The purpose of the analysis would not be to discount reading difficulties, of course. Poor reading remains a problem of central importance to both educators and researchers. The purpose of controlling for reading ability here would simply be to measure more accurately the association between test performance and a separate variable—instructional skill.)

In Spotlight on Research 9.2, a correlational study that relies heavily on partial correlations is described.

Types of Correlational Designs

If correlation does not prove causation, why would researchers ever choose a correlational design? Depending on the study, one or more of the following partially overlapping considerations may play a role:

- Correlational studies tend to be quicker and more convenient to carry out than experimental studies.
- Correlational studies provide information about naturally occurring relationships between variables, rather than the effects of artificially manipulated variables.
- Correlational studies provide information about relationships between variables over time that would be difficult to study through an experimental approach (e.g., the relationship between amount of TV watched as a child and attitudes toward violence during adolescence, which could be measured by interviewing adolescents about current attitudes and prior TV-viewing habits).
- Correlational studies provide information about relationships between variables that for ethical reasons cannot be manipulated (e.g., the relationship between the age of first intercourse and the likelihood of contracting a sexually transmitted disease).

Broadly speaking, there are two types of correlational design—relational designs and prediction designs—each corresponding to a different purpose for conducting the research.

Relational Designs

In a **relational design,** the researcher collects data (by means of surveys or tests, for example) and then calculates the correlations between variables. The purpose of a relational design is to quantify the extent to which two or more variables are interrelated. For example, relational studies have attempted to do the following:

- Determine the extent to which academic achievement in middle school is related to amount of time spent on homework.
- Determine how closely related binge drinking in college is related to peer pressure, social isolation, emotional maturity, and GPA.
- Determine the extent of association between self-esteem, social skills, and popularity in high school.

A relational design is reflected in a study by Schappe (2005), who wanted to know whether a performance assessment designed for preschoolers would yield information that is consistent with the impressions obtained by their teachers. The researcher collected data on three variables: preschool teachers' perceptions of their

Music Lessons and Academic Achievement: A Correlational Study

In the 1990s, experimental research suggested that people who listen to a 10-minute selection of Mozart immediately before taking the Stanford–Binet IQ test do better on spatial reasoning items than people who spend the 10 minutes either in silence, or listening to highly repetitive music (Rauscher, Shaw, & Ky, 1993, 1995). This finding, dubbed the "Mozart effect," generated a great deal of interest among educators as well as the general public. However, some attempts to replicate the effect were unsuccessful (e.g., Steele, Bass, & Crook, 1999), while other studies showed that the Mozart effect is simply attributable to the creation of greater arousal and a more positive mood—internal states that can be created by other kinds of music, and can benefit performance on a variety of tests.

Ideally, the question of whether the Mozart effect exists is addressed by an experimental design in which participants are randomly assigned to conditions (listening to Mozart, listing to another type of music, etc.). Other questions about the cognitive benefits of exposure to music are more suitably addressed through correlational designs. For example, we might wish to know whether formal instruction in music has long-term benefits for intellectual functioning. This question was addressed in a 2006 study by Glenn Schellenberg published in the *Journal of Educational Psychology**. By means of two experiments, Schellenberg examined whether the duration of music lessons in childhood would be related to IQ and academic achievement later in life.

In the first experiment, Schellenberg sampled 147 Canadian children ranging in age from 6 to 11. The approach to sampling was purposive (see Chapter 4), in the sense that children who had taken music lessons were targeted. Schellenberg described the predictor and criterion variables as follows:

Predictor variables were measured with a questionnaire. Parents were asked to provide details about their child's history of private or group music lessons taken outside of school.... The questionnaire also contained items about family income, linguistic background, country of birth, parents' education, and the child's involvement in nonmusical out-of-school activities.... As with music lessons, each activity was measured in months of involvement.

Criterion variables consisted of measures of intelligence, academic ability, and social adjustment. The WISC-III is a

test of childhood intelligence used widely in North America, with well-established reliability and validity.... Measures of academic achievement included the Kaufman Test of Educational Achievement—Brief Form [K-TEA] as well as school grades. The K-TEA is a standardized test of academic achievement from the United States that provides a composite score as well as scores on three subtests (Mathematics, Spelling, and Reading).

Parents of 125 children (85% of the sample) provided photocopies of school report cards, which are identical across all publicly funded schools in Ontario and thus comparable.... A composite school average was the average of each child's grades. Report cards also contained grades ... in nine areas that measured learning skills (Independent Work, Initiative, Homework Completion, Use of Information, Cooperation with Others, Conflict Resolution, Class Participation, Problem Solving, and Goal Setting to Improve Work). These grades were converted to a numerical scale (e.g., Excellent = 4, Needs Improvement = 1) and averaged to yield a composite measure of Learning Skills.

In one set of analyses, Schellenberg looked at the partial correlations between music lessons and each of the criterion variables while holding constant the most important predictor variables (nonmusical activities, family income, and parents' education). The partial correlations were small but significant for WISC-III scores (.25), K-TEA scores (.23), grades (.25), and Learning Skills (.22). In other words, months of involvement in music lessons was positively correlated with IQ, grades, and achievement scores after controlling for the effects of nonmuscial activities, family income, and parents' education.

In the second experiment, Schellenberg sampled 150 Canadian undergraduates from introductory psychology classes. Once again the approach to sampling was purposive, in the sense of focusing on individuals who had taken music lessons in childhood.

The predictor variables were quantified based on responses to a questionnaire. Students were asked about their history of music lessons. For each instrument they studied (including voice), they were also asked to indicate how long they had played it on a regular basis.... Compared to music lessons, regular playing was assumed to be a better reflection of students' actual commitment to musical training and to be a better indicator of musical interest and enjoyment. Thus, the predictor variable used in the statistical analyses was years of playing music regularly that accompanied private lessons (i.e., years of lessons plus additional years of regular playing), which had a strong association with years of music lessons, r = .94, p = .001. Participants were also asked about their age, ethnicity, linguistic background, and family income, as well as their parents' education, ethnicity, and linguistic backgrounds.

Criterion variables included measures of intelligence and academic achievement. Each student was administered the complete Wechsler Adult Intelligence Scale—Third Edition (WAIS-III), which has good reliability and validity. . . . High school average, based on self-report, served as a measure of academic achievement.

Small but significant partial correlations were found between years of playing music regularly and both WAIS-III scores (.21) and high school grade point average (.19) when family income, parents' education, and students' gender were held constant. In short, as in the first experiment, involvement in music was positively correlated with IQ and achievement after controlling for family income and parents' education. Although in both experiments other third variables are conceivable, the results are consistent with the possibility that music lessons have enduring cognitive benefits.

In closing, Schellenberg noted that the design of his study "does not allow for inferences of causation," and then discussed a variety of alternative explanations for his results:

One possible explanation is that individual differences in IQ influence the likelihood that a child takes music lessons. . . . More specifically, high-IQ children (and/or their parents) could be more motivated than other children. Thus, taking music lessons and playing music regularly for extended periods of time could be a consequence of motivation. Although this explanation is appealing in its simplicity, links between IQ and motivation in other domains (e.g., school in general, mathematics problems in particular, information-processing tasks, monetary gain, economic and professional status) tend to be weak or nonexistent. . . . It is also possible that high-IQ children enjoy music lessons more than their lower-IQ counterparts because they find it easier to read musical notation, to identify patterns in musical stimuli . . . and so on. In other words, high-IQ children may have more mental capacity to take music lessons as well as go to school because both activities are cognitively demanding. Although this perspective can account for the present findings as well as for previous correlations between

music lessons and intellectual functioning, it cannot explain previous experimental findings . . .

Schellenberg also discussed four versions of the possibility that formal instruction in music benefits IQ for reasons that are not specific to participation in music lessons per se: (1) music lessons are a school-like activity that benefit IQ in much the same way that school does; (2) music lessons are comparable to the learning of a foreign language, which is known to have cognitive benefits; (3) some particular skill or set of skills acquired through music lessons enhances IQ; and/or (4) exposure to music itself, rather than lessons per se, has cognitive benefits. Schellenberg noted that each of these four possibilities is consistent with the findings of published studies.

With respect to the possibility of third variable effects, Schellenberg discussed whether parents' IQ might have contributed to the relationship between music lessons and intellectual ability. (Parents' IQ was presumably only partially accounted for through the measures of their years of education.)

To illustrate, the correlation between IQ and years of education is about .55 . . . which means that only about 30% of the variance in parents' IQ was accounted for in the present study. In principle, the remaining 70% could account for individual differences among the present participants in IQ and in duration of musical involvement. It is less likely, however, that parents' IQ could account for the association between music lessons and academic performance that was independent of general intelligence. Moreover, parents' IQ cannot account for the positive results of a controlled experiment that included random assignment of young children to music lessons (Schellenberg, 2004).

Explanations of observed associations between music lessons and intellectual functioning are not necessarily mutually exclusive. . . . All or most of the proposed explanations could be correct to some degree because the underlying mechanisms might prove to be complex and interactive, perhaps even circular (Schellenberg, 2005). For example, parents with high IQs tend to have children with high IQs . . . who could be more likely than other children to undergo extended training in music, which could exaggerate individual differences in intellectual functioning. The true nature of the association between music lessons and intellectual abilities can be clarified only by future research.

*Schellenberg, E. G. (2006). Long-term positive associations between music lessons and IQ. *Journal of Educational Psychology, 98*(2), 457–468.

students' achievement, the students' scores on a specific performance assessment, and how well students liked the assessment. Schappe found that teachers' sense of their students' achievement was positively correlated with their students' scores on the assessment, but that neither of those variables was correlated with students' feelings about the assessment. The fact that teachers' perceptions and students' scores were directly correlated was taken as support for the usefulness of the performance measure Schappe used.

If you look back at the correlation matrix of Table 9.2, you will see the main results of the study just described. You should be able to tell that the correlation between teachers' perceptions of student achievement and students' scores on the performance assessment was .35, while the correlation between students' scores and their feelings about the assessment was .02, and the correlation between their feelings and teachers' perceptions was .08.

Prediction Designs

The Schappe (2005) study illustrates a relational design, because the goal is to determine the extent of correlation between variables measured at one point in time. In a **prediction design,** information about one variable or set of variables is used to predict the values of another variable or variables. The variables used to make predictions are often called the **predictor variables** (or "predictors"), while the variables being predicted are called the **criterion variables** (or "outcome variables"). For example, prediction studies have attempted to do the following:

- Predict college GPA on the basis of high school GPA, SAT scores, and senior class ranking.
- Predict the extent of peer victimization (i.e., being the target of bullying) on the basis of stature, social skills, and self-control.
- Predict reading fluency in first grade on the basis of IQ, vocabulary size, and phonological awareness.

In prediction studies, statistical methods are used to calculate precise estimates of the amount of variability in the criterion variable that can be predicted from variability in the predictor variables. The ultimate goal of these studies is to find the combination of predictor variables that provides the most information about variability in the criterion variable. For example, over time literacy researchers have identified variables that predict early reading fluency—although there are still some disagreements about which variables are most important, and about exactly how much each variable should be weighted in the models of prediction that are currently being developed.

INFERENCE IN PREDICTION STUDIES   Although prediction designs are correlational, researchers typically infer causality from the results. Whether or not causality is inferred is a matter of theoretical inclination and common sense. Although researchers would readily acknowledge that predictors such as high school GPA do not directly "cause" college GPA (there must be third variables here such as intrinsic motivation and academic skills), in peer victimization studies it is often assumed that key predictors are causally related to the extent of peer victimization. Being small, exhibiting poor social skills, and having difficulties controlling one's emotions when being teased all tend to invite bullying from other students. In the same way, some researchers would argue that being highly intelligent, knowing a great deal of vocabulary, and having good phonological awareness skills all contribute (in a

TABLE 9.3 Two Major Types of Correlational Studies

Type	General Approach
Relational design	Determination of correlations between variables
Prediction design	Use of information about variables to predict values of other variables

causal sense) to early reading fluency. This is not to say that researchers believe that all causal relationships are fully and unambiguously described in prediction studies. Although poor social skills may predispose a student to peer victimization, being bullied on a regular basis may diminish a student's social skills. And it is clear that a good vocabulary contributes to better reading fluency, which in turn increases the child's vocabulary. The point here is simply that prediction studies tend to be interpreted within a causal framework. This is a characteristic that distinguishes them from relational studies (see Table 9.3).

Both relational and prediction studies rely on correlations and, in some cases, partial correlations in order to achieve their goals. In Chapters 11 and 12, you will read about statistical techniques such as multiple regression, path analysis, and structural equation modeling that are used in prediction studies to describe the relationships between predictors and outcome variables. What these statistical techniques have in common is that they provide information about the strength of the relationship between predictors and outcome variables, and they generate formulae that allow values for outcome variables to be predicted (to some degree of confidence) given information about the predictors.

Descriptive Research Designs

The causal–comparative and correlational designs discussed so far all represent quantitative approaches to determining relationships between variables. In contrast, the purpose of a **descriptive design** is to simply describe phenomena in quantitative terms. (Descriptive designs in qualitative research are described in Chapters 13 and 14.) Simply describing "what is" represents one of the simplest and most straightforward goals one could have as a researcher, and for that reason descriptive studies have been a constant presence throughout the history of educational research.

Some of the research questions that can be addressed through descriptive studies include the following:

- What types of instructional methods are used by reading teachers in a particular school?
- Who do middle school students rely on for support when making the transition to high school?
- How many high school seniors fail to graduate?
- Where do migrant parents find information about educational services?
- Which countries demonstrate good student achievement in science and math?

As you can imagine, any study addressing one of the research questions above might include a causal–comparative and/or correlational component. For example, in a descriptive study on how many high school seniors fail to graduate, comparisons might be made between graduation rates for males versus females, and/or correlations may be calculated between graduation rates across schools and the teacher–student ratio within each school. This illustrates the idea that in actual practice we do not always see a clear distinction between a descriptive design and other types of nonexperimental quantitative research. Moreover, because all research, regardless of design, contains a descriptive component, the concepts discussed in this section are not unique to descriptive designs.

Types of Descriptive Designs

With respect to how data are collected, three types of descriptive designs can be identified: observational, survey, and content analysis (see Table 9.4). (Later in the chapter, I will introduce a further distinction based on how descriptive researchers measure change over time.)

OBSERVATIONAL DESIGNS   **Observation** is a desirable method of research in naturalistic settings. As a quantitative approach to data collection, the goal of observation is to carefully and systematically record information about specific behaviors. The observational researcher may attempt to record information without disturbing the participants, a technique sometimes referred to as "naturalistic observation" or "nonparticipant observation." Alternatively, the researcher may introduce some sort of change and then observe the participants' responses to the change, a technique that goes by many names, including "structured observation."

When recording observations, the observational researcher will make use of checklists, rating schemes, and/or coding schemes (see Chapter 5 for discussion). Some of these methods of data collection are used strictly by researchers, while others are also appropriate for use by teachers and/or parents to screen for developmental problems or other behavioral patterns of interest. Whatever method is used, it is essential for the observational researcher to decide in advance which behaviors will be observed and how they will be quantified. Advance preparation prevents the researcher from becoming distracted by the complexity of real-time behavior, and provides a consistent method for recording information.

Observational research is particularly susceptible to the experimenter and instrumentation effects described in Chapter 7. These threats to internal validity can be reduced through a well-planned, consistent approach to measurement, and through the audio- or videotaping of participants for later coding.

SURVEY DESIGNS   A **survey** is a self-report measure consisting of questions that can be administered in the form of a personal interview or a questionnaire.

TABLE 9.4 Major Types of Descriptive Designs

Type	Source of Data
Observational design	Direct observation
Survey design	Responses to self-report measure
Content analysis	Materials

Personal interviews can be conducted in person or over the phone. This approach to data collection allows the researcher the flexibility to clarify questions, ask for additional information, and otherwise deviate from a rigid script as necessary.

Questionnaires can be handed to participants, sent via e-mail, or made available on the Internet in an interactive environment. In some respects, they are preferable to personal interviews:

- Questionnaires can reach larger numbers of participants more quickly, easily, and cheaply than personal interviews can.

- Questionnaires are less susceptible than personal interviews to experimenter effects.

- Participants may respond more openly to questionnaires than to an interviewer, given the sense of greater confidentiality (although studies suggest that this is not universally the case).

In other respects, questionnaires can be more problematic than personal interviews. Because the researcher may not be present when the questionnaire is completed, there is a greater likelihood that participants will fail to understand questions or to follow directions properly. Moreover, the response rate for questionnaires may be low and/or biased. Whether a questionnaire is distributed on paper or electronically, the researcher faces a logistical challenge in getting people to respond—as well as the interpretive challenge of figuring out whether there was a systematic tendency for certain kinds of individuals to either respond or not respond to the questionnaire. Imagine a questionnaire on sexual behavior that has been completed and returned by only 60% of students in a particular high school. We might ask about the composition of the remaining 40%. If there is no single predominant reason for their failing to return the questionnaire, then the 60% who did return it constitute a representative sample. But what if most of the 40% of nonrespondents are sexually active but afraid that by returning the questionnaire they might be identified? What if the majority of them are highly conservative in their attitudes toward sexuality and found the questionnaire distasteful or irrelevant? What if they simply happen to be the students involved in the most extracurricular activities, and consequently felt too busy to respond? Each of these scenarios would indicate a nonrepresentative sample. A major challenge for the survey researcher is to figure out the characteristics of a group of people who, by definition, have not provided any information.

CONTENT ANALYSIS DESIGNS   **Content analysis** refers to the collection of information from materials rather than people. The materials may be written or recorded in a visual or auditory format. They may consist of legal documents, program requirements, textbooks, diaries, informal narratives, and so on. Like observational and survey studies, content analysis can be quantitative or qualitative, and more than one quantitative or qualitative approach may be used within a single study. Not all studies are "pure" representatives of single design, in other words. This point is illustrated by the descriptive study on school safety summarized in Spotlight on Research 9.3. The study in question was based on a review of historical documents as well as interviews with a subset of the individuals under study. For the most part, a quantitative approach to content analysis was adopted.

(Qualitative approaches to content analysis are discussed in Chapter 14.)

The Safe School Initiative: A Descriptive Study

The majority of educational studies are conducted by researchers, working individually or in collaborative groups. These researchers are typically affiliated with colleges or universities.

Researchers who work for federal, state, or local agencies also conduct and disseminate research on topics of immediate practical importance. Their research reports may not be published in peer-reviewed journals, but the findings contribute to our understanding of how to improve educational policy and practice. (See further discussion of professional reports in Chapter 3.)

Following the shootings at Columbine High School in 1999, the U.S. Secret Service and the U.S. Department of Education collaborated on the Safe School Initiative, a descriptive case study of 37 school attacks that took place in the United States between 1974 and 2000. The final report of this study appears in Vossekuil, Fein, Reddy, Borum, and Modzeleski (2002)*. Vossekuil and colleagues describe their objective and methodology as follows:

The objective of the Safe School Initiative was to attempt to identify information that could be obtainable, or "knowable," prior to an attack. That information would then be analyzed and evaluated to produce a factual, accurate knowledge base on targeted school attacks. This knowledge could be used to help communities across the country to formulate policies and strategies aimed at preventing school-based attacks . . .

For the purposes of this study, an incident of targeted school violence was defined as any incident where (i) a current student or recent former student attacked someone at his or her school with lethal means (e.g., a gun or knife); and, (ii) where the student attacker purposefully chose his or her school as the location of the attack. Consistent with this definition, incidents where the school was chosen simply as a site of opportunity, such as incidents that were solely related to gang or drug trade activity or to a violent interaction between individuals that just happened to occur at the school, were not included.

Under the study's research strategy, each incident of targeted violence was assigned to a study review team comprised of criminal investigators and social science researchers. At least two reviewers were assigned to each incident.

. . . Beginning with June 2000 and working back in time, researchers explored all relevant, searchable databases

maintained in the public domain or available by subscription, such as public news databases and professional publications, to identify incidents meeting the definition of the study population. Researchers also consulted with law enforcement officials and school violence experts to develop leads on incidents of school violence that might meet the criteria for inclusion in the study constituency.

In the end, researchers identified 37 incidents of targeted school violence involving 41 attackers that occurred in the United States from 1974, the year in which the earliest incident identified took place, through June 2000, when data collection for the study was completed . . .

Information on each incident of targeted school violence identified by Secret Service and Department of Education researchers was drawn principally from primary source materials concerning the incident. These primary source materials included investigative, school, court, and mental health records. In addition, study researchers conducted supplemental interviews with 10 of the perpetrators of incidents of the school-based attacks identified by the Secret Service and the Department of Education.

Each member of the review team assigned to a particular incident independently answered several hundred questions about each case, entering his or her answers to the questions in a codebook. Review team members were instructed to record information gathered from primary sources as it appeared in those sources, and not to engage in interpretation of facts presented.

Information regarding the attacker's demographic characteristics and personal history, including criminal and school history, also were coded. When each reviewer had completed his or her response to the questions, the review team met as a whole to compare responses and produce a single "reconciled" coding of the incident.

Based on this methodology, the researchers calculated a variety of descriptive statistics. Some of the statistics suggested clear trends. All of the attackers were male, for instance. In addition:

Almost all of the attackers were current students at the school where they carried out their attacks (95 percent, n = 39).

In most of the incidents, the attackers carried out the attack alone (81 percent, n = 30). In four of the incidents, the attacker engaged in the attack on his own but had assistance in planning the attack (11 percent, n = 4). In three incidents, two or more attackers carried out the attack together (8 percent, n = 3).

In over half of the incidents (54 percent, n = 22), the attacker had selected at least one school administrator, faculty member or staff member as a target. Students were chosen as targets in fewer than half of the incidents (41 percent, n = 15).

Most attackers had a grievance against at least one of their targets prior to the attack (73 percent, n = 30).

Although the attackers and their methods were clearly similar in some respects, they were also quite diverse in age, family background, and other demographic characteristics. Contrary to popular opinion, the attackers did not show a preponderance of academic failure, social isolation, or disciplinary problems:

The attackers in the largest grouping were doing well in school at the time of the attack, generally receiving As and Bs in their courses (41 percent; n = 17); some were even taking Advanced Placement courses at the time of the incident or had been on the honor roll repeatedly.

Very few of the attackers were known to be failing in school (5 percent, n = 2). Attackers also varied in the types of social relationships they had established, ranging from socially isolated to popular among their peers.

The largest group of attackers for whom this information was available appeared to socialize with mainstream students or were considered mainstream students themselves (41 percent, n = 17).

One-third of attackers had been characterized by others as "loners," or felt themselves to be loners (34 percent, n = 14).

However, nearly half of the attackers were involved in some organized social activities in or outside of school (44 percent, n = 18). These activities included sports teams, school clubs, extracurricular activities and mainstream religious groups.

Nearly two-thirds of the attackers had never been in trouble or rarely were in trouble at school (63 percent, n = 26).

One-quarter of the attackers had ever been suspended from school (27 percent, n = 11).

Only a few attackers had ever been expelled from school (10 percent, n = 4).

Most attackers showed no marked change in academic performance (56 percent, n = 23), friendship patterns (73 percent, n = 30), interest in school (59 percent, n = 24), or school

disciplinary problems (68 percent, n = 28) prior to their attack.

Although the statistics cited above suggest that most of the attackers were functioning well on the surface, in other respects there was evidence of distress:

Almost three-quarters of the attackers felt persecuted, bullied, threatened, attacked or injured by others prior to the incident (71 percent, n = 29).

Although most attackers had not received a formal mental health evaluation or diagnosis, most attackers exhibited a history of suicide attempts or suicidal thoughts at some point prior to their attack (78 percent, n = 32). More than half of the attackers had a documented history of feeling extremely depressed or desperate (61 percent, n = 25).

Almost all of the attackers had experienced or perceived some major loss prior to the attack (98 percent, n = 40). These losses included a perceived failure or loss of status (66 percent, n = 27); loss of a loved one or of a significant relationship, including a romantic relationship (51 percent, n = 21); and a major illness experienced by the attacker or someone significant to him (15 percent, n = 6).

For most attackers, their outward behaviors suggested difficulty in coping with loss (83 percent, n = 34).

The actual attacks tended to be planned in advance and concealed from both adults and targeted victims, although warning signs were detected by adults, and, in many cases, the attackers made their plans known to other students.

In nearly all of the incidents for which information concerning the attacker's conceptualization of the attack was available, researchers found that the attacker had developed his idea to harm the target(s) before the attack (95 percent, n = 39).

In addition, almost all of the attackers planned out the attack in advance of carrying it out (93 percent; n = 38). Moreover, there was evidence from the attacker's behavior prior to the attack that the attacker had a plan or was preparing to harm the target(s) (93 percent, n = 38).

Revenge was a motive for more than half of the attackers (61 percent, n = 25). Other motives included trying to solve a problem (34 percent, n = 14); suicide or desperation (27 percent, n = 11); and efforts to get attention or recognition (24 percent, n = 10).

More than half of the attackers had multiple motives or reasons for their school-based attacks (54 percent, n = 22). In addition, most of the attackers held some sort of grievance at the time of the attack, either against their target(s) or against someone else (81 percent, n = 33). Many attackers told other people about these grievances prior to their attacks (66 percent, n = 27).

In most cases, other people knew about the attack before it took place. In over three-quarters of the incidents, at least one person had information that the attacker was thinking about or planning the school attack (81 percent, n = 30). In nearly two-thirds of the incidents, more than one person had information about the attack before it occurred (59 percent, n = 22). In nearly all of these cases, the person who knew was a peer—a friend, schoolmate, or sibling (93 percent, n = 28/30).

Almost all of the attackers engaged in some behavior prior to the attack that caused others—school officials, parents, teachers, police, fellow students—to be concerned (93 percent, n = 38). In most of the cases, at least one adult was concerned by the attacker's behavior (88 percent, n = 36). In three-quarters of the cases, at least three people—adults and other children—were concerned by the attacker's behavior (76 percent, n = 31).

Experience using weapons and access to them was common for many attackers. Nearly two-thirds of the attackers had

a known history of weapons use, including knives, guns and bombs (63 percent, n = 26). Over half of the attackers had some experience specifically with a gun prior to the incident (59 percent, n = 24), while others had experience with bombs or explosives (15 percent, n = 6).

The Safe School Initiative represents a concerted effort to describe the characteristics of the 41 students who engaged in targeted school violence since 1974. A number of themes emerged from this descriptive study: most of the attackers felt persecuted by other students, expressed suicidal intent, exhibited behaviors that concerned adults, experienced a major loss, planned their attacks, and "advertised" their plans to at least one other person. Although this research does not allow educators to reliably identify attackers before they become violent—it is doubtful we could ever do so with complete accuracy—it does point to warning signs that should be taken seriously in educational settings.

*Vossekuil, B., Fein, R. A., Reddy, M., Borum, R., & Modzeleski, W. (2002). *The final report and findings of the Safe School Initiative: Implications for the prevention of school attacks in the United States.* Washington, DC: U.S. Department of Education, Office of Elementary and Secondary Education, Safe and Drug-Free Schools Program and U.S. Secret Service, National Threat Assessment Center.

Time-Related Change in Descriptive Designs

Many educational researchers are concerned in one way or another with developmental change. For example, educational research and practice have been influenced by more than a century of stage theories pertaining to drawing, spelling, reading, play behavior, perspective taking, moral development, cognition, and a variety of other capacities that were originally the focus of descriptive research in developmental psychology. Educational research also addresses more continuous forms of developmental change in areas such as cognition, learning, motivation, emotion, and social behavior, all of which are grounded in part on descriptive studies.

Developmental change is just one kind of time-related phenomenon of interest to educational researchers. Descriptive research designs (among others) are used to explore differences in populations over time, changes in the availability of educational resources, and the emergence and consequences of new policies and curricula. In short, descriptive research is not only concerned with how people and things are, but also with how people and things have changed and are changing.

In order to document time-related change, two types of descriptive designs can be used: cross-sectional and longitudinal. The distinction between these designs is independent of the method-based distinctions discussed earlier. A survey study, for example, can be cross-sectional or longitudinal, as can any of the other types of descriptive designs.

TABLE 9.5   Time-Related Designs in Descriptive Research

Design	General Approach
Cross-sectional	Collection of data from different age groups at one point in time
Longitudinal	
Panel study	Collection of data from same sample at different points in time
Cohort study	Collection of data from same population at different points in time
Trend study	Collection of data from same population at different points in time as membership in population changes

Cross-Sectional Designs

Cross-sectional designs are based on the collection of data at one point in time. Most studies can be described as cross-sectional. Survey research, for instance, is typically based on the administration of a survey on one occasion. However, the term "cross-sectional" is used here in the more specialized sense of data collection on one occasion that sustains inferences about time-related change. Change is implied by differences between groups that are observed through data analysis. For example, a study on the development of attitudes about substance abuse might focus on a sample of fifth-, eighth-, and eleventh-graders interviewed on one occasion. From the results of the interviews, the researcher would make inferences about the typical progression of attitudes from middle-school through high-school age.

In some cases, a cross-sectional study requires data collection on several occasions. A survey may need to be divided into two parts, for instance, and administered to children on consecutive days so that they do not become fatigued. This can still be considered a cross-sectional approach, because the purpose of collecting data on separate days is to obtain a complete dataset rather than documenting changes in children's attitudes from day to day. In a sense, data collection in this case still occurs on one "occasion."

Longitudinal Designs

Longitudinal designs are based on repeated collection of data over time, in order to document changes on key dimensions. Depending on the type of change of interest, the researcher will use one of three types of longitudinal design: a panel study, a cohort study, or a trend study, see Table 9.5.

PANEL STUDIES   In a **panel study,** the same sample is surveyed at two or more points in time in order to document age- or experience-related changes. For example, a group of students might be interviewed when they are in fifth, eighth, and then eleventh grade in order to survey their attitudes about substance abuse at each point in time. Panel studies provide the most direct information about individual change over time, because data from the same sample are acquired on separate occasions.

COHORT STUDIES   In a **cohort study,** the same population is surveyed at two or more points in time, but a different sample is drawn each time. Whereas a panel study is based on multiple surveys of the same sample, a cohort study is based on multiple surveys of different samples from the same population. For example, in a large school district, fifth-graders might be surveyed in 2010, then in 2013 eighth-graders from the same district would be surveyed, followed by the surveying of eleventh-graders from the district in 2016. Although the composition of the samples is different each time data are collected, researchers can gain a sense of how the population changes over time. Cohort studies serve essentially the same purpose as panel studies. Although panel studies provide more focused information about individual change, the results of cohort studies are more generalizable to a large population.

TREND STUDIES In a **trend study,** the same population is surveyed at two or more points in time as membership in the population changes. Whereas a cohort study requires the tracking of a population over time, a trend study does not "follow" a population but rather focuses on sampling new members as they enter the population. By means of this approach, researchers are able to document historical trends in the population. For example, since 1995 the National Center on Addiction and Substance Abuse (CASA) has surveyed 12- to 17-year-olds' attitudes toward substance abuse. Each year CASA surveys a new sample of teens, and in recent years some alarming trends have been observed. From 2002 to 2005, for instance, there was a 47 percent increase in the number of middle school students who report that drugs are used, kept, or sold at their schools. The extent of increase among high school students during this period of time was 41 percent.

Selecting A Descriptive Design

The descriptive researcher must decide whether to observe participants, administer surveys, examine documents and other materials, or some combination of these methods. At some point, the researcher must also choose whether to make use of a cross-sectional or longitudinal design. This decision will be influenced by the nature of the research question, and by the time and resources available for the study. The advantage of cross-sectional designs is their relative convenience because, by definition, data collection takes place on one occasion. Longitudinal studies tend to require more time and resources, and attrition becomes increasingly problematic as the duration of a longitudinal study increases. At the same time, longitudinal studies represent the most direct and widely respected approach for documenting change over time.

Time-Related Change Revisited

The distinction between cross-sectional and longitudinal designs transcends descriptive research. That is, any study can be described as cross-sectional or at least partially longitudinal. The other designs you have read about thus far (experimental, causal–comparative, correlational) are discussed in cross-sectional terms, but any one of these designs could incorporate longitudinal data collection. For example, Elbro and Petersen (2004) studied the effects of a phoneme awareness training program on the reading skills of a sample of Danish kindergartners who were identified as at risk for dyslexia. The experimental group consisted of at-risk kindergartners who participated in the 17-week program. One control group consisted of at-risk kindergartners who followed their usual classroom routine (which included some phoneme awareness training), while the other control group consisted of not-at-risk kindergartners who followed their usual routine. The reading skills of each group were measured in first, second, third, and seventh grades. Elbro and Peterson found that the at-risk experimental group outperformed the at-risk control group over time (although the dependent variables on which they showed superior performance were different at each grade), but that the not-at-risk control group showed the strongest reading skills throughout the duration of the study. In terms of design, Elbro and Peterson conducted a quasi-experimental study, in the sense that intact groups (at-risk or not-at-risk) were assigned to experimental and control conditions, but the study contains a longitudinal component, in that the effects of phoneme awareness on each group's reading skills were measured repeatedly through seventh grade. If you recall the different types of quasi-experimental designs discussed in Chapter 7, along with the three types of longitudinal designs discussed here, you will see that Elbro and Peterson conducted a nonequivalent control group panel study.

Final Remarks

Just as single-participant designs can address certain research questions more effectively than group designs (see Chapter 8), so there are questions that call for one of the three nonexperimental quantitative designs discussed in this chapter. The most appropriate design for a particular study will depend on the goals and research questions that frame the study. At the same time, the questions addressed by experimental and nonexperimental designs are not completely exclusive. Although some questions about gender differences cannot be addressed through true experimental designs, other topics could be addressed by any type of design. For instance, some research on the effects of changes in sleep habits is causal–comparative, in the sense of examining the effects of naturally occurring variability across children, whereas other studies are correlational, descriptive, or even experimental, as when children are assigned to conditions in which they voluntarily restrict or extend their sleep over a period of time (as you will see in Spotlight on Research 11.2).

A Look Ahead

In chapters 7 through 9 I presented an overview of quantitative research design. Chapters 10 through 12 focus on the analysis and reporting of data—the next step after designing and carrying out a quantitative study.

Applications: A Guide for Beginning Researchers

Here are some ideas from the chapter that will help you plan your research:

- If you plan to do nonexperimental quantitative research, you will have three basic types of designs to choose from.
- Each nonexperimental design is most appropriate for certain types of research questions.
- Choose a causal–comparative design if your interest is in comparing groups. Use matching and other techniques to minimize the impact of differences between groups on extraneous variables.

- Choose one of the correlational designs if your interest is in measuring relationships between variables. Do what you can to contend with interpretive limitations arising from the third-variable problem and other sources.
- Choose one of the descriptive designs if your interest is primarily in describing your participants.
- Regardless of which design you choose, determine in advance whether your plan for data collection is cross-sectional or longitudinal.

Chapter Summary

Causal–comparative, correlational, and descriptive designs provide quantitative information that may not be obtainable through experimental research.

Causal–comparative studies are carried out within the framework and terminology of experimental design. Threats to validity are countered by increasing sample size, obtaining homogeneous or stratified samples, comparing homogeneous subgroups, and/or controlling for group differences.

In a correlational study, variables are shown to be positively or negatively associated, or not associated at all. Correlations are reported in the form of correlation coefficients, correlation matrices, and/or scatterplots. Correlation implies but does not prove causation, since the association between variables may be coincidental, ambiguous as to the direction of causality, or attributable to a third variable. Partial correlation is one way to counter the third-variable problem. The two major types of correlational research are relationship designs and prediction designs.

Descriptive research includes observational designs, survey designs, and content analysis. Developmental change is measured by means of cross-sectional or longitudinal methods. Longitudinal approaches include panel, cohort, and trend studies.

The appropriateness of a particular experimental or nonexperimental design will depend on the goals and research questions that frame a study.

Key Terms

Causal–comparative design	**Curvilinear relationships**	**Criterion variables**
Correlational design	**Outlier**	**Observation**
Correlation coefficient	**Third-variable problem**	**Survey**
Descriptive design	**Partial correlation**	**Content analysis**
Pearson product–moment coefficient	**Suppressor effect**	**Cross-sectional designs**
Correlation matrix	**Relational design**	**Longitudinal designs**
Scatterplot	**Prediction design**	**Panel study**
Linear relationships	**Predictor variables**	**Cohort study**
		Trend study

Exercises

For questions 1–6, identify the type of design implied by each quotation as causal–comparative, correlational, or descriptive. (All quotations are taken from Santrock, 2008).

1. "Researchers have found strong links between self-esteem and happiness. The higher a person's self-esteem, the happier he/she tends to be . . ." (p. 98).

2. "The evidence is strong that reflective students learn more effectively and do better in school than impulsive students" (p. 133).

3. "In 2004, 17.8 percent of children were living in families below the poverty line . . ." (p. 147).

4. "12-year-olds were markedly better than 8-year-olds and slightly worse than 20-year-olds at allocating their attention in a situation involving two tasks . . ." (p. 269).

5. "Individuals with higher scores on tests designed to measure general intelligence tend to get higher-paying, more prestigious jobs . . ." (p. 125).

6. "As they begin to write, children often invent spellings of words . . ." (p. 376).

7. Which of the following designs is most easily undermined by preexisting differences between groups?

a) Correlational
b) Panel
c) Causal–comparative
d) Descriptive

8. What type of correlation would you expect to find between number of illnesses per school year and number of absences from school per year?

a) Positive
b) Negative
c) No correlation

9. What type of correlation would you expect to find between social awkwardness and popularity?

a) Positive
b) Negative
c) No correlation

10. Researchers find a positive correlation between the number of toys children have and their physical health. Which of the following seems most likely to be the third variable accounting for this correlation?

a) Parental permissiveness
b) Gender of parents
c) Parents' socioeconomic status
d) Parent motivation

11. What is the criterion variable in a study that attempts to determine the effects of exposure to televised violence on children's tolerance for aggression?

 a) Exposure to televised violence
 b) Age
 c) Aggressive behavior
 d) Tolerance for aggression

 For questions 12–14, identify the longitudinal study in each description as a panel, cohort, or trend study.

12. Over a 10-year period, the valedictorians of the three high schools in a local school district are interviewed.

13. Fifteen Hispanic kindergartners are sampled from a large school that is predominantly Hispanic. One year later, 15 Hispanic first-graders are sampled from the same school.

14. Twenty-six children with dyslexia are interviewed once per year from third through eighth grade.

15. *Critical thinking question:* When two variables are strongly correlated, would the fact that variable A definitely preceded variable B constitute strong evidence that variable A has a causal influence on variable B?

Answers to Exercises

 1. Correlational   **2.** Causal–comparative   **3.** Descriptive   **4.** Causal–comparative

 5. Correlational   **6.** Descriptive   **7.** c   **8.** a   **9.** b   **10.** c   **11.** d

 12. Trend study   **13.** Cohort study   **14.** Panel study

 15. *Possible answer:* No. The fact that variable A precedes variable B *is consistent with* the possibility that A has a causal influence on B. The fact that A precedes B *suggests that* A has a causal influence on B. But the temporal order of variables does not itself constitute strong evidence of causal influence. Other data, theoretical considerations, and/or common sense are needed in order to build a case that A causally influences B, and that there are no third variables responsible for their apparent relationship.

Suggestions for Further Reading

Research Article: Peskin, M. F., Tortolero, S. R., & Markham, C. M. (2006). Bullying and victimization among black and Hispanic adolescents. *Adolescence, 41*, 467–484.

This quantitative study provides a straightforward illustration of descriptive research design.

Application Article: Roberts, J. E., Burchinal, M. R., & Zeisel, S. A. (2002). Otitis media in early childhood in relation to children's school-age language and academic skills. *Pediatrics, 110*(4), 696–706.

This longitudinal study illustrates several of the correlational research concepts discussed in this chapter.

Extension Article: Caudill, B. D., Crosse, S. B., Campbell, B., Howard, J., Luckey, B., & Blane, H. T. (2006). High-risk drinking among college fraternity members: A national perspective. *Journal of American College Health*, *55*(3), 141–155.

This quantitative study is based on descriptive, causal–comparative, and correlational components.

CHAPTER 10

Descriptive Statistics

Gulfimages/Getty Images

Introduction

There are words, like "dentist," "final exam," and "skydiving," that strike terror in the hearts of some people. "Statistics" is one of those words. Part of the terror (or at least mild anxiety) that people feel when they hear the word stems from their belief that statistics is a kind of mathematics. Statistics is indeed a branch of mathematics, like algebra, geometry, or calculus, and it has played an important role in social science and educational research for more than a century. The term "statistics" also refers to specific procedures (e.g., the formula for calculating the class average on a test) and to the numerical results of those procedures (e.g., the actual class average). If you are one of those people who fears mathematics, it might not be very reassuring, at first, to learn that the next two chapters have a mathematical emphasis.

The good news is that the mathematical discussions in these chapters are ultimately driven by practical interests. Statistical procedures, like other research tools, are designed to help researchers better understand their topics. Although the formulae underlying statistical procedures may be difficult to grasp, the reasons for using these procedures, and the conceptual meaning of what they tell us, tend to be sensible. Consider, for example, a 1978 report claiming that in the United States, male symphony conductors live longer than other men. The evidence for this claim was that the average lifespan for males was 69.5 years, while the average lifespan for an informal sample of male symphony conductors was 73.4 years (Jaffe & Spirer, 1987). These two numbers (average lifespans) are exactly the kinds of statistics we want to consider in this situation. There seems to be a perfectly sensible link between the research question (do male conductors live longer?) and the way statistics on lifespan were calculated and compared.

Although statistics do not lie, they can be miscalculated, or misinterpreted. The "truthfulness" of a statistical procedure is largely dependent on conceptual issues—in particular, the correspondence between what a statistic can tell us, which numbers are used to calculate the statistic, and what we wished to know in the first place. Consider again the finding that male symphony conductors live longer. The individual who reported this finding claimed that there is something about being a conductor that "causes" one to live longer. However, as a later commentator observed, people rarely become conductors prior to age 30. The longevity of symphony conductors should not have been compared to that of the general population, because at least some people fail to live to age 30, thereby lowering the average lifespan calculated for nonconductors. The original research question should have been addressed by comparing the longevity of conductors to that of people who have already survived to the age of roughly 30. In short, what constitutes the "right" versus the "wrong" comparison in this case is not purely a matter of mathematics. We have to consider what we want to know, what the statistical procedure can tell us, and what kind of data should be analyzed.

Definition and Types of Statistics

Statistics can be defined as procedures for describing, integrating, and analyzing data. There are two main types: descriptive and inferential.

Descriptive statistics consist of numbers that summarize the characteristics of a sample. The number of boys in a particular history class, the average age of the boys, their scores on an IQ test, and the extent to which their IQ scores are related to their grades in the particular class are all examples of descriptive statistics. It is impossible to understand the results of a quantitative study without descriptive statistics. At the same time, most research questions cannot be addressed by descriptive statistics alone. The goal of most studies is to draw conclusions about the populations from which samples were drawn, and to achieve this goal inferential statistics are needed.

By definition, **inferential statistics** consist of mathematical procedures that allow researchers to generalize from samples to populations. (The term "statistics" refers to sample characteristics, while the term **parameters** refers to the characteristics of populations.) Inferential statistics are the focus of Chapter 11. In this chapter I provide an introduction to descriptive statistics.

Types of Descriptive Statistics

Depending on what we wish to know, we can make use of four types of descriptive statistics: measures of central tendency, variability, position, and relationship.

Measures of Central Tendency

In quantitative research, measurements of a variable yield numerical values. For example, if we administer an IQ test to 11 students, we will obtain 11 values (i.e., 11 test scores). By arranging those test scores from lowest to highest, we end up with a distribution of values, as in Table 10.1. A **distribution**, then, is an ordered set of values.

By looking at an entire distribution we may learn something. For example, once we have administered an IQ test we can examine the entire distribution of scores. We might notice that they seem especially low, or that they seem to cluster around a particular score, or that they seem distinctive in some other respect. But informal impressions cannot tell us much. In many cases, we would obtain more information by reducing the distribution to a single, representative value. Such values, known as **measures of central tendency**, are not only more informative but also easier to interpret than what we obtain by examining all the numbers in a distribution. The three measures of central tendency that researchers rely on most extensively are the mean, the median, and the mode.

TABLE 10.1 A Distribution of WISC-IV Scores

92	97	97	97	101	104	104	106	107	107	110

THE MEAN   A **mean**, or arithmetic average, is calculated by summing the values in a distribution and dividing the result by the total number of values. For example, the mean of the distribution of IQ scores in Table 10.1 is 102. (You can verify this for yourself by adding the numbers together and dividing by 11.) The mean is an appropriate measure of central tendency when the distribution is based on interval or ratio data, although in some cases researchers calculate means for Likert-scaled questionnaires and other measures that yield ordinal values. Calculations of means from ordinally-scaled data must be interpreted cautiously, because the data are treated as if they were obtained by means of an interval scale.

THE MEDIAN   The **median** is the midpoint of a distribution. That is, it is that point in the distribution above and below which an equal number of values are found. The median of the IQ scores in Table 10.1 is 104. If a distribution contains an odd number of values, the median will be a value that is actually found in the distribution, as in Table 10.1. If the distribution contains an even number of values, the median is defined as the mathematical average of the two middle values. Thus, in a distribution of IQ scores consisting of 84, 96, 100, and 104, the median would be 98. The median is an appropriate measure of central tendency for distributions based on ordinal data. Medians may also be reported for interval or ratio data, particularly when the mean and median are likely to be considerably different. With respect to annual income, for example, the mean is considerably higher than the median—the average American makes more money than the American in the middle. Although annual income represents a ratio scale, treating the variable ordinally is informative if we want to know what the midpoint is.

THE MODE   A **mode** is the most frequently occurring value in the distribution. In Table 10.1, the mode, or modal value, is 97. A distribution will always have a mean and a median, but if no value occurs more than once, there will be no mode. On the other hand, it is possible for a distribution to have two or more modes. The distribution of IQ scores below is "bimodal," because the scores 94 and 99 each occur exactly twice, and no other score occurs more than once:

$$90, 92, 94, 94, 95, 99, 99, 101, 103$$

The mode is most appropriate for nominal data, as when a researcher determines which ethnicity or gender is most prevalent in a particular school district. However, any kind of distribution can have a mode, and in some cases it is revealing when a particular value in the distribution is highly prevalent.

Usefulness of Central Tendency Measures

Notice that each measure of central tendency provides a different kind of information about the distribution it represents. The mean is the most widely used of the three, because it is based on every score in the distribution. In Table 10.1, for example, if the highest score had been 116 rather than 110, the mean would change, but the median and mode would remain the same. Owing to this "sensitivity" to individual values, the mean is more representative of the entire distribution than the median or the mode. On the other hand, when there are outliers, the relative sensitivity of the mean is problematic. One IQ score of 175 added to the data in Table 10.1 would raise the mean to 108 but would have no impact on either the median or the mode. Ultimately, the measures of central tendency that researchers report are determined by the focus of their research questions. In the process of evaluating the construct validity of an aptitude test, for example, researchers frequently consider the mean correlations between scores on the test and scores on established achievement tests. (That is, scores on these tests obtained by each individual in a sample are correlated, and the average correlation across the entire sample is then calculated.) However, researchers also recognize considerable variability in the extent to which ability and achievement are related. In such cases, the *median* correlations obtained across an entire sample are informative too (Das & Naglieri, 2001). This is analogous to the way that a very different perspective on annual income is obtained by considering the median rather than just the mean.

Measures of Variability

Measures of central tendency tell us nothing about variability, or how widely dispersed the scores in a distribution are. Consider the two groups of IQ scores in Table 10.2. As you can see, each group has the same mean, median, and mode (100), but it would be misleading to say that the distribution is the same in each case, since the scores obtained by Group B are more variable. The two most commonly used **measures of variability**, the range and the standard deviation, provide numerical descriptions of variability in a distribution.

THE RANGE   The simplest measure of variability is the **range**, which consists of the difference between the highest and lowest scores in a distribution. In Table 10.2, the range for Group A is only 2, while for Group B it is 20. The range is an easily calculated and readily understood statistic, but it is limited as an estimate of variability because it only takes into account two values in a distribution. This limitation is illustrated by a comparison of the two distributions in Table 10.3. Although the range for Groups C and D is the same, the variability in each group is clearly not. The variability in Group C is much greater, because with only two exceptions, all of the scores in Group D are within one point of the median of the distribution.

THE STANDARD DEVIATION   The most widely used measure of variability, the **standard deviation**, is more informative than the range, because it takes into account every value in the distribution. Informally speaking, the standard deviation tells you something about the average amount of variability in a distribution—in other words, the average amount that each value in the distribution varies from the mean. The more "spread out" the values are around the mean, the greater the

TABLE 10.2 Two Distributions of WISC-IV Scores with the Same Mean, Median, and Mode

Group A	Group B
99	90
100	100
100	100
101	110

TABLE **10.3** Two Distributions
of WISC-IV Scores with the Same Range

Group C	Group D
85	85
90	99
93	99
97	100
101	100
104	100
107	100
109	101
113	101
115	115

standard deviation. The standard deviation for a particular distribution can range from zero (in the unusual case that all the values in the distribution are the same) to an indefinitely large number. Every distribution of interval or ratio data will have one mean and one standard deviation. (Each distribution will also have one range and one median; it may or may not have a mode.)

The standard deviation is defined as the square root of the **variance**, or the average of the squared differences between each value and the mean of the distribution. In order to understand what this definition means, have a look at Table 10.4, which consists of four columns of numbers. A distribution of four IQ scores is given in the far left column of the table. These scores are 98, 102, 102, and 106. As you can see, the mean of this distribution is 102. In the second column of the table, the mean is repeated next to each one of the IQ scores. The difference between each score and the mean (i.e., the "difference scores") are presented in the third column of the table.

Now pause for a moment. Given that we want to know something about the average variability in this distribution, we might be tempted to add up the difference scores and then divide by the total number of scores. That seems like a straightforward way to calculate average variability, since each difference score tells you how much the IQ score varied from the mean. Notice though that adding the difference scores in this case yields a value of zero. This should give you a

TABLE **10.4** Steps in the Calculation of Variance and Standard
Deviation for a Distribution of WISC-IV Scores

Score	Mean	Difference Scores	Squared Difference Scores
98	102	−4	16
102	102	0	0
102	102	0	0
106	102	4	16

Sum of squared differences $= 32$
Variance $= 32/4 = 8$
Standard deviation $= \sqrt{8} = 2.83$

hint as to why the scores must be squared before they are summed. By squaring the difference scores, we guarantee that each one will be a positive number (unless it was zero to begin with). Working only with positive numbers ensures that an IQ score that is 10 points below the mean, for example, will have just as much influence on our calculation of variability as an IQ score that is 10 points above the mean. Intuitively, we know this is what we want, because both scores do vary an equal amount from the mean value.

Back now to our calculation. The rightmost column in Table 10.4 shows the squared difference scores. When these scores are summed and then divided by four, we obtain a value of 8. This is the variance of the distribution. The standard deviation is simply the square root of 8, or about 2.83. Given below is the entire standard deviation formula, along with the steps by which the formula is applied.

$$SD = \sqrt{\frac{\sum (X-M)^2}{N}} \qquad (10.1)$$

In this formula, SD is short for "standard deviation," Σ means "sum of," X refers to each raw score, M refers to the mean of the distribution, and N is the number of scores in the distribution. (As explained in Chapter 11, $N - 1$ is used in the denominator when the population SD is being estimated.) Computationally, the formula is applied by means of the following steps:

1. Calculate the mean of the distribution.
2. Subtract each score from the mean.
3. Square each result in step #2.
4. Add the results of step #3.
5. Divide the result of step #4 by the number of scores in the sample.
6. Calculate the square root of the result of step #5.

Refer back to Table 10.4 for a concrete illustration of these steps.

The mean and standard deviation are the most commonly reported descriptive statistics. Means in published reports are typically labeled either "M," or "$\overline{X}$." Standard deviations are identified by the acronym "SD" or by a lowercase sigma ("σ"). Typically, these statistics are reported together in tabular form, as in the study described in Spotlight on Research 10.1.

Measures of Position

Measures of central tendency and variability tell us about entire distributions, but at times we need information about individual values. In educational settings, for example, we may want to know how well one particular student performed on a test in comparison to his or her peers. **Measures of position** indicate the location of one value with respect to other values in a distribution. As with measures of central tendency, a measure of position is a single number that is more informative and economical than what we would get by scanning an entire distribution. The four most commonly used measures of position are the percentile rank, along with three types of standard scores: the z score, the T score, and the stanine.

Is There a Relationship Between Early Drawing and Early Writing?

Drawing and writing both require planning, physical coordination, and responsiveness to sensory feedback. Given the various similarities between these visual–motor skills, researchers have attempted to determine whether they are developmentally related. In a 2005 article published in *School Psychology International**, Fotini Bonoti, Filippos Vlachos, and Panagiota Metallidou explored whether the quality of children's drawings and their writing performance would be correlated, and whether right-handers would outperform left-handers in both kinds of tasks.

[W]e expected to find positive correlations between children's writing and drawing performance (Hypothesis 1). Specifically, we predicted that poor writers will present lower performance in drawing tasks, especially in those which demand advanced planning and spatial skills, given that previous findings related dysgraphia to difficulties in spatial accuracy (Smits-Engelsman et al., 1998).

The second aim of our study was to investigate if handedness intervenes and influences graphic performance as it is manifested in drawing and writing. . . . There is . . . empirical evidence that visual–motor skills affect handwriting and drawing performance (e.g. Maeland, 1992), as well as evidence which reports differences in right- and left-handed children's performance on visual–motor tasks (Gabbard et al., 1995; Karapetsas and Vlachos, 1997). Left-handers had lower performance in those tasks in comparison to right-handers. As regards the involvement of handedness, then, it was expected that right-handers would perform better than lefthanders in both writing and drawing tasks (Hypothesis 2).

Bonoti and colleagues sampled 91 left-handers and 91 right-handers from the second, fourth, and sixth grades in Volos, Greece. Several drawing and writing tasks were administered:

Children were asked to complete four different drawing tasks. More specifically they were asked to draw two simple favorite topics ("a man" and "a house") and two scenes in which the one object was partially occluded by another ("a man inside a boat" and "a tree in front of a house").

The writing skills of the students were examined individually with the writing scale of the Greek adaptation of the Luria–Nebraska Neuropsychological Battery (Golden,

1981). Concretely, students were examined in three writing tasks: spontaneous writing, copying and writing to dictation. During spontaneous writing the students were asked to write their full name as well as that of their mother. The students were also asked to copy small and capital letters, phonemes, words and sentences from a placard. Then, they were asked to write to dictation single letters, words and sentences. All children were tested individually in their own school by the researcher.

For each drawing task a four-point scale of assessment was developed. The scoring criteria were based on previous empirical data, which suggest a developmental pattern in the depiction of the topics used in the present study (Cox, 1992; DiLeo, 1983; Freeman, 1980; Moore, 1986).

More specifically, in the "man" task a score of 1 was given for a tadpole figure—that is a circle to which the limbs are attached—or a stick figure; a score of 2 for a conventional figure to which the limbs were depicted with single lines; a score of 3 for a conventional figure in which the limbs were drawn with double lines and a score of 4 was administered when the man was drawn with a continuous outline.

In the "house" task a score of 1 was given for the depiction of the main schema of the house; a score of 2 when the defining features of the house were drawn in a wrong way (i.e. the windows attached to the sides, the chimney perpendicular to the roof); a score of 3 when the above mentioned features were placed appropriately and a score of 4 for the depiction of a three-dimensional house.

In the "man inside a boat" task a score of 1 was given when the body of the man was drawn entirely inside the boat; a score of 2 when the body or/and the legs of the man could be seen through the boat (transparency); a score of 3 when the man was presented as standing on the boat and a score of 4 for a visually realistic depiction of the scene.

In the "tree in front of a house" task a score of 1 was given when the two objects were drawn side by side; a score of 2 when the house and the tree were placed vertically on the page; a score of 3 when the house could be seen through the tree (transparency) and a score of 4 when only the visible part of the occluded object was drawn.

Children's productions were evaluated in the three writing tasks depending on the placement of letters (if they leant in the horizontal line of the examination sheet or if they were found over or under this), their form (if corresponded with the classic form of letter or if small and capital letters were confused) and their composition (if their size and their place in the word was correct). The above criteria produced three individual degrees for each writing task, while their sum gave a total score for the writing. The scores differed depending on the student's age and oscillated from a 0 (no error) to 4 for the individual aspects of writing tasks. The total writing score was calculated as the sum of the scores in the three writing tasks divided by 3 in order to maintain the same scoring range (from 0 to 4).

All of the writing and drawing productions were scored independently by two judges, using the scoring criteria mentioned above. Agreement between the two raters ranged from 91–97 percent.

In the analysis we used two scores for drawing performance, one mean score for the performance on simple drawing tasks ("a man" and "a house") and one mean score for the more complex one ("a man inside a boat" and "a tree in front of a house").

The Pearson product–moment correlations between the drawing and writing task scores are presented in the table below.

Correlations marked with an asterisk were significantly different. (The concept of statistical significance is explained in Chapter 11, as are the *t*-tests you will see mentioned in a later excerpt from this study.) With respect to the correlational data, the researchers made the following observations:

It is important to notice here that we recoded the scores on the writing tasks and used a reversed scale in order to match with the scale we used for the drawing scores. Significant positive correlations between children's performance in drawing and performance in almost all the writing tasks were found. It seems, though, that the correlations between performance on the complex drawing tasks and writing were stronger in comparison to those between simple drawing tasks and writing tasks. Also, it is notable that no significant correlation between performance in simple drawing tasks and performance on the copying writing task was found.

In short, the correlational evidence provided some support for the researchers' first hypothesis (i.e., drawing and writing skill would be positively correlated). However, their second hypothesis, that right-handers would outperform left-handers, was not supported. The means (M) and standard deviations (SD) for right- and left-handers, and for the two groups combined, are presented in the table below. (You should be able to see, for example, that the Copying mean for left-handers was 0.91, and the standard deviation associated with that mean was 1.08.)

The researchers found no significant differences between right- and left-handers on any of these variables. However, in further analyses pertaining to their first hypothesis, the researchers did find that left-handers comprised the majority of the poorest writers in their sample.

	Writing Tasks		
	Spontaneous Writing	Copying	Writing to Dictation
Drawing Tasks			
1. Simple tasks	0.151★	0.125	0.178★
2. Complex tasks	0.152★	0.197★★	0.200★★

	Right-handers		Left-handers		Total	
Tasks	M	SD	M	SD	M	SD
Spontaneous writing	0.62	1.25	0.99	1.47	0.80	1.38
Copying	0.71	0.86	0.91	1.08	0.81	0.98
Writing to dictation	0.73	0.88	0.86	1.11	0.79	1.00
Writing (total)	0.69	0.80	0.92	1.08	0.80	0.96
Simple drawings	3.06	0.78	3.00	0.84	3.03	0.81
Complex drawings	3.23	0.87	2.98	1.00	3.11	0.94

In an attempt to investigate the possible differences in drawing performance between students who presented different levels of writing performance, we divided our sample into three subgroups according to their total writing score. Since children's mean performance on this writing test was 0.80 with a SD 0.96, the proficient subgroup consisted of the children who performed over the mean (0 to 0.80). The intermediate subgroup included children whose performance was up to two SD above the mean (scores 0.81 to 2.52) and in the poor writers' subgroup children with the worst performance in writing, that is at least two SD over the mean (scores 2.53 to 4). According to several studies the handwriting quality of children described as "poor hand-writers" can be characterized by inappropriate spacing between letters or words, incorrect shaping of letters, letter inversions and mixing of different letter forms (Rosenblum et al., 2003).

As a next step, we matched each child from the subgroup of poor writers with a child from the subgroup of proficient writers according to their sex, age, and hand preference. We applied a t-test analysis for paired groups with the mean scores on drawing as a dependent variable and the subgroup (proficient-poor) as the independent variable. Significant differences between the two groups were found only in the case of the complex drawing tasks [t(9) = 1.754, p = 0.117 for the simple drawings and t(9) = 3.846, p = 0.005 for the complex drawings]. . . . Proficient writers performed significantly better on these tasks as compared to poor writers. The most interesting finding, though, was that in the subgroup of poor writers almost all of the children were left-handers (eight children out of nine).

Bonoti and colleagues drew the following conclusions from their findings:

Our results showed that there are correlations between drawing scores and scores in all three writing tasks. This finding seems to reinforce claims about the common background on which both abilities are grounded. However, the stronger correlations found between drawing scores on complex tasks and handwriting scores might suggest the important role that spatial skills play on handwriting (Smits-Engelsman et al., 1998; Wann, 1987). It has been reported that complex drawing tasks require advanced spatial skills since the drawer has to depict the partial occlusion of the two objects from a particular viewpoint, taking into account the spatial relationship of the two objects (Thomas and Silk, 1990).

On the other hand, the weaker correlations found between copying and drawing scores can be attributed to the fact that during copying children are engaged in handwriting having a model in front of them, which facilitates them and, therefore, they do not have to make decisions about the process they need to follow. For example, they do not have to decide about the spatial arrangement of letters, the distance between them or their shape and size . . .

Despite the lack of a statistically significant difference between the two handedness groups in drawing and writing performance, we found a great proportion of left-handers among poor writers. This finding supports researchers (Natsopoulos et al., 1998) who suggest that lefthanders consist of heterogeneous subgroups of subjects lying at either extreme of abilities with significantly more subjects performing worse and significantly fewer subjects performing better as compared to right-handers.

Bonoti, F., Vlachos, F., & Metallidou, P. (2005). Writing and drawing performance of school age children. Is there any relationship? School Psychology International, 26(2), 243–255. Quoted with permission from the publisher.

PERCENTILE RANKS   A **percentile rank** indicates the percentage of values at or below a particular value. If 94% of a sample of eighth-graders obtain a raw score of 46 or lower on a test, for example, then a score of 46 on the test represents the 94th percentile. Percentile rankings are familiar to most of us because they are widely used to describe individual results on standardized tests administered in school settings.

In order to understand more about percentile ranks and other measures of position, you should keep in mind each measure of position is a transformation of some raw score. A **raw score** is simply a value that has not been transformed in any way. If a test consisting of 45 items is administered, the number of correct items obtained by one student will be that student's raw score on the test.

Percentile ranks are based on the conversion of raw scores to an ordinal scale. Because the ordinal scale in this case is the familiar one that ranges from 0 to 100%, percentile ranks are intuitively easy to understand, and are often compared across measures. Eligibility for the schoolwide program that serves gifted students, for example, is often based in part on scoring above a certain percentile on several tests of aptitude and achievement.

Although percentile ranks are easy to understand, they should be interpreted cautiously, owing to the fact that the underlying scale is ordinal. A student who scores at the 76th percentile on a test has outperformed a student who has scored at the 75th percentile, but it is impossible to tell how much better the first student performed simply by comparing percentiles. In some parts of a distribution, a small change in raw score will result in a large change in percentile rank, whereas in other parts of the distribution, the same extent of change in raw score may result in a smaller change in rank. For instance, at the low end of a distribution of test scores, where there are relatively few scores, a slight increase in score will be associated with a large increase in rank, while in the middle of the distribution, where the scores are clustered, a slight increase in score may have little or no impact on percentile ranking. Patterns such as this obscure our understanding of student progress when changes in percentile rank are compared across students whose initial scores represent different areas of the distribution. The fact that percentile ranks are based on an ordinal scale also tells us that they should not be combined (e.g., averaged).

A **standard score** indicates the distance of a particular value from some reference point in terms of standard deviation units. Each of the remaining measures of position I discuss in this section is a kind of standard score.

z **SCORES**   A *z* **score** is defined as the difference between a particular value and the mean of the distribution, expressed in standard deviation units. For example, if the mean IQ score for a distribution is 100, and the standard deviation is 15, an IQ score of 115 corresponds to a *z* score of 1.0, because 115 is one standard deviation above the mean. Here are some more examples, assuming a distribution mean of 100 and a standard deviation of 15:

- An IQ score of 130 will correspond to a *z* score of 2.0.
- An IQ score of 85 will correspond to a *z* score of −1.0.
- An IQ of 100 will correspond to a *z* score of 0.

Any raw score in a distribution of continuous values can be converted to a *z* score, regardless of the mean and standard deviation values. If the mean of a distribution is 76, and the standard deviation is 10, then a score of 86 would correspond to a *z* score of 1.0. (Whole numbers are used in these examples to illustrate the nature of a *z* score, but fractional values are much more common in actual studies.) The formula for calculating a *z* score is given below.

$$Z = \frac{(X - M)}{SD} \tag{10.2}$$

In this formula, X is one raw score, M is the distribution mean, and SD is the standard deviation.

You might be wondering why *z* scores are needed when percentile ranks accomplish the same thing (i.e., a description, in precise mathematical terms, of the relative position of a raw score in a distribution). The advantage of *z* scores is that they represent a ratio rather than ordinal scale. This allows comparisons to be made across tests that differ in format, length, difficulty, and content, or across more than one administration of the same test. If we want to evaluate a particular

The Academic Benefits of Inclusion: A Case Study

One provision of the Individuals with Disabilities Education Act (IDEA, 1997) is that students with disabilities should be included in regular classrooms to the greatest extent possible. This approach, referred to loosely as inclusion, can be contrasted with approaches in which students with disabilities are educated in separate, self-contained classrooms. Although some evidence suggests that inclusion is more beneficial, it is difficult to make systematic comparisons, owing in part to substantial variability across schools and districts in the way that inclusion is implemented. In a 2006 article published in *Psychology in the Schools**, Sara Signor-Buhl, Michael LeBlanc, and James McDougal attempted to surmount this problem by comparing inclusion and self-contained classroom approaches within one particular school district.

Specifically, the goal of this project was to evaluate the academic outcomes of children served in self-contained versus inclusive models of special education programming in a mid-size urban school district in Upstate New York. Within this specific school district, both self-contained and inclusion programs were provided to primary-grade students with mild disabilities. Two questions were posed: By using the data available to the district, can the academic progress of students served in self-contained and inclusion programs be compared? If so, what results would be generated? Therefore, this evaluation project was developed within a school district to examine the special education programming that was being offered to their students . . .

District records were reviewed for students in fourth-grade inclusion classrooms attending a midsize urban district in Upstate New York. . . . A comparison group was chosen by

selecting a group of students from self-contained classrooms within the same district. To compare academic outcomes of students in different instructional environments, it was important to ensure that each student selected had participated in a special education program for a reasonable amount of time. Therefore, participants who had not attended their respective self-contained or inclusive education program for at least 2 years prior to this study were excluded. In addition, participants with significant disciplinary difficulties based on documentation of a previous superintendent hearing and/or a manifestation review were excluded from this study to avoid possible confounding variables related to student misbehavior . . .

Intelligence test scores were used to control for cognitive differences between the inclusive setting and the self-contained setting groups. The Wechsler Intelligence Scale for Children, Third Edition *(WISC-III; Wechsler, 1991a) was chosen because it was widely used within the school district. If the WISC-III had not been previously administered, cognitive scores from other available measures were transformed to standard scores comparable to the WISC-III (e.g., $M = 100$, $SD = 15$) . . .*

Performance on the state-mandated high-stakes assessment of English and Language Arts (ELA) skills for all fourth-grade students was used as a measure of achievement for participants in the study. In addition to the ELA results, scores on individually administered achievement tests also were used as measures of academic progress.

Signor-Buhl and colleagues reported two sets of results. First, descriptive statistics were used to characterize the demographics of the sample. In the following description, "SD" stands for standard deviation, "N"

student's performance across several tests of aptitude, for instance, it would be misleading to consider the student's percentile ranks across tests. A more valid representation of the student's performance would be reflected in his or her z scores. This consideration informs the choice of statistics in the study described in Spotlight on Research 10.2.

The other two measures of position I discuss in this section each represent simple transformations of z scores.

T SCORES   A **T score** is the standard score obtained by multiplying a z score by 10 and adding 50. In other words, $T = 10(z) + 50$. The result is an interval scale ranging represents the entire sample size, and "n" is used for the size of a particular group:

> The mean age for the total sample was 11.16 years (SD = 1.06, N = 69), with the mean age of the self-contained group (11.42 years, SD = .68, n = 38) being slightly higher than the mean age of students in the inclusive setting (10.84 years, SD = .73, n = 31). Students in the self-contained group had a mean Full Scale IQ score of 76.19 (SD = 13.08, n = 37), and students in the inclusion group displayed a mean score of 79.32 (SD = 15.99, n = 28). Percentages of students in the self-contained and inclusion groups who qualified for free or reduced lunch status were 89.5 and 87.1%, respectively. Forty-seven percent of the self-contained group and 64% of the inclusion group were male students. The ethnicity of the students in both groups was consistent, with 35% of the students being White, 51% of the students being African American, and 14% of the students identified as Other. Finally, the average time that students in the inclusion group spent in their placement (3.78 years, SD = 1.79) was similar to the average time that students spent in the self-contained group (3.15 years, SD = 2.09).

Next, a technique known as analysis of covariance (ANCOVA), discussed in Chapter 11, was used to explore differences in the effects of inclusion versus self-contained classroom on achievement scores, after controlling for differences in IQ. The focus of this analysis was on the z scores for each measure of achievement. (The gist of the following passage should be clear, but some of the terms may be unfamiliar to you. If so, try rereading it after you finish the next chapter.)

> After controlling for IQ, the ANCOVA results indicated that students in inclusive classrooms performed significantly better on individual measures of reading achievement than

students in self-contained classrooms, $F(1,57) = 7.9$, $p = .007$. Students in self-contained classrooms attained a mean standard score of 65.35 (z = −2.31) on individual measures of reading achievement whereas students in the inclusive classrooms achieved a mean standard score of 73.61 (z = −1.76). After controlling for IQ, the children in the inclusion setting performed approximately .6 SDs better on measures of reading achievement, producing a moderate effect.

> ANCOVA also was used to examine differences in performance between the inclusion and self-contained groups on individual measures of math achievement. After controlling for IQ, students who participated in an inclusive classroom performed at a comparable rate to students who were in self-contained classes, $F(1,57) = .758$, $p = .39$. A small, but positive, effect (SD s = .18) was found for children in inclusive settings. Finally, results of the ELA assessment comparison suggested students in the inclusive classrooms performed better on the ELA than students in self-contained classrooms, $F(1,53) = 12.38$, $p = .001$. Comparison of mean scores against the four performance levels described within the ELA suggested that the self-contained group (M = 583) fell within the lowest performance level whereas the inclusion group (M = 614) fell one performance level higher.

The authors concluded that although their study is limited in its reliance on archival methodology and a single case, the results do suggest that inclusion is beneficial for students.

*Signor-Buhl, S. J., Leblanc, M., & McDougal, J. (2006). Conducting district-wide evaluations of special education services: A case example. *Psychology in the Schools, 43*(1), 109–115. Quoted with permission from the publisher.

from 20 to 80. (A z score of −3 equals a T score of 20, while a z score of 3.0 equals a T score of 80. Transformations for more extreme z scores are not usually calculated.) One reason for converting z scores to T scores is that z scores can be negative and contain decimals, and are therefore less sensible to nonexperts than T scores, which are always positive and represent whole numbers.

If you took an SAT test as part of the college admissions process, you may have wondered why the possible scores on each part of the test ranged from 200 to 800. Raw scores on the SAT and a number of other standardized tests are transformed by means of a formula similar to that for T scores: $100(z) + 500$. The result is a scale ranging from 200 to 800 (here again, transformations are not made for z scores more than three standard deviations above or below the mean). You should be able to see now that a score of 600, for example, would be one standard deviation above the mean, while a score of 700 would be two standard deviations above the mean.

STANINES   A **stanine** (short for "standard nine") is a standard score based on the division of a distribution into a 9-point ordinal scale. Each stanine from 2 to 8 spans exactly half of one standard deviation unit (see Table 10.5). The stanine score is created by doubling a z score, adding five, and rounding the result to the nearest whole number. That is, the formula for a stanine score is $2(z) + 5$. As Table 10.5 illustrates, the scores in a distribution that are closest to the average correspond to a stanine score of 5. In contrast to percentile ranks, z scores, and T scores, stanines indicate position within a group. For this reason, stanines are often reported with standard test results and used in school systems for ability grouping, and to help identify gifted students and other special groups.

Measures of Relationship

Measures of relationship indicate the extent of association between two or more variables. The most commonly used measure of relationship is the correlation coefficient, a descriptive statistic that summarizes the extent of association between two variables. When both of the variables are continuous, the **Pearson product–moment coefficient** is calculated. This is the widely used correlation coefficient that you read about in Chapter 9. Chapter 9 also made note of other coefficients that may need to be calculated, depending on whether each variable is categorical or continuous (see Table 9.1). The formula for the Pearson coefficient is given below.

In order to calculate the Pearson product–moment correlation coefficient, the values obtained for two continuous variables must be lined up in pairs. Then, each value is converted to a z score. The formula for the Pearson coefficient (r) can be written as follows:

$$r = \frac{\sum Z_x Z_y}{N} \tag{10.3}$$

In this formula, $\sum Z_x Z_y$ is the sum of the products of each pair of z scores, and N is the total number of pairs of values.

TABLE 10.5 Stanine Scores
and Corresponding z-Score Ranges

Stanine	z Score
9	Above 1.75
8	1.25 to 1.75
7	0.75 to 1.25
6	0.25 to 0.75
5	−0.25 to 0.25
4	−0.75 to −0.25
3	−1.25 to −0.75
2	−1.75 to −1.25
1	Below −1.25

To illustrate this formula, imagine that you want to know the correlation between years of experience as a kindergarten teacher and instructional effectiveness (as rated on a 9-point Likert scale by an independent observer). After the data are recorded for 10 teachers, we would pair the values obtained for each teacher as follows:

Years	Rating
1	3
2	2
2	3
2	3
3	4
4	6
5	5
6	7
6	9
9	8

Next, we would convert the values to z scores. The mean for years of experience is 4.0, and by using the formula in Eq. 10.1 (with the $N - 1$ denominator), we would find that the standard deviation is 2.5. The mean rating for instructional effectiveness is 5.0, and by using the same formula as before we would find that the standard deviation is 2.4. The resulting z scores are given below. Next to each pair of z scores is the product that results from multiplying them together. (All numbers are rounded up or down for convenience.)

Years	Rating	Product
−1.2	−0.83	1.00
−0.8	−1.25	1.00
−0.8	−0.83	0.66
−0.8	−0.83	0.66
−0.4	−0.42	0.17
0	0.42	0
0.4	0	0
0.8	0.83	0.66
0.8	1.67	1.33
2.0	1.25	2.50

Our last step in calculating the correlation is to sum the products and divide by 10. Doing so results in a Pearson coefficient of .79. This is a very high positive correlation. It appears that teaching experience is positively correlated with ratings of instructional effectiveness—the longer someone has been teaching, the more effective their instruction (as rated by an adult observer). Keep in mind, however, that our "study" was based on only 10 teachers. In Chapter 11 the issue of sample size is revisited, and the question of what can be inferred from such a small sample is addressed quantitatively.

In Table 10.6, the different types of descriptive statistics discussed in this chapter are summarized.

TABLE 10.6 Major Types and Examples of Descriptive Statistics

Type	Examples
Measures of central tendency	Mean, median, mode
Measures of variability	Range, standard deviation
Measures of position	Percentile rank, z score, T score, stanine
Measures of relationship	Correlation coefficient

Computer Applications and Descriptive Statistics

The formulae for descriptive statistics are easy to calculate for very small samples. However, the calculations needed for sample sizes in most published research would take a great deal of time (and introduce many opportunities for error). For reasons of both convenience and accuracy, researchers use statistical software programs to analyze their data, even when the focus is primarily or exclusively on descriptive statistics. Although special programs are available, or can be written, for particular statistical needs, most researchers find that their statistical needs can be met by commercially available software programs that can calculate a variety of descriptive and inferential statistics, along with other functions. The most popular statistical software programs are available through two companies, SAS (*www.sas.com*) and SPSS (*www.spss.com*). Spotlight on Research 10.3 leads you through the use of one such program to create a data file and generate descriptive statistics.

The Normal Curve

"Greetings from Lake Wobegone, where all the women are strong, all the men are good-looking, and all the children are above average."

—*Garrison Keilor*

Mr. Keilor's remark is funny in part because it violates some of our informal assumptions about distributions. We consider it unlikely that all members of any gender would be strong or beautiful, and that all of their children would exceed the state or national average with respect to some variable(s). Rather, we expect that the residents would exhibit variability, with some individuals above and others below average in strength, beauty, and numerous other dimensions. We might even expect a roughly equal number of individuals to be above versus below average, with most people falling at or near the middle.

Consider the following, seemingly unrelated activities:

- You measure the height of every child in the United States on his or her 11th birthday.

- You administer a well-designed spelling test to 15,000 second-graders whose native language is English, and then record the number of errors per child.

- You toss an ordinary coin 1,000 times, and after each set of 20 tosses you record the number of heads and tails obtained.

Using SPSS to Calculate Descriptive Statistics

Statistical Package for the Social Sciences (SPSS) provides several convenient ways of obtaining the descriptive statistics discussed in this chapter. The example illustrated here is based on the use of SPSS 17.0 Statistics for Windows. The purpose of this example is to lead you through the creation and analysis of a simple dataset. Data from the following sample of 12 kindergarten-age participants will be used:

Participant	Gender	Age in Months	IQ
1.	M	61	104
2.	F	66	97
3.	F	60	110
4.	M	67	102
5.	F	62	103
6.	F	67	100
7.	M	63	89
8.	M	66	113
9.	M	73	99
10.	F	65	92
11.	F	67	97
12.	M	62	101

To create a data file, click on the SPSS 17.0 Statistics for Windows icon and select the "Type in data" option. Next, click the "Variable View" option at the lower left of your screen. This will open a blank spreadsheet. What you should see at this point is captured in Screenshot 1 below.

Now you can define the variables in your dataset.

"Name" refers to the name you choose for each variable. In this example, there are three variables: gender, age, and IQ.

"Type" refers to the type of variable. When you click the gray square in the right side of the box, you will find several options. In this example, all variables are numeric, the default option provided by SPSS. (When you enter the data, you will assign one number to male and another number to females).

"Width" refers to the anticipated number of digits required. In this example, the variables are 1 digit (gender), 2 digits (age) and 3 digits (IQ). You will need to change the values accordingly, since SPSS provides default values of 8.

"Decimals" refers to the anticipated number of decimal places. No decimals are needed for this example, and so the choice here should be 0 for each variable.

SCREEENSHOT 1

SCREEENSHOT 2

"Labels" refers to whatever name you wish your variable to be specified by in the output file. This column can be left blank for this example. Likewise, "Values" and "Missing" need not be used in this example.

"Columns" refers to the actual size of the columns in which data are entered. In this example, the default value of 8 can be used.

"Measure" refers to the scale underlying each variable. In this example, gender is nominal, while the other variables should be classified as "Scale," which means either interval or ratio. (Click on the Scale icon in the Gender row to change the scale to nominal.)

After defining the three variables as described above, you will see the screen in Screenshot 2.

SCREENSHOT 3

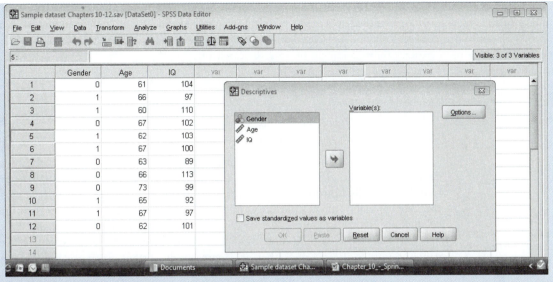

Look again at the options "Data View" and "Variable View" at the lower left of your screen. You can shift back and forth between these fields at any time. The "Data View" option provides the cells in which you enter the actual data. Click on that option now, and you will see three empty columns that already have the names you chose for your variables. Once you have entered the data (using 0 for male and 1 for female), you should see the screen captured in Screenshot 3.

Now use the drop-down menu to select "Analyze," "Descriptive Statistics," and then "Descriptives." You should now see the screen in Screenshot 4.

Double-click each variable, so that it moves to the "Variable(s):" box. Check the box labeled "Save standardized values as variables" to create z scores. Select the "Options" button and make sure that the Mean, Std. deviation, and Range options are chosen. Click on "Continue" and then "OK." You should now be looking at an output file that provides simple descriptive statistics, as in Screenshot 5 below. You should be able to see, for example, that the mean IQ for your sample is 100.58, with a standard deviation of 6.735.

The output file containing your descriptive statistics can be saved and opened again like any other file, or

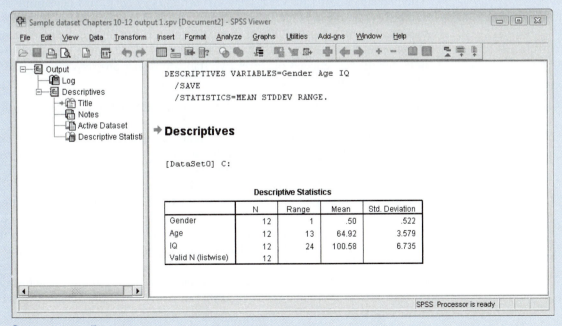

simply deleted. Once you have returned to your data file, you will notice that columns containing z scores for each variable have been created. Information on other descriptive statistics, such as percentiles, median, and mode, can be obtained by means of the "Frequencies" option available under "Descriptive Statistics."

Save the data file—you will be using it again in Chapter 11 to run inferential statistics (see Spotlight on Research 11.1).

What these activities have in common pertains to the distributions they would yield. You would find in each case that most of your observations fall near the middle of the distribution: most 11-year-olds would be average in height or close to the average value, most children would make an average or nearly average number of spelling errors, and most sets of coin tosses would yield 10 heads and 10 tails, or something close to that. You would also find fewer and fewer examples of each value as you look at values that are increasingly distant from the middle of the distribution. There would not be many six-foot-tall 11-year-olds, nor would there be many sets of coin tosses in which you obtained 19 heads and only one tail.

Characteristics of the Normal Curve

In each of the scenarios described above, the distribution would approximate the **normal curve** (also known as the "normal distribution" or "bell curve"), a symmetrical distribution that has several distinctive characteristics:

- The mean, median, and mode are the same.
- Half the values are above the mean, while the other half are below the mean. (This characteristic follows from the equivalence of the mean and the median.)
- The more distant a value is from the mean, the fewer the observations for that value.
- The percentages of scores that fall a given number of standard deviations above and below the mean is the same. (That is, the percentage of scores between the mean and one standard deviation above the mean is the same as the percentage of scores between the mean and one standard deviation below the mean. The same holds for the percentages of scores two standard deviations above and below the mean, and so on.)

Each of these characteristics contributes to the symmetrical appearance of the normal curve, as illustrated in Figure 10.1.

In Figure 10.1, the numbers on the x-axis are standard deviation units—in other words, z scores. The y-axis represents the number of observations for each value. (As you will see, the exact range of the y-axis is unimportant. All you need to remember is that higher points on the y-axis correspond to a greater number of observations for that value.) If you recall that a z score of 0 corresponds to the mean, you can see from Figure 10.1 that the mean of the normal distribution corresponds to the mode (the highest point of the curve). From the symmetry of the curve around the mean, you can also see that the mean corresponds to the median.

The normal curve is a theoretical construct. Researchers rarely if ever obtain perfectly normal distributions in their experiments. What is interesting, and important to the use of inferential statistics, is that in many cases, the greater the sample size, the more the distributions of scores *approximate* the normal curve.

FIGURE 10.1 The Normal Distribution

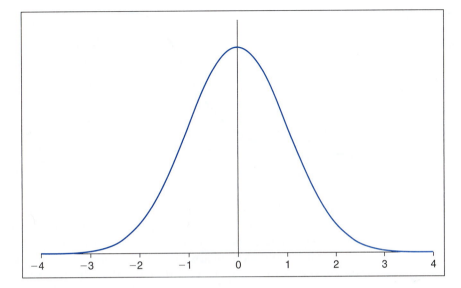

A concrete example may be useful in illustrating the properties of the normal curve. Imagine that we have administered a large number of IQ tests and have, to our surprise, obtained a perfectly normal distribution in which the mean is 100 and the standard deviation is 15. In this example, the curve depicted in Figure 10.1 represents a distribution of IQ test scores transformed into standard deviation units, so that an IQ score of 100 would correspond to a z score of 0, an IQ score of 115 would correspond to a z score of 1, and so on. You can see from the curve that more people obtained the mean score than any other score. The further a score is from the mean, the smaller the number of people who obtained the score. You would also find through calculation that the mean, median, and mode are the same value.

PERCENTILE RANKINGS AND z SCORES Recall that one of the characteristics of the normal curve is that the percentage of scores falling a certain number of standard deviations above and below the mean is the same. Here are a few of the details:

- 34.13% of scores fall between the mean and one standard deviation above the mean.
- 34.13% of scores fall between the mean and one standard deviation below the mean.
- 13.59% of scores fall between one and two standard deviations above the mean.
- 13.59% of scores fall between one and two standard deviations below the mean.
- 2.14% of scores fall between two and three standard deviations above the mean.
- 2.14% of scores fall between two and three standard deviations below the mean.
- 0.13% of scores fall three or more standard deviations above the mean.
- 0.13% of scores fall three or more standard deviations below the mean.

Returning to our example of a normal distribution of IQ scores, in which the mean is 100 and the standard deviation is 15, we can see that 34.13% of scores will fall between 100 and 115, and that 47.72% of scores will fall between 100 and 130. We can also see that 68.26% of scores fall between 85 and 115, and so on. Figure 10.2 provides an illustration.

FIGURE 10.2 Areas Under Curve for Normal Distribution of IQ Scores

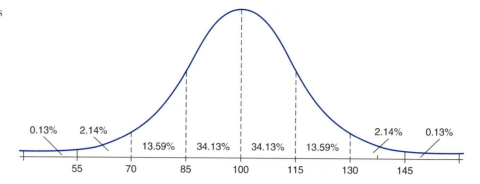

You should be able to see now that when the values of a variable are normally distributed, raw scores, percentile rankings, and z scores can be translated into each other. The mean value of a normal distribution is by definition the 50th percentile. A raw score that is exactly one standard deviation above this mean can be converted to a z score of 1.0, and either the raw score or the z score can be converted to the 84th percentile. (A z score of 1.0 corresponds to the 84th percentile because the mean score is greater than 50% of the scores, and one standard deviation above the mean consists of another 34.13% of the scores. That is, 50% + 34.13% = 84.13%, which can be rounded down to 84%. Simple calculations can be used to determine percentile rankings for z scores that are not whole numbers.) Thus, if the mean of a normally distributed set of test scores is 80 and the standard deviation is 8, then a score of 88 on the test would correspond to a z score of 1.0 and represent the 84th percentile. A score of 72 on this test would correspond to a z score of -1 and represent the 16th percentile. (z scores of greater than 3.0 or less than -3.0 are rarely observed when data are normally distributed. Only 0.26% of observations—less than three in a thousand—can be expected to fall above or below these values.)

The relationships among the normal curve and several of the descriptive statistics discussed in this chapter are summarized in Figure 10.3.

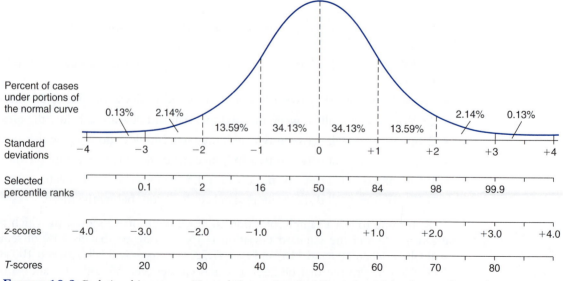

FIGURE 10.3 Relationships among Normal Curve, Standard Deviation Units, Percentile Ranks, z Scores, and T Scores

Other Distributions

Many of the statistical tests described in the next chapter depend on the assumption that the distribution of population values is normal. However, it is rare for sampling distributions to be perfectly normal. Two dimensions on which a distribution may vary from the type of normal curve described earlier are kurtosis and skew.

Kurtosis

Kurtosis refers to the extent to which values cluster around a particular point in a distribution. The normal distribution has a kurtosis value of 0. A positive value for kurtosis indicates a relatively high degree of cluster, while negative kurtosis indicates relatively little cluster (see Figure 10.4 for illustration). Roughly, the higher the kurtosis, the lower the standard deviation of the distribution. High values of kurtosis are problematic if the purpose of the measure is to distinguish among the individuals measured. We may conclude, for example, that a test is not sensitive enough if all of the scores cluster very tightly around a particular value. Low values of kurtosis may be problematic if we wish to characterize the distribution with a measure of central tendency such as the mean—a somewhat misleading figure given the extensive variability in the distribution.

Skew

Skewness, or skew, refers to the extent to which the distribution is asymmetrical. Because the normal distribution is symmetrical, it has a skewness value of 0. A **positively skewed distribution** is asymmetrical because there are more scores at the upper end of the distribution, resulting in the mean being greater than the median, and the median being greater than the mode. Distributions of reaction time, for example, tend to be positively skewed because there are lower limits to how quickly people can respond to a stimulus, but virtually no upper limit in how slowly they respond. A **negatively skewed distribution** is asymmetrical for the opposite reason: There are more scores at the lower end of the distribution, resulting in the mean being less than the median, and the median being less than the mode. An extremely difficult test, on which most students do poorly (and some give up altogether) might yield a negatively skewed distribution. Figure 10.5 illustrates distributions with positive and negative skew.

Numbers and Pictures

Although skewness indicates non-normality, not all symmetrical distributions are normal. One example would be a symmetrical bimodal distribution, as illustrated in Figure 10.6. It is important to remember that both descriptive statistics and graphic

FIGURE 10.4 Three Distributions Illustrating Different Degrees of Kurtosis

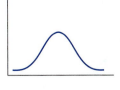
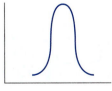
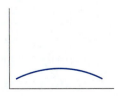

Normal curve   Strongly positive kurtosis   Strongly negative kurtosis

FIGURE 10.5 Distributions Exhibiting Positive Skew (a) and Negative Skew (b)

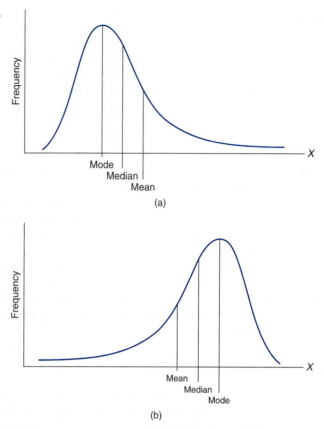

representations are helpful in understanding distributions. Descriptive statistics are the primary source of information, in part because graphs can be misleading (as discussed in Chapter 12), and in part because much of the information available in graphs is given in the statistical data or can be inferred from that data. At the same time, the graph of a distribution can reveal information that is not readily apparent from the descriptive statistics. You read about one example of this point in the discussion of scatterplots in Chapter 9. A second example is that descriptive statistics do not reveal information about local changes in frequencies—the "peaks" and "valleys" that can be seen when a distribution is graphed. A third example is the distribution with two modes shown in Figure 10.6.

By looking at the descriptive statistics associated with Figure 10.6 you would find that the mean and median of the distribution are both 4, and that the standard deviation is relatively large. But the peculiar shape of the distribution would not

FIGURE 10.6 Symmetrical Bimodal Distribution

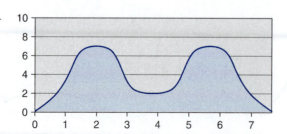

be fully apparent without a graph, and you might not realize how misleading it would be to use the mean as an expression of central tendency. Examining the graph would reveal a perfectly symmetrical bimodal distribution and perhaps call for further data analysis. For instance, you might suspect that your sample consists of two distinct groups of participants, each providing scores on some measure that are normally distributed around the group mean, thereby yielding two slightly overlapping normal distributions.

A Cautionary Note

USA Today has come out with a new survey—apparently, three out of every four people make up 75% of the population."

—David Letterman

You may have heard about (or personally witnessed) the misuse of descriptive statistics in media reports, commercials, and political campaigns. Misuse also occurs sometimes in educational settings. In 1979, for instance, the chief administrator of public schools in New York City reported a 45% dropout rate among high school students. However, "dropout rate" was operationalized in the chancellor's report as the difference between the number of graduating seniors and the number of students who had entered high school four years earlier. The result is an inflated estimate of dropout rate, because some students transferred to different school districts rather than dropping out, while other students counted as dropouts were actually enrolled in evening or work-study programs (Jaffe & Spirer, 1987). In 2008, almost three decades later, the U.S. Department of Education was still contending with inappropriate calculations of dropout rates used by some states.

Unfortunately, educational research is not immune to the misuse of descriptive statistics. Studies are often criticized on the grounds that key statistics were incorrectly applied or interpreted. This is not to say that the misuse is intentional. The issues tend to be highly technical, and in some cases there is simply a less-than-ideal match between the kinds of statistics used and the conclusions the researcher wishes to draw. It is not always easy to select the right statistics. For example, how should we operationalize the "typical" number of children per family in a particular school district? This seems like a straightforward question, but the mean, median, and mode are each "typical" in some sense, and thus none of these options is clearly right or wrong in itself. We have to consider whether we are most interested in the average family, the family in the middle, or the most commonly observed type of family. The selection and interpretation of a measure of central tendency, or any other type of statistic, ultimately rests on an understanding of what each statistic can tell us, and on exactly what it is we wish to know.

A Look Ahead

This chapter has presented an introduction to descriptive statistics, the foundation of quantitative research. Inferential statistics, which are essential to the process of generalizing from samples to populations, are taken up in Chapter 11. In Chapter 12

I explore the representation of statistical information by means of visual aids such as tables and graphs, as well as complex models.

Applications: A Guide For Beginning Researchers

Here are some ideas from the chapter that will help you plan your research:

- Choose the software program you will use to analyze data. Figure out how you will learn to use this program if you are not already familiar with it.
- Choose the descriptive statistics that best address each question you have about your data.
- At least some of the descriptive statistics you choose should provide information of direct relevance to your research question.

Chapter Summary

Descriptive statistics, the focus of this chapter, can be contrasted with inferential statistics. The main types of descriptive statistics include measures of central tendency, variability, position, and relationship.

Measures of central tendency and variability provide information about distributions. Specific measures of central tendency include the mean, median, and mode. Measures of variability include the range and the standard deviation.

Measures of position provide information about individual scores. Specific measures of position include percentile rank, along with three types of standard scores: the z score, the T score, and the stanine. Measures of relationship provide information about the extent of association between variables. A specific measure of relationship is the Pearson product–moment coefficient.

Descriptive statistics are usually calculated by means of computer software programs such as SAS and SPSS.

In a normal distribution, the mean, median, and mode are the same, as are the percentages of scores that fall a given number of standard deviations above and below the mean. As a result, raw scores, percentile rankings, and z-scores associated with a normal distribution can be translated into each other. A distribution may deviate from normality along the dimensions of kurtosis and skew.

The usefulness of a descriptive statistic depends on the nature of the statistic and what we wish to know.

Key Terms

Statistics	**Distribution**	**Median**
Descriptive statistics	**Measures of central tendency**	**Mode**
Inferential statistics		**Measures of variability**
Parameters	**Mean**	**Range**

Standard deviation	T score	Normal curve
Variance	Stanine	Kurtosis
Measures of position	Measures of relationship	Skewness
Percentile rank		Positively skewed distribution
Raw score	Pearson product–moment coefficient	
Standard score		Negatively skewed distribution
z score		

Exercises

For questions 1-7, refer to the following distribution of test grades:

$$60, 75, 77, 84, 85, 90, 92, 93$$

1. What is the mean?

2. What is the median?

3. What is the mode?

4. What is the range?

5. What is the standard deviation?

6. What is the z score corresponding to a grade of 84?

7. What is the T score corresponding to a grade of 84?

For questions 8–12, name the measure of central tendency or variability that would address the question most directly.

8. Which of five non-English languages is most commonly spoken among a sample of bilingual students?

9. What is the difference between the highest and lowest annual salaries for principals in a particular school district?

10. Which student, out of a classroom of 15 students, obtains the eighth highest test score?

11. How much do the parents in a particular school district tend to vary in annual income?

12. What is the average number of absences per year recorded for each student at a particular high school?

For questions 13–16, assume a normal distribution of test scores for which the mean is 90 and the standard deviation is 8.0.

13. What is the z score corresponding to a 74 on the test?

14. What is the percentile rank corresponding to a 74 on the test?

15. What is the raw score corresponding to a *z* score of 2.0?

16. What is the raw score corresponding to the 16th percentile?

17. *Critical thinking question:* A posttest-only control group design (see Chapter 7) is used to compare the effects of participation in a summer program at the local zoo on fifth-graders' knowledge of biology. Ninety-two fifth-graders from a particular school district who participate in the program are compared to a random sample of 92 fifth-graders from the same district who do not participate in the program. Knowledge of biology is measured at the outset of the school year by means of a test consisting of 30 multiple-choice questions. What descriptive statistics can be used to help evaluate whether participation in the summer program influenced students' knowledge of biology?

Answers to Exercises

1. 82   **2.** 84.5   **3.** There is no mode   **4.** 33

5. 10.34. Using the formula in Eq. 10.1, the standard deviation is calculated as follows:

X	M	X-M	$(X-M)^2$
60	– 82 =	– 22	484
75	– 82 =	– 7	49
77	– 82 =	– 5	25
84	– 82 =	2	4
85	– 82 =	3	9
90	– 82 =	8	64
92	– 82 =	10	100
93	– 82 =	11	121

$$\Sigma(X - M)^2 = 856$$
$$\Sigma(X - M)^2/N = 107$$
$$\sqrt{\Sigma(X - M)^2/N} = \mathbf{10.34}$$

6. 0.19. Using the formula in Eq. 10.2, $z = (84-82)/10.34 = \mathbf{0.19}$

7. 51.9. Using the formula given in the text, $T = 10(.19) + 50 = \mathbf{51.9}$

8. Mode   **9.** Range   **10.** Median   **11.** Standard deviation   **12.** Mean   **13.** −2.0

14. 2nd percentile   **15.** 106   **16.** 82

17. *Possible answer:* Mean test scores for students who did versus did not participate in the program can be compared. The median scores of the two groups could also be compared. If the program had a strong impact on the knowledge covered in the test, the mean and median would be higher for the students who participated in the program than for the other group. Ranges and standard deviations would give some indication of the extent of variability within each group. If the program had a strong impact, both measures of variability might be smaller for the group that participated in the program. Likewise, if the program had a strong effect, the distribution for the group that participated in the program might be more positively skewed. Finally, point biserial correlations could be computed between the dichotomous variable (group) and the continuous variable (test score).

Suggestions for Further Reading

Research Article: Burns, M. K., VanDerHeyden, A. M., & Jiban, C. L. (2006). Assessing the instructional level for mathematics: A comparison of methods. *School Psychology Review*, *35*(3), 401–418.

This empirical study relies on many of the statistical concepts discussed in this chapter, as well as reliability and validity concepts.

Application Article: Deutscher, B., Fewell, R. R., & Gross, M. (2006). Enhancing the interactions of teenage mothers and their at-risk children. *Topics in Early Childhood Special Education*, *26*(4), 194–205.

This experimental study makes use of several of the statistical concepts discussed in this chapter.

Extension Article: Sadler, P. M., & Good, E. (2006). The impact of self- and peer-grading on student learning. *Educational Assessment*, *11*(1), 1–31.

This empirical study makes use of numerous statistical concepts discussed in this chapter, as well as concepts from prior chapters such as meta-analysis, effect size, scatterplots, and partial correlation.

CHAPTER 11 Inferential Statistics

John Glustina/Getty Images

After studying this chapter, you will be able to answer the following questions:

- What is sampling error and why is it important?

- What is hypothesis testing?

- What is statistical significance and how is it determined?

- What are effect sizes and how are they determined?

- What are the major types of parametric statistics and how is each type used?

- What are nonparametric statistics and how can they be used?

This chapter will prepare you to do the following:

- Understand and evaluate the use of inferential statistics in published research

- Select appropriate inferential statistics for data analysis

- Interpret the results of inferential data analysis

Introduction to Inferential Statistics

As researchers, one of the main reasons for using statistics is to overcome a logistical barrier: We want to understand populations, but we can only study samples. Through intervention research, for instance, we try to figure out the best methods for teaching academic skills, enhancing motivation, or preventing bullying, and we hope to find the methods that work best among *all* students at a given age, but we can only test our interventions among particular groups. This would not be problematic if our samples were perfect microcosms of the populations from which they were drawn, but samples always diverge from their populations to a greater or lesser extent, and we cannot be certain about the extent of divergence. We have two ways to reduce the uncertainty. The first way, discussed at length in Chapter 4, is to ensure to the greatest extent possible that each sample is representative of the population from which it was drawn. The second way, and the focus of this chapter, is to make use of inferential statistics.

Inferential statistics are mathematical procedures for determining the likelihood that sample characteristics reflect population parameters. Through inferential statistics, researchers generalize from samples to populations and thereby advance one of the fundamental goals of quantitative scientific inquiry. If a study is based on an experimental or causal–comparative design, inferential statistics are used to decide whether differences between samples reflect actual population differences. In a correlational study, inferential statistics are used to estimate how strongly variables are associated in the actual population.

Guide to This Chapter

This chapter is divided into two parts. In the first part I sketch in the conceptual foundation for inferential statistics. In the second part I describe the main types of inferential statistics that researchers use. The content of the chapter is cumulative—later discussions make more sense in light of earlier ones—and you will find that as the chapter progresses, conceptual points are revisited in increasingly quantitative terms. These comments are not meant to alarm you but to provide some guidance as to how to approach the chapter. If you find parts of this chapter difficult, rereading the entire chapter may help. And if it seems like a particular discussion is simply restating an earlier one in more specific or mathematical terms, you are probably right.

To help illustrate the conceptual discussions in the first part of the chapter, I will periodically refer to a 2006 study looking at gender differences in cognition among 11- and 12-year-olds in the United Kingdom. The authors of the study, Steve Strand, Ian Deary, and Pauline Smith, obtained scores on the Cognitive Abilities Test (CAT) from a representative sample of roughly 324,000 students in the United Kingdom who were tested at ages 11 and 12. Scores were obtained for the entire CAT, and for three batteries, or subtests:

- Verbal reasoning (sentence completion, analogies, etc.)
- Quantitative reasoning (number series, equation building, etc.)
- Nonverbal reasoning (figure classification, figure analysis, etc.)

TABLE 11.1 CAT Battery Means by Gender (with Standard Deviations in Parentheses) in Strand, Deary, and Smith (2006)

CAT Battery	Boys	Girls
Verbal	98.4 (15.1)	100.6 (14.5)
Quantitative	99.4 (15.0)	98.9 (13.8)
Nonverbal	99.7 (14.8)	100.2 (13.9)
Total score	99.1 (13.5)	99.9 (12.7)

Mean scores for each of the three batteries, and for total score, are given separately for boys and girls in Table 11.1. (Standard deviations associated with each mean are given in parentheses.)

The researchers described the results in Table 11.1 as follows:

All sex comparisons are highly statistically significant; girls had a higher mean score than boys on the verbal battery, the non-verbal battery and [total] mean CAT score, and boys had a significantly higher mean score than girls on the quantitative battery.

(Strand et al., 2006, p. 470)

One of the main goals of the first part of this chapter is to illustrate what it means to describe a comparison, or any other finding, as "statistically significant."

Sampling Error

In the quotation at the outset of this chapter, Rutherford presents a rather dim appraisal of statistics. Roughly, what he meant is that we would not need (inferential) statistics to draw conclusions from experiments conducted with entire populations—these would be, in a word, "better" experiments. That may be true, but it is rarely possible for educational researchers and other social scientists to study entire populations. We will never find enough time, resources, or willingness among participants to study *everyone*. (Even the enormous sample obtained by Strand et al., 2006, only represents about 45% of the total 11- and 12-year-old UK population.) We must accept the fact that scientific knowledge about populations is based almost exclusively on results obtained with samples.

Sampling error refers to the discrepancy between sample and population characteristics. Each sample will tend to differ from the population from which it is drawn along most or all of the dimensions of central tendency and variability discussed in Chapter 10. Sampling error is not the researcher's fault (as is the case with sampling bias, as discussed in Chapter 4). Rather, the term "error" simply refers to the random differences that are inevitable when examining one subset of a population.

Suppose we were interested in studying the intelligence of American 16-year-olds and chose to administer an IQ test to a large number of samples, each consisting of 50 students selected at random from U.S. high schools. We would probably find that each sample has at least a slightly different mean from the rest, and that few if any of the samples reflect the exact mean of the 16-year-old American population (assuming that the latter is known). In short, we would find sampling error associated with the scores obtained from all or almost all of our samples. Considering that our goal is to generalize from sample to population, we might begin to worry.

Fortunately, sampling error is not a completely random phenomenon. The next sections of the chapter show that sampling errors are normally distributed and have the same standard deviation as the population. Later, you will find that these characteristics help us estimate population characteristics, the ultimate goal of most quantitative scientific inquiry.

Normal Distribution of Sampling Errors

If an infinite number of samples are obtained from a population, the sampling errors will be normally distributed. As a result, samples that are similar to the population in central tendency and other characteristics are more common than samples that reflect extreme sampling error, and we can make predictions about the incidence of different amounts of sampling error. To illustrate what the previous two sentences mean, imagine that we have an IQ test for which the population mean is 100 and the standard deviation is 15. We then take the following steps:

- Administer the test to a sample and record the mean score.
- Return the sample to the population and obtain a second sample.
- Administer the test to the second sample and record the mean score.
- Return the second sample to the population and obtain a third sample.
- Continue sampling, testing, and recording mean scores indefinitely.
- Create a distribution consisting of the mean scores obtained from all the samples.

We would find that as the number of samples increases, the distribution of scores we obtain will more closely approximate a normal curve. If we could test an infinite number of samples, the distribution of scores would be completely normal. In other words, assuming that the population mean is 100, we would find that samples with means of 100 would be most common. Samples with means of 101 or 99 would be very common too. We would also find that 68.26% of the samples have means between 85 and 115, while only 0.26% of the samples have means below 70 or above 130. These and other expected patterns reflect the characteristics of the normal curve discussed in Chapter 10 and revisited in Figure 11.1.

In order to show that sampling errors are normally distributed, we need to take two more steps:

- Calculate the sampling errors by subtracting the mean of each sample from the population mean.
- Create a distribution of all the sampling errors.

FIGURE 11.1 Areas Under Curve for Normal Distribution of IQ Scores

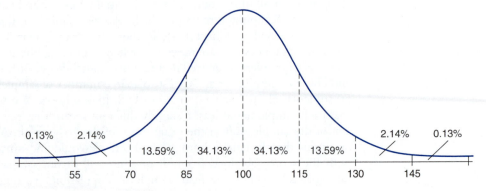

We now have a distribution consisting of an infinite number of scores. Each score is the sampling error that we obtained by subtracting one sample mean from the population mean. Importantly, we would discover that this infinitely large set of sampling error values is normally distributed. Sampling errors of zero would be most common (because samples with means of 100 would be most common). Sampling errors close to zero would be more common than larger sampling errors. And, the kinds of sampling errors we find would be predictable. We would find, for example, that 68.26% of the samples have sampling error values ranging from −15 to 15, since 34.13% of the samples would have means ranging from 85 to 100, while another 34.13% of the samples would have means ranging from 100 to 115. Other predicted outcomes can be calculated by looking at the details of Figure 11.1. Because the normal curve in this figure is symmetrical around the mean value, the mean of sampling errors would be zero. Given infinite sampling, we would find an equal number of samples scoring, say, 2.5 standard deviations above the mean as we would samples scoring 2.5 standard deviations below the mean. The same result would be obtained for any other possible score.

In the next few sections of the chapter, you will see further references to infinite sampling. Infinite sampling is not something we actually do, of course. Rather, it is an imaginary procedure that allows us to estimate our chances of obtaining a sample with particular characteristics, given all possible samples that could be obtained. (Each time infinite sampling is discussed, you should assume the sort of replacement described in the bullet items above: after each sample is obtained, it is returned to the population before another sample is taken.)

Same Variability as Population for Sampling Errors

The distribution of sampling errors reflects the same extent of variability as the population. In our IQ study, we would find that as the number of samples increases, the standard deviation of the distribution of sampling errors would more closely approximate that of the population. Given an infinite number of samples, the standard deviation of the sampling errors and that of the population would be identical.

Standard Error Estimates

The previous discussions were based on the assumption that the mean and standard deviation of the population are known. In actual practice, we rarely know those values. How, then, can we estimate sampling error if we do not know the true values from which the samples diverge? How can we know how wrong we are when we do not know the right answer?

Because sampling errors are normally distributed and reflect the same variance as the population, we are able to estimate the extent of sampling error reflected in a particular sample, even though the population values are unknown. Measure of variability called **standard error estimates** provide us with quantitative estimates of the extent to which sample characteristics diverge from population parameters. The importance of a standard error estimate is that it tells us the likelihood that we have correctly inferred population characteristics from sample data.

The type of standard error estimate of greatest relevance to this discussion is the standard error of the mean.

Standard Error of the Mean

The **standard error of the mean** can be defined as the standard deviation of the sampling errors for a particular population. In other words, it is an expression of the amount of variability we would expect to find in the sampling errors if we had measured an infinite number of samples from the population. If the mean IQ score of a population is 102, and everyone in that population happens to score between 101 and 103 on the IQ test, the standard error of the mean would be very small, because each time we took a sample from this population, we would find very little sampling error (since nobody in any sample we take could deviate more than one point from the mean). On the other hand, imagine that the mean IQ score in the population is 102 but the scores range from 35 to 180, and the scores are fairly evenly distributed across this range of values. Here we would expect to find a broad range of sampling errors, because the means of the samples we take could vary widely from sample to sample (and would in fact vary widely if an infinite number of samples are measured).

Although we cannot obtain an infinite number of samples from a population, and we rarely know the population parameters anyway, we can estimate the standard error of the mean on the basis of a single sample by using the formula below.

$$Se_x = \frac{SD}{\sqrt{N-1}}$$

(11.1)

In this formula, Se_x is the standard error of the mean, SD is the standard deviation of the sample, and N is the sample size.

You can see from the formula that as the standard deviation of the sample increases, the standard error of the mean will increase too. In other words, the more variability there is in a sample, the more variability we could expect to find in the distribution of sampling errors. In the case in which a population mean is 102 and every score falls between 101 and 103, any one sample of test scores we obtain would show very little variability (i.e., the sample standard deviation would be very low) and our standard error of the mean formula would correctly estimate very little variability in the distribution of sampling errors.

You can also see from the formula that as the sample size increases, the standard error of the mean will decrease. Intuitively, this makes sense. As the sample size approaches that of the population, the amount of variability that could exist in the sampling errors will decline. If we could measure several samples, each consisting of 99% of the same population, we would only find a tiny amount of sampling error, because the composition of each sample would be nearly identical. Any one sample we measure would be virtually identical to the population, and to any other sample we could have measured.

Now think back to the Strand et al. (2006) study introduced near the beginning of the chapter. As you can imagine, standard error estimates in this study would be quite small, owing to the vastness of the sample. For example, given that approximately 161,700 boys completed the Verbal battery of the CAT and the standard deviation for their scores was 15.1, the standard error of the mean we would calculate from the formula above is .038. We can be very confident that the mean Verbal score obtained for boys (98.4) is an accurate estimate of the population mean, because the average extent of sampling error we would expect to find, if we took an infinite number of samples from the population of 11- and 12-year-old UK students, would be less than one point. This is not to say that we could *never* obtain a wildly misrepresentative sample. We might sample 1,000 11- and 12-year-old boys, and find that their mean IQ is 116, then test another sample of 1,000 boys from the same UK population and find that their mean IQ is 86. But these findings would be a fluke. On average, the mean we would obtain for any sample will diverge .038 points from the population mean we infer.

You might be wondering then what we have inferred about the population mean. The mean Verbal score for boys in Strand and colleagues' study is 98.4, and the standard error of the mean is .038. Do these figures tell us that the population mean is 98.4 *plus* .038? Or 98.4 *minus* .038? The answer is neither, as you will see in the next section.

CONFIDENCE INTERVALS An important application of the standard error of the mean is the calculation of a **confidence interval**, the range of values within which the population mean is expected to fall, to some degree of likelihood. Sample data do not allow us to calculate the population mean, but rather how likely that mean will fall within a given range of values.

To understand what confidence intervals are, imagine that you have administered an IQ test to a sample of 101 16-year-olds and obtained a mean of 102 with a standard deviation of 20. Using Equation 11.1, you can calculate the standard error of the mean through the following steps:

- To obtain $N - 1$, subtract 1 from 101. The result is 100.
- To obtain $\sqrt{N - 1}$, calculate the square root of 100. The result is 10.
- To obtain $SD/\sqrt{N - 1}$, divide 20 by 10. The result is 2.

Now you know that the standard error of the mean for your sample of test scores is exactly 2. Assuming that the sample is normally distributed, you are ready to estimate something about the population mean, even though you have no information about the population other than what you have learned from the sample. What you can estimate now is the likelihood that the population mean will fall within a particular range of values. Recall, for example, that in a normal distribution, 68.26% of values will be found between one standard deviation above and below the mean. In our IQ study, we have estimated that the standard deviation of sampling errors is 2. Since the mean of our sample is 102, we can infer that there is about a 68% chance that the population mean falls between 100 and 104. To take another example, since only 0.13% of values in a normal distribution will be three standard deviations above or below the mean, we can infer that there is greater than a 99% chance that the population mean falls between 96 and 108. In sum, the standard error of the mean can be used to estimate a population mean to a given degree of probability.

At this point you should be able to see a tradeoff between precision and confidence in the estimation of population parameters. Narrower confidence intervals are desirable, because they provide us with more precise estimates concerning the population. In our IQ study, we would rather conclude that the population mean falls somewhere between 100 and 104 than between 96 and 108. But narrower confidence intervals are associated with lower probabilities—if we conclude that the population mean is between 100 and 104, we are more likely to be wrong than if we conclude that the population mean will range from 96 to 108. The more confidence we want to have in our estimate of a population parameter, the wider the confidence intervals will have to be. (And yet as we widen our confidence intervals, precision declines. We can be very sure that the population mean falls between 30 and 200, but that does not tell us much.)

Now we can answer our earlier question about how to estimate the mean Verbal score for the population of 11- and 12-year-old boys in the United Kingdom. Recall that the sample mean is 98.4 and the standard error of the mean is .038. The answer to our question depends on whatever tradeoff between precision and confidence we want to maintain. There is a 68.26% chance that the population mean falls between 98.362 and 98.438. That is a very precise estimate, but our confidence is not great. We ought to take advantage of the unusually tiny standard error of the mean and calculate our 99.74% confidence intervals (i.e., our confidence that the population mean will fall within three standard deviations above or below the sample mean). What we will find is a greater than 99% likelihood that the population mean will fall between 98.286 and 98.514.

Confidence intervals are a useful source of information in their own right. Increasingly, researchers are including confidence intervals in their results sections along with statistically significant effects. (The meaning of statistical significance is described a little later in the chapter.)

Hypothesis Testing

In the previous discussion, you learned how sample characteristics can be used to estimate population parameters, but only to a given degree of probability. We cannot "prove" anything meaningful about a population on the basis of our samples. Rather, the conclusions we draw always carry some extent of uncertainty.

In the case of the Strand et al. (2006) study, we enjoy precise estimates of CAT means along with a very small extent of uncertainty, but this is an unusual study, owing to the exceptionally large sample size. Most studies cannot incorporate such a sizeable proportion of the population, owing to resource limitations, design constraints (experimental research, for example, requires assignment to groups), the need for in-depth data collection from each participant, and other logistical constraints. Thus, most researchers have to make some hard decisions about the degree of uncertainty they are comfortable with. We have to decide when to trust a result, even though we could never be 100% certain that the result is no fluke. Statistics do not make this decision for us. Statistics only give us estimates of population values, along with estimates of uncertainty. It is up to us to decide whether two means are "genuinely" different, or two correlated variables are "genuinely" associated. (A "genuine" difference or association can be defined as one that we would find if we had obtained accurate measurements of the entire population.)

Traditionally, the decision-making process used to determine whether a result is "genuine" is **hypothesis testing**. As you will see, hypothesis testing requires the researcher to set some predetermined standard for evaluating a result obtained through sampling. This standard, called a significance level, provides a numerical estimate of confidence that the result is "genuine" rather than attributable to "chance" (i.e., sampling error).

Null and Alternative Hypotheses

Hypothesis testing is based on a distinction between two types of hypotheses, the null hypothesis and the alternative hypothesis:

- The **null hypothesis** states that a result is not genuine but rather attributable to sampling error.

- The **alternative hypothesis** states that the result is genuine.

Suppose we have obtained IQ scores from two samples, one consisting of 16-year-old Rhode Island students and the other consisting of 16-year-old Connecticut students. The null hypothesis holds that there is no genuine difference between the two populations in IQ, whereas the alternative hypothesis is that the two populations truly differ on this dimension. In theory, the null and alternative hypotheses are formulated before data are collected. Although it is not very common for researchers to refer explicitly to the two hypotheses in their reports, these hypotheses represent assumptions of great importance to the concept of statistical significance.

TYPES OF NULL HYPOTHESES   Many types of null and alternative hypotheses can be distinguished, depending on the design of the study and the research questions that are addressed.

In experimental research, the null hypothesis asserts that there are no differences between experimental and comparison groups—typically, the assertion is that group means are not different. In a literacy intervention study focusing on whether instructional method A or B has a greater impact on students' reading scores, the null hypothesis would be that instructional method has no impact, and thus any observed difference between methods (i.e., any observed difference between the reading score means for students exposed to each method) would be attributable to sampling error rather than to a genuine difference.

In causal–comparative research, the null hypothesis asserts that there are no differences between the naturally occurring groups under study. For example, in the Strand et al. (2006) study, one of the null hypotheses is that there are no gender differences in mean CAT scores (other than what can be attributed to sampling error), while the alternative hypothesis is that boys and girls genuinely differ on the dimensions measured by the test.

In correlational designs, the null hypothesis states that the variables are not associated—in the simplest case, this amounts to an assertion that the correlation coefficients are not greater than chance. In a study on the relationship between socioeconomic status (SES) and creativity, the null hypothesis would be that these two variables are unrelated, and thus any positive or negative correlation that is observed would be attributable to sampling error rather than a genuine association between variables. Likewise, if we want to know whether IQ scores in our Rhode Island sample are associated with SES, the null hypothesis would be that any correlation between IQ and SES in the Rhode Island sample would reflect sampling error, while the alternative hypothesis would be that the correlation is genuine.

Hypothesis testing is not confined to comparisons of means and evaluation of associations between variables. Strand and colleagues (2006), for example, also considered the null hypothesis that there are no gender differences in variance, with the alternative being that variance in scores is greater among boys than among girls, or vice versa. Keep in mind that each set of null and alternative hypotheses applies to one specific statistical test, so that many studies will have more than one set.

Evaluating the Null Hypothesis

In hypothesis testing, we do not prove that one of our hypotheses is correct. Instead, we either "reject" or "fail to reject" the null on the basis of the data that we collect.

1. By rejecting the null hypothesis, we assert that a particular effect observed in our sample is genuine. Although we cannot be 100% certain, we assert that to a given degree of confidence the observed difference between means (or correlation between variables) is found in the population.

2. By failing to reject the null, we assert that we cannot be sure that our result reflects a population parameter. This is not the same as confirming the null. Failure to observe a difference between two groups does not prove that there is no difference in the population. "Absence of evidence does not equal evidence of absence," as the saying goes.

In a study of whether Rhode Island and Connecticut 16-year-olds differ in IQ, we would reject the null hypothesis if the data we gather from students in each state led us to believe that the two populations genuinely differ. We would fail to reject the null hypothesis if the data led us to conclude no difference. The next section explains how we would go about making one of these decisions.

Significance Levels

The predetermined, quantitative standard for rejecting the null hypothesis is called the **significance level**. (This concept is referred to by many names, including "level of significance," "probability level," "alpha level," or simply "α." In this chapter, the terms "significance level" and "alpha level" will be used interchangeably.) By convention, the alpha level in most educational research is set at .05. This means that in order to reject the null hypothesis, statistical calculations must show that the chances of sampling error are 5 in 100 or less. In other words, in order to claim that a correlation or a difference between means is "genuine," statistical tests must show that the likelihood of that correlation or mean difference being a fluke is less than 5%. The alpha level thus defines a cutoff point. If our statistics show that the likelihood of sampling error is greater than 5%, the null hypothesis will not be rejected.

The significance level in some studies is set at .01, or even lower, depending on the nature of the study. In medical research, for instance, alpha levels of .01 are often considered too lax. At the same time, you will notice that alpha levels of .05 are most common, and that the specific analyses available through software programs such as SAS and SPSS tend to provide .05 as a default value.

STATISTICAL SIGNIFICANCE   The term **statistical significance** describes a finding for which the likelihood of error is calculated to be less than the alpha level. (As explained later in the chapter, the likelihood of error is expressed as a number, "p." If the p value is less than the alpha value, the effect is significant. If the p value is greater than alpha, the effect is not significant.) Within the framework of hypothesis testing, statistical significance is synonymous with rejection of the null hypothesis. Reporting a significant effect means you have decided that a result is "genuine" rather than attributable to chance—the result can be accepted provisionally as a fact about the population, in spite of there being a small degree of uncertainty. Look back at the quotation from the Strand and colleagues (2006) study. There the researchers note that girls did significantly better than boys on the verbal and nonverbal subtests of the CAT, and in overall score, while boys did significantly better than the girls on the quantitative subtest. We can conclude, to a given degree of certainty, that in the United Kingdom, 11- and 12-year-old girls are better at verbal and nonverbal reasoning, while boys are better at quantitative reasoning.

Later in the chapter, the concept of statistical significance will be revisited in more quantitative terms.

Outcomes of Hypothesis Testing

In classical hypothesis testing, there are four possible decisions we can make, two correct and two incorrect. Table 11.2 illustrates these four decisions.

CORRECTLY REJECTING THE NULL   Correctly rejecting the null hypothesis means that the researcher has decided that two means are genuinely different, or that two variables are genuinely correlated, and in fact they are. In practical terms, what this means is that the significant difference or correlation turns out to represent population characteristics. Do not be misled by the casualness or the finality of the phrase "turns out to." This phrase refers to the process, noted in Chapter 1, through which specific findings become accepted as scientific knowledge through replication by additional research (and through consistency between data and theory). The outcome of hypothesis testing—the decision that the researcher makes about a particular finding—is ultimately evaluated by an accumulation of evidence suggesting that the finding is correct, incorrect, or in need of refinement.

You now have a statistical perspective as to why scientific knowledge in education and the social sciences was described in Chapter 1 as provisional—that is, potentially fallible and always open to revision. Scientific knowledge is based largely on significant findings, but statistical significance is a characteristic of samples. All significant findings carry with them a small chance of error. As a particular finding is replicated over time, the chance of error will diminish but could never reach zero.

CORRECTLY FAILING TO REJECT THE NULL   Correctly failing to reject the null hypothesis represents an accurate decision. The researcher finds no group differences or associations between variables, and it turns out that none exist in the population. In the practical sense, this outcome is less desirable than the first one, because nonsignificant findings are rarely the centerpiece of scientific publications. Rather, in most published research, rejection of null hypotheses (i.e., significant effects) are typically what provide the strongest support for researchers' conclusions.

Correctly failing to reject the null hypothesis tends to be a happy outcome only with respect to specific effects that were unwanted anyway. An experimental researcher who has developed a curricular intervention probably hopes that the entire population of interest will benefit from it. Thus, the researcher may be happy to find no significant differences between students of different backgrounds in the extent to which they benefit from the intervention. (On the other hand, the researcher would be unhappy to find that students who participated in the intervention are later indistinguishable from a control group.)

TABLE 11.2   Four Possible Outcomes in Hypothesis Testing

		Actual State of Affairs	
		Null is True	Null is False
Researcher's decision	Reject null	Type I error	Correct decision
	Do not reject null	Correct decision	Type II error

INCORRECTLY REJECTING THE NULL (TYPE I ERROR)   Rejecting a null hypothesis that is actually true is referred to as **Type I error**. You might think of this type of error as a kind of oversensitivity, or "false alarm." The researcher decides that two means are truly different, or that two variables are genuinely correlated, when in fact (i.e., in the population) they are not. Type I error is possible in theory for any statistically significant finding, since significance is not a form of proof but rather an expression of confidence. Again, the ultimate determination of Type I error tends to be an accumulation of evidence suggesting that some prior result was spurious.

INCORRECTLY FAILING TO REJECT THE NULL (TYPE II ERROR)   Failure to reject a null hypothesis that is false is referred to as **Type II error**. You can think of this type of error as reflecting undersensitivity, in that the researcher fails to detect a genuine difference between means, or a genuine correlation between variables. Ultimately, a Type II error is implicated when later studies identify effects that were not observed in an earlier one.

Some researchers hold that Type II error tends to be less serious than Type I error. A published study in which a meaningful result has been overlooked will be less problematic than a study in which spurious effects are reported. Arguably, the extent to which each type of error is problematic depends on the nature of the study. Imagine that we want to compare the extent of side effects experienced by students with attention-deficit/hyperactivity disorder (ADHD) who take a new versus an established drug. Failure to detect an increased incidence of serious side effects from the new drug (Type II error) seems like a more serious problem than claiming, inaccurately, that the new drug is more risky than the old one (Type I error). On the other hand, if in truth the new drug has tremendous benefits but no side effects, Type I error would be highly problematic from the perspective of students who currently experience ADHD. The safest conclusion is that neither type of error is desirable.

BALANCING THE RISK OF TYPE I AND TYPE II ERROR   Earlier it was noted that in many studies the alpha level is set at .05. In actual practice the .05 cutoff is a convention, in the sense that researchers often assume this value without explicitly thinking through the assumptions of hypothesis testing. In theory, however, the selection of an alpha value represents a decision about the risk of Type I and II errors we are willing to take.

We want our alpha levels to be low enough to allow us reasonable confidence that any significant findings are genuine. But by setting the alpha level too low, we run the risk of Type II error. In comparisons between two groups in their mean scores on various tests, an alpha level of .000001 may prevent us from detecting some of the genuine differences between the groups. On the other hand, an alpha level that is set too high introduces the risk of a Type I error. An alpha of 0.5, for instance, would open the door to many spurious effects, because we would be willing to reject the null hypothesis any time there is better than a 50–50 chance that a result is simply a fluke.

Interim Summary

You know now that hypothesis testing is a decision-making process through which one determines whether the characteristics of a sample can be considered genuine, to some degree of confidence. You have also learned that hypothesis testing is carried out by means of four steps:

- State the null and alternative hypotheses.
- Set a level of significance.
- Conduct the relevant statistical tests.
- Decide whether or not to reject the null hypothesis.

The null hypothesis is not usually stated explicitly in a research report, but it provides a conceptual basis for quantitative analysis—roughly analogous to the way that the scientific method informs quantitative inquiry, even though, as noted in Chapter 1, most researchers do not explicitly state or follow in a strict order the steps of the scientific method when conducting research. Although some scholars reject one or more of the basic premises of hypothesis testing (such as a simple distinction between only two empirical outcomes), significance testing is ubiquitous in quantitative research and plays a foundational role. In actual practice, the process of determining statistical significance can be understood either within or separately from the formal structure of hypothesis testing.

Although you know now that the alpha level provides a criterion for determining significance, what has not been explained yet is how researchers decide whether an observed effect meets that criterion. How do we measure the likelihood that a difference between means is due to chance? How will we know that the likelihood is less than 5%, or 1%, or whatever value we happen to have set for our alpha level?

In the second part of the chapter, these questions are answered through discussion of the specific statistical test that researchers use. Here, I address these questions through an introduction to concepts that apply to all instances of significance testing.

Critical Regions

Once again, suppose that we wish to know whether the IQ scores of 16-year-old Rhode Island students are different from those of their Connecticut peers. Our null hypothesis states that there is no difference in IQ between the two groups, while the alternative hypothesis holds that the two groups genuinely differ. Assume we have selected an alpha level of .05, meaning that we will not claim that the two groups genuinely differ unless we can show that any differences we do observe have less than a 5 in 100 chance of being a fluke. Now imagine a theoretical distribution created by measuring the IQ scores of an infinite number of pairs of samples from each state, and then calculating the difference between each pair of mean scores. Our calculations would yield a normal distribution of difference scores, as depicted in Figure 11.2.

FIGURE 11.2 Normal Distribution of Scores Illustrating Critical Regions Associated with a .05 Alpha Level

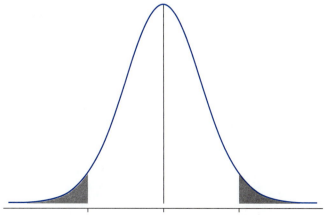

The unshaded area of the distribution in Figure 11.2 marks the 95% confidence interval (see earlier definition), because 95% of the difference scores will fall into this area. Each of the shaded areas in Figure 11.2 includes the most extreme 2.5% of the difference scores—altogether, 5% of the distribution.

The null hypothesis—the assertion that there are no genuine differences between the groups—is equivalent to the assertion that the two groups simply represent the same population rather than two different populations. If that were true, we would still expect to find extreme difference scores in the shaded areas 5% of the time during our infinite sampling procedure, owing to sampling error. Since we happen to be selecting just one pair of samples and calculating one difference score, there is a 5% chance that the difference score we obtain will fall into the shaded areas of the curve, even if there is no genuine difference between the groups. If the difference score we obtain actually does fall into one of these areas, we should reject the null hypothesis and conclude that the 16-year-olds from each state are significantly different in IQ (keeping in mind, of course, that we are acknowledging up to a 5% likelihood of error). If we obtain a smaller difference score—one that falls within the unshaded region of the curve—we should fail to reject the null hypothesis, because we cannot conclude that our results would be expected less than 5 in 100 times. (Perhaps we will come close. The difference score we observe may fall very close to one of the borders between the shaded and unshaded areas; we may find that the likelihood of a fluke is less than 9 in 100, for example. But if we have set the alpha at .05, an observed probability of .09 will not constitute a significant effect.)

The shaded areas of the curve in Figure 11.2 are referred to as **critical regions**—areas under the normal curve in which the probability of finding an observation is less than the alpha value. Critical regions provide a visual representation of the basis for determining statistical significance.

Notice that because our infinite sampling procedure always yields the normal distribution shown in Figure 11.2, the values that mark the critical regions will be the same from variable to variable when expressed as standard deviation units (z scores). Specifically, z scores of greater than 1.96 will constitute the highest 2.5% of scores in a normal distribution, while z scores of less than -1.96 will constitute the lowest 2.5% of scores. Z scores of 1.96 and -1.96 represent cutoff values for rejecting the null hypothesis when the alpha level is set at .05 That is, the 1.96 and -1.96 values mark the boundaries of the highest and lowest 2.5% of scores in any normally distributed variable (see Figure 11.3). In the appendix at the end of this book, Table A.1 lists the z scores corresponding to the areas under the normal curve.

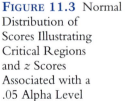

FIGURE 11.3 Normal Distribution of Scores Illustrating Critical Regions and z Scores Associated with a .05 Alpha Level

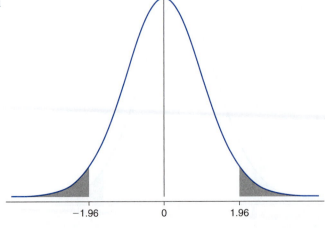

DIRECTIONALITY   The alpha level we choose can be used in one of two ways to establish critical regions.

1. With a **nondirectional test**, we make no assumptions in advance as to the direction of our results if the null hypothesis must be rejected. In our cross-state IQ comparison, the null asserts no differences in IQ between Rhode Island and Connecticut students. We need a nondirectional test because we cannot be sure in advance that if we reject the null, one group would exhibit higher scores than the other. If the null hypothesis asserts that two variables are uncorrelated, a nondirectional test is needed because the variables may turn out to be positively or negatively correlated. Even if we strongly suspect that one group will outperform the other, or that a correlation between variables will be positive, the opposite result is always possible.

Looking back at Figure 11.3, you can see a graphic illustration of the critical regions in a nondirectional test when the alpha level is set at .05.

2. If we are sure that the only alternative to the null hypothesis is an effect in one direction, we can conduct a **directional test**, as illustrated for an alpha level of .05 in Figure 11.4. (By comparing Figures 11.3 and 11.4, you can see why nondirectional tests are often referred to as "two-tailed tests," whereas directional tests are referred to as "one-tailed tests." In directional tests, only one "tail" of the distribution constitutes the critical region.)

Most tests of significance are nondirectional, because the researcher must remain open to more than one possible alternative to the null hypothesis. The literacy intervention researcher may hope to find that the experimental group ends up reading more fluently than the control group, but it is always possible that the control group will show superior reading performance at posttest. A correlational researcher may hope to find that the number of hours per week children read is positively correlated with their vocabulary size, but it is always possible (albeit unlikely) that a negative correlation will be observed.

The preceding examples illustrate why some social scientists believe that only nondirectional tests should be used for significance testing. Others believe that in some cases directional tests are appropriate. If you conduct a longitudinal study on normal growth in childhood, and you exclude from your sample the tiny percentage of children who fail to grow, owing to some disorder, then once you calculate the correlation between age and growth for a limited period of time (e.g., 60–64

FIGURE 11.4 Normal Distribution of Scores Illustrating Critical Regions and *z* Score for a Directional Test Assuming a .05 Alpha Level

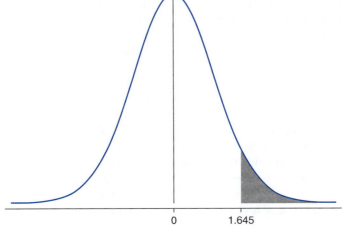

months), there are only two possible outcomes: (1) no correlation, because children do not undergo a significant amount of growth during this time period, or (2) a positive correlation, indicating significant growth over time. A negative correlation would be impossible, given your restriction on sampling, and thus a directional test is appropriate.

Although the directional test is not usually warranted, the advantage of using such a test is that a smaller z score would be needed to obtain a significant effect. As you can see in Figure 11.4, if we set our alpha level at .05, a z score of 1.645 is needed to reject the null in a directional test. In contrast, a z score of 1.96 would be needed for significance in the case of a nondirectional test in which you feel sure that only one direction of difference, if any, will be observed.

Actual Significance Values

By means of the statistical tests described later in the chapter, researchers calculate actual probabilities that the effects they observe are due to chance. These probabilities are called **p values**. A p value of .023 indicates that there is less than a 23 in 1000 chance that the observed effect is a fluke. If the alpha level is set at .05, then for each comparison between means (or each correlation) a p value of less than .05 indicates that the null hypothesis can be rejected, and the effect can be considered statistically significant. (In the Strand et al., 2006, study, the p values for comparisons of the means given in Table 11.1 were less than .0001.) The difference between the alpha level and the p value is that an alpha level sets a criterion for significance against which the actual p value is evaluated. When the p value is less than the alpha level, the effect is considered significant. Thus, the alpha value is a criterion established before data collection, while the p value is calculated after the data are in.

You will find that some researchers report exact p values, while others simply indicate that the p values are less than some particular probability (e.g., $p < .05$, $p < .01$, $p < .001$, and so on). In some cases, the number that the p values are described as less than is the alpha value, while in other cases, the researcher simply chooses the next largest round number. In other words, if the actual p value is .0008, some researchers might convey that value with the phrase $p < .05$, while other researchers might use the phrase $p < .001$.

Degrees of Freedom

One more concept of importance to the determination of statistical significance is **degrees of freedom**, or df, which refers to the number of values in a particular analysis that are free to vary, given a fixed parameter estimate. For example, by calculating the mean of a sample, you are creating an estimate of the population mean, and every value from the sample used to calculate the mean, except for one, can vary. To illustrate this idea, suppose that the sample consists of four scores: 2, 3, 5, and 6. The mean of the scores is 4. The first three values could be any possible score—they are free to vary. The final value is not free to vary, because it would have to be whatever number yields a sample mean of 4. If the first three numbers were 1, 3, and 5, for instance, the final value would need to be 7. This example illustrates the idea that the degrees of freedom associated with the calculation of a mean is always N − 1 (the number of values minus one).

Degrees of freedom must be calculated differently for each type of statistical test, because not all tests impose the same constraints on how many values can vary when a fixed parameter estimate is assumed. Sample size is not the only consideration. In all cases, however, degrees of freedom are taken into account when determining statistical significance. When a statistical test is conducted, the researcher (or, more commonly, the researcher's statistical software program) uses the outcome of the test *and* the degrees of freedom in order to determine the *p* value. All else equal, the greater the number of degrees of freedom, the more likely the test will yield a significant result. This should not surprise you, given the close relationship between degrees of freedom and size of distribution.

Effect Sizes

Here again is Strand and colleagues' summary of their results:

> *All sex comparisons are highly statistically significant; girls had a higher mean score than boys on the verbal battery, the non-verbal battery and [total] mean CAT score, and boys had a significantly higher mean score than girls on the quantitative battery.*

(2006, p. 470)

Notice that the authors use the phrase "highly statistically significant" to describe gender differences in mean CAT scores. The use of the term "highly" indicates that the actual *p* values were quite small—all *p*'s were less than .0001. These values tell us that there is less than a 1 in 10,000 chance that the observed gender differences were a fluke.

In the past, social science researchers were sometimes guilty of treating the *p* value as an indicator of the strength of an effect. Researchers exploring gender differences might conclude that a *p* value of .00002 indicates a greater difference between boys and girls than a *p* value of .02. In recent years, we have come to see this practice as a conflation of statistical significance and effect sizes. A highly significant result is one that is highly (if not completely) certain to be genuine. It is a result for which the likelihood of Type I error is very low, as in the case of Strand et al.'s study. But our confidence about the genuineness of a result is independent from the strength of that result.

Statistical Significance versus Effect Size

To illustrate the distinction between confidence and strength, consider the scenario in which a sprinter wins 37 100-meter races in a row and then claims to be the "fastest woman in the world." If her claim is operationalized in terms of 100-meter dash results, she may be right. But the magnitude of difference between her and her competitors is quite small. Most of the women she defeated in prior races finished each race less than a second slower than she did. Even though we can be quite confident that she is faster than the others, the actual extent of difference is tiny. This conclusion is analogous in a sense to what we can say about Strand et al.'s findings. Although the *p* values in their study were quite small, the differences between means were fairly small too (refer back to Table 11.1). In short, Strand and colleagues' results warrant a large extent of confidence about a small extent of difference.

In another sense, there is an important difference between what we can say about the sprinter and what can be said about Strand et al.'s data. For the sprinter, the tiny difference in speed has enormous practical consequences. In the Strand and

FIGURE 11.5 Distributions of Quantitative Test Scores for Males and Females

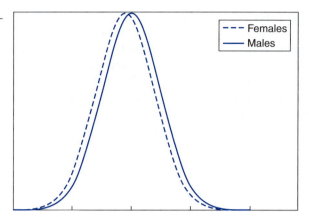

colleagues study, the mean differences are of somewhat less practical importance. These differences may be genuine (although the findings from the literature on gender differences are not settled), but the extent of practical import is qualified by the amount of variability within each group. Girls may be verbally superior to boys on average, but a large number of individual boys will score higher on the verbal subtest of the CAT than a large number of girls. Likewise, boys may obtain higher quantitative scores on average, but a large number of individual girls will score higher on the quantitative subtest than a large number of individual boys. The results for the quantitative measure are illustrated conceptually in Figure 11.5. As you can see, the mean of the distribution for males (solid line) will be slightly higher than that of the distribution for females (broken line), but the overlapping region is extensive.

Definition of Effect Size

In general, an **effect size** refers to the magnitude of a significant effect. The effect size is a specific number that constitutes an estimate of the strength of the effect. In an experimental study, the effect size tells you something about the extent to which participants were influenced by the experimental condition. In a correlational study, the effect size indicates the strength of the relationship between variables.

Smith and Glass (1997) first developed the concept of an effect size in the context of experimental research. Their formula for calculating effect size is given below. As you can see from the formula, effect size is strongly influenced by the absolute magnitude of difference between the experimental and control group means (the more they differ, the larger the effect size), but it is not identical to the magnitude of that difference. For example, extensive variability within the control group would diminish the effect size that is calculated.

$$\Delta = \frac{X_e - X_c}{SD_c} \tag{11.2}$$

In this formula, Δ is the effect size, X_e is the mean of the experimental group, X_c is the mean of the control group, and SD_c is the standard deviation of the control group.

Cohen (1988) developed a widely used alternative to Smith and Glass' formula that does not require a distinction between experimental and control groups. Cohen's formula for calculating effect size, referred to as **Cohen's *d*** (or simply *d*) is given below.

$$d = \frac{X_1 - X_2}{\sqrt{(SD_1{}^2 + SD_2{}^2)/2}} \qquad (11.3)$$

In this formula, d is the effect size, X_1 is the mean of the first group, X_2 is the mean of the second group, SD_1 is the standard deviation of the first group, and SD_2 is the standard deviation of the second group.

Note that when using this formula, it does not matter which group is designated as "first" or "second" so long as you are consistent. Thus, the formula is appropriate for use in both experimental and causal–comparative studies, as well as in any other kind of research in which means can be calculated from continuous variables. The numerator of the formula is the difference between means. As you can see, the magnitude of this difference once again influences effect size (the greater the difference, the larger the effect size). The denominator is the pooled standard deviation—an approximation of the average standard deviation obtained when the two groups are combined.

Interpretation of Effect Sizes for Mean Comparisons

Cohen's d is like a z score because it indicates the extent of difference between the two means in terms of standard deviation units. An effect size of .56 tells us that one mean is slightly more than half a standard deviation larger than the other one. An effect size of 1.0 indicates that one of the means is exactly one standard deviation higher than the other. (Keep in mind that the standard deviation being referred to here is the pooled standard deviation—the average value calculated from the two groups.)

Cohen (1988) recommended a set of standards for evaluating the effect sizes of mean comparisons. These standards are now widely assumed:

- Effect sizes ranging from .2 to .5 can be considered "small."
- Effect sizes ranging from .5 to .8 can be considered "moderate."
- Effect sizes that exceed .8 can be considered "large."

In the study by Strand et al. (2006), the results of mean comparisons were "highly" significant, but the effect sizes were very small. On average, boys and girls differed in their test scores—we can say that with a great deal of confidence—but the extent of difference was tiny. The largest effect size that Strand and colleagues reported for their mean comparisons was 0.15, for Verbal battery scores. You can calculate this effect size yourself by taking the data for Verbal scores from Table 11.1 and plugging those numbers into the formula for Cohen's d given above. Here is how to do it:

- Arbitrarily designate girls as the first group and boys as the second group.
- To obtain $SD_1{}^2$, square the standard deviation value for girls (14.5). The result is 210.25.
- To obtain $SD_2{}^2$, square the standard deviation value for boys (15.1). The result is 228.01.
- To obtain $\sqrt{SD_1{}^2 + SD_1{}^2/2}$, add the previous two values (210.25 and 228.01), divide by two, and then calculate the square root. The result is 14.803. This is the pooled standard deviation.
- To obtain $X_1 - X_2$, subtract the mean for boys (98.4) from the mean for girls (100.6). The result is 2.2. This is the difference between means.

- To obtain $X_1 - X_2/\sqrt{SD_1{}^2 + SD_2{}^2/2}$, divide the difference between means (2.2) by the pooled standard deviation (14.80). The result is 0.1486, which can be rounded up to 0.15.

In recent years, effect sizes for gender differences in academic skills, such as those reported in the Strand et al. study, have been diminishing. Carefully designed studies have not typically revealed effect sizes that exceed the "low" range.

Interpretation of Effect Sizes for Correlational Comparisons

Correlation coefficients, such as the Pearson product–moment coefficient, are in themselves estimates of effect size, because they indicate the strength of the relationship between two variables. (Again, whether or not the relationship is significant is a separate question.) Cohen (1988) recommended the following criteria for evaluating effect sizes that are expressed in the form of a correlation:

- Correlations ranging from .1 to .3 can be considered "small."
- Correlations ranging from .3 to .5 can be considered "moderate."
- Correlations that exceed .5 can be considered "large."

Interpretation of Effect Sizes: General Considerations

Types of effect sizes other than Δ, d, and r are discussed at a later point in the chapter. A useful quality of the various estimates of effect size is their independence from the particular measures on which they are based. Cohen's d, for example, expresses the magnitude of difference between means in terms of standard deviation units, and thus will have the same meaning regardless of what measures the means were derived from. For this reason, effect sizes are extremely helpful when contrasting or attempting to integrate studies that approach the same topic by means of different methodologies.

The usefulness of effect sizes is especially clear in quantitative meta-analyses. (See Chapter 2 for discussion.) Even though the studies reviewed in a meta-analysis rely on dependent measures that differ in length, difficulty, range of scores, and so on, effect sizes across studies can be compared and combined. In Spotlight on Research 2.3, for example, a meta-analysis of intervention studies on the benefits of self-determination strategies for individuals with disabilities is described. The median effect size across studies with group designs was found to be 0.6—an indication of moderate benefits.

Finally, a caveat. Cohen (1988) was careful to point out that it is risky to use the labels "small," "moderate," and "large" to compare effect sizes across studies that vary widely in methodology and intent. The effect size values themselves may be independent of particular measures, but our interpretation of the strength of an effect is a subjective judgment. When labeling an effect size, we should always remember both the specific value and, more broadly, what we can conclude about the relationship between variables.

Effect Sizes and Statistical Significance

Effect sizes are not just integral to the practice of meta-analysis. In recent years, the practice of reporting of effect sizes along with patterns of significance has become increasingly common, and at present most if not all editors of high-quality

TABLE 11.3 How to Read a Quantitative Results Section: A Guide for Beginners

- Make sure you understand what the research questions are and how key variables are operationalized.
- Read the descriptive statistics carefully in order to get a basic idea of the results.
- Keep in mind that most results sections include statistical tests that vary in importance. Try to distinguish between them. Rereading the abstract, reminding yourself of the research question, and skimming the first part of the discussion section can help you distinguish between tests of greater and lesser importance.
- Remind yourself of the purpose of statistical tests you are already familiar with. Try to identify the purpose of statistical tests you are not familiar with. Ask yourself whether the statistical test compares means, medians, variances, frequencies, or something else, and if so, how many values were compared. Ask yourself whether the statistical test attempts to quantify the extent of association between variables, and if so, which variables.
- Pay attention to statistical tests that do not yield significant results. Ask yourself whether any of the nonsignificant results bears on the research questions. Ask yourself whether the researcher would consider each nonsignificant result desirable or not.
- For each significant result, make note of the extent of significance that was obtained. Specifically, look at the size of the p values that are reported. Note whether alpha levels other than .05 were assumed.
- Relate each significant result to the descriptive statistics on which the statistical test was computed. Try to paraphrase each significant result nonquantitatively.
- For each significant result, look for information about effect sizes. Make note of the strength of each effect.
- Try to integrate the most important results. Look for patterns of significance across tests. Look for patterns of effect sizes across significant tests.
- Notice how the researcher summarizes the results in both the results and discussion sections. Check how well the researcher's conclusions fit the descriptive statistics as well as the results of specific statistical tests. Evaluate whether the researcher's conclusions are justified by observed patterns of significance and effect sizes.

journals require effect sizes to be included with descriptions of statistically significant findings. As you read through the results sections of scientific reports and encounter unfamiliar statistics—a common phenomenon, even for experienced researchers—two questions can always help guide you through the details:

- What effects were significant?
- What was the strength of the effects?

More specific advice about reading a quantitative results section is given in Table 11.3. The remainder of the chapter introduces some of the specific statistical tests that are most widely used in educational research.

Statistical Tests

You have now read about the conceptual basis of inferential statistics. In the remainder of the chapter I introduce some of the statistical tests that researchers use.

Statistical tests, or analyses, were traditionally carried out by means of the steps listed in the top half of Table 11.4. At present, virtually all researchers conduct analyses through the slightly different but vastly quicker set of steps given in the bottom half of the table.

Although researchers rarely calculate statistics by hand, a small amount of information about the mathematical basis of specific tests are provided in this section. With a few exceptions, the mathematical information is not sufficient for you to calculate these tests by hand—that would typically be an arduous task—but it will help you understand the purpose and meaning of each type of statistic.

Broadly, there are two types of statistical tests: parametric and nonparametric. Each type is based on a different set of assumptions about measurement, measures, and distributions of measured values.

Parametric tests are based on four assumptions:

- The participants have been randomly sampled.
- The measures reflect continuous variables (interval or ratio scales).
- The population data are normally distributed.
- The variances of any comparison groups are the same.

In actual practice, violation of some of these assumptions is considered tolerable, and it is expected that minor violations will not have a strong influence on the outcome of the statistical test. However, random sampling is critical, as is the assumption that key measures reflect continuous rather than discrete variables.

Nonparametric tests are based on three assumptions:

- The measures reflect discrete variables (nominal or ordinal scales).
- The population distribution is skewed or unknown.
- Any other basic parametric assumption has been strongly violated.

The practical importance of the differences between parametric and nonparametric tests will become clear by the end of the chapter. For many researchers, the most salient differences are simply whether key variables are continuous or discrete, and whether the distribution of population data is expected to be normal.

TABLE 11.4 Traditional and Contemporary Approaches to Statistical Analysis

Traditional Approach

1. Set an alpha value.
2. Choose a particular statistical test.
3. Use the computational formula for the test to calculate a statistic (a particular number).
4. Calculate the degrees of freedom.
5. Using the results of steps 3 and 4, consult a table to determine whether the outcome of the test is significant.

Contemporary Approach

1. Set an alpha value.
2. Choose a particular statistical test.
3. Enter commands into the software program that conducts the test.
4. Examine the output generated by the program to determine whether the outcome of the test is significant, and to determine the effect size.

Parametric Tests

In this section I describe three sets of statistical tests: t-tests, analyses of variance, and multiple regression. Each test serves a different purpose.

The *t*-Test

The **_t_-test** is used to decide whether two means are significantly different or not. When conducting a t-test, the traditional approach is to set an alpha level, use a formula to calculate a t value, note the degrees of freedom, and then consult a table to determine whether the t value is significant or not. (The table of critical t values is reproduced as Table A.2 in the appendix. This table must be consulted because as sample size decreases, the distribution of t values increasingly diverges from the normal curve.) At present it is much more common for the researcher to ask a software program such as SAS or SPSS to compute the t value and determine significance based on an alpha value assumed by the program or set by the researcher.

The two main types of t-test, independent and dependent, are distinguished from each other on the basis of the samples from which the means are obtained.

t-TEST FOR INDEPENDENT SAMPLES   The **_t_-test for independent samples** is used to determine whether or not means obtained from independent samples are significantly different. Independence in this case means that the composition of one sample is unrelated to the composition of the other. A t-test for independent samples would thus be appropriate for addressing the following questions:

- On a test of aggression, do boys obtain higher scores, on average, than girls?
- Which of two schools reported the greatest mean number of in-school suspensions per year over the past decade?
- Who tends to express more concern about student absenteeism—principals or teachers?
- Are the mean IQ scores of Rhode Island students significantly different from those of Connecticut students?

The t-test for independent samples is equal to the actual difference between two means divided by the difference that would be expected by chance, as illustrated by the formula below. (This formula illustrates the conceptual basis of the test. The actual formula that would be used to compute a t-test by hand is more complicated.) As you can see, larger differences between the means result in larger t scores, while larger standard error terms result in smaller t scores. The larger the t score, the more likely the difference between the means is significant. The likelihood of a significant difference also increases as the degrees of freedom increase, as can be seen in Table A.2 in the appendix of this book.

$$t = \frac{X_1 - X_2}{s_{x1-x2}} \tag{11.4}$$

In this formula, X_1 and X_2 are two means, and s_{x1-x2} is the standard error of the difference between the means.

A fairly common approach to the reporting of t-tests for independent samples is illustrated in the following passage. This passage is taken from the results section of a study on the benefits of a practice test developed for undergraduates enrolled in an instructional design and evaluation course.

One hundred forty-two students (67%) took the practice test between 1 and 13 times, with an average of 3.16 administrations per student. A t-test analysis for independent samples was used to compare the means of practice-test and non-practice-test groups. Students who took the practice test received an average grade of 80.74 on the graded in-class exams, while the mean for the students who took no practice test was 75.66. The mean difference of 5.07 points was statistically significant, t = 3.23, df = 210, p < .001, and was equivalent to one-half a letter grade (a low B versus a middle C) using the instructor's 10-point grading scale.

(Gretes & Green, 2000, pp. 48–49)

t-TEST FOR DEPENDENT SAMPLES   The **t-test for dependent samples** is used to determine whether means obtained from dependent samples are significantly different or not. What makes the samples "dependent" is that they have been closely matched on some dimension, or that they consist of the same individuals who provide two scores that are compared. In a true experimental design, a comparison of pre- and posttest means could be carried out by a t-test for dependent samples. Examples of other questions that can be addressed by this type of t-test include the following:

- Is the GPA of a particular group of students lower in 12th grade than it was in 9th grade?

- On a "resistance to peer pressure" survey, is students' resistance greater on average at the beginning or the end of the school year?

- When students at two different schools are carefully matched on gender and SES, do mean achievement scores differ across schools?

t-tests for dependent and independent samples are reported in the same way, as illustrated in the following passage from a study on college students' helping behavior in cooperative learning environments. Participants in this study were given the opportunity to help another group member under two different conditions: one in which the group member failed to participate for controllable reasons and another in which failure to participate could not be controlled. (Degrees of freedom are reported in parentheses, and exact p values are given.)

A paired-samples t test was conducted to evaluate whether the emotional responses of the 8 participants who experienced both conditions varied by causal condition. The t test was nonsignificant, t (7) = .55, p = .60. Results suggest that the 8 participants experienced similar emotions toward group members who failed to participate due to a controllable cause and those who failed to participate due to an uncontrollable cause.

An additional paired-samples t test conducted to evaluate whether the behavioral responses of the group indicating both causal conditions varied by causal condition was significant, t (7) = 3.50, p = .010. A participant's willingness to help varied according to causal condition. Participants were more likely to help a group member if the cause of nonparticipation was uncontrollable than if it was controllable.

(Ahles, 2006, p. 621)

An illustration of how to use a statistical software program to conduct a t-test is presented in Spotlight on Research 11.1.

Using SPSS to Calculate an Independent Samples *t*-Test

In the previous chapter, Spotlight on Research 10.3 led you through the use of SPSS 17.0 Statistics for Windows to create a dataset and then compute descriptive statistics. The same dataset can be used now to illustrate how a *t*-test can be carried out in SPSS. If you need to recreate this dataset, look back now at Spotlight on Research 10.3. Otherwise click on the Windows SPSS 17.0 icon and open your file.

Once you have opened (or recreated) your data file, you will see raw scores for three variables: gender, age, and IQ. (If you are reopening the file, you will also find *z* scores for these variables, which can be ignored for the present discussion.)

One question that might be asked about your data is whether there are gender differences in IQ. The simplest way to answer this question is by means of a *t*-test for independent samples.

To carry out the test, use the drop-down menu to select "Analyze," "Compare Means," and then "Independent-Samples T test...." You should now see the small window captured in Screenshot 1 below.

The space labeled "Test Variable(s)" is where you identify the variable whose means will be compared—in this case, IQ. The variable list can be seen on the left

side of the small window. Click on "IQ" one time so that it is highlighted, then click on the upper of the two arrows to move IQ over into the space underneath "Test Variable(s)." Next, click on "gender" one time so that it is highlighted, then click on the lower arrow so that this variable appears in the space under "Grouping variable." ("Grouping variable" is the term used in SPSS for the binary variable used in the *t*-test.) Once you have performed these actions, you will see the screen captured in Screenshot 2.

Notice that there are two question marks by your grouping variable "gender." You must define the two levels of this variable now. To do so, click on the "Define Groups" button, enter 0 for Group 1 and 1 for Group 2, then click on "Continue" to return to where you were. (The reason you enter 0 and 1 to define each level of gender is that these are the values you chose in your original dataset. Zero was the value arbitrarily chosen for boys, while 1 was the value chosen for girls.)

Notice that if you click on the "Options" button at the lower right of the window, you will see a smaller window giving you the option of choosing a particular confidence interval. You will see that the default is 95%—an alpha of .05, in other words. Once you are finished looking at this smaller window, click on "Continue" to return to where you were.

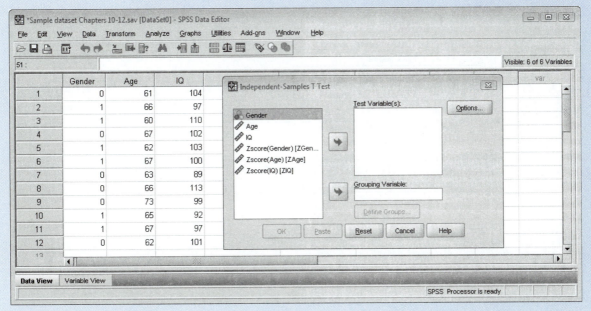

SCREEENSHOT 1

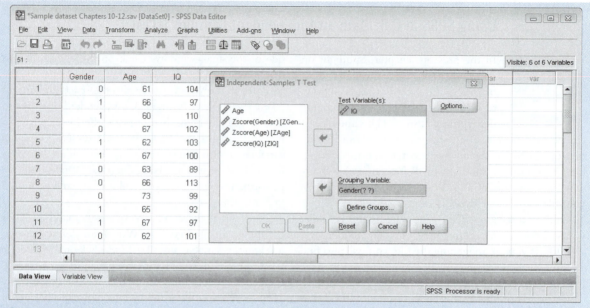

SCREEENSHOT 2

Once you click "OK," you will immediately obtain an output file. Once you maximize your view of this file (by clicking on the partially overlapping box icon at the far upper right of the window), you will see the screen captured in Screenshot 3 below:

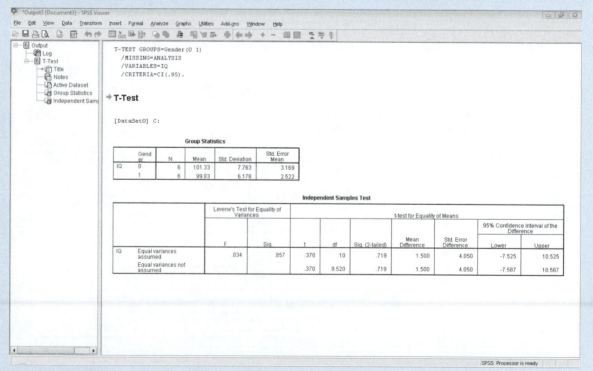

SCREEENSHOT 3

The first box of numbers, labeled "Group Statistics," provides some of the basic descriptive statistics for your two variables. You can see that the mean value for boys (101.33) is slightly higher than the value for girls (99.83). Your original question is whether this is a significant difference.

The second box of numbers, labeled "Independent Samples Test," provides the results of your *t*-test. You can see that if equal variances are assumed, the value of *t* is .37. Given that there are 10 degrees of freedom, this *t* value is not significant according to a two-tailed (i.e., nondirectional) test. You can tell that the *t* value is not significant because the *p* value given in the column labeled "Sig. (2-tailed)" is .719—vastly greater than your alpha level of .05. The means for boys and girls differed by less than 2 points, but the 95% confidence intervals provided at the end of the table define a 17-point spread.

Look around under the "Analyze" drop-down option and you will see some of the other statistical tests discussed in this chapter. SPSS has a help menu, tutorials, and other resources if you wish to learn more about conducting inferential tests with the program.

Save the data file—you will be using it one more time in Chapter 12 to create graphs (see Spotlight on Research 12.2).

Analysis of Variance

A *t*-test can be used to compare only two means at a time. **Analysis of variance (ANOVA)** is used to compare the means of two or more groups simultaneously. ANOVA techniques are prevalent in experimental and causal–comparative research. Typically, the ANOVA is used to determine whether one or more categorical independent variables have significant effects on a continuous dependent variable. Examples of questions that can be addressed through ANOVA techniques include the following:

- Will high-functioning autistic children respond more favorably on average to a behavioral intervention, a cognitive intervention, or a mixed cognitive-behavioral intervention?

- Which of the four main ethnic groups in a school district obtained the highest mean scores on the SAT last year? Are there gender differences within any of these groups?

- How much does student interest in a social studies class increase when a textbook chapter on American history is supplemented by a video, by a diary, or by nothing at all?

- Are there significant differences in job satisfaction between teachers in high-, medium-, and low-SES school districts? Is the job satisfaction reported by teachers in each type of district influenced by their gender and level of experience (novice vs. experienced)?

- In which year of high school do students exhibit the strongest identification with their school, and is the extent of student identification influenced by whether or not they participate in sports?

Each of the means compared in an ANOVA corresponds to a different group. For instance, if you have administered a job satisfaction survey to teachers in high-, medium-, and low-SES school districts, you will obtain three means, one corresponding to each district. If you also record each teacher's gender, you end up with six means—one for male teachers and one for female teachers within each district. In these examples, the groups are independent. When the groups are closely matched, or when more than one score is obtained from a single sample, a **repeated measures ANOVA** can be calculated.

FACTORS AND LEVELS IN ANOVA   The term "factor" is used in certain ANOVA procedures to describe the categorical independent variable. The term "level" is used to describe the categories within each independent variable. Thus, gender is a factor that has two levels. In a study in which SES is treated as an independent variable, dividing the sample into high-, medium-, and low-SES groups yields a factor with three levels.

CALCULATING THE ANOVA   ANOVA is based on the assumption that total variance in observations can be partitioned into variance between groups and variance within groups. (Recall from Chapter 10 that variance is the square of the standard deviation.) The general formula for determining ANOVA consists of dividing the mean variance between groups by the mean variance within groups, as shown below.

$$F = \frac{MS_B}{MS_W} \tag{11.5}$$

In this formula, F is the F ratio, MS_B refers to the mean squares between groups, and MS_W refers to the mean squares within groups.

$MS_B = SS_B/df_B$. That is, the mean squares between groups equals the sum of squares between groups divided by the between-group degrees of freedom (df_B = K − 1). (That is, the between-groups degrees of freedom is equal to the number of groups minus one.)

$MS_W = SS_W/df_W$. That is, the mean squares within groups consists of the sum of squares within groups divided by the within-group degrees of freedom (df_W = N − K). (That is, the within-group degrees of freedom is equal to the number of values minus the number of groups.)

The formula above yields an *F* ratio. Higher *F* ratios are more likely to be significant and, as you can see, the greater the variance between groups, the larger the *F* ratio. Greater variance within groups results in smaller *F* ratios. Intuitively, this makes sense. Imagine that the job satisfaction means obtained for three groups of teachers are very different from each other, but the teachers in each group provide satisfaction scores that are very close to their own group's mean. In this scenario, high between-group variability is combined with little variability within groups, and we would expect the resulting *F* ratio to be large and indicate significant differences. On the other hand, if the means for each group were very similar, and we found a lot of within-group variability, we would expect the *F* ratio to be small. Theoretically, the null hypothesis states that between-group and within-group variability is identical, resulting in no differences between groups.

In a published report, the results of an ANOVA are typically described like this: $F(1, 344) = 14.67$, $p < .0001$. The first number in the parentheses (1) is the between-subjects degrees of freedom, while the second number in the parentheses (344) is the within-subjects degrees of freedom. The actual *F* ratio is 14.67, and the *p* value is less than .0001. The result is "highly" significant—less than a 1 in 10,000 chance of Type I error has been estimated. The list of critical *F* values is given in the appendix as Table A.3.

EFFECT SIZES IN ANOVA   In ANOVA procedures, effect sizes are estimated by η^2 ("eta-squared"), a statistic that indicates what percentage of variation in the dependent variable is accounted for by variation in the independent variable. A typical description of the eta statistic can be seen in the following passage from a study with teenage mothers in which it was hoped that an intervention would result in the mothers' showing increased responsiveness to their children:

At posttesting, there were significant differences between mothers who received the intervention and mothers in the contrast group on the Responsiveness factor, $F(1, 92) = 6.64$, $p = .012$; partial $\eta^2 = .07$, with the intervention mothers scoring higher.

(Deutscher, Fewell, & Gross, 2006, p. 200)

In this passage, the term "partial" indicates that the η^2 value only pertains to the effects of the group, and not the effects of the other independent variable (time: pretest vs. posttest). The researchers found that at posttest, mothers who had participated in the intervention showed significantly more responsiveness toward their children than comparison group mothers, but that only 7% of variability in responsiveness could be accounted for by the group in which the mothers had participated. The effect of the intervention was significant but small, in other words.

Types of ANOVA

Five types of tests can be classified under the heading of analysis of variance, as summarized in Table 11.5 and described in further detail below.

ONE-WAY ANOVA   In experimental and causal–comparative designs, the **one-way ANOVA** is used to analyze the effects of one categorical independent variable on one continuous dependent variable. The one-way ANOVA determines whether there are any differences between the means obtained for each level of the independent variable. For example, in a study comparing the mean SAT scores of four different ethnic groups, SAT score is the dependent variable and ethnic group is the independent variable. One mean will be calculated for each of the four levels of ethnic group. The one-way ANOVA will yield an F ratio. The F ratio and the degrees of freedom will then be used to identify the p value—and, as you recall, if the p value is less than the alpha level, the means are significantly different.

When a one-way ANOVA (or any other type of ANOVA) is used to compare three or more means, you cannot tell from a significant F ratio which means are and are not significantly different from the rest. **Multiple comparisons** must be carried out between each pair of means. Examples of widely used multiple comparison statistics are the **Scheffé test**, which is appropriate when group sizes are equal or unequal, and the **Tukey HSD test**, which requires equal group sizes. (HSD stands for "honestly significant differences".) Effect sizes can also be calculated for each pair-wise comparison of means.

TABLE 11.5 Major Types of ANOVA Tests

Name of Test	Acronym	Number of Independent Variables	Number of Dependent Variables	Controls for Extraneous Variables?
One-way analysis of variance	ANOVA	1	1	No
Multifactorial analysis of variance	ANOVA	2 or more	1	No
Multivariate analysis of variance	MANOVA	1 or more	2 or more	No
Analysis of covariance	ANCOVA	1 or more	1	Yes
Multivariate analysis of covariance	MANCOVA	1 or more	1	Yes

As the number of comparisons in a study (and across studies) increases, the possibility of Type I error will increase. In other words, the more comparisons that are made, the greater the likelihood that any one will come out significant, just by chance. For this reason researchers sometimes use the **Bonferroni correction**, a formula that yields a more conservative estimate of the p value for a particular comparison.

To illustrate how the one-way ANOVA is presented in a results section, consider the following quotation:

A one-way ANOVA test found statistically significant differences amongst the initial geometry scores of students from the four schools investigated, F(3, 220) = 8.174, p < 0.000. The Tukey HSD (Honestly Significant Difference) post hoc analysis indicated statistically significant differences between school A and school C (p < 0.001); school A and school D (p < 0.001); and school B and school D (p < 0.042).

(Olkun, Altun, & Smith, 2005, p. 322)

You can tell from this quotation that type of school is the independent variable and geometry score is the dependent variable. There are three between-groups degrees of freedom and 220 within-groups degrees of freedom. The actual F ratio is 8.174, a significant value, and since four schools were studied, multiple comparisons were needed. (Multiple comparisons are sometimes referred to as "post hoc," as in this quotation, because they are carried out after the initial test of significance.) All comparisons between schools were significant, except that no differences were found between schools A and B, or between schools C and D. As a reader, you would need to look elsewhere in the text (perhaps in a table or figure) to find the specific means associated with each school. In other words, F tests and multiple comparisons only tell you whether any differences are significant. You must look at the actual means to determine the direction of difference. (This is true for all forms of ANOVA, not just the one-way variety.)

MULTIFACTORIAL ANOVA The **multifactorial ANOVA** evaluates the effects of two or more independent variables on one dependent variable. A two-way ANOVA includes two independent variables, a three-way ANOVA includes three independent variables, and so on. The independent variables may be called factors, and a distinction is made between two types. First, a **between–subjects factor** is one whose levels correspond to different groups. Gender is always a between-subjects factor. In a comparison between schools, school is a between-subjects factor. Second, a **within-subjects factor** is one whose levels represent distinctions within the same group. In an experimental design, testing at pre- and posttest represents a within-subjects factor, because all participants take the pretest and the posttest.

You will find that researchers vary in how explicitly they describe the structure of their ANOVAs. Between-subjects and within-subjects factors may or may not be explicitly distinguished. The number of levels associated with each independent variable may or may not be specified. In a study looking at the effects of gender and three levels of SES (low, medium, high) on some dependent variable, the researcher may refer to a 2 × 3 ANOVA, or, more specifically, to a 2 (gender) × 3 (SES) ANOVA. The "2" indicates that gender is a two-level independent variable, while the "3" indicates that SES has three levels. At the outset of the following passage, you can tell that Race is treated as a four-level independent variable in the study:

A 2 × 4 (Gender × Race) analysis of variance (ANOVA) was planned for data analysis. . . . When we found significant F values, we used post-hoc comparisons with Tukey's Honestly Significant Differences Test to explain differences among racial categories. Because we performed multiple tests to determine who was most helpful in the transition, we used the Bonferroni adjustment to control for Type 1 errors . . .

(Akos & Galassi, 2004, p. 104)

In a multifactorial ANOVA, F ratios are calculated for the effects of each independent variable separately, and in combination with each other. Recall from Chapter 7 that the term "main effect" refers to a significant effect of one independent variable, whereas the term "interaction" refers to a significant effect of two or more independent variables that cannot be reduced to the separate effects of each. The multifactorial ANOVA yields one F ratio for each potential main effect and interaction. (Notice that if any one of the independent variables has more than two levels, multiple comparisons will be needed for both main effects and interactions.) If we are studying the effects of gender and four types of ethnicity on SAT scores and obtain a main effect of ethnicity, a multiple comparison procedure such as the Scheffé test will be needed to compare the means for each possible pair of ethnic groups. Once again, effect sizes can be calculated for each comparison.

Spotlight on Research 11.2 describes a study in which multifactorial ANOVAs revealed interactions of central importance to the research question.

MULTIVARIATE ANOVA   The **multivariate analysis of variance (MANOVA)** evaluates the effects of one or more independent variables on two or more dependent variables. The use and interpretation of the MANOVA is essentially the same as for the multifactorial ANOVA, except that the analysis considers two or more dependent variables simultaneously.

ANALYSIS OF COVARIANCE (ANCOVA)   The **analysis of covariance (ANCOVA)** evaluates the effects of one or more independent variables on one dependent variable while controlling for the effects of potentially extraneous variables. Each variable that is controlled for is called a **covariate**. The number of possible covariates is large, if not endless. If we compare the effects of switching versus not switching schools in the middle of the year, we know that the effects of switching may be influenced by whether or not the child also changes residences, as well as the student's prior school performance, the quality of the new school, the supportiveness of the parents, and so on. We cannot identify and measure every possible covariate, and so we simply measure the most likely culprits and count on statistical analysis to control for their effects.

ANCOVA is often used in experimental research, since randomization procedures do not guarantee that the experimental and control groups are identical. ANCOVA procedures are especially useful in causal–comparative studies, since the researcher cannot control preexisting differences between groups. For example, Engec (2006) looked at how student mobility affects their scores on the Illinois Test of Basic Skills, or ITBS, a widely used norm-referenced test of achievement. For one set of analyses, Engec treated mobility as a three-level independent variable by dividing students into those whose families had either not moved, moved once, or moved two or more times during the school year. Student mobility was then used as the main independent variable in an ANCOVA in which grade in school was treated as the covariate.

"What a Difference an Hour Makes": The Effects of Restricting or Extending Children's Sleep

As you may know from personal experience, the effects of sleep deprivation can be quite unpleasant. Sleep deprivation is a problem in educational settings, particularly as children begin to enter puberty and experience a "phase delay"—the tendency to want to go bed later and get up later. Secondary-level teachers are quite familiar with the challenge of teaching first- and second-period classes. Studies confirm that sleep-deprived students experience negative effects such as poor school performance and increased absenteeism. However, there is very little experimental research with children on the relationship between more than one day of sleep deprivation and daily functioning.

In a 2003 article in *Child Development**, Avi Sadeh, Reut Gruber, and Amiram Raviv explored the effects of either restricting or extending fourth- and sixth-grade Israeli children's sleep for an hour on three consecutive nights. Children lived at home while participating in the experiment. The research was designed to test three hypotheses: (1) most children would be able to restrict or extend their sleep when asked by the researcher to do so for a 3-day period; (2) sleep restriction would result in better sleep quality than sleep extension; and (3) compared to sleep extension, sleep restriction would lead to an increase in fatigue and to compromised neurobehavioral functioning (NBF).

The study took place during one 6-day school week. At the outset of the experiment, each child's baseline NBF was measured. On Days 1 and 2, children slept as they regularly sleep. For the remainder of the experiment, each child was asked to go to bed either 1 hour later or 1 hour earlier. Doing so resulted in a "sleep-extension" group and a "sleep-restriction" group (since all children had to get up at the same time for school). Each day, children completed a diary report on the quality of their sleep and the extent of their alertness during the day. Quality of sleep was also monitored by a wristwatch-like device called an actigraph that children wore each night. Finally, NBF was measured again at the end of the study. The researchers referred to the timing of the second measurement of NBF as "intervention" to distinguish it from the earlier "baseline" measurement.

In this study, there are two main dependent variables: quality of sleep (measured by diary reports and the actigraph) and neurobehavioral functioning. In measuring

quality of sleep, the actigraph revealed the following information:

(a) sleep onset time, (b) morning rise time, (c) sleep period—total time from sleep onset time to morning awakening time, (d) true sleep time—sleep time excluding all periods of wakefulness, (e) sleep percent—percentage of true sleep time . . . (f) number of night wakings, and (g) quiet sleep—percentage of motionless sleep.

NBF was operationalized in terms of performance on the following tests administered by computer:

1. *Finger tapping test. Task: to tap as fast as possible with one finger on a single button. . . . Variable: maximum number of taps.*
2. *Simple reaction-time test. Task: to press a button as quickly as possible when a large square appears on the screen. . . . Variable: average reaction time.*
3. *Continuous performance test (CPT). Task: to respond as fast as possible to a specific animal presented and to avoid responding to any other animal. . . . Variables: average reaction time, omission errors (not responding to target stimulus), and commission errors (responding to non-target stimulus).*
4. *Symbol-digit substitution (SDS). Task: nine symbols and nine digits are paired at the top of the screen and the child is requested to press the digits on the keyboard corresponding to a test set of the nine symbols presented in a mixed order. . . . Variable: average response latency for completing each set.*
5. *Visual digit span test. Task: to recall presented sequences of digits and to repeat the sequences on the computer keyboard (forward) or to repeat the digits in reversed order (backward). . . . Variables: lengths of the longest span answered correctly forward and backward.*
6. *Serial digit learning test. Task: to recall a long sequence of single digits presented in succession. . . . Variable: an error score that is the sum of the errors over all trials attempted.*

The first set of data analyses used multivariate ANOVAs to evaluate the effects of sleep restriction or extension on quality of sleep:

To assess the effects of the experimental manipulation on the actigraphic sleep measures and the subjective reports, we used ANOVAs with gender, age (fourth and sixth grades), and group (sleep-restriction or sleep-extension group) as the between-subject vaiables, and period (baseline vs. intervention) as the within-subject independent variables. Actigraphic and subjective sleep measures were used as the dependent variables.

In this first set of analyses, the finding of most relevance to the researchers' original hypotheses would be an interaction between group and period, showing that while the two groups had comparable sleep quality at the outset of the study, by the end of the study (i.e., at "intervention"), quality of sleep would differ between the groups. This is indeed what Sadeh and colleagues found. The descriptive statistics and ANOVA results are given in the table below.

Sadeh and colleagues described the results from this table as follows:

Significant Group × Period interaction effects were found for the following actigraphic sleep measures . . . : sleep onset time, sleep period, sleep percent, true sleep time, quiet sleep, and number of night wakings. These interactions reflected the fact that sleep was significantly extended from baseline to intervention period in the sleep-extension group (by an average of 35 min) and that sleep was significantly shortened in the sleep-restriction group (41 min). . . . Sleep quality was significantly improved in the sleep-restriction group as manifested in increased sleep percent and quiet sleep and reduced number of night wakings following intervention, whereas the opposite changes occurred in the sleep-extension group.

Interactions were also found for the subjective (diary report) measures of sleep quality:

The Effects of Sleep Manipulation on Sleep Measures: Means (±SDs) and F Values

Sleep measure	Group		$F(1, 69)$ Time × Group
	Sleep restricted	Sleep extended	
Sleep onset time (hr)			139.17***
Baseline	22.23 ± .52	22.20 ± .73	
Intervention	23.01 ± .68	21.56 ± .59	
Morning rise time (hr)			2.47
Baseline	6.96 ± .36	6.81 ± .30	
Intervention	7.04 ± .43	6.74 ± .29	
Sleep period (min)			88.66***
Baseline	523.7 ± 29.7	516.3 ± 43.5	
Intervention	482.1 ± 36.2	551.0 ± 34.7	
True sleep time (min)			69.44***
Baseline	488.6 ± 29.3	487.7 ± 43.0	
Intervention	457.1 ± 38.3	516.9 ± 40.2	
Sleep percent (%)			8.50**
Baseline	93.33 ± 3.54	94.50 ± 3.74	
Intervention	94.78 ± 3.02	93.77 ± 3.48	
Night wakings (N)			10.46**
Baseline	1.64 ± 1.18	1.34 ± 1.22	
Intervention	1.20 ± 0.89	1.81 ± 1.25	
Quiet sleep (%)			6.03*
Baseline	70.00 ± 9.08	71.70 ± 9.97	
Intervention	71.55 ± 9.68	70.00 ± 8.68	

*$p < .05$.
**$p < .005$.
**$p < .001$.

Significant Group × Period interactions were also found on the following subjective measures . . . reported evening fatigue, $F(4, 61) = 8.61$, $p < .001$; predicted sleep latency, $F(4, 61) = 2.80$, $p < .001$; and reported sleep latency. . . . The significant interactions . . . indicated that compared with advancing sleep onset, delaying sleep onset resulted in increased evening fatigue and predicted and reported shorter sleep latency.

Several main effects of age and gender were also obtained for the quality of sleep measures:

Compared with the younger age group (fourth grade), older children (sixth grade) had delayed sleep onset time, $F(1, 69) = 41.25$, $p < .001$; shorter sleep period, $F(1, 69) = 35.65$, $p < .001$; shorter true sleep time, $F(1, 69) = p < .001$; and increased percentage of quiet sleep, $F(1, 69) = 6.7$, $p < .001$. Significant gender differences were also found. Compared with boys, girls had higher sleep percent, $F(1, 69) = 7.42$, $p < .001$, and higher quiet sleep percent, $F(1, 69) = 14.83$, $p < .001$.

The Effects of Sleep Manipulation (Group) on Neurobehavioral Functioning: Means (±SDs) and F Values

NES measure	Group			$F(1, 61)$ Time	$F(2, 61)$ Time × Group
	Sleep restricted	No change	Sleep extended		
Tapping				0.00	0.28
Baseline	149.8 ± 15.0	152.8 ± 20.4	151.2 ± 17.8		
Intervention	149.7 ± 14.9	152.2 ± 19.3	151.5 ± 18.6		
Simple RT				16.2**	3.94*
Baseline	431.4 ± 82.5	412.2 ± 73.1	414.2 ± 50.2		
Intervention	458.2 ± 77.1	461.7 ± 74.6	418.7 ± 58.4		
Symbol-Digit RL				18.7***	1.06
Baseline	2429 ± 399	2530 ± 504	2405 ± 411		
Intervention	2337 ± 415	2335 ± 421	2275 ± 390		
CPT-RT				0.98	6.74**
Baseline	641.0 ± 55.7	633.3 ± 45.4	615.8 ± 73.5		
Intervention	639.9 ± 61.1	650.1 ± 60.9	587.8 ± 67.8		
CPT-Om Err				0.02	0.28
Baseline	1.57 ± 1.17	1.43 ± 1.56	1.00 ± 0.63		
Intervention	1.32 ± 1.09	1.48 ± 0.90	1.00 ± 1.04		
CPT-Com Err				0.18	0.75
Baseline	0.89 ± 1.42	0.57 ± 1.04	0.48 ± 1.33		
Intervention	1.03 ± 1.29	0.83 ± 1.03	0.29 ± 0.46		
Digit span FW				0.05	3.25*
Baseline	5.61 ± 0.69	5.17 ± 0.83	5.43 ± 0.98		
Intervention	5.25 ± 0.89	5.22 ± 1.09	5.71 ± 0.90		
Digit span BW				4.83*	0.71
Baseline	4.14 ± 0.89	4.35 ± 1.07	4.43 ± 1.29		
Intervention	4.36 ± 1.16	4.52 ± 1.04	5.05 ± 1.32		
Digit learning ES				10.00**	0.23
Baseline	2.79 ± 2.69	3.43 ± 3.64	2.67 ± 2.13		
Intervention	2.04 ± 1.57	2.30 ± 2.30	1.71 ± 2.45		

Note. Intervention groups: neurobehavioral (NES) measures: tapping = number of finger tappings, RL = response latency, Om Err = omissions errors, Com Err = commissions errors, FW = forward, BW = backward, ES = error score.

*$p < .05$.

***$p < .005$.

***$p < .001$.

The remaining multivariate ANOVAs focused on the other main dependent variable: performance on the NBF tests. Before conducting these analyses, children were divided into three groups according to how successfully they actually restricted or extended their sleep:

Children who extended their sleep by an average of 30 min or more during the intervention days were defined as the sleep-extension group (SEG). Children who shortened their sleep by an average of 30 min or more were defined as the sleep-restriction group (SRG). Children who failed to extend or shorten their sleep by at least 30 min were defined as the no-change group (NCG). . . .

The analyses were based on ANOVAs with gender, age (fourth and sixth grades), and Group (SRG, SEG, and NCG) as the between-subject independent variables, and period (baseline vs. intervention) as the within-subject repeated independent variable. The [NBF] measures were used as the dependent variables . . .

The results of these analyses are summarized in the table on the previous page.

Here is how Sadeh and colleagues summarized the results given in the table:

Significant Group × Period interactions were found on three [NBF] measures . . . simple reaction time, digit forward, and the reaction time on the CPT. These interactions and the post hoc tests indicated that children who extended their sleep significantly improved their performance (from baseline to postintervention period) on the digit forward memory test, whereas the performance of the other groups did not change. On the CPT, children in the SEG significantly improved their reaction time, whereas the performance of children in the other groups (SRG and NCG) did not change significantly. On the simple reaction time test, performance of the children from the SRG and the NCG significantly deteriorated whereas the performance of the children from the SEG remained the same.

In sum, interactions obtained by means of multivariate ANOVAs pointed to several specific benefits of sleep extension, along with a number of deficits resulting from sleep restriction.

*Sadeh, A., Gruber, R., & Raviv, A. (2003). The effects of sleep restriction and extension on school-age children: What a difference an hour makes. *Child Development, 74*(2), 444–455. Quoted with permission from the publisher.

Engec (2006) found that student mobility had a significant impact on ITBS scores, after controlling for grade in school ($p < .001$). Tukey HSD tests showed that ITBS scores for students who had not moved were significantly higher than for students who had moved, and that scores for students who had moved once were significantly higher than for students who had moved two or more times during the school year. As you can see, the results of an ANCOVA are described and interpreted in the same way as for a regular ANOVA. (In the previous chapter, Spotlight on Research 10.2 contains a more detailed description of a study in which ANCOVA is used.)

MULTIVARIATE ANALYSIS OF COVARIANCE (MANCOVA) The **multivariate analysis of covariance (MANCOVA)** evaluates the effects of one or more independent variables on two or more dependent variables while controlling for the effects of some extraneous variable(s). The MANCOVA can be understood as a simple extension of the ANCOVA to analyses incorporating more than one dependent variable.

ANOVA and Regression

Although ANOVA techniques are widely used in educational research, their usefulness is limited somewhat by the need for categorical independent variables and continuous dependent variables. Many variables of interest to researchers—ability, achievement, affluence, age, and so on—are understood to be continuous dimensions but must be treated categorically if we want to study their relationship to continuous variables through ANOVA statistics. Because the ANOVA is based on assumptions about partitioned variance, it may be difficult to extrapolate from significant effects. If we explore whether parents who are classified as "low," "medium," or "high" in SES differ in the number of hours per day they read to their preschool children, we may find differences between the means for each SES group, but we cannot be sure what to conclude about more extreme groups ("lowest" and "highest"), nor can we be entirely sure of the effects of variability within each group, other than concluding that the extent of within-group variance was not enough to prevent significant differences between groups from being observed.

Regression statistics are an increasingly popular complement to ANOVA techniques. The popularity of regression stems in part from its flexibility. Like ANOVA, regression can be used in experimental and causal–comparative studies, but unlike ANOVA regression analyses are also appropriate for correlational designs (since, as you will see, regression is essentially a correlational method). Regression is used in all forms of quantitative design because there are no restrictions on whether key variables are categorical or continuous. In short, regression analyses can accomplish just about everything that ANOVA does, and more. (You might be wondering why ANOVA techniques continue to be popular. The results of ANOVAs tend to be easier to interpret, for one thing.)

Multiple Regression

The essence of regression is prediction, and prediction is of great interest to both researchers and educators. Consider the following examples:

- Policymakers want to know which methods of reading instruction, and which types of reading materials, together produce the strongest academic benefits.
- Educators want to know which high school students are most likely to flourish at the university level.
- Parents want to know what characteristics to look for when evaluating the relative desirability of public, private, and charter schools.
- Researchers want to know which variables have a substantial impact on the incidence of depression on different groups of adolescents.

Information about each of these topics has been obtained by means of **multiple regression** analyses. The purpose of multiple regression is to discover the combination and weighting of **predictor variables** that yield the highest possible correlation with a **criterion variable** (also called an "outcome" or "dependent" variable). The higher the correlation, the greater the accuracy with which values of the criterion variable can be predicted given information about the predictor variables. (**Simple regression** explores the relationship between one predictor and one criterion variable, but since most regression analyses incorporate more than one predictor, the focus of this section is on multiple regression concepts.)

Multiple regression is based on three assumptions:

- The predictor variables are uncorrelated with each other.
- Any relationship between predictors and criterion variable will be linear.
- Residuals (differences between predicted and observed values) will be normally distributed.

Minor violations of these assumptions are considered tolerable. To some extent, correlations between predictor variables and nonlinear relationships between predictors and criterion variables (as revealed in scatterplots) can be corrected statistically.

The most immediately useful results obtained through a regression analysis are sets of predictors, regression coefficients, and R^2 values. These three concepts are described below and illustrated through discussion of a study by Kirby, Parrila, and Pfeiffer (2003) on how well phonological awareness and word naming speed in kindergarten can predict reading performance through grade 5.

SETS OF PREDICTORS   In some cases, the researcher chooses all of the predictor variables that will be included in a regression analysis. The researcher might include all of the predictors at once, or use a hierarchical method in which predictors are entered individually (or in groups) in order to see how the addition of each predictor (or group of predictors) affects the strength of the relationship with the criterion.

In other cases, the researcher's statistical software program uses a **stepwise method** to select predictors with the greatest predictive power while excluding less helpful ones from the model. Several types of stepwise procedures are available, each relying on a different approach to identifying the strongest set of predictors.

Whether or not the researcher chooses the predictors included in the regression analysis, the analysis may focus on individual predictors, or it may also include one or more interaction terms. Each interaction between predictors is included in the form of a single term. Effects of covariates can also be controlled for in regression analyses, analogous to the way that covariates can be identified and controlled for in ANCOVA procedures.

In the Kirby et al. (2003) study, the researchers chose the variables used in their regression analyses. They used a hierarchical method in which the predictor variables were entered in groups. The first group consisted of three covariates: scores obtained at kindergarten age from two subtests of the Cognitive Assessment System (CAS) and a letter recognition test. Treating these variables as covariates allowed the researchers to control for mental ability (CAS scores) and for prior exposure to print (letter recognition test). The second group of variables entered into the regression analysis were the two main predictors: phonological awareness (PA) and word naming speed (NS). Using these two groups of predictors, three separate regression analyses were conducted, each focusing on a different criterion variable: word attack, word identification, and reading comprehension. (The criterion variables were measured by means of the Woodcock Reading Mastery-Revised test. Word attack and word identification were measured each year from kindergarten through grade 5, while reading comprehension was measured from grades 1 to 5.) Table 11.6 provides a summary of the variables used in Kirby et al.'s multiple regression analyses

REGRESSION COEFFICIENTS   A **regression coefficient** indicates how much a criterion variable changes on average given one unit of change in a predictor variable (when all other predictors are held constant). Depending on how the unit of change is defined, two types of regression coefficients can be distinguished. The **unstandardized coefficient** reflects the original unit on which the variable was measured, while the **standardized coefficient** indicates how much the criterion

TABLE 11.6 Multiple Regression Variables in Kirby, Parrila, and Pfeiffer (2003)

Predictors: Phonological awareness (PA), naming speed (NS)
Criterion variables: Word attack, word identification, reading comprehension
Covariates: Scores on two CAS subtests (FR and VSR), letter recognition test (LR)

variable changes given one standard deviation of change in the predictor. The standardized coefficient is commonly referred to as the **beta coefficient**, or β.

The beta coefficient provides a numerical estimate of the strength of the association between predictor and criterion variables when the effects of other predictors are held constant. Positive betas indicate a positive relationship between predictor and criterion. Negative beta values indicate a negative relationship between predictor and criterion. Beta coefficients can be calculated for individual predictors and/or for groups of predictors. p values are typically reported in order to indicate whether or not each positive or negative relationship between predictor(s) and criterion variable is significant.

Beta coefficients and other results from the multiple regression analyses in Kirby, Parrila, and Pfeiffer (2003) are given in Table 11.7. Each individual table within Table 11.7 presents the results for one of the three criterion variables. The results for Step 1 (covariates) and Step 2 (PA and NS) are presented separately in the three tables. The beta coefficients (labeled as β coefficients) are given for each grade and variable in each step of the multiple regression analysis. Significant coefficients are marked with an asterisk.

TABLE 11.7 Results of Hierarchical Multiple Regression in Kirby, Parrila, and Pfeiffer (2003) for Word Attack, Word Identification, and Reading Comprehension

| | | Step 1 | | | | Step 2 | |
| | | β Coefficients | | | | β Coefficients | |
Grade	R^2	LR	FM	VSR	ΔR^2	PA	NS
\multicolumn{8}{c}{(a) Word Attack as Criterion Variable}
K	.146***	.177*	.171*	.154	.155***	.504***	−.101
1	.205***	.324**	.137	.111	.217***	.570***	−.140
2	.292***	.392***	.113	.170	.102***	.344**	−.157
3	.263***	.385***	.085	.166	.067*	.153	−.247*
4	.252***	.369**	.082	.176	.092**	.256*	−.241*
5	.358***	.323**	.094	.349**	.055*	.088	−.260*
\multicolumn{8}{c}{(b) Word Identification as Criterion Variable}
K	.218***	.273**	.219**	.112	.203***	.540***	−.179*
1	.309***	.432***	.169*	.083	.255***	.591***	−.203**
2	.378***	.458***	.157	.153	.101***	.302**	−.209*
3	.354***	.400***	.127	.233*	.092**	.152	−.306**
4	.409***	.433***	.108	.269**	.097**	.113	−.347**
5	.377***	.368***	.144	.290**	.079**	.141	−.293**
\multicolumn{8}{c}{(c) Reading Comprehension as Criterion Variable}
1	.302***	.436***	.155	.081	.260***	.560***	−.261**
2	.390***	.488***	.158	.124	.080**	.225*	−.228*
3	.366***	.370***	.163	.253**	.064**	.064	−.284**
4	.509***	.422***	.166	.338***	.082**	.070	−.332***
5	.433***	.262**	.194*	.409***	.089**	−.015	−.366***
5[a]	.423***	.385***	.220*	.295**	.068*	.077	−.281**

[a] Gates–MacGinitie Reading Comprehension Test.

*$p < .05$. **$p < .01$. ***$p < .001$.

You can see that for word attack, for example, the beta coefficients for the covariate LR (letter recognition) in Step 1 are positive and significant at each grade. This tells you that at each grade, the letter recognition score that had been obtained at kindergarten is significantly positively related to scores on the word attack measure—the better the letter recognition skills in kindergarten, the better the word attack skills throughout elementary school. Scores for the other two covariates (FM and VSR, the two subtests of the CAS) were only significantly related to word attack in two cases. The beta coefficients given for Step 2 show that both of the main predictors of interest are significantly related to word attack at different ages. Scores on phonological awareness (PA) obtained at kindergarten significantly predicted word attack at kindergarten, first grade, and second grade. The relationship is positive—the higher the PA scores, the higher the word attack scores. From third to fifth grade, scores on word naming speed (NS) obtained at kindergarten significantly predicted word attack. Here, the negative beta coefficients tell us that the relationship is negative—higher naming speed scores in kindergarten are associated with lower word attack scores in third to fifth grade.

R^2 VALUES R^2 is the squared value of R, the correlation between a criterion variable and one or more predictors (taken together). The R^2 statistic indicates how much variability in the criterion variable can be predicted from variability in the predictor(s). A separate F test indicates whether or not the R^2 value is significant.

When the researcher chooses predictors, a R^2 value will be given for each predictor and each combination of predictors. If a stepwise procedure is used, information will be obtained as to how the overall R^2 value changes as each predictor is added or removed from the model. This information is important because in many cases a predictor will have a different impact depending on which additional predictors it is combined with.

If you look back at Table 11.7, you can see the R^2 values for each covariate at each grade in Step 1. You can also see in Step 2 the ΔR^2 values for the main predictors combined. These "delta R-squared" values indicate the change in R^2 obtained once the main predictors are introduced after the first step. Significant ΔR^2 values tell us that the predictor variables, taken together, account for a significant amount of variability in the criterion variable even after the association with the covariates is considered. For example, you can see that for word identification, each ΔR^2 value is significant at each age. Even after controlling for mental ability (CAS subtest scores) and prior exposure to print (LR scores), the combination of phonological awareness and naming speed in kindergarten predicts a significant amount of variability in word identification skills throughout elementary school.

On the whole, the results of the three multiple regression analyses given in Table 11.7 suggest that phonological awareness and word naming speed in kindergarten both predict reading performance throughout elementary school to some extent.

Nonparametric Tests

As noted earlier, nonparametric tests are appropriate when all measures are based on nominal or ordinal scales, when the population distribution is skewed or unknown, or when some other basic parametric assumption has been strongly violated. As you will see, the scale underlying key measures is the major determinant of whether a nonparametric test should be used.

Chi Square

Chi square, the most widely used nonparametric test, is used to analyze the frequencies of each level of a nominal variable. The data are counted rather than measured. For example, the numbers of boys versus girls at each of three schools might be tallied in order to determine whether the gender ratio is the same across schools.

The purpose of the chi-square analysis is to determine whether observed data differ from expected values. In general, the "expected" values represent the null hypothesis that the variables are unrelated (e.g., the ratio of boys to girls is the same across Schools A, B, and C). The alternative hypothesis is that the variables are related (e.g., compared to Schools B and C, the ratio of boys to girls is significantly higher in School A). Examples of questions that could be addressed through chi-square tests include the following:

- Are the proportions of gifted students the same in urban versus rural school districts? If not, in which type of school district are there proportionally more students labeled as gifted?

- Among high school students, is there an association between grade in school and plans after graduation (attending college vs. working)?

- When the attentional skills of students with ADHD are tested before and after a behavioral intervention, is the number of students who improve greater than the number who either stay the same or get worse?

The chi-square analysis yields a statistic, also pronounced "chi square" but written notationally as χ^2. Given the χ^2 value and the degrees of freedom, the researcher can determine from a table (or software program) whether the observed and expected values are significantly different or not. (The table of critical χ^2 values is given in the appendix as Table A.4.) A statistic known as Cramer's phi coefficient can provide information about effect size (i.e., the strength of association between variables).

The formula for a simple chi-square test is given below.

$$\chi^2 = \Sigma\left[\frac{(O-E)^2}{E}\right]$$

(11.6)

In this formula, Σ means "sum of," O refers to observed frequencies, and E refers to expected frequencies.

Suppose we want to know whether there is a relationship between gender and type of American history class taken by students in a particular high school. At this school there are two types of American history: regular and advanced placement (AP). Our first step is to find out how many boys and girls there are in each class and tabulate the results, as in Table 11.8. The boldface numbers in the table are observed frequencies, while the small numbers in parentheses are expected frequencies.

You might be wondering at this point how the expected frequencies were obtained. Although statistical software programs readily do this for us, we can obtain expected values for any one cell in a chi-square table by simply multiplying the total number of observed values in the column by the total number of observed values in the row, and then dividing by the total number of observed values overall. (In other words, $E = C_t R_t/T$.) In this example, the expected value for boys in regular history classes is obtained by multiplying the column total (202) by the row total (140) and dividing by the overall total (280). Notice that the expected values of boys and girls within each type of history class are equal—a reflection of the null hypothesis that gender and type of history class are unrelated.

TABLE 11.8 Numbers of Boys and Girls Enrolled in Regular and AP History Classes in One School District

	Regular history	AP history
Boys	**98** (101)	**42** (40)
Girls	**104** (101)	**36** (40)

TABLE 11.9 Numbers of Boys and Girls Enrolled in Regular and AP History Classes in Another School District

	Regular history	AP history
Boys	**110** (96)	**30** (44)
Girls	**82** (96)	**58** (44)

Using the formula in Equation 11.6, we can calculate the χ^2 value through the following steps:

1. Subtract each expected value from the corresponding observed value, as follows:

$$98 - 101 = -3$$
$$104 - 101 = 3$$
$$42 - 40 = 2$$
$$36 - 40 = -4$$

2. Square each result from the previous step. This yields 9, 9, 4, and 16.

3. Divide each result from the previous step by the expected value. This yields 9/101, 9/101, 4/42, and 16/36, which correspond to .089, .089, .095, and .444, respectively.

4. Sum the values from the previous step. The result is .717. This is the chi-square value.

5. Calculate the degrees of freedom. For chi-square analyses involving two variables, the degrees of freedom equal one less than the number of rows multiplied by one less than the number of columns. In other words, $df = (R - 1)(C - 1)$. In this example, the value for degrees of freedom is 1.

By looking at a table of chi-square values, such as Table A.4 in the appendix of this book, we would find that our calculated value is not significant. Now consider the data in Table 11.9. Here again, the district consists of 140 students of each gender, but the distribution of students across history classes differs. The χ^2 value in this case is 8.17 (you can check for yourself if you like). This value is significant at $p < .01$. Evidently, there is an association between gender and type of class this time: Boys are more likely to take regular history, whereas girls are more likely to take AP history.

Other Nonparametric Tests

The chi-square test is useful for examining relationships between nominal variables. Researchers use other tests when the data are ordinal. For example, the **Wilcoxon signed-rank** test functions like a *t*-test for dependent samples when the data are ordinal and paired. If an admissions officer were to provide two rankings for each applicant (one for prior achievement, the other for future potential), the Wilcoxon signed-rank test could be used to determine whether the two sets of rankings are significantly different or not. In contrast, the **Mann–Whitney test** serves the same purpose as a *t*-test for independent samples when the data are ordinal rather than truly continuous. The Mann–Whitney test could be used to determine whether two admissions officers' rankings of a set of applicants are significantly different or not. If there were more than two administrators, the **Kruskal–Wallis test** could be used (analogous to a one-way ANOVA) to determine whether or not their rankings are significantly different. Finally, if our interest were to determine amount of relationship rather than likelihood of difference, the **Spearman rank–order correlation** would tell us the extent of association between two sets of rankings. These are just a few of the nonparametric tests that are commonly used.

To close out this chapter, Table 11.10 summarizes the statistical tests previously discussed (along with the correlational statistics described in Chapter 9). Spotlight on Research 11.3 describes a study in which numerous parametric and nonparametric statistics are used.

TABLE 11.10 A Sample of Statistical Tests Commonly Used in Educational Research

Type of Test	Name of Test	Purpose of Test
Parametric	*t*-test for independent samples	Determine whether two independent means are different
Parametric	*t*-test for dependent samples	Determine whether two dependent means are different
Parametric	ANOVA	Determine whether two or more means are different
Parametric	ANCOVA	Determine whether two or more means are different while controlling for effects of at least one covariate
Parametric	Regression	Predict values of criterion variable from one or more predictor variables, with option of controlling for effects of at least one covariate
Parametric	Pearson product–moment correlation	Measure strength of association between two continuous correlation variables
Nonparametric	Point–biserial correlation	Measure strength of association between one continuous and one categorical variable
Nonparametric	Phi coefficient	Measure strength of association between two categorical (binary) variables
Nonparametric	Chi square	Determine whether categorical variables are related
Nonparametric	Wilcoxon signed-rank	Determine whether two dependent rankings are different
Nonparametric	Mann–Whitney	Determine whether two independent rankings are different
Nonparametric	Kruskal–Wallis	Determine whether two or more rankings are different
Nonparametric	Spearman rank–order correlation	Determine extent of association between two rankings

ADHD and Expressive Writing Limitations: A Causal–Comparative Study

It is well known that students with attention-deficit/hyperactivity disorder (ADHD) encounter serious academic challenges at school. However, few studies have explored whether children with ADHD have poorer writing skills in particular. Some studies suggest that given a finite period of time, children with ADHD tend to write less than their peers—not because they have fewer ideas or slower writing speed, but because their ability to plan and organize a written text is somewhat impaired. In a 2007 study reported in the *Journal of Learning Disabilities**, Anna Maria Re, Martina Pedron, and Cesare Cornoldi systematically explored differences between students with ADHD and matched controls in their expressive writing skills.

In the first of three experiments, Re and colleagues measured the writing skills of 24 sixth- and seventh-graders with ADHD and a control group consisting of 24 students matched by age, gender, and school. The study was conducted in Italy, and each group of students participated in two writing tasks, one eliciting pictorial description and the other measuring writing speed:

> *Children were administered the Description test from the BVSCO (Tressoldi & Cornoldi, 1991) in their classroom. This task is based on the presentation of a colored figure showing people at the zoo, with a variety of animals in their surroundings. Children receive a copy of the figure and a response sheet corresponding to the type of paper on which they are used to writing. They have 10 min to write a text on the basis of the following instruction: "Imagine that you have been at the zoo and you have to describe the scene you see in the picture to some friends who were not there." As a control, children were administered a writing speed subtest taken from the same BVSCO. This test requires writing, in letters, as many numbers as possible in 1 min, starting from uno (one) and proceeding with the subsequent numbers of the number series. There was no significant difference between the two groups' performance on this task.*

Two independent raters evaluated the expressive writing essays (the description of the people at the zoo) on four qualitative dimensions:

1. *adequacy, defined as the adequacy of the written text with respect to the task request;*
2. *structure, based on the organization of the text;*
3. *grammar, concerning the correct use of punctuation, subdivision in paragraphs, correct use of verb tenses, and correct concordance between gender and number of nouns, verbs, and adjectives (very important in Italian); and*
4. *lexicon, defined as the quantity of different words used.*

Means scores obtained by each group of students on these four qualitative "parameters" were compared through *t*-tests for independent samples:

> *The agreement of the two raters was high for each of the four parameters (i.e., adequacy, r = .89; structure, r = .84; lexicon, r = .83; and grammar, r = .78). Therefore, in the subsequent analyses, we only considered the ratings given by the first rater.*

> *Children with ADHD symptoms obtained significantly lower scores than controls on adequacy (ADHD, M = 2.62, SD = 0.78; controls, M = 3.92, SD = 0.87, t(46) = 5.41, p < .01), structure (ADHD, M = 2.25, SD = 0.99; controls, M = 3.04, SD = 0.99, t(46) = 2.76, p < .01), lexicon (ADHD, M = 1.92, SD = 0.93; controls, M = 3.29, SD = 1.30, t(46) = 4.21, p < .01), and grammar (ADHD, M = 1.83, SD = 0.82; controls, M = 3.12, SD = 1.11, t(46) = 4.58, p < .01). In other words, children with ADHD symptoms obtained lower scores than controls on all qualitative parameters.*

Re and colleagues also analyzed an objective measure of essay length. (The term "CI" in the following passage refers to confidence intervals, as described earlier in this chapter.)

> *We also computed the quantity of words written by every child, and we found that children with ADHD symptoms wrote significantly less, on average, than controls. In the group with children showing ADHD symptoms, the mean length of the text was 51.79 words (SD = 21; 95% CI = 42.92–60.66), with a range between 20 and 90. In the control group, the mean length of the text was 68.21 words (SD = 32.96; 95% CI = 54.29–82.12), with a range between 32 and 143. A t-test comparison between group means showed a significant difference, t(46) = 2.06, p < .05.*

A final set of analyses looked at percentages of three types of spelling errors: phonological errors (PhE), in which an adult's reading of a word would be incorrectly pronounced; nonphonological errors (NPhE), in which our reading of the word would be correctly pronounced even though the word is spelled incorrectly; and third-type errors, in which accents and other phonological marks are missing. (In the passage below, you will see that nonsignificant results are reported as $p > .05$.)

> Because the length of the essay was different for each participant, we computed the percentages of the three types of errors with respect to the total number of written words. We found that large groups of children had a very low percentage of errors, suggesting that a control for the normality of the distribution and the use of nonparametric tests would be appropriate. In fact, the Kolmogorov–Smirnov test, a statistical test for the evaluation of distribution normality, showed that the distributions deviated significantly from the normal distribution for all types of error ($p < .05$), so we used nonparametric tests. First, we compared the two groups on the overall percentage of errors with the nonparametric Mann–Whitney U test and found a significant difference between groups, $U = 97.50$, $p < .001$. In fact, the group with children showing ADHD symptoms made more than four times more errors than the control group, with a mean percentage of errors higher than 7% (ADHD, $M = 7.88$, $SD = 6.48$, range $= 0–24.24$; control, $M = 1.66$, $SD = 2.45$, range $= 0–9.38$).
>
> When we considered the three different types of errors separately, we could see that many children were perfectly accurate in one or more categories. For this reason, we decided to divide children into two categories according to whether they had made one or more errors of a particular type or no such errors. We made this division for the three types of error. The results showed that the two groups were significantly different only for the third type of error . . . whereas the differences between groups were slight both for PhE (62.5% of ADHD and 41.7% of controls made errors), $\chi 2(1, N = 48) = 2.09$, $p > .05$, and for NPhE (29.2% ADHD vs. 12.5% control), $\chi 2(1, N = 48) = 2.02$, $p > .05$. In contrast, there was a highly significant difference in the third error type, which was present for 87.5% of children with ADHD and only 29.2% of controls, $\chi 2(1, N = 48) = 16.8$, $p < .001$.

Re and colleagues summarized the results of this first experiment as follows:

> Study 1 confirmed that children with ADHD symptoms, despite showing an adequate standard of general abilities, presented expressive writing difficulties. Their problems were rather general, as they concerned all the measured aspects. Children with ADHD symptoms were rated as less proficient writers on all four basic parameters (adequacy, structure, lexicon, and grammar). They produced shorter texts and made a higher percentage of errors. These difficulties were not related to writing speed, because the two groups did not differ on this measure.

In their second experiment, Re and colleagues measured the writing skills of 163 second-through fifth-grade students—one group with ADHD and a control group once again matched on age, gender, and school. In this experiment, two writing tasks were administered—the same expressive writing task from the first experiment (image condition), and a modified version of that task in which instead of a picture children based their descriptions on the following verbal scaffold (scaffold condition):

> Try to imagine that you and another child have been to visit the zoo, where there were a lot of people and animals. At one point you stopped in front of a cage in which there were many parrots of different colors.

The same four dimensions of children's writing were analyzed as in the first experiment. The descriptive statistics are presented in the table on the next page, by group and writing condition (image vs. scaffold), followed by Re and colleagues' description of the main statistical analyses.

> Four 2×2 (Group $\times$ Task [verbal vs. picture]) ANOVAs were run for the different parameters. We did not find a significant difference between the two tasks, but we found differences between the two groups on all aspects: adequacy: $F(1, 324 = 261.50$, $MSE = 307.10$, $p < .001$, partial $\eta 2 = .447$; structure: $F(1324) = 213.18$, $MSE = 290.47$, $p < .001$, partial $\eta 2 = .397$; lexicon: $F(1324) = 239.52$, $MSE = 220.48$, $p < .001$, partial $\eta 2 = .425$; and grammar: $F(1324) = 249.17$, $MSE = 209.35$, $p < .001$, partial $\eta 2 = .435 \ldots$
>
> We also carried out a 2×2 (Group $\times$ Task) ANOVA to compare the length of the descriptions and found a significant difference between groups (ADHD: $M = 52.13$, $SD = 1.55$, 95% CI $= 49.09–55.18$; control: $M = 67.97$, $SD = 1.55$, 95% CI $= 64.92–71.01$; $F(1, 324) = 52.33$, $MSE = 780.88$, $p < .001$, partial $\eta 2 = .139$), but no significant difference between the two conditions. . . .

Study 2: Means and Standard Deviations on Four Basic Parameters of Expressive Writing in Two Conditions for ADHD and Control Groups

| | ADHD group[a] | | | | | | Control group[a] | | | | | |
| | Image condition | | | Scaffold condition | | | Image condition | | | Scaffold condition | | |
Parameter	M	SD	95% CI	M	SD	95% CI	M	SD	95% CI	M	SD	95% CI
Adequacy	2.87	0.84	2.73–3.00	2.98	0.91	2.84–3.12	4.15	0.65	4.05–4.25	4.16	0.66	4.06–4.26
Structure	2.77	0.70	2.67–2.88	2.82	0.68	2.72–2.93	3.88	0.81	3.75–4.00	3.88	0.79	3.76–4.01
Lexicon	2.39	0.66	2.29–2.49	2.39	0.58	2.30–2.48	3.40	0.66	3.30–3.50	3.39	0.75	3.27–3.50
Grammar	2.34	0.64	2.25–2.43	2.31	0.60	2.22–2.40	3.29	0.71	3.18–3.40	3.34	0.67	3.24–3.45

Note. ADHD = Attention−Deficit/Hyperactivity Disorder.
[a]$n = 163$.

[T]here was no difference in the number of words used to write the description of an image alone or with the aid of a verbal scaffold. That is, children with ADHD symptoms and controls wrote on average a similar number of words in the two tasks, but in general, as in Study 1, the children with ADHD symptoms wrote fewer words than the control group.

Finally, Re and colleagues analyzed the extent of spelling errors among each group, overall and for each type of error.

[C]hildren with ADHD symptoms made more errors than control children both in the condition with images (ADHD: $M = 3.6$, $SD = 2.6$, range = 0−13; controls: $M = 1.6$, $SD = 1.5$, range = 0−7, Mann−Whitney $U = 6,800$, $p < .001$) and in the condition with verbal scaffolding (ADHD: $M = 3.7$, $SD = 2.5$, range = 0−14; controls: $M = 1.7$, $SD = 1.6$, range = 0−9, Mann−Whitney $U = 6,178$, $p < .001$). In particular, in the condition with images, 22.7% of children with ADHD symptoms versus 13.5% of control children made PhE, $\chi 2(1, N = 326) =$ 11.95, $p = .001$; 36.2% of children with ADHD symptoms versus 23.9% of control children made NPhE, $\chi 2(1, N = 326) = 20.47$, $p < .001$; and 39.9% of children with ADHD symptoms versus 30.1% of controls made third-type errors, $\chi 2(1, N = 326) = 14.94$, $p < .001$. A similar result could be observed in the verbal scaffolding condition: 22.2% of children with ADHD symptoms versus 11.4% of controls made PhE, $\chi 2 (1, N = 326) = 17.24$, $p < .001$; 35% of children with ADHD symptoms versus 24.8% of controls made NPhE, $\chi 2(1, N = 326) = 13.90$, $p < .001$; and 43.4% of children with ADHD symptoms versus 32.3% of controls made third-type errors, $\chi 2(1, N = 326) = 20.77$, $p < .001$.

The results of a third study supported the conclusions of the first two: Children with ADHD score lower than age- and gender-matched controls on both qualitative and quantitative measures of writing quality.

*Re, A.M., Pedron, M., & Cornoldi, C. (2007). Expressive writing difficulties in children described as exhibiting ADHD symptoms. *Journal of Learning Disabilities, 40*(3), 244−255. Quoted with permission from the publisher.

A Look Ahead

In this chapter you studied the conceptual basis of inferential statistics and learned about a few of the most widely used statistical tests, as summarized in Table 11.10.

Chapter 12 focuses on the representation of statistical information in tables and figures, and includes a discussion of some of the more advanced correlational techniques currently popular in educational research. Introduction to these techniques extends the discussions of simple correlation in Chapter 9 and multiple regression in this chapter.

Applications: A Guide for Beginning Researchers

Here are some ideas from the chapter that will help you plan your research:

- Once you know what software program you will use to analyze data, figure out how you will learn to run inferential analyses with the program if you do not already know how to do so.
- Choose the inferential statistics that best address each question you have about your data. Review the statistical tests discussed in this chapter, but bear in mind that there are many others to choose from.
- At least some of the inferential statistics you choose should provide information of direct relevance to your research question.
- Interpretation of most inferential analyses will require more information than could be provided in this chapter.

Chapter Summary

If an infinite number of samples is obtained from a population, the sampling errors will be normally distributed. Sampling error can be estimated from a single sample through statistics such as the standard error of the mean. The standard error of the mean can be used in turn to calculate confidence intervals.

In hypothesis testing, a significance level is chosen as the standard for whether or not to reject the null hypothesis and determine that an effect is statistically significant. The researcher may correctly reject the null hypothesis, correctly fail to reject the null, incorrectly reject the null (Type I error), or incorrectly fail to reject the null (Type II error). Selection of a significance level (alpha) represents a decision about the extent of Type I and Type II error the researcher is willing to risk.

Tests of significance may be nondirectional or directional and are carried out through calculation of actual significance values (p values). Effect sizes associated with each statistical test are an important source of information that complements information about significance.

Inferential statistics consist of parametric and nonparametric tests. Widely used parametric tests include t-tests, analyses of variance (ANOVAs), regression procedures, and correlation coefficients. Widely used nonparametric tests include the chi-square analysis. Each type of statistic is based on different assumptions about the sample and population distributions, and each statistic yields a different kind of information. Computer software programs are used to calculate these statistics.

Key Terms

Inferential statistics	**Confidence interval**	**Significance level**
Sampling error	**Hypothesis testing**	**Statistical significance**
Standard error estimates	**Null hypothesis**	**Type I error**
Standard error of the mean	**Alternative hypothesis**	**Type II error**

Critical regions

Nondirectional test

Directional test

p values

Degrees of freedom

Effect size

Cohen's d

Parametric tests

Nonparametric tests

t-test

t-test for independent samples

t-test for dependent samples

Analysis of variance (ANOVA)

Repeated measures ANOVA

η^2

One-way ANOVA

Multiple comparisons

Scheffé test

Tukey HSD test

Bonferroni correction

Multifactorial ANOVA

Between-subjects factor

Within-subjects factor

Multivariate ANOVA (MANOVA)

Analysis of covariance (ANCOVA)

Covariate

Multivariate analysis of covariance (MANCOVA)

Multiple regression

Predictor variables

Criterion variable

Simple regression

Stepwise method

Regression coefficient

Unstandardized coefficient

Standardized coefficient

Beta coefficient

R^2

Chi square

χ^2

Wilcoxon signed-rank test

Mann–Whitney test

Kruskal–Wallis test

Spearman rank–order correlation

Exercises

1. Which of the following will tend to increase sampling error?

a) Increasing the sample size

b) Taking steps to obtain a more representative sample

c) Losing a large part of the sample through attrition

d) Obtaining a sample with the same gender distribution as the population

2. If the standard error of the mean estimated from a particular sample is extremely small (i.e., almost zero), what can we infer about the sample?

a) The standard deviation of the sample is very large, but the sample size is very small.

b) The extent of sampling error reflected in the sample may be very large.

c) The mean of the sample will almost certainly be very different from that of another sample drawn from the same population, but the standard deviations of each sample will be similar, if not identical.

d) The standard deviation of the sample is very small, the sample size is very large, or both.

3. The mean score on a test of creativity is 84, and the standard error of the mean is 6. Which of the following can be inferred about the population mean?

a) There is a 99.7% chance that the population mean falls between 66 and 102.

b) There is a 68.26% chance that the population mean falls between 83 and 85.

c) There is a 99.7% chance that the population mean falls between 78 and 90.

d) There is a 68.26% chance that the population mean falls between 72 and 96.

4. If you have set an alpha level at .05 and obtained a *p* value of .15, what can you conclude about the effect being tested?

a) The effect is significant.

b) The effect is not significant.

c) The effect is three times as likely as chance to be significant.

d) There is no possibility of Type II error.

5. In a study comparing the overall TIMSS scores of 12th-graders in the United States, Japan, and Taiwan, what is the null hypothesis?

a) The students of one country will have the highest scores, the students of another country will have the lowest scores, and the students of the third country will have scores exactly midway between the scores of the other two student groups.

b) There will be no differences in scores across the three countries.

c) The students of one country will obtain scores that are significantly different from the others, while no differences will be observed between students from the latter two countries.

d) American students will obtain the highest scores, followed by Japanese students and then by students from Taiwan.

6. Which of the following illustrates Type I error?

a) A researcher finds that teacher–student ratios are unrelated to teachers' job satisfaction, but it turns out that in fact these variables are closely related.

b) A researcher finds no differences between two states in their per capita spending on public school students, and it turns out that there are in fact no differences in per capita spending between these states.

c) A researcher finds significant differences between 11- and 12-year-olds on a test of hypothetical reasoning, but it turns out that the test has poor construct validity and there are in fact no differences in hypothetical reasoning between these two age groups.

d) A researcher finds a significant correlation between the socioeconomic status of parents and the number of books they purchase for their children, and it turns out that in fact these variables are closely related.

7. How would the risk of Type II error be affected when the alpha level for a particular test is lowered from .05 to .001?

a) The risk will increase.

b) The risk will decrease.

c) The risk will be unchanged.

d) It is impossible to say.

For questions 8–16, choose the statistic most likely to be used to address the question.

8. Is the extent of teachers' professional development activities related to the number of years they have been teaching and the affluence of their school district (as measured on a ratio scale)?

a) Chi square

b) One-way ANOVA

c) Multiple regression

d) ANCOVA

9. Is the percentage of automobile accidents involving teenage (as opposed to adult) drivers greater now than it was exactly 15 years ago?

a) *t*-test for dependent samples

b) Chi square

c) ANCOVA

d) Pearson product–moment correlation

10. Among U.S. teachers, is there an association between teaching level (elementary vs. secondary) and the proportions of female versus male teachers?

a) One-way ANOVA

b) Mann–Whitney test

c) ANCOVA

d) Chi square

11. How accurately can children's IQ be predicted given knowledge of their parents' IQ, educational levels, and socioeconomic status (annual income in dollars)?

a) *t*-test for independent samples

b) Pearson product–moment correlation

c) ANCOVA

d) Multiple regression

12. Are there gender differences in IQ?

a) Two-way ANOVA

b) *t*-test for independent samples

c) ANCOVA

d) Pearson product–moment correlation

13. Is the size of a Parent–Teacher Association related to the size of the school district in which it is located?

a) Pearson product–moment correlation

b) Multiple regression

c) *t*-test for independent samples

d) MANOVA

14. Following an alcohol awareness program, will the average resistance of teenagers to drinking-related peer pressure increase relative to their resistance before participation in the program?

a) Two-way ANOVA

b) Mann–Whitney test

c) Pearson product–moment correlation

d) *t*-test for dependent samples

15. Is children's motivation to succeed at school related to the size, ethnicity, and socio-economic status of their families?

a) Chi square

b) Kruskal–Wallis test

c) Multiple regression

d) Two-way ANOVA

16. Are there gender differences in mean achievement levels when differences in residence (rural vs. urban) are controlled for?

a) One-way ANOVA

b) ANCOVA

c) MANOVA

d) MANCOVA

17. *Critical thinking question*: In a study on the relationship between class size and disciplinary problems, a measure is used in which the extent of disciplinary problems is treated as a continuous variable. From a statistical perspective, how should class size be coded? Should it be treated as a continuous variable (number of students in a class), or as a discrete variable? If it is treated as a discrete variable, should there be two levels (large vs. small classes), three levels (large vs. medium vs. small classes), or should some other approach to categorization be used?

Answers to Exercises

1. c   **2.** d   **3.** a   **4.** b   **5.** b   **6.** c   **7.** a   **8.** c   **9.** b   **10.** d   **11.** d

12. b   **13.** a   **14.** d   **15.** c   **16.** b

17. *Possible answer*: From a statistical perspective, the best way to treat class size depends in part on the research question. If the researcher is interested in the general relationship between class size and disciplinary problems, treating class size as a continuous variable and running a correlational analysis would provide the most information about the relationship between the variables for different values of class size. In contrast, if the researcher has a hypothesis about particular class sizes, a categorical definition may be preferable. If the researcher believes that class sizes larger than 30 undermine discipline, then it might be preferable to contrast "large" classes (those with 30 or more students) with smaller ones through an ANOVA or regression analysis. The researcher can contrast "large" versus "small" classes, or introduce an additional distinction between "small" and "medium" if he or she has hypotheses about the distinction. Sample size might also be a consideration. If the sample is relatively small, there might be a loss of statistical power if "small" and "medium" classes are distinguished.

Suggestions For Further Reading

Research Article: Furrer, C., & Skinner, E. (2003). Sense of relatedness as a factor in children's academic engagement and performance. *Journal of Educational Psychology, 95*(1), 148–162.

This correlational study on the relationship between relatedness and school engagement among third- through sixth-graders presents an accessible illustration of multiple regression techniques.

Application Article: Reed, J. M., Marchand-Martella, N. E., Martella, R. C., & Kolts, R. L. (2007). Assessing the effects of the Reading Success Level A program with fourth-grade students at a Title I elementary school. *Education and Treatment of Children*, *30*(1), 45–68.

This pre-experimental study on the effects of a reading intervention illustrates the use of a variety of parametric and nonparametric statistics.

Extension Article: Floyd, R. G., Hojnoski, R. L, & Key, J. (2006). Preliminary evidence of the technical adequacy of the Preschool Numeracy Indicators. *School Psychology Review*, *35*(4), 627–644.

This quantitative study makes use of a variety of parametric and nonparametric statistics in the evaluation of the reliability and validity of a test of preschoolers' numerical skills.

Statistical Representation

Tim Pannell/©Corbis

After studying this chapter, you will be able to answer the following questions:

- How are tables used to represent single-variable data?

- What are the different types of graphs used to represent single-variable data?

- How are tables used to represent multivariate data?

- What are the different types of graphs used to represent multivariate data?

- What is statistical modeling?

- What are some of the more widely used statistical models?

This chapter will prepare you to do the following:

- Understand and evaluate tables and graphs in research reports

- Understand and evaluate statistical models in research reports

- Create appropriate tables and graphs for your own quantitative data

Introduction

In Chapters 10 and 11 you learned about the use and interpretation of statistics in quantitative research. In this chapter I discuss the representation of statistical data in tables and figures.

In a sense, most of what you studied in Chapter 10 concerns statistical representation. A mean represents a distribution. So do a median, a mode, and a standard deviation; in each case, a different aspect of the distribution is represented by a single number. What distinguishes the tables and figures discussed in this chapter is that they can represent large amounts of raw data, the results of statistical tests, and relationships between variables in a single visual display. The topics covered in this chapter range from the simple, single-variable table to the complex path diagram in which the strength of associations between variables is represented through a schematization of the results of multiple regression analyses.

Tables and Figures

A **table** consists of information organized by rows and columns, while a **figure** consists of a graphic portrayal of information. The focus of this chapter is on the use of tables and figures to represent quantitative information, although of course they are used for qualitative presentations too.

The ultimate purpose of a table or figure is the clear, accurate, and simple representation of large amounts of information. Tables and figures are a small but integral part of the results sections of most research reports, owing to their brevity and informativeness—in most cases, any other form of presentation would be harder or more time-consuming to grasp, or would occupy far too much space. A good table or figure is concise and stands alone, in the sense that readers can quickly discern, without referring back to the main text, what kind of information is conveyed and how the information is organized.

This first section of this chapter focuses on the representation of statistical information about individual variables, while the second section focuses on the more common scenario in which statistical information about two or more variables is depicted.

Single-Variable Representation

In this section, some of the most common types of single-variable representation are reviewed.

Single-Variable Tables

Single-variable tables are most commonly used to represent frequencies. Frequency information may be reported in a conventional frequency table, or in a stem-and-leaf display.

FREQUENCY TABLES   The number of observations for each level of a discrete (nominal or ordinal) variable is referred to as the **frequency**. Examples of frequency information for one discrete variable include the following:

- The numbers of boys and girls in a particular elementary school
- The numbers of first-, second-, and third-tier universities in a particular state
- The number of charter schools that have been in existence for more than 10 years
- The number of first-year students in four high schools who plan to take Advanced Placement (AP) classes

As described in Chapter 10, all of the observations for a particular variable can be arranged into a frequency distribution, which depicts frequencies in the form of raw numbers. Frequency data may also be represented as proportions or percentages. (Proportions and percentages will be referred to interchangeably in this chapter, since you can readily convert one into the other without using a calculator.) Research reports typically include whichever form of information is most meaningful and readily comprehended in a particular context. Often, more than one type of frequency information will be helpful. Raw numbers are commonly reported when describing sample characteristics. If you are reading about a sample of students from different schools, it is helpful to know how many students from each school participated. At the same time, your evaluation of the quality of the sample will depend on knowing what percentage of the entire student body of each school participated in the study. Information about percentages is also helpful when describing the characteristics of large samples or populations,

An example of a frequency table for a single nominal variable is given in Table 12.1.

For continuous variables, frequencies may be represented for particular intervals, or ranges of values, as in Table 12.2.

STEM-AND-LEAF DISPLAYS   Another tabular approach for representing the frequency distributions of continuous variables is the **stem-and-leaf display** (also called a stemplot), in which each score is divided into "leaves" (the final digit of each score) and "stems" (all digits but the leaf). The stems and leaves are arranged vertically, so that the frequencies of each score can be quickly grasped, as illustrated in Table 12.3.

In Table 12.3, the stems are separated from the leaves by vertical lines. Each raw score can be recreated by combining each stem with each leaf and multiplying by the unit (0.1). For example, the first line of data represents two scores: 0.7 and 0.9.

TABLE 12.1 Frequency Table for Single Nominal Variable

Numbers of first-year students in four high schools who plan to take AP classes

High School	N
Jackson	59
Walker	47
Donovan	52
Central	44

TABLE 12.2 Table Summarizing Frequencies for Single Continuous Variable

Numbers of participants falling within different WISC-IV score intervals

WISC-IV Score	N
81–85	2
86–90	5
91–95	11
96–100	36
101–105	28
106–110	9
111–115	2
116–120	1

The second line represents four scores: 1.4, 1.8, 1.8, and 1.9. As you can see, the highest score in the distribution was 9.9, and it appears to be an outlier.

Stemplots are useful in that they provide a quick sense of the shape of a distribution that cannot be obtained simply by examining the raw scores. The data in Table 12.3, for instance, seem roughly normally distributed. Now that software programs can quickly graph distributions, stemplots are not as common as they used to be.

Parts of a Graph

Graphs of all sorts (not just those that represent single-variable frequencies) consist of several parts. The **y-axis** (also called the vertical axis or the ordinate) is oriented vertically on the page. The **x-axis** (also called the horizontal axis or the abscissa) is oriented horizontally on the page, at a right angle to the y-axis and typically extending from the base of the y-axis toward the right. Together the x- and y-axes define a **grid** in which data are represented. One or both axes may contain **ticks**, or small perpendicular lines that subdivide the axis into appropriate units. Each axis will be labeled with the variable name and the graph. A **legend** may be included

TABLE 12.3 Stem-and-Leaf Display of Frequency Data

Frequencies of scores on creativity measure (possible range 0–10)

Unit = 0.1

```
0 — 7 9
1 — 4 8 8 9
2 — 0 1 1 2 4 5 5 7 7 7 8 9 9
3 — 0 0 1 2 2 3 3 4 4 6 8 8 8 9 9
4 — 1 1 2 2 2 3 3 5 5 5 7 7 8 8
5 — 0 0 0 1 2 2 3 4 4 5 5 6 6 6 7 7 8 9
6 — 0 1 1 1 2 2 4 4 5 5 6 6 7 8 8 9
7 — 0 1 1 2 3 3 3 3 4 4 5 5 6 7 7
8 — 1 3 3 3 5 6 6
9 — 9
```

to help identify variables or variable levels depicted in the graph. (Legends are not usually needed for single-variable representation, since the *x*- and *y*-axis labels provide sufficient information.) Finally, the graph will contain a title that indicates what kind of information is displayed.

Single-Variable Graphs

Frequencies and other information for single variables can be represented by means of four types of graphs: bar graphs, histograms, frequency polygons, and pie charts. In each type, except for pie charts, the *y*-axis depicts frequency information.

BAR GRAPHS   A **bar graph** uses columns to represent information about each level of a nominal variable. In the case of frequency data, the height of each bar gives a quick sense of the frequencies. The *x*-axis of a bar graph consists of each level of the variable, as in the example provided in Figure 12.1, which summarizes the data from Table 12.1 in graphic form. Notice that there are tick marks in the *y*-axis of this graph corresponding to each interval. The *y*-axis is unlabeled, although it appears from the title of the graph that it represents raw numbers of students. Horizontal grid lines are provided to help discern the values of each bar.

Bar graphs are used sometimes to depict the frequencies of ordinal rankings, or the scores or score intervals associated with interval or ratio data, although polygons are considered more suitable for the representation of continuous data.

HISTOGRAMS   A **histogram** looks the same as a bar graph, except that the vertical edges of the columns touch each other. Histograms may be used to graph nominal, ordinal, interval, or ratio data. Although each bar is distinct, which implies that the *x*-axis variable consists of discrete levels, the fact that the bars touch can be taken to imply a continuum. The bars themselves should be equal in width. When appropriate, the *x*-axis of a histogram consists of each possible score or score interval arranged from lowest to highest, as in Figure 12.2, which presents the data from Table 12.2 in the form of a histogram.

Although a vertical arrangement of bars is most common in bar graphs and histograms, as in Figure 12.2, horizontal orientations are sometimes used, depending on the preference of the researcher. An example of a horizontal orientation is provided in Figure 12.3.

FIGURE 12.1 Bar Graph Summarizing Frequencies from Table 12.1

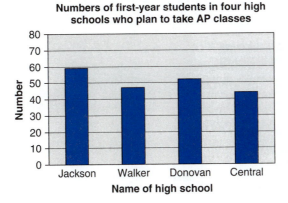

FIGURE 12.2 Histogram Representing Frequencies from Table 12.2

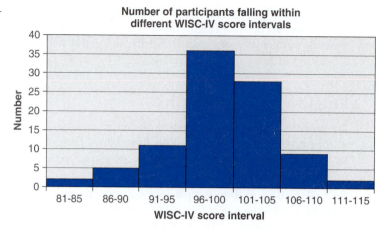

Number of participants falling within different WISC-IV score intervals

FREQUENCY POLYGONS A **frequency polygon** is the same as a histogram, except that points rather than columns are used to represent each x-axis value, and the points are connected by a line. The use of a line is helpful when it is assumed that the underlying variable is truly continuous. On the other hand, frequency polygons are not suitable for representing discrete variables, since the line in the graph clearly implies a continuum. You have already encountered examples of frequency polygons in my discussion of the normal curve in Chapter 10. Figure 12.4 presents the data from Table 12.2 (and the histogram from Figure 12.2) in the form of a frequency polygon. In this case, the histogram and the frequency polygon both suggest that the distribution roughly approximates a normal curve. Statistics such as the **Kolmogorov–Smirnov test** can be used to determine whether or not the frequency distribution for a single variable deviates significantly from normal.

PIE CHARTS The **pie chart** is a circular representation of a nominal or ordinal variable that has been divided into its constituents. Pie charts can be used to represent percentages of observations for each level of a single discrete variable. For example, Figure 12.5 presents the data from Table 12.2, Figure 12.2, and Figure 12.4 in the form of a pie chart. When using a pie chart to graph ordinal data, each level will be presented in order of increasing magnitude, either clockwise, as in Figure 12.5, or, very commonly, counter-clockwise.

FIGURE 12.3 Horizontally Oriented Histogram Representing Frequencies from Table 12.2

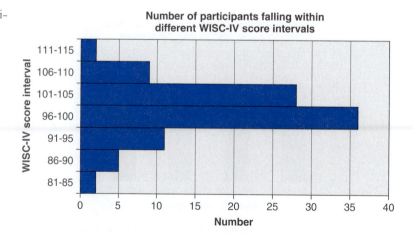

Number of participants falling within different WISC-IV score intervals

FIGURE 12.4 Frequency Polygon Representing Frequencies from Table 12.2

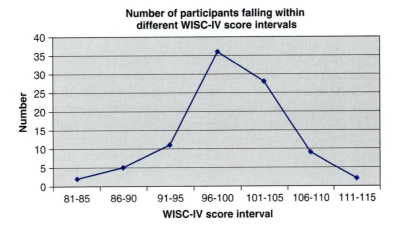

Selection of Graphs

Notice that rather than creating the pie chart in Figure 12.5, the *y*-axes in Figures 12.2 and 12.4 could have been modified so that the graphs give the percentage of the sample associated with each WISC–IV score interval. This illustrates one of many situations in which the researcher has some flexibility in the choice of graph to represent a particular distribution. It would be easier to discern the percentages of scores in each interval from a modified version of the histogram in Figure 12.2, or from the pie chart in Figure 12.5. On the other hand, the line graph in Figure 12.4 would be preferable if the goal is to show how closely the data approximate a normal distribution.

Notice that Figures 12.1, 12.2, and 12.4 could have also been modified so that they depict percentages of the target population rather than raw numbers. In Figure 12.1, for example, the percentages of first-year students at each school who are interested in AP classes could be quite revealing. If the schools differ in size,

FIGURE 12.5 Pie Chart Representing Frequencies from Table 12.2 in the Form of Percentages

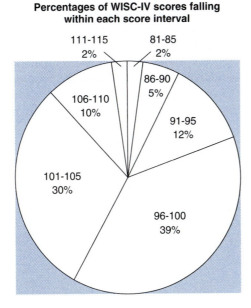

the raw frequency data might be misleading. Although Jackson students appear to show the greatest interest, Jackson might turn out to be the largest school. If so, student interest in AP classes might be proportionally less at Jackson than at the other schools. Of course, a statistical test such as the chi-square analysis described in Chapter 11 could determine whether there are significant differences in proportions of first-year students interested in AP classes across schools. But the figure itself should not be misleading. Raw numbers should not be reported in Figure 12.1 unless the schools are comparable in size, or unless information about frequencies is interesting in its own right, apart from information about proportions. (For example, an administrator who has to make hiring decisions might be most interested in actual frequencies of interested students.)

Multivariate Representation

The term **multivariate** refers to two or more variables. Tables and graphs are extremely useful for the representation of multivariate statistics.

Multivariate Tables

Multivariate tables can be used to represent frequencies, as well as a variety of other descriptive statistics and inferential test results.

FREQUENCIES   A **contingency table** depicts the relationship between two categorical variables. Frequency data (expressed as raw numbers, percentages, or proportions) is provided for each intersection of the levels of each variable. An example is given in Table 12.4.

What you see in Table 12.4 can be described as a 2 × 2 contingency table, because each variable has two levels. Along with the numbers of students in each cell (e.g., the numbers of girls who take AP history classes), the table provides marginal totals, which indicate how many students represented each level of each variable (e.g., 291 students took AP history classes). The grand total (in this case, 883) corresponds to the entire sample size.

Table 12.5 illustrates a 2 × 3 contingency table in which the data from Table 12.4 are again presented, but AP classes are further subdivided into "regular" versus those that have an additional TAG component. Because the same data are used, the totals in Table 12.4 can be reconstructed from the information in Table 12.5. Whether or not a researcher would provide the breakdown given in Table 12.5,

TABLE 12.4 2 × 2 Contingency Table

Numbers of high school boys and girls in a school district enrolled in regular versus AP history classes

	Regular History	AP History	TOTAL
Boys	310	128	438
Girls	282	163	445
TOTAL	592	291	883

TABLE 12.5 2 × 3 Contingency Table

Numbers of high school students in a school district enrolled in
history classes, by school, gender, and type of history class

| | Type of History Class | | |
Gender	Regular	AP Regular	AP-TAG
Boys	310	76	52
Girls	282	94	79

as opposed to the simpler summary in Table 12.4, depends on the level of detail appropriate to the study.

Frequency data for more than two variables may be represented side-by-side in a single table, as in Table 12.6, or in a hierarchical way, as in Table 12.7. In the latter table, high school completion rate data for the years 2003–2006 are reported overall, within four ethnic/gender groups, and by gender within each ethnic/racial group.

Finally, data for several categorical variables may be presented in the same table, as in Table 12.8, which presents information obtained from a large sample of smokers in 2005. Each of the health-related variables in the first column can be thought of as marking its own contingency table. For example, you can reconstruct a 3 × 2 contingency table relating educational level (high school vs. 2-year college vs. 4-year college) to history of depression (yes vs. no). You can reconstruct a comparable 3 × 2 contingency table relating educational level to whether or not a person smokes every day (yes vs. no), whether or not they smoke within 5 minutes of waking (yes vs. no), and whether or not one or more friends smoke (yes vs. no). The percentage of "yes" responses for each of these variables are given in the table, while the percentage of "no" responses simply equals 100% minus the percentage of "yes" responses for that category. As you can see, the researchers conducted simple chi-square analyses (of the sort described in Chapter 11) to determine whether each variable was related to educational level.

DESCRIPTIVE STATISTICS   Multivariate tables are commonly used to report descriptive statistics. You have seen numerous examples in previous chapters. These tables might simply present means and standard deviations for a few variables, or

TABLE 12.6 Table Summarizing Frequencies for Individual Variables

Percentages of 9th- through 12th-graders who reported being threatened or injured with a weapon on school property during the previous 12 months, by gender and race/ethnicity. (Adapted from National Center for Education Statistics Indicators of School Crime and Safety, 2006.)

| | | Gender | | Race/Ethnicity | | | | | | |
Year	Total	Male	Female	White	Black	Hispanic	Asian	American Indian	Pacific Islander	More Than One Race
1999	7.7	9.5	5.8	6.6	7.6	9.8	7.7	13.2	15.6	9.3
2001	8.9	11.5	6.5	8.5	9.3	8.9	11.3	15.2	24.8	10.3
2003	9.2	11.6	6.5	7.8	10.9	9.4	11.5	22.1	16.3	18.7
2005	7.9	9.7	6.1	7.2	8.1	9.8	4.6	9.8	14.5	10.7

TABLE 12.7 Table Summarizing Frequencies for Nested Variables

Percentages of 25- to 29-year-olds who completed high school, by race/ethnicity and sex, from 2003 to 2006. (Adapted from National Center for Education Statistics report.)

Year	Total Total	Total Male	Total Female	White Total	White Male	White Female	Black Total	Black Male	Black Female	Hispanic Total	Hispanic Male	Hispanic Female
2003	86.5	84.9	88.2	93.7	92.8	94.5	88.5	87.4	89.4	61.7	59.6	64.2
2004	86.6	85.2	88.0	93.3	92.1	94.5	88.7	91.2	86.6	62.4	60.1	65.2
2005	86.1	84.9	87.3	92.8	91.8	93.8	86.9	86.6	87.3	63.3	63.2	63.3
2006	86.4	84.4	88.5	93.4	92.3	94.6	86.3	84.2	88.0	63.2	60.5	66.6

they might be more longer and more informative, as in Table 12.9, which provides information on first-year students admitted to the University of California school system.

INFERENTIAL TESTS Tables are often used to report the results of statistical analyses when more than a few analyses have been conducted. Descriptive statistics and inferential tests may be reported together, as in Table 12.10, or the inferential

TABLE 12.8 Multiple Contingency Tables Combined (Adapted from Solberg, Asche, Boyle, McCarty, and Thoele, 2007)

Characteristics of smokers at baseline, by educational background: Minnesota HealthPartners enrollees, 2004–2005

Health-related variables	High School or Less (n = 242)	2-Year College[a] (n = 280)	4-Year College[b] (n = 334)
Self-reported overall health very good or excellent★★	37.2	56.6	57.7
Had a history of depression diagnosis	35.0	31.2	28.3
Smoking-related variables			
Smokes every day★★	76.9	64.3	47.0
No. of cigarettes smoked per day ★★			
0–10	58.4	66.9	81.7
11–20	28.2	28.4	15.6
≥20	13.5	4.7	2.7
Smokes within 5 min of waking★★	11.6	6.1	3.6
1 or more close friends smoke	99.2	99.3	99.1
1 or more quit attempts in past year	56.5	62.6	55.8
Seriously considering quitting in next 6 mo[c]	66.8	60.4	58.9

[a]The 2-year college group included those respondents who had completed at least some post-high school technical education but were not currently enrolled in any school and those that were enrolled in a 2-year college.

[b]The 4-year college group included those respondents who were enrolled in a 4-year college or university and those who had a college degree and were not currently enrolled in any school.

[c]After removal from analyses of those who had already quit.

★★$P < .001$ (Pearson χ^2 comparisons across columns).

TABLE 12.9 Table Presenting Various Descriptive Statistics (Adapted from Geiser and Studley, 2002)

High school GPA and SAT scores for UC students

Variable	N	Mean	SD	25th Percentile	Median	75th Percentile
High school GPA	77,893	3.84	0.41	3.56	3.86	4.14
SAT-I Verbal	77,893	588	93	530	590	650
SAT-I Math	77,893	625	89	570	630	690
SAT-I	77,893	1213	158	1110	1220	1330
SAT-II Writing	77,893	568	97	500	570	640
SAT-II Math	77,893	608	94	540	610	680
SAT-II Third Test	77,893	612	106	530	610	690
SAT-II	77,893	1789	240	1620	1790	1960

results may be presented in their own separate table (e.g., see Table 9.2 in Chapter 9 or Table 12.11 later in this chapter).

Multivariate Graphs

Graphic approaches to the representation of multiple variables include bar graphs, line graphs, and scatterplots.

BAR GRAPHS Bar graphs were discussed earlier as a means of representing frequency distributions for single nominal variables (e.g., the numbers of boys vs. girls in a particular class). Bar graphs can also be used to represent continuous values associated with each level of a discrete variable (e.g., the IQ scores of boys vs. girls in a particular class). The discrete variable is depicted on the x-axis, while the continuous variable corresponds to the y-axis. In experimental and causal–comparative research, the x-axis thus corresponds to the independent variable, while the y-axis presents the dependent variable values (frequencies, means, etc.). Bar graphs may be oriented horizontally or vertically, and the bars may be subdivided and/or filled in differently in order to represent additional, nested variables. For example, Figure 12.6 presents the results of a study exploring the relationship between oral reading fluency in English and time of school year, student's grade, and whether the student is a general education student or participates in a bilingual education as a Spanish-speaking English language learner (ELL).

The y-axis of the graph in Figure 12.6 depicts oral reading fluency means—specifically, the average number of words per minute students can correctly read out loud. The x-axis contains five sets of bars presenting data from grades 1–5. The set of bars corresponding to each grade consists of two subsets of three bars

TABLE 12.10 Table Showing Descriptive and Inferential Statistics (From Kim, 2007)

Average Number of books low- and middle-income children reported owning at posttest

Survey question (posttest)	Low income			Middle income			t	p
	M	SD	n	M	SD	n		
Mean number of books owned	2.97	1.38	62	4.15	1.10	213	−6.229	.000

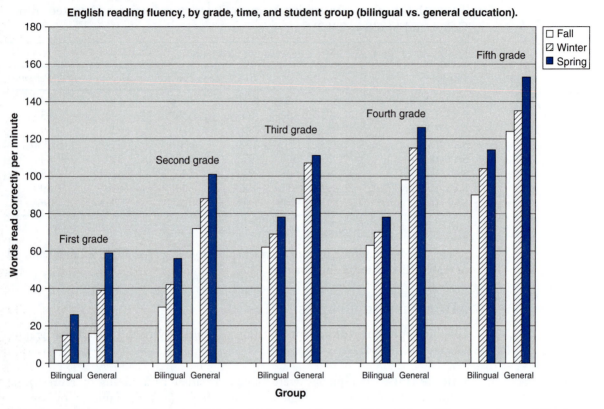

FIGURE 12.6 Bar Graph Illustrating Relationship between Four Variables (Adapted from Ramirez and Shapiro, 2006)

apiece. Within each grade, one subset of three bars provides data for students in bilingual programs, while the other subset of three bars provides data for students in general education programs. White bars represent data collected in the fall, bars with diagonal stripes represent data collected in the winter, and black bars represent data collected in the spring. As you would expect, improvement in reading fluency can be seen for all groups from fall to spring. Improvement is also evident from first through fifth grade. At the same time, at each grade, and at each time of testing, general education students obtained higher fluency scores than students in bilingual education programs. Analyses of variance revealed further information about patterns of significance:

The comparison between general and Spanish-speaking ELLs for reading passages in English revealed a significant main effect for time [F(2.238) = 236.01, p < .001, $\eta^2 = 0.665$], suggesting that all students showed significant growth in English oral reading fluency scores between October [fall] and May [spring]. There was a significant main effect for group [F(1,119) = 42.81, p < .001, $\eta^2 = 0.265$], with general education students reading more fluently in English than Spanish-speaking ELLs; and a significant interaction between time and group [F(2.238) = 10.62, p < .001, $\eta^2 = 0.082$]. The interaction showed that general education students had greater growth in reading fluency than the Spanish-speaking ELLs group. The three-way interaction between group, grade, and time was not significant [F(8,238) = 1.97, p = .051, $\eta^2 = 0.062$], suggesting that such a pattern was constant across grades.

[In sum] . . . general education students outperformed Spanish-speaking ELLs at all assessment periods and across grades. As Spanish-speaking ELLs moved up in grade,

FIGURE 12.7 Cumulative Frequencies Reported by Means of Bar Graph (From National Highway Transit Safety Administration, 2003)

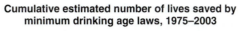

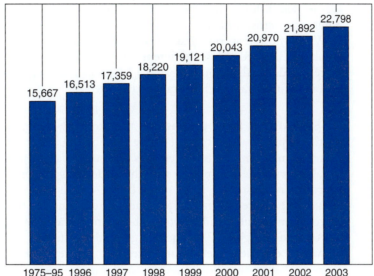

the number of words read correctly per minute increased steadily. In [the figure] it can also be noted that the pattern repeated itself across grade levels. Differences between general and Spanish-speaking ELLs were steadily larger from Grades 1–4, and then lessened at Grade 5. (Ramirez & Shapiro, 2006, pp. 363–364)

In the preceding example, a bar graph is used to depict information about group means. Information about standard deviations can be represented by means of patterns superimposed on the bars. Bar graphs can be used to represent other kinds of descriptive statistics for multiple variables, including simple or cumulative frequencies. For example, in Figure 12.7 each bar on the *x*-axis represents the cumulative total of those that precede it. This mode of presentation emphasizes the cumulative benefits of minimum drinking age laws.

A different approach to the representation of cumulative frequencies through bar graphs is given in Figure 12.8, in which each bar is subdivided into percentages of

FIGURE 12.8 Cumulative Frequencies Reported by Means of Bar Graph (Adapted from Wilson, 1999)

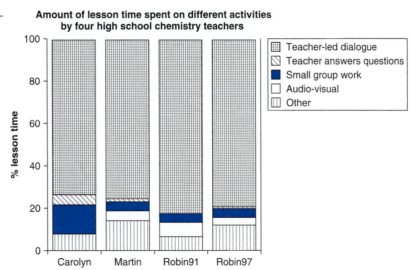

total lesson time spent on each of five types of activities. Examining each bar from the bottom up reveals the cumulative frequencies, and it is easy to see that although teacher-led dialogue was the predominant class activity, there were also individual differences across students in their participation in other activities.

When more than one graph is included in a research report, the same type of graph will be used unless a different type is called for by the nature of the statistics represented. Spotlight on Research 12.1 presents a study in which it was necessary for both bar graphs and line graphs to be used.

LINE GRAPHS **Line graphs** are an extremely common way of representing relationships between two or more variables. Lines rather than bars are used to represent continuous dimensions. In some cases, lines are used for ordinal variables with the assumption that the underlying dimension is continuous. This approach is illustrated in a study by de Bruin and Rudnick (2007) on the relationship between self-reported academic cheating and the personality dimensions of conscientiousness and excitement-seeking. The main results of the study are reproduced in Figure 12.9. The first graph in this figure shows a direct relationship between excitement-seeking and cheating: As the need for excitement increases,

FIGURE 12.9 Line Graphs Illustrating Relationships between Pairs of Variables (Adapted from de Bruin and Rudnick, 2007)

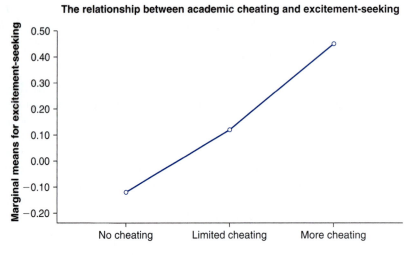

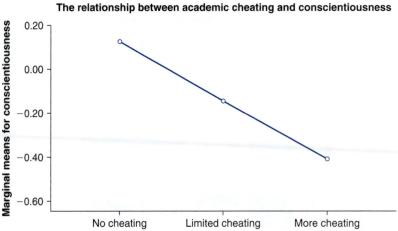

The Prediction of First-Year College GPA

As noted in Chapter 6, both researchers and educators are keenly interested in the predictive validity of SAT tests, since the primary function of these tests is to help identify students who will flourish at the undergraduate level. Predictive validity studies have shown that both SAT scores and high school GPA are related to first-year GPA in college (FGPA). However, SAT tests and high school classes do not measure exactly the same abilities. The possibility that high school grades and SAT scores are related to FGPA in different ways was explored in a 2006 College Board Research Report by Jennifer Kobrin and Rochelle Michel*.

Kobrin and Michel pointed out that although high school GPA and SAT scores are highly correlated, these variables tap into different constructs and will therefore be related to different levels of college GPA. The SAT measures reasoning ability and educational achievement, while high school GPA is a reflection of both achievement as well as "noncognitive" factors such as attendance, motivation, and effort. Kobrin and Michel proposed that among college students, noncognitive factors are more important to the determination of average grades, while reasoning ability and achievement have a greater impact on high grades. For this reason they predicted that high school GPA would be more predictive of moderately good FGPA, while SAT performance would be a stronger predictor of high FGPA.

Kobrin and Michel conducted their study with data from roughly 34,000 students who entered college in 1995. To analyze the data, the researchers used a type of regression analysis known as **logistic regression**, in which the criterion variable is discrete rather than continuous. Logistic regression is similar to ordinary regression (as discussed in Chapter 11), except that the focus is on predicting the likelihood of membership in each level of the criterion variable. Information about predictor variables can yield either an accurate or an inaccurate decision about whether each observation can be assigned to each level of the criterion; the logistic regression analysis quantifies the extent of accuracy.

Kobrin and Michel used a multiple logistic regression procedure in which SAT scores and high school GPA (HSGPA) served as predictor variables, and FGPA was the criterion. The researchers treated FGPA as a six-level ordinal variable, defined in terms of whether the student earned a first-year college GPA greater than or equal to 2.0, 2.5, 3.0, 3.25, 3.5, or 3.75. The logistic regression analysis indicated how accurately information about SAT scores and HSGPA could assign students to each of these six levels of "success" (as opposed to the "unsuccessful" category—students who obtained a FGPA of less than 2.0). Thus, the main research question was whether each level of FGPA would be more accurately predicted by SAT scores or HSGPA. Kobrin and Michel also considered demographic variables, in that their logistic regression analyses were performed on the entire group, as well as one of each gender and racial or ethnic subgroup.

Some of the main descriptive results are summarized in the contingency table below. Notice that in this particular table, the cells in each row are not independent of each other. Reading the rows from right to left provides cumulative frequency information.

The logistic regression results for the overall sample are presented in the figure on the next page. This bar graph illustrates the accuracy with which HSGPA and SAT scores, separately and in combination, predicted membership in each of the six levels of FGPA.

The table on the next page summarizes other results indicating whether SAT scores or HSGPA was the more accurate predictor for each criterion level and demographic subgroup.

Percentage of Students Achieving Various Levels of Success

| Subgroup | N | FGPA Greater than or Equal to: | | | | | |
		2.00	2.50	3.00	3.25	3.50	3.75
Females	18,209	89.7	73.4	47.3	31.4	17.8	6.7
Males	15,860	84.1	65.1	39.5	26.4	15.5	6.6
TOTAL N	34,069	29,672	23,689	14,870	9,894	5,706	2,267
TOTAL %	100	87.1	69.5	43.6	29.0	16.7	6.7

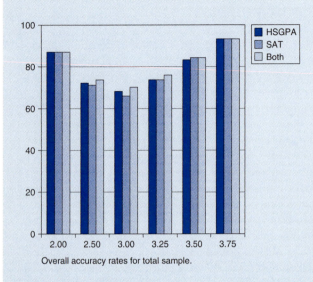

Overall accuracy rates for total sample.

In discussing this table, Kobrin and Michel called attention to differences in the predictive power of SAT scores and HSGPA at different levels of FGPA. The researchers noted that for FGPAs greater than or equal to 3.25 and 3.5, SAT scores were found to be more accurate predictors than HSGPAs were. For FGPAs at or above 2.5 to 3.0, however, HSGPAs showed greater accuracy.

The researchers conducted two additional logistic regression analyses, one for "successful" students (FGPA of 2.0 or greater) and another for "unsuccessful" students (FGPA less than 2.0). The results are summarized in the two figures below. As you can see, for most of the FGPA levels classified as "successful," SAT scores slightly outperformed HSGPAs in predicting successful students, while for the "unsuccessful" levels, HSGPAs showed

Summary of Results for Predicting Successful Students

| | FGPA Criterion Level | | | | | |
Subgroup	2.0	2.5	3.0	3.25	3.5	3.75
Total Sample	SAT	HSGPA	SAT	SAT	SAT	—
Females	SAT	HSGPA	HSGPA	SAT	SAT	—
Attending Very Selective Colleges	=	HSGPA	SAT	SAT	SAT	—
Attending Moderately Selective Colleges	SAT	HSGPA	SAT	HSGPA	SAT	SAT
Attending Least Selective Colleges	SAT	HSGPA	HSGPA	HSGPA	HSGPA	SAT

Note: An equal sign means that SAT and HSGPA were equally effective as predictors. Dash means that neither predictor was effective.

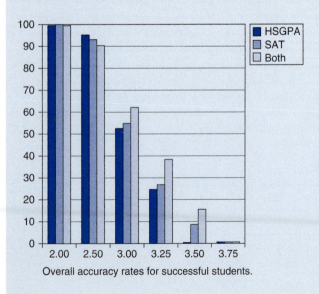

Overall accuracy rates for successful students.

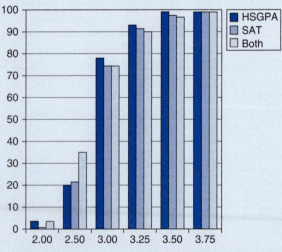

Overall accuracy rates for unsuccessful students.

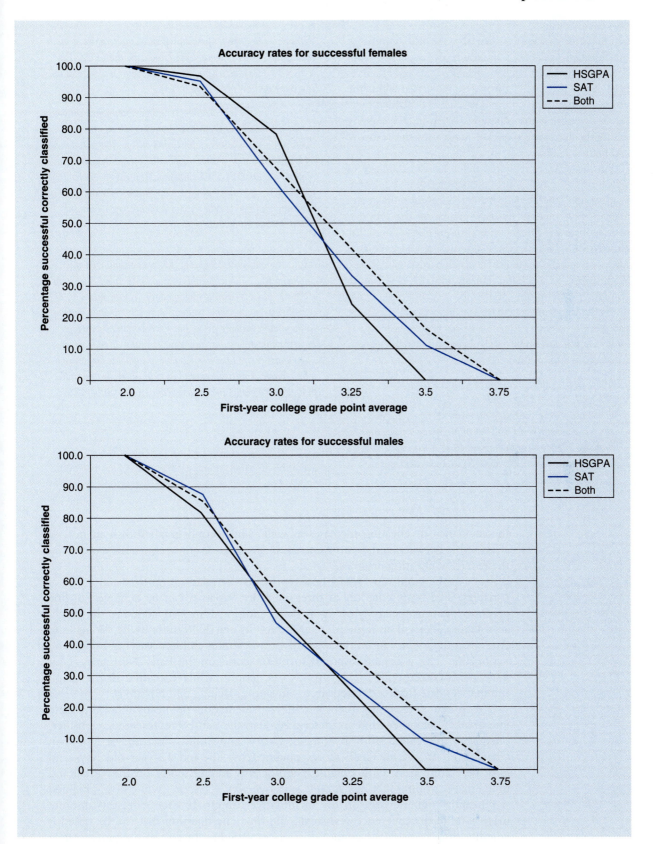

better performance. You can also see that within the successful group, FGPA increases are associated with declines in how accurately both SAT scores and HSGPAs predicted FGPAs, while the pattern is reversed within the unsuccessful group. Kobrin and Michel explained these results by noting that there was very little variability within the extreme groups (i.e., students with the lowest and highest FGPAs).

Further analyses explored differences in accuracy of classifications across some of the demographic subgroups. For example, the breakdown for successful females and males is presented in the two graphs on the previous page. Kobrin and Michel found, among other things, that either SAT scores or HSGPAs almost always predicted successful females more accurately than successful males. With respect to successful females, HSGPA was a more accurate predictor for FGPAs of 2.5 and 3.0, while the SAT was more accurate for FGPAs of 2.0, 3.25, and 3.5.

Following are some of Kobrin and Michel's main conclusions and caveats:

In the total sample, at all success-criterion levels except the 2.5 level, the SAT was equal to or slightly more accurate than HSGPA in predicting successful students, but generally less accurate than HSGPA in predicting unsuccessful students. However, at the highest FGPA level (3.75 or higher), neither the SAT nor HSGPA was able to predict successful students.

The SAT was a better predictor of successful females at moderately high FGPA levels (3.25 and 3.5) than HSGPA. The SAT was a better predictor of successful males at all but two criterion levels (3.0 and 3.75) . . .

[T]here are some caveats that should be noted when interpreting the results of these analyses. Because all of the students in the sample were admitted to college, these students were of higher ability than the population of college-bound seniors that take the SAT each year. It would be preferable to have a sample that included . . . students who applied but were not admitted to college, and students who were admitted to but did not attend college.

The fact that none of the models predicted any of the successful students at the highest college performance level is problematic. . . . One possible reason for the poor prediction is [that] students earning high grades in college make up a very diverse group; some students may take rigorous courses in the math or science fields that have demanding requirements, while others may take courses that tend to be graded more leniently and have less strict requirements for earning a high grade. Future research will focus on predicting individual course grades in the first year of college rather than FGPA.

*Kobrin, J. L., & Michel, R. S. (2006). The SAT as a predictor of different levels of college performance. *College Board Research Report, 2006–3*, 1–10.

the incidence of cheating increases as well. The second graph shows an inverse relationship between conscientiousness and cheating: As conscientiousness increases, the extent of cheating declines.

Each of the graphs in Figure 12.9 represents the relationship between a pair of variables. The representation of three or more variables can be achieved in line graphs by various means. Most commonly, additional lines are added to the graph, as in Figure 12.10. This figure depicts the results of a 2006 study by Ee, Wang, and Aunio on differences in numeracy skills across young children varying in age and nationality. The *y*-axis corresponds to mean scores on the Early Numeracy Test. The *x*-axis corresponds to age groups (see graph), while each line in the graph summarizes data from a different city (Singapore, Bejing, and Helsinki).

The previous examples focus on the representation of means in multivariate line graphs, but other kinds of descriptive statistics can be represented. Consider, once again, the 2006 study by Strand, Deary, and Smith, discussed at length in Chapter 11, in which CAT scores obtained by 11- and 12-year-old boys and girls were compared. Girls obtained significantly higher scores on the verbal and nonverbal reasoning subtests, as well as in overall CAT score, while boys obtained significantly higher scores on the quantitative subtest. In each case, the absolute magnitude of the difference was small, and thus one question that can be raised is whether the extent of the gender differences varied according to the performance

FIGURE 12.10 Line Graph Illustrating Relationship between Three Variables (Adapted from Ee, Wong, and Aunio, 2006)

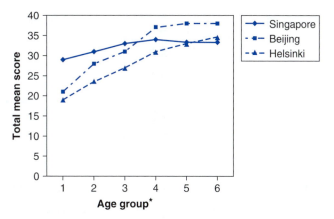

Total mean scores by age groups and cities.

*Age group corresponds to the following age ranges in months:
1 = 56–60, 2 = 61–66, 3 = 67–72, 4 = 73–78, 5 = 79–84, 6 = 85–90.

level of the students. We might ask, for example, whether the gender differences are attributable to the highest-performing students of one gender outperforming the highest-performing students of the other level, or whether the differences are equally distributed across performance levels. One way to address this question is to explore gender differences at performance levels as defined by stanines. (Recall from Chapter 10 that a stanine is a standard score in a distribution that has been divided into a 9-point ordinal scale, so that each stanine from 2 through 8 spans exactly half of one standard deviation unit.) Figure 12.11 presents Strand and colleagues' graphs illustrating the percentages of boys and girls in each stanine for each of the CAT subtests, as well as the overall score.

As you can see from Figure 12.11, the answer to our question is that gender differences are not equally distributed across performance levels. Moreover, the relationship between gender differences and performance level depends on the variable. The slightly higher overall mean obtained by girls on the verbal subtest, for example, is attributable to a combination of a higher percentage of boys scoring in the lower stanines combined with a slightly higher percentage of girls scoring in the upper stanines. For the quantitative subtest, the slightly higher overall mean obtained by boys is attributable to a difference in the percentages of boys who scored in the upper stanines (a difference that was large enough to outweigh the higher percentages of boys scoring in the lowest stanines). In short, for verbal skills the gender difference can be attributed to relatively large numbers of low-scoring boys and high-scoring girls. For quantitative skills, the most influential factor was the relatively high proportion of high-scoring boys. (Although the differences in the stanine graphs may seem large, a close look at the y-axes shows that the difference in percentages of boys and girls at each stanine is never very great—at most, only about a 20% difference for any one stanine.)

SCATTERPLOTS   In Chapter 9 you learned that a scatterplot is a graph in which the x-axis corresponds to one continuous variable, the y-axis corresponds to a second continuous variable, and each point in the graph represents one individual's score on both variables (look back at Figure 9.1 in Chapter 9 for an example). Scatterplots are useful for spotting outliers, and for gaining a sense of the relationship between variables—in some cases, the correlation coefficient alone cannot detect relationships between variables that are curvilinear or restricted to particular ranges.

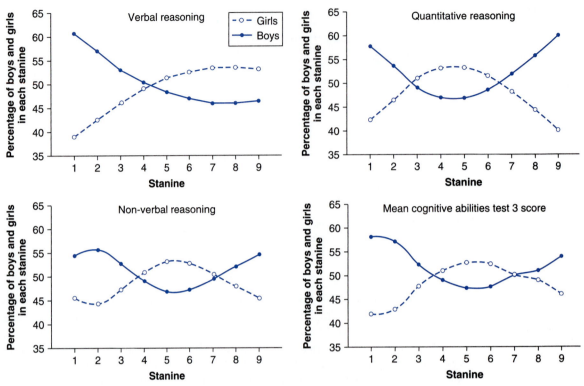

FIGURE 12.11 Relationship between Gender and Stanine in Strand, Deary, and Smith (2006)

Construction of Graphs

Regardless of whether single-variable or multivariate, histograms, bar graphs, and line graphs are constructed by means of the same general steps:

- Create a grid consisting of an *x*-axis and a *y*-axis. (Often, by convention, the ratio of *x*-axis to *y*-axis length is 3 to 4.)
- Subdivide the *x*-axis by levels (in the case of nominal variables), ranks (in the case of ordinal variables), or value intervals (in the case of continuous variables). For ordinal and continuous variables, arrange the values from left to right in order of magnitude (lowest to highest). Make sure that each subdivision of the axis is equal in extent. Do not skip levels or values.
- Subdivide the *y*-axis into equal values or value intervals. Do not skip values or intervals. Make sure the scale and range are appropriate.
- Mark the datapoints inside the grid.
- Construct a histogram, bar graph, or line graph.

Typically, researchers use software programs to create graphs and other figures, as illustrated in Spotlight on Research 12.2. However, the use of a computer program to create graphs does not guarantee that the graphs are appropriately constructed, or that the data they represent will be correctly interpreted. This point is revisited at the end of the chapter.

Using SPSS to Create a Bar Graph

The dataset you created for Chapters 10 and 11 can be used once again to illustrate how graphs are created in SPSS. (See Spotlights on Research 10.3 and 11.1 for further details.)

To begin, click on the Windows SPSS 17.0 icon and open your file. Click on the drop-down menu entitled "Graphs" and then "Legacy Dialogs" to obtain a list of graph-related options.

Imagine that you want to create a bar graph illustrating the mean IQ scores for each gender. Highlight and click the "Bar . . ." option. A small window entitled "Bar Charts" will open. Click on the icon labeled "Simple" and then click the button marked "Define." You should now see the window shown in Screenshot 1 below.

To assign gender to the *x*-axis, highlight the term "gender" at the top of the box on the left by clicking on the term once, then click on the arrow next to the centrally located box entitled "Category axis." The term "gender" should now appear in the box. To define the

y-axis in terms of IQ means, click on the small circle next to "Other statistic (e.g., mean)," then click on the term "IQ" near the top of the box on the left, and finally click on the uppermost arrow next to the term "Variable." The IQ term should now appear in the small box under the term "Variable." You should now see Screenshot 2.

To create a title for the graph, click on the button marked "Titles. . . ." Fill in an appropriate title in Line 1 (e.g., Mean IQ, by gender), then click the button marked "Continue" to return to where you were (Screenshot 2). Now click the button marked "OK" at the lower left, and you will obtain the output file containing your bar graph, as shown in Screenshot 3.

Double-click anywhere on the chart in order to open the Chart Editor. From here you can edit the appearance of the graph. For example, your graph would be improved by removing the unnecessary ticks from the *x*-axis, and by labeling each gender with a meaningful term rather than 0 and 1. To remove the ticks, click

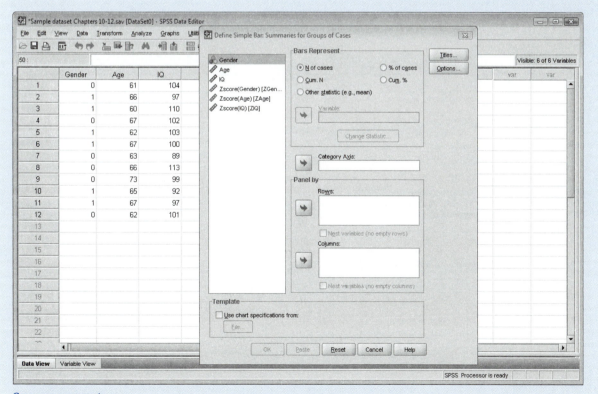

SCREEENSHOT 1

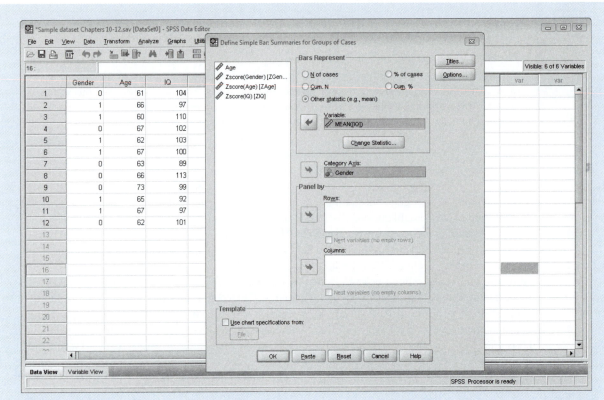

SCREEENSHOT 2

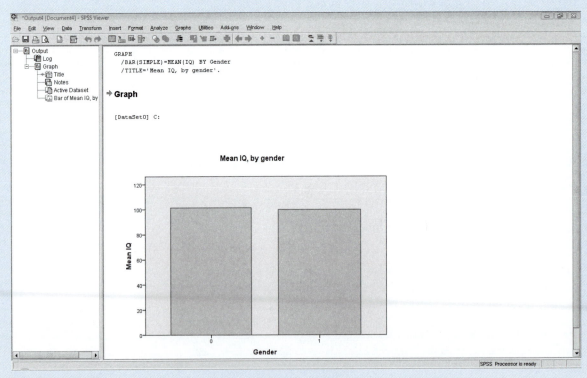

SCREEENSHOT 3

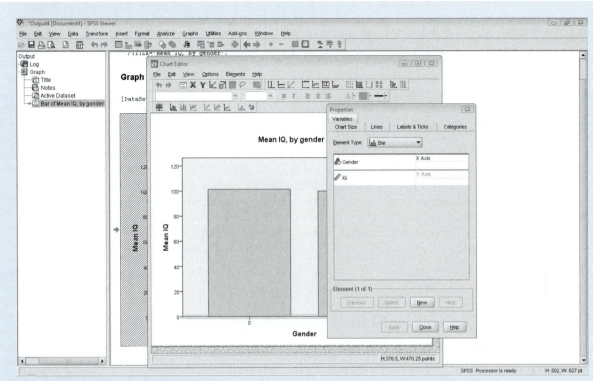

SCREEENSHOT 4

on the drop-down menu marked "Edit" and choose the option "**X** Select X Axis." This opens a separate window entitled "Properties," as in Screenshot 4 below.

Now click on the "Labels & Ticks" tab, and then click on the check mark in the box labeled "Display ticks." This removes the check mark and also the ticks in the graph. Now click on the buttons "Apply" and "Close" to return to where you were. To change the names of each

level of gender, double-click the 0 and type in the word "boys." Replace the 1 with the word "girls." (When you created the original data file, boys were arbitrarily designated with a 0 and girls were designated with a 1.) To exit the Chart Editor, click on the drop-down menu entitled "File" and then click on the "Close" option. You will be returned to the output file, where you can see the changes you made.

Modeling

In quantitative research, a **model** is a formal statement about the relationship between two or more variables. Either causal or correlational relationships can be articulated in a model. Models are usually expressed in statistical terms, but it is also common for researchers to use figures for purposes of illustration. In this section I focus on the use of figures in advanced model-building and model-testing analyses.

The three types of statistical analyses discussed in this section—path analysis, hierarchical linear modeling, and structural equation modeling—are all extensions of multiple regression. Recall from Chapter 11 that the general purpose of multiple regression is to identify the combination and weighting of predictor variables that yield the highest possible correlation with a criterion variable. Two of the most important results of a regression analysis are the beta coefficients, which indicate the direction and strength of the relationship between a predictor (or set of predictors) and a criterion variable when the effects of other predictors are held constant, and the R^2 values, which indicate how much variability in the criterion variable can be predicted from variability in the predictor or predictors. (See Chapter 11 for details.)

Path Analysis

Path analysis is an extension of multiple regression in which direct and indirect causal relationships among variables are identified. The result of a path analysis is a **path diagram**, which consists of variable names, arrows indicating the direction of causality, and, typically, path coefficients indicating how strongly one variable influences another when the influences of other variables are controlled for. (Path coefficients can be understood as beta coefficients and therefore range from −1.0 to 1.0.) A concrete example of path analysis is described in Spotlight on Research 12.3.

Hierarchical Linear Modeling

Hierarchical linear modeling, or HLM, is an extension of multiple regression to **nested variables** (i.e., variables that are hierarchically related). For example, a particular group of students is nested within a particular classroom, which is in turn nested within a particular school. The school is nested within a particular school district that is nested within a particular community. If we want to know what is responsible for the academic performance of this group of students, we may need to consider individual-level variables (e.g., students' IQ scores), classroom-level variables (e.g., quality of instruction), school-level variables (e.g., ethnic diversity), and community-level variables (e.g., affluence). Moreover, some of the variables we need to consider should be measured at more than one level. Instructional quality, for instance, may have distinct influences at both the individual and the school level. Ordinary multiple regression does not readily distinguish among the separate and combined influences of nested variables. Regression analyses that include nested variables may yield inaccurate results—beta coefficients tend to be lowered, for example. HLM is currently growing in popularity as a means of surmounting this limitation.

Table 12.11 gives an example of one way HLM results are reported. This table is taken from a study on class- and student-level predictors of the extent to which eighth-grade students are motivated to complete their homework, and the amount of effort they put into their homework. The predictors—divided into class- and student-level variables—are listed in the column at the left side of the table. (The variable "Homework quality" refers to student beliefs about how well the teacher prepared the homework assignments.) Beta coefficients (*b*) and standard error terms (*SE*) are provided for expectancy and value, which are two criterion variables reflecting students' motivation to complete their homework. (Roughly, expectancy refers to beliefs about the likelihood of succeeding on homework assignments while value refers to the perceived importance of the assignments.) The *b* and *SE* terms are also provided for another criterion variable, homework effort. These terms are given both with and without mediators (i.e., covariates). Expectancy and value are treated as the mediators in this analysis.

Prediction of College GPA Revisited

Studies on the prediction of college performance encompass a variety of predictor and criterion variables. The study described in Spotlight on Research 12.1, for example, examined how well first-year college GPA can be predicted from high school GPA and SAT scores. The study described in this Spotlight on Research stems from the same literature but explores a somewhat different set of variables.

In a 2005 study published in the *Journal of Developmental Education**, Joseph Maggio, William White, Susan Molstad, and Neelam Kher tracked 397 students from six universities who had attended prefreshman summer programs. As Maggio and colleagues point out, prefreshman programs were originally developed as a proactive method of helping to prepare at-risk students for college. The content of these programs varies widely, however, and there have been few studies exploring the characteristics of successful programs.

Among the predictors that Maggio and colleagues explored were student characteristics (age and high school GPA) as well as characteristics of the prefreshman summer program that each student attended (e.g., size and length of program). The two criterion variables of interest were college GPA and student retention (i.e., whether or not the student graduates).

Maggio and colleagues conducted a series of hierarchical regression analyses in order to measure the extent of the direct and indirect relationships between their predictor and criterion variables. One multiple regression explored how well student achievement (i.e., college GPA) could be predicted on the basis of high school GPA (HSGPA) and two characteristics of the prefreshman programs—size and length. The results of this analysis are given in the lower left table below. As you can see from the beta coefficients in the final column, the relationship between each of the three predictors and college GPA was significant. HSGPA was positively related to college GPA, while program size and length were negatively related. In other words, higher GPAs in high school predicted higher college GPAs, as did shorter and smaller prefreshman programs.

The next two tables (below right and following page) present the results of hierarchical multiple regression analyses looking at the extent to which student retention can be predicted from different combinations of program-related and student characteristics.

Based on the results of the multiple regression analyses, the path diagram on the next page was conducted.

Each path coefficient in the figure is the beta weight for the simple regression of one variable (the one at the end of the arrow) on another variable (the one at the beginning of the arrow) after controlling for the effects of the other variables in the model. For example, the coefficient linking high school GPA to student achievement is .344. Looking at the table at the lower left, you can see that .344 is the beta coefficient for the relationship between high school GPA

Summary of Regression Analysis for Precollegiate Student Characteristics and Program Characteristics Predicting Student Achievement ($N = 397$)

Variable	B	SE B	ß
Step 1			
HSGPA	.432	.071	.311**
Step 2			
HSGPA	.465	.067	.335**
Program Size	−.008	.001	−.330**
Step 3			
HSGPA	.477	.067	.344**
Program Size	−.008	.001	−.323**
Program Length	−.061	.030	−.097*

Note. $R^2 = .097$ for step 1: $R^2 = .205$ for step 2: $R^2 = .214$ for step 3. *$p < .05$. **$p < .01$.

Summary of Regression Analysis for Precollegiate Student Characteristics and Program Characteristics Predicting Student Retention ($N = 397$)

Variable	B	SE B	ß
Step 1			
Voluntary Peer/Professional Tutoring	−.744	.196	−.198**
Step 2			
Voluntary Peer/Professional Tutoring	−.807	.197	−.215**
Age	−.415	.175	−.124*

Note. $R^2 = .039$ for step 1; $R^2 = .054$ for step 2. *$p < .05$. **$p < .01$.

Direct, Indirect, and Total Effects on Student Retention (N = 397)

Model	Direct	Indirect	Total
		Effects	
Student Characteristics			
HSGPA	0	.128	.128
Age	−.124	0	−.124
Program Characteristics			
Voluntary Peer/ Professional			
Tutoring	−.215	0	−.215
Program Size	−.323	−.120	−.443
Program Length	−.097	−.036	−.133
College GPA	.372	0	.372

and achievement with all of the other variables in the model held constant. (In other words, it is the value for HSGPA in step 3, after the effects of all of the other predictors have been measured and controlled for.) To take another example, the −.124 coefficient linking age to retention comes from the beta coefficient in the final

step of the table at the lower right of the previous page, in which the relationship between age and retention is measured after the effects of other predictors are controlled for.

Maggio and colleagues summarized their results as follows. (You should be able to link this narrative summary to the details of the path diagram above, particularly the directions of the arrows and the positive or negative values of the path coefficients.)

The results of the analysis to predict student achievement and retention by pre-collegiate student characteristics and prefreshman summer program characteristics revealed that only HSGPA had a direct positive effect and that program size and program length had direct negative effects on college GPA. Furthermore, voluntary peer and professional tutoring and age had direct negative effects on student retention. These results comprise the major findings of the study.

The negative impact of program size on student achievement and retention indicated that the larger the size of prefreshman summer programs, the lower the cumulative college GPA of participants and the fewer total semesters participating students remained enrolled following the program. Although there have been no other studies investigating prefreshman

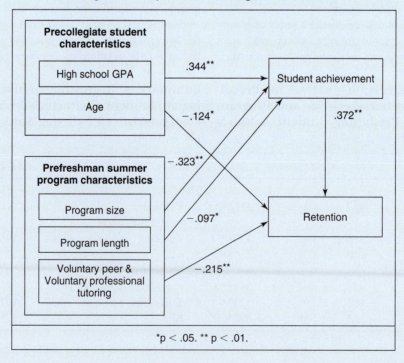

Path diagram for the prediction of college GPA and retention.

*p < .05. ** p < .01.

summer program size and its effect on student achievement and retention, the results of this study showed that program size was a significant characteristic of prefreshman summer programs.

A second key finding of the study was the direct negative effect of voluntary peer and professional tutoring services on student retention. The findings of this study suggested that the retention rates were lower for those students who participated in programs with only voluntary peer and professional tutoring services, which is consistent with previous tutoring study results.

Another significant finding of the study was the direct effect of high school GPA on student achievement. This positive direct effect indicated that the higher the participating students' high school GPAs then the higher their cumulative college GPAs were likely to be.

Many studies have shown significant relationships between high school GPA and student achievement (e.g., Mukulawendo, 1997; Rogers, 1990; Schade, 1977). This study confirmed what many collegiate educators and others who deal with freshman admissions have known: high school GPA is a consistent predictor of college GPA (Profozich, 1989; Smith, 1980).

An additional major finding was that program length had a direct negative effect on student achievement. The negative

direct effect indicated that students enrolled in programs that were longer in duration had lower GPAs . . .

[T]he results of this study were consistent with the theories of Tinto (1987) and Pascarella (1985) who postulated that early intervention is important to the success of students. Tinto suggested that the time prior to entry into the institution, when students separate themselves from past forms of associations and make the transition into the social and intellectual life of the institution, is critical. The direct negative impact of older age on student retention in this study confirmed earlier findings that early intervention was important to the success of students.

A final key finding in this study was that several prefreshman summer program variables did not reveal significant direct effects on student achievement or retention. Required on-campus residence, course credit availability, required enrollment, enrollment, counseling services, enrollment status, and social/recreational programming are characteristics that are common to many prefreshman programs, but none of these entered the equation in the regression analysis to explain the variance in student achievement and retention.

*Maggio, J. C., White, W. G., Molstad, S., & Kher, N. (2005). Prefreshman summer programs' impact on student achievement and retention. *Journal of Developmental Education, 29*(2), 2–33. Quoted with permission from the publisher.

Here are some of the researchers' original predictions:

[W]e expected homework quality to have a positive effect on homework motivation and homework effort at both the student level and the class level. Moreover, we expected homework motivation to have a statistically significant, direct effect on homework effort and to mediate the effects of homework quality.

(Trautwein, Lüdtke, Schnyder, & Niggili, 2006, p. 448)

The results of the HLM analysis in Table 12.11 largely support these predictions. When homework quality was treated as a class-level predictor (the first line in the table), you can see that the beta coefficients were positive and significant for the two motivational variables, expectancy and value. When homework quality was treated as a student-level predictor, the beta coefficients were once again positive and significant for expectancy and value. In short, at both the class and the student level, the more positively students viewed the quality of homework assignments they received, the more successful they expected to be on the assignments, and the more they valued the assignments.

As for effort, the beta coefficients for homework quality were significant and positive at both the class and student levels when no mediators were included. However, when the two motivational variables were included as mediators, only

TABLE 12.11 Table Illustrating HLM Results (From Trautwein, Lüdtke, Schnyder, and Niggli, 2006)

Predicting homework motivation and homework effort in French as a foreign language: Results from Hierarchical Linear Modeling

	Homework motivation				Homework effort			
	Expectancy		Value		Without mediators		With mediators	
Predictor	b	SE	b	SE	b	SE	b	SE
Class level								
Homework quality	.28*	.11	.44***	.08	.19**	.06	.06	.06
Homework control by teacher	−.19**	.06	−.03	.06	−.07	.06	−.04	.06
Student level								
Conscientiousness	.27***	.02	.20***	.02	.40***	.03	.33***	.02
Basic cognitive abilities	.09***	.02	−.02	.02	−.02	.02	−.03	.02
Gender: Male	−.09	.06	−.14**	.05	−.08	.04	−.04	.04
Homework quality	.09**	.03	.33***	.03	.19***	.02	.11***	.02
Homework control by teacher	.07*	.03	.03	.03	.14***	.03	.12***	.03
Parental provision of help	.11***	.03	.01	.03	.09***	.02	.07**	.02
Unwanted parental help	−.15***	.03	.02	.02	−.04	.03	−.03	.02
Expectancy							.11***	.02
Value							.22***	.03
R^2	.24		.34		.39		.43	

Note. $N = 1,501$ from 93 classes. b = unstandardized regression coefficient. SE = standard error of b.
*$p < .05$. **$p < .01$. ***$p < .001$.

the student-level measure of homework quality was significant. The positive relationship between perceived quality of homework assignments and the effort put forth to complete those assignments is seen at the student level, but at the class level expectancy and value are the more influential variables.

Structural Equation Modeling

Structural equation modeling, or SEM, is a broad set of statistical procedures that include multiple regression, path analysis, and other statistical tests as special cases. SEM is used to compare models to each other and to theoretical models developed by the researcher, in order to see which model best fits the data. SEM is also used to refine models to increase the fit with the actual data. Chi-square analyses are often used to evaluate fit, and the SEM results may be depicted in a path diagram (see Spotlight on Research 12.3). In recent years, SEM has grown in popularity, owing to its flexibility—it can accomplish the same goals as other statistics but is less constrained by some of their key assumptions.

Evaluating Statistical Representations

"Look for an overall pattern and also for striking deviations from that pattern."

Moore (1995)

This section of the chapter provides some general advice for evaluating tables and graphs. Some dimensions on which statistical representations can be evaluated are a matter of common sense. A good table or graph is accurate, readily understandable, informative without being cluttered, and relevant to the research report. In this section I focus on additional details of importance.

Interpreting Tables

Following are some simple guidelines for understanding a table as well as determining whether it is a reliable source of information.

- Carefully read the title, column title(s), row titles(s), footnotes, and other descriptive information in the table. Are all parts of the table labeled? Are the labels understandable?

- Examine the information presented in the table. Can you tell what the table is intended to represent? What patterns does the table illustrate? Are these patterns consistent with what is asserted in the main text?

- Note whether the table has been constructed properly. Are the divisions of the table appropriate to the underlying scale of the variables? Is all of the relevant information included in the table? Does the table show the information the researcher intended to present?

Interpreting Graphs

In the quotation at the outset of the chapter, Mark Twain notes that figures do not lie. Strictly speaking, Mr. Twain was correct. Figures do not lie. They do not "do" anything. But one can create a deceptive figure. Moreover, one can inadvertently mislead—or be mislead by—a figure that is improperly created.

A CAUTIONARY TALE   Consider the fictional data on school district expenditures per student in Figure 12.12. In this figure, the same data are depicted in four different graphs. The graph at the top left suggests that from 1994 through 2006, expenditures per student (in thousands of dollars) increased substantially. Moreover, the graph seems to indicate that expenditures increased every year. The graph at the top right tells a more qualified story. During two time periods (1994–1996 and 2004–2006), expenditures did not increase. The graph at the lower left raises the question of just how substantial the increase was. Given the new scale of the y-axis, the results seem much less dramatic. The graph at the lower right adds a further and particularly important qualification. Although the absolute amount of money being spent per student increased from 1994 through 2006, when adjustments are made for inflation, we find that the spending power of the money has been declining.

   This example illustrates some of the reasons for exercising caution when examining representations of statistical data, particularly in graphs. Changing the scale of the x- or y-axis, or changing the way one of the variables is coded, can have a huge impact on the appearance of a graph. Following are some guidelines for understanding and evaluating the reliability of graphs.

- Carefully read the title, legend, axis titles, subdivisions of axes, and any footnotes. Are all parts of the graph labeled? Is each label understandable and specific enough?

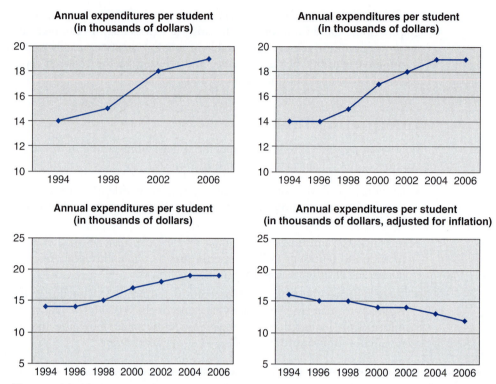

FIGURE 12.12   Four Graphs Representing Annual Expenditures per Student in a Fictional School District between 1994 and 2006

- Examine the information presented in the graph. Can you tell what the graph was intended to represent? What trends does the graph illustrate? What exceptions to those trends can be observed? Are these trends and exceptions consistent with what is asserted in the text?

- Note whether or not the *y*-axis is properly constructed. Are the intervals equally spaced? Do the axis values match the underlying scale? Is the range of values too large or too small, thereby misrepresenting the strength of some effect.

- Note whether or not the *x*-axis is properly constructed. Are the intervals equally spaced? Is the underlying dimension correctly represented? Is the range of levels or values too large or too small? Is the ratio of *x*- to *y*-axis length appropriate?

- Note whether the right type of graph has been used. Is the type of graph appropriate to the scale on which the variables were measured? Does the graph illustrate the findings that the researcher intends it to?

A Look Ahead

In Chapters 7–9 you learned about quantitative research design. In Chapters 10–12 you learned about quantitative data analysis and representation. The next three chapters shift into a discussion of qualitative research.

Applications: A Guide for Beginning Researchers

Here are some ideas from the chapter that will help you plan your research:

- Create tables and/or figures for your research report when you feel that they can provide brief, clear summaries of large amounts of information.
- Once you know what software program you will use to analyze data, figure out how you will learn to create tables and figures with this program if you do not already know how to do so.
- Be sure to review the guidelines for constructing tables and graphs summarized in this chapter before you begin.
- If you are interested in using one of the advanced modeling techniques described in this chapter, further study will be required.

Chapter Summary

Tables and figures may be used to represent single-variable or multivariate information. Frequency data for a single variable may be reported in a frequency table, in a stem-and-leaf display, or in one of four types of graphs: bar graph, histogram, frequency polygon, or pie chart. Choice of a particular table or graph depends on the nature of the data and what the researcher wishes to show.

Multivariate tables can be used to represent frequencies, other descriptive statistics, and the results of inferential tests. Multivariate graphs consist of bar graphs, line graphs, and scatterplots. Multivariate tables and graphs are commonly created by means of computer software programs.

Models of causal or correlational relationships between variables, based on multiple regression statistics, can be represented in tabular or graphic form. Three commonly used approaches to modeling are path analysis, structural equation modeling, and hierarchical linear modeling.

Although tables and graphs may differ widely in format and content, simple guidelines can be followed in the process of comprehending and evaluating them.

Key Terms

Table	Bar graph	Model
Figure	Histogram	Path analysis
Frequency	Frequency polygon	Path diagram
Stem-and-leaf display	Kolmogorov–Smirnov test	Hierarchical linear modeling
y-axis	Pie chart	Nested variables
x-axis	Multivariate	Structural equation modeling
Grid	Line graphs	
Ticks	Logistic regression	
Legend		

Exercises

1. A researcher is studying gender differences in achievement motivation (AM) among students in urban versus rural schools. AM is measured by means of an interval-scaled test. What type of graph would be most suitable for representing the data?

a) Line graph, with one pair of lines representing mean AM scores for males and females in urban schools, and the other pair of lines representing AM scores for males and females in rural schools.

b) Bar graph, with one pair of bars representing mean AM scores for males and females in urban schools, and the other pair of bars representing AM scores for males and females in rural schools.

c) Two pie charts, each representing the percentages of males and females within each stanine of AM scores for one type of school.

d) Frequency polygon, showing the numbers of males and females in each type of school obtaining each AM score.

2. Each eighth-grader in four different school districts is labeled as a "high," "medium," or "low" risk for academic failure. Which of the following would be the clearest way to illustrate differences in the proportions of the three risk groups across the four school districts?

a) Four pie charts

b) A line graph with four lines

c) A bar graph with 12 bars

d) A 3×4 contingency table

3. How could the graph below be improved?

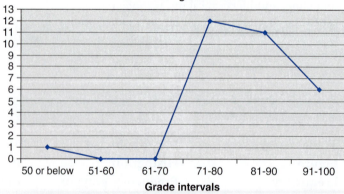

Numbers of students in a college chemistry class who fall within each grade interval

a) Increase the highest value of the y-axis so that it corresponds to the total number of students in the class (30).

b) Change the form of the graph so that the data are represented by a histogram.

c) Remove the outlier (the one score below 50) and reduce the range of the x-axis intervals.

d) All of the above

4. How could the graph below be improved?

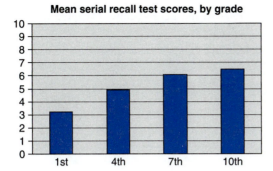

a) Change the form of the graph to a histogram, since an age-related trend is implied.

b) Arrange the bars horizontally rather than vertically, with the highest grade at the top.

c) Superimpose the bars, so that the improvement across grades is emphasized.

d) Change the form of the graph to a line graph, since values for intermediate grades can be accurately determined.

Questions 5 and 6 refer to the figure below, which depicts the percentages of different types of peer victimization that sixth-graders reported experiencing or witnessing during a school week. (Adapted from Nishina & Juvonen, 2005.)

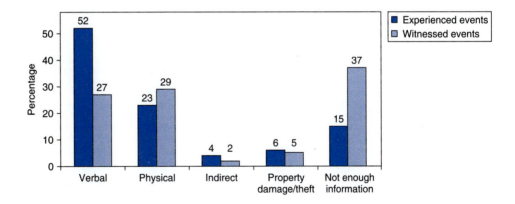

5. What percentage of witnessed events was physical?

a) 23

b) 27

c) 29

d) 52

6. Which of the following would also provide a clear and accurate depiction of these data?

a) Line graph

b) Contingency table

c) Pie chart

d) Cumulative frequency polygon

Questions 7 and 8 refer to the figure below. (Adapted from de Ramirez and Shapiro, 2006.)

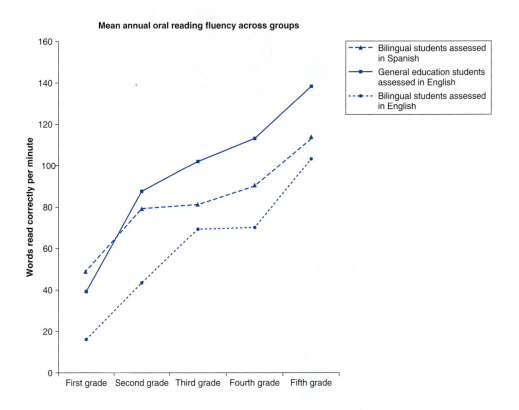

7. Roughly how many words per minute can second-grade bilingual students read, on average, when assessed in Spanish?

a) 30

b) 40

c) 80

d) 90

8. Which group seems to improve the most in oral reading fluency from first to fifth grade?

a) Bilingual students assessed in Spanish

b) General education students assessed in English

c) Bilingual students assessed in English

d) All groups improve to the same extent

Questions 9 and 10 refer to the path diagram below. (Adapted from Ray and Elliot, 2006.)

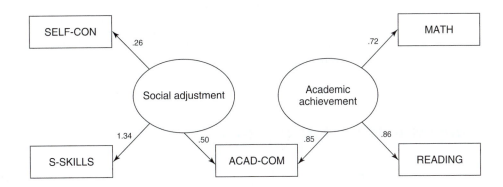

9. What does this path diagram indicate about the relationship between SELF-CON and Social Adjustment?

a) SELF-CON directly influences Social Adjustment.
b) Social Adjustment directly influences SELF-CON.
c) SELF-CON and Social Adjustment influence each other.
d) There is no relationship between SELF-CON and Social Adjustment.

10. On which variable does Academic Achievement have the strongest impact?

a) SELF-CON
b) ACAD-COM
c) MATH
d) READING

11. *Critical thinking question:* A researcher wishes to compare the scores on a math achievement test obtained by fourth-graders in three sets of schools. The researcher has designated each set of schools as "public," "private," and "charter," and the schools are matched on numerous variables. The researcher analyzes the data by conducting a 3 (type of school) × 2 (gender) ANOVA on math score means. Should the researcher report group means in a table or a bar graph? If a graph is used, should the x-axis represent gender, with three bars given for each gender (one bar per type of school), or should the x-axis represent type of school, with two bars given for each type of school (one bar per gender)?

Answers to Exercises

1. b   **2.** d   **3.** c   **4.** a   **5.** c   **6.** b   **7.** c   **8.** b   **9.** b   **10.** d

11. *Possible answer:* The means could be accurately depicted in either a table or a bar graph. A table would be preferable if the researcher wanted the means to be accompanied by other kinds of descriptive statistics (sample sizes, measures of variability, and so on) as well as the results of the ANOVA. A bar graph might have a stronger impact if there were unusual trends in the data. Group means could be accurately depicted in the graph regardless of whether the x-axis represents the means for each gender further subdivided by school (two sets of bars, with three bars per set), or the means for each school further subdivided by gender (three sets of bars, with two bars per set). The decision about how to structure the *x*-axis should be informed by the researcher's hypotheses. For example, if the researcher predicts an interaction between type of school and gender, such that boys outperform girls in public and charter schools, while girls outperform boys in private schools, evidence for (or against) the prediction would be easiest to see if the *x*-axis represents type of school, with pairs of bars depicting the gender breakdown corresponding to each type.

Suggestions for Further Reading

Research Article: Lawlor, D. A., Clark, H., Ronalds, G., & Leon, D. A. (2006). Season of birth and childhood intelligence: Findings from the *Aberdeen Children of the 1950s* cohort study. *British Journal of Educational Psychology, 76,* 481–499.

This causal–comparative report contains a variety of tables, histograms, frequency polygons, and multivariate line graphs.

Application Article: von Schrader, S., & Ansley, T. (2006). Sex differences in the tendency to omit items on multiple-choice tests:1980–2000. *Applied Measurement in Education, 19*(1), 41–65.

This causal–comparative study contains a substantial number of tables as well as some line graphs.

Extension Article: Braun, H., Jenkins, F., Grigg, W., & Tirre, W. (2006). *Comparing private schools and public schools using hierarchical linear modeling.* U.S. Department of Education, NCES-2006-461.

This analysis of 2003 NAEP data includes an introduction to and application of HLM techniques.

CHAPTER 13

Ethnographies and Case Studies

Pete Oxford/Minden Pictures, Inc.

After studying this chapter, you will be able to answer the following questions:

- What is qualitative research?

- What are the characteristics and purposes of ethnographic research?

- What are the different types of ethnographic designs?

- What other types of qualitative research are similar to ethnographic designs?

- What are the characteristics and purposes of case studies?

This chapter will prepare you to do the following:

- Understand and evaluate ethnographic research reports

- Understand and evaluate case studies

- Choose an ethnographic or case study design that best suits your research question

- Design an ethnography or case study

Introduction to Qualitative Research

One of the recurrent themes in this book is that research designs fit research questions. If you want to compare the effects of two new methods of ESL instruction on reading scores, an experimental or quasi-experimental approach would be appropriate. If you want to quantify the relationship between reading scores and the number of ESL classes students have taken, a correlational approach would be preferable. But if you want to reconstruct the experience of students in an ESL class—the pleasures and frustrations of studying a new language, the desire for acceptance by English-speaking peers, the concerns about assimilation outside class—then a qualitative design may be most suitable for your research question.

As noted in Chapter 1, qualitative research reflects nonquantitative epistemologies and methods. The information obtained from qualitative studies is expressed in narratives rather than numbers. The qualitative narrative consists of highly detailed descriptions of people, environments, and institutions, with emphasis on peoples' interactions and experiences as well as the meanings they construct. In order to create such "thick" descriptions, the qualitative researcher obtains a great deal of information, often through more than one method, and often with smaller samples than ordinarily found in quantitative studies. Because the qualitative researcher assumes that realities are constructed by individuals rather than objectively observed, the researcher may acknowledge his or her own fallibility in reconstructing the perspectives of participants.

These characteristics of qualitative designs are reflected in a study by Faye Mishna (2004), who interviewed five fourth- and fifth-graders about their experiences as victims of bullying. In the following sections, some of the basic features of qualitative research will be discussed using Mishna's study as an illustration.

Qualitative Research Questions

As noted in Chapter 1, qualitative research may begin with clearly formulated research questions and hypotheses or simply a focus of inquiry. As information is gathered, the qualitative researcher may revise the initial topic, develop and evaluate hypotheses, or otherwise respond to emerging trends with more flexibility than may be possible in quantitative studies. In Mishna's study, semi-structured interviews were used in which children were asked to define bullying and discuss their experiences. Although Mishna asked specific questions about type and location of bullying, she did not begin her study with a hypothesis but rather with a sense of the kinds of information that would be valuable.

Qualitative Sampling

Approaches to qualitative sampling are discussed at length in Chapter 4. As discussed in that chapter, qualitative sampling typically focuses on small numbers of individuals who are likely to be informative—both because of who they are, and because the researcher anticipates the opportunity to interact with and/or observe them extensively. By means of an intensity sampling procedure, Mishna used survey responses to identify five students who described themselves as victims of bullying but differed in the extent to which their victimization was physical, relational, or racial. One parent of each child, three of the children's teachers, and two administrators at the children's school were also interviewed about bullying.

Qualitative Analysis and Interpretation

The main approaches to measurement in qualitative research are introduced in Chapter 5 and revisited later in this chapter and in Chapter 14. Qualitative studies tend to incorporate multiple measures that yield substantial amounts of information. In contrast to most quantitative studies, some analysis and interpretation may take place while a qualitative study is still underway. After interviewing several students, for instance, the qualitative researcher may notice particular themes and change the question format so that later interviews elicit more information relevant to those themes. In other cases, as in Mishna's study, the researcher waits until information gathering is complete before beginning the qualitative analysis.

ORGANIZATION   Before data analyses can be completed, the qualitative researcher must organize the information he or she has obtained. This can be a daunting task, given that qualitative data tend to be informationally rich. The researcher may organize the information by hand, or make use of a family of computer software programs known as **CAQDAS** (computer-assisted qualitative data analysis software). Unlike the SPSS and SAS programs described in the chapters on quantitative designs, CAQDAS programs are not designed for statistical calculation. Rather, they help the researcher store, organize, label, relate, and retrieve information.

In Mishna's study, a software program called NVivo was used to organize the data. Like other programs, NVivo provides storage for text as well as images. Each unit of information (e.g., a sentence) can be labeled with one or many codes. The researcher can access data through these codes, relate different units of information, and create relational maps. (Further information about such programs can be found online at *www.qsrinternational.com*.)

CODING   Although qualitative researchers may use informal methods to identify themes in their data, a widely used tool in qualitative analysis is the formal **coding system** used to simplify the data by sorting it into categories. There are no fixed principles for doing so. Because the goal of coding is to identify recurrent themes in the data, the researcher proceeds inductively, assigning each element of the data to a category that seems meaningful. In a study on substance abuse among high school students, for instance, the qualitative researcher might analyze transcripts from interviews in which students talk about how they got involved with drugs. As the researcher reads through the transcripts, he or should would begin to make note of themes that are reflected in student comments. The researcher might circle particular comments, or make notes in the margins, each time a student expresses social rejection, alienation from parents, low self-esteem, peer pressure, boredom, curiosity, or some other category that strikes the researcher as potentially important.

In this example, the researcher has begun to analyze the data by means of **open coding**, in which specific elements (in this case, student comments) are assigned to categories. Other approaches to coding may be used as well. The researcher might use **axial coding** to identify relationships between several categories and one category of interest. For instance, the researcher might place susceptibility to peer pressure in a central position, and determine how other categories are related to it (e.g., statements implying low self-esteem might be labeled as having a causal influence on susceptibility to peer pressure, while certain descriptions of drug-taking behavior might be labeled as effects of peer pressure). The researcher might also use **selective coding**, which means looking for observations that fit particular categories. For instance, the researcher might reread the transcripts in order to document instances in which students expressed alienation from teachers.

Although some qualitative researchers use categories identified in prior studies, it is more common for them to proceed inductively, creating categories on the basis of the information obtained. This inductive attitude is reflected in the **constant comparative method**, an ongoing process in which categories are created as the data are examined, further data are sorted into these categories, and the categories are compared and perhaps combined or modified in some other way (Glaser & Strauss, 1967). The goal of the constant comparative method is to maximize within-category similarities and cross-category differences. For instance, if students in the previous scenario frequently voiced a sense of alienation from adults, the constant comparative method would help the researcher distinguish that experience from other forms of disaffection, and perhaps also to clearly distinguish between statements reflecting alienation from parents and other family members versus statements reflecting alienation from teachers and other professionals at school.

In Mishna's study, all participants were asked how they define bullying. Mishna used the constant comparative method to identify categories that emerged in the definitions, as well as in children's judgments about whether or not bullying had taken place in particular situations. The definitional categories that Mishna identified were power imbalance, intent to hurt, and whether an act of aggression is nonphysical or relational. The constant comparative method allowed Mishna to identify these four categories as distinct dimensions of children's definitions.

INTERPRETATION   Interpretation of qualitative results also tends to proceed inductively, and is often not clearly distinct from coding and other analytical steps. As I discuss later in the chapter, the researcher's interpretations are informed by awareness of his or her own biases and their influence on the findings. At some point the researcher will have reviewed the literature, so that prior research and theory is also brought to bear on the interpretation of current findings. **Negative case analysis** may be used, in which the researcher carefully reexamines the data for observations that would contradict any conclusions that have been drawn.

One of the themes that emerged in Mishna's study is the difficulty of ascertaining how people define bullying. Although all participants referred to a power imbalance in their definitions, both children and adults provided mixed responses as to whether intent to hurt is essential to the definition. Likewise, neither the children nor the adults consistently indicated that bullying could involve verbal and relational aggression. Mishna also found that children's definitions of bullying were not always consistent with the way they labeled particular incidents as bullying or not (e.g., when a friend is the aggressor). Mishna concluded that for children bullying is a complex and somewhat confusing concept.

Qualitative Research Reports

The general flow of information in a qualitative research report is similar to that of a quantitative report. The researcher begins with the statement of a problem and a discussion of prior research relevant to the problem. The researcher then describes his or her methods, results, and conclusions. The research report may be divided into sections with labels typical of quantitative reports, as in Mishna's study, but it is also common for qualitative reports to deviate from this fixed, clearly demarcated structure. As noted in Chapter 3, qualitative researchers may describe (and evaluate) their methods and findings without dividing these topics into separate sections. In this way, qualitative researchers indicate how their understanding of the methods and findings evolved during the process of gathering information.

Qualitative Research in This Book

Qualitative research is discussed throughout the book (except in Chapters 7–12, which have a purely quantitative focus) and it is my sole focus in this chapter and the next one. This chapter introduces ethnographies and case study designs (along with several related approaches), while Chapter 14 takes up content analysis and historical research. Roughly, these chapters correspond to a distinction between qualitative designs in which the main source of information is living participants versus qualitative designs in which information is gathered primarily from documents, artifacts, and other materials. In Chapter 15 I introduce mixed-method designs, which rely on both quantitative and qualitative methods.

Introduction to Ethnographic Research

Ethnographic research (or ethnography) is the qualitative study of individuals and groups who represent particular cultures. The researcher who carries out an ethnographic study is called an **ethnographer**.

Ethnographic studies take place in natural settings. Quantitative research may be carried out in natural settings too—in classrooms and playgrounds, at PTA meetings, and so on. What distinguishes most clearly between ethnographic and quantitative research is that the ethnographer attempts to reconstruct the behaviors, perspectives, and experiences of people from particular cultural groups. The ethnographer's "data" consists of detailed narrative descriptions rather than numbers. These descriptions, as you will see, tend to be richer and include a broader array of cultural and personal details than the results of a quantitative study.

Historical Underpinnings

The ethnographic approach was developed in the 19th and early 20th centuries by cultural anthropologists. At that time, colonialism had already brought Americans and Europeans into contact with cultures that differed greatly from their own. As travel became increasingly convenient, the field of anthropology developed in part through scholarly interest in these "unusual" cultures. Originally, anthropologists assumed that it was desirable to create objective descriptions of cultures that vary on a continuum from primitive (non-European) to advanced (European). This assumption has been discarded. Contemporary ethnographic research is based more or less explicitly on the idea that the researcher is a fallible observer whose observations are informed by his or her own cultural background, and that European culture does not represent the highest standard toward which other cultures are developing.

During the past half century, educational anthropologists as well as educational researchers interested in anthropology have adopted ethnographic approaches to the study of educational questions. These researchers are interested in the experiences of people from different cultures, and their definitions of culture have expanded to include groups such as students, teachers, classrooms, schools, and so on. The ethnographic approach has become a popular, if sometimes controversial, way to conduct educational research. Much of the controversy pertains to the acceptability of qualitative research as an alternative to what some believe to be the greater rigor of quantitative approaches—a topic I revisit later in the chapter, and then again in Chapter 18.

Definition of Culture

As you can tell, the concept of culture is central to ethnographic research. For our purposes, **culture** can be defined as the acquired behaviors, beliefs, meanings, and values shared by the members of a group.

According to this definition, culture is not just a characteristic of large, geographically defined regions (as in "Italian culture" or "the culture of the American Southwest"). When students in a particular community play their favorite dice game during recess, for example, they engage in specific behaviors that reflect beliefs about how to play the game. Their behaviors consist of physical movements as well as verbal exchanges. Each roll of the dice and other events during the game tend to have meaning to those familiar with the game, while those who are unfamiliar with this "dice culture" might not understand what each event means. These shared meanings might be specific to the game (*so-and-so is losing now*) or they might reflect a broader understanding of people and situations (*so-and-so is getting frustrated now, as he usually does when he fails to succeed*). The children as well as older members of the community may also have more or less explicitly articulated assumptions about the importance of the game and other leisure activities, about the proper mix of work and leisure, and so on. An ethnographic study might include a detailed description of the children's behaviors, a reconstruction of their beliefs about how the game should be played, an explanation of what meanings each player attributes to different game-related events, and a description of the role of the game and other leisure activities in the lives of the players and other members of the community. In sum, the dice-players could be viewed as a distinct culture within their own community, and if they were to relocate to another geographic region they would bring their culture with them.

Characteristics of Ethnographic Research

Ethnographic research has a number of distinctive characteristics. Most ethnographic studies reflect at least some of the characteristics in the following list.

- Information is gathered through direct observation of participants. Although the researcher may distribute surveys and examine artifacts, the foundation of ethnographic research is observation and perhaps also interviews with the participants themselves.

- Observations and interviews are carried out in natural settings. Information is not usually obtained in the researcher's lab or office. Instead, the researcher engages in **fieldwork**, which refers to the process of observing and interacting with participants wherever they live, work, study, obtain services, and/or recreate.
- Multiple methods of gathering information are used. These methods include observation, interviews, examination of documents, and so on, gathered in an attempt to create a detailed reconstruction of the lives and perspectives of the participants.
- The process of information gathering tends to be inductive. Rather than testing specific hypotheses, the researcher may obtain information in a somewhat unstructured way, allowing specific findings to guide further inquiry as well as the formulation of theoretical explanations.
- A large amount of information is obtained. Since the researcher may not know in advance what information will be most relevant, the early stages of information gathering will be relatively inclusive. As a result, ethnographic studies tend to be lengthy. Rather than gathering information on one or two occasions, the ethnographer may spend weeks, months, or even years interacting with participants.
- The researcher may acknowledge personal influence on the research process. Rather than interpreting the results impartially, the ethnographer may explicitly consider how his or her actions influence participants, and how his or her own cultural background informs the interpretation of the results.

These six characteristics are illustrated in a study by Chrispeels and Rivero (2001) on how parent education classes affect the way Latino parents view their role in their children's education. Chrispeels and Rivero observed families directly rather than obtaining information exclusively through surveys. The observations took place in natural settings, including the schools where parent education classes were conducted as well as the parents' homes. Multiple methods of gathering information were used, including videotaped observations of parents during class, in-depth interviews with individual families, distribution of questionnaires, and analysis of parent education documents. Information gathering during interviews was somewhat inductive, in the sense that parents often raised new topics, leading the interviews in unplanned directions A great deal of information was obtained over an 8-week period. And, in their write-up of the study, the researchers acknowledged the importance of conveying the parents' perspectives rather than imposing on them the values of the researchers (or anyone else). Here is how Chrispeels and Rivero summarized several of their findings:

> On the basis of 8 weeks of observing participants in the classes and the interview data, we would argue that a strong motivator propelling these parents to attend was their love and aspirations for a better life for their children. The parents reported that they believed that attending the classes was a demonstration of their commitment to their children's future. We believe this sense of hope for a brighter future is a unique aspect of role construction that also needs further study. Our data suggest that although parents responded to PIQE [the parent education classes] because of their aspirations, their aspirations were also impacted by the classes. After attending PIQE, parents realized it was not sufficient to just have dreams of a better future for their children, but that they had to assume a significant place and role in helping realize those dreams. In particular, they understood the relationship among literacy activities, homework, and the close monitoring of academic progress as essential steps needed

for higher education. Although PIQE instructors stressed that lack of financial resources need not be an obstacle to college attendance, some parents proactively opened a savings account to increase the possibility that their children would be able to go. These actions suggest that with further information about possible ways to support their children's school success, parents were able to respond and express their love and aspirations in more concrete forms.

In conclusion, our study suggests that through the information provided by PIQE, parents developed higher levels of engagement both with their child and with the school, especially the teacher. They were able to negotiate new relationships with their spouse, their children, and their children's teachers. As they gained an understanding of what is required for success in school and for admission to university, parents set more specific goals for their children. The final outcome was increased parent participation in the child's education both at home and at school, reflecting a much fuller range of types and levels of involvement.

(Chrispeels & Rivero, 2001; quoted with permission from Lawrence Erlbaum Associates, Inc.)

Ethnographic Methods

Following is the general sequence of steps in an ethnographic research study:

- Identify a research question or focus of inquiry
- Gain entry to a fieldwork site
- Establish trust and rapport with participants
- Gather information from participants
- Interpret the information obtained

Although this sequence of steps is roughly similar to those of a quantitative study, the details of each step clearly distinguishes ethnographic approaches. The initial focus of inquiry may be broad, in contrast to the narrowly focused research question in a quantitative study, so that the ethnographic researcher may begin the study in a state of receptiveness to virtually any sort of information. Gaining entry to a site and establishing a trusting relationship with participants may be more challenging for the ethnographic researcher, owing to the length of time that may be spent with participants, and to the fact that interactions will take place where the participants live. Finally, the processes of gathering and interpreting information may not be clearly distinguished. Whereas the quantitative researcher obtains and codes data, performs statistical analyses, and then interprets the results, the ethnographic researcher often attempts to make sense of new information "online," using this information for guidance in the development of hypotheses and in subsequent information-gathering activities.

In ethnographic studies, the three main approaches to gathering information are observation, interviews, and content analysis.

Observation

The simplest approach to gathering information is to simply observe. No equipment is needed other than your five senses and a notebook or some other tool for recording information. Observation is also highly flexible. Although tests, surveys, and other formal measures allow data collection to be focused, these methods are not usually flexible enough to accommodate responses that are lengthy, highly creative, or seemingly irrelevant. In contrast, observation is receptive to whatever the participants happen to reveal. Most ethnographic research is based at least in part on observational methods, owing to their simplicity and flexibility.

A distinction between participant and passive observation can be made on the basis of whether or not the researcher interacts with the individuals he or she is observing.

PARTICIPANT OBSERVATION   **Participant observation** occurs when the researcher interacts with participants in activities that the participants naturally engage in. The researcher's level of participation may range from a few casual conversations to a period of months working alongside the participants.

One advantage of participant observation is that it allows the researcher to interact with participants, rather than observing from a distance. Interaction helps put people at ease, facilitates the collection of richer information, and allows the researcher to guide the process of information gathering by asking questions, making comments, and otherwise gently influencing the flow of information.

The interactivity of participant observation also constitutes its main disadvantage. The researcher may unwittingly bias the results by eliciting some conversational themes or behaviors more than others. The participants themselves may feel inhibited, or wish to present themselves in an especially favorable light. In short, participant observation runs the risk of the experimenter and subject effects discussed in Chapter 7.

PASSIVE OBSERVATION   **Passive observation** occurs when the researcher does not interact with the participants that he or she is observing. The researcher may sit at the back of a classroom or school board meeting, for example, and make note of various activities without talking to anyone. The researcher actively looks and listens, of course. What is "passive" about the researcher's behavior is simply that he or she does not initiate interactions with participants.

Ordinarily, it is impossible to observe people without at least minimal interaction—eye contact, for instance, or a casual greeting. Thus, we can think of the distinction between participant and passive observation as simply a matter of degree. The extent of researcher participation varies greatly from study to study.

The advantage of passive observation is that in the ideal case it reveals "natural" behavior that is uninfluenced by the researcher's presence. This is assuming that the participants are unaware of, or have forgotten about, the researcher. In actual practice, participants may alter their behavior when observed, even if they are not interacting with the person who is observing them. Subject effects are a potential risk in any type of research, quantitative or qualitative.

Although passive observation does not allow the researcher to influence the conversations and behaviors that are observed, the likelihood of experimenter effects is less than it would be for participant observation. Whereas participant observers influence the information they obtain through their comments, actions, reactions to participants, and so on, the only experimenter effects created by passive observers stem from their own cultural biases. Passive observers filter information through the lens of their own culture (as do participant observers) but their actions do not contribute to the filtering process.

FIELD NOTES Both participant and passive observation tend to be accompanied by the recording of **field notes**, or detailed records of a situation. Even though it would be easier to observe participants without having to make notes, researchers know that human memory is fallible. Field notes help guard against the loss and/or distortion of information.

Field notes may be handwritten or recorded with an audiotape or some other portable device. If written down, field notes are created during observation, or as soon after the observation as possible. The notes will be thorough, concrete, and specific, and will typically include descriptions of the following:

- The date, time, location, and duration of the observation
- The characteristics of the immediate setting
- The appearance, behavior, and speech of participants
- The activities and interactions engaged in by participants
- The apparent subjective experience of participants
- Background information on participants and setting
- The researcher's own reflections, including background observations, interpretive comments, methodological considerations, ethical concerns, and notes on the researcher's own frame of mind.

The use of field notes to record these different kinds of information is illustrated in Spotlight on Research 13.1.

Interviews

Along with observation and the recording of field notes, the ethnographic researcher may interview participants. Interviews can be carried out in person, over the phone, by mail, or through a computer medium such as e-mail. One person at a time may be interviewed, or the researcher might interview an entire group simultaneously. The question format may be structured, semi-structured, or completely open-ended.

It can be difficult to conduct a successful interview. The participant may say too little or too much. Key information may be forgotten. Participants may struggle to express themselves if they are inhibited or young. Experimenter and subject effects are clear risks when interviews are used in ethnographic research, since researcher and participant will be somewhat familiar with each other.

Following are some general principles for ensuring a successful interview:

- *Be prepared.* If the question format is structured or semi-structured, know your questions in advance so that little or no reading from notes will be needed. Keep track of any personal information about participants that might influence the content of the interview. Be ready to audiotape or take notes in the least obtrusive way.
- *Begin slowly.* Unless you and the interviewee are already closely acquainted, some time may be needed to put the individual at ease. Make small talk and remain positive. Do not begin the interview if the individual seems anxious or unwilling to talk.
- *Explain your purpose.* The interviewee should be reminded of what to expect during the interview. The interviewee's willingness to speak freely may be facilitated if he or she is reminded that all responses will be kept confidential.

A Sample of Field Notes

In their 2007 book *Qualitative Research for Education**, Robert Bogdan and Sari Biklen provide a sample of field notes generated by an observer during one of his visits to a high school class in 1980.

The field notes begin with a description of the setting and other contextual information. The following passage illustrates some of the basic characteristics of field notes: A neutral tone, a careful rendering of concrete details, and a narrative flow. In addition, there is a clearly demarcated "O.C.," or observer comment, in which the observer pauses in his descriptions to record a personal reaction.

I arrived at Westwood High at five minutes to eleven, the time Marge told me her fourth period started. I was dressed as usual: sports shirt, chino pants, and a Woolrich parka. The fourth period is the only time during the day when all the students who are in the "neurologically impaired/learning disability" program, better known as "Marge's program," come together. During the other periods, certain students in the program, two or three or four at most, come to her room for help with the work they are getting in other regular high school classes.

It was a warm, fortyish, promise of a spring day. There was a police patrol wagon, the kind that has benches in the back that are used for large busts, parked in the back of the big parking lot that is in the front of the school. No one was sitting in it and I never heard its reason for being there. In the circular drive in front of the school was parked a United States Army car. It had insignias on the side and was a khaki color. As I walked from my car, a balding fortyish man in an Army uniform came out of the building and went to the car and sat down. Four boys and a girl also walked out of the school. All were white. They had on old dungarees and colored stenciled t-shirts with spring jackets over them.

One of the boys, the tallest of the four, called out, "oink, oink, oink." This was done as he sighted the police vehicle in the back.

O.C.: This was strange to me in that I didn't think that the kids were into the "police as pigs." Somehow I associated that with another time, the early 1970s. I'm going to have to come to grips with the assumptions I have about high school due to my own experience. Sometimes I feel like Westwood is entirely different from my high school and yet this police car incident reminded me of mine. . . .

In the next passage, the observer comment provides background information as well as interpretive comments. Although the main text continues to be neutral, concrete, and thorough, some interpretive comments and personal reactions are interspersed with the more objective observations. A distinction is made between direct quotation and approximations of dialogue. The physical description of the classroom is enhanced by a drawing of the seating arrangement.

I walked into Marge's class and she was standing in front of the room with more people than I had ever seen in the room save for her homeroom which is right after second period. She looked like she was talking to the class or was just about to start. She was dressed as she had been on my other visits—clean, neat, well-dressed but casual. Today she had on a striped blazer, a white blouse and dark slacks. She looked up at me smiled and said: "Oh, I have a lot more people here now than the last time."

O.C.: This was in reference to my other visits during other periods where there are only a few students. She seems self-conscious about having such a small group of students to be responsible for. Perhaps she compares herself with the regular teachers who have classes of thirty or so.

(continued)

- *Question carefully.* Avoid leading questions. Avoid "yes-or-no" questions unless they pertain to concrete details. Use open-ended questions, and then probe for details or request clarification as needed.

- *Listen closely.* Say as little as possible without awkwardness, ask questions if you do not understand a comment, and avoid interrupting the interviewee. Whenever possible, paraphrase the interviewee's comments and otherwise give the impression of attentiveness. Remember what the interviewee says so that if the need arises you can refer back to it later in the interview.

There were two women in their late twenties sitting in the room. There was only one chair left. Marge said to me something like: "We have two visitors from the central office today. One is a vocational counselor and the other is a physical therapist," but I don't remember if those were the words. I felt embarrassed coming in late. I sat down in the only chair available next to one of the women from the central office. They had on skirts and carried their pocketbooks, much more dressed up than the teachers I've seen. They sat there and observed.

Below is the seating arrangement of the class today.

Alfred (Mr. Armstrong, the teacher's aide) walked around but when he stood in one place it was over by Phil and Jeff. Marge walked about near her desk during her talk which she started by saying to the class: "Now, remember, tomorrow is a fieldtrip to the Rollway Company. We all meet in the usual place, by the bus, in front of the main entrance at 8:30. Mrs. Sharp wanted me to tell you that the tour of Rollway is not specifically for you. It's not like the trip to G.M. They took you to places where you were likely to be able to get jobs. Here, it's just a general tour that everybody goes on. Many of the jobs that you will see are not for you. Some are just for people with engineering degrees. You'd better wear comfortable shoes because you may be walking for two or three hours." Maxine and Mark said "Ooh," in protest to the walking.

She paused and said in a demanding voice: "OK, any questions? You are all going to be there. (Pause.) I want you to take a piece of paper and write down some questions so you have things to ask at the plant." She began passing out paper and at this point Jason, who was sitting next to me, made a tutting sound of disgust and said: "We got to do this?" Marge said: "I know this is too easy for you, Jason." This was said in a sarcastic way but not like a strong put-down.

O.C.: It was like sarcasm between two people who know each other well. Marge has known many of these kids for a few years. I have to explore the implications of that for her relations with them . . .

Notice that in the last observer comment, a note is made to explore the implications of a particular idea. This illustrates the inductive quality of ethnographic research. While making observations, the researcher gradually develops ideas, questions, and theoretical interpretations that will be subsequently explored.

*Bogdan, R. C., & Biklen, S. K. (2007). *Qualitative research in education: An introduction to theories and methods* (5th ed.). New York: Pearson Education, Inc. Quoted with permission from the publisher.

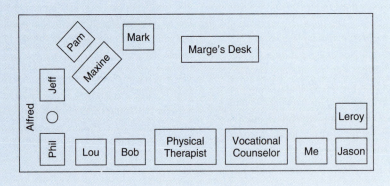

- **Keep on your toes.** Some topics may elicit a strong emotional response from interviewees. If the interviewee changes the subject, follow the new topic. If you feel it is important to lead the interviewee back to the original topic, do so gently.
- **Remain supportive.** Avoid challenging interviewees, or passing judgment on their opinions.

TABLE 13.1 Three Methods of Gathering Information
in Ethnographic Research

Method	Interaction with Participants?
Observation	May or may not rely on interaction with participants.
Interviews	Requires interaction with participants.
Content analysis	Often requires no interaction with participants.

Content Analysis

As in other types of qualitative research, the ethnographer may examine written documents as well as artifacts such as videotapes, diaries, artwork, and so on. Further details on these methods of gathering information are provided in Chapter 14.

The three main types of ethnographic methods described in this section are distinguished in part by the extent of interaction between researchers and participants, as shown in Table 13.1.

Combinations of Methods

Since the goal of ethnography is to provide a detailed reconstruction of peoples' lives and perspectives, more than one method of gathering information is typically necessary. Most ethnographers gather information through some combination of the three methods just described. A typical approach is illustrated in the following passage. In this study, Catherine Ashcraft (2004) documented the progress of a debate among members of a Colorado school district over a revision to the language of the district's policy on diversity:

> Data were collected during the six-month debate over the diversity policy, beginning in August of 1998 and ending in February of 1999. I attended the primary meetings where the diversity policy was discussed and took extensive field notes. A co-researcher and I also collected videotapes, agendas and written materials (e.g. copies of the strategic plan, the diversity statement and other working draft documents) from these meetings. In addition, we interviewed all board members for approximately an hour to 90 minutes. Data were then initially analyzed using a combination of qualitative and discourse analytic methods (Spradley, 1980; Tracy, 1995; Lareau, 1996). Field notes, agendas and other written materials were read and initial codes were determined to identify common themes and patterns. . . . I watched videotapes of meetings to enhance field notes, revise codes and identify key segments of the debate to be transcribed. (pp. 690–691)

By means of these various sources of information, Ashcraft was able to track the progress of the community's debate over whether district policy should call for schools to "respect" or to "value" diversity. The decision about which term to use created much controversy in the school district, in part because some individuals felt that schools should teach appropriate behaviors (i.e., respect) rather than personal beliefs (i.e., values). Multiple methods of data collection allowed Ashcraft to tease out various nuances of the debate and to offer her own opinions on the different positions.

Meta-Methods

Observation, interviews, and content analysis are three methods for gathering information in ethnographic research. Regardless of which method, or combination of methods, an ethnographer employs, two additional "meta-methods" are often used: triangulation and self-reflection. These can be referred to as meta-methods because each helps improve the accuracy of the information obtained through the three primary ethnographic methods. Triangulation is a way of cross-checking the accuracy of the researcher's sources of information, while self-reflection, or reflexivity, helps prevent the researcher from undermining the accuracy of that information. (Both of these meta-methods are widely used in qualitative research traditions other than ethnography.)

Triangulation

Ethnographic researchers understand that just as they themselves are fallible, biased observers, so the people they observe may be biased and otherwise fallible sources of information. This is especially likely given the types of research questions addressed in ethnographic studies. Although an individual might provide accurate and unbiased answers to a list of true–false survey questions on a neutral topic, the likelihood of inaccurate or biased responses is much greater in conversations about cultural and political themes, topics of immediate personal relevance, and so on. Moreover, one would expect some diversity in responses to questions about each person's unique perspective and experience. For these reasons, the ethnographic researcher often resorts to more than one source of information in order to establish a fact. This is called **triangulation**, a way of corroborating information by comparing the information obtained from multiple sources. Just as a quantitative researcher calculates interrater reliability estimates in order to determine how closely observers agree about a phenomenon, so ethnographic researchers engage in triangulation as a way of checking the reliability of statements that are made.

Reflexivity

As noted in Chapter 1, objectivity is a fundamental goal in science, in the sense that researchers seek impartial descriptions of the phenomena they study. For this reason, quantitative research reports tend to be written with a neutral, objective tone. The researcher remains a more or less invisible narrator who lays out each step of the research process while avoiding expression of personal interests and biases.

Ethnographic researchers are more likely to acknowledge that their own cultural assumptions and individual histories can be obstacles to the appreciation of other cultures. **Reflexivity** refers to conscious reflection on the effects of the researcher's own assumptions and biases on the ethnographic process. Although some ethnographers assume that with effort one can escape one's own subjectivity to a greater or lesser extent, others are more pessimistic about this possibility.

Although self-reflectiveness fosters specific methods, such as critical case analysis (discussed earlier in the chapter), in essence reflexivity is a general attitude that informs all aspects of the gathering and interpretation of information. Through a reflexive attitude, the researcher attempts to surmount personal biases, or to incorporate these biases into his or her narratives in an illuminating way.

REFLEXIVITY AS A WAY OF OVERCOMING PERSONAL BIASES   The researcher may take a reflexive or self-reflective attitude simply for the purpose of identifying personal biases that must be set aside in order to obtain more accurate information. Examples of this type of reflexivity can be seen in the following passages taken from two different studies:

> [E]ach researcher recognized the limitations in his or her experience and background and diligently sought to privilege the participants' perspective throughout all aspects of the study. For example, we employed very open-ended questions during the focus groups to enable participants to navigate us through their worlds. We attempted to ensure that we were really "listening" to students' words, facial expressions and their use of material culture, without interjecting our personal views. For example, as we explained the instructions for completing goal maps and collages, we asked participants to think of examples of how to complete the exercise, rather than imposing our own ideas. Any probing statements used during the focus groups were always statements derived from the student's own words (e.g. rephrasing their statements to qualify the meaning of what they had stated). These techniques, and our stance toward the research process, ensured that we remained self-reflexive and aware of our own biases in this research project. In sum, we attempted to "understand and capture the points of view of other people without predetermining those points of view."
>
> (Sirin, Diemer, Jackson, Gonsalves, & Howell, 2004, pp. 441–442)

> Bias and researcher subjectivity were concerns here. I handled this by stating my biases up front. I am a gay man who suffered six years of abuse at the hands of my classmates, teachers and even administrators from grades 7 through 12. I would like to end anti-gay bias in every US school so no other GLBTQ [gay, lesbian, bisexual, transgender, or queer) youth will ever have to go through what I went through. While interviewing Concerned Citizens, I took extra care to be very aware of my own subjectivities. I had the very real desire to understand the points of view and the rationales of those with whom I did not agree (i.e. opponents who believe that GLBTQ people and perspectives should not be included in all aspects of public schooling). This was not a difficult task for me and I allowed myself to be "steeped" in Concerned Citizens' logic to the point where it took a while for me to step back from it and begin to see it objectively. This was a good learning experience and made this research stronger.
>
> (Macgillivray, 2004, pp. 354–355)

REFLEXIVITY THAT INCORPORATES BIASES INTO THE NARRATIVE   The researcher may take a reflexive attitude in order to use his or her personal biases as a way of creating a more illuminating ethnography. Rather than trying to overcome personal biases, the researcher incorporates them into the ethnographic narrative in a useful way. In the following passage, for example, the researcher uses himself as a "metaphor" or representative for a broader set of attitudes toward Native Americans.

> [My book] Chronicles begins with my earliest recollections of Indians and racism and continues through my teenage years. I recount my romanticized view of Indians, my timidity to speak out against white school bullies, and my general indifference to and ignorance of local racism. Like Behar (1996) I tell several stories that analogize my feelings and reactions to those of other Whites. In effect, I am claiming to be a metaphor for some local Whites who

bear no intense malice towards the Mesquaki, but who have little interest in and knowledge of their way of life. By representing myself as a metaphor for Whites, it helps me be didactic without being too preachy and moralistic. The Chronicles is nuanced with personal memories to characterize and situate myself historically and ideologically. The autobiographical vignettes also help represent how the ethnographic text was produced through a series of personal encounters. Finally, the text is openly subjective, and I make judgmental remarks about events and actors. This allows me to break openly with the usual objectifying scientific voice.

(Foley, 2002, p. 483)

Types of Ethnographies

The term "ethnography" refers to a particular approach to conducting research, as well as to the product of the research (i.e., the published, or potentially publishable, description of individuals, groups, and/or activities that represent a particular culture). Different approaches to ethnography (in the sense of how the research is conducted) are reflected in different types of ethnographies (in the sense of how the results are written up).

Among the many different approaches to ethnographic study, several types can be identified based on their prevalence and on common themes within each type (e.g., Creswell, 2005; Van Maanen, 1988). Keep in mind as you read this section that different types of ethnography are not just reflective of different "styles" of research. Rather, each type corresponds to different epistemological and ethical assumptions about how qualitative research should be conducted, and there are scholarly debates both about how to categorize different approaches to qualitative research, and about which type is most appropriate.

In this section, a distinction is made between realist and critical ethnographies, followed by a discussion of other types. In a later section, qualitative approaches that are somewhat distinct from ethnographies are discussed.

Realist Ethnographies

The oldest approach to ethnographic study, **realist ethnography**, is presented as an objective account of a particular culture. The researcher attempts to collect data without influence from his or her personal, political, or ethical biases. Although aware that these biases exist, the researcher hopes that careful observation will yield unbiased and meaningful information. The researcher tends to use the third-person voice to describe his or her observations, and avoids personal reflections and judgments. The language of the resulting descriptions consists of standard categories (e.g., "family life," "status systems," etc.) rather than categories created by the researcher.

Although the realist ethnographer may seek to be a dispassionate observer, this does not mean that he or she avoids topics of political and social importance. Rather, the researcher strives for a dispassionate treatment of topics that he or she may happen to be passionate about. An example of a realist ethnography focusing on a politically sensitive topic is provided in Spotlight on Research 13.2.

Spotlight on Research 13.2

Latino Students and the "Burden of Acting White"

Educational researchers have long been interested in studying and attempting to remedy the disparity in academic achievement between black and white students. Many explanations for the achievement gap have been proposed. For example, the late educational anthropologist John Ogbu argued that after experiencing centuries of discrimination, the attitudes of African Americans toward school tend to be antagonistic because they realize that education is not a means of improving their social condition in the way that it is for whites. Fordham and Ogbu (1986) argued that because high achievement is associated with whiteness, African American students who succeed in school risk being abused by lower-achieving peers for "acting white." Fordham and Ogbu coined the phrase "the burden of acting white" to describe the tendency for African American students to avoid academic success or to conceal their accomplishments, either by pretending to do poorly or by adopting a "raceless persona."

In a 2005 study published in the *International Journal of Qualitative Studies in Education**, Nilda Flores-Gonzalez evaluated whether the "burden of acting white" theory applies to the experiences of Latino students in an urban high school. Flores-Gonzalez's study was motivated in part by recent research questioning whether Fordham and Ogbu's thesis is generally correct. According to some of these recent studies, many students of color do in fact wish to achieve academic success while still maintaining their ethnic or racial identity. Flores-Gonzalez's study can be characterized as a realist ethnography because she attempted to carefully gather information that would bear on the "burden of acting white" theory. That is, rather than explicitly discussing her own ethnicity, her personal interest in the issues, or the potential biases she might have brought to the research setting, Flores-Gonzalez attempted to let the facts speak for themselves.

Flores-Gonzales began the empirical part of her ethnography with a description of the site where information was gathered.

This paper is based on a year-long ethnographic study at Hernandez High School in Chicago. In all measures, Hernandez High is the typical inner-city high school, including a large minority and low-income population. At the time of my research, the student body was 83% Latino, 12% black, 3% Asian and 2% White. Among the total student population, 57.6% were Puerto Rican, 23% Mexican, 2.5% other Latino. Of the students, 70% were low-income and qualified for subsidized or free lunches. With a dropout rate hovering around 65% for the past 20 years, Hernandez High has one of the highest dropout rates in the city. The school's image is stigmatized by stories of academic mediocrity and gang violence.

Much of what Flores-Gonzalez observed at Hernandez High was based on a distinction between "school kids" and "street kids," which encompasses, among other things, a distinction in levels of academic achievement. The degree of segregation that Flores-Gonzalez observed between school and street kids is essential to the argument she ultimately develops.

At Hernandez High, there were two peer cultures—one school-oriented and the other street-oriented. The high achievers belong to the school-oriented peer culture while the low achievers are found mostly among the street-oriented peer culture. Because academic achievement and peer-group membership are interconnected, I refer to high achievers and low achievers as "school kids" and "street kids" respectively. In the school kid category, I include students ranging from high achievers (honor students) to those who are in "good" academic standing (at least a C-average). By contrast, the street kids include very low achievers (below C-average) who are marginally getting by at school, or who are failing. Besides grades, the main difference between the school kids and the street kids is that the former have never dropped out of school, while most of the latter have interrupted their schooling at least temporarily. Another difference between these groups is the orientation of their peer network: the school kids belong to a school-oriented peer group while the street kids are directly or indirectly connected to the street-oriented peer culture . . .

At Hernandez High, portions of the spatial and social structure allow high-achieving school kids to remain relatively separate from the low-achieving street kids. The main mechanisms that segregated school kids from street kids are academic tracking and extracurricular activities. Many of the high achieving school kids are found in the academic elite programs such as honors and college preparatory, while the low-achieving street kids conglomerate in general education and vocational tracks. Track placement has profound repercussions on peer culture membership because it acts as a gatekeeper, granting or denying access to unique opportunities to connect with school through relationships with teachers, participation in extracurricular activities and peer networks.

Tracking at Hernandez High resulted in the segregation of the highest-achieving school kids into the Scholars Program. This was a rather small and very selective college preparatory program, comprised of only about 35 students per grade—just enough students to fill a classroom. The program separates the "scholars," as participants are known, physically and socially from the rest of the school, and from other high achievers, by placing them in honors and advanced placement courses in English, social studies, sciences and mathematics. . . . The scholars were taught by the best teachers in the school and tended to develop close relationships with them. As a result of this physical and social segregation, the scholars comprised a tight-knit group which spent time together in the classroom, in program-related activities and outside of school.

Extracurricular programming was the other main mechanism that segregated school kids (both scholars and non-scholar high achievers) from the street kids. With a 19% student participation rate, Hernandez High was typical of most large high schools (Flores-Gonzalez, 2002). School kids had high rates of extracurricular participation (85%) compared to the lower rates (20%) of the street kids. While extracurricular activities are viewed as open systems where everyone has an equal chance to participate, the reality is that schools like Henrandez High impose guidelines and restrictions that curtail widespread student participation (Quiroz et al., 1996; Flores-Gonzalez, 2000). At Hernandez High, track placement, grades, enrollment in classes and skill level determined eligibility to extracurricular programs. For example, the scholars not only exceeded the C-average grade requirement for participation, but they also had access to highly selective extracurricular activities such as the Anchor Club and the Key Clubs, which required scholar status for membership. . . . Of course, recruitment was very selective, since the teacher sponsors encouraged only the "good" kids (that is, school kids) to join these programs. Students who were perceived to be troublemakers were simply not asked to join. . . .

As a result of academic tracking and extracurricular participation, school kids were kept separate from the street kids. . . . Unlike the selected few who found shelter in the academic and extracurricular programs, most students, especially low achievers, were segregated into physical and social spaces which left them exposed and unprotected from street peer culture.

After describing the conditions that segregated school and street kids, Flores-Gonzalez described some of the negative aspects of the street kids' academic experience:

At Hernandez High, students in the general education and vocational track lacked enthusiasm in academics because, according to several students, classes were dull, and because as long as students abided by the behavioral rules set by each teacher, they passed. According to the street kids, some teachers just sat at their desks, often reading a newspaper, and let the students do as they pleased as long as they did not make too much noise. Street kids also complained about the coldness, indifference and uncaring attitude of teachers, and suspected that teachers held them in low regard. For instance, Marisol began to be absent from school when her stepfather was dying from cancer because she was needed at home to care for her siblings, who were toddlers at the time. She went to school as often as she could but teachers would not accept her excuse because as one teacher boldly said "Well, he's not dead yet, so come down [to school]." Such experiences kept the street kids from being close to their teachers.

Participation in extracurricular programs was rare among the low achievers. While most stated that they had no desire to participate in such programs, upon further probing many reluctantly admitted that they did not meet the grade criteria, or did not know how to join. Many just assumed that they had to have a C average to even try-out, unaware that the school waved that requirement when students showed significant talent. It was clear that these students were not encouraged nor recruited to participate. Even those whose extraordinary skills caught the attention of a coach and were recruited despite their failing grades, were quickly dropped when they were identified as street kids. For instance, Jerry was recruited to play basketball although he was failing some classes. When Jerry's gang membership became obvious from his participation in gang-related fights at school, he was immediately dropped from the team. Ironically, basketball, by keeping him busy after school, may have been the only thing that could have saved him from diving more deeply into the gang . . .

As a result of lower academic tracking and fewer extracurricular opportunities, street kids had limited access and opportunity to interact with school kids. In the classroom, they interacted with other street kids. Carrying a lower academic load and lacking participation in extracurricular activities gave them more disposable time to hang out in the hallways with other street kids, to start trouble, and to be present when trouble started. Having little interaction with school kids because of academic and extracurricular tracking that segregated physical and social spaces for the two groups, the street kids' confrontations were overwhelmingly with other street kids . . .

Flores-Gonzalez noted that the segregation between the students extended to the means by which they achieved respect.

In the street-oriented culture of Hernandez High School, respect was the means to success. For the street kids, respect came from gaining a reputation for being tough and fearless. Social success was gained by being tough, daring and willing to fight. Joining a gang was the sure way of gaining respect, and it was also the one extracurricular activity that they could enter and excel in . . .

Because respect entailed "playing with danger," street kids almost always sought to prove their worth against other street kids. In street culture, one's status improves when one responds immediately to a threat and when one beats an equal or slightly tougher contender. Disregarding, walking away or blowing off a challenge is a sign of cowardice and disrespect to the challenger, and becomes an invitation to further and escalating confrontation. In addition, challenging an inferior contender does nothing to increase respect and may result in ridicule. . . . Among the students, school kids were perceived as meek and street un-savvy and therefore not able to defend themselves adequately. Thus there was nothing to be gained by challenging those who would not or could not defend themselves. As a result, altercations between street kids and school kids were rare. In addition, the school's academic and social separation of the groups ensured limited interaction and chances for confrontations between them.

Academic and social separation, and being labeled as an unworthy contender, help the school kids avoid being harassed by the street kids. But their concern with becoming popular also steered them away from street kids. For the school kids, popularity was to be known by the rest of the students, and it was achieved when others recognized you and knew your name. This recognition could come only by high academic performance and by participation in extracurricular activities. . . .

Being a scholar, a member of the honors program, bestowed upon students academic popularity. It also bestowed upon them a status above the rest of the students—including other school kids.

You could say they [non-scholars] call us nerds because we are in scholars. They separate us. You're [non-scholars] por cortar [into cutting], you are like the bad people. You've got the honor students, and usually scholars I see hang out

with those who have the same aspirations. They associate with other people. Don't get me wrong, but I think that they hang around people that have the same aspirations.

(Elizabeth)

As the quote above implies, at Hernandez High there was a clear distinction of who were school kids and who were street kids. Students and teachers knew these distinctions, and used them in their interactions with others. School kids, and especially the scholars, were perceived as "smart" and as having high aspirations. They also thought of themselves as different from the street kids, who they viewed as bad people, lazy people and low lives . . .

Knowing the "code of the street," the school kids understood that to avoid and to diffuse harassment from street kids, they had to present themselves as "unworthy" contenders. They build up their image as "school kids" by becoming nerds, wearing the school letters or "dressing Pentecostal." At Hernandez High, there was a "look" distinctive to Pentecostal kids. While both boys and girls wore conservative clothes, girls were easier to spot because they wore no make up, wore their hair long and untreated, wore homely skirts and dresses, and never wore pants. Although the boys tended to wear conservative clothes such as "dockers" and buttoned shirts, they could be seen walking around the school carrying their Bible outside their backpack.

Flores-Gonzalez concluded that there was little support for Fordham and Ogbu's thesis at Hernandez. High-achieving "school kids" occupied their own academic and social sphere in which achievement was considered desirable. Low-achieving "street kids" occupied a largely separate sphere in which their influence on the high achievers was relatively minimal.

Although all students at Hernandez High School were affected by street culture, violence was not random and did not affect the school kids and the street kids equally. The street kids were overwhelmingly the main targets of violence. While school kids experienced an initial period of harassment from street kids, they were quickly left alone and became "invisible" to street kids. This happened because according to the "code of the street" in the community I studied, reputations are built by challenging "worthy" opponents. Nothing is gained from challenging those who cannot defend themselves. To prey on the weak brings up questions about the perpetrator's reputation. As a result, hostility and violence happened mostly "within" the group (street kid against street kid) rather than "between" groups (street kid against school kid). The kind of harassment and aggression inflicted by the low achievers upon the high achievers that Ogbu and Fordham described was very rare at Hernandez High—and when it happened it had nothing to do with academic achievement or with accusations of "acting white." Indeed, between-group conflict was very rare at Hernandez High, since the school's academic and social structures segregated students into two separate peer cultures with little interaction between them. Put simply, school kids and street kids had little opportunity to interact because they inhabited separate academic and social spaces in the school. While some

of this sorting had happened already in the elementary school years, the emphasis on tracking at the high school level, and its accompanying unequal distribution of resources, widened the separation of these groups.

*Flores-Gonzalez, N. (2005). Popularity versus respect: School structure, peer groups and Latino academic achievement. *International Journal of Qualitative Studies in Education, 18*(5), 625–642. Quoted with permission from the publisher.

Critical Ethnographies

The **critical ethnography** advocates for a particular culture. Rather than seeking to present the facts objectively, the researcher assumes that all research is value-laden, and that the goal of ethnography is to identify and help ameliorate situations in which people experience disempowerment, inequality, repression, and/or victimization. By bringing these situations to light and helping to understand the forces that create them, the researcher hopes that participants will benefit. The researcher may also propose concrete solutions. In order to ensure that the ethnographic research does not further exploit participants, the researcher may be openly reflective about his or her influence on these individuals and on the way their lives are interpreted through the research. Thus, the critical ethnography may contain discussion of the researcher's own biases, and the interpretations that are made are often tentative.

An example of a critical ethnography is a study by Lorna Rivera (2003) on the role of popular education classes in the lives of 50 homeless and formerly homeless women in Massachusetts. At the time of data collection, the state had just passed a welfare reform "work-first" policy requiring individuals to obtain employment as soon as possible. This legislation forced the women, who had been welfare recipients, to drop out of their education classes and take low-paying jobs, thereby preventing them from finishing their education and finding better jobs. In her conclusion section, Rivera describes the situation while clearly taking the side of the women and recommending changes on their behalf:

This research highlights the contradictions in the belief that education is the path to economic success. By limiting access to adult literacy education through "work-first" welfare reform policies, social inequalities are produced and reproduced. The fastest-growing sector in Massachusetts' labor market is the services industry. Denying access to education for the women in this study ensured that they serve as a source of cheap labor. Kates (1999) writes, "There is a disconnect between a) economic trends that indicate education and training levels of workers should be raised and b) public assistance policies that have greatly reduced access to education and training for hundreds of thousands of women who are entering the workforce" (p. 1).

As Congress prepares to reauthorize the Personal Responsibility and Work Opportunity Act, it should increase access to education for those who need it most. Some women continued to attend popular education classes at The Family Shelter despite the "workfare" requirement. They hoped that the law would change and tried to advocate for changes. For example, Delila explained, "Look, I tell my friends, don't give up on education because welfare is pushing you. Okay? Yeah, the law is fine today, okay? There is a new law this minute, but who knows what's gonna happen [next year]? Things can change." Indeed, the time is ripe for change. (p. 48)

Other Ethnographic Approaches

There are numerous ethnographic approaches that can be distinguished to a greater or lesser extent from the realist and critical varieties. For example, the **ethnographic case study** focuses on a single individual, group, event, or process. Because the emphasis is on a particular case, cultural themes might not be explored to the extent they are in other forms of ethnography, although the details of the case will be interpreted within a cultural context. (Nonethnographic case studies are discussed separately in the final section of this chapter.)

Other types of ethnographic approaches are motivated by fundamental concerns about the realist assumption that the researcher can be an impartial, value-free observer. For example, the **autoethnography** consists of a mix of ethnography and autobiography, in which the researcher incorporates personal experiences into the narrative, and uses these experiences as a window into his or her own culture (and vice versa). The **confessional ethnography** also relies on personal reflections, but the focus is on the researcher's own reflections and experiences in the context of another culture. Critical approaches include the **feminist ethnography**, which documents, analyzes, and responds to the cultural disempowerment of women, and the **postmodern ethnography**, which focuses more broadly on the marginalization of individuals and groups in modern society, and attends very closely (and more or less pessimistically) to the claim that ethnography can provide a definitive account of a particular culture. These and other contemporary forms of ethnography are acutely reflexive, both in the epistemological sense and in their concern about the role of the ethnographer and his or her ethnography in political and cultural power relations.

The ethnographic approaches discussed in this chapter are summarized in Table 13.2. Most ethnographies are not perfectly illustrative of any particular type. Methods drawn from different types are common, and in some studies an ethnographic approach is combined with quantitative measures or formal content analysis.

TABLE 13.2 Types of Ethnographies

Type	Distinguishing Feature
Realist ethnography	Objective description
Critical ethnography	Advocacy for disempowered group
Ethnographic case study	Focus on single person or process
Autoethnography	Self-reflection in own cultural context
Confessional ethnography	Focus on own experience in another culture
Feminist ethnography	Advocacy for women
Postmodern ethnography	Focus on marginalization of individuals

Strengths and Weaknesses of Ethnographic Research

Although there are concerns among researchers, educators, and legislators that qualitative approaches are somehow less rigorous or scientific than quantitative approaches, the only thing we can say with reasonable certainty is that qualitative research is less quantitative. As you have read, particularly in Chapters 6 and 7, quantitative research can be highly rigorous and yet deeply flawed, as in the example of a carefully controlled experimental study that has poor internal validity. Rigor is no guarantee of quality, in other words. Ethnographic research has its own standards of rigor. An ethnography based on careful, thorough, detailed, and thematically integrated observations is both rigorous and preferable to a poorly designed quantitative study in which isolated behaviors are precisely quantified.

The characteristics for which ethnographic research is criticized can also be counted among its greatest strengths. For instance, the supposed lack of focus in many ethnographies is a reflection of the researchers' openness to patterns that do not fit their preconceived ideas. Openness gives the ethnographer considerable flexibility in the way that information is gathered, and allows for the possibility of unexpected results.

Although extensive interaction between ethnographer and participant may compromise the research findings owing to experimenter or subject effects, these effects are potential problems for almost any type of research. Each design and type of method introduces its own somewhat distinctive set of risks for experimenter and subject effects. The results of a Likert-scaled survey distributed by e-mail, for example, are less prone to experimenter effects than an ethnographic study, but the survey is also considerably less flexible and detailed than the living observer, and some people will find it easier to misrepresent themselves in an anonymous e-mail than during a face-to-face interaction.

Reflexivity is one way that the ethnographic researcher deals with the risk of experimenter and subject effects. Although it can be questioned whether we can fully overcome our biases (and those of participants) simply by acknowledging them and attempting to be impartial—and it can be questioned whether we can identify all possible instances of bias in the first place—the various forms of reflexivity count as a strength of ethnographic research.

Just as some research questions are most suitably addressed by quantitative research designs, other questions call for qualitative approaches such as ethnography, and these approaches continue to reveal important insights into educational questions.

Related Qualitative Approaches

Some approaches to qualitative research are distinct from ethnography yet share many of its fundamental premises and methodologies. Studies that reflect these approaches may use ethnographic designs, or their designs might diverge to some extent from a purely ethnographic approach. Three prominent examples are phenomenology, critical race theory, and the grounded theory approach.

Phenomenology

In a **phenomenological study**, the researcher attempts to describe the subjective experiences of participants. Drawing on both theory and methods from early 20th century philosophy and psychology, phenomenological studies are based on extensive interviews in which both researcher and participant attempt to give up habitual ways of interpreting experience and focus instead on how the participant directly experiences particular situations. Although ethnographic studies tend to have a phenomenological aspect, what distinguishes the phenomenological approach is more exclusive focus on the subjective experiences of participants and less attention to cultural themes.

Following is a description of the methods used by Bowles and Lesperance (2004) in a phenomenological study of three middle school victims of bullying.

Participants were offered a variety of creative methods (art expression pieces) to work on during . . . interviews to depict the experience of being bullied in an attempt to help them communicate more effectively.

Each participant was then interviewed on four separate occasions. The interviews were conducted and tape-recorded while participants worked on the art pieces. The first interview was initiated with a grand-tour question asking participants to describe themselves and their lives with the aim of forming a supportive and open relationship with each participant. The second interview began with the interviewer asking: "Tell me about being bullied. What has it been like for you?" Because adolescents can be hesitant in talking to adults, the interviewer restated questions and used silence and open-ended questions to more easily elicit information . . .

The taped interviews were transcribed verbatim. . . . [S]ignificant statements were extracted from the interviews. Duplicate statements were discarded and specific statements generalized. A complete list of significant statements was formulated and analyzed, and the meanings of these statements were "discovered and illuminated" . . .

Clusters of themes were isolated from these formulated meanings. These theme clusters were integrated into an exhaustive description of the findings. In paragraph form, the meanings of the isolated themes were discussed at length. These meanings were then summarized.

(Bowles & Lesperance, 2004, p. 96)

Through their analysis of the interviews, Bowles and Lesperance identified several themes pertaining to connection. Participants relied on parents as a source of strength, although they also experienced difficulties at home related to being bullied. Participants experienced a sense of isolation from peers and even a lack of connection to self resulting from an inability to stand up to the bullies. In their conclusions, Bowles and Lesperance emphasized that helping adolescents gain a sense of connectedness can strengthen their ability to cope with bullying.

Critical Race Theory

Studies informed by **critical race theory** are based on the assumption that racism is enduring and pervasive in society at large, as well as in particular components of society such as the educational system. The goal of critical race theory research is to identify various forms of racism and their effects on both the majority and the oppressed minority groups, and to develop ways to ameliorate these effects. Although some critical ethnographies have a racial focus too, at least some of the studies that fall under the heading of critical race theory rely primarily on nonethnographic methods such as content analysis.

Some of the assumptions and findings of studies motivated by critical race theory can be seen in a passage from a 2005 study on the treatment of black students in England:

> One of the most consistent findings in research on school-based selection processes is that, when asked to judge the potential, attitude and/or motivation of their students, white teachers tend to place disproportionate numbers of Black students in low ranked groups. . . . These decisions frequently have a cumulative effect whereby the initial decision compounds inequity upon inequity until success can become, literally, impossible. For example, where students are placed in low ranked teaching groups they frequently cover a restricted curriculum; their teachers have systematically lower expectations of them; and, in many high-stakes tests in England, they are entered for low "tiered" examinations where only a limited number of grades are available. In the lowest maths paper, for example, the best available grade is D: that is, less than the C grade that is commonly accepted as the minimum necessary for entry into the professions or further dedicated study at advanced level. In a study of these decisions in London secondary schools, it was Black students who were most likely to be placed in this situation: two-thirds of Black students in the schools under study (Gillborn & Youdell, 2000). It is difficult to think of a clearer example of institutional racism than a test, disproportionately taken by Black students, in which the highest possible grade is commonly judged to be a "failure." We have to ask whether such discriminatory processes would be permitted if their victims were white, and especially, middle class whites. Ernest R. House has noted an identical situation in the US in relation to the practice of "retaining students," i.e., holding them back a year:
>
>> Americans will support policies that are harmful to minorities that they would not tolerate if those same policies were applied to majority populations. In education, for example, Americans are strongly in favor of retention—retaining students at the same grade level for another year—even though the research evidence overwhelmingly shows strong negative effects . . . Retention programs are applied massively to minorities in large cities, but not to majority populations. (House, 1999, p. 2)
>
> [T]he English education system appears to be a clear case where the routine assumptions that structure the system encode a deep privileging of white students and, in particular, the legitimization, defence and extension of Black inequity. In terms of policy priorities race equity has been at best a marginal concern, at worst non-existent. In relation to beneficiaries the picture is more complex than usually recognized (some minoritized groups do relatively well), but the most consistent beneficiaries are white students and, in key respects, Black students' position is no better than it was when the whole reform movement began in the late 1980s. Finally, an examination of outcomes clearly shows that central reform strategies (such as the use of selection and hierarchical teaching groups) are known to work against race equity but are nevertheless promoted as "best practice" for all. These reforms are known to discriminate in practice (regardless of intent) and are, therefore, racist in their consequences. These three tests of the system are by no means exhaustive but they are sufficient to establish

the education system's active involvement in the defence and extension of the present regime of white supremacy in the contemporary British state.

(Gillborn, 2005, pp. 496–497; quoted with permission from Routledge)

Grounded Theory Approaches

Traditionally, researchers assumed that one of the main purposes for conducting research is to test a theory (see Chapter 2). According to this view, the researcher states the theory, collects data, and then decides whether the data support the theory or not. Critics of this view have argued that data collection and data interpretation cannot be so clearly distinguished from each other or from the researcher's theoretical assumptions. Theoretical assumptions influence the formulation of research questions and the selection of methods, which in turn influence the type of data that will be collected and the particular interpretations that are made.

One way that qualitative researchers have responded to these concerns is by means of the **grounded theory approach**, in which data collection is intended to engender rather than test a theory (Glaser & Strauss, 1967). The grounded theory researcher proceeds as inductively as possible, with no preconceived ideas at the outset of the study. As data are collected, the results guide the development of tentative explanations that are explored through further data collection. This is a cyclical process in which data are collected in order to evaluate and refine the emerging theory. Data collection ends when no new insights emerge, and the constant comparative method is used for data analysis. Some but not all ethnographies are based on a grounded theory approach, and this approach is used sometimes in studies that rely at least in part on nonethnographic methods.

The inductive quality of data collection in grounded theory approaches is illustrated by the following excerpt from a study on urban adolescents' career aspirations, in which the researchers took extra precautions to ensure data-driven conclusions:

> *[W]e [the research team] decided to collect all data from each participant before analyzing the materials so that we would not form theories from a partial data set. We also completed our literature review after we had collected the data so that we would avoid ''finding'' our a priori assumptions in the data set. The goal of the researchers was to understand the adolescent's experience through his or her own words. Through an inductive process, we individually looked for patterns in the data, which we then formulated into a coding schema; this schema was then revised using the constant comparative method. We then met to discuss the patterns that we had found individually. Through a series of discussions (and occasional argument) we reached a conclusion about the validity and meanings of our claims.*
>
> *(Sirin et al., 2004, p. 442)*

Based on this grounded theory methodology, the researchers found that adolescents' career aspirations were either facilitated or hindered by personal factors (such as self-reliance) as well as contextual factors (such as gender stereotypes). The types of factors that the researchers identified, and the distinction between personal and contextual factors, were not assumed in advance but rather emerged as the researchers attempted to understand their data.

Case Studies

Qualitative case studies have a long history in medicine and in social sciences such as psychology and sociology. Freud, for example, published a number of case studies in the late 19th and early 20th centuries that were influential in both content and methodology.

Several characteristics, taken together, distinguish the case study as a form of qualitative research:

- The research focuses on specific cases. The "case" is often an individual, but may be a group, such as a classroom, an organization, or a community, a set of objects such as documents or artifacts, or something more abstract such as an event, a process, or an issue.

- Information gathering is intensive, focused, and typically based on multiple methods. The goal is an in-depth understanding of the case. The difference between single-participant designs (Chapter 8) and case studies focusing on individuals is not only that data collection in case studies is mostly qualitative but also that the focus of the case study is not a specific behavior or behaviors but rather a more inclusive set of experiences, both past and present.

- The researcher attempts to understand the case in relation to real-life settings. Although the case is a "bounded system," in the sense that the researcher focuses on the case rather than its cultural context, efforts are made to provide information about local context.

Other characteristics of case studies, including approaches to sampling, measurement, analysis, and interpretation, draw on methods and assumptions that are shared by ethnographic research and other qualitative approaches. In practice there is not always a sharp distinction between ethnographic designs and qualitative case studies.

Types of Case Studies

One way to distinguish among case studies is to consider their fundamental purpose (Stake, 2003).

The **intrinsic case study** is fundamentally descriptive. Emphasis is placed on describing the particulars of the case rather than making generalizations. For this reason, the case that is sampled in an intrinsic case study will tend to be unusual in some respect.

The **instrumental case study** is carried out in order to gain insight into a broader issue. The case that is chosen for analysis may be typical or atypical, and data analysis will be interpretive rather than merely descriptive. Assumptions ranging from psychoanalysis to ethnography may be brought to bear on interpretation of the case. When the case is an educational program, the purpose of the case study may be to evaluate the merit and effectiveness of the program, and to make recommendations that influence program implementation. This illustrates program evaluation, a form of applied research discussed in Chapter 17.

The **collective case study** is an instrumental case study that is applied to multiple cases that sustain the researcher's generalizations. Here again data analysis will be interpretive.

The distinctions between the three types of case studies are simply intended as a heuristic, since in practice many studies do not fit neatly into one particular type (Stake, 2003). For example, in Spotlight on Research 13.3 you will be reading about a case study of a consistently high-performing school. The immediate purpose of this study was to figure out what factors contribute to the school's academic success. The actual research report reads like an intrinsic case study, because the researchers presented an exhaustive description of school facilities, personnel, and practices, without drawing comparisons, discussing theoretical issues, or otherwise diverging much from their description of the school. The researchers' attention was very narrowly focused on the case, in other words. At the same time, it was also clear that the ultimate goal of the study was to figure out what makes any school successful, a theme that was taken up in a general way in the final discussion. For this reason, the researchers can be said to have conducted an instrumental case study.

Advantages and Disadvantages of Case Studies

Case studies are an especially useful approach in the study of distinctive cases—the struggling student, the outstanding school, the unique PTA, and so on. The main advantage of a case study approach is the richness of information that results from intensive focus on a single case. A well-designed case study can provide a wealth of information about many different facets of an individual's experience. Reliance on a single case is, of course, a key limitation as well. It may be difficult to generalize from the results of a case study, since there is no comparison group (or additional case) against which the characteristics of the case can be understood. If generalization is indeed the goal of the case study, there is no guarantee that the case is representative. Case study researchers address these issues by relating their results to published theories and findings, and in some cases by conducting multicase studies in which the findings of different cases are compared.

The use of multiple methods in a case study, combined with a grounded theory approach, is illustrated in Spotlight on Research 13.3.

A Look Ahead

In this chapter, you read about qualitative research designs in which the main source of information is living, breathing individuals (see Table 13.3 for summary). In Chapter 14, I discuss qualitative approaches in which the information is gathered from documents and other materials.

TABLE 13.3 Major Types of Qualitative Research Based on Living Participants

Type of Research	Examples
Ethnography	Realist ethnography Critical ethnography
Case study	Intrinsic case study Instrumental case study Collective case study
Related	Phenomenology Critical race theory

Literacy Achievement in an Advantaged School: A Case Study

There is considerable research on the characteristics of schools that produce high achievement among disadvantaged students. However, even the schools that serve advantaged students produce a wide range of achievement. In a 2007 study published in the *Journal of Educational Psychology**, Michael Pressley, Lindsey Mohan, Lisa Raphael, and Lauren Fingeret examined the characteristics of Bennett Woods Elementary School, a school that consistently outperforms other schools in Michigan on tests of reading and writing, including schools that serve comparably advantaged students. The purpose of this case study was to determine what characteristics of Bennett Woods have such a strong influence on the students' reading and writing skills.

Bennett Woods is a relatively small elementary school located near Michigan State University. In 2005 Bennett Woods enrolled 296 kindergarten through fifth-grade students from primarily middle class backgrounds.

The school was selected because it had the highest 2004 combined language arts (i.e., reading and writing) achievement on the state test of schools in the area surrounding the university (which includes a medium-sized city, the surrounding suburbs, and a few middle-class villages): 95% of its students passed the Grade 4 reading test, and 91% passed the Grade 4 writing test. The state averages for 2004 were 79% and 48% passing for Grade 4 reading and writing, respectively. . . . Especially notable was the fact that there were many schools in the state serving decidedly more economically advantaged communities that did not score near the Bennett Woods level. The 2005 state test was administered while this study occurred, and Bennett Woods performed highly once again, with 98% passing Grade 4 reading and 84% passing Grade 4 writing (for the entire state, the 2005 passing rates were 82% and 46%, respectively).

Data collection for this case study was intensive, based on multiple methods, and reflective of the grounded theory approach discussed earlier in the chapter.

The lead researcher (Michael Pressley) was an experienced educational psychologist with an extensive background in elementary reading and writing education. He was in the school, either observing or interviewing teachers, for 122 hours (113 hours observing, 9 hours interviewing), which extended over 55 visits that were conducted from early

January through early June 2005. The second, third, and fourth researchers each spent approximately 50 hours in the school from January through May 2005, and most of their time was spent observing (i.e., only Lindsey Mohan participated in interviewing, doing so with Michael Pressley for one teacher). These observation hours, if anything, underestimate total time spent in the school, because time in the teachers' lounge or hallways, during lunch and recess, or at school assemblies was not recorded, although it typically resulted in informal conversations that were revealing about the school's functioning . . .

Observations were the primary data, complemented by interviews and document/artifact analyses, consistent with the types of data typically collected and considered in qualitative case studies and grounded theory analyses (Strauss & Corbin, 1998). The four researchers visited classes, usually for about an hour and typically on a prearranged appointment basis; they also reviewed and gathered documents and other artifacts during these visits (e.g., posters and displays in classrooms, completed student projects). The main question they sought to answer was "How does Bennett Woods Elementary School produce high reading and writing achievement in its students?" Usually, a single researcher observed instruction, but on some occasions two, three, or all four researchers watched the same lesson. The researchers were determined to be sensitive to any aspect of the teaching and learning observed that might impact student achievement. Observations continued until no new insights were emerging about factors that might contribute to achievement at Bennett Woods, consistent with grounded theory methodology (Strauss & Corbin, 1998) . . .

Nothing like a behavior checklist was used in this study. Rather, the researchers came to the school and attempted to record everything that might impact achievement. . . . [C]oding was open, and categories of observation were developed and refined as the study proceeded, consistent with grounded theory approaches.

Along with classroom observations, the researchers received briefings from principal and teachers; conducted formal interviews with teachers; engaged in less formal conversations with teachers, parents, and students; and reviewed documents such as school and district curriculum guides as well as materials in the classroom.

Reflexivity and triangulation are reflected in the following description of methodology:

Case study (e.g., Stake, 2005) and grounded theory (Strauss & Corbin, 1998) approaches recognize that researchers come to a study with background knowledge that can influence their points of view toward the object of study and that researchers have theoretical sensitivities (Strauss & Corbin, 1998). As detailed earlier, the researchers came to the study with disciplinary knowledge in education expected to heighten their sensitivity to school, curricular, and teaching variables that might account for achievement in the school. Beyond their general disciplinary knowledge, however, the researchers knew the previous research on effective schools that was reviewed briefly in the introduction to this article, and, thus, they came to this study with the expectation that they might find many interrelated elements contributing to student success at Bennett Woods Elementary School.

One check on the possibility that the investigators' a priori understandings might be driving their conclusions more than the data was the fact that every general conclusion had to be supported by multiple pieces of data and agreed to by all four researchers. That is, if one of the four researchers could not find evidence in their notes for a conclusion, and all four researchers did not ultimately concur that the conclusion held, it was not included in this report. Thus, a very stringent reliability standard was set with respect to the conclusions offered here. Specific examples to illustrate general conclusions, however, were drawn from the notes of individual researchers. All researchers agreed, however, that all examples typified what was seen at the school with regard to the general conclusion being illustrated.

In their results section, Pressley and colleagues commented favorably on a variety of dimensions, ranging from the facilities, administration, teachers, and other educational staff at Bennett Woods, to the parents and students themselves.

At the time of this study, Bennett Woods Elementary School was housed in a modern, bright building. The classrooms comfortably seated the students in each class with enough room for work tables and additional reading areas. All classrooms had bookcases for the many books available for students to read and the substantial curriculum materials in active use. All facilities were attractive, and the library was large and inviting. A point of emphasis is that there were books everywhere in this school, and every classroom had its own well-stocked library. No matter what measure of print richness might be applied to evaluate the Bennett Woods classrooms (e.g., Hoffman, Sailors, Duffy, & Beretvas, 2004; Wolfersberger, Reutzel, Sudweeks, & Fawson,

2004), the conclusion would be that the classrooms in the school were exceptionally print-rich environments. The school had a computer lab, which was complemented by a smaller lab dedicated to a program for struggling Grade 4 and Grade 5 students. . . . There were also several up-to-date computers in each classroom. The school was located near a major university and often availed itself of the resources of the university, including frequent field trips to plays, museums, and arboretum/garden settings on the campus . . .

Like any effective school (Teddlie & Reynolds, 2000), the school was clearly well administered. . . . The many little commotions that can occur in elementary schools (e.g., book club orders done incorrectly, teachers missing important meetings, Internet hookups being inefficient or down much of the time) were infrequent. Also consistent with effective schools, there was a clear academic emphasis, with detailed district and school guides available for each grade level with respect to each subject area, guides often mentioned by teachers as they discussed their content coverage. . . . The emphasis on academics was obvious during school-wide events that were academically focused (e.g., a March is Reading Month assembly, assemblies celebrating achievement, family science night) . . .

Several teachers pointed out that the majority of kindergarten students at Bennett Woods had good experiences during the preschool years that prepared them well for formal schooling. For example, many experienced homes in which there was a great deal of verbal interaction, including book reading. Several teachers were emphatic that having a large proportion of students prepared for school on arrival, who thrived in the school once there, permitted greater attention to the students who arrived not so well prepared or otherwise did not thrive given the regular curriculum and instruction. In fact, most classrooms had only a few (i.e., from 1 to 4) students who were progressing at rates that caused concern . . .

Teachers and staff at Bennett Woods Elementary School were clear in their praise of the principal, whom they felt had transformed the school in her 6 years there. The teachers remarked often that language arts had received much more emphasis since the current principal assumed her position. An important accomplishment during her tenure was the raising of the reading and writing test scores. In 2005, 2% of students failed the state reading test, compared with 27% of students the year before this principal arrived; in 2005, 84% of students passed the state writing test, compared with only 38% of students the year before this principal arrived. The school went from being a middle-of-the-heap school in language arts to a top performer in the state . . .

The principal delegated. She clearly allowed the most knowledgeable teacher in the building about reading, the reading specialist, to be in charge of much of the programming with respect to reading, although always in consultation both with the principal and the teachers. The principal also selected a teacher with extensive knowledge of writing instruction to lead the school in its writing instruction, sending the message that this teacher's view on writing was to be valued . . .

The principal had a clear academic focus. She was very aware of what went on in individual classrooms in the school; the researchers observed that she often dropped into classes. In a 2 1/2-hour exit interview with the lead researcher, the principal talked about most of the classes in the school, reflecting on her understanding of the general and differing philosophies of individual teachers and the way these philosophies played out (i.e., the principal was aware of specific practices in the classrooms, practices the interviewer had witnessed). As part of her academic focus, a high priority was to fund as much teacher professional development as possible; she pointed out with pride that her teachers averaged more than 60 hours of professional development each in 2004–2005 . . .

Professional development was an important vehicle for curricular and instructional improvement, and teachers not only attended in-service development programs but implemented what they learned in their classrooms. For example, when teachers explained their teaching to the researchers, they frequently mentioned how their instruction had been influenced by previous professional development. Everyone seemed to buy into the research-supported perspective that professional development was essential for the school to improve and that professional development in reading and writing instruction can change teaching in ways that impact student achievement . . .

The teachers believed so strongly in professional development that they often paid for professional development on their own. . . . Also circulating among faculty were materials associated with comprehension strategies instruction, including Harvey and Goudvis's (2000) Strategies That Work, Miller's (2002) Reading With Meaning, and Zimmermann and Hutchins's (2003) 7 Keys to Comprehension. The Harvey and Goudvis book was also the subject of a teacher book club, with several members of the faculty meeting biweekly to discuss the content of the book, a form of in-school professional development. . . . The communication practices among the teachers at Bennett Woods were reflective of an evolving teacher community (Grossman, Wineburg, & Woolworth, 2001). That is, many of the teachers were willing to seek out and implement new teaching methods in their classrooms, and these same teachers recognized that their colleagues were valuable resources for

their own intellectual renewal. Furthermore, it was striking that all of the professional development that the researchers witnessed or heard about was about language arts . . .

Shortly before this study began, the state announced new language arts standards for elementary students and that a new state test would be devised that would be based on the new standards. Bennett Woods teachers were on top of these developments. In late March, the reading specialist and informal writing specialist . . . attended a 2-day meeting focused on the new language arts standards and probable changes in the state test. They obtained the prototype new tests from the state and began to analyze them with respect to content. Shortly after, these two teachers led an all-morning teachers' meeting at the school to provide information to all of the teachers about the new test and changes.

The teachers did more than prepare their students for tests. They analyzed and used the assessment results to inform their instruction with individual students. The Gates–MacGinitie Reading Tests were given to every student in the school in spring 2005, and there were other tests targeted at particular grade levels. . . . The reading specialist analyzed the results of each reading test and provided the information in an understandable way to classroom teachers. The lowest performing students on these standardized reading assessments were targeted for remediation, and the reading specialist was in charge of seeing that this occurred. In her interview, the principal was emphatic that she believed that much of the school's success reflected such targeting of resources . . .

In addition to the classroom teachers, Bennett Woods Elementary School had support staff who worked extensively with the students who most needed it, including a reading specialist, an ESL specialist, a resource room teacher, and two instructional aids, both of whom were college educated and one of whom was a licensed teacher. At least four or five students in every class, except kindergarten, received some assistance from one or more support teachers. Students who needed the most support received as much as 90 min of such teaching a day, typically either tutoring or small-group instruction . . .

Among the support teachers, the reading specialist was most salient in promoting reading and writing achievement. Struggling readers met with her four times a week in 30-min, small-group sessions, each of which included all of the struggling readers in the child's classroom. These groups ranged in size from 2 to 7 students. At the primary level, the focus of the instruction was basic reading skills, with individual word recognition emphasized in Grade 1 and decoding of real text increasing in prominence with advancing grade level, *consistent with models of beginning reading intervention that work with many struggling beginning readers (see Torgesen, 2004). In Grades 4 and 5, the reading specialist delivered a computer-based program known as HOTS (i.e., Higher Order Thinking Skills; e.g., Pogrow, 1992), which emphasized problem solving and comprehension. For students at all grade levels, the reading specialist also provided some support for writing . . .*

There was an art teacher, a music teacher, and a physical education teacher, and the art and music teachers were especially active in connecting with the language arts curriculum . . .

The local university has a fifth-year, full year teaching intern program. Eight interns served Bennett Woods Elementary School while this study was being conducted, an unusually large number of interns for one school. . . . These eight interns de facto increased the teaching staffing considerably in the classrooms they were serving. The school demanded much from these interns, and they delivered, providing many carefully prepared lessons and participating in extracurricular activities with students.

The school had a full-time library specialist. Each class visited the library once a week; the librarian read a book or story and discussed books available in the library. After the story, students selected books to check out. The library specialist was aware of the content being covered in the classroom and had books on display reflecting current units being covered in the various classes. The specialist worked to expand the materials in the library and was the main point person in the school's adopt-a-book program, which encouraged students, parents, and staff to provide half the funding for a book, with matching funds to be provided by the school district . . .

The school invited parental participation, and most parents actively participated, which is consistent with evidence that parental involvement improves student achievement (e.g., Cooper, Charlton, Valentine, & Muhlenbruck, 2000; Miller & Kelley, 1991; Taylor & Pearson, 2004). For example, the family science night was packed with families and teachers participating in many science activities and reading the dozens of student-constructed science projects . . .

At all levels, many of the homework assignments were designed for students and parents to work on together; for example, rubrics went home so that parents could give meaningful support and feedback on their children's writing assignments. Completed work went home regularly in every classroom. . . . In every class, students took home daily planners, which reminded them of their homework but also provided a communication to the parent about what was

expected of the student. Many of the teachers also sent home weekly newsletters, which let the parents know what was happening in the classroom and included homework for the week as well as news of upcoming tests and other big events. Newsletters often included suggestions as to how parents could assist their children with schoolwork.

The school maintained a parent e-mail listserv, which provided messages to parents several times a month. About half the teachers in the school also maintained classroom Web sites, which contained a great deal of information about the curriculum and classroom events. Parents received report cards two times a year. Although parents received information about performance in all areas of the curriculum, the greatest amount of information was provided about reading and writing.

In summary, there were multiple lines of communications and opportunities for interaction between families and the school. Because the researchers always checked in and out of the office, they also had an opportunity to witness communications between the school office and families. The staff consistently knew the parents' children, listened carefully, and interacted constructively to respond to the parents' concerns . . .

Reading and writing definitely were the focus at Bennett Woods Elementary School, and there were three especially salient indicators of that focus: Students experienced many books, students were explicitly taught a great deal about reading, and students wrote a lot and were also taught much explicitly about writing as they did so.

Pressley and colleagues also reported extensively, and highly favorably, on specific practices related to reading and writing instruction, noting that "reading and writing definitely were the focus" at Bennett Woods. In their discussion section, the researchers outlined and commented on the grounded theory they developed.

The intent of a grounded theory analysis is to produce a theory and associated hypotheses, in this case about how a school serving a middle-class, relatively advantaged population produces high reading and writing achievement. The overarching hypothesis that emerges is that a large number of elements supporting achievement are aligned at the school—that is, the people, a strong literacy-focused curriculum, and a positive social environment. All of these factors in combination are required to produce the very high achievement at Bennett Woods Elementary School.

The first tenet of the theory is that the people of Bennett Woods Elementary School definitely mattered, with the principal, in particular, clearly making language arts achievement a high priority in the school and placing faculty who could co-lead in positions to do so. The principal also directed discretionary resources in ways to support reading and writing instruction, for example, providing funding for a huge expansion of the number of books in the library and for field trips connected to reading experiences (e.g., buses and tickets for several classes of students to attend a play at the university based on a well-known piece of children's literature). Other people at Bennett Woods Elementary School also mattered, including the faculty and staff, who definitely shared the principal's vision for language arts as a priority in a highly academically focused school, one in which state, district, and self-imposed expectations with respect to language arts teaching were embraced. The teachers' enthusiasm for learning more about language arts and how to deliver quality reading and writing instruction was apparent from their commitment to professional development and their reflection with their colleagues on the curriculum and its improvement for the next year and beyond. It also helps that the preponderance of Bennett Woods Elementary School students arrive at the school well prepared for kindergarten, which permits a generous allocation of available remediation resources to students who require assistance.

Next, the language arts curriculum was strongly balanced with respect to skills instruction and holistic reading and writing experiences. . . . At Bennett Woods Elementary School, the students receiving remediation received a large dose of skills instruction. More typically achieving students and those with strong reading skills received more holistic reading and writing instruction. That said, there was substantial teaching of reading and writing skills and strategies across the elementary grades, with teachers consistently explaining, modeling, and scaffolding the word recognition, comprehension, and composing strategies that are part of skilled reading and writing (Duffy, 2003). There were also strong connections across the curriculum from year to year, so that the language arts experienced by a student meshed as the student progressed though the grades. There was careful thinking

about what should happen in each grade with respect to every aspect of the curriculum and strong commitment by the faculty to deliver a curriculum that cohered across the years.

Last, Bennett Woods Elementary School students experienced a consistently positive environment, one that encouraged them to strive to grow as readers and writers. Their growth was fostered by instruction and demands matched to their individual needs and capacities, and students were encouraged to work in a self-regulated fashion. Caring teachers make a huge difference in students' lives (Noddings, 2003; Wentzel, 1997); Bennett Woods teachers genuinely cared about their students' academic and personal needs.

In summary, the successes at Bennett Woods Elementary School reflect years of immersion in a well thought-out curriculum that is delivered in an inviting way by teachers who work hard to figure out how to deliver the curriculum well, in ways that connect to the needs of all students. The curriculum has taken years to develop and is informed by the latest instructional advances being showcased in professional development, and the curriculum continues to improve as teachers reflect on their experiences and emerging demands and expectations. The principal, faculty, and staff were highly committed to all students at Bennett Woods Elementary achieving at as high a level as possible. One proof of the commitment is that a high proportion of class time was spent engaged in activities requiring high teaching effort (i.e., direct explanation, modeling, and scaffolding). Another is that the teachers worked overtime to participate in professional development that improved their teaching. [The result is] a well-qualified and determined faculty and staff delivering high-quality language arts curricula in ways likely to motivate students to engage in learning to read and write and in actual reading and writing.

*Pressley, M., Mohan, L., Raphael, L. M., & Fingeret, L. (2007). How does Bennett Woods Elementary School produce such high reading and writing achievement? Journal of Educational Psychology, 99(2), 221–240. Quoted with permission from the publisher.

Applications: A Guide for Beginning Researchers

Here are some ideas from the chapter that will help you plan your research:

- If you plan to take a qualitative approach to the study of people, decide which type of ethnography, case study, or related approach will be the most informative and logistically feasible way to address your research question or focus of inquiry.

- Once you have chosen a qualitative approach, think about the extent to which you want the gathering of information to be influenced by theoretical considerations and preliminary hypotheses.
- If you choose an ethnographic approach, you will need to plan on extensive gathering of information based on multiple methods, and you will need to have a plan for taking field notes.
- If you choose a case study approach, you will need to plan on extensive gathering of information about the case based on multiple methods.

Chapter Summary

Qualitative research is distinctive in the epistemological and methodological assumptions that inform the way research questions are posed, participants are sampled, and data are gathered, organized, coded, interpreted, and reported. The two types of qualitative research discussed in this chapter, ethnographies and case studies, are based on interactions with living participants.

Ethnographies emphasize cultural themes and are carried out in natural settings. Information gathering is intensive, and based on multiple methods that include observation, interviews, and/or content analysis. Field notes are integral to information gathering. Triangulation and reflexivity help the researcher obtain more accurate findings.

Two of the many types of ethnographic research designs are realist ethnographies and critical ethnographies. Qualitative approaches that draw on the assumptions and methods of ethnographic research are feminist ethnographies, critical race theory studies, and grounded theory approaches.

Case studies of individuals or groups are based on intensive, multiple methods of information gathering. Although each case is situated within a local context, cultural themes receive less emphasis than in ethnographic research. The three major types of case studies are intrinsic, instrumental, and collective.

Key Terms

CAQDAS

Coding system

Open coding

Axial coding

Selective coding

Constant comparative method

Negative case analysis

Ethnographic research

Ethnographer

Culture

Fieldwork

Participant observation

Passive observation

Field notes

Triangulation

Reflexivity

Realist ethnography

Critical ethnography

Ethnographic case study

Autoethnography

Confessional ethnography

Feminist ethnography

Postmodern ethnography

Phenomenological study

Critical race theory

Grounded theory approach

Intrinsic case study

Instrumental case study

Collective case study

Exercises

1. How would you describe the information-gathering method of a researcher who sits at the backs of various classrooms, silently jotting down notes about teacher–student interactions?

a) Autoethnography

b) Participant observation

c) Passive observation

d) Ethnographic case study

2. What concept is illustrated by the researcher who indicates that personal experience with dyslexia has sparked his interest in research on discrimination experienced by students with reading-related problems?

a) Triangulation

b) Reflexivity

c) Phenomenology

d) Grounded theory

For questions 3–5, indicate the type of study implied by each description.

3. A researcher identifies discriminatory practices targeting one particular ethnic group in a school district, describes the historical and cultural forces that created the discrimination, comments at length on the injustice of the situation, and offers his own recommendations for change.

a) Realist ethnography

b) Grounded theory approach

c) Critical ethnography

d) Autoethnography

4. A researcher interviews the directors of a variety of teacher certification programs in order to explore their attitudes about the impact of No Child Left Behind. The researcher has no preconceived notions about what she might discover, preferring instead to continue interviewing directors until key themes emerge.

a) Phenomenological study

b) Ethnographic case study

c) Autoethnography

d) Grounded theory approach

5. A researcher wishes to know more about the experiences of blind students who are included in general education classrooms. To this end, the researcher conducts both formal and informal interviews with a blind student at a local school. The researcher also sits near the blind student during classes as a passive observer, and interviews the student's teachers in between classes.

a) Ethnographic case study

b) Postmodern ethnography

c) Critical ethnography

d) Autoethnography

For questions 6–9, identify the type of method described.

6. After concluding that the education majors in her study all have strongly favorable attitudes toward Vygotskian theory, a researcher rereads the transcripts of interviews with the students in order to determine whether there are any reservations about Vygotsky's ideas.

a) Reflexivity

b) Participant observation

c) Negative case analysis

d) Constant comparative method

7. A researcher learns from a middle school student that drug dealers congregate in the school parking lot at lunchtime. Later, the researcher asks other students whether they have observed or heard about drug dealers coming to the parking lot. The researcher also asks the principal whether she has heard about this.

a) Triangulation

b) Semi-structured interviews

c) Field notes

d) Passive observation

8. An ethnographic researcher is analyzing a set of transcripts from interviews with high school students whose families recently emigrated to the United States. The researcher recalls from the interviews that the students frequently commented on the extent to which they miss their country of origin, as well as their feelings about being newcomers, their academic interests, and their aspirations for the future. The researcher begins coding each student's transcripts with respect to these four categories. The researcher then notices that most of the comments about academic interests are linked to future career aspirations, and so the researcher collapses these two categories before continuing to code the data.

a) Participant observation

b) Constant comparative method

c) Field notes

d) Negative case analysis

9. A researcher plays with a group of second-graders during their recess, while occasionally pausing to record information about negative social interactions between students.

a) Negative case analysis

b) Participant observation

c) Constant comparative method

d) Reflexivity

10. *Critical thinking question*: Why don't all ethnographic researchers make use of the purely inductive methods of the grounded theory approach? In other words, if the purpose of ethnography is to reconstruct peoples' experiences, why not begin every ethnographic study with no preconceived ideas, so that theoretical explanations can emerge from the data?

Answers to Exercises

1. c   **2.** b   **3.** c   **4.** d   **5.** a   **6.** c   **7.** a   **8.** b   **9.** b

10. *Possible answer*: Although a purely inductive method seems desirable in some cases, in other situations it makes sense for the ethnographic researcher to allow preexisting beliefs and interests to motivate the research. The ethnographer might wish to test a theory, or to explore a social problem such as discrimination that has already been extensively documented among a particular group. In such cases the ethnographer may remain open to unexpected themes that emerge during observation and interviews, but the collection of data will be focused by the need for information that bears on the theory or social problem.

Suggestions for Further Reading

Research Article: Skiba, R., Simmons, A, Ritter, S., Kohler, K., Henderson, M., & Wu, T. (2006). The context of minority disproportionality: Practitioner perspectives on special education referral. *Teachers College Record*, *108*(7), 1424–1459.

This critical ethnography focuses on the causes of disproportionate minority representation in special education.

Application Article: Levinson, M. P., & Sparkes, A. C. (2005). Gypsy children, space, and the school environment. *International Journal of Qualitative Studies in Education*, *18*(6), 751–772.

This ethnographic study conducted in England focuses on how Gypsy children's spatial orientations create difficulties for them in educational settings.

Extension Article: Eisenhart, M. (2001). Educational ethnography past, present, and future: Ideas to think with. *Educational Researcher*, *30*(8), 16–27.

This essay identifies and proposes solutions to three types of controversies pertaining to ethnography and key ethnographic concepts.

CHAPTER 14

Content Analysis and Historical Research

Digital Vision/Getty Images

After studying this chapter, you will be able to answer the following questions:

- What is content analysis and when is it used?

- How are content analyses conducted?

- What are the strengths and weaknesses of content analysis designs?

- What is historical research and when is it used?

- How are historical materials evaluated and interpreted?

- What are the strengths and weaknesses of historical research designs?

This chapter will prepare you to do the following:

- Understand and evaluate content analysis in research reports

- Understand and evaluate historical research studies

- Choose a content analysis or historical approach that best suits your research question

- Design a content analysis or historical research study

Introduction to Content Analysis

In ethnographic research, as in most quantitative studies, no data are available until the researcher makes observations, conducts interviews, administers tests, or gathers information in some other way. The data are obtained directly from participants—the living, breathing people who agree to be observed, interviewed, or tested. In **content analysis**, the immediate focus of the research is not people but materials such as textbooks or letters. These materials constitute the data. The researcher does not gather the data but rather analyzes and interprets it. Through content analysis the researcher can describe materials, people, situations, and programs, and engage in inferences about associations and causal patterns. In short, content analysis is an indirect way of addressing virtually any topic that can be studied through other research designs. Content analysis is also the most suitable way of addressing certain research questions. For example, if we want to know how students with learning disabilities are portrayed in educational psychology textbooks, the best way to find out is to examine the books directly.

Content analysis has been widely used among social scientists since the early 20th century. A content analysis may be carried out by means of quantitative, qualitative, or mixed-methods approaches. Analyses of student essays, for example, may include frequencies and means for different types of grammatical and spelling errors, as well as qualitative descriptions of recurrent themes. Some content analyses blur the quantitative–qualitative distinction—frequency data are reported, as in descriptive research, but the overall approach to analysis is qualitative. My focus in this chapter is on studies that rely exclusively or at least primarily on qualitative approaches to content analysis. Typically, a qualitative content analysis involves the restatement of a longer narrative (the original text) in terms of a shorter one (the content analysis) in which key themes are identified and analyzed.

The Goals of Content Analysis

Broadly, most content analyses reflect at least one of three goals (Krippendorf, 2003):

- To reveal something about the materials
- To reveal something about the creators of the materials
- To reveal something about the context in which the materials were created

Imagine that you are studying the portrayals of students with learning disabilities (LD) in several textbooks widely used in undergraduate teacher certification classes. Any one or more of the three goals mentioned above could motivate your study. If you wish to identify common themes in the way students with LD are portrayed, so that you can characterize the images of these students that prospective teachers are exposed to, then your goal is to reveal something about the materials. If you wish to reconstruct the thinking of the textbook authors, in the sense of identifying their theoretical biases, stereotypes, and unstated assumptions, then your goal is to reveal something about the creators of the materials. But if you wish to make a case that views of students with LD among contemporary experts reflect a number of themes in special education research and theory, then your goal is to reveal something about the scholarly context in which the materials were created.

The Content of Content Analysis

Although sometimes referred to as document analysis, I use the term "content analysis" here to emphasize the fact that documents are not the only type of material that the researcher examines. A distinction can be made between personal documents, public records, and other materials:

- Personal documents include diaries, letters, postcards, e-mail messages, and transcripts of online interactions.
- Public records include textbooks, curriculum standards, meeting minutes, news-paper articles, and websites.
- Other materials include photographs, audiotapes, videos, artworks, and cultural artifacts.

Personal documents are created for oneself, for another person, or for a small group known to the author. The document is typically not disseminated beyond the individual or group. In contrast, the author of a public record intends to reach a larger group of individuals, many of whom the author may not know. The distinction between personal and public is not always clear-cut, as in the case of teachers' lesson plans, which are created for personal use, shared with school personnel, and in some cases may end up in a public database. The same can be said of the "documents" created by research participants. For example, one of the early uses of content analysis in psychology and education was for analyzing responses to the Thematic Apperception Test (see Chapter 5). A participant's responses were conveyed to the interviewer, who was known to the participant, but then shared with the scientific community in aggregate form.

Content analysis is especially useful for examining textbooks, student writings, statements of policy, and other materials of central importance to educational practice. For example, the study described in Spotlight on Research 14.1 focuses on children's storybooks as a way of revealing the images of teachers that inform the public consciousness.

How to Conduct a Content Analysis

The general sequence of steps in a content analysis are summarized below. These steps are not always distinct or followed in a strict order, but they indicate where the researcher must make important decisions.

1. Identify research question or focus of inquiry.
2. Identify types of materials to be reviewed.
3. Develop method of sampling materials.
4. Obtain permission to sample materials.
5. Develop coding categories, or other method of analysis
6. Analyze materials.
7. Interpret results.

As you can see, content analyses are carried out by means of roughly the same kinds of sampling, coding, and interpretive steps as in other types of qualitative design.

Images of Teachers in Children's Picture Storybooks: A Content Analysis

Children enter school with various conceptions about what teachers are like. Their conceptions—and misconceptions—are based in part on the portrayals of teachers in children's literature. In a 2005 study published in the journal *Education**, Sarah Sandefur and Leeann Moore presented the results of a content analysis of children's picture storybooks. The study was motivated by Sandefur and Moore's realization that picture storybooks often present unflattering portrayals of teachers. In the storybooks that the researchers were already familiar with, they noticed that teachers were often depicted as witches, dragons, drill sergeants, "incompetent fools," and other undesirable characters. Sandefur and Moore noted that these portrayals of teachers may have a negative impact on children's expectations and behavior when they first come to school. More broadly, these portrayals contribute to what Sandefur and Moore refer to as the public's frequent suspicion of the efficacy of teachers. One of the main goals of their study was to increase awareness of negative portrayals of teachers in children's literature, so that teachers are better equipped to deal with the impact of these portrayals.

Sandefur and Moore's content analysis focused on 62 children's picture storybooks published from 1965 through the present. A total of 96 teacher images from these books were initially coded in terms of five categories:

1. *Appearance.* This category included details about the teachers' apparent age and race, gender, body type, clothing, name, and so on.
2. *Language.* This category included statements made by the teacher.
3. *Subject.* This category included the academic subjects taught by the teacher.
4. *Approach.* This category included indicators of a philosophy of teaching, "including whether children were seated in rows, were working together in learning centers, were reciting memorized material, whether the teacher was shown lecturing...."
5. *Effectiveness.* This category included signs of how well or how much students learned from the teacher, as well as their emotional response to the teacher.

Sandefur and Moore's findings were clear, and somewhat disturbing:

> The teacher in children's picture storybooks is overwhelmingly portrayed as a white, non-Hispanic woman ...

> The teacher in picture storybooks who is sensitive, competent, and able to manage a classroom effectively is a minority ...

> The negative images outnumbered the positive images. Teachers who were dictatorial, used harsh language with children were distant or removed, or allowed teasing among students comprised 42% of the [teacher images] ...

> The teacher in children's picture storybooks is static, unchanging, and flat. [T]eachers in picture storybooks are never shown as learners themselves, never portrayed as moving from less effective to more effective ...

> The teacher in children's picture books is polarized.... [A]pproximately 84% of the teachers represented in our sample are either very good or horrid ...

> The teacher in children's picture books does not inspire in his or her students the pursuit of critical inquiry. The overwhelming majority of texts which represent teachers in a positive light ... show them as kind caregivers who dry tears ... resolve jealousy between children ... restore self-esteem.... However, few teachers are presented as having a substantial impact on a child's learning.

Sandefur and Moore concluded that students and teachers—and society at large—would benefit from the realization of how unfavorably teachers are presented in children's picture storybooks. The researchers also commented on the benefits of more positive representations of teachers and school in children's literature:

> The picture storybook has the potential to encourage a child to anticipate the valuable discoveries that are possible in the school setting; it can also demonstrate to parents how school ought to be and how teachers support children in cognitive and psychosocial ways. Children's literature can also provide positive enculturation for preservice teachers and validation for inservice teachers of the possibilities inherent in their social contributions.

*Sandefur, S. J., & Moore, L. (2004). The "nuts and dolts" of teacher images in children's picture storybooks: A content analysis. *Education, 125*(1), 41–55.

Sampling

Although content analysis focuses on materials, sampling considerations are essentially the same as in research with human participants. Obtaining access to personal documents may require approval from an Institutional Review Board as well as permission from the individuals who own the documents. (Permission is not required for public records.) The sampling options available for a content analysis are the same as those available for research with humans. If a representative sample is desired, as in the study described in Spotlight on Research 14.1, the researcher may choose either a probability or a nonprobability approach to achieving representativeness. If the researcher's goal is not representativeness but rather to illuminate the characteristics of a special case, critical case or extreme case sampling may be used in the selection of materials. Even snowball sampling is possible in a content analysis, as when the researcher uses the reference list of one text to identify other sources. (Refer back to Chapter 4 for details on these and other approaches to sampling.)

Coding and Interpretation

The coding and interpretation of data in a content analysis also tends to be carried out in the same way as in other qualitative studies. As discussed in Chapter 13, an approach such as the constant comparative method may be used to identify distinct categories or themes through a largely inductive process. Alternatively, the researcher may attempt to find instances of themes that he or she already believes to be important. For example, Smith (2006) looked at how students with disabilities are represented in classroom management textbooks. Smith's content analysis was based on a distinction between competence- and deficit-orientations toward students with disabilities:

> *Competence-orientation means that educators perceive students, including those with cognitive and communication impairments, as whole and complex persons and teach with the students' strengths in mind . . .*

> *Deficit-orientation refers to the attitudes of educators who tend to teach to a medical model of repairing the (often) irreparable individual. Their descriptions of students foster ranking, sorting, and diagnosing. Such medical model descriptions obscure the abilities of students who may have unique approaches to communicating understanding, wants, and needs. (p. 93)*

Here is how Smith described the process through which the classroom management texts were coded:

> *I began by inspecting each text for inclusion of students with disabilities, how students with disabilities were described, and the context and locations of these students in the book. Guiding questions initially included the following:*
>
> - *What was said about students with disabilities?*
> - *What was the context and language of their inclusion in the text?*
> - *Were competence- or deficit-oriented language and examples used?*

I took notes and developed and expanded themes relating to competence- and deficit-orientation. As part of this process, I took notes on recurring features in structure and content. (p. 95)

With respect to competence-orientation, for example, coding was based on the following questions: Did the text include substantial disability-related guidelines in the chapters? Did the text include students with disabilities in illustrative case examples? Was disability segregated in a separate section or chapter? Did the text use people-first language? Overall, was the text competence-oriented?

The results of Smith's content analysis suggested that four themes are prevalent in classroom management textbooks:

- Students with disabilities are treated as "aliens" (in that they are often discussed in separate chapters and contrasted with normal students).
- Students with disabilities are likely to fail academically.
- Students with disabilities are best handled and treated by special education experts (rather than teachers).
- Some types of disabilities are not mentioned in some texts.

Reliability and Validity in Content Analysis

Interrater reliability, or consistency across observers (see Chapter 6), may play an important role in a content analysis. The information obtained through the content analysis can be considered reliable insofar as two observers of the same materials would record the same information (e.g., by means of the same coding scheme).

Three types of validity that can be considered when evaluating a content analysis: Face validity, social validity, and empirical validity (Krippendorf, 2004).

Face validity refers to the plausibility of the content analysis, while social validity refers to the extent to which the content analysis focuses on socially important issues. (These two forms of validity are discussed in Chapter 6 with respect to quantitative measures.) As with any other form of research, informal judgments about face validity and social validity may increase (or decrease) our confidence in the results of a content analysis.

Empirical validity takes on many different forms. For example, "semantic validity" refers to the extent to which the themes identified in the content analysis accurately describe the way important terms and ideas are used in the materials. Semantic validity is thus a form of content validity, as defined in Chapter 6. Evidence for semantic validity gives us confidence in the coding scheme used for the content analysis. Such evidence may be obtained through theoretical considerations or empirical methods such as consultation among collaborating researchers.

Strengths and Weaknesses of Content Analysis

A strength of content analysis is its focus on physical materials. Materials can be examined and reexamined at one's leisure. Materials do not become impatient, tired, inhibited, or prone to subject effects. Experimenter effects are not possible either (unless the researcher's biases foster over- or underattention to particular details, or some other kind of distorted reading). Some materials—those that fall under the heading of public records—do not even require permission to be examined.

The reliance of content analysis on preexisting materials also happens to be a potential limitation. Although the researcher can select what to study from available materials, the researcher cannot determine what materials are available. And although the researcher can always reexamine materials and discover new meanings, he or she cannot persuade the materials to say more than they already do. As a result, there may be limitations on the generalizability of content analysis findings. The problem here is not that the researcher is unable to develop a method of obtaining a representative sample of existing materials, but rather that the existing materials themselves may fail to be representative of the population of interest. Limitations in the representativeness of existing materials is an especially common problem when historical documents are reviewed. (None of this is a problem, of course, when the goal of the content analysis is to describe a highly unusual case rather than to make generalizations.)

One way of enhancing generalizability is to link the content analysis closely with prior scholarship. Findings that are consistent with prior research and theory enhance the generalizability of the content analysis, as illustrated in Spotlight on Research 14.2.

Introduction to Historical Research

In qualitative traditions, **historical research** is a means of describing and interpreting the past. Although the results of historical research may be interesting in their own light, most historical studies are based on the premise that a better understanding of the past can foster greater insight into the present. This premise is illustrated by Laurel Tanner's book *Dewey's Laboratory School* (1997), which describes a famous experimental school that existed from 1896 through 1904. As Tanner unfolds the details of the creation and functioning of Dewey's school, she continually draws out implications for contemporary educational practice, arguing that the school embodied many of the ideals for educational practice that we currently aspire to but do not quite attain.

Distinctions Between Historical Research and Other Approaches

Although historical research relies heavily on content analysis, the two constructs can be distinguished. Content analysis is a method that can be used in many types of studies, including historical research. When a study relies exclusively, or nearly exclusively, on content analysis, the study itself can be called a content analysis. In other words, the term "content analysis" can be used to describe either a method or a type of design in which that method predominates. As a type of design, content analysis tends to focus on contemporary situations. Historical research, in contrast, focuses exclusively on prior events. Another difference between content analysis (as a type of design) and historical research is that the latter may rely at least in part on interviews with people who are asked about their recollections of the past.

Critical Thinking in Online Discussion Threads?

Online learning environments are becoming increasingly popular in higher education. Although online instruction has numerous benefits, one challenge faced by instructors as well as students is how to make sense of a potentially overwhelming number of postings in group discussion formats (particularly when the entire class is involved). A source of concern for all is the quality of the interactions. Do the contributors to group discussions engage each others' ideas in a receptive yet critical way, or is the group discussion simply a dumping ground for unreflective, random opinions, dominated by a few voices? This question was explored in a 2007 study published in the *Quarterly Review of Distance Education* by Kim Dooley and Leah Wickersham*.

In prior research, Dooley and Wickersham found that in small online learning communities, interaction between participants was fairly balanced and reflected a considerable amount of critical thinking. This finding motivated their current study, which focused on whole class discussion among 28 graduate students enrolled in a 2½ week online course. The topic for discussion was the "strengths and challenges of learner-centered instruction," and the discussion guidelines were fairly simple:

> [The] students read a chapter from the textbook in addition to related research articles on learner-centered instruction prior to participating within the discussion forum. The instructor required that each student submit an original posting in response to the forum question and reply to at least one thread. Although learners were not given the critical thinking skills framework, the instructor informed students that grading of the discussion forums was based on quality of discussion and not quantity of postings.

In their content analysis of the ensuing discussions, Dooley and Wickersham found evidence of critical thinking as well as some less desirable characteristics. In discussing these characteristics, the researchers related the present findings to those of their earlier study focusing on small online learning communities.

> Content analysis of the whole class discussion transcripts revealed that critical thinking was present; however, three distinct patterns emerged: discussions were more often off topic, certain students tended to dominate, and there was more disconnect between and among the critical thinking indicators with fewer intense interactions.

> [T]here were 146 postings for the whole class discussion. Of those, 97 were on-topic and 49 were off-topic (34%). One student who widened the discussion by posting a reference to schools not wanting authentic assessment related to individual growth . . . resulted in another student's response that was off-topic.

> > "Just to add a little personal bit into the picture as to how over rated letter/number grades can be, my 17-year-old daughter has Mono and has not been to school in almost two weeks and next week is the last week . . . at a time when she needs to be fully resting, she is twisted in panic knots . . . "

> This statement resulted in a long discussion about stress and grades. Although instructors working with adult learners do not necessarily need to cut off discussion that is off-topic, these diversions can disorient the flow away from the primary objective. In a traditional classroom, it is easier for the instructor to pull everyone back together and redirect the discussion. In an asynchronous environment, discussion that is off-topic confuses the learner who joins later and has no idea where the discussion went askew. The researchers did not find evidence of this pattern in the analysis of the discussions within the smaller virtual learning communities (Wickersham & Dooley, 2006).

Although other types of qualitative design, such as ethnographies, also explore peoples' recollections of prior events, the focus of those designs tends to be on current experiences and situations. In contrast, historical research deals with events that have already taken place. The ethnographer may inquire about the past in order to achieve a better understanding of the present. The historical researcher attempts a better understanding of the past, in hopes that the past contains useful lessons for the present.

A phenomenon that is not unique to the online environment is the domination of discussions by one or two students. One student alluded to this in a posting about learner-centered instruction in relation to working in groups. "Unfortunately I see the alpha member monopolizing, and the followers sitting back although each member is responsible for completing certain activities" . . . This phenomenon was also present in the whole class discussion . . .

The alpha student in this class was consistently engaged from the beginning to the end of every topic. This student not only posted most frequently (28 times), but also influenced whether or not the discussion stayed on-topic. Discussion domination directly influenced the previous pattern of off-topic discussion. To illustrate this point, a discussion was analyzed from a topic posted by the alpha student that was not related. Eleven individuals were pulled off-topic and diverged away from the original objective of the discussion. . . . The alpha student pattern was not prevalent in the small virtual learning communities previously studied (Wickersham & Dooley, 2006).

The final pattern that emerged from this analysis was that the overall critical thinking indicators were less integrated and synthesized in the whole group discussion. Students incorporated fewer critical thinking skills in one posting, but over numerous postings included one or two critical thinking skills within their statement. Responses during the whole class discussion were scattered and disjointed. The following is an example of a posting that incorporated relevant and important statements, linked ideas, facts, and notions, used outside relevant material, brought in a new idea, discussed the advantages and disadvantages of solutions, and widened the discussion by bringing in a larger perspective.

> *"Many of my ideas regarding education mirror John Dewey's idea of experiential learning and I believe it to be the most effective for the individual learner and for society. . . . Simply put, the educator must help guide the student on their journey to relate the subject to*

his/her own values, thoughts and pre-conceived ideas. . . . Once a student can do that . . . learning can truly commence. . . . The student's experiences bring in the importance of their community into education. . . . The challenges that face learner centered instruction are based in fear. Administrators who do not want their teachers to deviate from the standard curriculum; Administrators who fear giving up control of their school . . . to students; Educators who may not be comfortable utilizing and promoting different types of learning styles; and fear of changing the type of instruction by which the community has become accustomed to . . . "

This example had potential for quality interaction and dialog with others. Instead, only three postings resulted, one of which was the original author. Respondent 25 welcomed outside knowledge by stating: "WOW . . . all I can say about your explanation is that it is perfect. I guess as a third grade teacher, I have not given much thought to a high school student's future in the real world." We continued to see this pattern of welcoming of new knowledge but nothing more in terms of critical thinking within postings/interactions.

Not only did discussion fail to incorporate many of the critical thinking skills within one posting, learners also found it difficult to follow the thread of discussion with 28 individuals with one forum. One student even stated: "This discussion has gotten rather large and it is hard to follow a post when you have slept (or not!) since you read it all" (6). This pattern was not evident when smaller virtual learning communities were formed (Wickersham & Dooley, 2006).

In sum, a content analysis approach allowed Dooley and Wickersham to identify some of the shortcomings of whole class online discussion formats.

*Dooley, K. E., & Wickersham, L. E. (2007). Distraction, domination, and disconnection in whole-class, online discussions. *Quarterly Review of Distance Education, 8*(1), 1–8. Quoted with permission from the publisher.

Types of Historical Materials

The materials used in historical research can be classified as either primary or secondary sources.

- **Primary sources** are original materials created by observers or participants in an event. These materials include letters, minutes, reports, photographs, videotapes, artifacts, and eyewitness accounts.

- **Secondary sources** are materials created by individuals who were not present at the event being described. These materials include biographies, history textbooks, and critical reviews.

The book by Laurel Tanner described earlier is an example of a secondary source. In order to create the book, Tanner reviewed a combination of primary and secondary sources. Primary sources included weekly reports submitted by the teachers of the laboratory school, accounts written by former teachers and students, and Dewey's own letters and formal writings concerning the school. Secondary sources included biographies of key individuals as well as commentaries on the school written by observers.

Evaluation of Historical Materials

The evaluation of historical materials depends in part on making a determination of their authenticity and their accuracy.

External criticism pertains to the authenticity of a historical document. The purpose of external criticism is to determine whether or not the purported author, date of publication, and other details of publication are accurate. There are several possibilities:

- The document is completely genuine.
- The document is largely genuine but there are inaccuracies (e.g., the dating of the document is slightly inaccurate).
- The document is a **variant source**, or altered copy of the original. The alteration may be minor or major, and may consist of additions, deletions, or other changes.
- The document is a forgery.

Internal criticism pertains to the accuracy of the statements expressed in a historical document. The purpose of internal criticism is to determine how credible the document is. There are several possibilities:

- The document is completely accurate.
- The document is largely accurate but contains a few minor inaccuracies.
- The document contains a significant number of inaccurate statements or key omissions (e.g., because the writer was biased).
- The document is intentionally deceptive.

Both external and internal criticism are carried out through a combination of careful scholarship, triangulation (corroboration among sources), and common sense.

Historical Interpretation

External and internal criticism are not the only interpretive activities on the part of the historical researcher. In order to reconstruct the lives, events, and perspectives of the past, the researcher must make inferences about how people thought and acted in particular situations. Historical research consequently has an interdisciplinary flavor. It is common for historical researchers to make use of theories and concepts from social scientific disciplines such as psychology, sociology, anthropology, and economics.

Typically, the interpretive efforts of the historical researcher are based on careful reading and thinking about a variety of primary and secondary sources. Consider, for example, the following passage from Tanner's book:

> *Articles written by the Dewey teachers show a clear understanding of his idea that the school should build on the child's experience and the relation of this conception to the teacher's own area of expertise. In the lead article of the first number of the* Elementary School Record, *Lillian Cushman (1900) applied Dewey's developing theories to her field of art. It is only by giving an artistic expression to their own life experiences that children can get any real aesthetic training, she told readers:*
>
>> *[S]ubject matter will arise out of [the child's] life and interests. While a part of these are common to all, others are modified by the local environment and by the activities of the school. Our six-year-old children whose studies are grouped about the activities of the farm, model in clay the vegetables and fruits, the domestic animals, the farmer himself plowing, sowing or engaged in any other occupation which may interest them'' (p. 6).*
>
> *Dewey's influence on Cushman is evident. Art, like other disciplines, grows out of the experiences of individuals, and like other disciplines its technical aspects are best learned when the individual has a real need . . .*
>
> *It should be noted here that in Dewey's experimental school aesthetic experience was not a special kind of activity confined to art. As Dykhuizen (1973) pointed out in his Dewey biography, Dewey held ''that the consummatory fulfillment in aesthetic experience is potential in all experience'' (p. 260). Solving a problem, writing a story, playing a game to completion are examples. In our day as in Dewey's, this kind of pleasure is universal and, as Forshay (1995) has observed, is a key to enriching children's school experiences.*
>
> *(Tanner, 1997, pp. 45–46, quoted with permission from the publisher)*

Notice that in developing a point about the aesthetic experience in Dewey's school, Tanner weaves together a primary source (Cushman's observations), a secondary source (Dykhuizen's biography), and an informed opinion (Forshay's observation).

Although reliance on multiple sources of information is commonplace in historical research, the experienced researcher has the interpretive skills (and the background knowledge) to generate many questions and speculative hypotheses even about a single document. Imagine, for example, what you might glean from the pages of the early reader given in Figure 14.1.

A careful look at primary sources such as this early reader can suggest something about reading instruction in the United States in the late 1930s and early 1940s. You can see that emphasis is placed on orthographically regular, one-syllable words. There is a heavy reliance on repetition. An effort has been made to present a scenario that would be familiar to children. At the same time, the dialogue is stilted and highly unnatural. The main characters in the story are white and, apparently, middle class. Jerry expresses interest in the stereotypically ''male'' toys depicted at the top of the page, but not in the doll. Although a historical research study on early reading instruction in the 1930s would probably be based on a review of numerous early readers, as well as scholarly publications and commentary generated

Figure 14.1 Two Pages from a 1941 Reading Primer

by reading teachers of the day, the historical research study might be motivated initially by a single example. A primer such as the one in Figure 14.1 suggests a variety of research questions. For example:

- How are the reading methods championed in different historical periods reflected in (or excluded from) the content of early readers?
- What kinds of compromises are made between the naturalness and orthographic simplicity of early readers in different historical periods?
- To what extent are early readers of different historical periods dominated by images of white, middle-class people and traditional gender roles?

In a historical research study, each of these questions would most likely be followed by an additional question: "And what are the implications for current reading instruction?"

Strengths and Weaknesses of Historical Research

We cannot say that historical research is a more or less suitable approach to studying historical research questions—by definition, it is the only approach. But we can discern some of its strengths and weaknesses as a type of research design.

Like content analysis, the focus of historical research on documents and other materials is both a strength (in that subject effects are impossible) as well as a weakness (in that the extent of available information will be limited). The authenticity of a historical source may be questionable and difficult to ascertain through external criticism, and the historical record may be too sparse to evaluate the accuracy of the source through internal criticism. Generalizability is a particular problem in historical research (assuming the goal is to make generalizations rather than illuminate particular cases). Whereas a content analysis of contemporary textbooks is limited only by the researcher's method of sampling, a content analysis of

Thirty-Six Children, Forty-Three Years Ago

A glimpse at the experiences of a new teacher in the 1960s is provided by Herbert Kohl in his 1967 book, *Thirty-Six Children**. In this widely read book, Kohl, a white graduate from Columbia University's Teachers College, describes his first teaching job at an all-black school in Harlem, just a few blocks away from the university. Although many of Kohl's observations would be familiar to new teachers today, his book serves as a historical document that illuminates, among other things, the quality of urban schools in the 1960s, and the disparity in cultural background between a white, Ivy League graduate and a classroom of black students growing up in a low-income urban environment. Here are a few of Kohl's recollections about his first day on the job:

> The children entered at nine and filled up the seats. They were silent and stared at me. It was a shock to see thirty-six black faces before me. No preparation helped. It is one thing to be liberal and talk, another to face something and learn that you're afraid . . .

> "What would you like to learn this year? My name is Mr. Kohl."

> Silence. The children looked up at me with expressionless faces, thirty-six of them crowded at thirty-five broken desks . . .

> Silence, a restless movement rippled through the class. They don't understand? There must be something that interests them, that they care to know more about.

> A hand shot up in the corner of the room.

> "I want to learn more about volcanoes. What are volcanoes?"

> The class seemed interested. I sketched a volcano on the blackboard, made a few comments, and promised to return.

> "Anything else? Anyone else interested in something?"

> Silence, then the same hand.

> "Why do volcanoes form?"

> And during the answer:

> "Why don't we have a volcano here?"

> A contest. The class savored it, I accepted. Question, response, question. I walked toward my inquisitor, studying his mischievous eyes, possessed and possessing smile. I moved to congratulate him, my hand went happily toward his shoulder. I dared because I was afraid.

> His hands shot up to protect his dark face, eyes contracted in fear, body coiled, ready to bolt for the door and out, down into the streets.

> "But why should I hit you?"

> [H]e looked torn and puzzled. I changed the subject quickly and moved on to social studies—How We Became Modern America . . .

> "Can anyone tell me what was going on about 1800? Remember, you studied it last year. Why don't we start specifically? What do you think you'd see if you walked down Madison Avenue in those days?"

> A lovely hand, almost too thin to be seen, tentatively rose.

> "Cars?"

> "Do you think there were cars in 1800? Remember that was over a hundred and fifty years ago. Think of what you learned last year and try again. Do you think there were cars then?"

> "Yes . . . no . . . I don't know."

> She withdrew, and the class became restless as my anger rose.

> At last another hand.

> "Grass and trees?"

> The class broke up as I tried to contain my frustration.

(continued)

curricular materials used in the early 19th century is limited to those materials that have been preserved, and there are many reasons why preservation might yield a nonrandom selection of materials.

Recent historical documents and records are less prone to some of the limitations described above. For example, Spotlight on Research 14.3 presents an excerpt from

"I don't know what you're laughing about—it's the right answer. In those days, Harlem was farmland, with fields and trees and a few houses. There weren't any roads or houses like the ones outside, or streetlights or electricity. There probably wasn't even a Madison Avenue."

The class was outraged. It was inconceivable to them there was a time their Harlem didn't exist.

"Stop this noise and let's think. Do you believe Harlem was here a thousand years ago?"

A pause, several uncertain "noes."

"It's possible that the land was green, then. Why couldn't Harlem also have been green a hundred and fifty or two hundred years ago?"

No response. The weight of Harlem and my whiteness and strangeness hung up in the air as I droned on, lost in my righteous monologue. The uproar turned into sullen silence. A slow, nervous drumming began at several desks; the atmosphere closed as intelligent faces lost their animation . . .

The cultural gap between Kohl and his students was not lessened by the textbooks available to the class:

There were two full sets of sixth-grade readers available. . . . Yet accepting these readers put me in an awkward situation. The books were flat and uninteresting. They only presented what was pleasant in life, and even then limited the pleasant to what was publicly accepted as such. The people in the stories were all middle-class, and their simplicity, goodness, and self-confidence were unreal. I couldn't believe in this foolish ideal and knew that anyone who had ever bothered to observe human life couldn't believe it. Yet I had to teach it, and through it make reading important and necessary. Remembering the children, their anxiety and hostility, the alternate indifference, suspicion, and curiosity they approached me with, knowing how essential it is to be honest with children, I felt betrayed by the books into hypocrisy.

As Kohl tried out different strategies for engaging the students, he gradually learned more about teaching and the nature of the teacher–student relationship. On the second day, for example, sensing that the students needed a break, Kohl offered them 10 minutes between lessons to do whatever they wanted.

The class looked fearful and amazed—freedom in school, do what you want? For a few minutes they sat quietly and then slowly began to talk. Two children walked to the piano and asked me if they could try. I said of course, and three more children joined them. It seemed so easy; the children relaxed. I watched closely and suspiciously, realizing that the tightness with time that exists in the elementary school has nothing to do with the quantity that must be learned or the children's needs. It represents the teacher's fear of loss of control and is nothing but a weapon used to weaken the solidarity and opposition of the children that too many teachers unconsciously dread.

Along with the many mistakes he so candidly documented, one of Kohl's early and enduring insights was the importance of teachers getting to know their students—a somewhat innovative idea at the time his book was written:

I am convinced that the teacher must be an observer of his class as well as a member of it. He must look at the children, discover how they relate to each other and the room around them. There must be enough free time and activity for the teacher to discover the children's human preferences. Observing children at play and mischief is an invaluable source of knowledge about them—about leaders and groups, fear, courage, warmth, isolation. Teachers consider the children's gym or free play time their free time too, and usually turn their backs on the children when they have the most to learn from them.

I went through a year of teacher training at Teachers College, Columbia, received a degree, and heard no mention of how to observe children, nor even a suggestion that it was of value. Without learning to observe children and thereby knowing something of the people one is living with five hours a day, the teacher resorts to routine and structure for protection . . .

*Kohl, H. (1967). *Thirty-six children*. New York: New American Library. Quoted with permission from the publisher.

a book that is only four decades old, yet functions in some ways as a historical document, owing to societal changes that have occurred since it was written. The authenticity, accuracy, and generality of a book such as this is relatively easily verified through examination of other written records from the time as well as more recent scholarly publications, most of which have been preserved.

A Look Ahead

Chapters 13 and 14 introduced some of the most prominent qualitative research designs. In the next chapter I discuss mixed-methods research, in which quantitative and qualitative methods each play a significant role within the same study.

Applications: A Guide for Beginning Researchers

Here are some ideas from the chapter that will help you plan your research:

- If you plan to take a qualitative approach to the study of materials, think about the extent to which you want your gathering and analysis of information to be influenced by theoretical considerations and preliminary hypotheses.
- Plan on extensive gathering of information based on multiple methods.

Chapter Summary

The goal of a content analysis is to reveal something about a set of materials, the individuals who created the materials, or the context in which the materials were created. The materials may be personal documents, public records, or something else. Coding and interpretation of data tend to be carried out in the same way as in other qualitative approaches, and the validity and reliability of the content analysis can be evaluated.

Historical research focuses on primary and secondary sources, and may include interviews with living participants. External and internal criticism are used to determine the authenticity and accuracy of a source.

Key Terms

Content analysis	**Secondary sources**	**Internal criticism**
Historical research	**External criticism**	
Primary sources	**Variant source**	

Exercises

For questions 1–4, indicate whether the materials can be described as personal documents, public records, or other materials.

1. Newsletters created by a national organization of science educators.

2. A series of memos written by the governor of a state to the director of the state board of education.

3. A set of 19th century lithographs illustrating children in classroom settings.

4. A blog maintained by the principal and assistant principal of a middle school.

5. Which of the following best describes a problem that may arise when a researcher compares two different sets of curricular materials in order to determine which set is more pedagogically sound?

a) Subject effects

b) History effects

c) Attrition

d) Selection bias

6. Which of the following illustrates internal criticism?

a) Reviewing the literature to determine whether there is evidence that a particular source has been forged.

b) Checking whether historical sources agree about the sequence of events that occurred on a particular day.

c) Evaluating the moral implications of an argument developed in a particular source.

d) Determining whether the year of publication attributed to a source in a database is the same as the year printed on the source.

7. *Critical thinking question*: What kinds of experimenter effects are possible in a historical research study?

Answers to Exercises

1. Public records   **2.** Personal documents   **3.** Other materials

4. Public records   **5.** d   **6.** b

7. *Possible answer*: Some experimenter effects could stem from cultural biases. For example, the researcher might inadvertently misrepresent a statement, owing to lack of knowledge about the context of the statement, or because the language and concepts underlying the statement are unfamiliar. Or, the researcher might pay too much attention to "special" characteristics and inadvertently downplay the extent of similarity between historical and current circumstances. Other types of experimenter effects would be less directly reflective of cultural bias. For example, the researcher might give more weight to information that supports a hypothesis, while discounting contradictory information. There are many possibilities.

Suggestions for Further Reading

Research Article: Raskind, M. H., Margalit, M., & Higgins, E. L. (2006). "My LD": Children's voices on the Internet. *Learning Disabilities Quarterly, 29*, 253–268.

This qualitative content analysis examines messages posted on a public website by children with LD.

Application Article: Gordon, L. E., & Ellingson, L. (2006). In the eyes of the beholder: Student interpretations of sexuality lessons. *Sex Education, 6*(3), 251–264.

This qualitative content analysis focuses on themes that emerged in essays written by students in undergraduate sexuality classes.

Extension Article: Adams, J. (2007). Then and now: Lessons from history concerning the merits and problems of distance education. *Simile, 7*(1), 1–14.

In this historical research study, qualitative content analysis is used to describe changes in distance education between 1898 and 1941.

CHAPTER 15

Mixed-Methods Designs

BananaStock/Jupiter Images Corp

After studying this chapter, you will be able to answer the following questions:

- What are mixed-methods designs and what purposes do they serve?

- What are the major types of mixed-methods designs?

- How are mixed-methods studies conducted?

- How are the results of mixed-methods studies evaluated?

This chapter will prepare you to do the following:

- Understand and evaluate mixed-methods research reports

- Select the mixed-methods design that best suits your research question

- Design a mixed-methods study

I arrived in Montreal for the American Educational Research Association (AERA) conference and stood in line at the airport shuttle bus for over an hour. I admit to eavesdropping to the people standing behind me. They were each attending the AERA and began by asking each other what they did. The first speaker, a woman, said she did quantitative research and was using a new statistical, structural modeling approach. She stopped short of saying what she was using the modeling for. [She] then asked her conversational partner what he did. He replied ... that he was studying Foucault's concept of meditation. Without missing a beat, the woman said, "oh, you do qualitative research." And from that point on, the discussion turned to personality characteristics, and that you either love or hate statistics, and either love or hate French theorists. But nowhere in this discussion did either one reveal to the other what they were learning about their subject matter.

What might have happened if these educational scholars had not sought the safe terrain of either side of this unnecessary divide...? One of the most regrettable consequences of not crossing anxious borders is that we miss out on each other's knowledge.

LUTTRELL, 2005, pp. 192-193

Quantitative and Qualitative Traditions

Here are three observations about quantitative and qualitative research designs that I have made at various points in the book thus far:

- Quantitative and qualitative designs are based on different epistemologies, methods, and approaches to analysis and interpretation.
- Quantitative and qualitative designs each have their own somewhat unique strengths and limitations.
- One type of research is not superior to the other. Rather, quantitative and qualitative designs are each suitable for addressing partially different sets of research questions.

My prior discussions also suggest that any given study can be classified as either quantitative or qualitative. In actual practice, these are not exclusive categories. Many quantitative research reports include informal, qualitative observations, just as many qualitative studies include a small amount of frequency information or other numerical data. Adding quantitative information to a qualitative study, or vice versa, can enhance the completeness and accuracy of the research. Even so, most studies are readily classified as either quantitative or qualitative, because one approach is clearly predominant, whereas the other one is not essential to the study but merely a source of minor additional information. Quantitative and qualitative approaches represent two largely distinct traditions, separated by key assumptions, outright disagreements, and, all too often, isolation and disdain.

At present, an epistemological gap still largely separates the two traditions, but there is not much physical distance between them: Quantitative and qualitative researchers occupy the same academic departments, present their research at the same major conferences, and publish articles in the same peer-reviewed journals (in spite of the fact that some departments, conferences, and journals are devoted exclusively to one tradition). Although tension was heightened in the first few years of the 21st century by federal legislation that favors quantitative over qualitative methods (see discussion in Chapter 18), progress has been made in the acceptance of one tradition by representatives of the other, and there is growing disenchantment with the idea that any one tradition is privileged. Moreover, in recent years there has been an increasing prevalence of **mixed-methods designs**, in which quantitative and qualitative methods are integrated, and each method plays an essential role in the study. Mixed-methods research, a genuine and coherent amalgam of two different research traditions, is the focus of this chapter.

Introduction to Mixed-Methods Designs

Although there are disagreements about exactly what constitutes a mixed-methods design, studies bearing this label represent a mix of quantitative and qualitative approaches to developing research questions, obtaining samples, gathering and coding data, and/or analyzing and drawing conclusions from the data (Tashakkori & Creswell, 2007). A mixed-methods study incorporates the relative strengths of quantitative and qualitative designs. The research process tends to be labor-intensive, since each approach is integral to the study rather than a minor addition, and expertise is required in both quantitative and qualitative traditions in order to conduct the study successfully.

In their comprehensive *Handbook of Mixed Methods in Social and Behavioral Research* (2003), Tashakkori and Teddlie note that the inclusion of quantitative and qualitative methods in a mixed-methods study serves at least one of three general purposes:

- The results of one method corroborate or extend the results obtained by the other method.
- The results of one method rule out alternative explanations for the results obtained by the other method.
- The combination of both methods enables the exploration of various aspects of a phenomenon.

What each of these purposes has in common is a meaningful integration of quantitative and qualitative methods—the two methods are interrelated rather than used to make isolated contributions to the study. Later in the chapter, other ways of classifying the various purposes of mixed-methods research are described.

Types of Mixed-Methods Designs

Although mixed-methods research was already being conducted in the early part of the 20th century, formal approaches to mixed-methods design were not suggested until the 1950s (Tashakkori & Teddlie, 2003). In this section I introduce some of the basic distinctions of relevance to the classification of these designs.

TABLE 15.1   Major Types of Mixed-Methods Designs

Type of Design	Alternative Name	Definition
Explanatory	QUAN-qual	Quantitative data is gathered first and predominates
Exploratory	QUAL-quan	Qualitative data is gathered first and predominates
Triangulation	QUAN-QUAL	Quantitative and qualitative data are gathered simultaneously and integrated

In some mixed-methods studies, quantitative and qualitative data are obtained from the same measure. For example, a survey might be used in which responses to Likert-scaled questions are coded quantitatively, while responses to open-ended questions pertaining to the same topic are coded qualitatively.

In other studies, quantitative and qualitative data collection are carried out separately and later integrated. Each quantitative and qualitative component in these studies is referred to as a **phase** (or "strand"), and the phases may be concurrent (carried out at the same time, by means of separate measures) or sequential (one before the other).

Depending on the timing of the phases, a further distinction can be made between three types of mixed-methods designs: explanatory, exploratory, and triangulation (see Table 15.1).

EXPLANATORY DESIGNS   An **explanatory design** consists of quantitative data collection followed by the gathering of qualitative information. Because quantitative data collection comes first, and remains somewhat predominant, this type of design is also called **QUAN-qual**. Generally, the role of qualitative information gathering in an explanatory design is to help explain the results of quantitative data collection.

An explanatory design is illustrated in a 2006 study by Igo, Riccomini, Bruning, and Pope on Internet text comprehension among seventh- and eighth-grade students with learning disabilities (LD). Igo and colleagues wanted to know whether students' comprehension would be affected by the way they take notes, and by the extent to which their note-taking strategies match the format through which their comprehension is tested. Fifteen students were asked to take notes from a website either by copying and pasting, or by typing or writing out paraphrases of what they read. Experimenter-designed multiple-choice and cued recall tests were subsequently administered.

In the quantitative phase of the study, Igo and colleagues (2006) tested between two hypotheses. The "depth of processing" hypothesis holds that students would perform better on each test when they typed or wrote paraphrases rather than simply copying and pasting. The "transfer-appropriate" hypothesis holds that students would perform better on the multiple-choice test when they cut and pasted their notes, while showing better performance on the recall test when they took notes by means of paraphrasing. The quantitative findings supported the transfer-appropriate hypothesis—mean scores on the multiple-choice test were significantly higher when students had cut and pasted notes, while the means on the cued recall test were significantly higher when students had typed or written paraphrases. Test performance was also better when students had written rather than typed their notes.

In the qualitative phase of the study, Igo and colleagues (2006) examined the content of each student's notes, and interviewed the students about their note-taking preferences. The students' typed and written notes consisted primarily of verbatim content, interspersed with a small number of short paraphrases that were relatively poor in quality—a pattern that further disconfirms the depth of processing hypothesis. Student interviews revealed an overwhelming preference for the copy-and-paste method of note taking, with most students preferring this method because it required no spelling and grammar. A number of students also described difficulties with typing.

In summarizing these findings, Igo and colleagues (2006) elaborated on how the qualitative phase of their study complemented the quantitative one:

> The . . . qualitative interview themes, coupled with an analysis of student notes, offer a sound explanation of the transfer-appropriate processing effects found . . . in the quantitative phase of this study. First, as indicated by the analysis of notes, most students created verbatim notes; they tended to write (or type) one or two words at a time while trying to match their notes to the main text. Verbatim note taking has been linked to shallow processing. . . . Further, during the interviews, students consistently described the need to monitor spelling while typing and writing notes. As such, they most likely would have had to shift their mental efforts away from the meaning of the text from time to time as they took notes, which can result in diminished encoding of the text ideas. . . . Finally, some students described the added distraction of searching the keyboard for letters while they took notes. This, too, forces students to shift their mental efforts to a task unrelated to the message in the text. The qualitative phase of this study also helps explain why students performed slightly better on tests for topics that were noted by writing than by typing. For example, although students indicated that spelling was a concern in both the writing and typing conditions, three students noted that they were able to write their notes more quickly than typing them. Similarly, five students described feeling less pressure to spell correctly while writing than while typing. Together, these two findings could account for the slightly higher performance on written topics, as each suggests that less time was spent on distracting tasks. (p. 98)

EXPLORATORY DESIGNS   An **exploratory design** consists of qualitative information gathering followed by quantitative data collection. This type of design is also called **QUAL-quan**. Typically, the role of qualitative data collection in an exploratory design is to offer preliminary guidance for quantitative data collection. In a 2006 study, for example, Okpala and Ellis examined perceptions of teacher quality among 218 business students at a historically black college in the southeastern United States. In the qualitative phase of the study, students were surveyed about their views on the basis of teacher quality by means of two open-ended questions:

Question 1: "Describe what a quality teacher means to you."
Question 2: "Identify the four most important teacher quality components."

Through qualitative analysis, five themes emerged in students' responses to both questions: caring for students, teaching skills, content knowledge, dedication to teaching, and verbal skills.

In the quantitative phase of the study, each theme was categorized, and the researchers calculated the percentages of students who mentioned each category.

Although the "caring for students" category was mentioned most frequently in response to each question, there were clear differences in prevalence across questions: 39% of students mentioned caring for students in response to the first question, while 83% mentioned this category in response to the second question. Although only 5% of students mentioned verbal skills in response to the first question, while 75% of students listed this category in response to the second question. In fact, none of the five categories was mentioned by fewer than two-thirds of the students in response to the second question. One of the contributions of the quantitative phase of Okpala and Ellis's (2006) study was to illustrate that when students are asked to describe quality teachers in any way they wish (Question 1), there is no single theme that predominates across students' responses, but when they are asked to list important components of teacher quality (Question 2), the same themes consistently emerge.

TRIANGULATION DESIGNS A **triangulation design** consists of simultaneous collection of quantitative and qualitative data. In this type of design, also called **QUAN-QUAL**, the researcher compares and integrates the results of quantitative and qualitative data collection, and perhaps bases further data collection on the initial findings. The quantitative and qualitative data corroborate each other—hence the name "triangulation" design (see Chapter 13 for discussion of triangulation in ethnographic research). A triangulation study focusing on teacher attitudes toward English Language Learners is described in Spotlight on Research 15.1.

Mixed-Methods Analysis and Interpretation

The design of a mixed-method study may be quite simple. For example, the researcher might gather qualitative information through passive observation, develop and administer a survey on the basis of the observations, and then analyze the results of the survey quantitatively. In this case, a QUAL-quan design is used in which the qualitative and quantitative phases are distinct and based on single measures. Other mixed-method studies reflect more elaborate designs based on multiple phases in which data are analyzed, interpreted, integrated, and then serve as the basis for additional data collection.

Mixed-methods designs are suitable for most research questions that can be examined by means of either quantitative or qualitative approaches alone. In an influential typology, Creswell (2005) summarized some of the different approaches reflected in mixed-methods procedures and analyses. Part of this typology is given in Table 15.2.

There are many different reasons for conducting mixed-methods research and, consequently, many different ways of classifying the purposes of the studies. In the introductory section of the chapter, a broad distinction was made between mixed-methods designs in which one method corroborates the other, rules out alternative explanations for the other, or allows the phenomenon under study to be explored from a different perspective. The typology given in Table 15.2 illustrates a more analysis-oriented distinction among different purposes. Later in the chapter, in Spotlight on Research 15.3, you will read about a third approach to distinguishing among the different purposes for mixed-methods designs.

Teacher Attitudes toward ELLs: A Triangulation Mixed-Method Study

As the number of immigrants in the United States increases, the extent of negativity toward individuals who are not fluent in English is increasing too. Unfortunately, even teachers may develop negative attitudes toward the English Language Learners (ELLs) who are—or may someday be—in their classes. In a 2004 study published in the *NABE Journal of Research and Practice,** Anne Walker, Jill Shafer, and Michelle Iiams used a triangulation design to study mainstream teacher attitudes toward ELLs.

Walker and colleagues emphasize that teacher attitudes are critical to the educational experience of ELL students:

Attitudinal assessment is important because teachers' attitudes and beliefs about language-minority children play a crucial role in determining the educational outcomes for this population of students (Valdes, 2001). Teachers who hold negative, ethnocentric or racist attitudes about ELLs, or who believe in any of the numerous fallacies surrounding the education of language-minority students, often fail to meet the academic and social needs of these students (Tse, 2001; Valdes, 2001; Youngs & Youngs, 2001) and work to maintain the hegemonic legitimacy of the dominant social order. . . .

Mainstream teachers from 28 North Dakota school districts participated in Walker and colleagues' study. (The researchers defined "mainstream teachers" as elementary teachers or secondary teachers of core content classes.) Three research questions were explored:

1. What are mainstream teachers' attitudes toward ELLs?
2. What factors affect teachers' attitudes toward ELL students?
3. How do teacher attitudes vary according to the demographic background of the teachers' schools and communities?

Walker and colleagues justified their use of a mixed-methods approach in terms of some of the strengths characteristic of quantitative and qualitative methods, and in terms of how each method would play a role in addressing their research questions:

Quantitative data was needed to determine the extent and degree of teacher attitudes towards ELLs, and to cross-analyze data in terms of multiple demographic factors.

Quantitative data was also needed to both generalize and contrast findings to teachers and schools throughout the state. Qualitative data, on the other hand, was needed to more deeply understand the factors influencing teacher attitudes. . . . Furthermore, anecdotal information was needed to describe and demonstrate the manner in which teacher attitudes towards ELLs played out in the classrooms and schools under study.

The primarily quantitative measure that Walker and colleagues used consisted of a Likert-scaled survey:

A 14-question survey using a 5-point Likert Scale was developed which elicited responses related to the extent and nature of teacher attitudes towards ELLs. Survey questions were developed both on the basis of the literature review and on the authors' previous conversations with both mainstream and ELL teachers from across the state. These survey statements addressed the following themes: (1) teacher attitudes about ELLs as students, (2) teachers' sense of self-efficacy in working with ELLs, (3) the impact of ELLs on the teacher's job responsibilities, (4) knowledge/opinions on English language acquisition and best practices in ELL education, and (5) the perceived school receptivity towards ELLs.

The survey also elicited information on variables such as whether or not the teacher had been trained in working with ELL students. The qualitative measure that Walker and colleagues used consisted of an open-ended interview format:

The second instrument employed in this study was an open-ended interview protocol designed for practicing ELL teachers. Protocol questions, based on research information and author experience, focused on (1) the extent and nature of existing ELL services provided in their schools, (2) perceived school and teacher attitudes towards ELLs, (3) the perceived obstacles and challenges these ELL teachers faced in providing a quality school-wide ELL program, and (4) ways in which negative teacher attitudes manifested themselves in the school setting. The interview protocol was designed so that the qualitative data provided by ELL teachers could be used to validate the survey results in terms of the extent and nature of negative teacher attitudes towards ELLs and to provide rich description of how negative attitudes detrimentally impacted the quality of education provided for ELLs in the surveyed schools.

The quantitative results of relevance to the first research question were disturbing, and a paradox emerged:

[O]nly 18% of all teachers (n = 77) felt that ELLs academically performed well in school. The vast majority of teachers either believed that ELLs perform poorly in school (30%, n = 124) or responded neutrally to the question (52%, n = 218). Furthermore, 16% of teachers (n = 68) felt that ELLs come from countries with inferior educational systems . . .

70% (n = 288) of mainstream teachers were not actively interested in having ELLs in their classroom. Fourteen percent (n = 58) directly objected to ELL students being placed in their classrooms and 56% (n = 230) responded neutrally to the idea.

Twenty-five percent of teachers (n = 103) felt that it was the responsibility of ELLs to adapt to American culture and school life while 30% (n = 121) responded neutrally.

Twenty percent of teachers (n = 83) directly objected to adapting their classroom instruction for ELLs, and another 27% (n = 110) were neutral on this issue.

Additionally, while 87% (n = 368) of teachers had never received any professional development or training in working with ELLs, 51% (n = 212) said they would not be interested in training even if the opportunity was available.

[G]iven the extent and nature of the negative statistics presented above . . . the next two statistical findings were surprising in their positiveness:

62% (n = 254) of teachers felt that their schools openly welcomed ELLs and embraced their native cultures and languages.

78% (n = 318) of teachers felt that language-minority students bring needed diversity to schools.

How do we begin to explain this paradox? Perhaps political correctness dictates teachers to comment positively on issues of diversity. To outright state that a school does not welcome new cultures, languages, and diversity smacks of racism and prejudice. It is far safer to complain about ELLs in terms of academic preparation and performance, and the added challenges they add to the classroom. . . . When teachers are asked questions that move beyond the school level, questions that probe at a teacher's ownership of their own classroom, political correctness ultimately falls aside . . .

Walker and colleagues addressed their second research question through qualitative data analysis from comments written in the surveys and from interviews. Much of the teachers' negativity could be traced to both time constraints and inadequate training.

[M]any of the respondents who negatively answered questions about teaching ELLs in the mainstream classroom offered the rationale that there were already too many other school demands placed upon their time. . . . Teachers who answered negatively to wanting professional development in the area of ELL education echoed similar thoughts . . .

Eighty-seven percent of survey respondents reported never having received any training or professional development in working with English Language Learners . . .

Mainstream teachers who have never had training in working with ELLs often feel overwhelmed when an ELL is first placed in their classroom. Unprepared teachers in our study reported feeling helpless and having no idea of where to begin . . .

The qualitative observation that training is an important variable led Walker and colleagues to run quantitative statistical analyses. Specifically, *t*-tests were conducted to compare the responses of teachers who had versus did not have ELL training.

Statistical results demonstrated that teachers who reported having at least some training in ELL education were more likely to: (1) want ELLs in their class, (2) be more receptive to the idea that ELLs bring needed diversity to the school, and (3) hold a stronger belief that mainstream teachers need to adapt their instruction for limited proficient students . . .

Walker and colleagues also found that when ELL teachers were interviewed, their observations about the mainstream teachers corroborated the findings that had been obtained through directly surveying and interviewing the latter group.

When we asked ELL teachers the interview question, "What do you see as the largest obstacles in implementing a quality ELL program in your school?" almost all of the responses included negative teacher attitudes. The ELL teachers repeatedly mentioned the unwillingness of many classroom teachers to make adaptations, or to have ELLs placed in their classroom . . .

[O]ne of the frustrations cited by ELL teachers was the problem of both administrators and mainstream teachers believing in misnomers about effective ELL education. The survey results highlighted two common misnomers in second language acquisition believed by both teachers and by the US public. Fifteen percent of respondents (n = 61) felt that ELLs learn better if they are prohibited from using their native language in school. The vast majority of teachers (46%, n = 189) responded neutrally to this statement. Seven percent of teachers (n = 30) believed that ELLs should be fluent in English after only one year of ELL instruction, and 27% (n = 108) were neutral. The prevalence of these fallacies have been documented by other researchers (Tse, 2001) . . .

In attempting to understand both teacher resistance to professional development (51% of respondents) and the belief that certified ELL teachers are unnecessary in the education of English Language Learners (17% of respondents, n = 73), a previously unconsidered factor emerged. As one teacher articulated: "Teachers don't need specialized ESL training; common sense and good intentions work fine." Allusions to "common sense" were reflected in numerous teacher comments. . . . As most experts in ELL education would agree, common sense and good intentions are important in working with ELLs, but [without specialized training] relying solely on common sense can lead to common mistakes that detrimentally impact student learning (Nieto, 1995).

Walker and colleagues addressed their third research question by contrasting the attitudes of teachers at low-incidence schools, rapid-influx schools, and schools serving migrant students. Both qualitative and quantitative data were cited. (Refer back to Chapter 11 for discussion of the chi-square statistics reported below.)

Teachers in low-incidence schools in this great plains state have historically experienced little diversity in their classrooms. The conservative culture of many rural communities, as well as the Norwegian and German/Russian heritages brought by immigrants over a century ago, remain prominent throughout the state . . .

Despite this conservative and homogenous background, teachers from low-incidence schools on average appeared to hold relatively neutral attitudes about ELLs. . . . Specifically, low-incidence teachers were the most likely to believe that ELLs tend to perform well academically and to disagree with the statement that ELLs usually come from places with inferior educational systems . . .

Teachers in low-incidence schools also positively believed that their schools welcomed ELLs ($\chi^2(4, n = 410) = 25.94$, $p < .001$). As one teacher remarked, "There have never been any ESL students at our school, but I would assume any student with any difference would be welcomed and supported!"

Walker and colleagues attributed the positivity of these attitudes to the fact that the few ELLs teachers in low-incidence schools have been exposed to were either foreign exchange students from Europe who had moderately proficient English skills and somewhat similar cultural norms, or a small number of students from immigrant families. Although teachers in low-incidence schools were positive on the whole, quantitative analyses showed that they were also the least likely among the three groups to want an ELL placed in their classroom, or to obtain training for working with ELL students.

Teachers in rapid-influx school districts experienced two large waves of refugees from Africa and Eastern Europe in the 1990s. Existing residents became concerned about increasing crime rates and the cost of social services, and many teachers felt that refugee students created discipline problems in the classroom.

The refugees brought other challenges to the rapid-influx schools. Many of the students had little previous formal education; a sizeable number of the junior high and high school refugees were illiterate. The ELL teachers, let alone the mainstream teachers, felt extremely inadequate in helping these students . . .

However, despite the huge challenges, the average attitudes of the mainstream teachers remained relatively neutral to positive. . . . Perhaps the most startling statistic is that 83% (n = 151) of the mainstream teachers in the rapid-influx schools still agreed that ELLs bring needed diversity to the schools, and 74% (n = 135) believed ELLs were welcomed by their schools. Rapid-influx teachers were the most likely to want language-minority students in their classroom [as compared with] the other two demographic groups of teachers ($\chi^2(4, n = 414) = 30.83$, $p < .001$), as well as the most interested in training ($\chi^2(4, n = 419) = 28.99$, $p < .001$) and believing that schools should hire ELL teachers ($\chi^2(4, n = 420) = 12.17$, $p < .05$). They also believed the most strongly in making adaptations for English Language Learners ($\chi^2(4, n = 409) = 18.15$, $p < .01$).

Rapid-influx teachers appeared to realistically understand many of the factors surrounding a language-minority student's acquisition of English and their academic achievement. They were the most likely to understand that English fluency is not achieved in a single year ($\chi^2(4, n = 407) = 20.23$, $p < .001$). They were also the most articulate about understanding that language acquisition is largely dependent on the individual. . . . Rapid-influx teachers frequently qualified their survey responses by saying "it depends" on factors such as the student's prior schooling and their experiences before coming to the US. In stark contrast, low-incidence and migrant-serving teachers did not differentiate between students of different backgrounds. Their attitudes and beliefs appeared to have been shaped by working primarily with only one ethnic group of students, high-status Western Europeans or marginalized Mexican Americans, respectively. Based on the absence of comments qualifying their responses to different ethnic groups, low-incidence and migrant-serving teachers appeared to have generalized these attitudes and beliefs to all English Language Learners.

Finally, teachers in the migrant-serving schools expressed the most negative attitudes.

Teacher attitudes regarding English Language Learners in the migrant-serving schools in this study range from neutral to highly negative. Migrant-serving teachers, for example, were significantly more likely than low or rapid-influx teachers to view language-minority students as poor academic performers and as coming from "places with inferior educational systems." Teachers serving migrant students tended to disagree with the idea that ELLs bring needed diversity to their schools. . . . Compounded with deficit-theory beliefs about ELLs, is the fact that many migrant-serving teachers object to making adaptations for ELLs in the mainstream classroom . . .

Forty-two percent ($n = 15$) of teachers in the migrant-serving schools were either neutral toward or not interested in ELL professional development, even though Hispanic students with a range of English proficiency levels sometimes comprised upwards of 20% of the schools' population during harvest season. Myths and misconceptions about ELL education appeared to have skewed some teachers' attitudes about professional development. One teacher explained her reluctance to participate in professional development by stating, "It would require learning Spanish. I don't know if I want to do that." This presents a conundrum. Professional development works to clear up harmful myths and misconceptions. But if those very myths and misconceptions cause teachers to resist professional

development, then professional development alone is not a viable solution . . .

Migrant-serving teachers in our study were the most likely to admit, compared with low-incidence and rapid-influx teachers, that their schools did not welcome language-minority students and did not embrace their culture or language ($\chi^2(4, n = 410) = 32.49$, $p < .001$). This could be interpreted as an encouraging statistic, suggesting many teachers of migrant students are at least cognizant of their negative attitudes. On the opposite hand, this could be an extremely discouraging statistic if ethnocentric and racist teacher attitudes are so ingrained that teachers feel comfortable candidly expressing them in public. One teacher offered this puzzling but telling comment: "Our school welcomes the students but as a whole doesn't welcome the culture and language . . . "

Why do teachers of migrant students tend to hold these particular negative attitudes more so than other teachers? . . . Migrant students in this region of the state typically attend school only for the first 6–8 weeks in the fall, until the potato and sugar beet harvests are completed. They are among the poorest children in the state. . . . Their culture often places family concerns before education, and migrant children may miss school in order to take care of younger siblings or other family responsibilities. . . . They are often referred to as long-term English Language Learners, because their English acquisition is hindered by frequently changing schools and limited opportunities for interaction with native English speakers. . . .

Walker and colleagues concluded from the low-incidence school data that most teachers do not start out with negative attitudes toward ELL students. Although they tend to have very little training and are vulnerable to misinformation, the attitudes of teachers who have relatively little experience with ELLs tend to be positive and optimistic. The rapid-influx school data show that negative attitudes begin to emerge when untrained (and unsupported) teachers must deal with ELLs, even though teachers in rapid-influx areas have the most realistic understanding of the challenges for educating ELLs. Finally, the migrant-serving school data suggest that when negative attitudes remain unchallenged over long periods of time, highly negative attitudes toward the minority group may diminish their already limited chances for a quality education.

*Walker, A., Shafer, J., & Iiams, M. (2004). "Not in my classroom": Teacher attitudes towards English Language Learners in the mainstream classroom. *NABE Journal of Research and Practice*, 2(1), 130–160. Quoted with permission from the publisher.

TABLE 15.2 Some Analysis and Interpretation Procedures Associated with Each Type of Mixed-Methods Design (Adapted from Creswell, 2005)

Type of Design	Examples of Analytic and Interpretive Procedures
Explanatory (QUAN-qual)	*Following up on extreme cases*: Qualitative information is used to help make sense of extreme cases identified through quantitative measures.
	Explaining results: Qualitative interviews are used to help illuminate responses to surveys and other quantitative measures.
	Using a typology: Qualitative themes are identified on the basis of factor analyses of quantitative data.
Exploratory (QUAL-quan)	*Locating an instrument*: Quantitative measures are found that reflect themes identified through qualitative data collection.
	Developing an instrument: Quantitative measures are created on the basis of themes identified through qualitative information gathering.
	Using extreme qualitative cases: Quantitative surveys are used to shed light on extreme cases identified through qualitative information gathering.
Triangulation (QUAN-QUAL)	*Quantifying qualitative data*: Comparisons are made between quantitative and qualitative information on frequencies of particular events or behaviors.
	Qualifying quantitative data: Comparisons are made between quantitative factors identified through factor analysis and themes identified by means of qualitative methods.
	Consolidating data: Quantitative and qualitative information are combined to form new variables.

How to Conduct Mixed-Methods Research

Following is the general sequence of steps in a mixed-methods study:

- Formulate, at least tentatively, the goal of the study.
- Determine whether a mixed-methods design is appropriate. Access to both quantitative and qualitative data is needed, as is expertise in both types of research. It should be clear in advance what a mixed-methods approach would contribute over and above a carefully designed study that relies on just one method.
- Choose a particular mixed-methods design (explanatory, exploratory, or triangulation). The choice of design, as always, will depend on the nature of the research question and the availability of participants. The intended prominence of quantitative versus qualitative data collection also determines the type of design.

- Develop the quantitative and qualitative research questions. How explicitly each question is formulated will depend on the type of design. For sequential designs (explanatory or exploratory), the research question underlying the second phase of data collection may be tentative at the outset of the study.

- Work out the specific details of the design. Careful planning is needed for a triangulation design, since data collection using different methods will be carried out simultaneously. Some flexibility is possible and may even be essential for the second phase of each of the sequential designs.

- Gather, analyze, and interpret data. The extent to which these are distinct steps, and the specific approaches taken, will depend on the type of design.

Evaluation of Mixed-Methods Research

As noted earlier, mixed-methods research builds on the relative strengths of quantitative and qualitative approaches. The researcher's choice of measures and analytic procedures reflects assumptions about what each type of method contributes to the overall design.

Contributions of Quantitative Methods

Quantitative methods contribute precision. If you wish to study the incidence of aggressive behavior in a playground setting, quantitative measures can be developed and implemented in a consistent way across participants. Rather than observing that "some" or "many" participants in the study exhibited aggression, quantitative analysis tells you exactly how many participants behaved aggressively, and whether the frequency is significantly greater among boys versus girls, on Fridays versus Mondays, when distinguishing between physical and verbal aggression, and so on. Precise measurement and analysis in turn contribute to the generalizability of the results, as may other aspects of quantitative approaches such as the logic of experimental design (see Spotlight on Research 15.2 for an illustration).

Contributions of Qualitative Methods

Qualitative methods contribute contextual information about individuals and settings. If the extent of aggressive behavior revealed by your quantitative measure is especially high or low among particular groups, at particular times, or overall, qualitative interviews may reveal some of the contributing factors. Moreover, the interviews might reveal information about questions that cannot be readily addressed in quantitative measures. What the observer perceives as aggressive behavior may not be interpreted as an act of aggression by the aggressor and/or the target of the behavior. Further discussion with participants may provide a deeper understanding of their subjective experiences.

The study described in Spotlight on Research 15.2 illustrates how precision and contextual insight are provided by each phase of an explanatory mixed-methods design.

Should Students Choose Their Own Groups for Collaborative Work?

When teachers assign group projects, they often take the lead in dividing their classes into groups, even though students express interest in selecting the groups themselves. We might ask what would happen if students got what they wanted in this case. Would students be satisfied with their self-chosen groups, and would they still wish to have a choice in the future? In a 2004 study published in the *Journal of Instructional Psychology**, Sidney Mitchell, Rosemary Reilly, Gillian Bramwell, Frank Lilly, and Anthony Solnosky studied the consequences of allowing high school students to choose their own groups for lab projects in science classes. The researchers used an explanatory mixed-methods design that incorporated elements of both experimental research as well as qualitative interviews. The goal of the study was to describe changes in student attitudes once they have been allowed to choose their own lab groups.

Mitchell and colleagues focused on the five classes of one high school science teacher in Quebec. Participants consisted of 139 10th- and 11th-graders divided across two "low-achieving" (LA) classes, two "normal-achieving" (NA) classes, and one "high-achieving" honors (HO) class. The study was carried out over a 6-week period during which students participated in two labs. The quantitative phase of the study reflected a pretest–posttest nonequivalent control group design (a type of quasi-experimental design described in Chapter 7). The pretest consisted of a quantitative attitudinal measure known as the Classroom Life Scale, or CLS, a list of statements that students rate as being more or less reflective of their own attitudes. The rating scale for each statement ranges from 1 (completely false) to 5 (completely true).

The CLS consists of several subscales measuring students' attitudes on cooperativeness, feelings of alienation, academic self-esteem, academic support, goal and resource interdependence, external motivation, cohesion, grading practices, independent learning, competitive learning, controversy, valuing homogeneity and heterogeneity. Two additional questions were included; these dealt with preferences for choosing group members (e.g., "I prefer to choose the students I work with" or "I prefer the teacher choose the students I work with").

Following the pretest, students either chose group membership or were assigned to groups for the first of the two labs. Once both labs were completed, the data were analyzed quantitatively, and qualitative interviews were then conducted to help illuminate the quantitative results.

Allocation of classes to student-selected (S-s) or teacher-selected (T-s) groups was done purposively, to ensure that at least one LA and one NA class was S-s and their cohorts were T-s; the honors class experienced both conditions (T-s/S-s). T-s classes acted as controls as this was the standard instructional approach employed by the teacher . . .

Each lab was approximately three weeks in length, with three one-week units in each lab. Groups were composed of three students and each was assigned a specific task role: experimenter, recorder, and materials coordinator. Students were in these groups for three units of instruction (i.e., one lab), and after each unit was completed they had to change roles within the group (normally one week). This ensured that all students had the opportunity to work in all roles. At the end of the first lab students were required to change groups. In S-s groups the only criteria was at least one person had to change to a new group or all three could change. Even though only one person was required to change groups, all members were still required to choose (e.g., who stays and who goes?). In the T-s groups the teacher assigned students to new groupings and all three members changed. After all students were in new groups they followed the same procedure for groupwork concerning task roles. At the end of the second lab, the CLS was administered again.

After the second administration of the survey, the researchers from McGill began analysis. Preliminary aggregated results were first shared with the teacher. These results led to additional questions and the decision was made to conduct focus groups with students who had selected their own groups in the hopes that their insights could shed some light on the data and supplement the quantitative results.

Mitchell and colleagues hypothesized that students who were allowed to choose their own groups would develop negative attitudes toward making such choices in the future. CLS responses were analyzed in order to evaluate this hypothesis. (See Chapter 11 for an explanation of the ANOVA statistics reported below.)

A 3 (group) × 2 (test) repeated measures multivariate analysis of variance revealed a significant multivariate main effect for test (pretest/posttest) . . . $F(2, 118) = 54.20$, $p < .001$, $\eta^2 = .32$ and a significant interaction for group . . . × test . . . $F(2, 118) = 12.31$, $p < .001$, $\eta^2 = .17$. As predicted, students in the S-s and T-s/S-s groups experienced a negative shift in their overall preferences for choosing groupmates from pretest to posttest . . .

As there were two low-achieving classes, two normally achieving, and one honors class we decided to explore if there were differences between the classes on the question of preference regardless of treatment condition. Results indicate that low-achieving students demonstrated a sharper decline in preference for choosing groupmates than the other students in the other classes. A 5 (class) × 2 (test) repeated measures multivariate analysis of variance revealed a significant multivariate main effect for test . . . $F(2, 116) = 47.39$, $p < .001$, $\eta^2 = .29$, and a significant interaction for class . . . × test . . . $F(4, 116) = 6.51$, $p < .001$, $\eta^2 = .183$.

Finally, as there was a shift in attitudes toward preference in the S-s groups we decided to explore if choice had an influence on overall liking for cooperative learning. We tested the subscale dealing with overall liking for and willingness to engage in cooperative learning. A 3 (group) × 2 (cooperative learning) repeated measures multivariate analysis of variance revealed that choice did not have a negative effect on liking cooperative learning. In fact, attitudes toward cooperative learning were more positive on posttest regardless of group . . . $F(1, 118) = 3.94$, $p < .05$, $\eta^2 = .032$.

After quantitative data analysis was complete, Mitchell and colleagues interviewed focus groups consisting of six to eight students from each class.

To illuminate grouping preferences, three questions were posed to the focus groups: 1) What were some of the reasons you wanted to choose your own group?; 2) What happened to change your preferences?; and 3) Why did females have a bigger shift in their opinion? Finally, students were also asked to provide recommendations for future groupings. This methodology was chosen to: 1) elicit perceptions, feelings, attitudes, and ideas concerning group selection; 2) gain the assistance of the students in interpreting the results; and

3) provide a versatile, dynamic source of data directly from participants . . .

Three themes emerged from the focus group interviews: control and responsibility, the potential for conflict, and achievement versus feelings.

Emergent themes for wishing to choose groups were centered on the students' desire for control and responsibility. Students tended to see themselves as better judges than the teacher of a "good" group member since they knew each other outside of class. . . . Students in the honors science class also expressed a desire for control that would insure equal responsibility for grades, since these would be important for their future education. . . . In addition, a developmental theme that reflected the adolescent's life stage (i.e., a desire for autonomy) was also expressed. Choosing their group meant being more adult . . .

Students also tended to question an assumed link between academic ability and good group skills. One male student remarked, "Marks aren't always the best way to choose groups. Grades don't tell you how well people will work together." It appears that students, like teachers, were searching for those criteria and qualities that might insure group success.

When asked about the shift in attitude toward choosing groups, many students pointed to the dawning realization of the potential conflict between a "good friend" and a "good team member." . . . Part of this was the tendency to socialize rather than work. A young man admitted, "With friends there can be lots of talking. With people you don't know there is nothing else to do except work." . . .

A surprising and forceful perspective was the attitude that the emotional dynamics could undermine the group process and success, as well as inflict harm on others, by rejecting or hurting those who are not known. "I'm too shy to say to someone I don't know that they aren't working hard enough. Friends accept you. You can say stuff like that and they won't think you're mean," one female student remarked . . .

In addition, the students expressed awareness that, in reality, they lacked the skill in judging effective team members. Several students repeated the following sentiment: "It's hard to tell who to choose. Who will put in the effort, and who won't? I don't know how to tell how well we'll work together." Members of the science classes also admitted that maybe the teacher did have more expertise in choosing groups . . .

Trends in focus group responses for males and females differed, demonstrating the emergence of rigid gender-stereotyping common in small group activity in high school settings (Hurley, 1996; Lafrance, 1991; Rehling, 1996; Sommers, 1992). Male students tended to characterize themselves as more assertive and able to cope with the conflict in groups. One young man remarked, "Guys are totally honest. They don't care. They say what they think." . . . Female students also repeated these stereotypes, noting, " . . . Guys are more willing to speak up and tell off those who aren't willing to do their share. Not a lot of girls are assertive."

Young women in the honors science class tended to reflect the attitude that "Girls don't like to waste time. They want to be in a group that's going to work hard." Young women in the other science classes tended to focus on feelings and connections with others, mirroring the theory found in the literature on adolescent women's development (Brown & Gilligan, 1992; Gilligan, 1990; Kaplan, Klein, & Gleason, 1991). Hurting friends was a major concern for one female student, "You cannot take the chance of not choosing your friends." Another thought that future connections with their friends would be disrupted if they were put in a position of having to choose or not choose them . . .

Mitchell and colleagues also commented on how tracking affected students' attitudes and experiences.

Differences in the responses were also observed across the tracked classes, which further supports the evidence for an interaction effect between achievement ability and the context of group work (Townsend & Hicks, 1995). . . . LA students came to the realization that one's friends did not necessarily make effective groupmates. LA students recommended a shift from a student-centered class to a more teacher-centered class with a stronger emphasis on lecturing. Although the questionnaire results did not yield significant findings on this point, discussion did reveal that several students in the low-achieving classes did not want to work in groups and this was independent of treatment condition (S-s or T-s). One young man captured the sentiment of many of the students when he stated, "Why would I want to work with them [others in the class]? We're all in the same boat. They can't help me. The teacher should just teach." This statement is further indication that low-achieving students in tracked classrooms are placed at a disadvantage.

One of the primary arguments for employing heterogeneous groups is that it benefits low-achieving students who are able to learn from their more capable peers (Webb & Palinscar, 1996). Under these conditions, low-achieving students benefit from a form of scaffolded instruction from their more capable peers. While this may be a positive outcome in classrooms where students of all achievement levels co-exist. It is not the case when students are tracked according to achievement. In tracked classrooms the low-achieving students are forced to work with others of similar achievement. As a result, the benefits of working with more capable peers are lost in tracked classrooms.

Mitchell and colleagues concluded that high school students should be allowed to choose their own groups on some occasions, but that the effectiveness of doing so will depend on many factors. Clearly, some students, at least in some classes, would rather let the teacher choose.

*Mitchell, S. N., Reilly, R., Bramwell, F. G., Lilly, F., & Solnosky, A. (2004). Friendship and choosing groupmates: Preferences for teacher-selected vs. student-selected groupings in high school science classes. Journal of Instructional Psychology, 31(1), 20–32.

How to Evaluate a Specific Mixed-Methods Study

The following questions will help guide you when evaluating the quality of a mixed-methods study.

- Do the researchers provide a rationale for combining quantitative and qualitative methods? Is the rationale clear?

- Does each method make a significant contribution to the study? Rationale aside, are the quantitative and qualitative components truly essential to the design, or is one just an afterthought or minor addition to the other?

- What type of mixed-methods design was used? Are the quantitative and qualitative methods clearly integrated, or are they merely operating "in parallel"?

- Exactly how were the two types of methods integrated? Did integration take place at the level of research questions, sampling, data collection and analysis, and/or interpretation?

An additional question is whether each method is properly carried out, according to the partially separate standards of quantitative and qualitative research. In a mixed-methods study, each method may compensate for the general limitations of the other type, but it cannot fix method-specific limitations. For example, a qualitative phase may provide the richness of description that quantitative measures cannot provide, but the study cannot be good if the quantitative measures are deeply flawed, owing to poor reliability and validity (see Chapter 6). Likewise, a quantitative approach may provide precise statistical comparisons that qualitative approaches cannot provide, but the study cannot be good if the qualitative component is deeply flawed, owing to subject and observer effects (see Chapter 13). One method cannot fix specific flaws in the way the other one is implemented, in other words. In a good mixed-methods study, each method simply contributes something that the other method does not readily contribute.

General Evaluation of Mixed-Methods Designs

Mixed-methods research does not, simply by its existence, bridge the gap between quantitative and qualitative traditions. Researchers who have a strong preference for one tradition may not be swayed by the importance of incorporating methods from the other. Moreover, just as quantitative and qualitative designs each have limitations, so mixed-methods research is limited in its own somewhat distinct ways. Limitations of mixed-methods designs include the need for labor-intensive data collection and analysis, as well as the need for two largely distinct research traditions to be integrated rather than simply pasted together. Mixed-methods studies are sometimes criticized on the grounds of insufficient or superficial integration of components. This criticism is countered by the small but growing number of books and articles in which the conceptual and methodological rationale for mixed-methods approaches is carefully analyzed. Examples of this type of analysis can be seen in Table 15.2, and in Spotlight on Research 15.3.

A Look Ahead

Chapters 7–14 introduced quantitative and qualitative research designs. In this chapter I described how these two traditions can be meaningfully integrated.

In the next three chapters, you will read about educational research designs that are purely applied in focus. The topic of Chapter 16 is action research, which may incorporate qualitative or quantitative elements (or both).

Why Mix Methods? A Typology for Special Education Research

In a 2006 article published in *Learning Disabilities: A Contemporary Journal**, Kathleen Collins, Anthony Onwuegbuzie, and Ida Sutton present a typology of reasons for conducting mixed-methods research in special education. Through this typology, you can see why researchers develop mixed-methods approaches, and you can obtain guidance in the creation of your own mixed-methods design.

As a first step in developing their typology, Collins and colleagues conducted a thorough review of existing literature.

Our original intent was to determine a typology of reasons for conducting mixed-methods research from articles published in special education journals. However, because a limited number of mixed-methods studies have been conducted by special education researchers (Collins et al., 2006), we quickly came to the conclusion that this body of literature would not yield a comprehensive typology. Thus, we decided to use the following two sources . . . (a) the 494 published journal articles identified by Collins, Onwuegbuzie, and Jiao (2005) that used the phrase "mixed method(s)" published between 2000 and 2005 across 14 major electronic databases (e.g., PsycINFO, CINAHL, ERIC) representing the fields of psychology, sociology, social services, education, business, and nursing and allied health; and (b) theoretical/methodological/conceptual articles and books on mixed methods, including those presented in the previous section (e.g., Greene et al., 1989), that had been published between 1973 (e.g., Sieber, 1973) and the time when the present article was written.

With respect to our second list of articles, we obtained methodological articles in the area of mixed methods either from literature databases or by attending methodological paper presentations at state . . . regional . . . national . . . and international . . . conferences over the last decade.

In addition to searching the literature database and collecting methodological articles from professional meetings, we used the "snowballing" approach to obtaining methodological manuscripts. Specifically, (a) the reference list of every methodological paper was extracted via the snowballing strategy, and (b) was examined to determine if it contained relevant articles that we had overlooked. This technique led to the identification of several additional articles. The method also helped us to validate our choice of articles . . .

Collins and colleagues then carried out a content analysis of the literature. The focus of the content analysis was on reconstructing why researchers conduct mixed-methods research. Four themes emerged: participant enrichment, instrument fidelity, treatment integrity, and significance enhancement.

Participant Enrichment

Participant enrichment represents the mixing of quantitative and qualitative techniques for the rationale of optimizing the sample. . . . In the field of special education, it is not unusual for researchers to study populations who exhibit a heterogeneous set of characteristics that differentially impact individuals' instructional responsiveness (e.g., individuals with learning disabilities). . . . In such cases, the researcher could conduct a qualitative and/or quantitative pilot study to determine the best ways to identify members of these various populations. For example, the researcher could use snowballing techniques to identify additional participants by asking existing participants to nominate potential population members. . . . Alternatively, documents such as case records that could be examined to obtain quantitative information (e.g., test scores, referral rates, prevalence rates) could be used to identify potential participants.

In special education research, it is also not unusual to study populations that represent a unique subset of the general population in terms of characteristics such that it is difficult to recruit them (e.g., students with multiple disabilities and/or low incidence disabilities). Again, interviews could be used to assess both suitability and willingness to participate in the study . . .

[P]articipant enrichment techniques only lead to a mixed-methods study if either (a) both quantitative and qualitative techniques are used at one or more phases of the study (e.g., pre-study phase, post-study phase), or (b) an approach (e.g., qualitative) is used to enrich the sample that is different from the approach used in the main study (e.g., quantitative).

Instrument Fidelity

[T]he instrument fidelity theme or rationale refers to steps taken by the researcher to maximize the appropriateness and/or utility of the instruments used in the study, whether quantitative or qualitative. For example, a researcher might

conduct a pilot study either to assess the appropriateness and/or utility of existing instruments with a view to making modifications where needed, or creating and improving a new instrument. Alternatively, in studies that utilize an evolving design, the researcher could assess instrument fidelity on an ongoing basis and make modifications, where needed, at one or more phases of the inquiry. . . .

Instrument fidelity also applies to cases where the instrument is the researcher himself/herself. This might involve the researcher using quantitative and/or qualitative techniques to maximize her/his ability to collect relevant data that indicate fidelity. As is the case for participant enhancement, use of instrument fidelity techniques only lead to a mixed-methods study if either (a) both quantitative and qualitative techniques are used at one or more phases of the study (e.g., pre-study phase, post-study phase), or (b) an approach (e.g., qualitative) is used to assess or obtain instrument fidelity that is different from the approach used in the main study (e.g., quantitative).

Treatment Integrity

Treatment integrity represents the mixing of quantitative and qualitative techniques for the rationale of assessing the fidelity of interventions, treatments, or programs. This rationale is particularly pertinent for research in special education in which an intervention is administered either randomly or non-randomly to some or all participants. . . . In order for an intervention to possess integrity, it must be implemented as intended . . .

With respect to quantitative assessment of treatment integrity, a fidelity score can be obtained by calculating the percentage of the intervention component that was implemented fully or estimating the average (e.g., mean) degree to which the treatment or program was implemented (Gersten, Fuchs, Coyne, Greenwood, & Innocenti, 2005). Qualitative assessment of treatment integrity could involve the use of tools such as interviews, focus groups, and observations. Clearly, the use of both quantitative and qualitative techniques for assessing treatment integrity would yield the greatest insights . . .

Whatever technique(s) is used to assess treatment integrity, it is essential to determine whether the level or degree of implementation is consistent across different conditions and intervention providers. . . . As before, use of treatment integrity techniques only lead to a mixed-methods study if either (a) both quantitative and qualitative strategies are used

at one or more phases of the study (e.g., pre-study phase, post-study phase), or (b) an approach (e.g., quantitative) is used to assess treatment integrity that is different from the approach used in the main study (e.g., qualitative).

Significance Enhancement

Significance enhancement represents mixing quantitative and qualitative techniques for the rationale of enhancing researchers' interpretations of data. A researcher can use qualitative data to enhance statistical analyses, quantitative data to enhance qualitative analyses, or both. Even though researchers working with quantitative data traditionally use statistical analyses and those working with qualitative data are more apt to utilize qualitative data analyses, quantitative and qualitative data analysis techniques may be used side-by-side to enhance the interpretation of significant findings in special education research (Onwuegbuzie & Leech, 2004) . . .

[For example] in concurrent mixed analyses, quantitative and qualitative data are collected at approximately the same point in time, and the data analysis typically does not occur until all the data . . . have been collected. Questionnaires that extract both quantitative and qualitative data may be subjected to concurrent mixed analyses.

For example, let us suppose that researchers were interested in examining the relationship between levels of anxiety and academic performance among elementary school students identified as having a learning disability. These investigators could administer a Likert-format scale measuring self-concept that has been found consistently to possess adequate psychometric properties. Then, they could correlate scores from the anxiety measure with a set of achievement scores. A correlation that was both statistically and practically significant would suggest an important relationship between these two variables; however, because of the correlational design used, causal statements would not be justified. Including one or more open-ended items asking students to describe the role that anxiety plays in their perceptions of instructional effectiveness could enhance the meaningfulness of this relationship. That is, the extent to which respondents indicate that anxiety negatively impacts their levels of performance would provide the researchers with more justification to make causal statements. Thus, the inclusion of qualitative data analyses would enable students not only to answer questions of who, where, how many, how much, and what is the relationship between specific variables, they also would be able to address why and how questions.

Concurrent mixed analyses also can be used in the quantitative phase of studies by qualitizing data, a common term used by mixed-methods researchers to denote a process by which quantitative data are converted into data that may be analyzed qualitatively (Tashakkori & Teddlie, 1998). One way of qualitizing data is to use narrative profile formation (i.e., modal profiles, average profiles, holistic profiles, comparative profiles, normative profiles), wherein narrative descriptions are constructed from statistical data.

Collins and colleagues described numerous other examples of the themes identified in their content analysis, then outlined a Rationale and Purpose (RAP) model in which the four themes are used to account for the development of mixed-models designs. Each theme (or "rationale type") may reflect how a particular researcher converted a mono-method study (exclusively quantitative or qualitative) into a mixed-methods one.

For example, a quantitative study may be transformed to a mixed-methods study via the participant enrichment rationale if the researcher uses qualitative techniques to identify obstacles to the recruitment and consent of participants or to prebrief them (i.e., before), to replace participants who dropped out of the study (i.e., during), or to debrief participants (i.e., after). Further, a qualitative study may be transformed to a mixed-methods study via the integrity fidelity rationale if the researcher uses quantitative techniques to assess the interrater reliability of observers before the study, during the study, or after the study.

A quantitative study may be transformed to a mixed-methods study via the treatment integrity rationale if the researcher uses qualitative techniques to refine interventions during a pilot study (i.e., before), to gain

more information about the intervention (i.e., during), or to determine the level of implementation of an intervention (i.e., after). A qualitative study may be transformed to a mixed-methods study via the significance enhancement rationale if the researcher uses quantitative techniques to use quantitative findings from a pilot study to inform the qualitative procedures (i.e., before), to triangulate the qualitative findings (i.e., during), or to determine the effect size of qualitative results (i.e., after). These are only a few examples of the myriad ways of illustrating how qualitative approaches can convert a mono-method study to a mixed-methods investigation and how quantitative approaches can convert a mono-method study to a mixed-methods inquiry.

Once the rationale type(s), purpose(s) for mixing, and the mixing phase(s) of the investigation have been selected, the researcher can use the research question(s) to determine the paradigm emphasis (i.e., deciding whether to give the quantitative or qualitative components of the study the dominant status or give both components equal status). Thus, decisions made regarding the rationale type(s), purpose(s) for mixing, mixing phase(s), and paradigm emphasis lead to the determination of the major elements of the research design. . . . We call this a Rationale and Purpose (RAP) model for designing mixed-methods studies. By using our RAP model, which involves making four sets of decisions, special education researchers will get the most out of their mixed-methods research designs.

*Collins, K. M. T., Onwuegbuzie, A. J., & Sutton, I. L. (2006). A model incorporating the rationale and purpose for conducting mixed-methods research in special education and beyond. *Learning Disabilities: A Contemporary Journal, 4*(1), 67–100. Quoted with permission from the publisher.

Applications: A Guide for Beginning Researchers

Here are some ideas from the chapter that will help you plan your research:

- Decide whether a truly mixed-methods approach is the best design for addressing your research question, or whether it would be best to conduct a quantitative study enhanced by a small amount of qualitative information (or vice versa).
- Choose the type of mixed-methods design that most effectively addresses your research question.
- Ensure that the quantitative and qualitative phases of your research are integrated and complement each other.

- Ensure that each phase of your mixed-methods design meets the standards of quality for that particular approach (quantitative or qualitative).

Chapter Summary

Qualitative and quantitative studies reflect distinct epistemologies and methods even though each type of study may incorporate elements of the other. In contrast, qualitative and quantitative methods both play an essential and integrated role in a mixed-methods design. The methods may be carried out simultaneously or sequentially. One method may predominate or each may play an equally central role. The ordering and prominence of each method yields three major types of mixed-methods designs: explanatory, exploratory, and triangulation.

Different ways of classifying the purposes of mixed-methods studies are described throughout the chapter. In each study, quantitative methods contribute precision while qualitative methods provide contextual depth. Each method contributes distinctive advantages but cannot compensate for flaws in the implementation of the other method. Evaluation of mixed-methods studies are based on general considerations as well as method-specific criteria.

Key Terms

Mixed-methods designs	**Explanatory design**	**QUAL-quan**
Phase	**QUAN-qual**	**Triangulation design**
	Exploratory design	**QUAN-QUAL**

Exercises

For questions 1–4, refer to the following passage:

The results of two studies of leadership in education are reported here. The purpose of the first study was (a) to determine [quantitatively] the degree to which educational leaders were perceived to use transformational and transactional leadership behaviors, and (b) to determine which behaviors were best able to predict follower satisfaction and leader effectiveness. The second study was designed as a qualitative follow-up to the first. Its purpose was to clarify aspects of transformational leadership that could not be explained on the basis of the quantitative data coded earlier.

(*Kirby, Paradise, & King, 1992, p. 204*)

1. What type of design seems to have been used?

a) Explanatory mixed-methods
b) Exploratory mixed-methods
c) Triangulation mixed-methods
d) Quantitative

2. How many phases were there?

a) One

b) Two

c) Three

d) Four

3. What specific approach to data analysis seems to have been used? (The following options are taken from Table 15.2.)

a) "Developing an instrument"

b) "Comparing results"

c) "Explaining results"

d) "Consolidating data"

4. If this study truly employed a mixed-methods design, which of the following is most likely to be true?

a) The details of both studies were planned in advance so that it would not have mattered which study was conducted first.

b) The details of the measures used in the second study were not finalized until the results of the first study were analyzed.

c) The details of neither study was planned out very specifically in advance.

For questions 5–7, refer to the following description:

> *A researcher conducts interviews of a sample of kindergarten teachers as to what they consider helpful instructional resources. Using a qualitative coding scheme, the researcher identifies nine resources that appear to be of greatest importance to the teachers. The researchers construct a survey that consists of these nine resources along with nine other instructional resources discussed in the research literature (but not mentioned very often by the teachers in this study). The survey is administered to a new sample of kindergarten teachers. These teachers are asked to indicate, on a 7-point scale, the instructional importance of each resource in the survey. The researcher then conducts statistical comparisons between ratings for each set of nine resources, including an analysis of whether teachers' ratings are influenced by their age and years of teaching experience.*

5. What type of design seems to have been used?

a) Explanatory mixed-methods

b) Exploratory mixed-methods

c) Triangulation mixed-methods

d) Quantitative

6. What specific approach to data analysis seems to have been used? (The following options are taken from Table 15.2.)

a) "Developing an instrument"

b) "Comparing results"

c) "Explaining results"

d) "Consolidating data"

7. Would it make sense if the researcher had interviewed the new sample of teachers after they completed the survey, in order to learn more about their survey responses? If interviews such as this were included, how many phases would the study have?

a) Yes; two

b) No; two

c) Yes; three

d) No; three

8. *Critical thinking question*: A biased (i.e., nonrepresentative) sample limits the generalizability of any kind of study. In what ways might biased sampling be especially problematic for mixed-methods designs?

Answers to Exercises

1. a   **2.** b   **3.** c   **4.** b   **5.** b   **6.** a   **7.** c

8. *Possible answer*: First, if the results of quantitative and qualitative data collection corroborate each other, the researcher may feel confident about the generality of the results. But since the sample is biased, the results might only reflect a small segment of the population. Second, the researcher might be misled by either the quantitative or the qualitative findings if the sample resembles the rest of the population in response to only one type of measure. For example, the relationship between political affiliation and views on education-related legislation such as the No Child Left Behind Act, as measured by a simple quantitative survey, may yield expected results, but if the sample is biased, qualitative interviews may yield a relatively narrow range of themes.

Suggestions for Further Reading

Research Article: Frederickson, N., Reed, P., & Clifford, V. (2005). Evaluating Web-supported learning versus lecture-based teaching: Quantitative and qualitative perspectives. *Higher Education, 50,* 645–654.

This triangulation mixed-methods study compares the effects of a graduate-level class delivered either in traditional lecture format or through Internet-based methods.

Application Article: Simons, L., & Cleary, B. (2005). Student and community perceptions of the "value-added" for service-learners. *Journal of Experiential Education, 28*(2), 164–188.

This explanatory mixed-methods study focuses on the perceptions of students who participated in service learning as part of an undergraduate course requirement.

Extension Article: Sammons, P., Siraj-Blatchford, I., Sylva, K., Melhuish, E., Taggart, B., & Elliot, K. (2005). Investigating the effects of pre-school provision: Using mixed methods in the EPPE Research. *International Journal of Social Research Methodology, 8*(3), 207–224.

This UK study on the cognitive and social effects of preschool illustrates how the mixed-methods approach can be applied to a longitudinal design.

Image Source/Getty Images

CHAPTER 16

Action Research

After studying this chapter, you will be able to answer the following questions:

- What is action research and why is it conducted?

- What are the basic methods used in action research studies?

- What are the two types of action research?

- How should action research be evaluated?

This chapter will prepare you to do the following:

- Understand and evaluate action research reports

- Select an action research design that best suits your research question

- Design an action research study

As noted in Chapter 1, educational researchers rarely seek knowledge for its own sake. Instead, researchers hope to contribute to both scientific knowledge as well as educational practice. The quantitative, qualitative, and mixed-methods designs you read about in Chapters 7–15 all reflect a combination of scientific and practical goals.

In this chapter and the two that follow, you will learn about approaches to research that have a purely applied focus. Although the studies that employ these approaches may contribute to scientific knowledge, the primary goal of the research is to evaluate and improve the situations of particular individuals, groups, and programs. Ideally, the results of purely applied research have immediate benefits for participants.

Introduction to Action Research

Action research, my focus in this chapter, is way for teachers and other educational practitioners to study and attempt to solve the everyday problems they encounter. The general characteristics of action research are given below. As you can see, action research is conducted by practitioners who address educational problems in a local setting (such as a classroom or school) by introducing changes in the setting and reflecting on the results. The most distinctive aspect of action research is that practitioners carry out the research themselves, rather than merely participating in the studies, offering guidance to academic researchers from the sidelines, or reading about the results in a professional journal.

Action research is:

- Conducted by practitioners
- Designed to address specific educational problems
- Carried out in local settings
- Carried out by introducing changes and reflecting on the results

Later in the chapter you will find that some kinds of action research focus on highly specific problems and settings, while other varieties focus on broader changes that may lead to the empowerment of individuals and organizations. Although many different kinds of practitioners conduct action research, the approach is of particular interest to teachers who find conventional forms of educational research to be abstruse, impractical, or otherwise not particularly relevant to their specific classroom needs. Hence even though teachers are not the only type of action researcher, there are many references in the action research literature to the "teacher-researcher."

Consider a 2005 study by Tonia Villano, a social studies teacher who was concerned that her fifth-graders were finding it difficult to understand key passages in their textbooks. Villano addressed this problem by sharing picture books with the students prior to their reading more advanced descriptions of the same material in the textbook. Villano found that student interest and comprehension were enhanced by the use of the picture books, which provided students with factual information as well as a conceptual foundation for textbook material. Given the success of the picture books, Villano's next step was to determine whether poetic material could also serve as a useful prelearning strategy. She chose to read and discuss "A Seaman's Shanty," for example, as well as the first stanza of the "Star Spangled Banner" as an introduction to textbook material on the War of 1812. Villano found that discussions of the poetic material also helped to stimulate student interest and learning.

Villano's study illustrates action research because it was conducted by a practitioner (a fifth-grade social studies teacher) who attempted to address a specific problem (student difficulty in comprehending textbook material) in a local setting (one fifth-grade classroom) by introducing change in the setting (using picture books and poems for prelearning) and evaluating the results. Villano's extension of her results with picture books to poetic material reflects another important characteristic of action research: the ongoing, iterative process of using the results of one change or set of changes as a basis for introducing further changes and evaluating their effects. Action research often reflects an ongoing process of refinement as the practitioner seeks increasingly desirable solutions to educational problems.

Although the roots of action research can be traced to the educational philosophies of John Dewey and others, the term "action research" and the basic principles of this approach were formulated by social psychologist Kurt Lewin in the 1940s. Lewin was interested in developing better methods for problem solving through group discussion and, in most general terms, the principles he outlined inform current action research methods.

Action Research Methods

Although most action research is qualitative, the methods used may be quantitative, qualitative, or mixed. In this section, the general sequence of steps in action research is outlined. This sequence, reflected in the work of Lewin, Kemmis (1994), Mills (2003), and others, consists of reflection, planning, action, and further reflection.

Reflection

The first step in action research is for the practitioner to identify a problem by reflecting on something he or she has observed in an educational setting. In the study described earlier, Villano observed that her fifth-grade class was struggling to understand their textbooks. Upon reflection, she decided that this problem is both serious and resolvable. Other kinds of problems that might give rise to an action research study include the following:

- Social isolation on the part of an immigrant student
- Poor motivation among students in a certain class
- The need for a particular teacher to receive additional training
- Insufficient access to vocational resources among a particular class of seniors
- Discrimination against certain groups of students and families in a school district
- Conflict between administrators and teachers concerning a new policy

Planning

Once the practitioner has identified a problem, the next step is to develop a plan of action. In developing the plan, the practitioner may conduct a literature review, consult with experts, and/or confer with colleagues. The resulting plan consists of a concrete set of steps for addressing the problem, including a strategy for introducing change as well as a method for collecting information about the effects of the change. Villano, for example, chose specific picture books and poems as part of a preplanned strategy for helping students, and she decided in advance to make informal assessments of how much students benefited.

Action

Once the practitioner has developed a plan of action, the next step is to act—to introduce pertinent changes and observe the results. Although Villano did not use formal measures, some action researchers systematically collect data by means of quantitative and/or qualitative measures administered during the "action" stage of their research. More broadly, the main approaches to data collection in action research have been referred to as the "three Es": experiencing, enquiring, and examining (Mills, 2003).

- Experiencing consists of participant or passive observation carried out by the practitioner.
- Enquiring consists of interviews with participants, or the administration of tests or some other measures.
- Examining consists of content analysis of written records, student work, lesson plans, newsletters, artifacts, and so on.

The action researcher may make use of one, two, or all three of these methods of data collection. The specific methods are usually qualitative and informal, although there are exceptions. For example, some action research studies make use of experimental or causal–comparative designs, in which participants are divided into experimental and comparison groups, and statistical comparisons among means or frequencies are reported.

The fact that action research tends to be qualitative and informal is not a limitation per se. Teachers are trained to be teachers, not researchers, and action research is an extension of what good teachers naturally do: reflecting on problems in the classroom, trying out solutions, evaluating the results of the solutions, and continuing to reflect on how to better serve the needs of the students. Action research that benefits students is successful research.

Reflection

Once the practitioner has introduced a change or changes and collected information, the next step is to reflect on what the results mean. The practitioner evaluates how effectively the original problem was addressed by asking whether students benefited, and by attempting to understand what happened if they did not. The practitioner may also attempt to communicate successful results to colleagues, experts, and other interested parties. Disseminating the results of action research may not advance scientific knowledge, but it can foster improvements in the way that teachers and other practitioners serve their students. In Villano's case, the use of picture books and poems as prelearning strategies appeared to be quite effective in both sparking interest and enhancing learning. Villano published a report of her research in *The Reading Teacher*, a peer-reviewed journal written primarily for the practicing teacher.

In Spotlight on Research 16.1 you can read about an action research study in which the basic steps of action research are clearly delineated.

Reducing Acting-Out Behavior through Practical Action Research

In a 2004 study reported in *Teaching Exceptional Children**, Sharon Schoen and Jen Nolen described an action research study in which Nolen attempted to decrease the extent of acting-out behavior of one of her sixth-graders, a 12-year-old boy who participated in both general and special education classes. Schoen and Nolen divided their report of the study into four steps: framing the question, collecting data, taking action, and reflecting on the action.

Step 1: Framing the Question

Framing the question in this study was relatively easy, since it was already clear to Nolen what sorts of problems the student was creating.

Edward is a sixth-grader in a public, urban school. He participates in general education with pullout special education instruction in reading and math. The student is classified as learning disabled, and he currently resides in a foster care home. Edward excels in the area of art and enjoys assisting classmates. When focused on his work, he completes tasks appropriately. Distractions in the class and reactions to peers, however, often precipitate acting-out behaviors. Obviously, such outbursts interfere with learning, both for Edward and his classmates. The problem necessitated thoughtful action.

Step 2: Collecting Data

In their collecting data step, Schoen and Nolen describe how they gathered preliminary information on the student, consulted with colleagues, and conducted a literature review in which four different theoretical bases for intervention were identified:

Focused observations . . . gleaned over a 5-day period clarified the problem behavior. Edward's acting-out behavior converged into patterns of misbehavior. These persistent patterns revealed categories of Edward's typical actions, including slamming materials, yelling at teacher/peers, muttering under his breath, storming out of the room, destroying his work, and tuning out (head down on the desk).

Interviews with the social worker, special education teacher, and student provided further insights. . . . Edward was

reportedly removed from his biological parent's home at the age of 9 due to neglect, violence, and maternal drug addiction. Edward had been placed in two foster care situations since that time. Several supplemental treatments were in place, including psychological counseling, behavior therapy, medication, and art therapy. The social worker strongly discouraged any use of punishment as consequences and encouraged the idea of self-regulation strategies . . .

We selected interventions from four different theoretical bases to maximize efficiency and effectiveness.

Social learning theory places emphasis on learning through example. Modeling, or observing the responses of another person, can have as much effect as direct instruction (Grusec, 1992: Schoen, 1989). Teachers can foster such observational learning by modeling expectations for their students, using peers to demonstrate desired behavior, or coupling competent learners in cooperative learning arrangements, for instance (Woolfolk, 1999). In Edward's case, vicarious learning held potential because we had observed him emulating peer behavior . . .

The humanistic theory, on the other hand, focuses on the student becoming a responsible, caring, feeling person. The teacher sets the example by emphasizing values, such as consideration, cooperation, respect, individuality, and honesty (Johnson, 1999). Consequently, personal needs, interests, and preferences are integral to instruction. We found that Edward's keen interest in drawing could readily be incorporated into many tasks. Moreover, choices in lesson activities permitted greater freedom in decision making in the teaching/learning process. High-interest lessons hold the potential for maximizing on-task behavior and minimizing the impact of classroom distractions. These ideas must be tempered, nevertheless, by the practical reality that such modifications may be inconsistent with the teacher's values and preferences or may be arduous to implement with particular classroom structures . . .

The cognitive theory builds on the foundation that knowledge is learned and that changes in knowledge make changes in behavior possible. Cognitive strategies emphasize rational thinking, self-talk, self-instruction, problem-solving, self-management, and social skills training. For the latter, social skills training might comprise mutually developed classroom rules, stress management techniques, cooperative learning strategies, and conflict resolution approaches. . . . Edward's cognitive level of development warranted consideration of strategies that tap rational thinking. The student's impulsive tendencies might be tempered by a problem-solving technique, in particular, that encourages him to reflect on the problem, generate solutions to the problem, prioritize potential solutions, and implement his plan . . .

The behavioral approach posits that new behaviors are learned by reinforcement that increases the likelihood of a response. Personalized rewards are essential for success. Through interview and observation, it was ascertained that Edward's desired behavior might be increased by rewards that include drawing time, computer time, classroom jobs, or socialization time. . . . Close, ongoing monitoring of any technique was key to the outcome of the interventions.

Step 3: Taking Action

For their plan of action, Schoen and Nolen developed interventions based on each of the four theoretical perspectives described earlier.

Social Learning Theory. We targeted observational learning and vicarious reinforcement as intervention strategies. Peer models demonstrated the desired behaviors of on-task performance and self-control. Clear expectations also promoted the distinction between appropriate and inappropriate outlets of frustration. In addition, we highlighted literary connections that illustrated regulated reactions to frustration.

Humanistic Learning Theory. Systematic observation revealed the activities that were associated with problematic behaviors, as well as the preferences and interests of the student. We then modified assignments so that we could maintain instructional objectives, yet still incorporate an area of individual interest (Kern, 2001). We readily found ways to encourage Edward to draw pictures as a part of his lessons. Creative writing also maintained Edward's attention . . .

Cognitive Learning Theory. Problem solving and social skills training constituted new units of instruction for the class as a whole. Social-learning stories and literature provided the context for practicing a 5-step problem-solving strategy. The generic components of problem-solving included

- *Recognition of the problem*
- *Definition of the problem*
- *Generation of possible solutions*
- *Evaluation of each solution*
- *Design of the plan of action*

In addition, the class revisited and refined classroom rules in a mutual effort to engender a stronger sense of community. . . .

Behavioral Learning Theory. We devised a behaviorally oriented form of self-management checklists, coupled with positive reinforcement, and we tailored it to fit Edward's acting-out and off-task behavior. A recording system directed Edward's attention to four prompt questions: Did I yell out? Did I stay on-task? Did I act respectfully to the other students and teachers? Did I use proper outlets to calm down? Edward used a check plus, check, and check minus to self-evaluate these areas. . . . We implemented the system during reading, math, and transition periods and determined the integrity of his self-assessment through intermittent observations.

Step 4: Reflecting on the Action

In this final step, Schoen and Nolen recorded and reflected on the results of their intervention. The researchers reported their data in a type of graph that is prevalent in the single-participant approach (see Chapter 8), and they concluded that their intervention was a success.

The management of behavior is a complex endeavor that requires clarity, individualization, reflection, and consequences. The eclectic use of strategies from multiple theory families can maximize effectiveness in the classroom [as in this study] . . .

The figure below illustrates the effect of such an approach, in the form of an intervention package, on Edward's behavior. Within a relatively short period of time, Edward's mean baseline level of 17.5 minutes of off-task behavior decreased to a mean intervention level of 5 minutes across a 15-day time span. It is not unusual for behaviors to temporarily rebound during intervention. Unusual events or behavior bursts may occur during the process of changing behavior. Nevertheless, in this case, improvement was effective. Gains were substantiated by interrater agreements of 86% and 87% during baseline and intervention phases.

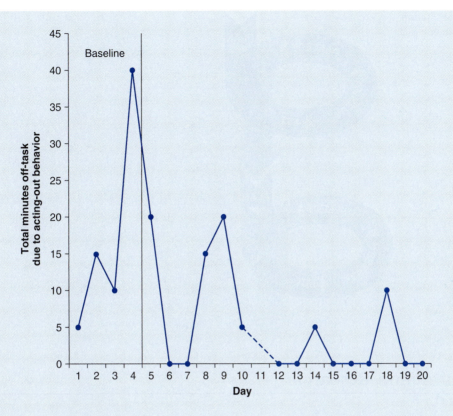

*Schoen, S. F., & Nolen, J. (2004). Decreasing acting-out behavior and increasing learning. *Teaching Exceptional Children, 37*(1), 26–29.

The Action Research "Spiral"

In the Schoen and Nolen study described in Spotlight on Research 16.1, the action research steps are clearly distinguished. In actual practice, action research is not always carried out through a neatly defined sequence of steps. Moreover, some action research studies have an iterative, or cyclical, quality. After reflecting on the results, the practitioner may revisit the original problem or address a closely related one, and develop a new plan of action. The new plan then leads to another sequence of action and reflection. For example, once a teacher has made one change in her curricular materials and found it to be beneficial, she might make an additional change to see whether the benefits increase. Or, if one change is found to have no effect, another change might be substituted. In the Villano study described earlier, the discovery that picture books could be part of a successful prelearning strategy led the teacher-researcher to see whether poetic material would work too. Thus, the steps through which action research is conducted are sometimes referred to as a "spiral," indicating an ongoing process of planning, acting, and reflecting, followed by another round of planning, action, and reflection as practice evolves and the educational environment improves (Kemmis, 1994; Mills, 2003). The action research spiral is illustrated in Figure 16.1.

FIGURE 16.1 Action
Research Spiral

Types of Action Research

Although terminology varies from writer to writer, a fundamental distinction can be made between practical and participatory action research.

Practical Action Research

Practical action research attempts to improve the situations of students, teachers, and other participants in the educational process through the development and evaluation of solutions to specific, local problems. The researcher is not a professor who visits an educational setting to collect data, but rather one or more educational practitioners, such as a teacher or principal. The action research conducted by these practitioners tends to be narrow in scope. Often, the research consists of a teacher introducing a series of changes in his or her classroom and then evaluating the effects of those changes, as in the Villano study. Although informal qualitative approaches are most common, quantitative data may be reported too (as in the study summarized in Spotlight on Research 16.1).

Participatory Action Research

Participatory action research (PAR) attempts to empower students, teachers, families, and other participants in the educational process. Although this approach reflects the same assumptions underlying practical action research, PAR is based on the additional assumption that educational researchers should help individuals in educational settings who are oppressed or exploited. PAR emerged in the 1960s as an amalgam of different theoretical perspectives on social injustice, and it continues to be informed by a liberal political emphasis. This emphasis is reflected in a predominance of qualitative methods, since qualitative approaches tend to be more holistic and incorporate more of an individual's situation and worldview into descriptions of results (see Chapter 13 for further discussion). Another important feature of PAR is that it tends to be collaborative, in the sense of involving participants in the process of studying themselves rather than just using them as a source of data (or as a target for the dissemination of findings). A key assumption is that allowing participants to influence the direction of the research not only gives them a sense of autonomy but also helps them acquire concrete strategies for helping themselves. The collaborative nature of PAR is illustrated by the study summarized in Spotlight on Research 16.2.

How to Conduct an Action Research Study

Following is a list of questions you might ask yourself in the process of planning and carrying out an action research study.

- Is action research the right approach? Are you interested in studying a local problem as opposed to a general topic?

- Are you interested in making immediate changes? Do you want to go beyond understanding the problem and actually begin to resolve or diminish it?

- Do you have some control over the situation? Are you in a position to make changes and evaluate the results?

- What is your focus of inquiry? What problem do you wish to study, and what kinds of solutions might you consider?

- Is your general interest in practical or participatory action research?

- Is there any published research, theory, or practical advice that bears on the problem?

- Do your colleagues, or other practitioners in your field, have suggestions about how to proceed?

- What other preliminary information do you need? Is this information readily accessible?

- What is your initial plan? How will you gather information and evaluate the results of any changes you introduce? Will the design of the study be formal or informal?

- Once the results are in, what changes will you implement, and what further investigation might be needed? At what point will the action research spiral end?

The last set of questions should be answered tentatively, since the nature of action research dictates that not all of the details can be worked out in advance. However, it is important for the action researcher to think about what might be possible. Constraints on time and resources may limit the duration and scope of the study. There may also be constraints on the kinds of changes that can be more or less permanently implemented. These and other practical considerations should have some influence on initial planning.

Curriculum Redesign through Participatory Action Research

The Individuals with Disabilities Education Act (IDEA) requires schools to ensure that all students with disabilities can benefit from the general curriculum. Schools may provide access to the general curriculum through special education classes and/or by including students with disabilities in general education classrooms. Improving the educational experiences of these students in a general education science class was the focus of a 2006 study by Stacy Dymond and colleagues.

Dymond and colleagues' study, published in *Research and Practice for Persons with Severe Disabilities**, focused on students with significant cognitive difficulties (SCD). The study was based on the assumption that general education classrooms at the high school level are less than ideal for meeting the basic requirements of IDEA, and should be redesigned so that they serve both special needs students as well as the rest of the student population.

Traditional instruction tends to emphasize whole group lecture and seatwork, often limiting the opportunities for students who do not learn well through these methods. In the past, approaches for helping students with SCD gain access in inclusive settings have focused on adapting the curriculum to meet the needs of the student (Ryndak, 1996; Snell & Brown, 2000). A relatively new trend is the concept of universal design for learning (UDL), which posits that the curriculum should be designed from the very beginning to incorporate the diverse needs of all students (Hitchcock, Meyer, Rose, & Jackson, 2002; Renzaglia, Karvonen, Drasgow, & Stoxen, 2003; Rose & Meyer, 2002) . . .

[However], strategies for universal design have not adequately addressed the needs of students with SCD. Many of the examples in the literature focus on the use of computer technology with limited attention to other methods for enhancing the learning of students with SCD. There is a need to determine the extent to which universal design can be used to sufficiently help students with SCD access and achieve in the general education curriculum in inclusive high school classrooms. To date, there have been no systematic, data-based investigations of UDL as a method for creating whole class change.

The purpose of Dymond and colleagues' 1-year PAR case study was to describe the experiences of school personnel (teachers, students, etc.) who participated in redesigning a high school science class. The redesign involved changes to lesson plans and the movement of students with SCD into general education classrooms. Here is how the researchers described the setting and participants in their study, as well as the problem they hoped to address:

One high school located in a small city in the Midwest was chosen for investigation. . . . Student ethnicity was primarily White (67.8%) but also included 24.2% Black, 5.6% Asian/Pacific Islander, 1.2% Hispanic, and. 2% Native American. . . . Twenty percent of the student body was identified as having a disability . . .

This study occurred in one general education science course entitled Unified Science. . . . The course was taught in a traditional manner. . . . Students generally enrolled in the course during ninth grade although it was open to students at any grade level. The course was considered to be the lowest level science course offered at the school that counted toward graduation credit. . .

During the course of this study, the majority of the students who were observed as members of the course were those who were at risk for failure. . . . Additionally, because it was a co-taught course, there was a larger number of students with mild disabilities (including learning disabilities and social and emotional disorders) in the course than would be expected . . .

The general education teacher appeared to be devoted to the students in the course . . . yet her expectations for these students were not high. She rarely gave homework assignments because she believed the students would not complete them. Moreover, the teaching format and expectations for learning were established for those learners who she expected to do the least well. This was evidenced in her class presentations where she gave students worksheets with blanks to fill in based on the transparency on the overhead projector. Students were required to copy down highlighted words from the transparency onto their worksheets . . .

Unified Science was selected for redesign because of the general education teacher's interest in improving her ability to meet the needs of students with disabilities enrolled in the course. Two of the four sections taught by the general education teacher were targeted for intervention. Both sections were co-taught with the same special education teacher. Each section included students with mild disabilities (i.e., learning disabilities, behavior disorders, autism, mild mental retardation, other health impaired), students with SCD (i.e., moderate or severe mental retardation), and students without disabilities . . .

Students with SCD were purposefully assigned to each section of the course by the research team (i.e., university researchers, school personnel). Each section included (a) one student with SCD without physical disabilities and (b) one student with SCD with severe physical disabilities (i.e., nonambulatory, used wheelchair). Prior to this investigation, these students received all of their education in a self-contained classroom, nonacademic integrated settings (e.g., lunch, physical education), the community, and job sites . . .

Participants in this study included the Unified Science general education teacher, the Unified Science special education co-teacher . . . and the special education case manager of students with severe disabilities (hereafter referred to as the ''special education teacher'') . . .

An action research spiral, in which the sequence of planning, acting, and reflecting is repeated several times, was illustrated in the methods by which the researchers redesigned the lesson plans.

The study was conducted using a PAR approach. . . . This approach was chosen because the overarching purpose of the full study (of which this case study was a part) was to develop a process for universally designing high school science courses and evaluate the effectiveness of that process in assisting students with and without SCD to gain access to the general curriculum.

Prior to the beginning of the school year, the research team convened across 3 days to discuss the Unified Science curriculum . . . and refine the research design. In addition, the group discussed the literature on UDL, explored strategies for promoting UDL, and engaged in hands-on activities to apply the concepts of UDL. On the last day, the team engaged in a MAPS process (Vandercook, York, & Forest, 1989) to create a vision and action plan for designing a UDL science course.

As the school year began, weekly research team meetings were held for two hours after school to plan for the redesign, share information about student needs, reflect on the redesign process, and problem solve around a variety of issues. A series of questions were developed to guide the discussion of strategies for redesigning the course. . . . The research team reviewed the traditional lesson plan typically used by the general education teacher to address the topic and then used the . . . questions to redesign the lesson in ways

hypothesized to increase student engagement and participation in the curriculum.

Following is a sample of questions used by the research team to guide discussion about redesign.

- How will I vary the curriculum (add and delete) to accommodate the learning needs of diverse students?
- How will I sequence skills so that each concept/skill . . . contributes to understanding of the main idea?
- How does the lesson/unit relate to outcomes for students outside of school (now and in the future)?
- How will I teach the students to be reflective learners/problem solvers?
- How will I incorporate a variety of heterogeneous groupings . . . to facilitate active learning/engagement?
- How will I provide an appropriate level of instructional support to the range of students . . . in the class?
- How will I provide students with choices related to materials, grouping . . . and self-directed . . . activities?
- How will I increase the amount of active engagement and problem solving required . . . in the lesson/unit?
- How will the lesson be structured so that all students can be involved in . . . collaboration and teamwork?
- What type of instructional technology will I use?
- What types of assistive technology support will I provide to maximize student performance?
- How will I assess student learning using multiple methods that promote ongoing authentic assessment?
- How will I use ongoing assessment data to refine my instruction for the rest of the lesson/unit?
- How will I assess the application of skills learned through this lesson/unit in out-of-class settings?

As the research team became more effective at addressing the . . . questions within each lesson plan, the process was refined (in Week 5) to allow more efficient planning and increased attention to other UDL questions. During research team meetings on Wednesdays, the general education teacher shared the traditional lesson plan with the research team. The following day the general education teacher and co-teacher met separately to identify ideas for redesigning the lesson. The university researchers also gathered to identify redesign ideas. On Fridays, the general education teacher and one of the university researchers convened to redesign the lessons based on ideas generated from both groups. This draft lesson plan was given to the special education teacher so that she could identify any additional strategies needed to include students from her caseload in a meaningful manner. The following Wednesday, during the research team meeting, the lesson plan was modified to address the needs of specific students (if needed) and finalized for implementation the following week. In summary, the process involved redesigning the whole class content first and then thinking about student specific needs that were still present despite the redesign.

The intervention began during the second month of the school year. . . . The intervention was staggered across the two sections of the course. During the first half of the year, the intervention occurred in Section 1 whereas Section 2 was taught in the same manner it had been taught in previous years. Beginning in semester two, both sections of the course received the intervention. Staggering the intervention allowed the research team time to develop, pilot, and refine the redesign process prior to applying it to both course sections.

As in most case study research (see Chapter 13), a variety of data were collected.

Each of the three teachers was interviewed pre- and post-intervention to determine how they defined access to the general curriculum for students with SCD. . . .

During the second semester, the general education teacher kept an electronic journal of her perceptions of the redesign process and its impact on her classroom. Twelve journal entries were obtained.

At the beginning of weekly research team meetings during the second semester, teachers were asked to reflect on the redesign process and how students with SCD participated in the course . . .

Minutes from weekly research team meetings were recorded by one university researcher and disseminated by e-mail to all team members. . . . A total of 31 meeting minutes were collected.

Two types of lesson plans were collected each week. The first was a traditional lesson plan (created by the general education teacher) that detailed how the course was typically taught. The second was a redesigned lesson plan (created by the research team) that modified the traditional lesson plan by applying the principles of UDL. . . . A total of 9 traditional and 19 redesign lesson plans were collected.

At the conclusion of the school year, the teachers participated in a focus group to determine their perceptions of the redesign process . . .

Data analyses were based on content analysis techniques (as described in Chapter 14).

A content analysis procedure (Merriam, 1998) was used to initially analyze and organize the data. Each data set (e.g., process interviews, lesson plans) was analyzed separately using the same process. This process consisted of having a team of two to three researchers read and re-read the data to identify units of meaning related to the development, implementation, and evaluation of the redesign process. Each unit of meaning was assigned a code. Once the codes were finalized, one researcher coded the data . . .

A constant comparative method (Glaser & Strauss, 1967) was used to develop categories within data sets as well as themes that cut across the multiple sources of data within the case. The development of categories was an emergent process. Categories were hypothesized as the codes were developed, and then refined and confirmed by all researchers once the data were coded. These categories were then compared across data sets to determine areas of convergence and divergence within the data. These comparisons led to the grouping of categories into themes related to the experiences of school personnel with the redesign process. Triangulation (Denzin, 1978) of the data was sought by using multiple sources of data (i.e., interviews, focus groups, documents) and multiple researchers in the analysis process (including a mixture of researchers directly and not directly involved with data collection).

The results were described qualitatively across different areas of change. In terms of teacher participation, Dymond and colleagues found that general and special education teachers acquired a greater sense of responsibility for special education students. Teachers, co-teachers, and paraprofessionals strongly emphasized the importance of teamwork following the redesign.

In terms of curricular materials, the redesign led to more usage of nontraditional materials and computer technologies, along with an increase in student opportunities for selecting and making use of such materials. As for the effectiveness of UDL strategies, teachers were mainly positive about the impact for all students and not just those with SCD.

Teachers reported that students enjoyed the variety of interesting materials available for the "hands-on" activities. Visual organizers . . . were helpful for many students who required modifications to the core content or additional support to complete tasks. Providing demonstrations of how to complete a lab as well as visual models of activity products at *various stages of completion helped many students work more independently and follow directions. Without these supports, some students would [previously] "jump in" without attending to the directions and have to re-do their work to correct for errors, thus lengthening the amount of time spent on the activity.*

Several changes to student grouping were found effective. One of the first changes the team made was to rearrange the seating chart so that students with SCD were seated next to their peers (as opposed to next to each other in the back of the room), and students without SCD who did not work well together were separated. The teachers noted that the changes resulted in students completing more work and increased interactions between students with SCD and their peers. Changes were also made to student grouping during class activities. During traditional instruction, students worked individually most of the time. Labs were generally completed with a partner of the student's choice. With the redesign process, students were strategically grouped to increase active engagement and provide sufficient support for learning. Teachers learned to pay attention to students' working relationships and determine which students worked well together. They found that spending time up front to predetermine group decreased the amount of non-task-related talking, increased student participation in activities, and eliminated having some students not chosen for a partner. Students were excited about working in groups, although some did not initially like being grouped with certain classmates.

Student outcomes following the redesign, particularly in the area of social relationships, were highly positive.

Three of the four students with SCD developed social skills and learned appropriate means for interacting with others. The general education teacher noted that one student with SCD "wants to communicate a lot more" whereas the co-teacher commented that another student with SCD was "getting more comfortable just being around people . . . she's not so nervous . . . it's not a big deal for her to just get up and walk around the room any more." A third student with SCD became more skilled at reading the social cues of others. The special education teacher found that this student learned, "Okay, they don't want to talk to me, they're totally not interested, I just need to leave them alone right now."

The teachers believed that students without disabilities learned to display more caring behaviors toward their peers

with SCD. The special education teacher was awed by the types of caring and kindness she observed from high school boys who interacted with the male student with the most severe, multiple disabilities.

> *"By the end of the school year, [peer] was wiping [student with SCD's] mouth and it's just like, wow, you know, this is so cool. . . . It brought out some really caring characteristics from some students that might not demonstrate those so easily. . . . You know, this is starting to happen and I wish it could have happened three months ago."*

Students with and without disabilities learned to work effectively together on science projects. The co-teacher felt this was the most positive outcome of the redesigned course. In fact, all of the teachers seemed surprised that high school students with and without disabilities enjoyed working together. Friendships were noted to emerge in each class only after the redesign was implemented. They attributed the development of these friendships to the structured opportunities students had to work with each other during class.

Other effects of the redesign included greater enthusiasm about school among students with SCD, as well as increased participation and better test performance among the other students. Although teachers expressed concerns about the time required to create the redesign, they acknowledged the positive benefits experienced by all. Dymond and colleagues concluded with a set of recommendations for classroom redesign:

- Create a realistic time frame for change
- Involve all stakeholders in the redesign process
- Use lesson plans to develop and communicate the UDL changes
- Ensure that appropriate supports are available to complete the changes
- Provide structure to support students in redesigned activities
- Evaluate the impact of the redesign

*Dymond, S. K., Renzaglia, A., Rosenstein, A., Chun, E. J., Banks, R. A., Niswander, V., et al. (2006). Using a participatory action research approach to create a universally designed inclusive high school science course: A case study. *Research and Practice for Persons with Severe Disabilities, 31*(4), 293–308. Quoted with permission from the publisher.

Evaluation of Action Research

Action research appears in peer-reviewed journals geared to a scientific audience, as well as in practitioner journals (e.g., *The Reading Teacher*), and in journals that are specific to action research, including *Action Research* and *Wisdom of Practice: An Online Journal of Action Research*. Published action research studies vary from informal projects conducted by classroom teachers to extensive, formally designed studies involving collaborations between practitioners and researchers (as in the study described in Spotlight on Research 16.2). Regardless of design, some basic questions can be asked that will help you evaluate each particular action research study you encounter:

- Is the problem clearly stated?
- Is the problem specific and meaningful?
- Did the researcher incorporate well-established research that bears on the problem?
- Was the plan of action a sensible way to address the problem?
- If the plan of action incorporated a particular quantitative, qualitative, or mixed-methods approach, was the approach implemented properly?
- Did the action researcher engage in reflection throughout the research process?
- Were participants treated ethically?
- Were there sensible criteria for deciding whether participants benefited?
- Did participants seem to benefit from the changes that were introduced?
- Were any beneficial changes implemented as part of regular practice?

General Evaluation of Action Research

Any type of design can be implemented in an action research study. For example, Spotlight on Research 16.3 presents the results of a study that employed mixed methods in the context of a one-shot case study design (see Chapter 7 for definition).

In actual practice, most action research studies are informal in design and execution. For this reason, action research has been criticized on the grounds of methodological weakness. Although it is true that many action research studies lack the methodological rigor of a well-designed experiment or ethnography, their informality reflects a limitation rather than a flaw.

You might be wondering at this point what the difference is between a limitation and a flaw. Quantitative research is limited in that it does not provide rich narrative descriptions. Qualitative research is limited in that it does not yield statistical analyses. But these are not flaws. Rather, they mark the boundaries of what each type of research is intended to do. So long as the results section of a quantitative study is primarily quantitative, and so long as a qualitative study does not purport to show evidence of statistically significant differences, each approach can make the kind of contribution it was designed to make, and neither approach could be described as inherently flawed.

The same kinds of observations can be made about action research. Action research is not intended to contribute to scientific knowledge. The sole purpose is to provide immediate benefits to specific individuals in a local educational setting. If an action research study achieves that purpose, it is a successful study. Thus,

Identifying Gifted Students Prior to English-Language Proficiency

Gifted students are an important sub-group within any population of students, including those who represent linguistic and cultural minorities. Serving the needs of gifted students until they become proficient in English is a challenge for the classroom teacher, since these students might not be recognized as gifted until their language skills allow them to succeed on whatever measures of giftedness their schools use.

In a 2002 study reported in *Roeper Review**, Ronda Uresti, Jeanie Goertz, and Ernesto Bernal described how the first author, an ESL teacher in a south Texas elementary school, implemented a method for facilitating achievement among her first-graders. One of the main goals for implementing the method was to help identify and support gifted students before they master English. Here is the researchers' description of the problem and the setting:

Uresti was an English-as-a-Second-Language (ESL) teacher in a school where typically bright CLD [culturally and linguistically different] students were not nominated for the district's gifted and talented (GT) program until they were well into the third or fourth grade, after they had become fluent enough in academic-level English to demonstrate their abilities to their teachers in that language. By that time, they were in a sense "behind" the native speakers of English in the district who had been selected for the GT program by the second grade. Mrs. Uresti learned about this situation while studying for a master's degree in gifted education, and she believed that she could adapt a particular GT approach she had studied [known as the] Autonomous Learner Model (ALM) . . .

This case study took place in a first grade classroom located in a mixed urban and rural school district in south Texas. This intact group consisted of 24 Hispanic students, 12 native speakers of Spanish who were learning English and 12 who were either English-Spanish bilinguals or English monolinguals. None of the students had been identified as needing special educational or GT services when the school year began . . .

Uresti and colleagues addressed the following research question: "Can the ALM be successfully adapted to facilitate sufficiently high student achievement in an ESL classroom to promote the early identification of CLD and other students for the district's GT program?" Uresti implemented the ALM through a variety of changes to her instructional methods and classroom activities.

The ALM, developed by Betts (1985) and Betts and Kercher (1999), was designed to teach learners the skills and sense of responsibility to initiate their own learning and evaluate its outcomes. . . . The ALM consists of five dimensions: Orientation, Individual Development, Enrichment Activities, Seminar, and In-depth Study. The gifted learner advances through the five dimensions to become an autonomous learner.

Three dimensions of the ALM—Orientation to the Center, Individual Development, and Enrichment Activities—were implemented in this trial. The Orientation to the Center began for the class as students experienced some group building and group problem-solving activities halfway through the fall semester. Group building involved affective exercises like "Temperature Reading," an activity in which children share their emotional "temperatures" and learn to read one another's thermometers. Group problem solving allowed the children to decide on a problem and work toward a solution as a group. The students chose to study classroom discipline. Their solution included ways to remind friends of classroom rules politely. The teacher took their lead, and in the end they rewrote the classroom rules and consequences in a cooperative group of the whole, with the teacher acting as scribe, and added a constitution that outlined the rights of all the students.

The second dimension of the ALM, Individual Development, consisted of activities that promote self-understanding. Each student completed a simple learning style inventory and kept a daily journal, activities designed to create the foundation for the children to transition into a less structured environment. The teacher and students first created a center together. After that, a rotating schedule was developed that permitted five to six children at a time to run their own centers while the others continued with the regular class.

To implement the third dimension of the program, Enrichment Activities, the teacher set up individual interviews to assist each child in choosing a topic for individual enrichment . . .

Once students selected a topic, they determined what questions needed to be asked and whom to address. The students were given mini-lessons on how to write a question that would elicit responses beyond "yes" or "no": who, what, what if, when, where, why, and how. Eli, a student who created a center about Jupiter, began the research process by writing questions about his topic The teacher initially acted as scribe. . . . Later in the year the first grade students were all able to write the written questions, albeit with creative spellings, with little or no assistance.

The students then began collecting data. The Center provided the People Forms, where the learners listed people who may have information on the topic. For example, Eli listed astronomers and NASA personnel who might be able to help him with the Jupiter project. The teacher taught students how to use the telephone book to find the names, addresses, and phone numbers of their sources.

Mock interviews were conducted among classmates before they spoke with specialists from their topical area. They wrote down key questions. (Spoken and written English were thus practiced by the English-language learners.) . . .

Once the People Forms were completed, students thought about other sources of information. Eli, for example, listed library materials and Internet searches to get specialized information on his topic. He also planned additional information-gathering activities: 1. Visit a local planetarium. 2. View a video about Jupiter. 3. Observe a Jupiter simulator.

The students gathered what for first graders appeared to be an immense amount of materials for their centers. Each student was given a soda flat that stored materials and doubled as a resource file for notes, clippings, pictures, completed interview forms, and other materials related to the topic that he or she studied. Eli surfed the Internet, browsed the computerized card catalog, read books, interviewed a local astronomer, and read about the Jupiter simulator at the Ames Research Laboratories . . .

The next step was to complete the Activity Cards. Eli used a verb chart and a product chart to facilitate his work. The verb list served as a suggestion source about the process, and the product list had ideas for ways to present the information.

The final steps, Presentation and Evaluation, not only put closure to the students' Center experiences but also gave them opportunities to reflect on how they learned, so that they were able to talk to other students about formulating questions, gathering and organizing information, and developing a final product. Each student selected an audience. Eli decided to read aloud the book he had written and then discussed facts about Jupiter. . . . All the children chose to present to the class and some went on to present to their

families, church groups, and clubs such as the 4-H and local Kennel Club. . . .

Finally, each of the students and Mrs. Uresti completed evaluation forms. The students' own evaluations helped them reflect on their progress, and the teacher gave feedback on the skills each student utilized in the Center process. These exercises also seemed to educe ideas for the students' next Center topic.

The quantitative results of the study were encouraging. Each student was given either the Iowa Test of Basic Skills (ITBS-M) or the Spanish Assessment of Basic Education (SABE-2). (The particular test taken by each student depended on the student's level of English proficiency.) Uresti and colleagues found that students scored above average on the language and reading subtests of each test, with mean percentiles ranging from 50 (ITBS-M reading) to 72 (SABE-2 reading).

The results of qualitative analyses were also encouraging:

For a first grade class in this school to achieve, on average, scores as high as the middle range on nationally standardized tests was an unusual, but happy event. There is, of course, no way to ensure that these good mean scores were due directly to the abbreviated implementation of the model, as the assignment of students was beyond the control of the teacher and because pretests were not administered nor comparison samples obtained. What we believe that we know "for sure" is that the atmosphere in Mrs. Uresti's classroom changed radically during the last 24 weeks of school, when she began using centers and individualized projects and instruction, and that the parents noticed changes in their children's behaviors and attitudes as well.

A surprising advantage of the Center was the effect it had on the students who were learning English as a second language. ESL students became willing to take certain risks with their English language development . . .

The Center allowed for high-level abilities to be demonstrated through behaviors that are characteristic of many Hispanic children, such as analogous reasoning and quick learning through experience. Some Mexican American children are taught in their homes to avoid individual competition, independence, and self-direction. The Orientation and Individual Development dimensions gave these children a chance to become comfortable making their own choices and exercising new levels of independence in their learning at school, apparently without sacrificing their familial protocol or having to engage in direct competition . . .

The teacher received positive phone calls and letters from parents who welcomed the opportunity for their students to do something new, something beyond traditional assignments. Parents also reported that their students were eager to attend school each day because they wanted to continue with their Center activities. One mother thanked Mrs. Uresti, because her son had gone from being a discipline problem at school to a star student who loved school. It should be noted that the parents, whose incomes were marginal to poor, were very supportive of their students' independent study activities, which in many cases involved family trips of several hundred miles.

The school principal expressed doubt when first approached about the implementation of the Center from the ALM. He was concerned that young students require more direct teaching to be successful and would waste important learning time. However, he was ultimately pleased to see an increase in the use of higher order thinking skills, greater motivation, and better scores on nationally standardized achievement tests than he had seen in a long time. Use of the described techniques actually gave the teacher the time to work with students who needed extra help or who required a more structured learning environment . . .

One of the practical consequences of this action research study was the inclusion of three students in the school's GT program, several years before they would have been considered in ordinary circumstances, owing to their limited English proficiency.

Finally, Mrs. Uresti nominated five of the first grade children for the GT program. She submitted a portfolio on each of the children, which documented their levels of achievement on the standardized tests and included samples of their work on the projects in her class. The students were then tested with the Raven's Progressive Matrices, a test of general intelligence that does not require reading or speaking. Three of the five students were subsequently selected for the GT program. Significantly, all three were CLD students, one of whom had begun the first grade year as limited English proficient. An informal followup of these three GT children a year later indicated that they were all doing well at the magnet GT elementary school in the district.

*Uresti, R., Goertz, J., & Bernal, E. M. (2002). Maximizing achievement for potentially gifted and talented and regular minority students in a primary classroom. *Roeper Review, 25*(1), 1–11. Quoted with permission from the publisher.

action research is not flawed, but simply limited to a particular purpose, just like other forms of research.

Throughout the book it has been emphasized that one type of research design is not inherently superior to another, but rather that each design is suitable for addressing a partially different set of research questions. This idea can be stated more broadly: Each way of conducting research is suitable for a somewhat different purpose. The purpose of action research is to make immediate improvements in educational settings. The immediacy of change distinguishes action research from other types of designs. Most quantitative, qualitative, and mixed-methods research is designed to effect change through a slower process of dissemination of results to practitioners, policymakers, and parents. Some action researchers hope to effect change through these forms of dissemination too, but what they all share is a commitment to improving the situations of specific individuals during the very process of conducting research.

A Look Ahead

In this chapter you read about the type of purely applied research that is conducted by practitioners and leads to immediate changes in local educational settings. In the next chapter I focus on program evaluation, in which researchers formally evaluate educational settings and other types of education-related programs.

Applications: A Guide for Beginning Researchers

Here are some ideas from the chapter that will help you plan your research:

- Decide whether action research is logistically feasible and the best approach for addressing your practical question of interest.
- Choose the type of action research that best addresses your question of interest.
- Choose the quantitative, qualitative, or mixed-method approach that you will use in your action research. Do what you can to ensure that your research meets the standards of quality associated with each individual approach.
- Think about how specifically you want to plan the action research "spiral" in advance of data collection.

Chapter Summary

Action research is carried out by practitioners in local settings for the purpose of improving specific educational conditions.

Action research consists of a "spiral" of reflection, planning, action, and further reflection. This sequence of steps is more or less iterative.

The two main types of action research are practical and participatory. The ultimate goal of any action research study will be to have an immediate impact on educational practice. The immediacy of the impact distinguishes action research from other approaches.

Key Terms

Action research	Practical action research	Participatory action research

Exercises

For questions 1–5, indicate whether the study appears to exemplify practical action research or participatory action research.

1. *"We recruited twenty-two practitioners in Adult and Community Education (ACE) . . . to assist us in exploring how 'generic skills and attributes' are fostered in the context of adult and community education and to theorize pedagogies of ACE in the light of the changed demographic of those who access ACE programs (especially disaffected young people and older unemployed men)."* (Sanguinetti, Waterhouse, & Maunders, 2005, p. 271)

2. *"In this study, conducted during one academic term, I used only oral assessment [instead of written tests] to determine the students' progress in a unit of work on physical and human resources . . . I expected that the students would benefit in [many] ways."* (Superville, 2001, p. 122)

3. *"My goal in this study was to collaborate with two third-grade teachers . . . who taught children from lower socioeconomic levels. I planned to mentor them through development of techniques that would promote student engagement and learning using the processes of action research. As a conceptual framework, I used Lather's ideas . . . with the spirit of carrying out research 'that is explicitly committed to critiquing the status quo and building a more just society' (Lather, 1986, p. 258)."* (Morton, 2005, p. 54.)

4. *"During the 3-year teaching innovation, the researcher continuously modified the teaching design and her attitudes towards teaching, based on the students' reactions and her understanding of learning theories."* (Chang, 2005, p. 410)

5. *"In my first introduction to the volunteer youth research team I explained that I did not believe myself to be an expert about out-of-school youths in the refugee camps, but that I considered the youths themselves as the experts. I stated that I wanted to support them in choosing what research should be done and how it should be done as well as how it should be used. As a way of further introduction I offered the youths a two-day introductory workshop in research design and methods, and facilitated a process whereby the youth team determined the goals and questions for the research as well as appropriate methods for accomplishing it and our own code of conduct."* (Cooper, 2005, p. 470)

6. Which of the following is essential to any action research study?

a) Quantitative data collection

b) Qualitative content analysis

c) Triangulation

d) Reflection

7. What is the most common reason for conducting a literature review before engaging in an action research study?

a) To determine how the study will contribute to the scientific literature

b) To help clarify the design of the study

c) To obtain ideas about practices that might be effective during the action phase of the study

d) To ascertain whether the study needs to be grounded in quantitative or qualitative data collection

8. *Critical thinking question:* Given the fact that action research leads to immediate improvements in the lives of students and other participants in the educational process, why isn't all research action research? In other words, why conduct research that requires a longer time for the results to disseminate to practitioners, policymakers, and parents?

Answers to Exercises

1. Participatory action research   **2.** Practical action research

3. Participatory action research   **4.** Practical action research

5. Participatory action research   **6.** d   **7.** c

8. *Possible answer*: Although immediacy of benefits is a unique strength of action research, "slower" forms of research are needed too. Quantitative, qualitative, and mixed-methods studies that yield scientific knowledge and promote theory development provide a foundation for action research. Studies with formal designs may yield more generalizable results than action research does. Replicating the results of a study before implementing them on a widespread basis may be desirable, particularly when the implementation would have a strong impact on the well-being of students and teachers.

Suggestions for Further Reading

Research Article: Goodnough, K. (2006). Enhancing pedagogical content knowledge through self-study: An exploration of problem-based learning. *Teaching in Higher Education, 11*(3), 301–318.

This study illustrates several action research concepts in the context of higher education.

Application Article: Graham, L. (2001, April). From Tyrannosaurus to Pokemon: Autonomy in the teaching of writing. *Reading*, pp. 18–26.

This practical action research study incorporated the efforts of a group of teachers.

Extension Article: Warrican, S. J. (2006). Action research: A viable option for effecting change. *Journal of Curriculum Studies, 38*(1), 1–14.

This article uses a participatory action research study as a basis for reflections on the conditions under which action research can effect meaningful change.

CHAPTER 17

Program Evaluation

NewsCom

After studying this chapter, you will be able to answer the following questions:

- What are program evaluations and why are they conducted?

- Who conducts program evaluations?

- What are some of the methods and specific purposes of program evaluation?

- What are the main types of program evaluation?

This chapter will prepare you to do the following:

- Understand and evaluate published program evaluations

- Begin to plan a program evaluation

When I came to Columbus [in 1929] I worked with faculty members ... in departments that had a required course for students, e.g. botany, zoology, and agriculture. The faculty were having large numbers of failures and they wanted help, and so it seemed important to find out how much students were learning. The instructors would usually say: "We'll give them a test." Then I would point out the problem: "What do you want tested? The typical so-called achievement test is simply a test of what students remember about things that appear in their textbooks, and surely that isn't what you're after ... you are not just teaching them to memorize." This conclusion led us to talk about what the instructors' objectives were, that is, what they really hoped their students would be learning.... Because the term "test" usually was interpreted as a collection of memory items, I suggested the use of the term "evaluation" to refer to investigating what students were really learning.

(RALPH TYLER, 1981, quoted with permission from the publisher)

Historical Background

In Chapter 1 you read about the impact of federal legislation on educational research and classroom practice. One consequence of legislation such as No Child Left Behind (NCLB) is the provision of federal funds to programs that have been "demonstrated to be effective through rigorous scientific research" (U.S. Department of Education, 2003, p. 18). Influential and controversial phrases such as "rigorous scientific research" are discussed in the last chapter of this book. Here let's consider the term "demonstrated." Who conducts demonstrations of program effectiveness, what methods are used, and where do the results go?

NCLB is a reauthorization of the **Elementary and Secondary Education Act (ESEA)**. The ESEA, passed in 1965, was the first federal law to mandate substantial funding for public schools. Broadly, the purpose of ESEA was to provide disadvantaged students with access to a quality educational experience from kindergarten through 12th grade. Title I of ESEA, for example, allocated roughly $1 billion per year to schools with high concentrations of low-income students, and served as the impetus for Head Start as well as a variety of other programs and subsequent legislation.

Since ESEA funding came from tax dollars, systems of accountability were needed to determine whether funded programs actually provided benefits for students. ESEA required that all school districts and educational programs receiving federal support must spend part of the money on evaluating their own effectiveness (although the law did not provide specific guidelines for how each district or program should conduct evaluations).

The passage of ESEA fostered a substantial increase in the evaluation of educational programs. However, evaluations have been carried out as long as educational programs have existed, because parents, educators, and policymakers have always been curious about program effectiveness. As a formal approach, program evaluation is linked to the rise of educational testing. Beginning in the 1840s, for example, Horace Mann promoted the assessment of teaching and learning in the Boston schools, and his influence resulted in the widespread implementation of comprehensive written exams for high school students. By the turn of the 20th century, the expansion and improvement of educational testing had become a major focus of research in psychology and education. Formal tools for conducting program evaluation already existed by the time ESEA was passed, even though school administrators were not always aware of these tools.

A historical impetus for program evaluation that predated the ESEA and contributed to its development is the work of Ralph Tyler in the 1930s and 1940s. Tyler directed the evaluation activities of the "Eight-Year Study" (1942) in which 30 high schools were encouraged to redesign their curricula and to allow the performance of their students in both high school and college to be studied (see *www.8yearstudy.org*). Among other things, the Eight-Year Study drew attention to the role of evaluation in curricular reform. In his best-selling book, *Basic Principles of Curriculum and Instruction* (1949), Tyler recommended four principles for the development of an educational curriculum, the fourth of which pertains to evaluation:

- Define appropriate learning objectives.
- Introduce useful learning experiences.
- Organize learning experiences to have the maximum effect.
- Evaluate the curriculum and revise whatever is ineffective.

The influence of these four principles extends beyond curricular issues. Contemporary emphasis on evaluating the content and impact of educational programs reflects Tyler's influence, both in a general way, and through his specific publications and professional activities such as chairing the committee that developed the National Assessment of Educational Progress (NAEP; see Chapters 1 and 6 for brief discussion). The term "evaluation," as used in this chapter, is also one of Tyler's contributions.

Introduction to Program Evaluation

Program evaluation is the process of evaluating the merit and effectiveness of educational programs. Evaluations are research-based, but unlike other forms of research the goal is not simply to understand programs but also to arrive at judgments about their impact and worth. The programs that are evaluated may be labeled as such (preschool programs, bully prevention programs, teacher training programs, and so on), but program evaluation also focuses on schools, professional organizations, curricula, and standards—in short, any organized system for the delivery of educational services. A program evaluation may address one aspect of a program, an entire program, or a set of programs implemented at a regional or national level. In the Eight-Year Study, for example, 30 high schools that were interested in trying out curricular reform were sampled from 12 different states. (Further details about this study will be introduced throughout the chapter.)

Before continuing, it may help to keep in mind a distinction between assessment and evaluation. As discussed in Chapter 5, assessment is a way of documenting student characteristics with respect to a set of goals or standards. Assessment contributes to judgments about academic progress, student placement, and other practical considerations. Evaluation is a way of judging the merit and effectiveness of programs with respect to a set of goals or standards. Thus, there are two important differences between assessment and evaluation:

- Assessment yields specific measurements and judgments pertaining to specific characteristics, whereas evaluation also enables judgments about overall merit.
- Assessment enables judgments about people, whereas evaluation enables judgments about programs.

Assessment plays a role in many program evaluations, but as you can see the two concepts are not completely synonymous.

Direct versus Indirect Evaluation

The focus of an evaluation is ultimately on program merit and effectiveness, and for this reason program evaluation has always been linked to educational reform. Effectiveness is a necessary condition for merit and may be studied directly and/or indirectly.

Studying effectiveness directly means that evaluators try to determine whether the stated objectives of a program have been achieved. Studying effectiveness indirectly means that the evaluators try to determine whether preconditions to meeting the stated objectives have been achieved. For example, the stated objectives of many bully prevention programs include reduction of the incidence of bullying in school settings. When evaluating such a program, the researcher might address effectiveness directly through the following research questions:

- What is the incidence of bullying before and after students participate in the program?
- Are there differences in how much the incidence of bullying changes after participation in the program versus participation in other programs?

The objectives of many bully prevention programs also include changing the attitudes students have about bullying. In an evaluation of these programs, effectiveness might also be directly addressed through the following question:

- How did attitudes toward bullying change following participation in the program?

Along with such questions, or instead of them, the researcher might evaluate effectiveness indirectly by exploring other questions of relevance. For example, the researcher might evaluate program **integrity**, or fidelity, which is the extent to which the program is being implemented as intended. Other indirect but important questions about effectiveness include the following:

- To what extent did participants enjoy the program and remember its basic message?
- How closely is program content aligned with a widely respected set of bully-prevention principles?
- How cost-effective is the expenditure of time and resources on various program activities?
- What elements appear to be lacking in the program?

A given program evaluation may address one question about effectiveness or a range of questions. In the Eight-Year Study, for instance, the effectiveness of curriculum changes were directly evaluated by addressing questions about students' overall performance in high school, about the content of specific information they were retaining from year to year, and about how well they did in college on a variety of dimensions. Alternatively, as the following description illustrates, an evaluation may focus on both direct and indirect indicators of effectiveness.

> *The purpose of this study was to evaluate the effectiveness of the Peace Pal elementary school peer mediation program in its fifth year of operation. This study answered the following five evaluation questions, which were derived from the goal and objectives of the program: Does student knowledge pertaining to conflict, conflict resolution, and mediation increase as a result of Peace Pal training? Do peer mediation sessions result in the successful resolution of student conflict? Do the number of school-wide out-of-school suspensions decrease with the implementation of the Peace Pal program? Do disputing students who participate in peer mediation sessions view the sessions as valuable? Do peer mediators perceive the Peace Pal program as valuable?*
>
> *(Cantrell, Parks-Savage, & Rehfuss, 2007, p. 476)*

In this description, you can see that effectiveness is evaluated directly (*Do peer mediation sessions result in the successful resolution of student conflict?*) as well as indirectly (e.g., *Do peer mediators perceive the Peace Pal program as valuable?*). The importance of the distinction between direct and indirect evaluation is further illustrated by the study discussed in Spotlight on Research 17.1.

Who Conducts Program Evaluations?

Most educational program evaluation is carried out by educational researchers. Some of these individuals are professors who conduct evaluations either as part of their regular research program or in the capacity of paid consultants. Other evaluators work in the private sector and make use of prior training in research methods. An **internal evaluator** is an existing employee of the program being evaluated, while an **external evaluator** is hired specifically to do the evaluation.

Program evaluation may be carried out by a group of individuals convened specifically for the purpose of conducting the evaluation, as in the case of the Eight-Year Study. Program evaluations are also carried out by established organizations consisting of experts in educational measurement and evaluation. For example, the Center for Evaluation and Education Policy at Indiana University conducts program evaluations and offers evaluation-related services. (Further information, as well as descriptions of specific evaluations, is available online at *http://ceep.indiana.edu/new.*) The program evaluation may take place at one point in time, or the researchers may follow a program and its participants longitudinally. The High/Scope Perry Preschool Project and the Carolina Abecedarian Project are two examples of preschool programs for which program evaluations were carried out over a period of decades. Longitudinal studies of the graduates of these programs showed, from a variety of evaluative and methodological perspectives, that early educational enrichment can have lasting benefits for children from disadvantaged backgrounds.

Evaluating the Effectiveness of a Sexual Assault Prevention Program

Sexual assault prevention at the undergraduate level is critical, given estimates that as many as 20–25% of women and 3% of men are sexually assaulted while in college. The effectiveness of one particular prevention program was evaluated in a 2007 study published in the *Journal of American College Health* by Emily Rothman and Jay Silverman*.

Rothman and Silverman noted that the vast majority of evaluation studies on the effectiveness of sexual assault prevention programs have measured effectiveness indirectly, rather than considering impact on actual incidence of assaults.

Although researchers have completed more than 60 unique college sexual assault prevention program evaluation studies, we have identified only 4 published studies in which researchers assessed sexual assault victimization as an outcome, and researchers in only 1 of these found a positive effect. Other evaluations have measured changes in participants' knowledge about sexual assault, attitudes toward rape victims, acceptance of rape myths, and levels of self-efficacy and anxiety.

Rothman and Silverman studied the effectiveness of a program more directly, in terms of its impact on actual incidence of assault. The researchers also examined whether incidence of reported assaults varied across subgroups of students who differ in sexual orientation (heterosexual, homosexual, or bisexual) and in alcohol use (abstinent, alcohol users, or binge drinkers).

Rothman and Silverman conducted their study at a large northeastern university where a sexual assault prevention program had been recently implemented. The program, mandatory for all first-year students, consists of a drama presentation during orientation entitled "Sex Signals" as well as a small-group educational workshop led by trained sexual assault prevention specialists.

"Sex Signals" is a 2-person show produced by an Illinois-based drama company that has been performed at more than 300 colleges in the United States. The show uses humor and audience participation to educate male and female students about gender role stereotypes, communication styles, and acquaintance rape. Staff members of the college sexual assault prevention office developed and facilitated the

90-minute small group educational workshop. The content of the workshop included a discussion of the definition of rape, the college's definition of sexual assault, criminal and college-specific consequences for perpetrators, personal risk reduction, peer intervention (e.g., helping friends avoid risky situations), improving communication in dating relationships, and basic statistics about sexual assault. The small group workshops took place on weekday evenings in the students' residence halls and were attended by 10 to 20 students each.

Rothman and Silverman were interested in comparing students who had versus had not participated in the prevention program. Since the program was mandatory for first-year students, the researchers compared sophomores from two different classes.

- The intervention group consisted of sophomores from the class of 2007 who were asked to recall incidents of sexual assault during their freshman year. All of these students had participated in the prevention program at the outset of the freshman year.

- The comparison group consisted of sophomores from the class of 2006 who were also asked to recall incidents of sexual assault during their freshman year. (None of these students had participated in the prevention program, since it had not been created yet.)

In all, there were 1,244 students in the intervention group and 744 students in the comparison group. Students in both groups participated in an online survey asking about sexual orientation, substance use, and experiences with sexual assault both prior to and during their first year of college.

We measured sexual assault victimization prior to and during college using 4 items from the revised Sexual Experiences Survey (SES). The revised SES is a 10-item scale often used with college students and has demonstrated good internal consistency (for women, $\alpha = 0.74$; for men, $\alpha = 0.89$), test–retest reliability ($r = .93$), and construct validity. Because of space limitations on the survey, we used 4 of the original items and modified the wording of 2 by changing the words sex play to sexual contact. We also asked whether each event occurred while the respondent was a college student and made the items gender-neutral—the original version assumes the respondent is a woman and asks only about *male assailants. These items had good internal consistency in our sample (for women, α = 0.74; for men, α = 0.79). For the purpose of this study, we defined sexual assault as any positive response to the 4 items on our modified version of the revised SES. [The items are as follows.]*

1. *Have you ever had sexual contact (touching, kissing, but not intercourse) when you didn't want to because you were overwhelmed by continual arguments and pressure?*

2. *Have you ever had sexual contact (touching, kissing, but not intercourse) when you didn't want to because a person threatened or used some degree of physical force (twisting your arm, holding you down, etc.) to make you?*

3. *Have you had sexual intercourse when you didn't want to because a person threatened or used some degree of physical force (twisting your arm, holding you down, etc.) to make you?*

4. *Have you had sexual intercourse when you didn't want to because that person gave you alcohol or drugs and you were too intoxicated to resist?*

We assessed sexual orientation (heterosexual/nonheterosexual) by asking students about the sex of their dating and sexual partners. We asked students "Do you 'date' or 'hook up with' men, women, both, or neither?" We classified men who indicated that they dated or hooked up with men or both men and women as nonheterosexual. We also classified women who indicated that they dated or hooked up with women or both men and women as nonheterosexual.

We measured alcohol use and binge drinking by single items from the Youth Risk Behavior Survey (YRBS) that have demonstrated test–retest reliability. We asked students "In the past 30 days, on how many days did you have at least one drink of alcohol?" and "In the past 30 days, on how many days did you have 5 or more drinks in a row (that is, within a couple of hours)?" (κ = 0.71 and 0.76, respectively). We classified students who indicated no alcohol consumption in the past 30 days as alcohol abstinent.

Rothman and Silverman found that the intervention group experienced slightly but significantly less sexual assault during their first year of college than the comparison group did. The researchers also found significant differences between certain subgroups.

Seventeen percent of the comparison group and 12% of the intervention group reported experiencing sexual assault during their first year of college. . . . After we controlled for differences in gender, and alcohol and binge drinking between these 2 groups, we found that the comparison group had 1.74 times the odds of reporting that they were sexually assaulted during their first year of college than did the intervention group. . . . After identifying specific demographic subgroups within the intervention and comparison groups, we observed a decreased prevalence of sexual assault victimization among men, women, heterosexuals, and those without a prior history of sexual assault victimization among the intervention group compared with its comparison counterparts. . . . We did not have a sufficient number of nonheterosexuals to detect a statistically significant difference in the prevalence of sexual assault among those exposed and unexposed to the prevention program; however, gay, lesbian, and bisexual students exposed to the program were 50% less likely to report being sexually assaulted during their first year of college than were their counterparts in the comparison group (18% and 27%, respectively . . .). Students with a prior history of sexual assault victimization who were exposed to the program were more likely to report that they had been sexually assaulted during their first year of college than were students with a prior history who were not exposed to the program (21% and 7%, respectively . . .).

We stratified the sample by gender and level of substance use to examine possible program effects for each of these subgroups. We detected statistically significant program effects for male alcohol users and women who used no alcohol in the past 30 days. . . . Alcohol-using men in the comparison group had 1.8 times the odds of sexual assault victimization as alcohol-using men in the intervention group. . . . Alcohol abstinent women in the comparison group had 3.2 times the odds of sexual assault victimization as alcohol abstinent women in the intervention group . . .

Rothman and Silverman concluded that the sexual assault prevention program they evaluated had small but genuine benefits, and that it seems to have been effective among homosexual as well as heterosexual students—thereby underscoring the importance of gender-neutral language in program presentations and materials.

*Rothman, E., & Silverman, J. (2007). The effect of a college sexual assault prevention program on first-years students' victimization rates. Journal of American College Health, 55(5), 283–290. Quoted with permission from the publisher.

Purposes of Program Evaluation

There are many different ways to classify program evaluations. In this section, distinctions will be made on the basis of five dimensions: the intended audience for the evaluation, the scale of the program, the extent of collaboration between evaluators and program, the level of analysis in the evaluation, and the timing and general purpose of the evaluation.

Intended Audience

Some program evaluations are carried out primarily for the benefit of the program and its participants. Internal evaluators, or paid external consultants, conduct the evaluation and prepare technical reports for program administrators. There may be no attempt to publish the results in a scientific journal or to disseminate the results to the public. Rather, the purpose of the program evaluation is to help administrators improve the quality of the program. Such evaluations may be requested voluntarily by administrators, or they may be mandated by internal policy or by local or federal law.

At the other end of the spectrum, some program evaluations contribute to scientific knowledge, help administrators improve their programs, and provide useful information to policymakers, advocacy groups, and the general public. Such is the case with the High/Scope Perry Preschool Project and, independently, the Carolina Abecedarian Project. These projects explored the effects of providing stimulating preschool environments to children from economically disadvantaged backgrounds. In conjunction with other research and evaluation evidence, longitudinal studies of the graduates of these programs over a period of decades converged on the following outcomes:

- Project administrators and funding agencies learned that the benefits of the programs last into adulthood, and they gained a clearer sense of areas in which effectiveness could be enhanced.

- Scientists in fields such as child development and education learned that some effects of poverty can be prevented or reversed, and they consequently intensified their study of how to best help disadvantaged children.

- Policymakers and advocacy groups learned that intervention programs can have long-lasting benefits for disadvantaged children, and as a result they worked toward supporting or mandating funds for additional programs.

- The general public learned that early childhood intervention programs can help break the cycle of poverty, and in consequence some citizens became more receptive to the idea of spending tax dollars on such programs.

Scale of Program

Whereas a small evaluation will focus on a single program, large-scale evaluations may explore the effectiveness of regional or national programs, such as all the delinquency prevention programs in a particular district, all the doctoral programs in a given field, or how all the practitioners of a given specialty implement national standards of practice. In the Eight-Year Study, suggestions for about 200 high schools were considered, from which a sample of 30 public and private schools ranging in size were selected on the basis of their interest in curricular innovation.

Extent of Collaboration

The extent of collaboration between researcher and program personnel can range from nonexistent (the researcher evaluates publicly available documents) to a full partnership in which evaluator, program personnel, and participants all have a roughly equal extent of influence over the research process. In the Eight-Year Study, the principals and teachers of the 30 schools were given the freedom to make whatever innovations they chose. (Participating colleges agreed to waive the usual requirements for high school coursework when evaluating applications from study participants, thus freeing the high schools to experiment with curriculum.) At the same time, representatives from the schools met with researchers on an annual basis to share ideas and receive feedback, and there were some similarities in the philosophies and new practices that gradually emerged across schools.

Level of Analysis

A given program evaluation may place greater emphasis on either participant outcomes or program characteristics, or it may reflect roughly equal emphasis on each.

PARTICIPANT FOCUS   An evaluation may explore how the attitudes, behaviors, material conditions, and/or experiences of participants are influenced by the program. Although information about the content and implementation of the program will be considered in the evaluation, the focus is on the participants. An example of such an evaluation in which quantitative methods were used was described in Spotlight on Research 17.1. A qualitative example would be the **responsive evaluation**, in which concerns and issues of personal relevance to participants are documented.

The Eight-Year Study reflected a participant focus, and might be thought of as an explanatory mixed-methods study, in the sense that although the analyses were grounded in a large variety of quantitative measures, the evaluators encouraged the use of any measure that was appropriate to the behavior being measured, including qualitative observations, anecdotes, and interviews.

PROGRAM FOCUS   A program evaluation may place more emphasis on the goals, administration, and/or resource allocation of the program than it does on how the participants turn out (as you will see later in Spotlight on Research 17.2). Although the ultimate purpose of such an evaluation is to increase the effectiveness with which participants are served, and although effectiveness data may be gathered, the focus of this kind of program evaluation is on the program. For example, in a **needs assessment** the evaluator identifies the resources, personnel, and practices that a program would need in order to achieve a desired state.

MIXED FOCUS   In many cases, participants and program are of roughly equal importance in the evaluation. For example, in a **cost–benefit analysis**, effectiveness measured at the level of participants is related to expenditures at the program level. In the case of the High/Scope Perry Preschool Project, Barnett (1996) studied data on graduates from the program at age 27 and weighed the per capita cost of the program against the economic benefits that had been documented. Benefits included higher salaries, less reliance on special educational and welfare services, and lower incidences of crime among graduates of the program. Barnett found that for every tax dollar spent on the program, $7.16 in tax dollars were saved.

Timing and Purpose of Evaluation

In terms of the timing and general purpose of a program evaluation, a broad distinction can be made between formative and summative evaluation (Scriven, 1967).

FORMATIVE EVALUATION   **Formative evaluation** takes place as a program is being developed. The purpose of formative evaluation is to gather information that will improve the merit and effectiveness of the program. Formative evaluation may result in radical changes to a program, or even discontinuance if serious problems with the program are revealed. Often, although not necessarily, the researchers who conduct formative evaluation are internal evaluators.

The use of formative evaluation is reported in a 2006 case study by Goei, Boyson, Lyon-Callo, Schott, Wasilevich and Cannarile. Goei and colleagues described how the Asthma Initiative of Michigan and the Michigan Department of Community Health developed an asthma management program for use in Michigan public schools. A team of 125 experts worked together to develop this program, which is called the Michigan Asthma School Packet, or MASP. The first step in the formative evaluation was to review existing programs in other states and select effective characteristics from those programs. The second step was to mail surveys to a variety of school employees, including principals, teachers, administrative assistants, custodians, and school nurses. Open-ended telephone surveys were then conducted with a separate sample of school personnel in order to illuminate earlier results.

Three themes emerged across both the quantitative and the qualitative survey responses:

1. School employees lack time to read most of the health information they receive.
2. School employees do not perceive asthma as a threat to their students.
3. School employees overestimate their ability to deal with asthma.

Each of these themes contributed to the development of the MASP. In order to address the first theme, the final version of the MASP consisted primarily of brief, visually striking booklets that conveyed only essential information. To address the second theme, MASP booklets stressed the seriousness of the problem and included the tag line "Asthma: It's more serious than you think". To address the third theme, the MASP booklets included asthma IQ quizzes and a "what to do" section. A page from one of the MASP booklets illustrating how underestimation of threat and overconfidence were addressed is reproduced in Figure 17.1.

SUMMATIVE EVALUATION   **Summative evaluation** consists of the evaluation of a completed program, often by external evaluators. Most of the research discussed in this chapter falls under the heading of summative evaluation, in part because formative evaluation studies are more likely to be oriented toward program development than publication.

In the original formulation of the concept, the purpose of summative evaluation was to compare a program to existing alternatives in terms of effectiveness (Scriven, 1967). For example, the results of the Eight-Year Study included comparisons of the college performance of students who had graduated from the 30 high schools versus students who had graduated from other high schools that had not engaged in curricular reform. The students in the two groups were carefully matched on age, race, SAT scores, community background, and personal as well as career interests.

FIGURE 17.1 Sample Page from MASP

IF YOU DON'T THINK **NOT** BEING

ABLE TO BREATHE

IS BAD, TRY IT SOMETIME.

To get a better idea, try breathing through a straw— it's even worse than the double negative you just read. Sadly, each school day children sit in classrooms filled with things that trigger attacks. Dust, molds, furry class pets, even perfume can all cause asthma symptoms. Worse still, a recent survey found that many school workers don't think asthma is really that serious. At the same time, triggers abound.

<u>Do you know what they are?</u>

it's more serious than you think.

Some of the main findings of this comparison are summarized in Figure 17.2. One conclusion drawn from the findings was that preparation for college does not depend on a set curriculum. Students who had attended the high schools in which curricular experimentation took place were better off in some ways than students who had attended high schools with a fixed, traditional curriculum.

The effectiveness of a program may be evaluated by comparing participants to nonparticipants, as in the Eight-Year Study results summarized in Figure 17.2, and in the causal–comparative study described earlier in Spotlight on Research 17.1. Spotlight on Research 17.2 illustrates how multiple program comparisons serve a primarily descriptive purpose rather than yielding direct comparisons of effectiveness.

FIGURE 17.2
College Performance of Students from the Thirty Schools in the Eight-Year Study

In comparison to students who had attended traditional schools, students from the 30 schools . . .

. . . had higher grades in college, both overall and in all subjects except foreign language.

. . . received more academic honors and more nonacademic honors each year.

. . . did not differ in areas of study, in the number of times they were placed on probation, in the extent of their social adjustment, or in their time management skills.

. . . were more often judged to be precise, systematic, and objective, to have a great deal of intellectual curiosity, to have developed clear ideas about the meaning of education, and to have demonstrated considerable resourcefulness in handling new situations.

. . . had about the same problems of adjustment as the comparison group, but approached their solution with greater effectiveness;

1. Participated somewhat more frequently, and more often enjoyed appreciative experiences, in the arts; participated more in all organized student groups except religious and "service" activities;

2. Had a somewhat better orientation toward the choice of a vocation;

3. Demonstrated a more active concern for what was going on in the world.

Spotlight on Research 17.2

Student Assessment in Criminal Justice Programs: A Summative Evaluation

Periodic assessment of learning is a legal requirement at the K–12 level but not in higher education. Although standardized national- and state-level tests are required for various kinds of licensure and certification, the law does not require universities to monitor the academic achievement of their students in any particular way. However, concerns about accountability in higher education are leading some educators and policymakers to call for national tests.

In a 2006 article in *Justice Quarterly**, Laura Moriarty pointed out that if national tests are imminent, institutions might begin the assessment process now rather than waiting for it to be mandated. To this end, she conducted a descriptive evaluation of how undergraduate programs in criminal justice carry out student assessment.

Moriarty surveyed a random sample of 162 criminal justice programs at 2- and 4-year colleges across the United States.

The web-based survey was designed and administered using SurveyMonkey, a tool used to create web surveys. There are six sections that include 30 open- and closed-ended questions: (1) general information about the institution such as size and type of the criminal justice program, (2) learning objectives developed by the program, (3) assessment instruments used by the program, (4) methods of analyzing the assessment data, (5) application of learning assessment results such as changes made to the criminal justice major based on results, and (6) institutional environment such as the resources available to the criminal justice program for conducting assessment activities.

One of Moriarty's findings was that not very many programs have developed and fully implemented learning objectives for their students.

When asked "At what stage is your program in developing learning objectives for your criminal justice majors?" we found that 23 or 19 percent have not yet developed student learning objectives. Of those responding (n = 122), more than half (53 percent) indicate that they have implemented a set of learning objectives. This means that there is still a great deal of work that needs to be done for a large number of units. About one-quarter (24.5 percent) of those who responded are somewhere in the assessment process, with about 3 percent just beginning to talk about learning objectives, almost 14 percent being in the process of formulating learning objectives, and about 8 percent having formulated a set of learning objectives that have been adopted but not implemented. About 19 percent are in the process of reviewing or revising a previously adopted set of learning objectives.

Moriarty observed a great deal of variability in terms of whether programs use assessments to measure student learning and, if so, in the way the assessments are created and administered.

Over half (52 percent) [of the programs] have identified an assessment instrument and have implemented it, while almost 20 percent are reviewing or revising previously implemented instruments. The other 29 percent have not had any discussions about assessment instruments (7.3 percent), have discussed an assessment instrument but have not decided on it (14 percent), or have decided on an assessment instrument but have not yet implemented it (7.3 percent) . . .

The assessment instruments were developed by the full department in regular meetings (33 percent), by a department subcommittee (27 percent), by the chair working alone (12 percent), adopted from another source (9 percent), or at a departmental retreat (6 percent). About 3 percent did not know how the assessment instruments were developed, and 10 percent indicated "other" . . .

For the most part, the chair (36 percent) or a designated faculty member (33 percent) or the faculty in general (17 percent) is the person/people who is/are responsible for gathering and analyzing the data generated by the learning assessment instruments. The departmental secretary is responsible in about five percent of the programs or "other" (e.g., assessment committee/director) in 9 percent of the programs. Data are gathered for assessment purposes each semester or term (45 percent), once a year (42 percent), on a multi-year cycle (10 percent), or other . . .

We are often very concerned about "unfunded mandates," and so we asked the programs to indicate if institutional resources have been made available to assist with assessment: More than one-quarter (26 percent) have no resources available, with about another quarter (24.2 percent) having few resources, more than one third (36.4 percent) have some resources, and about 14 percent have substantial resources available. When asked to clarify what kinds of resources are available, the following were available in rank order: on-campus workshops (25 percent), travel to off-campus workshops or conferences (22 percent), none (17 percent), on-campus centers on teaching and learning (15 percent), course release time (10 percent), financial compensation (6 percent), and "other" . . . (5 percent).

Moriarty found much less variability in what motivated institutions to conduct student assessments in the first place.

The external and internal pushes for assessment are apparent in this research, with 88 percent of the programs indicating that the regional accrediting organization has made student learning assessment a high or somewhat high priority. Almost 94 percent indicate that the institutional administration has made student learning outcomes a high or somewhat high priority.

In terms of specific learning objectives and assessments, some themes were apparent among those institutions that provided information.

We provided a list of student learning objectives and asked the programs to indicate which ones are included in the program's list of student learning objectives. The top three learning objectives include developing critical thinking skills (96 percent), developing writing skills (89 percent), and comprehending to the level of familiarity the major theories and analytical approaches in criminal justice (88 percent). Two thirds (66 percent) to almost three quarters indicate the following as student learning objectives included in the programs: comprehend to the level of familiarity the major sub-fields of criminal justice (74 percent), develop inter-personal communication skills (70 percent), understand ethnic, gender, or cultural dimensions of problems and policies related to criminal justice (69 percent), and comprehend criminal justice research (66 percent). More than half or half of the programs indicated the following: Develop skills in making public presentations (55 percent), develop information technology skills (55 percent), knowledge of general management and administrative principles applicable to criminal justice (50 percent), acquire practical experience in areas of criminal justice (50 percent), and develop reading skills (50 percent). The other items on the list were used in more than one third of the programs: employ quantitative and statistical approaches to solve criminal justice problems/issues (44 percent), design and conduct criminal justice research projects (41 percent), develop a fundamental understanding of cognate disciplines like political science, sociology, psychology, or public administration (41 percent), and understand the international dimensions of problems and policies related to criminal justice (36 percent) . . .

Respondents were given a wide array of assessment techniques to indicate if they used these techniques in their programs and then to rate the effectiveness of each technique . . .

The top seven assessment measures in terms of usage include: grades in course work (80 percent), survey of students (79 percent), internship (75 percent), observation by faculty members (72 percent), survey of departmental alumni (69 percent), survey of employers/internship supervisor (67 percent), and senior seminar or capstone course (66 percent), with two-thirds or more of the programs indicating that these instruments are used in their programs. The top seven assessment measures in terms of their effectiveness in evaluating student objectives include: survey of employer/internship supervisor (92 percent), major field test (92 percent), survey of students (91 percent), case-study analyses (91 percent), rubrics (90 percent), post-test only (90 percent), and internship (89 percent), with about 90 percent or more of the programs indicating these techniques are very effective or somewhat effective.

In summarizing the results, Moriarty noticed a troubling pattern.

> *Interestingly enough, the top three learning objectives for the programs are to develop critical thinking skills . . . develop writing skills . . . and to be familiar with major theories and analytical approaches in criminal justice . . . while the most often used method to assess these learning objectives is grades in major course work. Arguably, grades are not the best measure of critical thinking skills or writing skills. They may be a good measure of familiarity with major theories and analytical approaches, but when grades are used as an assessment tool, we are often left to ponder just what the students did not understand. When a student receives a ''B'' in a theory class, exactly which theories or theorists or paradigms or schools of thought is the student having difficulty mastering?*
>
> *If we believe that assessment is an ongoing process that incorporates reflection and revision, then we need to make sure that we are not just checking the assessment box as done, and moving forward without really addressing whatever is problematic in terms of student learning. If the students are not getting it, how do we work to help them get it?*

In spite of this concern, Moriarty noted that many programs are using their assessment results to improve their offerings, by making changes such as modifying courses and revising course offerings. She closed with a set of recommendations.

- *Course-embedded assessments can be used for individual-, course-, program-, and institutional-level assessment of student learning through appropriate analysis and aggregation. Selected assignments can be designated within major courses to serve as threshold, milestone, or capstone assessments . . .*

- *Individual student learning can be tracked constantly on campuses through course-level assessments, particularly if faculty learn about good formative and summative assessment practices. Administrative support for faculty development is important.*

- *Student development takes time so representative samples of student work, gathered at carefully chosen points in a curriculum, can be sufficient to create a program or institutional picture of student learning. Choose the sample points after analyzing the curriculum to find points at which . . . students will likely have had sufficient opportunity to learn what is being assessed.*

- *Given that evaluation is the highest level of the cognitive domain, students themselves should be challenged to learn assessment techniques in which they assess work in exactly the same ways used by experts in the particular domain. Not only does this raise the level of student learning, but it can also provide cycles of self- and peer-formative assessment, relieving faculty of part of the formative assessment workload (Association of American Colleges and Universities, 2005, p. 8).*

*Moriarty, L. J. (2006). Investing in quality: The current state of assessment in criminal justice programs. *Justice Quarterly, 23(4)*, 409–427. Quoted with permission from the publisher.

Standards for Program Evaluation

In Chapter 5 you read about how several professional organizations collaborated in the production of the *Standards for Educational and Psychological Testing*, an authoritative guide to measurement and testing in educational research. Through a roughly analogous process, the American Educational Research Association, the National Education Association, and 14 other organizations jointly participated in the creation of standards for program evaluation. Under the guidance of the Joint Committee on Standards for Educational Evaluation, these organizations worked together during the 1980s to create a volume now titled *Program Evaluation Standards* (1994). This authoritative volume includes four sets of criteria for effective evaluation: utility, feasibility, propriety, and accuracy. These four criteria and the standards associated with each are reproduced in Figure 17.3. (You can view the

Utility Standards

The utility standards are intended to ensure that an evaluation will serve the information needs of intended users.

U1 Stakeholder Identification Persons involved in or affected by the evaluation should be identified, so that their needs can be addressed.

U2 Evaluator Credibility The persons conducting the evaluation should be both trustworthy and competent to perform the evaluation, so that the evaluation findings achieve maximum credibility and acceptance.

U3 Information Scope and Selection Information collected should be broadly selected to address pertinent questions about the program and be responsive to the needs and interests of clients and other specified stakeholders.

U4 Values Identification The perspectives, procedures, and rationale used to interpret the findings should be carefully described, so that the bases for value judgments are clear.

U5 Report Clarity Evaluation reports should clearly describe the program being evaluated, including its context, and the purposes, procedures, and findings of the evaluation, so that essential information is provided and easily understood.

U6 Report Timeliness and Dissemination Significant interim findings and evaluation reports should be disseminated to intended users, so that they can be used in a timely fashion.

U7 Evaluation Impact Evaluations should be planned, conducted, and reported in ways that encourage follow-through by stakeholders, so that the likelihood that the evaluation will be used is increased.

Feasibility Standards

The feasibility standards are intended to ensure that an evaluation will be realistic, prudent, diplomatic, and frugal.

F1 Practical Procedures The evaluation procedures should be practical, to keep disruption to a minimum while needed information is obtained.

F2 Political Viability The evaluation should be planned and conducted with anticipation of the different positions of various interest groups, so that their cooperation may be obtained, and so that possible attempts by any of these groups to curtail evaluation operations or to bias or misapply the results can be averted or counteracted.

F3 Cost Effectiveness The evaluation should be efficient and produce information of sufficient value, so that the resources expended can be justified.

Propriety Standards

The propriety standards are intended to ensure that an evaluation will be conducted legally, ethically, and with due regard for the welfare of those involved in the evaluation, as well as those affected by its results.

P1 Service Orientation Evaluations should be designed to assist organizations to address and effectively serve the needs of the full range of targeted participants.

P2 Formal Agreements Obligations of the formal parties to an evaluation (what is to be done, how, by whom, when) should be agreed to in writing, so that these parties are obligated to adhere to all conditions of the agreement or formally to renegotiate it.

P3 Rights of Human Subjects Evaluations should be designed and conducted to respect and protect the rights and welfare of human subjects.

(continued)

standards and related information online at *www.mich.edu/evalctr/jc.*) As you can see, the standards encompass a range of dimensions, including the qualifications of the evaluator, the quality and relevance of the evaluation, the ethical treatment of participants, and the dissemination of evaluation results.

FIGURE 17.3
continued

P4 Human Interactions Evaluators should respect human dignity and worth in their interactions with other persons associated with an evaluation, so that participants are not threatened or harmed.

P5 Complete and Fair Assessment The evaluation should be complete and fair in its examination and recording of strengths and weaknesses of the program being evaluated, so that strengths can be built upon and problem areas addressed.

P6 Disclosure of Findings The formal parties to an evaluation should ensure that the full set of evaluation findings along with pertinent limitations are made accessible to the persons affected by the evaluation and any others with expressed legal rights to receive the results.

P7 Conflict of Interest Conflict of interest should be dealt with openly and honestly, so that it does not compromise the evaluation processes and results.

P8 Fiscal Responsibility The evaluator's allocation and expenditure of resources should reflect sound accountability procedures and otherwise be prudent and ethically responsible, so that expenditures are accounted for and appropriate.

Accuracy Standards

The accuracy standards are intended to ensure that an evaluation will reveal and convey technically adequate information about the features that determine worth or merit of the program being evaluated.

A1 Program Documentation The program being evaluated should be described and documented clearly and accurately, so that the program is clearly identified.

A2 Context Analysis The context in which the program exists should be examined in enough detail, so that its likely influences on the program can be identified.

A3 Described Purposes and Procedures The purposes and procedures of the evaluation should be monitored and described in enough detail, so that they can be identified and assessed.

A4 Defensible Information Sources The sources of information used in a program evaluation should be described in enough detail, so that the adequacy of the information can be assessed.

A5 Valid Information The information-gathering procedures should be chosen or developed and then implemented so that they will assure that the interpretation arrived at is valid for the intended use.

A6 Reliable Information The information-gathering procedures should be chosen or developed and then implemented so that they will assure that the information obtained is sufficiently reliable for the intended use.

A7 Systematic Information The information collected, processed, and reported in an evaluation should be systematically reviewed, and any errors found should be corrected.

A8 Analysis of Quantitative Information Quantitative information in an evaluation should be appropriately and systematically analyzed so that evaluation questions are effectively answered.

A9 Analysis of Qualitative Information Qualitative information in an evaluation should be appropriately and systematically analyzed so that evaluation questions are effectively answered.

A10 Justified Conclusions The conclusions reached in an evaluation should be explicitly justified, so that stakeholders can assess them.

A11 Impartial Reporting Reporting procedures should guard against distortion caused by personal feelings and biases of any party to the evaluation, so that evaluation reports fairly reflect the evaluation findings.

A12 Metaevaluation The evaluation itself should be formatively and summatively evaluated against these and other pertinent standards, so that its conduct is appropriately guided and, on completion, stakeholders can closely examine its strengths and weaknesses.

The *Program Evaluation Standards* do not specify which particular designs or methods should be used in an evaluation. Emphasis is placed on thoroughness, validity and reliability, systematicity, and clear and unbiased reporting of results—standards that can be met by virtually any specific quantitative, qualitative, or mixed-methods design. For example, the study summarized in Spotlight on Research 17.3 illustrates an experimental approach to the evaluation of a truancy prevention program.

Evaluation of a Truancy Prevention Program: An Experimental Approach

Truancy, defined as unexcused absences from school, is a major problem in the United States. In a 2007 study published in *Preventing School Failure**, Janiece DeSocio and colleagues developed, implemented, and evaluated a pilot program for preventing truancy at one high school in the Northeast.

The intervention program that DeSocio and colleagues developed was based on the assumption that health services and teacher mentoring can have an impact on truancy rates.

Although health problems are identified as root causes of truancy, a review of literature found little evidence of comprehensive health assessments and services being integrated within programs for truancy prevention/intervention. Given the gap in existing models, enrollment in school-based health services was incorporated as a key feature of this intervention.

Truancy is also associated with factors within the school environment. Characteristics of school environments that inhibit truancy include attending to individual student needs, engaging students in supportive relationships, establishing incentives for attendance, promptly addressing student absences, minimizing punitive responses, and forming alliances with health and human services to address the problems of students and their families (Roderick et al., 1997; Rohrman, 1993; U.S. Department of Education, 1996a). It was anticipated that enlisting teachers as mentors from within the students' school would impact the school culture and help build positive attitudes and truancy intervention skills from within.

The health services component of DeSocio and colleagues' intervention program was provided by the school-based health center (SBHC), which offers comprehensive health services to students and would ordinarily be voluntary.

Enrollment in the SBHC was a condition of participation for students in the intervention group. Students participated in usual SBHC enrollment procedures, which included completing a health questionnaire, a health interview, and a physical examination by a nurse practitioner. With student and parent or guardian consent, the health questionnaire

was part of data collection for students in the intervention group. Pediatric and psychiatric nurse practitioners provided health services and followed-up on identified health risks and problems.

Clinic hours of one psychiatric nurse practitioner were expanded to serve students in this project in anticipation of the greater mental health needs among students with high absenteeism. The psychiatric nurse practitioner functioned as health liaison to the project team and participated in family meetings to provide consultation regarding health barriers affecting students' school performance . . .

The mentoring component of the program was extensive and was based primarily on teacher support.

An invitation to participate as student mentors was extended to all teachers in the school. Interested teachers were asked to submit a brief written statement about why they were interested in serving as a student mentor and what they believed could help students with high absenteeism develop positive attitudes toward school. Seven teachers were selected on the basis of their enthusiasm for working with students and their positive beliefs and ideas about helping students. Teachers who were selected as mentors participated in an orientation to the philosophy and activities of the intervention. Four to five students were randomly assigned to each teacher . . .

The primary role of mentors was to build a relationship with each student to engender processes of self-development and promote school engagement. In large schools, students find it easy to cultivate anonymous identities that allow them to miss school with little notice by school officials (Roderick et al., 1997). To counteract this sense of anonymity, mentors informed students they would look for them each school day and would follow up if they were absent. Mentors established predictable times for daily student check-ins and one-on-one interactions. Efforts were made to encourage each student's special interests as a way to link school attendance to personal aspirations. Small grants from the school were used to create opportunities to promote students' special interests. For example, one student showed exceptional ability in art and a small grant was used to pay for individual art lessons after school.

Mentors facilitated two after-school tutoring sessions weekly to assist students with homework and encourage positive peer relationships. They helped students improve study habits and connected them with services for special learning needs.

Students with chronic patterns of truancy usually elicit frustration and lowered expectations from teachers and staff and may, thereby, contribute to a growing sense of alienation between students and teachers. Mentor advocacy within the school helped interrupt this negative cycle and was an important aspect of the intervention. For example, when a student reported problems with a teacher or a particular class, the mentor would offer to mediate by checking in with the teacher to gain a better understanding of the student's problems and would set up meetings with the student and teacher to explore options for resolving the problems. Teachers in the school soon became aware of which students had mentors, and because they had existing relationships with teacher colleagues who were serving as mentors, they would seek them out for help in resolving problems . . .

Group meetings were held with mentors and members of the project team throughout the intervention period. These group meetings were an essential source of support for mentors as they experienced the highs and lows of working with youth who had serious academic and attendance problems. . . .

In addition to home visits to obtain consent, the project coordinator called families to offer encouragement or inquire about students' whereabouts when they were absent from school. When a mentor did not find a student at the usual check-in time, they called the coordinator for assistance in locating the student. Support was essential for teachers to function in the mentor role and continue to meet other teaching responsibilities. Many students formed their strongest in-school connection with the project coordinator whose office was conveniently located in the main school corridor, encouraging drop-in visits by students on their way to and from classes.

Parents participated in the development of a school reentry plan with the youth and the project coordinator. Re-entry plans addressed practical issues such as acquiring alarm clocks and negotiating school transportation, as well as restructuring family routines to support school attendance. Telephone contacts with the coordinator were encouraged and additional home visits were conducted if families were without telephones or did not return telephone calls. Public transportation tokens were offered to families to support their participation in two in-school meetings held during the intervention semester, for the purpose of discussing student progress.

All students in the study were under 16 years of age and had a history of 15 or more unexcused absences during the prior year. These students were experiencing serious problems with academics and attendance, and were at risk for dropping out of school. Students were randomly assigned to one of three groups:

- Intervention group (n = 29). These students participated in the truancy prevention program described above.

- Unable-to-enroll group (n = 37). These students had been contacted by the researchers but were unable to participate in the intervention program.

- Control group (n = 37). These students received usual school services and had no contact with the researchers.

As a baseline measure, DeSocio and colleagues calculated group means for four variables during the semester prior to the intervention program: least number of days absent from a class, greatest number of days absent from a class, number of classes failing, and grade point average (GPA). The results of an ANOVA indicated that the three groups did not differ significantly on any of these variables at baseline.

Following the intervention, means for the four dependent variables were once again calculated. The means and ANOVA results are summarized in the table on the next page.

Although no significant differences emerged for the two grade-related variables (number of classes failing and grade point average), the intervention group showed significantly lower absenteeism means than the other two groups. In a separate analysis, DeSocio and colleagues found that by the end of the academic year, only two students in the intervention group had left school, as compared with six students from the unable-to-enroll group and 11 students from the control group. The researchers concluded that their program, although still in the piloting stage, has some benefits for the at-risk population they wish to help.

Comparison of Interventions, Unable-to-Enroll, and Control Group on School Performance Measures in Third Grading Period, N = 92

| School performance measures | Groups[c] | | | | | | Source of variance (SS) | | | | | |
| | Intervention (*n* = 28) | | Unable to enroll (*n* = 33) | | Controls (*n* = 31) | | | | | | | |
	M	*SD*	*M*	*SD*	*M*	*SD*	Between	Within	Total	*F*	*df*	*p*
Least days absent	4.5[a]	4.2	9.0[b]	7.1	9.4[b]	6.1	429.594	3229.482	3659.076	5.92	2	.004**
Most days absent	28.0[a]	13.3	34.2[b]	11.5	34.4[b]	11.4	781.601	11,003.834	11,785.435	3.16	2	.047*
Number classes failing	5.2	2.5	6.0	2.0	5.7	1.9	11.019	401.851	412.870	1.22	2	.30
Grade point average	0.67	0.78	0.33	0.61	0.39	0.63	1.908	40.371	42.278	2.10	2	.13

Note. N = 92. Means with different subscripts differed significantly.
*Significant group difference based on alpha set at .05. **Significant group difference based on alpha of .01.

*DeSocio, J., VanCura, M., Nelson, L.A., Hewitt, G., Kitzman, H., & Cole, R. (2007). Engaging truant adolescents: Results from a multifaceted intervention pilot. *Preventing School Failure, 51*(3), 3–11. Quoted with permission from the publisher.

Ethical Considerations in Program Evaluation

As a form of research, program evaluation is subject to the same ethical constraints as any other kind of study (see Chapter 4 for details). However, the fact that in some cases the evaluator is being paid to conduct the research introduces some ethical issues that do not ordinarily arise in other types of research. Two of the fallacies that paid evaluators must take special care to avoid are "clientism" and "contractualism" (Howe, 1995).

Clientism is the assumption that because the client (i.e., the program representative) has paid for the evaluation, the evaluator should do whatever the client wants. Although the evaluating researcher must create an evaluation that serves the needs of the program (see standard P1 in Figure 17.3), it is also essential that the researcher creates an ethically sound evaluation. The researcher should not allow findings to be distorted or the privacy of participants to be violated if pressured to do so by a program administrator (see, for example, standards A1, A11, and P3 in Figure 17.3).

Much the same can be said for **contractualism**, the assumption that the evaluator must follow the terms of the contract to the letter. Although the evaluating researcher must honor the contract (see standard P2 in Figure 17.3), in extreme situations, such as the discovery of child abuse, it may be necessary to violate the original terms of the contract.

How to Plan a Program Evaluation

Following is a list of steps that are taken in planning an evaluation. The list is not definitive, nor are the steps distinct or carried out in exactly the order given here. For the most part, the list is comparable to lists you have seen in earlier chapters describing how to carry out a particular type of research. The list also contains steps that are common to other types of research but receive special emphasis in program evaluation.

- Identify a program or programs. Will your evaluation focus on a single program or on a set?

- Formulate the broad goals of the evaluation. Is your evaluation intended to benefit one or more programs and their participants, or are you trying to also reach a broader audience that includes researchers and policymakers?

- Conduct a literature review. What general or specific guidance can you obtain from prior research and theory?

- Tentatively formulate your research questions and research design. Will your research questions focus on program characteristics, participant outcomes, or a balance of the two? How do your research questions connect with program objectives? What type of quantitative, qualitative, or mixed-methods design seems most suitable and feasible for addressing your research questions?

- Determine the extent of your collaboration with the program(s). Will you be evaluating publicly available documents or collaborating with program administrators? If the evaluation will be collaborative, what are the details of the partnership?

- Determine the availability of resources. What kinds of materials are available? What kinds of information can be gathered from program administrators and participants? Are there specific ethical constraints over and above those normally encountered in human subjects research?

- Establish a timeline. Are there time constraints imposed by program administrators and/or practical circumstances, or is there flexibility in the timing of data collection and reporting?

- Review the general standards for evaluation. Are any of the widely accepted evaluation standards in Figure 17.3 especially critical? Will any of these standards be particularly difficult to meet?

- Review any specific evaluation criteria. Do program administrators have a particular interest in certain kinds of information or themes? What kinds of decisions are the administrators hoping to make?

Evaluating a Program Evaluation

You should keep two questions in mind when evaluating a particular evaluation study. First, how well does the study meet the standards of the particular quantitative, qualitative, or mixed-methods design that was used? Second, how well does the study meet the standards of program evaluation? The answer to the first question depends on the evaluative criteria for different types of research design discussed in earlier chapters. The answer to the second question depends on how well the evaluation study meets the standards embodied in Figure 17.3 and in other authoritative sources, such as the American Evaluation Association's *Guiding Principles for Evaluators*, an extensive series of volumes focusing on different aspects and types of program evaluations.

A general strength of program evaluation research is its capacity to directly influence educational practice in local settings. Whether the goal is to help create a new program or to evaluate and refine an existing program, evaluation research can have an immediate and focused impact. The more appropriate the design and implementation of the evaluation study, the greater the practical benefits for program and participants.

Depending on the particular study, a program evaluation may have limited generalizability. The researcher's ability to create a methodologically sound study with good external validity may be limited by time constraints, by the availability of participants and resources, and by the needs of the particular program being evaluated.

Some limitations on the program evaluation as a form of scientific inquiry may be imposed by the need to obtain findings of highly specific relevance to a particular program. Although the emphasis of this chapter has been on program evaluation as a form of research, ultimately the goal of the evaluation is to support judgments and decisions about program practice.

A Look Ahead

You have now read about the major approaches to conducting educational research—quantitative designs (Chapters 7–12), qualitative designs (Chapters 13 and 14), mixed-methods designs (Chapter 15)—as well as two very different applied approaches to research that can employ virtually any kind of design—action research (Chapter 16) and program evaluation (Chapter 17). The final chapter of the book discusses further issues of importance to the way that educational research is translated into practice, and provides some guidance in the development of your own research.

Applications: A Guide for Beginning Researchers

Here are some ideas from the chapter that will help you plan your research:

- Decide whether a program evaluation is something you want to participate in. Identify the more experienced individuals who will help you plan and carry out this research.
- Help understand the needs of the program as well as the timeline and other logistics of the evaluation.
- Help choose the quantitative, qualitative, or mixed-methods approach that will be used in the evaluation.
- Help ensure that the program evaluation meets both general standards as well as program needs.

Chapter Summary

The development of program evaluation was prompted by federal legislation as well as prior scholarly work. Currently, program evaluations vary widely in scope and in the types of research designs that are used. The general purpose of a program evaluation is to evaluate the merit and effectiveness of an educational program.

Program evaluation differs from assessment. Each specific program evaluation may focus directly and/or indirectly on the merit and effectiveness of a program. The researchers who carry out an evaluation may be internal or external evaluators.

Different types of program evaluations can be distinguished on the basis of the intended audience for the evaluation, the scale of the program, the extent of collaboration between evaluators and program personnel, the level of analysis in the evaluation (participant, program, or mixed), and the timing and general purpose of the evaluation (formative or summative).

Authoritative standards for conducting program evaluations are highly influential. Evaluation of a particular program evaluation will be informed by these standards as well as by considerations specific to the research design that was used.

Key Terms

Elementary and Secondary Education Act (ESEA)

Program evaluation

Integrity

Internal evaluator

External evaluator

Responsive evaluation

Needs assessment

Cost–benefit analysis

Formative evaluation

Summative evaluation

Clientism

Contractualism

Exercises

1. Which of the following is an accurate statement?

a) Program evaluation relies exclusively on quantitative methods.

b) A variety of quantitative, qualitative, and mixed-methods designs are used in program evaluation.

c) Program evaluation is a form of action research that relies on quantitative and/or qualitative methods.

d) Qualitative methods are the preferred approach in program evaluation.

2. Measurement of which of the following variables would constitute the most direct test of the effectiveness of an after-school program at reducing absenteeism?

a) Rates of absenteeism before and after participation in the program

b) Attitudes toward school before and after participation in the program

c) Explanations of reasons for absenteeism before and after participation in the program

d) Enjoyment of the program

3. What type of program evaluation might result in radical changes to a program while it is in the process of being created?

a) Cost–benefit analysis

b) Needs assessment

c) Responsive evaluation

d) Formative evaluation

4. Which of the following types of program evaluation relies exclusively on qualitative methods?

a) Cost–benefit analysis

b) Formative evaluation

c) Responsive evaluation

d) Needs assessment

5. A program evaluation that inadvertently violates participants' privacy fails to meet what kind of standards?

a) Utility standards

b) Feasibility standards

c) Propriety standards

d) Accuracy standards

6. Decisions about how to write up and disseminate the results of a program evaluation should be most directly informed by what kind of standards?

a) Utility standards

b) Feasibility standards

c) Propriety standards

d) Accuracy standards

7. *Critical thinking question*: Could there be a program evaluation of program evaluations?

Answers to Exercises

1. b **2.** a **3.** d **4.** c **5.** c **6.** a

7. *Possible answer*: Yes. Studies could evaluate the methods used in program evaluations in a particular area, in order to characterize the evaluations on dimensions such as accuracy, or to indicate the extent to which evaluation activities are aligned with standards such as those of the *Program Evaluation Standards* (see Figure 17.3). Longitudinal studies on the merit and effectiveness of program evaluations in a particular area could ascertain the extent to which evaluations have led to program-related changes, and perhaps yield cost–benefit analyses relating the benefits of these evaluations to the resources that were needed to conduct them. These are just a few of the ways the process of program evaluation could itself be evaluated. (Studies such as those described here are in fact conducted.)

Suggestions for Further Reading

Research Article Yearwood, D. L., & Abdum-Muhaymin, J. (2007). Juvenile structured day programs for suspended and expelled youth: An evaluation of process and impact. *Preventing School Failure, 51*(4), 47–59.

This explanatory mixed-methods study presents an evaluation of structured day programs for juvenile delinquents in North Carolina.

Application Article Shoenfelt, E. L., & Huddleston, M. R. (2006). The Truancy Court Diversion Program of the family court, Warren Circuit Court Division III, Bowling Green, Kentucky: An evaluation of impact on attendance and academic performance. *Family Court Review, 44*(4), 683–695.

This quasi-experimental study describes the effects of an intervention program on elementary and middle school students.

Extension Article Hannan, C. K. (2007, February). Exploring assessment processes in specialized schools for students who are visually impaired. *Journal of Visual Impairment and Blindness*, pp. 69–79.

This qualitative study evaluates the assessment procedures used in schools for the blind across the United States.

CHAPTER 18

Research Into Practice

Gabe Palmer/©Corbis

Introduction

This last chapter is meant to help you gain a better understanding of the vast and shifting field of educational research. If you plan to conduct a research project, this chapter will help you locate your own study in the contemporary scene. The title of the chapter, "Research into Practice," has two meanings, each corresponding to a different part of the chapter.

Since educational research has a strongly applied focus, a topic of interest to all researchers is how their work might impact educational practice. In the first part of the chapter I focus on concerns and disagreements about how research should influence practice, as well as recommendations for bridging the research–practice gap.

In the second part of the chapter I discuss how to translate what you have learned from this book into practice. Here "practice" does not mean educational practice but rather the practice of conducting research. This part of the chapter begins with a discussion of different areas and approaches in educational research. Then, building on material I have introduced throughout the book, the chapter closes with guidance for carrying out each stage of a research project from planning through publication.

Research and Practice

The history of public education and the history of educational reform are closely intertwined. Educators, political leaders, and parents have always striven to improve the quality and relevance of the educational system—sometimes cooperatively, sometimes with extreme antagonism within and across groups. Scholars have had a voice too, offering critical opinions from the perspectives of philosophy, religion, precedent, and common sense. Researchers, in contrast, are latecomers to this history. As noted in Chapter 1, educational research is barely a century old.

Although a fundamental goal of research is to acquire scientific knowledge, what educational researchers have always shared with other stakeholders in the educational system is an interest in improving educational practice. The practical interests of educational researchers continue to expand as the field grows and becomes more differentiated. It would be impossible to characterize the state of the field at present, or to touch on all the issues of both general and specific importance to educational researchers. Instead, this part of the chapter addresses one of the themes that has a more or less visible presence across the entire field. The theme can be expressed in the form of a question: What is the proper relationship between research and practice? This question takes on a somewhat different form in different areas of research, and there is much variability in the answers that are either directly stated or implied.

The Research–Practice Gap

As you will see, there are many levels of discussion about how research findings should influence practice, as well as concerns that the extent of influence is insufficient. The sense that research findings have not sufficiently informed educational practice is sometimes referred to as the **research–practice gap**. Broadly, the research–practice gap can be attributable to three sources.

- Limited accessibility: The practitioner has insufficient access to research reports.
- Limited comprehensibility: The practitioner cannot understand the research.
- Limited usability: The practitioner does not find the research relevant or practical.

Examples of each of these sources are given in Table 18.1. These examples consist of more or less widely accepted claims that have been made about the disconnect between research and practice.

Notice that with respect to each of the three sources, one could hold the researcher or the practitioner (or both) responsible for the disconnect.

TABLE 18.1 Examples of the Three Main Sources of Research–Practice Disconnect

Limited accessibility

Researchers publish their findings in peer-reviewed journals and other scientific outlets. Practitioners rely on practitioner outlets, the Internet, and other informal sources for information.

Practitioners are too busy to seek out research reports, and would receive no professional support for such efforts.

Research on key topics is sparse or methodologically weak.

Limited comprehensibility

Research reports are written in the language of social science and statistics, and are filled with literature-specific jargon that practitioners cannot understand.

Successful interventions are not described concretely enough to be implemented.

Descriptions of empirical findings are couched in excessive amounts of theory, dogma, and/or conjecture.

Limited usability

It is inherently difficult to import scientific findings into the diverse and constantly shifting conditions of a classroom.

Interventions that have been shown to be successful may require too much time, money, and resources to be implemented.

The process of conducting formal studies and disseminating the results relegates the practitioner to the role of consumer with little or no input into the research process.

Educators are readily influenced by trends, hype, and policies mandated at the local, state, and federal levels.

- You could attribute limited accessibility to the researcher's failure to communicate research findings in outlets that practitioners rely on, or you could say that the practitioner has not tried hard enough to seek out the research.

- You could attribute limited comprehensibility to poor communication skills on the researcher's part, or you could say that the practitioner is inadequately trained in research methods.

- You could attribute limited usability to the researcher's failure to consider practitioner needs when designing studies, or you could say that the practitioner is unable or unwilling to appreciate how the findings can be implemented.

Rather than assigning blame, it makes more sense to recognize that researchers and practitioners have traditionally had somewhat different goals and methods, in spite of sharing a common interest in improving educational practice. One way to advance that common interest is to find ways in which the research–practice gap can be bridged.

Literature-Specific Bridges

There are many recommendations for integrating specific research areas and specific practices. Rather than trying to do justice to the diversity of areas and recommendations in this section, I merely present one example pertaining to each of the three sources of disconnect.

ACCESSIBILITY   Some of the literature-specific recommendations for bridging the research–practice gap focus on making research findings more accessible to practitioners. For example, Sharp (2005) offers a number of suggestions for increasing the accessibility of school improvement research to classroom teachers, including the following:

- Ensure that someone at the school takes the lead in encouraging the use of research.

- Ensure that the research is relevant and used by teachers in a collaborative way.

- Provide support for teachers to access research reports and attend conferences.

- Build a critical mass of teachers who use research and can inspire others to do so.

- Connect teachers with teacher-researchers at their own schools or other institutions.

- Ensure that teachers have opportunities to share what they are learning and doing.

This is a promising list that could apply to virtually any research literature. At the same time, some of the suggestions on the list underscore the fact that the research–practice gap is exacerbated by limited resources. Many schools and school districts lack the funding to send teachers to conferences. Teachers themselves may not have the time to attend conferences, to make connections with teacher-researchers at other institutions, or to otherwise become more active as consumers of research.

Lack of resources is also a problem for researchers themselves. Chard (2004) has pointed out that because educational research has never been as extensively funded as research in the hard sciences or medicine, those who conduct intervention studies often have little to offer teachers who implement their interventions. The teachers who agree to participate in these studies will be the ones who are most highly interested in exploring innovative practices. As a result, the effectiveness of the interventions per se may be overestimated. In short, limitations in the resources available to researchers may not only prevent key research from being carried out, but may also impose limitations on the generalizability of those studies that are conducted.

COMPREHENSIBILITY   Some literature-specific recommendations focus on encouraging researchers to disseminate their results to practitioners in a more comprehensible way. For example, there is considerable evidence that large-scale assessment data, such as the results of testing mandated by NCLB or obtained through NAEP assessments, are a source of confusion and misunderstanding among educators, policymakers, and parents. Obviously, it is impossible to make effective use of results if one cannot understand them. Goodman and Hambleton (2004) reviewed the test score reports created by 11 states, as well as two Canadian provinces and three commercial test publishers, and came up with a list of suggestions, some of which are given below.

- Use devices such as headings, boxes, and spacing to organize reports into different components.
- Include a highlights section presenting an overall summary of results.
- Use comprehensible, jargon-free, and redundant descriptions.
- Use narrative descriptions, as well as numerical and graphic displays.
- Tailor reports to specific audiences (e.g., one report for parents, another for teachers).
- Describe the skills and knowledge that the test assesses, the expected levels of test performance, the skills and knowledge that the particular student seems to possess, and the results of relevant comparison groups.

The recommendation that researchers tailor reports to specific audiences could reduce the research–practice gap with respect to any literature. Researchers know that teachers tend to receive little or no exposure to research methods as part of their certification training. Consequently, researchers must continue to find ways to translate their findings into more accessible terms if they wish to have more of an impact on educational practice.

USABILITY   In many areas, research is unlikely to impact practice because researchers focus on problems, methods, and interventions of limited relevance to practitioners, or because researchers create interventions that are relevant but highly impractical given the constraints on time and resources that practitioners face. Interest in improving usability is at the heart of Snell's (2003) suggestions to researchers in the area of instructional interventions for students with disabilities:

- Engage in social validation by describing research goals, methods, and interventions with practitioners prior to conducting the research. (Social validity is defined in Chapter 6.)
- Involve practitioners in the design and assessment of interventions, to ensure a contextual fit between the intervention and the needs, skills, and resources of practitioners.
- Ensure that the research is methodologically sound, usable, and disseminated in an accessible way.

Many recommendations address accessibility, comprehensibility, and usability simultaneously. For example, curriculum-based measurement (CBM) was originally developed as a way of allowing special education teachers to obtain immediate feedback on student achievement (Deno, 1985, 2003). Although not without critics, CBM has become popular, owing to accessibility (researchers make programs available to teachers), comprehensibility (teachers readily learn how CBM procedures work), and usability (measures of achievement are curriculum-based, require very little time to administer, and yield immediate results). The essay reviewed in Spotlight on Research 18.1 also illustrates the idea that recommendations specific to the special education literature may simultaneously pertain to the three sources of research–practice disconnect.

Literature-Independent Bridges

Many suggestions for bridging the research–practice gap are expressed in a literature-independent way, or described in the context of a particular literature but readily generalized (as illustrated in Spotlight on Research 18.2 later in the chapter). Action research, as well as some of the qualitative approaches you studied in Chapter 13, simply collapse the distinction between researcher and practitioner. As for research carried out by researchers, Carnine (1997) proposed that three characteristics of a research study determine the extent of its influence on practice:

- The trustworthiness of a study is determined by its methodological soundness, which, if recognized by practitioners, fosters confidence in the results.
- The usability of a study refers to both its relevance to practitioners as well as the clarity with which it is described. Practitioners will immediately recognize the importance of usable research. (What Carnine refers to as "usability" is a combination of what I referred to earlier in this chapter as usability and comprehensibility.)
- The accessibility of a study refers to how quickly and easily practitioners can obtain the results. Accessible research is more likely to be put into practice.

These characteristics are relevant in a general way to bridging the research–practice gap. Working out the details is the challenging part. What Carnine (1997) refers to as trustworthiness is the focus of the "EBR wars" described later in the chapter. Usability depends in part on practitioners having enough time and resources to implement key findings. Accessibility depends on researchers having time to keep up with research (and having access to primary or secondary sources).

Carnine (1997) predicted that demand among practitioners for trustworthy, usable, and accessible research will lead to changes in the relationships among different educational groups. What Carnine called "influence producers" (e.g., professional organizations and teachers' unions) will become more closely tied to "knowledge producers" (e.g., researchers) and insist that the knowledge producers conduct research that is trustworthy, usable, and accessible. Carnine also suggested that these changes would be fostered by greater emphasis on practice in promotion and tenure decisions, in the content of articles published in peer-reviewed journals, and in the criteria for external funding. Some of the changes that Carnine predicted have occurred in the decade since his article was published, although there are still concerns about the research–practice gap, as well as debates about trustworthiness.

Implementing Special Education Research

Since the passage of the Individuals with Disabilities Education Act (IDEA), special education research has been considered increasingly important to the instruction of students with disabilities. In a 2006 article in the *High School Journal**, Calvin Cannon reviewed some of the obstacles to the implementation of special education research findings, and offered a number of suggestions as to how these findings can better serve classroom practice.

Building on a distinction discussed by Vaughn, Klinger, and Hughes (2002), Cannon suggested that the research–practice gap in special education can be attributed to "teachers' fault" and "researcher's fault" explanations.

One explanation is that some teachers choose approaches to instruction that are familiar to them as opposed to utilizing approaches that are more effective. They may continue this approach even when they know how to implement the more effective approaches and have experience and evidence that support their effectiveness. Other factors that need to be considered are: 1) teacher time, 2) perceived responsibility for new tools, 3) perceived fit with ongoing activities, and 4) the limits of applicability of any single instructional tool (Stone, 1998). The basic questions that need to be addressed include: Why do some teachers continue to choose less effective practices? What supports and resources are necessary to alter this practice? What questions should we be asking and understanding to better modify this practice?

The opposing explanation for the ineffective use and continued application of research-based practices is that researchers design practices that do not satisfactorily reflect the realities of classroom teaching and the constraints teachers have on their use (Gersten et al., 1997; Malouf & Schiller, 1995). It is assumed that many researchers study what they are interested in rather than what teachers need. This assumption implies that researchers design materials that they "impose" on teachers, which reflect the interests of the researchers rather than the classroom needs of the teacher (Richardson, 1990). This also implies that researchers are not responsive to the needs of teachers, perhaps, because they do not adequately engage them in the developmental process. In this case, researchers treat teachers as "subjects" in their studies, and they have unrealistic and high demands about what teachers "should" do. Furthermore, instructional practices developed to improve outcomes for specific standards (e.g., those

with disabilities), may not serve the class as a whole, or may not be practical to implement in large groups (Vaughn & Schumm, 1996). The question of whether, when, and how the teacher should focus on the special needs of the unique child versus serving the group of students is the most common enduring dilemma faced by teachers in classrooms as they are organized today (Richardson & Anders, 1998, p. 86).

One of the lessons for researchers attempting to implement and sustain intervention practices is the importance of ongoing communications. Researchers must be open to input along the way from teachers, principals, students as well as their successes and failures (Fuchs & Fuchs 1998; Stone, 1998). Without this type of openness, continued and effective intervention practices are not possible (Tharp & Gallimore, 1998). When two partners enter into a collaborative process such as the teacher and researcher relationship, there is a responsibility for sensitivity and responsiveness on the part of both parties. Therefore, it is necessary to dramatically reduce the number of teachers who have participated in research projects and ended up with negative feelings regarding the process.

Simply providing teachers with access to innovative instructional strategies is not sufficient to alter existing patterns of teaching (Goldenberg & Gallimore, 1991; Richardson, 1990; Showers, Joyce, & Bennett, 1987). A structure and system must be in place so that when teachers try out new methods of teaching, they receive feedback from a peer or a person knowledgeable in the new strategies or innovations (Cruickshank, 1985; Gersten et al., 1992). In addition, it is critical that teachers have regular opportunities to discuss the impact of the new practices on student learning in a supportive, collaborative atmosphere (McLaughlin, 1990; Showers et al., 1987). McLaughlin (1990) suggested that successful changed efforts need to involve individuals who can supply the continuing and sometime unpredictable support teachers needed.

Cannon notes that a key determinant of whether teachers continue to implement research-based practices is whether there are observable benefits for students, particularly those who have disabilities or otherwise pose special challenges for the teacher.

One of the earliest findings from the research on innovation and change was that the major reason teachers continued to use innovative practice was that it improved performance for difficult-to-teach students (Berman & McLaughlin,

1976). Researchers have found that prior attitudes to proposed changes were not good indicators of implementation success. In fact, attitudes often changed dramatically when teachers observed changes in their students' learning performances. Therefore, attitudinal changes often followed behavioral changes. It is important to realize that in judging the effectiveness of a lesson many teachers depend more on observable student behavior than on quantitative assessments (Morine-Dershinmer, 1978–1979). In fact, in many cases, teachers do not even look at curriculum-based measurement data unless these data serve as a focus for a discussion with a consultant (Gersten, Morvant, & Brengelman, 1995). Finally, it is important for those in special education to understand that, for many classroom teachers, enhanced performance of students with learning disabilities or other low-performing students is only one concern among many (Gersten & Woodward, 1992) . . .

A series of studies (Gersten, Carnine, Zoref, & Croonin, 1986; Guskey, 1984; Sparks, 1988) found that a critical determinant of teachers' attitudes toward change was not previous attitudes toward change or beliefs, as was generally thought, but rather, whether new practices led to confirmed gains in student achievement. These researchers found that previous attitudes to proposed changes were not good predictors of implementation success. In fact, attitudes frequently changed dramatically when teachers saw changes in their students' learning performance. Therefore, attitudinal shifts often followed behavioral shifts. Furthermore, this focus on student learning is crucial given that "intensive collaboration—planning, exchanging materials, and regulating pupil performance—does not automatically translate into observable changes in classroom practices and may, if pushed too hard, actually eat into time for ongoing instructional work in class" (M. Huberman, 1993, p. 13). By concentrating on the impact of instruction on learners and helping teachers to more carefully appraise student learning during instruction, those involved in collaborative efforts can help teachers become more observant and reflective as they teach (Cruickshank, 1985).

Cannon also observed that the interventions researchers create and evaluate may be too narrow or too broad to be effectively implemented.

Many special education interventions presently being recommended may be simply too narrow in scope. If one intervention concentrates on only one child and is based on a narrow conception of teaching, it is unlikely to engage a teacher in a serious way. This would be equally true for the research findings on wait time or guided practice, which, in spite of their

empirical support, rarely found their way into routine practice. Again, the scope may not have been sufficient to truly engage teachers.

Conversely, far too many interventions have faltered due to their overly broad, ambitious scope. The erratic implementation of cognitively derived approaches toward teaching math (Ball, 1990) and reading may well result from the radical shifts required in both teaching behaviors and conceptual understanding, as well as the elusiveness of the specific nature of desired changes in teaching. Bereiter and Kurland (1981–82) pointed out how the intricate instructional management systems and discourse structures promoted by many reformers tend to be implemented well by only a small segment of teachers, and thus rarely produce benefits for students, particularly those with serious learning difficulties.

Finally, Cannon observed that researcher–teacher collaboration and the provision of essential tools to teachers are critical to bridging the research–practice gap.

As a result of the failure of traditional in-service training to effect change in classroom practice, contexts are needed that enable teachers and others to work together in the classroom. Some specific contexts such as teacher-researcher participation (Fuchs & Fuchs) have resulted in sustained interactions between teachers and trainers. Each of these contexts cultivated interactions over at least one school year, if not longer; and in some cases they seemed successful in increasing teacher participation in this form of professional development in subsequent years. Additionally, other potentially important contexts for extending professional development experiences into the classroom include professional development schools (Calder, 1990) and other teacher preparation models where classroom experience and teaching opportunities with systematic feedback are frequently provided (e.g., Sharpe, Hawkins, & Ray, 1995).

Teachers need proficiency with the instructional tools they will utilize. Present evidence suggests that general education teachers do not have deep understanding of the principles and concepts underlying their tools (Vaughn et al., 2000) nor do they have a large inventory of alternative strategies and practices to apply to meeting the different needs of students (Fuchs & Fuchs). One possible reason is that teachers are rarely required to implement instructional practices to high levels of quality. Another possible explanation is that teachers and educational leaders may use practices supported by little or weak evidence of their effectiveness. Still another possible explanation is that professional development experiences fail to combine teaching of the theoretical principles of learning with the practical classroom demonstrations that display implementation to high standards.

Cannon closes with a call for revising the boundary between research and practice through greater collaboration between researchers and teachers, noting that just as teachers can learn from researchers, so researchers can learn from the way teachers listen to and value the perspectives of their students—a good model for listening in turn to teachers and discovering their needs and concerns.

Cannon, C. (2006, April/May). Implementing research practices. High School Journal, pp. 8–13. Quoted with permission from the publisher.

Literature-Specific Debates

The problem of how research and practice should be integrated is not merely an issue of bridging the gap between them. Within particular literatures, there are also debates about the practical implications of prior studies. Although these debates are often informed by more general considerations about how research can and should influence practice, the debates turn on disagreements about how to interpret and apply particular research findings. A famous example is the so-called "reading wars." In this example, research genuinely does influence practice to an extent, but in ways that researchers either consider highly desirable or undesirable, depending on their perspective and on the particular examples of practice they are considering.

The Reading Wars

Briefly, the **reading wars** consist of a set of long-standing debates about how to teach young children to read. One group of disputants, the phonics advocates, stress bottom-up practices in which phonics is taught first and plays a central role in the early reading curriculum. The emphasis of phonics instruction is on word decoding skills that allow children to analyze individual words into constituents such as letters that are then combined. In strong opposition to phonics approaches are whole language advocates, who prefer a top-down approach in which children are engaged in meaningful reading and writing activities even before they can isolate phonemic constituents. The emphasis of whole language approaches is on reading for meaning, a process that may include decoding but is driven by recognition of whole words and context-driven inferences about word meanings. Disputants in the reading wars also include advocates of "balanced" approaches, who call for various forms of integration between phonics and whole language in early reading instruction.

The reason that the various disagreements have been referred to as "wars" rather than simply "debates" is the sense among many disputants that their own approach is most effective, and that alternative approaches hinder children's progress and may even be permanently damaging. The phonics approach has been criticized for deadening children's interest in reading, for example, while the whole language approach has been criticized for inadequately preparing children to read advanced texts. In short, many researchers and educators feel that children's well-being is at stake. The debates are not just about which approaches to reading instruction are outstanding versus merely adequate, but also about which approaches should be excluded from the classroom because they are harmful.

TEACHING CHILDREN TO READ   The reading wars are fueled in part by how the relevant literatures are interpreted. For example, a recent flash point is *Teaching Children to Read* (2000), a report from the National Reading Panel (NRP) prompted by a Congressional request to evaluate the current state of research-based knowledge on the most effective approaches to reading instruction. The 14 experts who constituted the NRP concluded on the basis of a quantitative meta-analysis that effective reading instruction focuses on five areas:

- Phonemic awareness (the ability to identify and manipulate sounds in words)
- Phonics (the ability to recognize sound–letter correspondences and blend letters to pronounce words)
- Oral fluency (the ability to read out loud, with guidance and feedback)
- Vocabulary (knowledge of word meanings)
- Text comprehension (strategies for understanding, summarizing, and recalling text)

Phonics advocates argue that the NRP report vindicates their position. In particular, they point to the NRP's conclusion that phonemic awareness and systematic phonics instruction are clearly efficacious in the teaching of reading, and can therefore be considered essential to good reading instruction. Although the NRP experts could not draw conclusions about specific teaching methods, they did provide some guidance as to what would and would not constitute appropriate implementation. For example, with respect to phonemic awareness training, the NRP experts recommended that students be taught letters as well as phonemes, while cautioning that length of instruction should be determined by situational factors, characteristics of individual students, and common sense rather than any specific number of hours suggested by the research evidence.

Whole language advocates argue that the conclusions of the NRP report are deeply flawed and should have little or no impact on classroom practice. One set of concerns stems from the criteria that the panel used for including studies in their meta-analysis. Although criteria such as publication in peer-reviewed journals are noncontroversial, the NRP's sole reliance on studies using experimental or quasi-experimental designs is considered problematic given that some qualitative and descriptive studies provide evidence for whole language views. A second concern pertaining to inclusion criteria is that whereas thousands of articles were identified, very few were actually included in the NRP meta-analyses. For example, the meta-analyses included only 52 studies on phonemic awareness and 38 studies on phonics. The fact that only a small proportion of published studies were analyzed suggests to some critics that the results should not inform classroom practice. A third inclusion-related concern is that many of the studies in the meta-analysis operationalized reading progress in undesirably narrow ways, such as the ability to sound out pseudowords or the ability to spell, rather than consistently focusing on comprehension of meaningful passages. Some researchers hold that reanalysis of pertinent NRP-reviewed data, as well as analyses of other studies, indicate that when the dependent measure is meaningful comprehension, whole language approaches have stronger effects on reading progress.

Along with concerns about how the meta-analysis was conducted are concerns about dissemination of the results to practitioners. The actual NRP report, although clearly written, is over 500 pages long. Also available is a 34-page summary booklet that was not written by the NRP experts. The booklet, which is much more accessible than the full report, has been criticized on the grounds of inaccuracy.

Although it is inevitable that some of the complexities of a large report will not survive brief summarization, the concern among whole language advocates is that the efficacy of certain practices such as systematic phonics instruction are overemphasized in the booklet.

Disagreements about the results of the NRP report constitute one of the most recent battles in the reading wars. As you can see, the focus of the disagreements is ultimately practical, since virtually all of the disputants would hope to decide, once and for all, what reading teachers should be doing in their classrooms.

Literature-Independent Debates

The combatants in the reading wars are united at least in their desire to serve children and teachers. These researchers share a basic assumption that reading instruction should be informed by pertinent research on topics such as the efficacy of different instructional methods, the best approaches for modifying instruction to fit the characteristics of individual learners, and the best methods of involving parents in the learning process. In fact, most researchers regardless of area assume that educational practice should be informed by research, even if they disagree about how specific findings should translate into specific practices. This is not to say that there is a complete consensus that practice should be research-based. A postmodernist, for example, might argue that a close look at the assumptions grounding any research call for restraint in the application of scientific "truths" to educational problems. The concerns here are both epistemological and ethical. As I noted in Chapter 13, the postmodernist doubts that science has privileged access to reality, arguing instead that realities are constructed by individuals and groups and are inherently subjective. Imposing the results of a research study on classroom practice may therefore be ethically problematic, because the results are not grounded in objective reality but rather in the values of the researcher and the entire culture of educational research. A common objection to the postmodernist view is that it does not provide much guidance as to what educational practice should be based on, if not educational research and other value-laden bodies of knowledge and experience.

Generally speaking, few researchers would find it controversial to say that educational practice should be based at least in part on evidence. Controversies arise over the question of what types of evidence are desirable. Some of these literature-independent debates seem like "wars" too, because of claims that certain approaches to conducting research are not rigorous enough to merit a significant influence on educational practice.

The EBR Wars

Evidence-based research, or **EBR**, may sound like a redundant and noncontroversial phrase—what research is not evidence-based?—but specific definitions of such phrases have fueled current debates about how to bridge the research–practice gap. The phrase "scientifically based research," or SBR, tends to be synonymous with EBR and equally central to the debates. The focus of this section is on just one point of contention: the question of whether experimental and quasi-experimental designs are the best approaches to carrying out educational research.

FEDERAL DEFINITIONS OF RESEARCH   As you may recall from Chapters 1 and 17, one consequence of the No Child Left Behind Act of 2002 is that federal spending is targeted to educational programs whose effectiveness has been demonstrated through scientifically based research. The phrase "scientifically based research" is used more than 100 times in the NCLB legislation. The definition of this phrase, as provided in the legislation, is reproduced in Figure 18.1. As you can see, almost nobody would quarrel with some aspects of the definition, such as the requirement of items B(v) and B(vi) that scientifically based research be presented in a detailed and clear way in peer-reviewed journals. Of greater concern to some researchers is that in item B(iv), scientifically based research is equated with experimental or quasi-experimental designs.

The NCLB Act is not the only federal document in which differential treatment of research designs can be observed. In 2003, the Institute of Education Sciences published a guide for helping educational practitioners identify research based on rigorous evidence. The purpose of the guide is captured in the following quotations from the Executive Summary:

> *This Guide seeks to provide educational practitioners with user-friendly tools to distinguish practices supported by rigorous evidence from those that are not. . . .*

> *If practitioners have the tools to identify evidence-based interventions, they may be able to spark major improvements in their schools and, collectively, in American education.*

Once again, there is nothing controversial about the general goals of this guide. Everyone would like educational practice to be based on rigorous evidence, assuming that the alternative is "carelessly assembled" or "fundamentally flawed" evidence. But these are not the alternatives that the IES intended. Controversies are fanned by the view of rigorousness expressed in this guide, as shown in the page reproduced in Figure 18.2. Here again, preference is given to designs that are experimental rather than quasi-experimental (the latter are referred to

FIGURE 18.1 Definition of "scientifically based research" in the NCLB Act

"The term 'scientifically based research'" —

(A) *means research that involves the application of rigorous, systematic, and objective procedures to obtain reliable and valid knowledge relevant to education activities and programs; and*

(B) *includes research that* —

   (i) *employs systematic, empirical methods that draw on observation or experiment;*

   (ii) *involves rigorous data analyses that are adequate to test the stated hypotheses and justify the general conclusions drawn;*

   (iii) *relies on measurements or observational methods that provide reliable and valid data across evaluators and observers, across multiple measurements and observations, and across studies by the same or different investigators;*

   (iv) *is evaluated using experimental or quasi-experimental designs in which individuals, entities, programs, or activities are assigned to different conditions and with appropriate controls to evaluate the effects of the condition of interest, with a preference for random-assignment experiments, or other designs to the extent that those designs contain within-condition or across-condition controls;*

   (v) *ensures that experimental studies are presented in sufficient detail and clarity to allow for replication or, at a minimum, offer the opportunity to build systematically on their findings; and*

   (vi) *has been accepted by a peer-reviewed journal or approved by a panel of independent experts through a comparably rigorous, objective, and scientific review.*

How to evaluate whether an educational intervention is supported by rigorous evidence: An overview

Step 1. Is the intervention backed by "strong" evidence of effectiveness?

<u>Quality</u> of studies needed to establish "strong" evidence:

- Randomized controlled trials (defined on page 1) that are well-designed and implemented (see pages 5-9).

+

<u>Quantity</u> of evidence needed:

Trials showing effectiveness in —
- Two or more typical school settings,
- Including a setting similar to that of your schools/ classrooms.

(see page 10)

= "Strong" Evidence

Step 2. If the intervention is not backed by "strong" evidence, is it backed by "possible" evidence of effectiveness?

Types of studies that can comprise "possible" evidence:

- Randomized controlled trials whose quality/quantity are good but fall short of "strong" evidence (see page 11); and/or

- Comparision-group studies (defined on page 3) in which the intervention and comparison groups are *very closely matched* in academic achievement, demographics, and other characteristics (see pages 11–12).

Types of studies that do <u>not</u> comprise "possible" evidence:

- Pre-post studies (defined on page 2).

- Comparison-group studies in which the intervention and comparison groups are not closely matched (see pages 12–13).

- "Meta-analyses" that include the results of such lower-quality studies (see page 13).

Step 3. If the answers to both questions above are "no," one may conclude that the intervention is not supported by meaningful evidence.

FIGURE 18.2 Excerpt from "*Identifying and Implementing Educational Practices Supported by Rigorous Evidence: A User-Friendly Guide (2003)*" (Available at *www.ed.gov/rschstat/research/pubs/rigorousevid /index.html*)

in the document as "comparison–group studies"). Step 3 seems to indicate very clearly that other sorts of designs are not considered sources of "meaningful" evidence.

The IES has worked very hard in recent years to help bridge the research–practice gap. For example, the IES-sponsored **What Works Clearinghouse** (WWC) is motivated by the desire to present useful research findings to various stakeholders in the educational process:

> *The What Works Clearinghouse was established in 2002 by the U.S. Department of Education's Institute of Education Sciences to provide educators, policymakers, researchers, and the public with a central and trusted source of scientific evidence of what works in education.*
>
> *The WWC aims to promote informed education decision making through a set of easily accessible databases and user-friendly reports that provide education consumers with high-quality reviews of the effectiveness of replicable educational interventions (programs, products, practices, and policies) that intend to improve student outcomes.*
>
> *(http://ies.ed.gov/ncee/wwc)*

These are laudable goals, but the WWC website also states clearly that "To be eligible for WWC review, a study must be a randomized controlled trial or a quasi-experiment."

RESEARCHERS' REACTIONS   Some researchers are glad that the federal government supports their view of rigorous evidence-based research. Others are offended by this view but consider it laudable that the government cares enough about educational practice to take such a proactive role in bridging the research–practice gap. Still others question the motives of those who equate EBR with a narrow range of research designs. Ultimately, the EBR wars are driven by epistemological and methodological disagreements that turn on whether any form of research other than experimental or quasi-experimental design can yield "rigorous" or "meaningful" results that merit being put into practice.

A fairly common alternative to a narrow construal of EBR is expressed in the following passage from Mayer (2003), who suggests some constraints on what constitutes good evidence without excluding particular research designs:

> *[M]y opinion is that recommendations for practice should be tightly based on evidence. By tightly based, I mean that you can make a reasoned argument for a specific recommendation based on the available evidence. By evidence, I mean specific empirical data that are directly relevant to a recommendation for practice. Acceptable sources of evidence include a full range of scientific methods ranging from controlled experiments to systematic observations in natural contexts—as long as they generate data that directly inform a particular recommendation for practice. Unacceptable sources of evidence include invoking the names of experts as supporters of a particular practice (which I call the "expert says" approach), invoking the name of a particular "ism" such as "constructivism" as supporting a particular practice (which I call the "doctrine says" approach), or making sweeping generalizations about the literature that go beyond the results of real studies (which I call the "research says" approach).*
>
> *In my opinion, research should be issue-driven, not method-driven. In short, researchers should select research methods that can test hypotheses or answer research questions. Thus, researchers should be able to choose from a variety of methods ranging from controlled experiments to observational studies, and to choose from a variety of dependent measures ranging from quantitative to qualitative.*
>
> *(Mayer, 2003, p. 361–362)*

Interestingly, Mayer (2003) also lauds experimental design as one of the greatest scientific advances of the 20th century and an "unsurpassed" tool. There are many examples like this of researchers who clearly prefer one approach yet recognize the need for others—see, for example, Spotlight on Research 7.1, in which Michael Pressley, who also relied heavily on experimental designs in his own research, acknowledges the limitations of such designs. Such views are consistent with those expressed in this book. Experimental designs are indeed unsurpassed at establishing cause–effect relationships between variables that are manipulable and readily quantified. But not all variables are manipulable or readily quantified, and not all questions a researcher can ask are reducible to simple cause–effect relationships. Each kind of research design discussed in Chapters 7–9 and 13–16 are suitable for a somewhat different set of research questions. Each design can do things the other cannot. (And, concomitantly, each has its own particular weaknesses.) No approach should be considered a privileged form of research. Rather, each approach is privileged only with respect to specific research questions. Again, to use Mayer's formulation, "research should be issue-driven, not method-driven."

While Mayer and Pressley commented favorably on experimental designs without calling for the exclusion of other approaches, Spotlight on Research 18.2 summarizes the views of a researcher who prefers qualitative approaches but sees a place for quantitative designs.

The Contemporary Scene

Concerns about the research–practice gap and debates about how research should influence practice are ubiquitous in contemporary educational research. To an extent, different approaches to research can be distinguished on the basis of the researchers' explicitly or implicitly held positions on research–practice issues. This section of the chapter provides some guidance in how to make further distinctions among areas and approaches in contemporary research. As you will see, there are many possible typologies.

It is daunting, even for experienced researchers, to step back from their areas of specialization and survey the entire field. There is so much research in so many areas that experts even find it difficult to keep up with the work being done in their own area of expertise. You can be sure, then, that this section of the chapter is not meant to provide you with a comprehensive sketch of the contemporary state of educational research. Rather, it simply gives you some ideas about how different types of educational research can be distinguished. Discussed in this section are distinctions embodied in university programs and professional organizations, as well as those that are reflected in research reports. Making these distinctions is important to both understanding research as well as positioning your own study in the contemporary scene.

University Programs

Distinctions between academic departments, and between programs within a department, illustrate some of the broad divisions in the field of education and educational research. For information about these distinctions you can look at individual universities or at comprehensive reviews such as *www.gradschools.com*. To illustrate, below are the specialization areas used by *U.S. News and World Report* guide in distinguishing among doctoral programs in education (see *http://grad-schools. usnews.rankingsandreviews.com/usnews/edu/grad/rankings/edu/eduindex_brief.php*).

Administration/Supervision
Counseling/Personnel Services

Evidence-Based Research in Adult Education

The "EBR wars" are created by disagreements about the kinds of evidence that are rigorous and therefore suitable for informing practice. Most disputants would agree at least that the goal of obtaining evidence is to determine what practices are most effective. In a 2006 article published in *Adult Education Quarterly**, John Dirkx argues that if we maintain a careful focus on finding out what works in practice, we can avoid some of the extreme views that EBR discussions have engendered.

Here is how Dirkx summarizes two basic positions on EBR:

Proponents of EBR, such as Michael Feuer, argue that practitioners are looking to the research community for strategies that effectively address their lingering practice problems. According to EBR proponents, the kind of knowledge they need is derived from research demonstrating particular characteristics. Chief among these characteristics are "rigorous, systematic, and objective methods" (Redfield, 2004, p. 24), preferably involving evidence derived from conducting randomized experiments, the "gold standard" of research. Acceptable alternatives include quasi-experimental designs using equating procedures or studies that employ regression discontinuity design. The intent of EBR and "what works" is to provide the educational consumer with confidence in being able to identify forms of practice that have been demonstrated, through application of this rigorous methodological approach, to produce intended, desired effects on student learning. To this end, the U.S. Department of Education's Institute of Education has funded the What Works Clearinghouse (WWC; www.whatworks.edu.gov) to help evaluate and synthesize studies that meet these research criteria . . .

Critics of EBR, such as Elizabeth St. Pierre, argue that the stress on EBR has more to do with political and ideological agendas than it does with improving the quality of educational experiences for students. They question the epistemological assumptions reflected in this approach to research and knowledge and suggest that an obsession with experimental research methodologies for demonstrating particular strategies that work in practice oversimplifies the complexity of practitioner knowledge. Such approaches also implicitly contribute to the control of education by politicians and corporate leaders (Olson, 2003), a claim that finds support in Alan Schoenfeld's (2006) description of his brief tenure with the WWC. St. Pierre charges that EBR . . . brushes aside qualitative methodologies and alternative epistemologies that have emerged in educational research over the past 30 years as "unscientific." Proponents of EBR largely ignore the ways in which knowledge and processes of coming to know are deeply embedded within the social, cultural, political, and economic relationships that constitute the various contexts of educational research.

Writing from the perspective of an adult education researcher, Dirkx advocates what he calls "insider research," a process of involving practitioners in collaborative research and in generating knowledge about their own practices. Dirkx considers insider research preferable to the traditional "outsider" approach in which findings obtained by researchers are disseminated to practitioners.

Although insider research does not necessarily imply qualitative versus quantitative approaches, it nonetheless stresses problems and questions that arise within and among practitioners as they engage their work in the field. This perspective is intended to address the limitations of an outsider, technical-rational approach to research on

Curriculum/Instruction
Educational Psychology
Education Policy
Elementary Education
Higher Education Administration
Secondary Education
Special Education
Vocational/Technical
Education Methodology

practice in adult education. As Clandinin and Connelly (1995) suggest, practitioners often experience outsider knowledge as a stream of conclusions that reach them through various informational sources and that transmit prepositional and theoretical knowledge with little or no awareness of contextual nuances of their practice landscape. Insider research seeks to honor and give voice to complexity and the multilayered nature of understanding that adult educators hold about the various dimensions of their practice, such as their students, the curriculum, teaching strategies, and issues of gender, race, class, and other social issues . . .

Although Dirkx is receptive to quantitative methods, he stresses the value of qualitative approaches in which the stories practitioners share provide information about practice that is more immediately useful, owing to its "insider" perspective, than the decontextualized findings of outsider research. For example, he has this to say about a 2002 text by Jane Vella titled *Learning to Listen, Learning to Teach:*

In this text, Vella describes 12 principles for helping adults learn. In presenting and elaborating these principles, however, Vella uses stories from her experience worldwide in planning and teaching programs for adult learners and their communities. Each principle is couched within a story that reveals its particular context, demands, uncertainties, complexities, and ambiguities. Rather than sitting apart and decontextualized from the messy fray of educational practice, the principle itself seems to organically arise from within the story she narrates. Students and practitioners respond quite favorably to this presentation of educational "theory" because they are able to immediately grasp and relate the principle to the particular aspects of practice for which it is intended . . .

Dirkx points out that research based on practitioner narratives has had much success within fields such as psychotherapy, medicine, and education. Although he calls for more case studies based on these narratives, he does not dismiss EBR as a viable approach. Rather, he simply wishes to see EBR play a circumscribed role:

I am not suggesting that the practice-based, insider research model represents the only way we should do research in adult and continuing education. An EBR perspective is useful and can play an important role in helping to inform and shape policy. If, however, our primary interests are to understand and improve practice (however that is defined), particular practice questions that involve matters of the curriculum or of teaching and learning, EBR methods will necessarily play a more limited role.

I am not suggesting that simply telling stories about our practice is a satisfactory formulation of an alternative to EBR, although it might represent a very good beginning. I am suggesting, however, more widespread use of systematic approaches to the use of reflection and narrative with one's own practice, to encourage and train more practitioners to study their own practices, to suggest that we as academics begin by taking seriously our own teaching as a context for scholarly research, and to mentor our graduate students in such an approach to the study of the field. In short, I am suggesting that we consider featuring more prominently case methodologies that stress the practitioner as researcher, not unlike that which characterizes much of the field of psychotherapy and other professional disciplines.

*Dirkx, J. M. (2006). Studying the complicated matter of what works: Evidence-based research and the problem of practice. *Adult Education Quarterly, 56*(4), 273–290. Quoted with permission from the publisher.

Professional Organizations

The divisions of major professional organizations also illustrate how the field of educational research, as well as specific areas within the field, are subdivided. For example, below are the 12 major divisions of the American Educational Research Association. Also within the AERA you will find over 100 special interest groups.

Division A: Administration, Organization and Leadership
Division B: Curriculum Studies

Division C: Learning and Instruction
Division D: Measurement and Research Methodology
Division E: Counseling and Human Development
Division F: History and Historiography
Division G: Social Context of Education
Division H: School Evaluation and Program Development
Division I: Education in the Professions
Division J: Postsecondary Education
Division K: Teaching and Teacher Education
Division L: Educational Policy and Politics

As indicated on the AERA website:

> *Special Interest Groups (SIGs) provide a forum within AERA for the involvement of individuals drawn together by a common interest in a field of study, teaching, or research when the existing divisional structure may not directly facilitate such activity. The Association provides the SIG's program time at the Annual Meeting, publicity, scheduling, staff support, viability, and the prestige of AERA affiliation.*

In short, from the major divisions and SIGs of AERA you can gain a sense of some of the research communities in the field of education.

Research Reports

By looking at research reports you can see many dimensions along which educational research can be distinguished, including their purposes, designs, populations, settings, methods and analyses, and theories and topics.

PURPOSES   Although most educational studies have an applied focus, a distinction can be made between studies that hope to make a contribution to basic knowledge versus those that are purely applied. Action research and program evaluation are two forms of purely applied research that may have a relatively immediate impact on practice.

DESIGNS   As you now know, educational research is based on quantitative, qualitative, or mixed-methods designs, a distinction that reflects somewhat different traditions, epistemologies, methods, analytic approaches, and writing styles. Within each general type of design you will find important distinctions at the level of design (e.g., experimental vs. quasi-experimental) as well as at deeper levels of assumptions about epistemology and method (e.g., realist vs. critical ethnography).

POPULATIONS   Educational research can be differentiated by type of population studied. Following are some key distinctions.

- Studies that focus on human participants versus those that focus on physical materials and abstract entities (e.g., programs).
- Studies that focus on a single age or grade of student versus those that include multiple ages, grades, or groupings (e.g., elementary vs. secondary).
- Studies that focus on students versus those that focus on parents, administrators, policymakers, and/or other groups.

- Studies that use cross-sectional versus longitudinal approaches to study changes in people and programs over time.
- Studies that focus on a single ethnicity, nationality, or race versus those in which multiple ethnicities, nationalities, or races are distinguished.
- Studies that focus on the general education student versus those that focus exclusively on special populations (vs. those in which both types of student are included).

SETTINGS   The majority of educational research focuses on the people and programs associated with public, private, and charter schools from preschool through secondary school levels. A substantial amount of postsecondary research also concerns undergraduate and graduate education, continuing studies, and distance learning. Studies are conducted in the classroom and in other educational settings, including PTA meetings, school board hearings, and online environments. Some educational studies are conducted in homes, in researchers' labs, or in public settings such as social service agencies.

METHODS AND ANALYSES   Many researchers have favorite designs, measures, and approaches to data analysis that reflect their training and specific areas of expertise. For example, a researcher with a strong foundation in multiple regression will tend to design studies in which regression modeling is the primary analytical approach to addressing the research question. The research question will concern predictive relationships between variables, and the variables will be measured quantitatively. A researcher trained in ethnographic methods will develop culturally oriented research questions and design studies that are based on qualitative measures and analyses.

You will also find that many fields and topics of research have their own methodological conventions. For example, as you saw in Chapter 8, single participant experimental research relies heavily on graphs to present time-dependent results (even though tabular approaches would convey the same information). And as you found in Chapter 13, ethnographic approaches commonly incorporate triangulation and reflexivity into the process of gathering and evaluating information.

THEORIES AND TOPICS   Each research study is carried out within a theoretical framework and may constitute a test of a specific theory or an attempt at theory-building. Each study also focuses on a specific topic. Specific topics can be identified by browsing journals, and by observing both the organization and the details of handbooks and other authoritative secondary sources. Also helpful are content analyses and other approaches to the study of graduate programs, professional organizations, and professional journals, as illustrated in Spotlight on Research 18.3.

Planning and Conducting A Study

Now that you have finished this book and, in this chapter, read about some of the general issues and specific distinctions that structure the field of educational research, you are ready to begin your research. This final section of the chapter

Learning About a Discipline through Content Analysis

As discussed in Chapter 14, content analysis allows researchers to conduct detailed observations and analyses of physical materials. Content analyses of empirical articles published in peer-reviewed journals are periodically conducted in many fields in order to identify trends in particular disciplines, and to illuminate the editorial practices of journals within those disciplines. These content analyses provide a small window into the particular areas, theoretical perspectives, and topics reflected in the research.

An example of a journal-related content analysis is presented in a 2005 study by Chin-Chung Tsai and Meichun Wen, published in the *International Journal of Science Education**. Tsai and Wen's content analysis focused on three leading science education journals: *International Journal of Science Education, Science Education,* and *Journal of Research in Science Teaching*. The researchers reviewed 802 articles published in these journals between 1998 and 2002. (All articles published in the journals during this 5-year period were reviewed except for editorials, commentaries, responses, and book reviews.)

Tsai and Wen's content analysis addressed three questions:

1. *How did authors from different countries contribute to the publications of these selected journals from 1998 to 2002?*
2. *How did the types of research published in the journals vary across these five years?*
3. *How did the research topics published in the journals vary across these five years?*

The first question was addressed by counting the number of articles submitted by authors from each country (with a formula to allocate authorship when authors of the same article came from different countries).

With respect to the second question, each article was classified into one of five types:

(1) empirical research article, such as quantitative and qualitative research; (2) position paper, which held a specific position in a certain issue of science education; (3) theoretical paper, which proposed a new theory or theoretical framework in the field of science education; (4) review, which summarized research literatures without proposing a strong position; and (5) other (e.g. a description of science curricula of a specific country).

Classification of each article into one of nine categories allowed the researchers to address the third

question. (With respect to the following classification, as well as the previous one, interrater reliability was above .85.)

1. *Teacher Education. Preservice and continuing professional development of teachers; teacher education programs and policy; field experience; issues related to teacher education reform; teacher as researcher/action research.*
2. *Teaching. Teacher cognition; pedagogical knowledge and pedagogical content knowledge; forms of knowledge representation (e.g. metaphors, images, etc.); leadership; induction; exemplary teachers; teacher thinking; teaching behaviors and strategies.*
3. *Learning—Students' Conceptions and Conceptual Change (Learning—Conception). Methods for investigating student understanding; students' alternative conceptions; instructional approaches for conceptual change; conceptual change in learners; conceptual development.*
4. *Learning—Classroom Contexts and Learner Characteristics (Learning—Context). Student motivation; learning environment; individual differences; reasoning; learning approaches; exceptionality; teacher–student interactions; peer interactions; laboratory environments; affective dimensions of science learning; cooperative learning; language, writing and discourse in learning; social, political, and economic factors.*
5. *Goals and Policy, Curriculum, Evaluation, and Assessment. Curriculum development, change, implementation, dissemination and evaluation; social analysis of curriculum; alternative forms of assessment; teacher evaluation; educational measurement; identifying effective schools; curriculum policy and reform.*
6. *Cultural, Social and Gender Issues. Multicultural and bilingual issues; ethnic issues; gender issues; comparative studies; issues of diversity related to science teaching and learning.*
7. *History, Philosophy, Epistemology and Nature of Science. Historical issues; philosophical issues; epistemological issues; ethical and moral issues; nature of science; research methods.*
8. *Educational Technology. Computers; interactive multimedia; video; integration of technology into teaching; learning and assessment involving the use of technology.*
9. *Informal Learning. Science learning in informal contexts (e.g. museums, outdoor settings, etc.); public awareness of science.*

Regarding their first question, Tsai and Wen found that the majority of articles were contributed by researchers from four English-speaking countries: the United States, Canada, Australia, and the United Kingdom.

Frequencies and Percentages of Research Topics from 1998 to 2002 (*n* = 802 papers)

Research topic	1998–2002	1998	1999	2000	2001	2002
Teacher Education	56 (7.0%)	13 (7.9%)	12 (7.0%)	12 (7.7%)	11 (7.1%)	8 (5.2%)
Teaching	55 (6.9%)	8 (4.8%)	11 (6.4%)	10 (6.4%)	8 (5.1%)	18 (11.7%)
Learning—Conception	198 (24.7%)*	55 (33.3%)*	40 (23.4%)*	41 (26.3%)*	30 (19.2%)*	32 (20.8%)*
Learning—Contexts	144 (17.9%)*	21 (12.8%)	34 (19.9%)*	28 (17.9%)*	29 (18.6%)	32 (20.8%)*
Goals, Policy, Curriculum	109 (13.6%)	22 (13.3%)	20 (11.7%)	17 (10.9%)	25 (16.0%)	25 (16.2%)
Culture, Social and Gender	115 (14.3%)	27 (16.4%)*	27 (15.8%)	15 (9.6%)	31 (19.9%)*	15 (9.7%)
Philosophy and History	68 (8.5%)	11 (6.7%)	14 (8.2%)	17 (10.9%)	12 (7.7%)	14 (9.1%)
Educational Technology	27 (3.4%)	5 (3.0%)	5 (2.9%)	11 (7.1%)	3 (1.9%)	3 (1.9%)
Informal Learning	30 (3.7%)	3 (1.8%)	8 (4.7%)	5 (3.2%)	7 (4.5%)	7 (4.6%)

*Top two topics.

Frequencies and Percentages of Research Topics in Individual Journals (*n* = 802 papers)

Research topic	SE	FRST	IFSE
Teacher Education	15 (8.3%)	19 (7.4%)	22 (6.0%)
Teaching	18 (10.0%)	24 (9.3%)	13 (3.6%)
Learning—Conception	37 (20.6%)*	41 (15.9%)	120 (33.0%)*
Learning—Contexts	30 (16.7%)*	50 (19.4%)*	64 (17.6%)*
Goals, Policy, Curriculum	28 (15.6%)	29 (11.2%)	52 (14.3%)
Culture, Social and Gender	24 (13.3%)	59 (22.9%)*	32 (8.8%)
Philosophy and History	18 (10.0%)	27 (10.5%)	23 (6.3%)
Educational Technology	2 (1.1%)	8 (3.1%)	17 (4.7%)
Informal Learning	8 (4.4%)	1 (0.4%)	21 (5.7%)

Regarding their second question, Tsai and Wen found that over 80% of the articles in each year were empirical research reports.

Following are the results with respect to the third question:

"Learning—Conception" consistently ranked in the top two topics from 1998 to 2002, with an average of 24.7% of the total research articles. Despite its popularity with science educators, however, this category had a declining trend within these years, decreased from 33.3% in 1998 to 20.8% in 2002 (see table below). Science educators also showed interests in "Learning—Context" topics, such as cooperative learning, affective domains, and interactions within learning environments, with an average of 17.9% articles classified in this category during these five years. Furthermore, issues about "Culture, Social, and Gender" have also attracted attention by science educators. Surprisingly, the papers about the research issues of "Teacher Education," "Teaching," and "Educational Technology" did not contribute much to the total quantity of published articles.

In addition to the analysis by year, the research topics were examined by journal, presented in the table below. The Table reveals that the first and second ranks of topics for IJSE and SE were "Learning—Conception" and "Learning—Context." The category "Learning—Conception," with the aforementioned popularity, comprised one-third (33.0%) of research articles in IJSE. For JRST specifically, "Culture, Social, and Gender" and "Learning—Context" were the top two research topics published in the journal. Among these three journals, this analysis of publication topics showed similarities in emphasis on learning and differences in other highlighted areas. The journal scope, editorial policies and the identities of the Editors might play a role in the publication topics. For future studies, it is also worth asking the journal Editors for their comments on the results.

*Tsai, C.-C., & Wen, M. L. (2005). Research and trends in science education from 1998 to 2002: A content analysis of publication in selected journals. *International Journal of Science Education, 27*(1), 3–14. Quoted with permission from the publisher.

provides a brief guide in how to plan and carry out an educational research study. Although the guide is presented as a straightforward list of recommendations, there is no recipe or formula for conducting meaningful research that can be followed mechanically. Rather, you will have to make a number of decisions. The list in this section indicates some of the most important decisions you will have to make, in roughly the order you will need to make them. The exact order of decisions will vary from researcher to researcher and, as you will see, these decisions are not made independently of each other. Reviewing published research, to take just one example, is something that you may need to do throughout the process of planning and conducting a study.

Your Interests

Think about what interests you. How do you hope to have an influence on educational practice? Is there some practical problem you want to investigate? Perhaps one of the studies you read about in this book raised some questions. Perhaps you saw something in a media report, or recalled something from your own experience in school, that makes you curious. Perhaps there is simply a topic you wish to know more about. Conducting a literature review, or at least skimming through books and journals, are good ways of finding a general topic if you are not sure what your interests might be.

The Timeline

Think about your timeline. Do you have a deadline, such as a due date for a thesis proposal or write-up of results? You need to budget time for each step of the research process, including your literature review, the planning of the study, the process of Institutional Review Board review, the identification of a site and sampling of participants, the gathering and analysis of data, and the writing-up of the results. It may be difficult to predict the timing of these steps. Your Institutional Review Board may not meet over the summer. Permission from a school may be slow and indeterminate. Participants may be hard to recruit.

The Literature Review

Conduct a literature review. As you make use of the various methods of identifying primary and secondary sources, you may find that a thorough review is very time-consuming. Unlike some of the other steps in conducting a research study, the literature review is one that may be ongoing as you work out the details of design, measurement, and analysis.

Approach and Design

Think about the overall approach and design of your study. Will it be "formal" research, action research, or program evaluation? Will the design be quantitative, qualitative, or mixed-methods? If you use a qualitative design such as a grounded theory approach, what will be your starting point? Regardless of design, what variables are you most interested in measuring? How might those variables be operationalized? What might your hypotheses be? Designing your study is a very important step, one that merits taking time to do carefully. A poorly designed study cannot be "fixed" once the data have been collected.

Feasibility

Think about the feasibility of your design. Is the estimated timeline consistent with any time constraints you have? Are you likely to have access to the participants and/or materials you wish to study? Are other personnel besides yourself needed to conduct the study, and if so do you have access to such individuals? Do you have (or will you be able to gain) expertise in the approach to measurement you will be using? Do you have (or will you be able to gain) the expertise and computer support needed to analyze your data? The more specifically you plan out your study, the more clearly you can identify areas in which advance preparation is needed, and the more likely you are to anticipate logistical problems.

Measurement

Select the measures or approaches to measurement you will be using. Will the measures be exclusively quantitative or qualitative, or will there be a mix? Will you be using established measures or creating your own? If they are established measures, do you need to purchase them? Whether established or created by you, how can you be assured that you will be using your measures in a reliable and valid way? Do the measures you plan to use provide appropriate operationalizations of the variables you wish to study? What is your plan, firm or tentative, with respect to data analysis?

Procedure

Work out the details of your procedure. Will the procedure be highly scripted, as in most quantitative research and some qualitative studies, or will you be using a qualitative approach in which some procedural details emerge as you go? Be as specific as you can in outlining your procedure, so that you can gain more information about the likely time commitment and feasibility of the study. If your study includes human participants, conduct a "dry run" of the study in which at least one person you know plays the role of participant, so that you can practice using study measures and identify any logistical problems in advance. You may need to conduct a pilot study with a small number of actual participants.

Sampling

Develop a sampling plan. What approach to sampling will you use? What sample size do you hope to obtain? Where will participants come from? You may need to make preliminary inquiries about the availability of participants. As with other aspects of your procedure, the plan for sampling should be as specific as possible in order to estimate the duration of the study and to ensure that data collection is logistically feasible.

Setting

Identify the setting where your study will take place. Where will you recruit participants? If you plan to conduct a content analysis, what materials do you intend to use, and where are these materials located? Whether you plan to study people or materials, your IRB application may need to include a letter of permission from someone in a position of authority at the setting where you intend to gather data.

IRB Approval

Contact your Institutional Review Board. What procedures do you need to follow to complete an IRB application? At the very minimum, you can expect to submit a project description and any consent and/or assent forms you will be using. During the planning of your study, you will have already been thinking about how to ensure the ethical treatment of your sample, but the process of obtaining IRB approval is a necessary step between the stages of planning the study and actually sampling participants.

Data Collection

Run the study. If pilot testing is needed, do so, analyze the data, and modify your materials and/or procedure before continuing. As you gather information, make sure that you keep the information organized and take appropriate precautions to protect participant confidentiality. Create backup copies of data as appropriate.

Data Analysis

Analyze your data. You may do this throughout the study, as in some qualitative approaches, or at the end as in most quantitative and some qualitative research. Analysis at any point may reveal a need to collect more data.

Disseminating the Results

Write up the results. Check first into the guidelines for style and content for your particular write-up. If you are writing a paper that will fulfill a graduate school requirement, be sure to check with your advisor or some other relevant person to ensure that you are on the right track. If you are writing for an academic journal or other scholarly source, get advice from an advisor or other experienced colleague as to where you should submit your report. In the case of a journal article, once you have selected a journal you should check the author guidelines included in each issue. These guidelines describe any requirements for format and content, as well as guidelines for submission. It will also be helpful to read through some of the articles published recently in the journal. Notice the range of topics, the length and breadth of articles, and the kinds of methods used. Be honest with yourself as to whether your own article would fit. You should be able to tell at least whether your study is comparable in length, scope, topic, and methodological approach. It is more difficult to tell whether your study is strong enough to merit publication in a particular journal. Here again, advice from a more experienced person might be helpful. (Hopefully this book was of assistance too!)

Chapter Summary

Educational research is informed by the need to link research with practice. The research–practice gap can be attributed to limitations in accessibility, comprehensibility, and usability. Both literature-specific and literature-independent recommendations for bridging the gap have been proposed.

Along with concerns about the research–practice gap are debates about how specific findings should inform specific practices. The "reading wars" encompass literature-specific disagreements about how early literacy instruction should reflect the results of reading research. The "EBR wars" reflect literature-independent disagreements about the types of research that merit an impact on practice.

Contemporary educational research can be understood in terms of different views of the research–practice relationship, and through distinctions across different areas and approaches to research. These distinctions can be seen in university programs and professional organizations, and in characteristics of research reports such as intended purposes, designs, populations, settings, methods and analyses, and theories and topics.

Conducting your own research study depends on a series of decisions and actions pertaining to personal interests, anticipated timeline, literature review, approach and design, feasibility, measurement, procedure, sampling, setting, IRB approval, data collection, data analysis, and dissemination of results.

Key Terms

Research–practice gap   EBR   What Works
Reading wars   Clearinghouse

Exercises

For questions 1–3, choose the source of research–practice disconnect illustrated in the quotation.

1. "I don't read studies that might relate to my teaching, because I don't understand statistics and some of the jargon that scientists use."

a) Accessibility
b) Comprehensibility
c) Usability

2. "I need practical solutions for my biggest classroom concerns, but all the studies in my field that I've read talk about intervention programs that my principal would never support."

a) Accessibility
b) Comprehensibility
c) Usability

3. "I'd like to know if there's research on the instructional methods I use, but I'm not sure where to find it."

a) Accessibility
b) Comprehensibility
c) Usability

4. *Critical thinking question:* After reading this book, what kind of approach to conducting research or research design do you consider preferable?

Answers to Exercises

1. b   **2.** c   **3.** a

Suggestions for Further Reading

Research Article: López, M. G., & Tashakkori, A. (2004). Narrowing the gap: Effects of a two-way bilingual education program on the literacy development of at-risk primary students. *Journal of Education for Students Placed at Risk, 9*(4), 325–336.

This quasi-experimental study addresses a research-practice controversy about the instructional practices most suitable for kindergartners with limited English proficiency.

Application Article: Snell, M. E. (2003). Applying research to practice: The more pervasive problem? *Research and Practice for Persons with Severe Disabilities, 28*(3), 143–147.

This essay explores causes and solutions for the research–practice gap in special education.

Extension Article: Riley-Tillman, T. C., Chafouleas, S. M., Eckert, T. L., & Kelleher, C. (2005). Bridging the gap between research and practice: A framework for building research agendas in school psychology. *Psychology in the Schools, 42*(5), 459–473.

This theoretical paper develops a framework for bridging the research–practice gap in the field of school psychology.

Appendix

TABLE A1   *Z* Scores Corresponding to Areas Under the Normal Curve

Column 2 gives the proportion of the area under the entire curve that is between the mean ($z = 0$) and the positive value of z. Areas for negative values of z are the same as for positive values, since the curve is symmetrical.

Column 3 gives the proportion of the area under the entire curve that falls beyond the stated positive value of z. Areas for negative values of z are the same, since the curve is symmetrical.

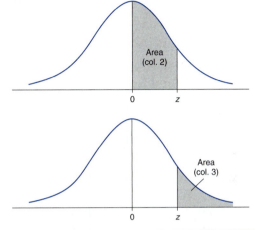

z	Area Between Mean and z	Area Beyond z	z	Area Between Mean and z	Area Beyond z	z	Area Between Mean and z	Area Beyond z
1	2	3	1	2	3	1	2	3
0.00	.0000	.5000	0.20	.0793	.4207	0.40	.1554	.3446
0.01	.0040	.4960	0.21	.0832	.4168	0.41	.1591	.3409
0.02	.0080	.4920	0.22	.0871	.4129	0.42	.1628	.3372
0.03	.0120	.4880	0.23	.0910	.4090	0.43	.1664	.3336
0.04	.0160	.4840	0.24	.0948	.4052	0.44	.1700	.3300
0.05	.0199	.4801	0.25	.0987	.4013	0.45	.1736	.3264
0.06	.0239	.4761	0.26	.1026	.3974	0.46	.1772	.3228
0.07	.0279	.4721	0.27	.1064	.3936	0.47	.1808	.3192
0.08	.0319	.4681	0.28	.1103	.3897	0.48	.1844	.3156
0.09	.0359	.4641	0.29	.1141	.3859	0.49	.1879	.3121
0.10	.0398	.4602	0.30	.1179	.3821	0.50	.1915	.3085
0.11	.0438	.4562	0.31	.1217	.3783	0.51	.1950	.3050
0.12	.0478	.4522	0.32	.1255	.3745	0.52	.1985	.3015
0.13	.0517	.4483	0.33	.1293	.3707	0.53	.2019	.2981
0.14	.0557	.4443	0.34	.1331	.3669	0.54	.2054	.2946
0.15	.0596	.4404	0.35	.1368	.3632	0.55	.2088	.2912
0.16	.0636	.4364	0.36	.1406	.3594	0.56	.2123	.2877
0.17	.0675	.4325	0.37	.1443	.3557	0.57	.2157	.2843
0.18	.0714	.4286	0.38	.1480	.3520	0.58	.2190	.2810
0.19	.0753	.4247	0.39	.1517	.3483	0.59	.2224	.2776

527

TABLE A1   *Continued*

z 1	Area Between Mean and z 2	Area Beyond z 3	z 1	Area Between Mean and z 2	Area Beyond z 3	z 1	Area Between Mean and z 2	Area Beyond z 3
0.60	.2257	.2743	1.00	.3413	.1587	1.40	.4192	.0808
0.61	.2291	.2709	1.01	.3438	.1562	1.41	.4207	.0793
0.62	.2324	.2676	1.02	.3461	.1539	1.42	.4222	.0778
0.63	.2357	.2643	1.03	.3485	.1515	1.43	.4236	.0764
0.64	.2389	.2611	1.04	.3508	.1492	1.44	.4251	.0749
0.65	.2422	.2578	1.05	.3531	.1469	1.45	.4265	.0735
0.66	.2454	.2546	1.06	.3554	.1446	1.46	.4279	.0721
0.67	.2486	.2514	1.07	.3577	.1423	1.47	.4292	.0708
0.68	.2517	.2483	1.08	.3599	.1401	1.48	.4306	.0694
0.69	.2549	.2451	1.09	.3621	.1379	1.49	.4319	.0681
0.70	.2580	.2420	1.10	.3643	.1357	1.50	.4332	.0668
0.71	.2611	.2389	1.11	.3665	.1335	1.51	.4345	.0655
0.72	.2642	.2358	1.12	.3686	.1314	1.52	.4357	.0643
0.73	.2673	.2327	1.13	.3708	.1292	1.53	.4370	.0630
0.74	.2704	.2296	1.14	.3729	.1271	1.54	.4382	.0618
0.75	.2734	.2266	1.15	.3749	.1251	1.55	.4394	.0606
0.76	.2764	.2236	1.16	.3770	.1230	1.56	.4406	.0594
0.77	.2794	.2206	1.17	.3790	.1210	1.57	.4418	.0582
0.78	.2823	.2177	1.18	.3810	.1190	1.58	.4429	.0571
0.79	.2852	.2148	1.19	.3830	.1170	1.59	.4441	.0559
0.80	.2881	.2119	1.20	.3849	.1151	1.60	.4452	.0548
0.81	.2910	.2090	1.21	.3869	.1131	1.61	.4463	.0537
0.82	.2939	.2061	1.22	.3888	.1112	1.62	.4474	.0526
0.83	.2967	.2033	1.23	.3907	.1093	1.63	.4484	.0516
0.84	.2995	.2005	1.24	.3925	.1075	1.64	.4495	.0505
0.85	.3023	.1977	1.25	.3944	.1056	1.65	.4505	.0495
0.86	.3051	.1949	1.26	.3962	.1038	1.66	.4515	.0485
0.87	.3078	.1922	1.27	.3980	.1020	1.67	.4525	.0475
0.88	.3106	.1894	1.28	.3997	.1003	1.68	.4535	.0465
0.89	.3133	.1867	1.29	.4015	.0985	1.69	.4545	.0455
0.90	.3159	.1841	1.30	.4032	.0968	1.70	.4554	.0446
0.91	.3186	.1814	1.31	.4049	.0951	1.71	.4564	.0436
0.92	.3212	.1788	1.32	.4066	.0934	1.72	.4573	.0427
0.93	.3238	.1762	1.33	.4082	.0918	1.73	.4582	.0418
0.94	.3264	.1736	1.34	.4099	.0901	1.74	.4591	.0409
0.95	.3289	.1711	1.35	.4115	.0885	1.75	.4599	.0401
0.96	.3315	.1685	1.36	.4131	.0869	1.76	.4608	.0392
0.97	.3340	.1660	1.37	.4147	.0853	1.77	.4616	.0384
0.98	.3365	.1635	1.38	.4162	.0838	1.78	.4625	.0375
0.99	.3389	.1611	1.39	.4177	.0823	1.79	.4633	.0367

TABLE A1 *Continued*

z 1	Area Between Mean and z 2	Area Beyond z 3	z 1	Area Between Mean and z 2	Area Beyond z 3	z 1	Area Between Mean and z 2	Area Beyond z 3
1.80	.4641	.0359	2.20	.4861	.0139	2.60	.4953	.0047
1.81	.4649	.0351	2.21	.4864	.0136	2.61	.4955	.0045
1.82	.4656	.0344	2.22	.4868	.0132	2.62	.4956	.0044
1.83	.4664	.0336	2.23	.4871	.0129	2.63	.4957	.0043
1.84	.4671	.0329	2.24	.4875	.0125	2.64	.4959	.0041
1.85	.4678	.0322	2.25	.4878	.0122	2.65	.4960	.0040
1.86	.4686	.0314	2.26	.4881	.0119	2.66	.4961	.0039
1.87	.4693	.0307	2.27	.4884	.0116	2.67	.4962	.0038
1.88	.4699	.0301	2.28	.4887	.0113	2.68	.4963	.0037
1.89	.4706	.0294	2.29	.4890	.0110	2.69	.4964	.0036
1.90	.4713	.0287	2.30	.4893	.0107	2.70	.4965	.0035
1.91	.4719	.0281	2.31	.4896	.0104	2.71	.4966	.0034
1.92	.4726	.0274	2.32	.4898	.0102	2.72	.4967	.0033
1.93	.4732	.0268	2.33	.4901	.0099	2.73	.4968	.0032
1.94	.4738	.0262	2.34	.4904	.0096	2.74	.4969	.0031
1.95	.4744	.0256	2.35	.4906	.0094	2.75	.4970	.0030
1.96	.4750	.0250	2.36	.4909	.0091	2.76	.4971	.0029
1.97	.4756	.0244	2.37	.4911	.0089	2.77	.4972	.0028
1.98	.4761	.0239	2.38	.4913	.0087	2.78	.4973	.0027
1.99	.4767	.0233	2.39	.4916	.0084	2.79	.4974	.0026
2.00	.4772	.0228	2.40	.4918	.0082	2.80	.4974	.0026
2.01	.4778	.0222	2.41	.4920	.0080	2.81	.4975	.0025
2.02	.4783	.0217	2.42	.4922	.0078	2.82	.4976	.0024
2.03	.4788	.0212	2.43	.4925	.0075	2.83	.4977	.0023
2.04	.4793	.0207	2.44	.4927	.0073	2.84	.4977	.0023
2.05	.4798	.0202	2.45	.4929	.0071	2.85	.4978	.0022
2.06	.4803	.0197	2.46	.4931	.0069	2.86	.4979	.0021
2.07	.4808	.0192	2.47	.4932	.0068	2.87	.4979	.0021
2.08	.4812	.0188	2.48	.4934	.0066	2.88	.4980	.0020
2.09	.4817	.0183	2.49	.4936	.0064	2.89	.4981	.0019
2.10	.4821	.0179	2.50	.4938	.0062	2.90	.4981	.0019
2.11	.4826	.0174	2.51	.4940	.0060	2.91	.4982	.0018
2.12	.4830	.0170	2.52	.4941	.0059	2.92	.4982	.0018
2.13	.4834	.0166	2.53	.4943	.0057	2.93	.4983	.0017
2.14	.4838	.0162	2.54	.4945	.0055	2.94	.4984	.0016
2.15	.4842	.0158	2.55	.4946	.0054	2.95	.4984	.0016
2.16	.4846	.0154	2.56	.4948	.0052	2.96	.4985	.0015
2.17	.4850	.0150	2.57	.4949	.0051	2.97	.4985	.0015
2.18	.4854	.0146	2.58	.4951	.0049	2.98	.4986	.0014
2.19	.4857	.0143	2.59	.4952	.0048	2.99	.4986	.0014

TABLE A1 *Continued*

z	Area Between Mean and *z*	Area Beyond *z*	*z*	Area Between Mean and *z*	Area Beyond *z*	*z*	Area Between Mean and *z*	Area Beyond *z*
1	**2**	**3**	**1**	**2**	**3**	**1**	**2**	**3**
3.00	.4987	.0013	3.10	.4990	.0010	3.20	.4993	.0007
3.01	.4987	.0013	3.11	.4991	.0009	3.21	.4993	.0007
3.02	.4987	.0013	3.12	.4991	.0009	3.22	.4994	.0006
3.03	.4988	.0012	3.13	.4991	.0009	3.23	.4994	.0006
3.04	.4988	.0012	3.14	.4992	.0008	3.24	.4994	.0006
3.05	.4989	.0011	3.15	.4992	.0008	3.30	.4995	.0005
3.06	.4989	.0011	3.16	.4992	.0008	3.40	.4997	.0003
3.07	.4989	.0011	3.17	.4992	.0008	3.50	.4998	.0002
3.08	.4990	.0010	3.18	.4993	.0007	3.60	.4998	.0002
3.09	.4990	.0010	3.19	.4993	.0007	3.70	.4999	.0001

TABLE A2 Critical Values of Student's *t*

The first column identifies the specific *t* distribution according to its degrees of freedom. Other columns give the value of *t* that corresponds to the *area beyond t* in one or both tails, according to the particular column heading. Areas beyond negative values of *t* are the same as those beyond positive values, since the curve is symmetrical.

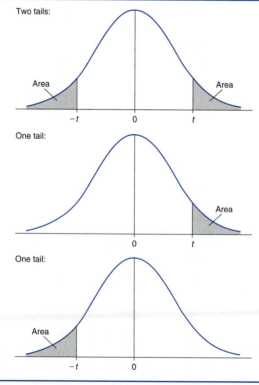

Source: From Statistical Tables for Biological, Agricultural and Medical Research, Sixth Edition, R.A. Fisher and F. Yates, copyright © 1963. Reprinted by permission of Pearson Education Limited.

TABLE A2 *Continued*

	Area in *Both* Tails					
	.50	.20	.10	.05	.02	.01

			Area in *Both* Tails			
df	.25	.10	.05	.025	.01	.005
1	1.000	3.078	6.314	12.706	31.821	63.657
2	0.816	1.886	2.920	4.303	6.965	9.925
3	0.765	1.638	2.353	3.182	4.541	5.841
4	0.741	1.533	2.132	2.776	3.747	4.604
5	0.727	1.476	2.015	2.571	3.365	4.032
6	0.718	1.440	1.943	2.447	3.143	3.707
7	0.711	1.415	1.895	2.365	2.998	3.499
8	0.706	1.397	1.860	2.306	2.896	3.355
9	0.703	1.383	1.833	2.262	2.821	3.250
10	0.700	1.372	1.812	2.228	2.764	3.169
11	0.697	1.363	1.796	2.201	2.718	3.106
12	0.695	1.356	1.782	2.179	2.681	3.055
13	0.694	1.350	1.771	2.160	2.650	3.012
14	0.692	1.345	1.761	2.145	2.624	2.977
15	0.691	1.341	1.753	2.132	2.602	2.947
16	0.690	1.337	1.746	2.120	2.583	2.921
17	0.689	1.333	1.740	2.110	2.567	2.898
18	0.688	1.330	1.734	2.101	2.552	2.878
19	0.688	1.328	1.729	2.093	2.539	2.861
20	0.687	1.325	1.725	2.086	2.528	2.845
21	0.686	1.323	1.721	2.080	2.518	2.831
22	0.686	1.321	1.717	2.074	2.508	2.819
23	0.685	1.319	1.714	2.069	2.500	2.807
24	0.685	1.318	1.711	2.064	2.492	2.797
25	0.684	1.316	1.708	2.060	2.485	2.787
26	0.684	1.315	1.706	2.056	2.479	2.779
27	0.684	1.314	1.703	2.052	2.473	2.771
28	0.683	1.313	1.701	2.048	2.467	2.763
29	0.683	1.311	1.699	2.045	2.462	2.756
30	0.683	1.310	1.697	2.042	2.457	2.750
40	0.681	1.303	1.684	2.021	2.423	2.704
60	0.679	1.296	1.671	2.000	2.390	2.660
120	0.677	1.289	1.658	1.980	2.358	2.617
∞	0.674	1.282	1.645	1.960	2.326	2.576

TABLE A3   Critical Values of F

The values of F are those corresponding to 5% (Roman type) and 1% (**boldface** type) of the area in the upper tail of the distribution. The specific F distribution must be identified by the number of degrees of freedom characterizing the numerator and the denominator of F.

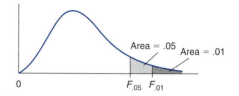

| Degrees of Freedom: Denominator | \multicolumn{16}{c}{Degrees of Freedom: Numerator} | | | | | | | | | | | | | | |
	1	2	3	4	5	6	7	8	9	10	11	12	14	16	20
1	161	200	216	225	230	234	237	239	241	242	243	244	245	246	248
	4,052	**4,999**	**5,403**	**5,625**	**5,764**	**5,859**	**5,928**	**5,981**	**6,022**	**6,056**	**6,082**	**6,106**	**6,142**	**6,169**	**6,208**
2	18.51	19.00	19.16	19.25	19.30	19.33	19.36	19.37	19.38	19.39	19.40	19.41	19.42	19.43	19.44
	98.49	**99.00**	**99.17**	**99.25**	**99.30**	**99.33**	**99.34**	**99.36**	**99.38**	**99.40**	**99.41**	**99.42**	**99.43**	**99.44**	**99.45**
3	10.13	9.55	9.28	9.12	9.01	8.94	8.88	8.84	8.81	8.78	8.76	8.74	8.71	8.69	8.66
	34.12	**30.82**	**29.46**	**28.71**	**28.24**	**27.91**	**27.67**	**27.49**	**27.34**	**27.23**	**27.13**	**27.05**	**26.92**	**26.83**	**26.69**
4	7.71	6.94	6.59	6.39	6.26	6.16	6.09	6.04	6.00	5.96	5.93	5.91	5.87	5.84	5.80
	21.20	**18.00**	**16.69**	**15.98**	**15.52**	**15.21**	**14.98**	**14.80**	**14.66**	**14.54**	**14.45**	**14.37**	**14.24**	**14.15**	**14.02**
5	6.61	5.79	5.41	5.19	5.05	4.95	4.88	4.82	4.78	4.74	4.70	4.68	4.64	4.60	4.56
	16.26	**13.27**	**12.06**	**11.39**	**10.97**	**10.67**	**10.45**	**10.27**	**10.15**	**10.05**	**9.96**	**9.89**	**9.77**	**9.68**	**9.55**
6	5.99	5.14	4.76	4.53	4.39	4.28	4.21	4.15	4.10	4.06	4.03	4.00	3.96	3.92	3.87
	13.74	**10.92**	**9.78**	**9.15**	**8.75**	**8.47**	**8.26**	**8.10**	**7.98**	**7.87**	**7.79**	**7.72**	**7.60**	**7.52**	**7.39**
7	5.59	4.47	4.35	4.12	3.97	3.87	3.79	3.73	3.68	3.63	3.60	3.57	3.52	3.49	3.44
	12.25	**9.55**	**8.45**	**7.85**	**7.46**	**7.19**	**7.00**	**6.84**	**6.71**	**6.62**	**6.54**	**6.47**	**6.35**	**6.27**	**6.15**
8	5.32	4.46	4.07	3.84	3.69	3.58	3.50	3.44	3.39	3.34	3.31	3.28	3.23	3.20	3.15
	11.26	**8.65**	**7.59**	**7.01**	**6.63**	**6.37**	**6.19**	**6.03**	**5.91**	**5.82**	**5.74**	**5.67**	**5.56**	**5.48**	**5.36**
9	5.12	4.26	3.86	3.63	3.48	3.37	3.29	3.23	3.18	3.13	3.10	3.07	3.02	2.98	2.93
	10.56	**8.02**	**6.99**	**6.42**	**6.06**	**5.80**	**5.62**	**5.47**	**5.35**	**5.26**	**5.18**	**5.11**	**5.00**	**4.92**	**4.80**
10	4.96	4.10	3.71	3.48	3.33	3.22	3.14	3.07	3.02	2.97	2.94	2.91	2.86	2.82	2.77
	10.04	**7.56**	**6.55**	**5.99**	**5.64**	**5.39**	**5.21**	**5.06**	**4.95**	**4.85**	**4.78**	**4.71**	**4.60**	**4.52**	**4.41**
11	4.84	3.98	3.59	3.36	3.20	3.09	3.01	2.95	2.90	2.86	2.82	2.79	2.74	2.70	2.65
	9.65	**7.20**	**6.22**	**5.67**	**5.32**	**5.07**	**4.88**	**4.74**	**4.63**	**4.54**	**4.46**	**4.40**	**4.29**	**4.21**	**4.10**
12	4.75	3.88	3.49	3.26	3.11	3.00	2.92	2.85	2.80	2.76	2.72	2.69	2.64	2.60	2.54
	9.33	**6.93**	**5.95**	**5.41**	**5.06**	**4.82**	**4.65**	**4.50**	**4.39**	**4.30**	**4.22**	**4.16**	**4.05**	**3.98**	**3.86**
13	4.67	3.80	3.41	3.18	3.02	2.92	2.84	2.77	2.72	2.67	2.63	2.60	2.55	2.51	2.46
	9.07	**6.70**	**5.74**	**5.20**	**4.86**	**4.62**	**4.44**	**4.30**	**4.19**	**4.10**	**4.02**	**3.96**	**3.85**	**3.78**	**3.67**
14	4.60	3.74	3.34	3.11	2.96	2.85	2.77	2.70	2.65	2.60	2.56	2.53	2.48	2.44	2.39
	8.86	**6.51**	**5.56**	**5.03**	**4.69**	**4.46**	**4.28**	**4.14**	**4.03**	**3.94**	**3.86**	**3.80**	**3.70**	**3.62**	**3.51**
15	4.54	3.68	3.29	3.06	2.90	2.79	2.70	2.64	2.59	2.55	2.51	2.48	2.43	2.39	2.33
	8.68	**6.36**	**5.42**	**4.89**	**4.56**	**4.32**	**4.14**	**4.00**	**3.89**	**3.80**	**3.73**	**3.67**	**3.56**	**3.48**	**3.36**
16	4.49	3.63	3.24	3.01	2.85	2.74	2.66	2.59	2.54	2.49	2.45	2.42	2.37	2.33	2.28
	8.53	**6.23**	**5.29**	**4.77**	**4.44**	**4.20**	**4.03**	**3.89**	**3.78**	**3.69**	**3.61**	**3.55**	**3.45**	**3.37**	**3.25**
17	4.45	3.59	3.20	2.96	2.81	2.70	2.62	2.55	2.50	2.45	2.41	2.38	2.33	2.29	2.23
	8.40	**6.11**	**5.18**	**4.67**	**4.34**	**4.10**	**3.93**	**3.79**	**3.68**	**3.59**	**3.52**	**3.45**	**3.35**	**3.27**	**3.16**

Source: From *Statistical Methods*, G.W. Snedecor and W.G. Cochran. Reprinted by permission of the publisher.

TABLE A3 *Continued*

Degrees of Freedom: Denominator	1	2	3	4	5	6	7	8	9	10	11	12	14	16	20
18	4.41	3.55	3.16	2.93	2.77	2.66	2.58	2.51	2.46	2.41	2.37	2.34	2.29	2.25	2.19
	8.28	**6.01**	**5.09**	**4.58**	**4.25**	**4.01**	**3.85**	**3.71**	**3.60**	**3.51**	**3.44**	**3.37**	**3.27**	**3.19**	**3.07**
19	4.38	3.52	3.13	2.90	2.74	2.63	2.55	2.48	2.43	2.38	2.34	2.31	2.26	2.21	2.15
	8.18	**5.93**	**5.01**	**4.50**	**4.17**	**3.94**	**3.77**	**3.63**	**3.52**	**3.43**	**3.36**	**3.30**	**3.19**	**3.12**	**3.00**
20	4.35	3.49	3.10	2.87	2.71	2.60	2.52	2.45	2.40	2.35	2.31	2.28	2.23	2.18	2.12
	8.10	**5.85**	**4.94**	**4.43**	**4.10**	**3.87**	**3.71**	**3.56**	**3.45**	**3.37**	**3.30**	**3.23**	**3.13**	**3.05**	**2.94**
21	4.32	3.47	3.07	2.84	2.68	2.57	2.49	2.42	2.37	2.32	2.28	2.25	2.20	2.15	2.09
	8.02	**5.78**	**4.87**	**4.37**	**4.04**	**3.81**	**3.65**	**3.51**	**3.40**	**3.31**	**3.24**	**3.17**	**3.07**	**2.99**	**2.88**
22	4.30	3.44	3.05	2.82	2.66	2.55	2.47	2.40	2.35	2.30	2.26	2.23	2.18	2.13	2.07
	7.94	**5.72**	**4.82**	**4.31**	**3.99**	**3.76**	**3.59**	**3.45**	**3.35**	**3.26**	**3.18**	**3.12**	**3.02**	**2.94**	**2.83**
23	4.28	3.42	3.03	2.80	2.64	2.53	2.45	2.38	2.32	2.28	2.24	2.20	2.14	2.10	2.04
	7.88	**5.66**	**4.76**	**4.26**	**3.94**	**3.71**	**3.54**	**3.41**	**3.30**	**3.21**	**3.14**	**3.07**	**2.97**	**2.89**	**2.78**
24	4.26	3.40	3.01	2.78	2.62	2.51	2.43	2.36	2.30	2.26	2.22	2.18	2.13	2.09	2.02
	7.82	**5.61**	**4.72**	**4.22**	**3.90**	**3.67**	**3.50**	**3.36**	**3.25**	**3.17**	**3.09**	**3.03**	**2.93**	**2.85**	**2.74**
25	4.24	3.38	2.99	2.76	2.60	2.49	2.41	2.34	2.28	2.24	2.20	2.16	2.11	2.06	2.00
	7.77	**5.57**	**4.68**	**4.18**	**3.86**	**3.63**	**3.46**	**3.32**	**3.21**	**3.13**	**3.05**	**2.99**	**2.89**	**2.81**	**2.70**
26	4.22	3.37	2.98	2.74	2.59	2.47	2.39	2.32	2.27	2.22	2.18	2.15	2.10	2.05	1.99
	7.72	**5.53**	**4.64**	**4.14**	**3.82**	**3.59**	**3.42**	**3.29**	**3.17**	**3.09**	**3.02**	**2.96**	**2.86**	**2.77**	**2.66**
27	4.21	3.35	2.96	2.73	2.57	2.46	2.37	2.30	2.25	2.20	2.16	2.13	2.08	2.03	1.97
	7.68	**5.49**	**4.60**	**4.11**	**3.79**	**3.56**	**3.39**	**3.26**	**3.14**	**3.06**	**2.98**	**2.93**	**2.83**	**2.74**	**2.63**
28	4.20	3.34	2.95	2.71	2.56	2.44	2.36	2.29	2.24	2.19	2.15	2.12	2.06	2.02	1.96
	7.64	**5.45**	**4.57**	**4.07**	**3.76**	**3.53**	**3.36**	**3.23**	**3.11**	**3.03**	**2.95**	**2.90**	**2.80**	**2.71**	**2.60**
29	4.18	3.33	2.93	2.70	2.54	2.43	2.35	2.28	2.22	2.18	2.14	2.10	2.05	2.00	1.94
	7.60	**5.42**	**4.54**	**4.04**	**3.73**	**3.50**	**3.33**	**3.20**	**3.08**	**3.00**	**2.92**	**2.87**	**2.77**	**2.68**	**2.57**
30	4.17	3.32	2.92	2.69	2.53	2.42	2.34	2.27	2.21	2.16	2.12	2.09	2.04	1.99	1.93
	7.56	**5.39**	**4.51**	**4.02**	**3.70**	**3.47**	**3.30**	**3.17**	**3.06**	**2.98**	**2.90**	**2.84**	**2.74**	**2.66**	**2.55**
32	4.15	3.30	2.90	2.67	2.51	2.40	2.32	2.25	2.19	2.14	2.10	2.07	2.02	1.97	1.91
	7.50	**5.34**	**4.46**	**3.97**	**3.66**	**3.42**	**3.25**	**3.12**	**3.01**	**2.94**	**2.86**	**2.80**	**2.70**	**2.62**	**2.51**
34	4.13	3.28	2.88	2.65	2.49	2.38	2.30	2.23	2.17	2.12	2.08	2.05	2.00	1.95	1.89
	7.44	**5.29**	**4.42**	**3.93**	**3.61**	**3.38**	**3.21**	**3.08**	**2.97**	**2.89**	**2.82**	**2.76**	**2.66**	**2.58**	**2.47**
36	4.11	3.26	2.86	2.63	2.48	2.36	2.28	2.21	2.15	2.10	2.06	2.03	1.98	1.93	1.87
	7.39	**5.25**	**4.38**	**3.89**	**3.58**	**3.35**	**3.18**	**3.04**	**2.94**	**2.86**	**2.78**	**2.72**	**2.62**	**2.54**	**2.43**
38	4.10	3.25	2.85	2.62	2.46	2.35	2.26	2.19	2.14	2.09	2.05	2.02	1.96	1.92	1.85
	7.35	**5.21**	**4.34**	**3.86**	**3.54**	**3.32**	**3.15**	**3.02**	**2.91**	**2.82**	**2.75**	**2.69**	**2.59**	**2.51**	**2.40**
40	4.08	3.23	2.84	2.61	2.45	2.34	2.25	2.18	2.12	2.07	2.04	2.00	1.95	1.90	1.84
	7.31	**5.18**	**4.31**	**3.83**	**3.51**	**3.29**	**3.12**	**2.99**	**2.88**	**2.80**	**2.73**	**2.66**	**2.56**	**2.49**	**2.37**
42	4.07	3.22	2.83	2.59	2.44	2.32	2.24	2.17	2.11	2.06	2.02	1.99	1.94	1.89	1.82
	7.27	**5.15**	**4.29**	**3.80**	**3.49**	**3.26**	**3.10**	**2.96**	**2.86**	**2.77**	**2.70**	**2.64**	**2.54**	**2.46**	**2.35**
44	4.06	3.21	2.82	2.58	2.43	2.31	2.23	2.16	2.10	2.05	2.01	1.98	1.92	1.88	1.81
	7.24	**5.12**	**4.26**	**3.78**	**3.46**	**3.24**	**3.07**	**2.94**	**2.84**	**2.75**	**2.68**	**2.62**	**2.52**	**2.44**	**2.32**
46	4.05	3.20	2.81	2.57	2.42	2.30	2.22	2.14	2.09	2.04	2.00	1.97	1.91	1.87	1.80
	7.21	**5.10**	**4.24**	**3.76**	**3.44**	**3.22**	**3.05**	**2.92**	**2.82**	**2.73**	**2.66**	**2.60**	**2.50**	**2.42**	**2.30**
48	4.04	3.19	2.80	2.56	2.41	2.30	2.21	2.14	2.08	2.03	1.99	1.96	1.90	1.86	1.79
	7.19	**5.08**	**4.22**	**3.74**	**3.42**	**3.20**	**3.04**	**2.90**	**2.80**	**2.71**	**2.64**	**2.58**	**2.48**	**2.40**	**2.28**

TABLE A3 *Continued*

Degrees of Freedom: Denominator	1	2	3	4	5	6	7	8	9	10	11	12	14	16	20
						Degrees of Freedom: Numerator									
50	4.03	3.18	2.79	2.56	2.40	2.29	2.20	2.13	2.07	2.02	1.98	1.95	1.90	1.85	1.78
	7.17	**5.06**	**4.20**	**3.72**	**3.41**	**3.18**	**3.02**	**2.88**	**2.78**	**2.70**	**2.62**	**2.56**	**2.46**	**2.39**	**2.26**
55	4.02	3.17	2.78	2.54	2.38	2.27	2.18	2.11	2.05	2.00	1.97	1.93	1.88	1.83	1.76
	7.12	**5.01**	**4.16**	**3.68**	**3.37**	**3.15**	**2.98**	**2.85**	**2.75**	**2.66**	**2.59**	**2.53**	**2.43**	**2.35**	**2.23**
60	4.00	3.15	2.76	2.52	2.37	2.25	2.17	2.10	2.04	1.99	1.95	1.92	1.86	1.81	1.75
	7.08	**4.98**	**4.13**	**3.65**	**3.34**	**3.12**	**2.95**	**2.82**	**2.72**	**2.63**	**2.56**	**2.50**	**2.40**	**2.32**	**2.20**
65	3.99	3.14	2.75	2.51	2.36	2.24	2.15	2.08	2.02	1.98	1.94	1.90	1.85	1.80	1.73
	7.04	**4.95**	**4.10**	**3.62**	**3.31**	**3.09**	**2.93**	**2.79**	**2.70**	**2.61**	**2.54**	**2.47**	**2.37**	**2.30**	**2.18**
70	3.98	3.13	2.74	2.50	2.35	2.23	2.14	2.07	2.01	1.97	1.93	1.89	1.84	1.79	1.72
	7.01	**4.92**	**4.08**	**3.60**	**3.29**	**3.07**	**2.91**	**2.77**	**2.67**	**2.59**	**2.51**	**2.45**	**2.35**	**2.28**	**2.15**
80	3.96	3.11	2.72	2.48	2.33	2.21	2.12	2.05	1.99	1.95	1.91	1.88	1.82	1.77	1.70
	6.96	**4.88**	**4.04**	**3.56**	**3.25**	**3.04**	**2.87**	**2.74**	**2.64**	**2.55**	**2.48**	**2.41**	**2.32**	**2.24**	**2.11**
100	3.94	3.09	2.70	2.46	2.30	2.19	2.10	2.03	1.97	1.92	1.88	1.85	1.79	1.75	1.68
	6.90	**4.82**	**3.98**	**3.51**	**3.20**	**2.99**	**2.82**	**2.69**	**2.59**	**2.51**	**2.43**	**2.36**	**2.26**	**2.19**	**2.06**
125	3.92	3.07	2.68	2.44	2.29	2.17	2.08	2.01	1.95	1.90	1.86	1.83	1.77	1.72	1.65
	6.84	**4.78**	**3.94**	**3.47**	**3.17**	**2.95**	**2.79**	**2.65**	**2.56**	**2.47**	**2.40**	**2.33**	**2.23**	**2.15**	**2.03**
150	3.91	3.06	2.67	2.43	2.27	2.16	2.07	2.00	1.94	1.89	1.85	1.82	1.76	1.71	1.64
	6.81	**4.75**	**3.91**	**3.44**	**3.14**	**2.92**	**2.76**	**2.62**	**2.53**	**2.44**	**2.37**	**2.30**	**2.20**	**2.12**	**2.00**
200	3.89	3.04	2.65	2.41	2.26	2.14	2.05	1.98	1.92	1.87	1.83	1.80	1.74	1.69	1.62
	6.76	**4.71**	**3.88**	**3.41**	**3.11**	**2.90**	**2.73**	**2.60**	**2.50**	**2.41**	**2.34**	**2.28**	**2.17**	**2.09**	**1.97**
400	3.86	3.02	2.62	2.39	2.23	2.12	2.03	1.96	1.90	1.85	1.81	1.78	1.72	1.67	1.60
	6.70	**4.66**	**3.83**	**3.36**	**3.06**	**2.85**	**2.69**	**2.55**	**2.46**	**2.37**	**2.29**	**2.23**	**2.12**	**2.04**	**1.92**
1000	3.85	3.00	2.61	2.38	2.22	2.10	2.02	1.95	1.89	1.84	1.80	1.76	1.70	1.65	1.58
	6.66	**4.62**	**3.80**	**3.34**	**3.04**	**2.82**	**2.66**	**2.53**	**2.43**	**2.34**	**2.26**	**2.20**	**2.09**	**2.01**	**1.89**
∞	3.84	2.99	2.60	2.37	2.21	2.09	2.01	1.94	1.88	1.83	1.79	1.75	1.69	1.64	1.57
	6.64	**4.60**	**3.78**	**3.32**	**3.02**	**2.80**	**2.64**	**2.51**	**2.41**	**2.32**	**2.24**	**2.18**	**2.07**	**1.99**	**1.87**

TABLE A4 Critical Values of χ^2

The first column identifies the specific χ^2
distribution according to its number of degrees
of freedom. Other columns give the proportion
of the area under the entire curve that falls
above the tabled value of χ^2.

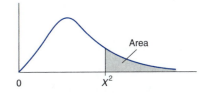

df	.10	.05	.025	.01	.005
			Area in the Upper Tail		
1	2.71	3.84	5.02	6.63	7.78
2	4.61	5.99	7.38	9.21	10.60
3	6.25	7.81	9.35	11.34	12.84
4	7.78	9.49	11.14	13.28	14.86
5	9.24	11.07	12.83	15.09	16.75
6	10.64	12.59	14.45	16.81	18.55
7	12.02	14.07	16.01	18.48	20.28
8	13.36	15.51	17.53	20.09	21.96
9	14.68	16.92	19.02	21.67	23.59
10	15.99	18.31	20.48	23.21	25.19
11	17.28	19.68	21.92	24.72	26.76
12	18.55	21.03	23.34	26.22	28.30
13	19.81	22.36	24.74	27.69	29.82
14	21.06	23.68	26.12	29.14	31.32
15	22.31	25.00	27.49	30.58	32.80
16	23.54	26.30	28.85	32.00	34.27
17	24.77	27.59	30.19	33.41	35.72
18	25.99	28.87	31.53	34.81	37.16
19	27.20	30.14	32.85	36.19	38.58
20	28.41	31.41	34.17	37.57	40.00
21	29.62	32.67	35.48	38.93	41.40
22	30.81	33.92	36.78	40.29	42.80
23	32.01	35.17	38.08	41.64	44.18
24	33.20	36.42	39.36	42.98	45.56
25	34.38	37.65	40.65	44.31	46.93
26	35.56	38.89	41.92	45.64	48.29
27	36.74	40.11	43.19	46.96	49.64
28	37.92	41.34	44.46	48.28	50.99
29	39.09	42.56	45.72	49.59	52.34
30	40.26	43.77	46.98	50.89	53.67
40	51.81	55.76	59.34	63.69	66.77
50	63.17	67.50	71.42	76.15	79.49
60	74.40	79.08	83.30	88.38	91.95
70	85.53	90.53	95.02	100.42	104.22
80	96.58	101.88	106.63	112.33	116.32
90	107.56	113.14	118.14	124.12	128.30
100	118.50	124.34	129.56	135.81	140.17

Source: From E. Pearson and H. Hartley, *Biometrika Tables for Statisticians,* ©1976, Vol. I, pp. 137, Table 8, by permission of the Oxford University Press on behalf of the Biometrika Trust.

Glossary

45 CFR 46 The Code of Federal Regulations for the Protection of Human Subjects, in which the ethical standards and related guidelines for research are embodied.

A Measurements taken at baseline in a single-participant research design.

A-B design A single-participant research design in which measurements are taken at baseline (A) and then again during treatment (B).

A-B-A design A single-participant research design in which measurements taken at baseline (A) and then again during treatment (B), following which the researcher withdraws the treatment and measures the participant again.

A-B-A-B design A single-participant research design in which measurements taken at baseline (A) and then again during treatment (B), following which the researcher withdraws the treatment, measures the participant again, and then adds a final treatment.

Abstract A brief summary of a study that describes the main research questions, the general design, the nature of the participants and procedure, the key findings, and the most important conclusions.

Achievement test A test that measures how well an individual has mastered some particular knowledge or skill.

Action research An applied approach in which practitioners conduct studies in their own educational settings and make immediate use of the results.

Age equivalent The average score on a test obtained by individuals of a particular age.

Alternating treatment design A single-participant design in which the effects of more than one treatment are compared.

Alternative hypothesis The assumption during hypothesis testing that there is a genuine difference or relationship between variables.

Analysis of covariance (ANCOVA) A statistical procedure that evaluates the effects of one or more independent variables on one dependent variable while controlling for the effects of potentially extraneous variables.

Analysis of variance (ANOVA) A set of statistical procedures used to evaluate the effects of one or more independent variables on one dependent variable.

Applied research Research that focuses on questions of immediate practical interest.

Aptitude test A test that measures how well an individual is likely to perform in the future on some particular dimension(s).

Archival measure A measure that relies on information obtained from inanimate, preexisting materials.

Assent Oral agreement to participate in research.

Assessment The inclusive process of gathering, recording, analyzing, and interpreting information. Assessment activities include the creation and administration of a measure, the scoring and interpretation of whatever information the measure yields, and the formulation of conclusions about what to do with the information.

Attitudinal test A test that measures beliefs, attitudes, or feelings about a specific topic.

Attrition The loss of participants from a study.

Autoethnography A type of qualitative research that embodies both ethnography and autobiography, in which the researcher incorporates personal experiences into the narrative, and uses these experiences as a window into his or her own culture (and vice versa).

Axial coding An approach to coding data in which relationships between several categories and one category of interest are identified.

B A treatment, during which measurements are also made, in a single-participant design.

Bar graph A form of graphic representation in which columns are used to represent information about each level of a nominal variable.

Baseline The natural characteristics of an individual prior to experimental intervention.

Baseline-treatment design A general category of single-participant designs that consist of measurements taken at baseline (A) and at treatment (B), during which measurements are also made.

Basic research Research that is conducted in order to acquire concrete knowledge, and ultimately to contribute to theory.

Behavioral measure A measure that is based on observations made by the researcher.

Between-subjects factor A categorical variable whose levels correspond to different groups.

Bonferroni correction A formula that yields a more conservative estimate of the p value for a particular statistical comparison.

Boolean operator   A term such as AND, OR, or NOT that allows keywords to be used in ways that either narrow or expand a search.

Computer-Assisted Qualitative Data Analysis Software (CAQDAS)   A family of computer software programs used for qualitative data analysis.

Carryover effects   Effects that continue to be observed during the withdrawal phase in a single-participant design.

Case study   An approach to conducting research that provides an in-depth exploration of an individual. The individual may be a person, program, institution, or anything else that can be treated as a single unit.

Causal-comparative research   A type of quantative research design in which the effects of naturally occurring differences in categorical variables are studied.

Checklist   A form used in observational research in which the experimenter indicates whether or not each behavior on a list is observed.

Chi square (χ^2)   A nonparametric statistical test used to analyze the frequencies or proportions of each level of a nominal variable by comparing observed to expected values.

Clientism   The assumption in program evaluation that because a client has paid for an evaluation, the evaluator should do whatever the client requests.

Cluster sampling   An approach to sampling in which entire groups rather than individuals are sampled.

Coding system   An approach to simplifying data by sorting it into categories.

Coefficient of equivalence   A correlation coefficient that reflects the extent of equivalent forms reliability.

Coefficient of stability   A correlation coefficient that expresses the extent of test–retest reliability.

Coefficient of stability and equivalence   A correlation coefficient that indicates both test–retest reliability and equivalent forms reliability.

Cohen's d   A formula for calculating effect size when two groups are compared.

Cohort study   A type of longitudinal research design in which the same population is surveyed at two or more points in time, but a different sample is drawn each time.

Collective case study   A type of instrumental case study that relies on multiple cases to sustain the researcher's generalizations.

Comparison group   The group in an experimental study that receives a different treatment from the experimental group.

Compensatory demoralization   A threat to internal validity in which control or comparison group participants become discouraged because they feel that the experimental group is receiving more desirable treatment.

Compensatory equalization of treatment   A threat to internal validity in which the control group's behavior is influenced by resources they receive that are intended to be similar to what the experimental group receives.

Compensatory rivalry   A threat to internal validity in which control or comparison group participants perform above their usual level because they believe they are in competition with the experimental group.

Concurrent validity   The extent to which scores on a test are related to scores on a similar, previously validated measure administered at the same time.

Confidence interval   The range of values within which a population mean is expected to fall.

Constant comparative method   An ongoing process in qualitative data analysis in which categories are created as the data are examined, further data are sorted into these categories, and the categories are compared and perhaps combined or modified in some other way.

Construct   An unobservable psychological entity that has been proposed in order to account for observable behavior.

Construct underrepresentation   A source of diminished validity that occurs when a test fails to measure part of what it is intended to measure.

Construct validity   The extent to which a test measures the construct it is intended to measure.

Construct-irrelevant variance   A source of diminished validity in which test results are influenced by variables that the test was not intended to measure.

Constructivism   The epistemological assumption that realities are constructed by individuals rather than objectively observed.

Content analysis   An approach to research that focuses on the analysis and interpretation of materials.

Content validity   The extent to which a test measures the content it is intended to measure.

Contractualism   The assumption in program evaluation that the evaluator must follow the terms of the contract to the letter.

Control   Anything the researcher does to exclude the effects of an extraneous variable.

Control group   Participants in an experimental study who are not treated any differently than usual.

Convenience sampling   An approach to sampling that focuses on whoever is available in a particular place at a particular time.

Correlation coefficient   A number that represents the magnitude of correlation between two variables.

Correlation matrix   A table in which the correlation coefficients are presented.

Correlational design   A type of quantitative research design in which the goal is to quantify the extent of association between variables.

Cost–benefit analysis   Relationship between effectiveness measured at the level of participants and expenditures measured at the program level.

Counterbalanced design   A type of quasi-experimental design in which all groups receive all treatments and are posttested after each treatment.

Covariate   A variable whose influence on a dependent variable is controlled through statistical procedures.

Criterion-referenced tests   Tests in which raw scores are compared to some predetermined standard rather than to the performance of other test-takers.

Criterion-related validity   The extent to which test scores are related to another measurement of relevance known as the criterion.

Critical case sampling   An approach to sampling in qualitative research in which the researcher selects a single case—such as an individual, document, program, event, or organization—or a small number of highly similar cases.

Critical ethnography   A type of ethnographic research in which the researcher both describes and advocates for a group rather than trying to minimize the impact of his or her own values on the research process.

Critical race theory   A theoretical perspective based on the assumption that racism is enduring and pervasive in society at large, as well as in particular components of society such as the educational system.

Critical regions   Areas under the normal curve in which the probability of finding an observation is less than the alpha value.

Cronbach's alpha   A statistical estimate of internal consistency that equals the average correlation of all possible split-half correlations.

Cross-sectional design   Any research design based on the collection of data at one point in time.

Culture   The acquired behaviors, beliefs, meanings, and values shared by the members of a group.

Curvilinear relationship   A relationship between two continuous variables in which a positive correlation is observed for one range of values, while a negative correlation is observed for a different range of values.

Data   Units of information.

Data saturation   Information that has become redundant in a qualitative study.

Database   A searchable, computer-based collection of primary and secondary sources.

Deduction   A form of logic in which specific conclusions are drawn from more general statements.

Degrees of freedom   The number of values in a particular analysis that are free to vary, given a fixed parameter estimate.

Dependent variable   A variable that may be affected by an independent variable.

Descriptive design   A type of quantitative research in which the goal is to simply describe phenomena in quantitative terms.

Descriptive statistics   Numerical indices that briefly summarize the characteristics of a sample.

Design   The general plan for carrying out a research study.

Differential selection   A threat to internal validity arising from preexisting differences between groups.

Diffusion   A threat to internal validity arising from communication between groups that results in sharing of information and resources between them.

Discussion   The section of a research article in which the results of the study are summarized, interpreted, and evaluated.

Dissertation   A formal report submitted as part of the requirements for a doctoral degree.

Distribution   An ordered set of numerical values.

Ecological validity   The extent to which experimental results can be generalized to a broader set of environmental conditions.

Education Resources Information Center (ERIC)   An online database consisting of the world's largest repository of educational research reports.

Educational testing   The use of tests for evaluating aptitude, achievement, and other academically relevant characteristics of students.

Effect size   A number that indicates the magnitude of a statistically significant effect.

Electronic mailing list   An electronic medium through which subscribers can receive announcements, post questions, and interact with members of an organization or group who have common interests.

Empiricism The epistemological assumption that knowledge is grounded in observation.

Epistemology Philosophical analysis of the nature of knowledge, how knowledge is acquired, and what constitute valid sources of knowledge.

Equivalent forms Two or more alternate versions of a test that measure the same characteristic to the same degree of precision.

Equivalent forms reliability The extent of consistency in responses to alternate forms of the same measurement.

Eta-squared (η^2) A statistic that indicates the percentage of variation in a dependent variable that is accounted for by variation in the independent variable.

Ethnographer A researcher who carries out an ethnographic study.

Ethnographic research A type of qualitative research that consists of attempts to provide rich, narrative descriptions of cultural or social groups based on extensive field work.

Experimental design A type of experimental research design in which one or more independent variables are manipulated, and the effects of the manipulation on one or more dependent variables are measured.

Experimental group The group in an experimental research design that experiences a change or changes introduced by the researcher.

Experimenter effect A threat to internal validity arising from unwanted influence the researcher has on a study.

Experimenter-designed test A test created by a researcher for a particular study.

Explanatory design A type of mixed-methods research design in which quantitative data collection guides and is augmented by qualitative information gathering.

Exploratory design A type of mixed-methods research design that consists of qualitative information gathering that guides and is augmented by quantitative data collection.

External criticism Critical analysis that focuses on the authenticity of a historical document.

External evaluator The individual who is hired specifically for the purpose of conducting a program evaluation.

External validity The extent to which experimental findings can be generalized beyond the original study.

Extraneous variables Any variable other than the independent variable(s) that affects the dependent variable in an experimental study.

Extreme case sampling An approach to sampling in qualitative research in which the researcher seeks cases that are unusual in some respect.

Face validity The extent to which a test appears to measure what it intends to measure.

Factor analysis A statistical approach that allows researchers to identify those items (i.e., factors) on a test for which responses tend to be relatively similar and thus imply an underlying construct.

Factorial design An experimental research design in which the effects of two or more categorical independent variables are studied.

Falsifiability The desirable quality of hypotheses that are expressed clearly and specifically enough that we know what kinds of evidence would refute them.

Feminist ethnography A type of ethnography that documents, analyzes, and responds to the cultural disempowerment of women.

Field notes Written or audiotaped records of a qualitative researcher's impressions during fieldwork.

Fieldwork An approach to information gathering in qualitative research that consists of observing and interacting with participants wherever they live, work, study, obtain services, and/or recreate.

Figure A graphic portrayal of information.

Focus of inquiry The general topic of interest in a qualitative research study.

Formative evaluation A type of program evaluation that takes place as programs are being developed.

Frequency The number of observations for each level of a discrete variable.

Frequency polygon A form of graphic representation in which points are used to represent each x-axis value, and the points are connected by a line in order to represent frequencies.

Grade equivalent The average score obtained by individuals of a particular grade.

Grounded theory approach An approach to information gathering in qualitative research in which rather than testing a theory, the researcher attempts to set aside preconceived ideas so that theoretical explanations can be constructed as information is gathered.

Guttman scale A set of unidimensional statements arranged hierarchically, so that if an individual agrees with a particular statement, he or she should agree with all previous statements.

Hawthorne effect Any changes in behavior that occur when individuals are aware of receiving special attention during their participation in a research study.

Hierarchical linear modeling (HLM) A statistical approach that is an extension of multiple regression to nested variables.

Histogram A form of graphic representation that consists of a bar graph in which there is no space between the vertical edges of the columns that represent frequencies.

Historical research A type of research design that relies on documents, artifacts, and other materials as well as interviews in order to describe and interpret past events.

History A threat to internal validity in which unexpected events that are not part of an experimental manipulation influence the dependent variable.

Homogeneous sampling An approach to sampling in qualitative research in which the researcher selects individuals who are highly similar in background, experience, and/or other characteristics.

Hypothesis An informed guess about the outcome of a research study.

Hypothesis testing A decision-making process used to determine whether or not the results of statistical analysis are consistent with hypothesized outcomes.

Independent variable The variable that is manipulated in an experimental research study.

Individual-referenced test A test in which the score that an individual obtains at one point in time is compared to the score that the individual obtains at a different point in time.

Induction A form of logic that relies on experience as a source of knowledge and proceeds from specific observations to general conclusions.

Inferential statistics Mathematical procedures that sustain generalizations from samples to populations.

Informed consent The process of informing individuals in advance about the nature of a study and their rights as research participants, and then seeking their permission to participate.

Institutional Review Board (IRB) The group of individuals that must review and approve a research study in advance of data collection in order to ensure that the study meets ethical standards for research with humans.

Instrumental case study A type of case study that is conducted in order to gain insight into a broader issue.

Instrumentation A threat to internal validity arising from changes in performance that result from changes in the measurement used.

Integrity The extent to which a program is being implemented as intended.

Intensity sampling An approach to sampling in qualitative research in which the researcher selects participants who allow the research question to be studied from different perspectives.

Interaction The combined influence of two or more independent variables on a dependent variable, which cannot be reduced to the separate influence of each independent variable.

Interrater reliability The extent to which two or more individuals are consistent in their observations of some variable.

Internal consistency reliability The extent of consistency observed in response to related items on a test.

Internal criticism Critical analysis that focuses on the accuracy of the statements expressed in a historical document.

Internal evaluator An evaluator who is an existing employee of a program that is being evaluated.

Internal validity The extent to which a dependent variable is affected by manipulation of the independent variable in an experimental study.

Interval scale A scale that yields ranked data with continuous underlying dimensions and equal intervals.

Intrinsic case study A type of case study that focuses on describing the particulars of a case rather than making generalizations.

Introduction The section of a research article that provides an overview of the study, a literature review, and any research questions and hypotheses.

Keyword A distinctive word or phrase that appears in a document.

Kruskal-Wallis test A statistical procedure for determining whether two or more rankings are different.

Kuder-Richardson 20 An estimate of internal consistency that corresponds to the average correlation of all possible split-half correlations for responses to a particular test administered on one occasion.

Kurtosis The extent to which values cluster around a particular point in a distribution.

Likert scale A type of ordinal or interval scale that allows respondents to indicate the extent of their agreement with a series of statements.

Line graphs A form of graphic representation in which relationships between two or more variables are represented by means of lines that correspond to continuous dimensions.

Linear relationship A relationship between two variables that is consistently positive or negative across all values of the variables, so that the graph of their relationship will approximate a straight line.

Literature The research and theory that address a particular topic.

Logistic regression A form of regression in which the criterion variable is discrete rather than continuous.

Longitudinal design Any research design based on repeated collection of data over time, in order to document changes on key dimensions.

Main effect The effect of one independent variable on a dependent variable.

Mann–Whitney test A nonparametric statistical test used to compare two independent rankings.

Matching The creation of groups that are comparable with respect to some variable(s).

Maturation A threat to internal validity arising from changes that naturally occur in participants over time.

Maximum variation sampling An approach to sampling in qualitative research in which the researcher selects participants who reflect the entire range of variation on some dimension of interest.

Mean The arithmetic average of the numbers in a distribution.

Measure of central tendency A single number that typifies all values in a distribution.

Measure of position A single number that represents the location of one value with respect to other values in a distribution.

Measure of relationship A single number that represents the extent of association between two or more variables.

Measure of variability A single number that summarizes the extent of variability in a distribution.

Measurement The process of recording information.

Measurement error The extent to which an individual's true score on a test is obscured by factors such as how the test is administered or scored.

Measures The tools that researchers use to record information about variables.

Median The exact midpoint of a distribution.

Meta-analysis A statistical approach to summarizing quantitative research on a topic.

Method The section of a research article that provides information on the participants, materials, and procedures of a study.

Mixed-methods design A type of research design in which quantitative and qualitative methods are integrated, and each method plays an essential role.

Mode The most frequently observed value in a distribution.

Model A formal statement about the relationship between two or more variables.

Monograph A book by a single author or group of authors focusing on a specific topic.

Multifactorial analysis of variance An ANOVA that evaluates the effects of two or more independent variables on one dependent variable.

Multiple comparisons Statistical procedures that follow the application of ANOVA to determine which means are significantly different from each other.

Multiple regression A form of regression that examines the relationship between two or more predictor variables and the criterion variable(s).

Multiple-baseline design A type of single-participant research design in which additional participants are added to the study, or additional variables are measured, so that more than one baseline is available.

Multivariate analysis of covariance (MANCOVA) A type of ANOVA that evaluates the effects of one or more independent variables on two or more dependent variables while controlling for the effects of some extraneous variable(s).

Multivariate ANOVA (MANOVA) A type of ANOVA that evaluates the effects of one or more independent variables on two or more dependent variables.

National Research Act Federal legislation passed in 1974 that led to the establishment of a national commission charged with the development of ethical guidelines for research with humans.

Needs assessment The process by which a program evaluator identifies the resources, personnel, and practices that a program would need in order to achieve a desired state.

Negative case analysis A procedure in which the qualitative researcher carefully reexamines the data for observations that would contradict any conclusions that have been drawn.

Negatively skewed distribution A distribution that is asymmetrical because there are more scores at the lower end of the distribution.

Nested variables A set of variables that are hierarchically related.

Nominal scale A scale that yields categorical data in which the values of the variable have no quantitative meaning, and there are no intermediates between these values.

Nonequivalent control group design A randomized pretest–posttest control group design in which participant groups are based on preexisting differences rather than random assignment.

Nonparametric statistics Statistical tests that are appropriate when all measures are based on nominal or ordinal scales, when the population distribution is skewed or unknown, or when some other basic parametric assumption has been strongly violated.

Nonparticipant observation The recording of information by a researcher who does not interact with participants in the study.

Nonprobability sampling An approach to sampling in which the likelihood that each member of a population will be chosen is unknown.

Nonproportional stratified sampling An approach to sampling in which the goal is to simply represent different subgroups.

Norm Information about test scores from a large group that has taken the test.

Norm-referenced test A test for which raw scores can be compared to norms.

Normal distribution A symmetrical, bell-shaped distribution that has several distinctive characteristics, including the equivalence of mean, median, and modal values.

Novelty effect A threat to external validity in which new experiences in an experimental condition create a sense of enthusiasm.

Null hypothesis The assumption during hypothesis testing that there is no difference or relationship between variables.

Objective personality measure A measure that requires individuals to describe themselves on specific dimensions of interests.

Observer effect A threat to internal validity that occurs when knowledge of the researcher's presence causes individuals to change their behavior.

One group pretest–posttest design An experimental research design in which one group is pretested, exposed to an experimental treatment, and then posttested in order to measure the effects of the treatment.

One-shot case study An experimental research design in which a single group is exposed to an experimental treatment and then posttested.

One-way analysis of variance (ANOVA) A type of ANOVA used to analyze the effects of one categorical independent variable on one continuous dependent variable.

Open coding An approach to data coding in which specific elements are assigned to categories.

Open-ended interview A verbal interaction between researcher and participant in which the topics of discussion are not formally constrained.

Operational definition A definition of a concept expressed in terms of how it is measured.

Ordinal scale A scale that yields categorical, ranked data.

Outlier A datapoint that does not fit the overall pattern of a distribution.

p value The actual probability that an observed effect is attributable to chance.

Panel study A type of longitudinal study in which the same sample is surveyed at two or more points in time in order to document age- or experience-related changes.

Parameter A characteristic of a population.

Parametric statistics Statistical procedures appropriate for continuous variables that meet conditions such as normal distribution of population data.

Partial correlation A statistical procedure that yields a correlation coefficient between two variables after the effects of a third variable or variables have been statistically removed.

Participant observation The recording of information by a researcher has meaningful interactions with the individuals being observed.

Participatory action research A type of action research that is intended to empower individuals who have been exploited or marginalized, in part by actively involving these individuals in researching the challenges they experience.

Path analysis An extension of multiple regression in which direct and indirect causal relationships among variables are identified.

Path diagram The representation of the results of a path analysis, consisting of variable names, arrows indicating the direction of causality, and path coefficients.

Pearson product–moment coefficient A correlation coefficient suitable for indicating the extent of association between two continuous variables.

Peer review The process by which experts in a particular field review a scientific manuscript and make suggestions to an editor, who then makes a decision about whether or not to publish the manuscript.

Percentile rank The percentage of values at or below a particular value.

Performance assessment A form of assessment that focuses on creative activities and products that students generate in specific, real-life contexts.

Performance measure A measure that records how an individual performs on a test, or in some situation in which specific behaviors are elicited.

Personal measure A measure that records information about attitudes, beliefs, or feelings with respect to specified topics, or about individual characteristics such as demographic background, motivation, or personality.

Personality test A test that measures one or more dimensions of personality.

Phase The period of quantitative or qualitative data collection in a mixed-methods study.

Phenomenological study A type of qualitative research in which the researcher attempts to describe the subjective experiences of participants.

Population The entire group of individuals that a study is intended to investigate.

Population validity The extent to which experimental results can be generalized to a larger group of individuals.

Position paper A closely reasoned argument for a particular idea, practice, etc.

Positively skewed distribution A distribution that is asymmetrical because there are more scores at the upper end of the distribution.

Positivism The philosophical assumption that reality consists of facts and causal processes that are independent of observers and thus can be revealed through scientific observation.

Postmodern ethnography A type of ethnography that focuses on the marginalization of individuals and groups in modern society, and provides critical analysis of the claim that ethnography can provide a definitive account of a particular culture.

Posttest A measure administered to the experimental and control (or comparison) groups after an experimental manipulation.

Power analysis A way of identifying the exact group sizes needed to obtain certain amounts of statistical power and desired effect sizes for particular analyses.

Practical action research A type of action research that is intendend to help the practitioner create improvements in his or her immediate educational setting.

Prediction design A type of correlational design in which information about one variable or set of variables is used to predict the values of another variable or variables.

Predictive validity The extent to which scores on a test are related to some variable that is subsequently measured.

Predictor variables The variables used to make predictions.

Preexperimental design A set of experimental research designs that are based on a single group.

Pretest A measure administered to the experimental and control (or comparison) groups before an experimental manipulation.

Pretest–treatment interaction A threat to external validity that arises from interaction between participation in the pretest and the experimental treatment.

Primary source A firsthand report created by participants in an event, by observers, or by researchers who conducted a study that is being reported.

Probability sampling An approach to sampling in which each member of a population has a known probability of being chosen.

Professional report A description of research written for parents, teachers, school administrators, policymakers, or the agencies that funded the research.

Program evaluation A systematic approach to judging the merit and effectiveness of educational programs.

Projective personality measure A type of measure that provides ambiguous stimuli for individuals to interpret, under the assumption that their underlying beliefs, desires, and anxieties will be unconsciously projected into their interpretations.

Proportional stratified sampling A type of sampling in which the goal is for the proportion of each subgroup in the sample to be the same as the proportion in the population.

Purposive sampling An approach to sampling in which the researcher samples whoever he or she believes to be representative of a given population.

Qualitative research A variety of approaches to research that are based on nonquantitative methods that yield rich, narrative information about individuals and/or phenomena of interest.

Quantitative research A variety of approaches to research in which research questions are posed, hypotheses are formulated, quantitative data are gathered, and conclusions are drawn from statisical analysis.

Quasi-experimental design A type of experimental research design in which random assignment cannot be used because experimental, comparison, and/or control groups correspond to preexisting groups.

Quota sampling An approach to sampling in which exact numbers of individuals who reflect certain characteristics are sampled.

Random assignment A procedure for assigning participants to groups in which each participant is equally likely to be assigned to the experimental or the comparison (or control) group.

Range A number that represents the difference between the highest and lowest scores in a distribution.

Rating scale A measure in which particular behaviors are rated along some dimension of interest.

Ratio scale A scale that yields ranked data with continuous underlying dimensions and equal intervals, and that contains a zero point.

Raw score The untransformed quantitative data obtained by means of a scale.

Reading wars A set of long-standing debates about the best methods for teaching young children to read.

Realist ethnography A type of ethnography in which the researcher attempts to be as impartial as possible in describing a group of interest.

Reflexivity A process by which the qualitative researcher reflects on his or her own assumptions in order to help prevent them from influencing his or her understanding of participants.

Regression coefficient A numerical estimate of how much a criterion variable changes on average given one unit of change in a predictor variable.

Relational design A type of correlational design in which the goal is to quantify the extent to which two or more variables are interrelated.

Reliability The extent to which measurement is consistent.

Representative sample A sample that accurately reflects the characteristics of the population from which it is drawn.

Research question A clearly stated, testable question.

Responsive evaluation An approach to program evaluation in which concerns and issues of personal relevance to participants are documented.

Results The section of a research article that provides information about the outcome of data collection, including descriptive and inferential statistics.

Sample The individuals who actually participate in a study.

Sampling bias Systematic divergence between sample and population characteristics.

Sampling error Random divergences between sample and population characteristics.

Scale A set of options that structure the way a variable is recorded by a measure.

Scatterplot A simple graph in which the x-axis corresponds to one variable, the y-axis corresponds to the other variable, and each point represents one individual's score on both variables.

Scheffé test A multiple comparison statistic that is appropriate whether group sizes are equal or unequal.

Scientific method An approach to conducting resarch in which the scientist establishes a hypothesis, deduces and tests specific predictions from the hypothesis through careful observation, and then determines through induction whether the initial hypothesis was supported.

Search engine Software that allows the user to search a database for sources that fit particular criteria.

Secondary source A secondhand description of a primary source, or a description created by individuals who were not present at the event being described.

Selection–maturation interaction A threat to internal validity arising from differential selection effects that result specifically from maturation.

Selection–treatment interaction A threat to external validity arising from an interaction between participant characteristics and the experimental treatment.

Selective coding An approach to data coding in which the coder searches for observations that fit particular categories.

Self-presentation bias A threat to internal validity arising from participants trying to present themselves in a positive light.

Semantic differential scale A measure in which an individual's attitudes, beliefs, or feelings are represented by a set of continua, the extremes of which are marked by bipolar adjectives.

Setting–treatment interaction A threat to external validity arising from interaction between the experimental setting and the experimental treatment.

Significance level The predetermined, quantitative standard for rejecting the null hypothesis following statistical analysis.

Simple random sampling An approach to sampling in which each member of the population has an equal and independent chance of being selected for participation in the study.

Simple regression   A stastical procedure that quantifies the relationship between one predictor and one criterion variable.

Skewness   The extent to which a distribution is asymmetrical.

Snowball sampling   An approach to sampling in qualitative research in which the researcher approaches one or more individuals, and then asks help from these individuals in order to obtain additional participants.

Social validity   The extent to which the results of a research study are relevant to audiences beyond the scientific community.

Solomon three-group design   A type of experimental design based on random assignment of participants to one experimental group and two control groups.

Spearman rank–order correlation   A statistical procedure that yields a numerical estimate of the extent of association between two rankings.

Split-half reliability coefficient   A numerical estimate of internal consistency based on the correlation between responses to half of the items on a test with responses to the other half of the items.

Standard deviation   A numerical estimate of the average variability in a distribution that is based on all scores in the distribution.

Standard error estimate   A numerical estimate of the extent to which sample characteristics diverge from population parameters.

Standard error of the mean   The standard deviation of the sampling errors for a particular population.

Standard error of measurement   A numerical estimate of how much an obtained score is likely to differ from an individual's true score.

Standard score   A number that represents the distance of a particular value from some reference point in terms of standard deviation units.

Standardized coefficient   A numerical estimate of the extent to which a criterion variable changes given one standard deviation of change in the predictor variable.

Standardized test   A type of test, developed over time by experts, that is administered and scored in the same way across test-takers.

Stanine   A standard score that is based on the division of a distribution into a nine-point ordinal scale.

Statistical regression   A threat to internal validity arising from the tendency for participants who make extreme scores on pretest measures to score nearer to the mean at posttest.

Statistical significance   The likelihood that a result is geniune rather than attributable to chance, because the likelihood of error is calculated to be less than the alpha level.

Statistics   Procedures for describing, integrating, and analyzing data.

Stem-and-leaf display   A type of graphic representation of scores in which each score is divided into its final digit (leaf) and the remaining digits (stems).

Stepwise method   A type of regression procedure in which predictors with the greatest predictive power are selected while less helpful ones are excluded in the process of creating a model.

Stratified sampling   An approach to sampling in which subgroups of a population are identified, and random sampling is carried out within each subgroup.

Structural equation modeling (SEM)   A set of statistical procedures that include multiple regression, path analysis, and other types of analyses.

Subject effect   A threat to internal validity arising from changes in participant attitudes and behavior that result from participation in the research.

Summative evaluation   A type of program evaluation that is carried out on existing programs.

Suppressor effect   A type of third variable effect in which two variables are more closely related than indicated by the simple correlation between them.

Survey   A self-report measure consisting of questions that can be administered in the form of a personal interview or a questionnaire.

Systematic sampling   An approach to sampling in which every nth individual is selected from a list of the population.

T score   A standard score that is obtained by multiplying a z score by 10 and adding 50.

t-test   A statistical procedure used to decide whether two means are significantly different or not.

Table   A representation of information organized by rows and columns.

Target population   The population of interest identified in a particular study.

Test   A systematic method of obtaining data from individuals.

Test–retest reliability   The extent to which a measure is consistent over time.

Testing   A threat to internal validity arising from improvement in performance that results from familiarity with a test.

Theory A set of interrelated concepts that are used to explain and make predictions about specific phenomena.

Thesis A formal report submitted as part of the requirements for a doctoral degree.

Third variable problem The creation of a spurious correlation between two variables as a result of the influence of a third variable.

Time-series design A type of quasi-experimental research design in which pretesting and posttesting are carried out repeatedly.

Treatment A change introduced by the researcher in an experimental research design.

Trend study A type of longitudinal study in which the same population is surveyed at two or more points in time as membership in the population changes.

Triangulation The use of more than one perspective or information source in order to establish a fact.

Triangulation design A type of mixed-methods research design in which qualitative and quantitative data collection take place simultaneously.

True experimental design A type of experimental research design in which there is random assignment of participants to an experimental group and at least one control and/or comparison group.

Tukey HSD test A multiple comparison statistic that requires equal group sizes.

Type I error The rejection of a null hypothesis that should not be rejected.

Type II error The failure to reject a null hypothesis that should be rejected.

Typical case sampling An approach to sampling in qualitative research in which the researcher seeks cases that are typical of the phenomenon under study.

Validity The extent to which interpretation of test scores is appropriate, in light of existing evidence and theory.

Variable Any dimension on which different values can be measured.

Variant source An altered copy of an original source.

What Works Clearinghouse (WWC) A government-sponsored website motivated by the desire to present useful research findings to various stakeholders in the educational process.

Wilcoxon signed-rank test A nonparametric statistical test for determining whether two dependent rankings are different.

Withdrawal phase The point in a single-participant research design following treatment when the participant is measured under the same conditions as baseline.

Within-subjects factor A categorical variable whose levels represent distinctions within the same group.

z score A standard score that represents the difference between a particular value and the mean of the distribution, expressed in standard deviation units.

References

Abbas, T. (2006). A question of reflexivity in a qualitative study of South Asians in education: Power, knowledge, and shared ethnicity. *Ethnography and Education, 1*(3), 319–332.

Adi-Japha, E., Levin, I., & Solomon, S. (1998). Emergence of representation in drawing: The relation between kinematic and referential aspects. *Cognitive Development, 13(1)*, 25–51.

Ahles, P. M. (2006). Explaining helping behavior in a cooperative learning classroom setting using attribution theory. *Community College Journal of Research and Practice, 30,* 609–626.

Akos, P., & Galassi, J. P. (2004). Gender and race as variables in psychological adjustment to middle and high school. *Journal of Educational Research, 98*(2), 102–108.

Albus, D., Thurlow, M., Liu, K., & Bielinski, J. (2005). Reading test performance of English-language learners using an English dictionary. *Journal of Educational Research, 98*(4), 245–254.

Alexander, H. A. (2006). A view from somewhere: Explaining the paradigms of educational research. *Journal of Philosophy of Education, 40*(2), 205–221.

Altshuld, J. W., & Thomas, P. M. (1991). The teaching of evolution: 25 years of growth and change. *Theory Into Practice, 30*(1), 22–29.

American Psychological Association. (2001). *Publication manual of the American Psychological Association.* Washington, DC: American Psychological Association.

Amrein-Beardsley, A., Foulger, T. S., & Toth, M. (2007). Examining the development of a hybrid degree program: Using student and instructor data to inform decision-making. *Journal of Research on Technology in Education, 39*(4), 331–357.

Andrews, M. L., & Ridenour, C. S. (2006). Gender in schools: A qualitative study of students in educational administration. *Journal of Educational Research, 100*(1), 35–43.

Apthorp, H. S. (2006). Effects of a supplemental vocabulary program in third-grade reading/language arts. *Journal of Educational Research, 100*(2), 67–79.

Arce, J. (2004). Latino bilingual teachers: The struggle to sustain an emancipatory pedagogy in public schools. *International Journal of Qualitative Studies in Education, 17*(2), 227–246.

Arndt, S. A., Konrad, M., & Test, D. W. (2006). Effects of the self-directed IEP on student participation in planning meetings. *Remedial and Special Education, 27*(4), 194–207.

Ashcraft, C. (2004). "It's just semantics?": Investigating a school district's decision to respect or value diversity. *International Journal of Qualitative Studies in Education, 17*(5), 685–706.

Astiz, M. F. (2006). School anatomy in the province of Buenos Aires, Argentina: Evidence from two school districts. *Comparative Education, 42*(2), 203–223.

Ates, S., & Stevens, J. T. (2003). Teaching line graphs to tenth grade students having different cognitive development levels by using two different instructional modules. *Research in Science and Technological Education, 21*(1), 55–66.

Bacon, F. (1620/1863). *Novum Organum. [New organon: Or, true directions concerning the interpretation of nature.]* Boston: Taggard and Thompson.

Bandura, A. (1965). Influence of models' reinforcement contingencies on the acquisition of imitative responses. *Journal of Personality and Social Psychology, 1,* 589–595.

Barnett, W. S. (1996). *Lives in the balance: Age-27 benefit-cost analysis of the High/Scope Perry Preschool Program* (Monographs of the High/Scope Educational Research Foundation, 11). Ypsilanti, MI: High Scope Press.

Baser, M. (2006). Effect of conceptual change oriented instruction on students' understanding of heat and temperature concepts. *Journal of Maltese Education Research, 4*(1), 64–79.

Bell, N. L., Rucker, M., & Finch, A. J., Jr. (2002). Concurrent validity of the Slosson Full-Range Intelligence Test: Comparison with the Wechsler Intelligence Scale for Children–Third Edition and the Woodcock–Johnson Tests of Achievement–Revised. *Psychology in the Schools, 39*(1), 31–38.

Belsky, J. (1985). Experimenting with the family in the newborn period. *Child Development, 56 (2),* 407–414.

Berg-Weger, M., Rubio, D. M., & Tebb, S. S. (2000). The caregiver well-being scale revisited. *Health and Social Work, 25*(4), 255–263.

Beron, K. J., & Farkas, G. (2004). Oral language and reading success: A structural equation modeling approach. *Structural Equation Modeling, 11*(1), 110–131.

Best, B. (2006). Deliberate self-harm in adolescence: A challenge for schools. *British Journal of Guidance and Counselling, 34*(2), 161–175.

Birenbaum, M., Tatsuoka, C., & Xin, T. (2005). Large-scale diagnostic assessment: Comparison of eighth graders' mathematics performance in the United States, Singapore and Israel. *Assessment in Education, 12*(2), 167–181.

Blake, J., Macdonald, S., Bayrami, L., Agosta, V., & Milian, A. (2006). Book reading styles in dual-parent and single-mother families. *British Journal of Educational Psychology, 76,* 501–515.

Blatchford, P., Bassett, P., Goldstein, H., & Martin, C. (2003). Are class size differences related to pupils' educational progress and classroom processes?: Findings from the Institute of Education class size study of children aged 5–7 years. *British Educational Research Journal, 29*(5), 709–730.

549

Bliss, S. L., & Skinner, C. H. (2006). Enhancing an English language learning fifth-grade student's sight-word reading with a time-delay taped-words intervention. *School Psychology Review, 35*(4), 663–670.

Bogdan, R. C., & Biklen, S. K. (2007). *Qualitative research in education: An introduction to theories and methods* (5th ed.). New York: Pearson Education.

Bondy, E. (2002). Warming up to classroom research in a professional development school. *Contemporary Education, 72*(1), 8–13.

Bonini, N. (2006). The pencil and the shepherd's crook. ethnography of Maasai education. *Ethnography and Education, 1*(3), 379–392.

Bonoti, F., Vlachos, F., & Metallidou, P. (2005). Writing and drawing performance of school age children. Is there any relationship? *School Psychology International, 26*(2), 243–255.

Boe, E. E., & Shin, S. (2005). Is the United States really losing the international horse race in academic achievement? *Phi Delta Kappan, 86(9)*, pp. 688–695.

Boon, R. T., Burke, M. D., Fore, C., & Burke, S. H. (2006). Improving student content knowledge in inclusive social studies classrooms using technology-based cognitive organizers: A systematic replication. *Learning Disabilities: A Contemporary Journal, 4*(1), 1–17.

Bowles, C. L., & Lesperance, L. (2004). Being bullied in adolescence: A phenomenal study. *Guidance and Counseling, 19*(3), 94–102.

Bracht, G. H., & Glass, G. V. (1968). The external validity of experiments. *American Educational Research Journal, 5*, 437–474.

Brand, S., Felner, R., Shim, M., Seitsinger, A., & Dumas, T. (2003). Middle school improvement and reform: Development and validation of a school-level assessment of climate, cultural pluralism, and school safety. *Journal of Educational Psychology, 95*(3), 570–588.

Brendgen, M., Bukowski, W. M., Wanner, B., Vitaro, F., & Tremblay, R. E. (2007). Verbal abuse by the teacher during childhood and academic, behavioral, and emotional adjustment in young adulthood. *Journal of Educational Psychology, 99*(1), 26–38.

Brewer, T. M. (2003). The "grand paradox" in teacher preparation and certification policy. *Education Policy Review, 104(6)*, 3–10.

Bridgeman, B., Cline, F., & Hessinger, J. (2004). Effect of extra time on verbal and quantitative GRE scores. *Applied Measurement in Education, 17*(1), 25–37.

Brookhart, S. M., & Durkin, D. T. (2003). Classroom assessment, student motivation, and achievement in high school social studies classes. *Applied Measurement in Education, 16*(1), 27–54.

Brophy, J. E. (1983). Research on the self-fulfilling prophecy and teacher expectations. *Journal of Educational Psychology, 75*, 631–661.

Brown, E., Avery, L., VanTassel-Baska, J., Worley II, B. B., & Stambaugh, T. (2006). Legislation and policies: Effects on the gifted. *Roeper Review, 29*(1), 1–33.

Bui, K. (1995). Educational expectations and academic achievement among middle and high school students, *Education, 127*, 328–331.

Byrnes, J. P. (2003). Factors predictive of mathematics achievement in white, black, and hispanic 12th graders. *Journal of Educational Psychology, 95*(2), 316–326.

Calderhead, W. J., Filter, K. J., & Albin, R. W. (2006). An investigation of incremental effects of interspersing math items on task-related behavior. *Journal of Educational Behavior, 15*(1), 53–67.

Camp, D.7, & Aldridge, J. (2007). Rethinking dyslexia, scripted reading, and federal mandates: The more things change, the more they stay the same. *Journal of Instructional Psychology, 34*(1), 3–12.

Campbell, P. H., & Anketell, M. (2007). Suggestions for statewide measurement systems: Pennsylvania's experience. *Topics in Early Childhood Special Education, 27*(1), 34–48.

Campbell, D. T., & Stanley, J. C. (1963). *Experimental and Quasi-Experimental Designs for Research*. Chicago: Rand McNally.

Cannon, C. (2006, April/May). Implementing research practices. *High School Journal*, pp. 8–13.

Cantrell, R., Parks-Savage, A., & Rehfuss, M. (2007). Reducing levels of elementary school violence with peer mediation. *American School Counselor Association, 2005*(2), 1–13.

Carifio, J., Jackson, I., & Dagostino, L. (2001). Effects of diagnostic and prescriptive comments on the revising behaviors of community college students. *Community Journal of Research and Practice, 25*, 109–122.

Carmona, C., Buunk, A. P., Peiro, J. M., Rodriguez, I., & Bravo, M. J. (2006). Do social comparison and copying styles play a role in the development of burnout?: Cross-sectional and longitudinal findings. *Journal of Occupational and Organizational Psychology, 79*, 85–99.

Carnine, D. (1997). Bridging the research-to-practice gap. *Exceptional Children, 63*(4), 513–521.

Carpentier, P. J., Jong, A. J., Dijkstra, B., Verbrugge, A. G., & Krabbe, P. (2005). A controlled trial of methylphenidate in adults with attention deficit/hyperactivity disorder and substance use disorders. *Society for the Study of Addiction, 100*, 1868–1874.

Carr, J. (2005). Stability and change in cognitive ability over the life span: A comparison of populations with and without

Down's syndrome. *Journal of Intellectual Disability Research*, *49*(12), 915–928.

Carreon, G. P., Drake, C., & Barton, A. C. (2005). The importance of presence: Immigrant parents' school engagement experiences. *American Educational Research Journal*, *42*(3), 465–498.

Cashwell, T. H., Skinner C. H., & Smith, E. S. (2001). Increasing second-grade students' reports of peers' prosocial behaviors via direct instruction, group reinforcement, and progress feedback: A replication and extension. *Education and Treatment of Children*, *24*(2), 161–175.

Chafouleas, S. M., & Riley-Tillman, T. C. (2005). Accepting the gap: An introduction to the special issue on bridging research and practice. *Psychology in School*, *42*(5), 455–458.

Chang, W. (2005). The rewards and challenges of teaching innovation in university physics: 4 years' reflection. *International Journal of Science Education*, *27*(4), 407–425.

Choi, H. J., & Park, J. H. (2006). Difficulties that a novice online instructor faced. *Quarterly Review of Distance Education*, 7(3), 317–322.

Choudhury, N., & Gorman, K. S. (1999). The relationship between reaction time and psychometric intelligence in a rural Guatemalan adolescent population. *International Journal of Psychology*, *34*(4), 209–217.

Chrispeels, J. H., & Rivero, E. (2001). Engaging Latino families for student success: How parent education can reshape parents' sense of place in the education of their children. *Peabody Journal of Education*, *76*(2), 119–169.

Cillessen, A. H. N., & Mayeux, L. (2004). From censure to reinforcement: Developmental changes in the association between aggression and social status. *Child Development*, *75*(1), 147–163.

Clement, J. M. (2004). A call for action: Applying science education research to computer science instruction. *Computer Science Education*, *14(4)*, pp. 343–364.

Cohen, R., Kincaid, D., & Childs, K. E. (2007). Measuring school-wide positive behavior support implementation: Development and validation of the benchmarks of quality. *Journal of Positive Behavior Interventions*, *9*(4), 203–213.

Collins, K. M. T., Onwuegbuzie, A. J., & Jiao, Q. G. (2006). Prevalence of mixed-methods sampling designs in social science research. *Evaluation and Research in Education*, *19*(2), 83–101.

Collins, K. M. T., Onwuegbuzie, A. J., & Sutton, I. L. (2006). A model incorporating the rationale and purpose for conducting mixed-methods research in special education and beyond. *Learning Disabilities: A Contemporary Journal*, *4*(1), 67–100.

Cook, T. D., & Campbell, D. T. (1979). *Quasi-Experimentation: Design and Analysis for Field Settings*. Chicago: Rand McNally.

Cooper, E. (2005). What do we know about out-of-school youths?: How participatory action research can work for young refugees in camps. *Compare*, *35*(4), 463–477.

Crawford, L., Tindal, G., & Carpenter II, D. M. (2006). Exploring the validity of the Oregon extended writing assessment. *Journal of Special Education*, *40*(1), 16–27.

Creswell, J. W. (2005). *Educational research: Planning, conducting, and evaluating quantitative and qualitative research* (2nd edition). Upper Saddle River, NJ: Pearson.

Cronbach, L. J. (1951). Coefficient alpha and the internal structure of tests. *Psychometrika*, *16(3)*, 297–334.

Cronbach, L. J. & Meehl, P. E. (1955). Construct validity in psychological tests. *Psychological Bulletin*, *52*, 281–302.

Crozier, G. (1996). Black parents and school relationships: A case study. *Educational Review*, *48*(3), 1–14.

Cukierkorn, J. R., Karnes, F. A., Manning, S. J., Houston, H., & Besnoy, K. (2007). Serving the preschool gifted child: Programming and resources. *Roeper Review*, *29*(4), 1–13.

Cusumano, D. L. (2007). Is it working?: An overview of curriculum based measurement and its uses for assessing instructional, intervention, or program effectiveness. *The Behavior Analyst Today*, *8*(1), 24–34.

Dale, N., Baker, A. J. L., Anastasio, E., & Purcell, J. (2007). Characteristics of children in residential treatment in New York State. *Child Welfare*, *86*(1), 5–27.

Darwin, F. (Ed.) (1899). *The life and letters of Charles Darwin, Volume 1*. London: John Murray.

Das, J. P. & Naglieri, J. A. (2001) The Das-Naglieri Cognitive Assessment System in practice. In Andrews, Saklofsky, & Janzen (Eds.) *Handbook of Psychoeducational Assessment* (pp. 33–63). San Diego, CA: Academic Press.

Davenport, D., & Jones, J. M. (2005, April/May). The politics of literacy. *Policy Review*, pp. 45–57.

DeBray, E. H. (2005). Introduction to the special issue on federalism reconsidered: The case of the No Child Left Behind Act. *Peabody Journal of Education*, *80*(2), 1–18.

De Bruin, G. P., & Rudnick, H. (2007). Examining the cheats: The role of conscientiousness and excitement seeking in academic dishonesty. *South African Journal of Psychology*, *37*(1), 153–164.

Dedrick, R. F., & Watson, F. (2002). Mentoring needs of female, minority, and international graduate students: a content analysis of academic research guides and related print material. *Mentoring and Tutoring*, *10*(3), 275–289.

DeLeon, P. (1999). The missing link revisited: Contemporary implementation research. *Policy Studies Review*, *16*(3/4), 311–338.

Delyser, D. (2003). Teaching graduate students to write: A seminar for thesis and dissertation writers. *Journal of Geography in Higher Education*, *27*(2), 169–181.

Demerath, P. (2006). The science of context: Modes of response for qualitative researchers in education. *International Journal of Qualitative Studies in Education, 19*(1), 97–113.

Demoss, M., & Nicholson, C. Y. (2005, July/August). The greening of marketing: An analysis of introductory textbooks. *Journal of Education for Business*, pp. 338–346.

Deno, S.L. (1985). Curriculum-based measurement: The emerging alternative. *Exceptional Children, 52*, 219–232.

Deno, S.L. (2003). Developments in curriculum-based measurement. *Journal of Special Education, 37*, 184–192.

de Ramirez, R., & Shapiro, E. S. (2006). Curriculum-based measurement and the evaluation of reading skills of Spanish-speaking English language learners in bilingual education classrooms. *School Psychology Review, 35*(3), 356–369.

DeSimone, J. R., & Parmar, R. S. (2006). Middle school mathematics teachers' beliefs about inclusion of students with learning disabilities. *Learning Disabilities Research and Practice, 21*(2), 98–110.

DeSocio, J., VanCura, M., Nelson, L. A., Hewitt, G., Kitzman, H., & Cole, R. (2007). Engaging truant adolescents: Results from a multifaceted intervention pilot. *Preventing School Failure, 51*(3), 3–11.

Deutscher, B., Fewell, R.R., & Gross, M. (2006). Enhancing the interactions of teenage mothers and their at-risk children: Effectiveness of a maternal-focused intervention. *Topics in Early Childhood Special Education, 26*(4), 194–205.

Dewey, J. (1938/1997). *Experience and Education*. New York: Touchstone.

Dweck, C. S., & Leggett, E. L. (1988). A social-cognitive approach to motivation and personality. *Psychological Review, 95*, 256–273.

Dickinson, D. K., McCabe, A., Anastasopoulos, L., Peisner-Feinberg, E. S., & Poe, M. D. (2003). The comprehensive language approach to early literacy: The interrelationships among vocabulary, phonological sensitivity, and print knowledge among preschool-aged children. *Journal of Educational Psychology, 95*(3), 465–481.

Dipardo, A., & Schnack, P. (2004). Expanding the web of meaning: Thought and emotion in an intergeneration reading and writing program. *Reading Research Quarterly, 39*(1), 14–37.

Dirkx, J. M. (2006). Studying the complicated matter of what works: Evidence-based research and the problem of practice. *Adult Education Quarterly, 56*(4), 273–290.

Donmoyer, R. (2006). Take my paradigm … please!: The legacy of Kuhn's construct in educational research. *International Journal of Qualitative Studies in Education, 19*(1), 11–34.

Donnor, J.K. (2005). Towards an interest–convergence in the education of African-American football student athletes in major college sports. *Race, Ethnicity and Education, 8*(1), 45–67.

Donovan, L., Hartley, K., & Strudler, N. (2007). Teacher concerns during initial implementation of a one-to-one laptop initiative at the middle school level. *Journal of Research on Technology in Education, 39*(3), 263–286.

Dooley, K. E., & Wickersham, L. E. (2007). Distraction, domination, and disconnection in whole-class, online discussions. *Quarterly Review of Distance Education, 8*(1), 1–8.

Dorans, N. J. (2002). The recentering of SAT scales and its effects on score distributions and score interpretations. *College Board Research Report, 2002-11*, 1–21.

Drummond, K. V., & Stipek, D. (2004). Low income parents' beliefs about their role in children's academic learning. *Elementary School Journal, 104*(3), 197–213.

Duckworth, A. L., & Seligman, M. E. P. (2006). Self-discipline gives girls the edge: Gender in self-discipline, grades, and achievement test scores. *Journal of Educational Psychology, 98*(1), 198–208.

Duhon, G. J., Noell, G. H., Witt, J. C., Freeland, J. T., Dufrene, B. A., & Gilbertson, D. N. (2004). Identifying academic skill and performance deficits: The experimental analysis of brief assessments of academic skills. *School Psychology Review, 33*(3), 429–443.

Dymond, S. K., Renzaglia, A., Rosenstein, A., Chun, E. J., Banks, R. A., Niswander, V., etal. (2006). Using a participatory action research approach to create a universally designed inclusive high school science course: A case study. *Research and Practice for Persons with Severe Disabilities, 31*(4), 293–308.

Ebrahim, F. (2006). Comparing creative thinking abilities and reasoning ability of deaf and hearing children. *Roeper Review, 28*(3), 140–147.

Ee, J., Wong, K. Y., & Aunio, P. (2006). Numeracy of young children in Singapore, Beijing and Helsinki. *Early Childhood Education Journal, 33*(5), 325–332.

Eisenhart, M. (2001). Educational Ethnography past, present, and future: Ideas to think with. *Educational Researcher, 30*(8), 16–27.

Elbro, C., & Petersen, D. K. (2004). Long-term effects of phoneme awareness and letter sound training: An intervention study with children at risk for dyslexia. *Journal of Educational Psychology, 96*(4), 660–670.

Ender, M. G., & Gibson, A. A. (2005). Invisible institution: The military, war, and peace in pre-9/11 introductory sociology textbooks. *Journal of Political and Military Sociology, 33*(2), 249–266.

Engec, N. (2006). Relationship between mobility and student performance behavior. *Journal of Educational Research, 99*(3), 167–178.

Espin, C. A., Weissenburger, J. W., & Benson, B. J. (2004). Assessing the writing performance of students in special education. *Exceptionality, 12*(1), 55–66.

Finn, J. D., & Pannozzo, G. M. (2004). Classroom organization and student behavior in kindergarten. *Journal of Educational Research, 98*(2), 79–92.

Finn, K. V., & Frone, M. R. (2004). Academic performance and cheating: Moderating role of school identification and self-efficiency. *Journal of Educational Research, 97*(3), 115–122.

Flores-Gonzalez, N. (2005). Popularity versus respect: School structure, peer groups and Latino academic achievement. *International Journal of Qualitative Studies in Education, 18*(5), 625–642.

Foley, D. E. (2002). Critical ethnography: The reflexive turn. *Qualitative Studies in Education, 15*(5), 469–490.

Fox, C. L., & Boulton, M. J. (2006). Friendship as a moderator of the relationships between social skills problems and peer victimization. *Aggressive Behavior, 32,* 110–121.

Freedman, S. W., & Delp, V. (2006). *Students "latch on": Rethinking applications of Vygotskian and Bakhtinian theories for teaching and learning in an untracked English class.* Paper presented at the annual meeting of the American Educational Research Association, San Francisco, April.

Gallagher, A., Bennett, R. E., Cahalan, C., & Rock, D. A. (2002). Validity and fairness in technology-based assessment: Detecting construct-irrelevant variance in an open-ended, computerized mathematics task. *Educational Assessment, 8*(1), 27–41.

Gallagher, C. J. (2003). Reconciling a tradition of testing with a new learning paradigm. *Educational Psychology Review, 15*(1), 83–99.

Geiser, S., & Studley, R. (2002). UC and the SAT: Predictive validity and differential impact of the SAT I and SAT II at the University of California. *Educational Assessment, 8*(1), 1–26.

George, N. A., Craven, M., William-Myers, C., & Bonnick, P. (2003). Using action research to enhance teaching and learning at the University of Technology, Jamaica. *Assessment and Evaluation in Higher Education, 28*(3), 240–250.

Gillborn, D. (2005). Education policy as an act of white supremacy: Whiteness, critical race theory and education reform. *Journal of Education Policy, 20*(4), 485–505.

Glaser, B. G., & Strauss, A. L. (1967). *The discovery of grounded theory: Strategies for qualitative research.* Chicago: Aldine.

Glaser, R. (1963). Instructional technology and the measurement of learning outcomes: Some questions. *American Psychologist, 18,* 519–521.

Glass, G. V. (1976). Primary, secondary, and meta-analysis of research. *Educational Researcher, 5,* 3–8.

Goei, R., Boyson, A. R., Lyon-Callo, S. K., Schott, C., Wasilevich, E., & Cannarile, S. (2006). Developing an asthma tool for schools: The formative evaluation of the Michigan Asthma School Packet. *Journal of School Health, 76*(6), 259–263.

Good, T. L., Burross, H. L., & Mccaslin, M. M. (2005). Comprehensive school reform: A longitudinal study of school improvement in one state. *Teachers College Record, 107*(10), 2205–2226.

Goodman, D. P., & Hambleton, R. K. (2004). Student test score reports and interpretive guides: Review of current practices and suggestions for future research. *Applied Measurement in Education, 17*(2), 145–220.

Gresham, F., Sugai, G., & Horner, R. H. (2001). Interpreting outcomes of social skills training for students with high-incidence disabilities. *Exceptional Children, 67(3),* 331–344.

Gretes, J. A., & Green, M. (2000). Improving undergraduate learning with computer-assisted assessment. *Journal of Research on Computing in Education, 33*(1), 46–54.

Griffiths, Y. M., & Snowling, M. J. (2002). Predictors of exception word and nonword reading in dyslexic children: The severity hypothesis. *Journal of Educational Psychology, 94*(1), 34–43.

Gulliksen, H. (1950). *Theory of Mental Tests.* Hillsdale, NJ: Erlbaum.

Guitar, B., & Marchinkoski, L. (2001). Influence of mother's slower speech on their children's speech rate. *Journal of Speech, Language, and Hearing Research, 44,* 853–861.

Guzzetti, B. J., & Gamboa, M. (2004). Zines for social justice: Adolescent girls writing on their own. *Reading Research Quarterly, 39*(4), 408–436.

Haertel, E. H., & Herman, J. L. (2005). A historical perspective on validity arguments for accountability testing. In J. L. Herman & E. H. Haertel (Eds.) *Uses and misuses of data for educational accountability and improvement.* (The 104th yearbook of the National Society for the Study of Education, Part 2, pp. 1–34). Malden, MA: Blackwell.

Haggarty, L., & Postlethwaite, K. (2003). Action research: A strategy for teacher change and school development. *Oxford Review of Education, 29*(4), 423–448.

Hall, G. S. (1883). The contents of children's minds. *Princeton Review, 2,* 249–272.

Hamilton, C., & Shinn, M. R. (2003). Characteristics of word callers: An investigation of the accuracy of teachers' judgments of reading comprehension and oral readings. *School Psychology Review, 32*(2), 228–240.

Hancock, D. R. (1994). Motivating adults to learn academic course content. *Journal of Educational Research, 88*(2), 102–108.

Harker, R. M., Dobel-Ober, D., Akhurst, S., Berridge, D., & Sinclair, R. (2004). Who takes care of education 18 months on? a follow-up study of looked after children's perceptions of support for educational process. *Child and Family Social Work, 9,* 273–284.

Held, M. F., Thoma, C. A., & Thomas, K. (2004). "The Jones show": How one teacher facilitated self-determined transition planning for a young man with autism. *Focus on Autism and Other Developmental Issues, 19*(3), 177–188.

Hemsley-Brown, J., & Sharp, C. (2003). The use of research to improve professional practice: A systematic review of the literature. *Oxford Review of Education, 29*(4), 449–470.

Hertberg-Davis, H. L., & Brighton, C. M. (2006). Support and sabotage: Principals' influence on middle school teachers' responses to differentiation. *Journal of Secondary Gifted Education, 17*(2), 90–102.

Hewitt, M. P., & Smith, B. P. (2004, October). The influence of teaching-career level and primary performance instrument on the assessment of music performance. *Journal of Research in Music Education, 52*(4), 314–327.

Hezlett, S. A., Kuncel, N. R., Vey, M., Ahart, A., Ones, D. S., Campbell, J. P., & Camara, W. (2001). The effectiveness of the SAT in predicting success early and late in college: A comprehensive meta-analysis. In D. Ones & W. Camara (Chairs), Predicting success in college: New findings on some old concerns. Symposia presented at the annual conference of the National Council on Measurement in Education, Seattle, WA, April.

Hiebert, E. H. (2005). State reform policies and the task textbooks pose for first-grade readers. *Elementary School Journal, 105*(3), 245–266.

Hong, G., & Raudenbush, S. W. (2005). Effects of kindergarten retention policy on children's cognitive growth in reading and mathematics. *Educational Evaluation and Policy Analysis, 27*(3), 205–224.

Horodynski, M. A., & Gibbons, C. (2004). Rural low-income mothers' interactions with their young children. *Pediatric Nursing, 30*(4), 299–306.

Hoy, W. K., Tarter, C. J., & Hoy, A. W. (2006). Academic optimism of schools: A force for student achievement. *American Educational Research Journal, 43*(3), 425–446.

Hruska, B. (2007). The construction of bilingualism in an American context: Three levels of analysis. *Ethnography and Education, 1*(3), 345–364.

Hughes, S. A. (2005). Some canaries left behind?: Evaluating a state-endorsed lesson plan database and its social construction of who and what counts. *International Journal of Inclusive Education, 9*(2), 105–138.

Igo, L. B., Riccomini, P. J., Bruning, R. H., & Pope, G. G. (2006). How should middle-school students with LD approach online note taking?: A mixed-methods study. *Learning Disability Quarterly, 29*, 89–100.

Jaffe, A. J. & Spirer, H. F. (1987). *Misused statistics: Straight talk for twisted numbers.* New York: Dekker.

Johnson, P. B. (1994). Alcohol expectancies and reaction expectancies: Their impact on student drinking. *Journal of Alcohol and Drug Education, 40*(1), 57–68.

Jussim, L., Smith, A., Madon, S., & Palumbo, P. (1998). Teacher expectations. In J. E. Brophy (Ed.), *Advances in research on teaching: Expectations in the classroom (pp. 1–48).* Greenwich, CT: JAI Press.

Kalil, A., & Kunz, J. (2002). Teenage childbearing, marital status, and depressive symptoms in later life. *Child Development, 73*(6), 1748–1760.

Kane, M. T. (2001). Current concerns in validity theory. *Journal of Educational Measurement, 38*(4), 319–342.

Karchmer, R. A. (2001). The journey ahead: Thirteen teachers report how the internet influences literacy and literacy instruction in their K–12 classrooms. *Reading Research Quarterly, 36*(4), 442–466.

Katzenmeyer, C. G. (1991). Signing into the same old tune: Federal evaluation and policy and the program effectiveness panel. *Theory Into Practice, 30*(1), 69–73.

Ketterlin-Geller, L.R., Yovanoff, P., & Tindal, G. (2007). Developing a new paradigm for conducting research on accommodations in mathematics testing. *Exceptional Children, 73*(3), 331–347.

Kirby, J. R., Parrila, R. K., & Pfeiffer, S. L. (2003). Naming speed and phonological awareness as predictors of reading development. *Journal of Educational Psychology, 95*(3), 453–464.

Kirby, P. C., Paradise, L. V., & King, M. I. (1992). Extraordinary leaders in education: Understanding transformational leadership. *Journal of Educational Research, 85*(5), 303–311.

Klingner, J. K., Scanlon, D., & Pressley, M. (2005, November). How to publish in scholarly journals. *Educational Researcher,* pp. 14–20.

Kobrin, J. L., & Michel, R. S. (2006). The SAT as a predictor of different levels of college performance. *College Board Research Report, 2006-3,* 1–10.

Kohl, H. (1967). *Thirty-six children.* New York: New American Library.

Kuhn, D., & Dean, D. (2005). Is developing scientific thinking all about learning to control variables? *Psychological Science, 16*(11), 866–870.

Kupperman, J., & Wallace, R. (1998). *Evaluating an intercultural internet writing project through a framework of activities and goals.* Paper presented at the annual meeting of the American Educational Research Association, San Diego.

Larzelere, R. E., Kuhn, B. R., & Johnson, B. (2004). The intervention selection bias: An underrecognized confound in invention research. *Psychological Bulletin, 130*(2), 289–303.

Lay, A. R. (2005). Interpretations of Islamic practices among non-Qatari students living in the University of Qatar's ladies hostel. *Dialectical Anthropology, 29*, 181–219.

Leach, J. M., Scarborough, H. S., & Rescorla, L. (2003). Late-emerging reading disabilities. *Journal of Educational Psychology, 95*(2), 211–224.

Leafstedt, J. M., Richards, C. R., & Gerber, M. M. (2004). Effectiveness of explicit phonological-awareness instruction for at-risk English learners. *Learning Disabilities Research & Practice, 19*(4), 252–261.

Lee, V. E., & Bryk, A. S. (1986). Effects of single-sex secondary schools on student achievement and attitudes. *Journal of Educational Psychology, 78*(5), 381–395.

Leff, S. S., & Lakin, R. (2005). Playground-based observational systems: A review and implications for practitioners and researchers. *School Psychology Review, 34*(4), 475–489.

L'Engle, K. L., Jackson, C., & Brown, J. D. (2006). Early adolescents' cognitive susceptibility to initiating sexual intercourse. *Perspectives on Sexual and Reproductive Health, 38*(2), 97–105.

Levin, T., & Wadmany, R. (2006). Teachers' beliefs and practices in technology-based classrooms: A developmental view. *Journal of Research on Technology in Education, 39*(2), 157–181.

Levinson, M. P., & Sparkes, A. C. (2005). Gypsy children, space, and the school environment. *International Journal of Qualitative Studies in Education, 18*(6), 751–772.

Lewis, M. E. (2004). A teacher's schoolyard tale: Illuminating the vagaries of practicing participatory action research (PAR) pedagogy. *Environmental Education Research, 10*(1), 89–114.

Li, D. (2007). Story mapping and its effects on the writing fluency and word diversity of student with learning disabilities. *Learning Disabilities: A Contemporary Journal, 5*(1), 77–93.

Lienemann, T. O., Graham, S., Leader-Janessen, B., & Reid, R. (2006). Improving the writing performance of struggling writers in second grade. *The Journal of Special Education, 40*(2), 66–78.

Lindquist, B., Carlsson, G., Persson, E. K., & Uvebrant, P. (2005). Learning disabilities in a population-based group of children with hydrocephalus. *Acta Paediatrica, 94*, 878–883.

Lu, L. F. L., & Jeng, I. (2006). Knowledge construction in inservice teacher online discourse: Impacts of instructor roles and facilitative strategies. *Journal of Research on Technology in Education, 39*(2), 183–202.

Luttrell, W. (2005). Crossing anxious borders: Teaching across the quantitative–qualitative "divide." *International Journal of Research and Method in Education, 28*(2), 183–195.

Lyytinen, P., Eklund, K., & Lyytinen, H. (2005). Language development and literacy skills in late-talking toddlers with and without familial risk for dyslexia. *Annals of Dyslexia, 55*(2), 166–192.

Macgillivray, I. K. (2004). Gay rights and school policy: A case study in community factors that facilitate or impede educational change. *International Journal of Qualitative Studies in Education, 17*(3), 347–370.

Maggio, J. C., White, W. G., Molstad, S., & Kher, N. (2005). Prefreshman summer programs' impact on student achievement and retention. *Journal of Developmental Education, 29*(2), 2–33.

Masko, A. (2005). "I think about it all the time": A 12-year-old-girl's internal crisis with racism and its effects on her mental health. *The Urban Review, 37*, 329–350.

Masse, L. N., & Barnett, W. S. (2003). A benefit cost analysis of the Abecedarian early childhood intervention. *National Institute for Early Education Research*, pp. 1–50.

Mayer, R. E. (2003). Learning environments: The case for evidence-based practice and issue-driven research. *Educational Psychology Review, 15*(4), 359–366.

McCall, R. B., Beach, S. R., & Lau, S. (2000). The nature and correlates of underachievement among elementary schoolchildren in Hong Kong. *Child Development, 71*(3), 785–801.

McGinty, D. (2005). Iluminating the "black box" of standard setting: An explanatory qualitative study. *Applied Measurement in Education, 18*(3), 269–287.

Messick, S. (1995). Validity of psychological assessment: Validation of inferences from persons' responses and performances as scientific inquiry into score meaning. *American Psychologist, 50(9)*, 741–749.

McHatton, P. A., Zalaquett, C. P., & Cranson-Gingras, A. (2006). Achieving success: Perceptions of students from migrant farmwork families. *American Secondary Education, 34*(2), 25–39.

Miller, K. J., Fitzgerald, G. E., Koury, K. A., Mitchem, K. J., & Hollingsead, C. (2007). Kid tools: Self-management, problem-solving, organizational, and planning software for children and teachers. *Intervention in School and Clinic, 43*(1), 12–19.

Mills, G. E. (2003). *Action research: A guide for the teacher researcher*. Upper Saddle River, NJ: Merrill/Prentice Hall.

Mishna, F. (2004). A qualitative study of bullying from multiple perspectives. *Children and Schools, 26*(4), 234–247.

Mitchell, S. N., Reilly, R., Bramwell, F. G., Lilly, F., & Solnosky, A. (2004). Friendship and choosing groupmates: Preferences for teacher-selected vs. student-selected groupings in high school science classes. *Journal of Instructional Psychology, 31*(1), 1–17.

Mitchell, S. N., Reilly, R., Bramwell, F. G., Solnosky, A., & Lilly, F. (2004). Friendship and choosing groupmates: Preferences for teacher-selected vs. student-selected groupings in high school science class. *Journal of Instructional Psychology, 31*(1), 20–32.

Mohler-Kuo, M., Lee, J. E., & Wechsler, H. (2003). Trends in marijuana and other illicit drug use among college students: Results from 4 Harvard School of Public Health college alcohol studies surveys: 1993–2001. *Journal of American College Health, 52*(1), 17–24.

Moriarty, L. J. (2006). Investing in quality: The current state of assessment in criminal justice programs. *Justice Quarterly, 23*(4), 409–427.

Morton, M. L. (2005). Practicing praxis: Mentoring teachers in a low-income school through collaborative action research and transformative pedagogy. *Mentoring and Tutoring, 13*(1), 53–72.

Mowbray, C. T., Collins, M., & Bybee, D. (1999). Supported education for individuals with psychiatric disabilities: Long-term outcomes from an experimental study. *Social Work Research, 23*(2), 1–33.

Murata, R. (2002). What does team teaching mean?: A case study of interdisciplinary teaming. *Journal of Educational Research, 96*(2), 67–77.

Murdock, T. B., & Bolch, M. B. (2005). Risk and protective factors for poor school adjustment in lesbian, gay, and bisexual (LGB) high school youth: Variable and person-centered analyses. *Psychology in the Schools, 42*(2), 159–172.

Nathanson, C., Paulhus, D. L., & Williams, K. M. (2004). The challenge to cumulative learning: Do introductory courses actually benefit advanced students? *Teaching of Psychology, 31*(1), 5–9.

National Center for Educational Statistics Indicators of School Crime and Safety (2006). NCES Number 200003. Washington, DC: U. S. Department of Education.

National Institute of Child Health and Human Development. (2000). *Report of the National Reading Panel. Teaching children to read: An evidence-based assessment of the scientific research literature on reading and its implications for reading instruction* (NIH Publication No. 00-4769). Washington, DC: U.S. Government Printing Office.

Nishina, A. & Juvonen, J., (2005). Daily reports of witnessing and experiencing peer harassment in middle school. *Child Development, 76*, 345–450.

Norris, C., & Dattilo, J. (1999). Evaluating effects of a social story intervention on a young girl with autism. *Focus on Autism and Other Developmental Disabilities, 14*(3), 180–186.

Norris, M. L., Boydell, K. M., Pinhas, L., & Katzman, D. K. (2006). Ana and the internet: A review of pro-anorexia websites. *International Journal of Eating Disorders, 39*(6), 443–447.

Ntenza, S. P. (2006). Investigating forms of children's writing in grade 7 mathematics classrooms. *Educational Studies in Mathematics, 2006*(61), 321–345.

Oczkus, L., Baura, G., Murray, K., & Berry, K. (2006). Using the love of "poitchry" to improve primary students' writing. *The Reading Teacher, 59*(5), 475–479.

Okpala, C. O., & Ellis, R. (2006). The perceptions of college students on teacher quality: A focus on teacher qualifications. *Education, 126*(2), 374–383.

O'Leary, M. (2001). The effects of age-based and grade-based sampling on the relative standing of countries in international comparative studies of student achievement. *British Educational Research Journal, 27*(2), 187–200.

Olkun, S., Altun, A., & Smith, G. (2005). Computers and 2d geometric learning of Turkish fourth and fifth graders. *British Journal of Educational Technology, 36*(2), 317–326.

Papanastasiou, C., & Papanastasiou, E.C. (2004). Major influences on attitudes towards science. *Educational Research and Evaluation, 10*(3), 239–257.

Parker, R. M. (1993). Threats to the validity of research. *Rehabilitation Counseling Bulletin, 36*, 130–138.

Parks, G. (2000, October). The High/Scope Perry Preschool Project. *Juvenile Justice Bulletin*, pp. 1–7.

Patrick, M. R., Snyder, J., Schrepferman, L. M., & Synder, J. (2005). The joint contribution of early parental warmth, communication and tracking, and early child conduct problems on monitoring in late childhood. *Child Development, 76*(5), 999–1014.

Patton, M. Q. (1990). *Qualitative research and evaluation methods* (3rd ed.). Thousand Oaks, CA: Sage.

Pearson, L. C., & Moomaw, W. (2005). The relationship between teacher autonomy and stress, work satisfaction, empowerment, and professionalism. *Educational Research Quarterly, 29*(1), 37–53.

Penfield, R. D., & Miller, J. M. (2004). Improving content validation studies using an asymmetric confidence interval for the mean of expert ratings. *Applied Measurement in Education, 17*(4), 359–370.

Petrill, S.A., Deater-Deckard, K., Thompson, L. A., DeThorne, L. S., & Schatschneider, C. (2006). Reading skills in early readers: Genetic and shared environmental influences. *Journal of Learning Disabilities, 39*(1), 48–55.

Picus, L. O., Marion, S. F., Calvo, N., & Glenn, W. J. (2005). Understanding the relationship between student achievement and the quality of educational facilities: Evidence from Wyoming. *Peabody Journal of Education, 80*(3), 71–95.

Power, T. J., Blom-Hoffman, J., Clarke, A. T., Riley-Tillman, T. C., Kelleher, C., & Manz, P. H. (2005). Reconceptualizing intervention integrity: A partnership-based framework for linking research with practice. *Psychology in Schools, 42*(5), 495–507.

Preis, J. (2006). The effect of picture communication symbols on the verbal comprehension of commands by young children with autism. *Focus on Autism and Other Developmental Disabilities, 21*(4), 194–210.

Pressley, M. (2003). A few things reading educators should know about instructional experiments. *The Reading Teacher, 57*(1), 64–71.

Pressley, M., Mohan, L., Raphael, L. M., & Fingeret, L. (2007). How does Bennett Woods Elementary School produce such high reading and writing achievement? *Journal of Educational Psychology, 99*(2), 221–240.

de Ramirez, R. D., & Shapiro, E. S. (2006). Curriculum-based measurement and the evaluation of reading skills of Spanish-speaking English language learners in bilingual education classrooms. *School Psychology Review, 35*, 356–369.

Rauscher, F. H., Shaw, G. L, & Ky, K. N. (1993). Music and spatial task performance. *Nature, 365*, 611.

Ray, C. E., & Elliot, S. N. (2006). Social adjustment and academic achievement: A predictive model for students with diverse academic and behavior competencies. *School Psychology Review, 35*(3), 493–501.

Re, A. M., Pedron, M., & Cornoldi, C. (2007). Expressive writing difficulties in children described as exhibiting ADHD symptoms. *Journal of Learning Disabilities, 40*(3), 244–255.

Ready, D. D., LoGerfo, L. F., Burkam, D. T., & Lee, V. E. (2005). Explaining girls' advantage in kindergarten literacy learning: Do classroom behaviors make a difference? *The Elementary School Journal, 106*(1), 21–38.

Reagon, K. A., Higbee, T. S., & Endicott, K. (2006). Teaching pretend play skills to a student with autism using video modeling with a sibling as model and play partner. *Education and Treatment of Children, 29*(3), 517–528.

Resnick, L. B. (2006). Do the math: Cognitive demand makes a difference. *Research Points, 4*(2), 1–4.

Rickford, A. (2001). The effect of cultural congruence and higher order questioning on the reading enjoyment and comprehension of ethnic minority students. *Journal of Education for Students Placed At Risk, 6*(4), 357–387.

Ridings-Nowakowski, J. (1981). An interview with Ralph Tyler. In G. F. Madaus & D. L. Stufflebeam (Eds.) *Educational Evaluation: Classic Works of Ralph Tyler.* Boston: Kluwer.

Riley-Tillman, T. C., & Chafouleas, S. M., Eckert, T. L., & Kelleher, C. (2005). Bridging the gap between research and practice: A framework for building research agendas in school psychology. *Psychology in Schools, 42*(5), 459–473.

Rivera, L. (2003). Changing women: An ethnographic study of homeless mothers and popular education. *Journal of Sociology and Social Welfare, 30*(2), 31–51.

Robbins, S. B., Allen, J., Casillias, A., & Peterson, C. H. (2006). Unraveling the differential effects of motivational and skills, social, and self-management measures from traditional predictors of college outcomes. *Journal of Educational Psychology, 98*(3), 598–616.

Rogers, T., Marshall, E., & Tyson, C. A. (2006). Dialogic narratives of literacy, teaching, and schooling: Preparing literacy teachers for diverse settings. *Reading Research Quarterly, 41*(2), 202–224.

Rosenthal, B. S. (1995). The influence of social support on school completion among Haitians. *Social Work in Education, 17*, 30–39.

Rosenthal, R., & Jacobson, L. (1968). *Pygmalion in the classroom.* New York: Holt, Rinehart & Winston.

Rosenthal, R. (1974). *On the social psychology of the self-fulfilling prophecy: Further evidence for Pygmalion effects and their mediating mechanisms.* New York: MSS Modular.

Rosenthal, R., & Rosnow, R. L. (1974). *Artifact in behavioral research.* New York: Academic Press.

Rothman, E., & Silverman, J. (2007). The effect of a college sexual assault prevention program on first-years students' victimization rates. *Journal of American College Health, 55*(5), 283–290.

Rothstein, A. S., Falvo, R. C., & Wirtzer, J. (1992). Evaluating postsecondary education and employment for high school graduates with physical disabilities. *Education, 114*(3), 451–458.

Rous, B., McCormick, K., Gooden, C., & Townley, K. F. (2007). Kentucky's early childhood continuous assessment and accountability system: Local decisions and state supports. *Topics in Early Childhood Special Education, 27*(1), 19–33.

Royer, R. (2002). Supporting technology integration through action research. *The Clearing House, 75*(5), 233–237.

Rumberger, R. W., & Palardy, G. J. (2005). Does segregation still matter?: The impact of student composition on academic achievement in high school. *Teachers College Record, 107*(9), 1999–2045.

Russell, J. (2006). What's to be done with the fox?: Inuit teachers inventing musical games for Inuit classrooms. *Curriculum Inquiry, 36*(1), 15–33.

Sadeh, A., Gruber, R., & Raviv, A. (2003). The effects of sleep restriction and extension on school-age children: What makes a difference an hour makes. *Child Development, 74*(2), 444–445.

Safer, A. M., Farmer, L. S., Segalla, A., & Elhoubi, A. F. (2005). Does the distance from the teacher influence student evaluations. *Educational Research Quarterly, 28(3)*, 27–34.

Sak, U. (2004). A synthesis of research on psychological types of gifted adolescents. *The Journal of Secondary Gifted Education, 15*(2), 70–79.

Sandefur, S. J., & Moore, L. (2004). The "nuts and dolts" of teacher images in children's picture storybooks: A content analysis. *Education, 125*(1), 41–55.

Sanders, M. G. (1999). Schools' programs and progress in the national network of partnership schools. *Journal of Educational Research*, *92*(4), 220–229.

Sanguinetti, J., Waterhouse, P., & Maunders, D. (2005). Pedagogies on the edge: Researching complex practice in youth and adult community education. *Studies in Continuing Education*, *27*(3), 271–287.

Schäfer, M., Korn, S., Brodbeck, F. C., Wolke, D., & Schulz, H. (2005). Bullying roles in changing contexts: The stability of victim and bully roles from primary to secondary school. *International Journal of Behavioral Development*, *29*(4), 323–335.

Schappe, J. F. (2005). Early childhood assessment: A correlation study of the relationships among student performance, student feelings, and teacher perceptions. *Early Childhood Education Journal*, *33*(3), 187–193.

Schellenberg, E. G. (2006). Long-term positive associations between music lessons and IQ. *Journal of Educational Psychology*, *98*(2), 457–468.

Schoen, S. F., & Nolen, J. (2004). Decreasing acting-out behavior and increasing learning. *Teaching Exceptional Children*, *37*(1), 26–29.

Schoenfeld, A. H. (2004). The math wars. *Educational Policy*, *18*(1), 253–286.

Schweinhart, L. J., & Wallgren, C. R. (1993). Effects of a Follow Through program on school achievement. *Journal of Research in Childhood Education*, *8*, 43–56.

Schweinhart, L. J., & Weikart, D. P. (1980). *Young children grow up: The effects of the Perry preschool program on youths through age 15*. Ypsilanti, MI: High/Scope Press.

Schweinle, A., Meyer, D. K., & Turner, J. C. (2006). Striking the right balance: Students' motivation and affect in elementary mathematics. *Journal of Educational Research*, *99*(5), 271–293.

Scriven, M. (1967). The methodology of evaluation. In R. W. Tyler, R. M. Gagné, & M. Scriven (Eds.), *Perspectives of curriculum evaluation*, pp. 39–83. Chicago, IL: Rand McNally.

Self-Brown, S. R., & Mathews S. (2003). Effects of classroom structure on student achievement goal orientation. *Journal of Educational Research*, *97*(2), 106–111.

Shabani, D. B., & Carr, J. E. (2004). An evaluation of response cards as an adjunct to standard instruction in university classrooms: A systematic replication and extension. *North American Journal of Psychology*, *6*(1), 85–100.

Shank, G., & Villella, O. (2004). Building on new foundations: Core principles and new directions for qualitative research. *Journal of Educational Research*, *98*(1), 46–55.

Shann, M. H. (1998). Professional commitment and satisfaction among teachers in urban middle schools. *Journal of Educational Research*, *92*(2), 67–73.

Sharp. C. (2005). How can LEAs help schools to use research for school improvement? *Management in Education*, *18(3)*, 12–15.

Siegel, L. S. (1988). Evidence that IQ scores are irrelevant to the definition and analysis of reading disability. *Canadian Journal of Psychology*, *42*, 201–215.

Signor-Buhl, S. J., Leblanc, M., & Mcdougal, J. (2006). Conducting district-wide evaluations of special education services: A case example. *Psychology in the Schools*, *43*(1), 109–115.

Simmerman, S., & Swanson H.L. (2001). Treatment outcomes for students with learning disabilities: How important are internal and external validity? *Journal of Learning Disabilities*, *34*(3), 221–236.

Simonite, V. (2003). The impact of coursework on degree classifications and the performance of individual students. *Assessment and Evaluation in Higher Education*, *28*(5), 459–460.

Simonite, V. (2004). Multilevel analysis of relationship between entry qualifications and trends in degree classifications in mathematical sciences 1994–2000. *International Journal of Mathematical Education in Science and Technology*, *35*(3), 335–344.

Sireci, S. G. (1998). Gathering and analyzing content validity data. *Educational Assessment*, *5*(4), 299–321.

Sirin, S. R., Diemer, M. A., Jackson, L. R., Gonsalves, L., & Howell, A. (2004). Future aspirations of urban adolescents: A person-in-context model. *International Journal of Qualitative Studies in Education*, *17*(3), 437–459.

Smagorinsky, P., Cook, L. S., & Reed, P. M. (2005). The construction of meaning and identity in the composition and reading of an architectural text. *Reading Research Quarterly*, *40*(1), 70–88.

Smith, M. L., & Glass, G. V. (1977). Meta-analysis of psychotherapy outcome studies. *American Psychologist*, *32*, 752–760.

Smith, G., & Smith, J. (2005). Regression to the mean in average test scores. *Educational Assessment*, *10*(4), 377–399.

Smith, J. B., Maehr, M. L., & Midgley, C. (1992). Relationship between personal and contextual characteristics and principals' administrative behaviors. *Journal of Educational Research*, *86*(2), 111–118.

Smith, R. M. (2006). Classroom management texts: A study in the representation and misrepresentation of students with disabilities. *International Journal of Inclusive Education*, *10*(1), 91–104.

Snell, M. (2003). Applying research to practice: The more pervasive problem? *Research and Practice for Persons with Severe Disabilities*, *28*, 143–147.

Solberg, L. I., Asche, S. E., Boyle, R., McCarty, M. C., & Thoele, M. J. (2007). Smoking and cessation behaviors among young adults of various educational backgrounds. *American Journal of Public Health, 97*(8), 1421–1426.

Spear-Swerling, L. (2004). Fourth graders' performance on a state-mandated assessment involving two different measures of reading comprehension. *Reading Psychology, 25,* 121–148.

Spencer, R., Porche, M. V., & Tolman, D. L. (2003). We've come a long way–maybe: New challenges for gender equity in education. *Teachers College Record, 105*(9), 1774–1807.

Stake, R. E. (1995). *The art of case study research.* Thousand Oaks, CA: Sage.

Standards for Educational and Psychological Testing. (1999). Washington, DC: American Psychological Association.

Stanovich, K. E. (1988). Explaining the differences between the dyslexic and the garden-variety poor reader: The phonological-core variable-difference model. *Journal of Learning Disabilities, 21*(10), 590–612.

Steele, K. M., Bass, K. E., & Crook, M. D. (1999). The mystery of the Mozart effect: Failure to replicate. *Psychological Science, 10*(4), 366–369.

Steiner, B., & Schwartz, J. (2007). Assessing the quality of doctoral programs in criminology in the United States. *Journal of Criminal Justice Education, 18*(1), 53–86.

Sternberg, R. J. (2004). Theory-based university admissions testing for a new millennium. *Educational Psychologist, 39*(3), 185–198.

Stevens, S.S. (1951). Mathematics, measurement and psychophysics. In S.S. Stevens (Ed.), *Handbook of experimental psychology* (pp. 1–49). New York: Wiley

Stokking, K., Leenders, F., Jong, J. D., & Tartwijk, J. V. (2003). From student to teacher: Reducing practice shock and early dropout in the teacher profession. *European Journal of Teacher Education, 26*(3), 329–350.

St. Pierre, E. A. (2006). Scientifically based research in education: Epistemology and ethics. *Adult Education Quarterly, 56*(4), 239–266.

Strand, S., Deary, I. J., & Smith, P. (2006). Sex differences in cognitive abilities test scores: A UK national picture. *British Journal of Educational Psychology, 76,* 463–480.

Sullivan, C. J., & Maxfield, M. G. (2003). Examining paradigmatic development in criminology and criminal justice: A content analysis of research methods syllabi in doctoral programs. *Journal of Criminal Justice Education, 14*(2), 269–285.

Sulzby, E., & Teale, W. (1991). Emergent literacy. In R. Barr, M. Kammil, P. Mosenthal, & D. Pearson (Eds.), *Handbook of reading research* (2nd ed., pp. 727–757). New York: Longman.

Superville, L. K. (2001, May/June). Oral assessment as a tool for enhancing students' written expression in social studies. *The Social Studies,* pp. 121–125.

Tan, K. H. K., & Prosser, M. (2004). Qualitatively different ways of differentiating student achievement: a phenomenographic study of academics' conceptions of grade descriptors. *Assessment and Evaluation in Higher Education, 29*(3), 267–282.

Tanner, L. (1997). *Dewey's laboratory school: Lessons for today.* New York: Teachers College Press.

Tashakkori, A., & Creswell, J. W. (2007). Exploring the nature of research questions in mixed methods research. *Journal of Mixed Methods Research 1,* 207–211.

Tashakkori, A., & Teddlie, C. (2003). *Handbook of mixed methods in social and behavioral research.* Thousand Oaks, CA: Sage.

Taylor, B. M., Pearson, P. D., Peterson, D. S., & Rodriguez, M. C. (2005). The Ciera school change framework: An evidence-based approach to professional development and school reading improvement. *Reading Research Quarterly, 40*(1), 40–69.

The National Commission for the Protection of Human Subjects of Biomedical and Behavioral Research. (1979). *The Belmont Report: Ethical Principles and Guidelines for the Protection of Human Subjects of Research.* DHEW Publication No. (OS) 78-0012. Washington, DC: The U.S. Government Printing Office.

The National Commission on Excellence in Education. (1983). *A Nation at Risk: The Imperative for Educational Reform.* Washington, DC: U.S. Department of Education.

Thombs, D. L., Olds, R. S., Osborn, C. J., Casseday, S., Glavin, K., & Berkowitz, A. D. (2007). Outcomes of a technology-based social norms intervention to deter alcohol use in freshman residence halls. *Journal of American College Health, 55*(6), 325–332.

Tierney, W. G. (2002). Get real: Representing reality. *Qualitative Studies in Education, 15*(4), 385–398.

Trautwein, U., Lüdtke, O., Schnyder, I., & Niggili, A. (2006). Predicting homework effort: Support for a domain-specific, multilevel homework model. *Journal of Educational Psychology, 98*(2), 438–456.

Tsai, C.-C., & Wen, M. L. (2005). Research and trends in science education from 1998 to 2002: A content analysis of publication in selected journals. *International Journal of Science Education, 27*(1), 3–14

Tuan, H. L, Chin, C. C., & Shieh, S. H. (2005). The development of a questionnaire to measure students' motivation towards science learning. *International Journal of Science Education, 27*(6), 639–654.

Uresti, R., Goertz, J., & Bernal, E. M. (2002). Maximizing achievement for potentially gifted and talented and regular minority students in a primary classroom. *Roeper Review, 25*(1), 1–11.

Vartanian, L. R., Schwartz, M. B., & Brownwell, K. D. (2007). Effects of soft drink consumption on nutrition and health: A systematic review and meta-analysis. *American Journal of Public Health*, *97*(4), 667–675.

Villano, T. L. (2005). Should social studies textbooks become history?: A look at alternative methods to activate schema in the intermediate classroom. *The Reading Teacher*, *59*(2), 122–130.

Van Maanen, J. (1988). *Tales of the field: On writing ethnography*. Chicago, IL: University of Chicago Press.

von Bothmer, M. I., & Fridlund, B. (2005). Gender differences in health habits and in motivation for a healthy lifestyle among Swedish university students. *Nursing and Health Sciences, 7(2)*, 107–118.

Von Schrader, S., & Ansley, T. (2006). Sex differences in the tendency to omit items on multiple-choice tests: 1980–2000. *Applied Measurement in Education*, *19*(1), 41–65.

Vossekuil, B., Fein, R. A., Reddy, M., Borum, R., Modzeleski, W. (2002). *The final report and findings of the Safe School Initiative: Implications for the prevention of school attacks in the United States*. Washington, DC: U.S. Department of Education, Office of Elementary and Secondary Education, Safe and Drug-Free Schools Program and U.S. Secret Service, National Threat Assessment Center.

Walker, A., Shafer, J., & Iiams, M. (2004). "Not in my classroom": Teacher attitudes towards English Language Learners in the mainstream classroom. *NABE Journal of Research and Practice*, *2*(1), 130–160.

Walsh, D. S. (2007). Supporting youth development outcomes: An evaluation of a responsibility model-based program. *Physical Educator*, *64*(1), 1–10.

Walsh, M. E., Barrett, J. G., & DePaul, J. (2007). Day-to-day activities of school counselors: Alignment with new directions in the field and the ASCA national model. *Professional School Counseling*, *10*(4), 1–12.

Wentzel, K. R. (1998). Social relationships and motivation in middle school: The role of parents, teachers, and peers. *Journal of Educational Psychology*, *90*(2), 202–209.

Whitehurst, G. J. (2002, Summer). Improving teacher quality. *Spectrum: The Journal of State Government*, pp. 12–15.

Whitehurst, G. J. & Lonigan, C. J. (1998). Child development and emergent literacy. *Child Development*, *69*, 848–872.

Williams, J. P., Lauer, K. D., Hall, K. H., Lord, K. M., Gugga, S. S., Bak, S. J., etal. (2002). Teaching elementary school students to identify story themes. *Journal of Educational Psychology*, *94*(2), 235–248.

Wilson, J. M. (1999). Using words about thinking: Content analysis of chemistry teachers' classroom talk. *International Journal of Science Education*, *21*(10), 1067–1084.

Wong, K. K., & Nicotera, A. C. (2004). *Brown v. Board of Education* and the Coleman Report: Social science research and the debate on educational equality. *Peabody Journal of Education*, *79*(2), 122–135.

Woodward, J. (2006). Developing automaticity in multiplication facts: Integrating strategy instruction with timed practice drills. *Learning Disability Quarterly*, *26*, 269–289.

Worthen, B. R., & Sanders, J. R. (1991). The changing face of educational evaluation. *Theory Into Practice*, *30*(1), 3–12.

Wright-Gallo, G. L., Higbee, T. S., Reagon, K. A., & Davey, B. J. (2006). Classroom-based functional analysis and intervention for students with emotional/behavioral disorders. *Education and Treatment of Children*, *29*(3), 421–436.

Yaden, D. B., & Tardibuono, J. M. (2004). The emergent writing development of urban Latino preschoolers: Developmental perspectives and instructional environments for second-language learners. *Reading and Writing Quarterly*, *20*, 29–61.

Yalon-Chamovitz, S., Mano, T., Jarus, T., & Weinblatt, N. (2006). Leisure activities during school break among children with learning disabilities: Preference vs. performance. *British Journal of Learning Disabilities*, *34*, 42–48.

Yenilmez, A., Sungur, S., & Tekkya, C. (2006). Students' achievement in relation to reasoning ability, prior knowledge and gender. *Research in Science and Technological Education*, *24*(1), 129–138.

Yoo, J., Brooks, D., & Patti, R. (2007). Organizational constructs as predictors of effectiveness in child welfare interventions. *Child Welfare*, *86*(1), 53–78.

Young, I. P. (2005). Predictive validity of applicants' reference information for admission to a doctoral program in educational leadership. *Educational Research Quarterly*, *29*(1), 16–25.

Zajacova, A., Lynch, S. M., & Espenshade, T. J. (2005). Self-sufficiency, stress, and academic success in college. *Research in Higher Education*, *46*(6), 677–706.

Index